DAVITT
AND IRISH REVOLUTION
1846–82

DAVITT

AND

IRISH REVOLUTION

1846–82

by

T. W. MOODY

CLARENDON PRESS · OXFORD

1981

Oxford University Press, Walton Street, Oxford OX2 6DP
London Glasgow New York Toronto
Delhi Bombay Calcutta Madras Karachi
Kuala Lumpur Singapore Hong Kong Tokyo
Nairobi Dar es Salaam Cape Town
Melbourne Auckland
and associate companies in
Beirut Berlin Ibadan Mexico City

Published in the United States by
Oxford University Press, New York

British Library Cataloguing in Publication Data

Moody, T. W.
Davitt and Irish revolution, 1846-1882.
1. Davitt, Michael 2. Politicians–Ireland –Biography 3. Fenians–Biography
I. Title
322.4'2092'4 DA952.D/

ISBN 0-19-822382-X

Typeset by Graphic Services,
Printed in Great Britain at the
University Press, Oxford
by Eric Buckley
Printer to the University

To
the memory of Eileen Davitt
and to
Cahir and Robert Emmet Davitt
children of Michael Davitt

CONTENTS

ILLUSTRATIONS

between pages 296–7

MAPS

at end of volume

ABBREVIATIONS

Many short titles other than those listed below are used in the footnotes. In such cases the full title and the date of publication are given in the first citation. In dates from 1801 to 1899 the first two digits are omitted where the month and year are given: for example 20 Sept. 81. When a year is not stated after a month, the year last mentioned is to be understood.

Arnold-Forster, Irish journal	The Irish journal of Florence Arnold-Forster
B.L.	British Library (formerly British Museum)
Bessborough comm. rep.	*Report of her majesty's commissioners of inquiry into the working of the Landlord and Tenant (Ireland) Act, 1870* [C2779], H.C. 1881, xviii
C.C.C. minutes, lxxii	*Central criminal court, sessions paper; Besley, mayor; seventh session, . . . 1870; minutes of evidence, . . .*, vol. lxxii (London, [1870]).
C.C.	Catholic curate
C. C. O'Brien. *Parnell*	Conor Cruise O'Brien, *Parnell and his party* (Oxford, 1957; 2nd, corrected impression, 1964)
C.P.	Commissioners of Dublin Metropolitan Police
Cashman	D. B. Cashman, *The life of Michael Davitt, founder of the Land League, to which is added The secret history of the Land League* (London, [1882])
Chamberlain, *Political memoir*	Joseph Chamberlain, *A political memoir, 1880-92*, ed. C.H.D. Howard (London, 1953)
D	Michael Davitt
DA/1 [etc.]	Davitt's autobiographical writings (Davitt papers, series V), no. 1 [etc.]
DL/1 [etc.]	Material in Davitt's papers relating to legal proceedings (Davitt papers, series IV), no. 1 [etc.]
DN/1 [etc.]	Davitt's diaries and note-books (Davitt papers, series II), no. 1 [etc.]
DP/A [etc.]	Davitt's letters and papers (Davitt papers, series I), packet A [etc.]
D.A.B.	*Dictionary of American biography* (20 vols, New York and London, 1928-37)

D.N.B.	*Dictionary of national biography* (reprint, with corrections, 22 vols, London, 1921-2 etc.)
D.P.B.	*Devoy's post bag, 1871-1928*, ed. William O'Brien and Desmond Ryan (2 vols, Dublin, 1948, 1953)
Defence	*The 'Times'-Parnell commission: speech delivered by Michael Davitt in defence of the Land League* (London, 1890)
Denvir, *Life story*	John Denvir, *The life story of an old rebel* (Dublin, 1918)
Devoy	John Devoy, 'Davitt's career', XVII parts, in *Gaelic American*, 9 June-30 Nov. 1906 [cited by part] I 9 June — X 11 Aug. II 16 June — XI 18 Aug. III 23 June — XII 8 Sept. IV 30 June — XIII 15 Sept. V 7 July — XIV 29 Sept. VI 14 July — XV 13 Oct. VII 21 July — XVI 20 Oct. VIII 28 July — XVII 3 Nov. IX 4 Aug.
Devoy, *Recollections*	John Devoy, *Recollections of an Irish rebel . . .. a personal narrative* (New York, 1929)
F.J.	*Freeman's Journal*
Fall	Michael Davitt, *The fall of feudalism in Ireland: or the story of the Land League revolution* (London and New York, 1904)
H.C.	House of Commons [in the citation of parliamentary papers]
H.-C.	Head constable of the Royal Irish Constabulary
Hamilton, *Diary*	*The diary of Sir Edward William Hamilton*, ed. D. W. R. Bahlman (2 vols, Oxford, 1972)
Healy, *Letters and leaders*	T. M. Healy, *Letters and leaders of my day* (2 vols, London, [1928])
I.G.P.	Inspector general of police, Royal Irish Constabulary
I.H.S.	*Irish Historical Studies* (Dublin, 1938-)
I.W.	*Irish World* (New York)
Irish crisis	*The Irish crisis of 1879-80: proceedings of the Dublin Mansion House Relief Committee* (Dublin, 1881)
Kimberley comm. rep., i [etc.]	*Report of the commissioners appointed to inquire into the workings of the penal servitude acts*, vol. i, i-lxvi [C2368], H.C. 1878-9, xxxvii, 1-66, vol. ii, 1-700 [C2386-I], H.C. 1878-9, xxxvii, 67-770, vol. iii, 700-1340 [C2386-II], H.C. 1878-9, xxxviii
Leaves	Michael Davitt, *Leaves from a prison diary* (2 vols, London, 1885)

Lyons, *Dillon*	F. S. L. Lyons, *John Dillon: a biography* (London, 1968)
Lyons, *Parnell*	F. S. L. Lyons, *Charles Stewart Parnell* (London, 1977)
McCaffrey, 'Irish federalism'	L. J. McCaffrey, 'Irish federalism in the 1870s: a study in conservative nationalism' in *Transactions of the American Philosophical Society*, new series, lii, pt 6 (Philadelphia, 1962)
MacDonagh, *Home rule*	Michael MacDonagh, *The home rule movement* (Dublin, 1920)
N.L.I.	National Library of Ireland
O'Connor, *Memoirs*	T. P. O'Connor, *Memoirs of an old parliamentarian* (2 vols, London, 1929)
O'Connor, *Parnell movement*	T. P. O'Connor, *The Parnell movement* (2nd edition, London, 1886)
O'Donnell, *Irish parl. party*	F. H. O'Donnell, *A history of the Irish parliamentary party* (2 vols, London, 1910)
O'Leary, *Recollections*	John O'Leary, *Recollections of fenians and fenianism* (2 vols, London, 1896)
P.L.G.	Poor law guardian
P.P.	Parish priest
P.R.O.	Public Record Office of England, London
P.R.O.I.	Public Record Office of Ireland, Dublin
Palmer, *Land League*	N. D. Palmer, *The Irish Land League crisis* (New Haven, 1940)
Personal histories	Queen *v.* Parnell and others (1880–81): personal histories of the traversers (Dublin: V. B. Dillon & Co., solicitors for the traversers)
Prison life	*The prison life of Michael Davitt, related by himself* (London, 1878)
R. B. O'Brien, *Parnell*	R. Barry O'Brien, *The life of Charles Stewart Parnell, 1846–1891* (2 vols, London, 1898)
R.I.C.	Royal Irish Constabulary
Reid, *Forster*	T. Wemyss Reid, *Life of . . . W. E. Forster* (2 vols, London, 1888)
Ryan, *Fenian memories*	M. F. Ryan, *Fenian memories*, ed. T. F. O'Sullivan (Dublin, 1945)
S.P.O.	State Paper Office, Dublin Castle
S.C.P.	*Special commission act, 1888: reprint of the shorthand notes of the speeches, proceedings, and evidence taken before the commissioners appointed under the above named act* (12 vols, London, 1890)

Sullivan, *Recollections*	T. D. Sullivan, *Recollections of troubled times in Irish politics* (Dublin, 1905)
T.C.	Town commissioner
Thom 1870 [etc.]	*Thom's Irish Almanac and Official Directory of the United Kingdom . . . for the year 1870* [etc.] (Dublin, 1870-)
Thornley, *Butt*	D. A. Thornley, *Isaac Butt and home rule* (London, 1964)
W. O'Brien, *Recollections*	William O'Brien, *Recollections* (London, 1905)

INTRODUCTION

THIS book is intended to cover the career of Michael Davitt in the context of two Irish revolutionary movements, the Irish republican or fenian movement and the Land League movement, which during 1879–82 interacted on each other with momentous results. Davitt was the son of working-class parents, who, evicted from a minute agricultural holding in the west of Ireland, emigrated with their young family to win a hard living in industrial Lancashire. He was unknown to the public till, in 1870, at the age of 24, he was sentenced to fifteen years penal servitude. His offence was trafficking in arms as a member of the Irish Republican Brotherhood, or the fenian organisation, which, secret, oath-bound, and recruited from the Irish working-classes, was dedicated to overthrowing British rule in Ireland by armed force and establishing a democratic Irish republic. When after seven years in penal servitude he was released from Dartmoor on ticket of leave at the end of 1877, Davitt was still generally unknown as a person, but was widely known among Irishmen as a symbol of unflinching resistance to British authority. In the course of the following year he became the most challenging figure in Irish politics next to Charles Stewart Parnell, and the pioneer, with John Devoy, of a new policy for the fenian movement.

The new policy called for a departure from high fenian orthodoxy, with its commitment to armed rebellion as the only means of ultimately achieving national independence, and its contemptuous rejection of open and constitutional action to that end. There had already been one such 'new departure', in the support given by John O'Connor Power, Patrick Egan, and other fenian opportunists to the home rule movement during its early years under Isaac Butt's leadership (1870–77). The Davitt–Devoy 'new departure' of 1878 was a more ambitious and wide-ranging scheme, which was initiated with the backing of

American fenianism: it proposed that the I.R.B. as such should cooperate, on specified conditions, with home-rulers of the combative kind typified by Parnell, in a united effort to obtain national self-government and a radical settlement of the land question at an early date. This idea did not become a political reality, but it helped to prepare the minds of nationalists for a different 'new departure' (the third in the series) with more limited and practical aims: a popular front for the immediate purpose of protecting Irish tenant farmers against their landlords and the ultimate object of converting the tenants into owners of their holdings. This was Davitt's response in 1879 to an economic crisis that threatened the tenant farmers with bankruptcy, eviction, and starvation. He became the founder, chief organiser, and inspiring genius of the Land League, through which, under the presidency of Parnell, mass resistance was successfully directed against the landlords. No such organised mass-movement had ever been seen in Ireland before. Conducted, under Davitt's inspiration, within the law but in a spirit of 'aggressive moral force', the 'land war' brought about a revolution in the psychological relations between landlords and tenants, which was quickly followed by a revolution in their legal relations affected progressively by acts of parliament beginning with the Gladstone act of 1881. In the long run the aims of the Land League were achieved in the liquidation of the old landlords as a class and the transformation of their former tenantry into owner-occupiers.

Davitt was engaged in the 'land war' for less than two years; his ticket of leave was revoked and he was sent back to penal servitude in February 1881 while the struggle was at its height. But as 'father of the Land League' he had already earned a secure place in Irish history. When he was again released from prison in May 1882, the agrarian crisis was over. The landlords remained, but Gladstone's land act of 1881 had established the principle of dual ownership of the soil by landlords and tenants; the tenants were visibly reaping the fruits of this decisive victory of the Land League; and the national movement was being firmly swung back by Parnell to a moderate and constitutional course. Davitt rejected this policy. He held that Parnell had paid too high a price for too limited a concession when, by refusing to compromise with the government, he might have secured the complete 'abolition of landlordism', which Davitt now interpreted to mean national ownership of the land. But the solid majority of the nation followed Parnell's lead, and Davitt assumed the role of freelance nationalist. The last twenty-four of his sixty years were crowded with many-sided public activity in Ireland, Great Britain, and far beyond, but he was never again to occupy the key position in Irish national politics that had been his in 1879-81. The year 1882 was thus a turning-point in his career.

This book, for which my research began many years ago, is based on all the primary sources known and available to me, both in manuscript and in print.

First among these sources are Davitt's private and unpublished papers, which were placed at my disposal without any conditions by the late Eileen Davitt, Michael's daughter and literary executor. The Davitt papers—letters, diaries, note-books, accounts, press-cutting books, and miscellaneous material—are an uneven and incomplete collection, especially for the years covered by this book. There are no original letters or papers before 1870, no diaries or note-books before 1878, and for the period of the land war personal records are all too scanty. This paucity of evidence is not accidental: people in the circumstances of Davitt's parents are not apt to accumulate letters and papers, and men involved in a revolutionary movement as Davitt was from 1865 to 1870 have reason not to do so. After his release from Dartmoor and until his marriage in 1886 he never had a permanent home; and, as he was a key figure in the land agitation till his re-arrest in February 1881, his personal life tended to be submerged in feverish public activity that left him little time for writing personal letters or keeping a diary. Nevertheless Davitt's papers are an indispensable source for his life from 1870 onwards, and for the period before 1870 they contain retrospective autobiographical information.

Besides his unpublished papers we have a mass of information about Davitt in his published writings—pamphlets (beginning with his *Prison life of Michael Davitt, related by himself* (1878)), books, articles, letters and other contributions to newspapers, and reports of speeches, interviews, and other oral statements. The bulk of this writing only appeared after 1882, but it has a good deal to say retrospectively about his earlier career. In this fact lies part of the difficulty and the fascination of the subject. For his retrospective explanations of some of his actions and attitudes are incompatible with the contemporary evidence. There is a crucial example of this in two accounts he gave of the new departure of 1878 and the land war, the first in 1889 before the *Times*-Parnell commission (published in book form as his *Defence of the Land League*), the second in 1904 in his last and greatest book, *The fall of feudalism in Ireland: the story of the Land League revolution*. In 1889 he was seeking to refute charges of intimidation, outrage, and ulterior motives brought by *The Times* against the land-leaguers for their conduct of the land agitation. The result was a powerful defence of the Land League as an instrument of moral force for the liberation of the Irish peasantry from an intolerable system, and of himself in conceiving, initiating, and directing it. This approach identifies Davitt's outlook of 1889 with that of 1878–81, which was very different, and in so doing begs a number of questions. His final account of the matter was written in a more relaxed mood, at a time when the fruits of the land war were being conspicuously harvested by the accelerating progress of peasant proprietorship. He was much less concerned with the reputation of the Land League than with its achievements, and his *Fall of feudalism*, by comparison with his *Defence of the Land League*, is detached and dispassionate. It is better history, and on the whole nearer in spirit to the events it relates. But it, too, involves problems of interpretation, especially in relation to the new departure of 1878 and the growth of Davitt's thought on the land question. To conclude from all this that Davitt was not a scrupulous witness would be to misread a character in which passionate concern for truth and justice was combined with resilience of mind, receptivity to new ideas, sensitivity to new situations, and a tendency to wishful thinking. In the course of his troubled life he felt compelled from time to time, in the light of altered views and priorities, to re-think all that had gone before, and to try to express it as a self-consistent whole. The problems that this has created are all the more complex when the process brings his testimony into conflict with that of contemporaries, above all Devoy. Yet the unravelling of such source-problems, though it involves difficulties of presentation as well as interpretation, is itself part of the story of Davitt's life and personality.

Next to Davitt's own writings, the most valuable materials for his life are to be found in the archives and official publications of governments and of other bodies public and private; in contemporary newspapers, pamphlets, and studies; and in the memoirs, narratives, and private papers of Davitt's contemporaries. Thus the earliest documentary evidence of Davitt's existence (no baptismal record having survived) is the census returns of 1851 for Haslingden; and before the date of the earliest surviving letter written by him (15 December 1869) we have evidence in police reports in the State Paper Office, Dublin Castle, of his fenian activities in Lancashire which led to his arrest and conviction for treason-felony in 1870. There are comparatively full records of his trial, and for his imprisonment (1870–77, 1881–2) there is valuable material in printed sources and in home office papers in the Public Record Office, London.

For Davitt's share in the new departure of 1878 and the origins of the Land League, the writings of John Devoy are the most important private source. Devoy was Davitt's collaborator in 1878, but quarrelled with him in 1882, and, holding that he had sacrificed the interests of fenianism to those of agrarian revolution, became his most implacable enemy. Devoy's contribution to the Davitt story began in his book, *The land of Eire* (New York, 1882), written before the quarrel, and culminated in a series of articles 'Davitt's career', published, ostensibly as an obituary tribute, in Devoy's newspaper, the *Gaelic American* (9 June–3 November 1906). These and other publications of Devoy are in large measure substantiated and complemented by his private correspondence (published as *Devoy's post bag* (2 vols, 1948, 1953), the most important corpus of printed material relating to the fenian movement. Even where they are most deeply tainted by partizanship Devoy's writings have unique value, partly because they cover a phase of Davitt's life for which his own surviving papers are scanty, and partly because Devoy was so intelligent and well informed. Anything that Devoy says about Davitt, especially in the context of the new departure of 1878 and the origins of the Land League, has to be scrutinised and weighed against Davitt's own account of the same matters; but even where it is demonstrably in error it cannot be disregarded, for the error itself may be part of the story of Davitt's relationship with Devoy. Devoy's writings are thus both secondary works and sources for Davitt's life; and his papers include many letters from Davitt of 1878–80 that reveal an aspect of Davitt's personality not otherwise documented.

A little book with the misleading title, *The life of Michael Davitt, with a history of the rise and development of the Irish National Land League*, by D. B. Cashman, was published in America in 1881.[1] It is in no sense a 'life' but a collection of extracts from speeches and other statements by Davitt largely derived from newspapers, together with an abridged version of his first pamphlet, *The prison life of Michael Davitt* (1878), strung together by partizan and hagiographical narrative. An enlarged edition[2] included 'The secret history of the Land League', which is simply a report of interviews given by Davitt to a representative of the New York *Daily World* and published in that paper on 9 and 16 July 1882. The book is of great value as a quarry of raw material, and the enlarged edition was long kept in print in a cheap popular series by the Glasgow firm of Cameron and Ferguson.

The official records of the Land League have not survived as such, and this is a serious gap in the archival evidence for the land war. But

[1] Boston: Murphy and McCarthy.

[2] Glasgow and London: Cameron and Ferguson [1882].

there is a complete series of reports of meetings of the central Land League in the *Freeman's Journal*, and meetings are also recorded in other newspapers. A fragmentary mass of letters and papers received at the headquarters of the league and of its auxiliary and successor, the Ladies' Land League, from local branches all over the country, together with minute books and other records of some of the branches themselves, has survived and is now in the National Library. And there is a vast quantity of material relating to the land war in newspapers, in police reports and other records of the chief secretary's office, in documents assembled for the prosecution of Parnell and others for conspiracy in 1880–81, in parliamentary papers, in the proceedings of the *Times*-Parnell commission of 1888–9, and in private letters and papers.

The only previous biography of Davitt, by Francis Sheehy-Skeffington, was published in 1908.[1] It is described by its author as 'a primer of Davitt' by one of his disciples: 'my twofold object in writing it has been to revivify Davitt's ideas amongst the Irish people, and to spread an appreciation of them amongst the people of Great Britain'. Considering that the book rests on a narrow base of printed sources, mainly newspapers and books by and relating to Davitt, and that it was completed within eighteen months of Davitt's death, it is remarkably good: well-informed and well organised, intelligent, sensitive, and readable.[2] But while Skeffington tries always to be accurate and fair, he is uncritical alike of his subject and his sources. The book is on a small scale, precise dates are few, and there are neither references nor bibliography. Skeffington's approach is not that of the historian but of the disciple he avows himself to be. It is not so much the Davitt of history that he presents as a Davitt conceived in accordance with his own fervent convictions—socialist and nationalist, pacifist, agnostic and anti-clerical. His book is a primary source of Davitt mythology, but at the same time it conveys a true sense of the strength and nobility of Davitt's character. One quality above all, moral courage, Skeffington shared with Davitt in full measure.[3]

The only other general work on Davitt deals with his career to 1891 in parallel with Parnell's. M. M. O'Hara's *Chief and tribune: Parnell and Davitt*, published in 1919,[4] is also based on printed sources. Though

[1] *Michael Davitt: revolutionary, agitator, and labour leader* (London: T. Fisher Unwin).

[2] A reprint, with an admirable introduction by F. S. L. Lyons, was published in 1967 (London: MacGibbon and Kee).

[3] Skeffington also wrote the article on Davitt in the *D.N.B., 1901–11* (1912). This is better history than his book.

[4] Dublin and London: Maunsel and Co.

not a work of scholarship it is written in an analytical and critical spirit. It augments Skeffington's narrative at some points, and while it is often inaccurate and reproduces myths it offers valuable new insights.

Apart from these two books, and articles on Davitt's life in Haslingden that have appeared in Lancashire newspapers, contributions to his biography are represented mainly by special studies of my own, published from 1942 onwards. But being so much a part of the general history of Ireland, Davitt figures prominently in the historiography of the period 1878–82; and while the bulk of what is thus written about him is derivative, a great deal has been done to establish and explain the political, social, and economic context in which he lived.

The general background is presented in two masterly syntheses, fully abreast of recent scholarship—F. S. L. Lyons's *Ireland since the famine* (1971) and L. M. Cullen's *An economic history of Ireland since 1660* (1972). Among special studies N. D. Palmer's pioneer book, *The Irish Land League crisis* (1940) has helped to lay a solid foundation for the years 1879-81. Conor Cruise O'Brien has elucidated the politics of the Parnell decade in relation to social forces in his *Parnell and his party, 1880–90* (1957). The late David Thornley treated the home rule movement under Butt's leadership on similar lines in his *Isaac Butt and home rule* (1964). B. L. Solow's *The land question and the Irish economy, 1870–1903* (1971), E. D. Steele's *Irish land and British politics . . . 1865–1870* (1974), J. S. Donnelly's *The land and the people of nineteenth-century Cork* (1975), and W. E. Vaughan's as yet unpublished 'Landlord and tenant relations in Ireland . . ., 1850–78' (Ph.D. thesis, University of Dublin, 1973) have opened a new era in the investigation of the land question. J. J. Lee's *The modernisation of Irish society, 1848–1918* (1973), nominally a short general history, is in large part a series of original and challenging essays on land and politics between 1848 and 1882. Two authoritative biographies by F. S. L. Lyons, *John Dillon* (1968) and *Charles Stewart Parnell* (1977), supply collateral information and illumination on Davitt. R. F. Foster's *Charles Stewart Parnell: the man and his family* (1976) includes comprehensive chapters on Fanny Parnell and on Anna Parnell and the Ladies' Land League. The behaviour of the catholic clergy towards the land war is methodically expounded by C. J. Woods in 'The catholic clergy and Irish politics, 1879–92' (Ph.D. thesis, University of Nottingham, 1968). Attitudes and reactions of the catholic bishops are displayed by Emmet Larkin in *The Roman Catholic Church and the creation of the modern Irish state, 1878–1886* (1975); and they are exemplified in a special case by Mark Tierney's *Croke of Cashel* (1976). The American dimension of the new departure and the politics of the land war has been interpreted with wit and learning by T. N. Brown in *Irish-American nationalism* (1966).

I had the benefit, prior to its publication, of Sam Clark's sociological analysis and elucidation of the land war (though my own approach is quite different) in his *Social origins of the Irish land war: rural social structure and collective action in nineteenth-century Ireland* (Princeton, 1979). Paul Bew's valuable work, *Land and the national question in Ireland* (1978), appeared too late (1979) for me to use.

All the material used, and also material for further study, are listed in the bibliography.

T. W. Moody
25 Trinity College
Dublin

December 1979

ACKNOWLEDGEMENTS

I have pleasure in acknowledging my indebtedness to many individuals and institutions for the help they have given me in my work for this book over many years. Special thanks are due to the Library of Trinity College, Dublin, and to W. E. Mackey, William O'Sullivan, and Margaret Chubb; to the National Library of Ireland, and to the late R. J. Hayes, to Patrick Henchy, and Alf MacLochlainn; to the State Paper Office of Ireland, and to Breandán MacGiolla Choille; to the Public Record Office of England, the Home Office, and H. G. Pearson; to the Free Library of Philadelphia; to a long line of research students and members of my former seminar on modern Irish history, and particularly those who have worked for me as research assistants—W. E. Vaughan, Brian M. Walker, R. F. Foster, C. J. Woods, Jacqueline Hill, and Elizabeth Malcolm; to Mary Davies for her expert care in drawing the maps; to Mary Griffiths for her painstaking work on the statistical tables and other material; to Peggy Morgan for her skill and patience in typing the greater part of the book; to J. S. Donnelly, Richard Hawkins, Dáithi Kelly, W. J. Lowe, Leon Ó Broin, Patrick O'Meara, and Rev. William O'Neill. On problems of agriculture, landlord-tenant relations, and statistical data I have received most generous cooperation from W. E. Vaughan.

My attention was first drawn to the Davitt papers many years ago by my friend, Robin Dudley Edwards.

I am grateful to the late Eileen Davitt and to her brothers, Judge Cahir and Dr Robert Emmet Davitt, for their confidence, understanding, and patience. They have never in any way sought to influence my treatment of their father's life and they have always been ready to answer my inquiries. For material relating to Davitt's connection with Lancashire I am much indebted to John Dunleavy, of Haslingden. I gained insight into the Davitt diaspora in America from the late Michael Davitt Crowley and his sister, the late Mary Ellen Crowley, of Scranton, Pennsylvania, nephew and niece of Michael Davitt, and from his grand-niece, Kathleen Burns, of New York, who put her abundant and scholarly knowledge of her family history at my disposal.

I owe a debt of gratitude to the Leverhulme Research Foundation, whose Fellowship I enjoyed in 1964–6; to the Institute for Advanced Study, Princeton, where, in 1965, I spent an invigorating interval of study-leave after thirty-two years of continuous teaching; to the Grace Lawless Lee fund of Trinity College, Dublin, for a grant in aid of my research, and to Trinity itself for innumerable blessings.

To the provost of Trinity College I am very specially indebted. As undergraduate, research student, colleague, head of the house, and constant friend, Leland Lyons has given me inspiration, encouragement, and help, tangible and intangible, over half a lifetime, to which I am happy to pay this affectionate tribute.

To my wife, who has borne with my Davitt preoccupation for so long, and without whose understanding and active cooperation the book could not have been brought to completion, no praise from me could be too high.

I

Childhood and youth, 1846–65

THE village of Straide has outwardly changed little since Michael Davitt[1] was born there on 25 March 1846.[2] The name (Irish *sraid*, Latin *stratum*) means 'street', and like many another Irish village Straide is merely one broad street, thinly lined with houses. It has a small catholic church, built early in the present century, but the only historic building is the nearby church of a ruined friary, founded for the Franciscans by Jordan de Exeter in the early thirteenth century and transferred to the Dominicans about 1252.[3] The tomb of the founder, in the chancel, is a notable example of its kind, being set in a niche canopied with richly flamboyant tracery.[4] Otherwise it is as the earliest home of Michael Davitt that Straide has earned a place in history. It stands in a flat, featureless landscape, set in the great undulating plain that sprawls through the centre of Connacht from Killala Bay on the north to Galway Bay on the south and spills out to the west coast at Clew Bay. The blue cone of Nephin can be seen far away to the north-west, but otherwise there is nothing visible from Straide to hint of the mountain grandeur of west Connacht. The village lies in the town-land of Straide in the parish of Straide or Templemore, which is part of the barony of Gallen, itself part of the six baronies making up the county of Mayo.[5]

[1] There is almost no contemporary material among Davitt's papers before 1870. This chapter is therefore based largely on (a) retrospective information supplied by Davitt himself, mainly his evidence before the penal servitude commission of 1878, his 'Jottings in solitary' (DA/1, pp 1-20, written in Portland prison on 20 Sept. 81), his evidence before the *Times*-Parnell commission (1889), and three chapters (to 1857) of an incomplete autobiography (DA/2, written in 1894); (b) census returns and other public records; (c) contemporary newspapers; (d) D. B. Cashman's *Life of Michael Davitt* [1882], pp 16-20; (e) recollections by contemporaries. Davitt's dating is often imprecise and inconsistent.

[2] The register of the R.C. parish of Straide for the period has not survived. Davitt's references in his papers (1870-1906) to the year of his birth show a variation of three years, 1846-8, but the balance of his evidence is decisively in favour of 1846, and this date is confirmed by the evidence of the census returns of 1851 and 1861 for Haslingden, Lancs. (see below, p. 5). 1846 is the date finally sanctioned by Davitt (*Who was who, 1897-1916*, p. 185).

[3] Aubrey Gwynn and R. Neville Hadcock, *Medieval religious houses: Ireland* (1970), pp 220, 230, 241, 259.

[4] H. G. Leask, *Irish churches and monastic buildings*, iii (1960), pp 167-8, plate XXVI a.

[5] See maps I-II.

Mayo ('God help us' the western Irish commonly add in speaking of it) forms the northwest quarter of the province of Connacht; it still contains in its vast peat bogs, its gaunt bare mountains, and its lonely peninsulas and islands some of the wildest, most remote, and most barren country in Ireland. Nearly half the county was bog and mountain or under water. The great bulk of the population was located along a coastal fringe and in the lowlands south of Killala Bay and east of Clew Bay, the rest of the interior being largely uninhabited.[1] In 1871, 28 per cent of this population, outside the few towns, lived in housing of the worst type—one-roomed cabins, rated as class IV by the census commissioners. Only one other county, Kerry, had a higher percentage of class IV housing. Of the profitable land more than two-thirds was pasture, and less than a third under crops, mainly potatoes, oats, and turnips. The general poverty of Mayo was reflected in the average valuation of its agricultural holdings—£9 in 1871, the lowest for any county in Ireland.[2] The average size of holdings in 1871 (38 acres) was above the average for Connacht (36 acres) and not much below the national average (41 acres), but these figures conceal more than they reveal. For in this, the poorest county in Ireland, the distribution of land between holdings of various sizes was egregiously uneven. Eighty-six per cent of the tenants occupied holdings of not more than 30 acres, and this multitude of small and poor tenants were crowded on 35 per cent of the total acreage of all holdings. On the other hand 14 per cent of the tenants, with holdings of over 30 acres, occupied 65 per cent of the total acreage of all holdings. On the upper levels the contrast was still more extreme: tenants with holdings of over 100 acres, representing 3.37 per cent of all tenants, occupied 46 per cent of the total acreage. This total included some hundreds of large grazing farms.

The distribution of population was no less uneven. Population density for the county as a whole was low—124 persons to the square mile in 1851, 115 in 1881—but for holdings of 30 acres and below, in 1881, it was 284, while on those above 30 acres it was 102. The general poverty of Mayo was such that most of it was scheduled as 'congested' by the congested districts board, the special administration set up in 1891 to promote the welfare of the impoverished regions of the west; the criterion of a congested district was an electoral division in which the valuation per head of population was less than £1 10*s*.

[1] T. W. Freeman, *Ireland, a general and regional geography* (4th ed., revised, 1972), pp 414–20 and map (a) in folder II.

[2] The counties ranking next to Mayo according to the valuations of their agricultural holdings were Donegal and Leitrim (£10), Galway (£13), Cavan and Sligo (£14).

Extreme pressure of population on natural resources and extreme dependence on the potato for survival explain why Mayo suffered a greater human loss (29 per cent) during the famine decade (1841-51) than any other county except Roscommon (32 per cent). But its percentage loss during the next three decades (11 per cent)[1] was much smaller than the national average (21 per cent),[2] and this was mainly because its emigration rate was relatively low—well below the national average per 1000 of the population in each decade.[3] That so many poverty-ridden tenants were able to survive in Mayo was due to another distinctive feature of its economy: of all Irish counties Mayo supplied by far the largest number of seasonal migrants for harvest work in England and Scotland. From being one-fifth of the national total in 1841 they amounted to about one half in 1880 (10,198 out of 22,900). Of these 10,198 migrants, about 44 per cent were farmers, of whom 90 per cent had holdings of 5 acres and above. All these migrants earned an essential part of their living in Britain and could not otherwise pay their rents.[4]

Mayo was a county of large estates and absentee landlords. Nearly half of it was owned by twenty landlords with above 10,000 acres each, most of whom resided in England. Nine of these, headed by Viscount Dillon, the marquis of Sligo, the earl of Lucan, and Sir Roger Palmer, together drew an income of £100,000 from the county in 1880, and spent under one-tenth of it on improvements. Lord Lucan, lord lieutenant of the county, who paid only occasional visits to his mansion at Castlebar, endeavoured to maintain a strict authoritarian regime on his estate (61,000 acres), from which he had evicted pauperised tenants in large numbers during and after the great famine. He earned fame outside Ireland as commander of the cavalry at Balaclava (25 October 1854), but was known locally as the 'old exterminator'. The Dillon estate (83,700 acres in Mayo, 5,400 in Roscommon) was for forty years managed benevolently by an agent, Charles Strickland, who resided in part of the otherwise unoccupied family mansion, Loughglynn House, Castlerea, County Roscommon. He kept rents low, recognised tenant right, and avoided evictions. Yet

[1] 275,000 in 1851, 245,000 in 1881.

[2] 6,552,000 in 1851, 5,175,000 in 1881.

[3] Emigrants per 1000 of the population of Mayo:—1851-60: 106; 1861-70: 110; 1871-80: 102; of Ireland: 1851-60: 178; 1861-70: 147; 1871-80: 115.

[4] *Census of Ireland, 1851-1881*; *Agricultural statistics, Ireland, 1871* [C762], H.C. 1873, lxix; *Agricultural statistics, Ireland, 1880: report and tables relating to migratory agricultural labourers* [C2809], H.C. 1881, xciii, 807-24; *Royal commission on congestion in Ireland, appendix to the ninth report: minutes of evidence (taken in Co. Mayo, 21 August-3 September 1907)* [Cd 3845], H.C. 1908, xli, 487-845; W. E. Vaughan and A. J. Fitzpatrick, *Irish historical statistics, population 1821-1971* (1978).

three-quarters of the tenants annually migrated to England to earn their rent. Lord Sligo had a reputation similar to Lord Lucan's, and seldom visited his estate (115,000 acres) or resided at Westport House, his splendid Georgian mansion. Among other large landowners of Mayo, Charles Howe Knox (24,400 acres) of Ballinrobe and Sir Robert Lynch Blosse (17,600 acres) were resident, and considerate of their tenants.[1]

The parish of Straide lies near the centre of the county. It is traversed by the highroad from Ballina, the chief town of north Mayo, to Westport, on Clew Bay; and the village of Straide is about half way between the two. The nearest towns are Foxford, about five miles north on the road to Ballina, Bellavary, about ten miles south, Swinford, about ten miles east, and Castlebar, the county town of Mayo, about ten miles on the road to Westport. The distance by road from Dublin is about 150 miles. Straide parish is spread about the east and south of Lough Conn, where the plain is composed of carboniferous limestone covered by glacial deposits in the form of small rounded hills or drumlins. There is good pasture and arable on their slopes, with bogs and marshes on the level ground and in the hollows. Much of the area is rough grazing, and tillage accounts for only about one-tenth of the improved land.[2] Despite a population loss of 44 per cent during the famine decade, the population density of the parish was high for Mayo (171 to the square mile in 1851, 172 in 1881). The population of Straide townland suffered a loss of 26 per cent in the same decade—from 321 in 1841 to 236 in 1851. It rose slightly during the next decade—to 253 in 1861—but plunged to 127 by 1871 and fell to 100 in 1881. The valuation of the townland was the highest in the parish, but averaged only £1 9*s*. per head in 1851 and £1 7*s*. in 1861. With the fall in population during the next two decades the valuation per head rose to £2 14*s*. in 1871 and to £3 9*s*. in 1881. This explains why the townland was not one of the areas in the county scheduled as 'congested' in 1891. The fall in population was paralleled by a fall in the number of houses: from 60 in 1841 to 45 in 1851, to 25 in 1871, and to 21 in 1881.[3] The houses that disappeared from Straide after 1841 included the birthplace of Michael Davitt.

[1] *Return of owners of land . . . in the several counties . . . in Ireland . . .* [C1492], H.C. 1876, lxxx, pp 375-81; *Thom 1878*, pp 739-40; B. H. Becker, *Disturbed Ireland* (1881), pp 36-48; Finlay Dun, *Landlords and tenants in Ireland* (1881), pp 201-2, 214, 222-34, 252-5; J. H. Tuke, *Irish distress and its remedies* (1880), pp 53, 86-7; G. J. Shaw-Lefevre, *Incidents of coercion: a journal of visits to Ireland in 1882 and 1888* (1888). For Lord Lucan see Cecil Woodham-Smith, *The reason why* (1953).

[2] Freeman, *Ireland*, pp 417-18.

[3] *Census of Ireland, 1851-1881; Royal commission on congestion in Ireland, appendix to the ninth report* [Cd 3845], H.C. 1908, xli, 758-60.

Michael Davitt was the second child of Martin Davitt and his wife Catherine. Both parents were of local, peasant stock, but otherwise nothing is known of their ancestry. Martin was born about 1814, probably in Straide parish. Catherine's maiden name was Kielty, and she came from the neighbouring parish of Turlough, where she was born about 1820,[1] in the village of that name near the round tower that stands on the road between Castlebar and Bellavary and is still one of the best-preserved in Ireland. Davitts were rooted in this part of Mayo, and Catherine herself was a Davitt on her mother's side.[2] The Davitts were probably descended from the Gaelic family of MacDevitt of Inishowen, in County Donegal, whose eponymous ancestor was a David O'Doherty who died in 1208. A branch of the MacDevitts had migrated to Mayo in the seventeenth century. But it is also possible that the Davitts were not of Gaelic but of Anglo-Norman stock and that their name was derived from a David Burke.[3] Whatever their origin, the society to which these Davitts belonged was as Gaelic—Michael would have said as Celtic—as it could be. The popular speech of the western half of Ireland at this time was still Irish, and Martin and Catherine Davitt used Irish as their native tongue.[4] This was typical of the environment in which Michael's life began.

Martin Davitt had the reputation of being a 'scholar', which meant that he had received a good primary education, probably from a hedge schoolmaster. He was bi-lingual, and besides being an accomplished *seanchai*, or Irish storyteller, he read books in English, especially on Irish and American history. Mild, patient, and kind-hearted, he had tenacity and great powers of endurance, and did not lack courage or resource. As a young man, in the thirties of the century, he had been all too prominent in one of those agrarian secret societies that were

[1] The birth dating derived from the following sources is shown in brackets: Census returns, township of Haslingden, Lancs., 1851, in P.R.O., H.O. 107/2250/477/4a, f. 47 (Martin 1808-9, Catherine 1815-16); Census returns, Haslingden, 1861, in P.R.O., R.G. 9/3061/477/4B, f.21^{v} (Martin 1814-15, Catherine 1820-21); passenger list of R.M.S. *Cuba,* Captain E. R. Moodie master, 13 Apr. 1870 (Washington D.C., National Archives, Passenger arrival lists, Port of New York) (Martin 1819-20, Catherine 1824-5); *Manayunk Sentinel*, 22 July 80 (Catherine 1820-21); Catherine's gravestone, Manayunk (1819-20). From this conflicting evidence 1820 emerges as the probable date of Catherine's birth, and of the three possible dates for Martin's—1808-9, 1814-15, 1819-20—the mean is to be preferred: family tradition makes him older than his wife when they married, and he is not likely to have lived longer than she.

[2] DA/1, pp 1-2; DN/7, 16, 17 July 80.

[3] Edward MacLysaght, *More Irish families* (1960), pp 79-80. Davitt cherished the belief that he was descended from the MacDevitts of Inishowen (DA/1, p. 2). But at Derry, in January 1890, he was told by a Mr Devitt that he was not a Celt but a Norman, his name being derived from a David Burke. 'This', Davitt wrote, 'would be a devil of a come-down if true' (DN/24, 24 Jan. 90).

[4] DA/1, pp 1-3.

the traditional response of the more high-spirited among the Irish peasantry to the insecurity and oppressiveness of the land system. Threatened with prosecution, he had fled to England, where Connachtmen were accustomed to go in search of seasonal employment, and he often recalled being in London at the time of Queen Victoria's coronation (1837). Returning to Mayo he appears to have lived more circumspectly. He married Catherine about 1840,[1] and for the next few years, though only a yearly tenant of a few acres, was able to provide a tolerable living for his wife and their growing family.[2] Their first child, Mary, was born in 1841.[3] Michael, born five years later, was followed by Anne in 1848 and Sabina in 1850.[4]

Catherine Davitt, a woman of strong character and intelligence, was the dominant partner. Without formal education, she could neither read nor write, and was never entirely at ease in speaking English. But she spoke Irish with fluency and power, and a delight in speaking it that never left her, though half her life was to be spent in exile. Her conversational style was vigorous and colourful, and she loved to clinch an argument or enforce a command with an Irish proverb. She had a rich imagination, quick sympathy, and an excellent memory. She was shrewd and humorous, strong-willed and stout-hearted, passionate and proud; and she had the same faculty of patient endurance as her husband. Tall and well-proportioned, with jet-black hair, large, deep-set, alert eyes, and firm mouth, she was distinguished-looking rather than handsome.[5] Physically she seems to have been more robust than her husband. Michael resembled her in his physical characteristics—his fine figure, strong features, and dark colouring—and in his passionate and imaginative nature, but his love of book-learning and the more reflective and subtle qualities of his mind he seems to have inherited from his father. From both parents he learnt fortitude, a high sense of duty, and the unstudied piety of the Irish catholic world to which they belonged.

There is no record of Martin Davitt's holding in Straide—of its precise location, its area, the name of the landlord, the rent, or the nature of the tenancy. But some authentic information can be extracted from a rental of 1854 relating to a sale in the encumbered estates court: this shows that the whole townland was then part of the estate of John Knox, of Castlerea, Killala, County Mayo, and

[1] The date is inferred from that of the birth of their first child; see note 3.

[2] DA/1, pp 1-3; DA/2, pp 7-8; *Fall*, p. 222.

[3] Census returns, township of Haslingden, Lancs., 1851, in P.R.O., H.O. 107/2250/477/4a, f. 47; census returns, Haslingden, 1861, in P.R.O., R.G. 9/3061/477/4B, f. 21^{v}; certificate of marriage of Neil Padden and Mary Davitt, 16 May 63, in Haslingden Register Office.

[4] Census returns, as above.

[5] DA/1, pp 2-3; DA/2, pp 1-2.

others, and was held under a lease dated 22 February 1741 for 999 years. The tenants nearly all held from year to year and the holdings were all very small. Three holdings together occupied an area of about 21 statute acres adjoining the village and including the site traditionally regarded as that of Michael Davitt's birthplace.[1] Of these holdings one was occupied by John Davitt (spelt Devitt) and two by Michael McDonnell, in succession severally to Henry Davitt and J. McDonnell. Both were yearly tenants, and their tenancies were terminable every 1 May. John Davitt's rent was £4 4*s*. 6*d*; Michael McDonnell's was £4 4*s*. 6*d*. for Henry Davitt's former holding and £8 9*s*. for J. McDonnell's. No other Davitts appear in the rental.[2]

The John Davitt named in the rental was Martin Davitt's brother, and it is almost certain that Henry Davitt was another brother. Both recur later in the Davitt story, but whereas John remained at Straide and is buried there, Henry emigrated.[3] It is highly probable that Martin Davitt once occupied the holding acquired by J. McDonnell, which Michael McDonnell in turn acquired in addition to Henry Davitt's holding. This would mean that Martin, John, and Henry Davitt once occupied adjoining farms, which is inherently probable. If they did, the 21 acres together held by John Davitt and Michael McDonnell in 1854 may represent the former holding of the father of the three Davitt brothers. Whatever the precise explanation, it can hardly be doubted that Martin Davitt's holding lay in this parcel of 21 acres. Two years later, the valuation lists for the parish show that this land, together with other parts of the Knox estate, had been bought by Henry Joynt. John Davitt and Michael McDonnell were still tenants. A Bridget Davitt also held a fraction of an acre in Straide townland, but otherwise there were no Davitts among the occupiers in Straide parish. In the neighbouring parish of Turlough, from which Catherine Davitt came, four Davitts are listed–Patrick, George, and two named Michael. Patrick held about 7 acres, Michael about 5, while the second Michael and George each had only a cottage.[4]

That Michael was born a peasant's son in 1846, at the height of the great famine, is profoundly significant; for, in cooperation with Parnell, it was to be his greatest achievement to arouse the sense of solidarity, inspire the will to resist disaster, and provide the leadership that the Irish peasantry so conspicuously lacked during the famine

[1] See map III.

[2] *Incumbered estates court rentals, 1850–85* ('O'Brien rentals'), vol. 29, June 54, p. 22, in P.R.O.I., ID 23 27.

[3] See below, p. 169.

[4] *General valuation of rateable property in Ireland, county of Mayo, union of Castlebar* (1857), parish of Turlough (pp 102–25), parish of Templemore (pp 144–53).

years. The man who was to be his partner in this revolution, Charles Stewart Parnell, was born only three months later in a very different setting: the son of an amiable country gentleman, his birthplace was Avondale House, a comfortable medium-sized mansion standing in one of the loveliest wooded estates of County Wicklow. But perhaps the contrast between the parents of Davitt and of Parnell is more significant than the contrast in their family circumstances. Parnell's mother, like Davitt's, was the dominant partner, and as his father died when he was only thirteen he grew up very much under his mother's influence. An American of Irish descent she was an imperious, headstrong, selfish, and eccentric woman, singularly unfit for the responsibilities of her large family. In terms of human values, Davitt was more fortunate in his parents than Parnell and had a better upbringing.

The Davitts survived the great famine, not without distress and privation. For a time Martin Davitt was able to mitigate the loss of his potato crop by obtaining an appointment as overseer of roads under a local relief scheme. Emerging from the famine impoverished and in arrears of rent, he went to England in the summer of 1849[1] as a 'harvester', or migratory labourer. The money he brought home did not, however, suffice to meet both the current rent and the accumulated arrears which his landlord demanded. He was served with an ejectment notice. A temporary settlement was then arranged which left him in possession for another year, but in 1850[1] (probably September), having failed to clear off his arrears, he was evicted. In conformity with an established pattern, the eviction involved the pulling down and burning of the Davitts' cottage by the landlord's agents. The incident was typical of a general movement among landlords immediately after the great famine, and especially in Munster and Connacht, to clear their estates of pauperised small tenants.[2] In terms of the utilitarian economics then in vogue the landlords were justified in thus using their legal powers to improve their incomes; to their victims such as the Davitts they were robbers and home-destroyers, and the law that sanctioned their 'hellish work' was self-condemned.[3] The eviction became permanently stamped on Davitt's consciousness:

I was then but four and a half year's old, yet I have a distinct remembrance (doubtless strengthened by the frequent narration of the event by my parents in

[1] Davitt assigns these events to 1850 and 1851 respectively (DA/1, p. 4), but I have adjusted his dating in accordance with the incontrovertible evidence of the 1851 census returns that the Davitts were in Haslingden in March 1851; see below, p. 11. *Who's who* gives 1852 as the date of the eviction (*Who was who, 1897–1916*, p. 185), and so does *Fall*, p. 222.

[2] A. M. Sullivan, *New Ireland* (15th ed. [1882]), ch. XI; *Fall*, pp. 67–8; J. H. Whyte, *The independent Irish party, 1850–9* (1958), pp 4–5; below, appendix D.

[3] DA/1, pp 3–5; *S.C.P.*, ix, 352, x, 557; *Defence*, p. 202; *Fall*, p. 222.

after years) of that morning's scene: the remnant of our household furniture flung about the road; the roof of the house falling in and the thatch taking fire; my mother and father looking on with four young children, the youngest only two months old, adding their cries to the other pangs which must have agitated their souls at the sight of their burning homestead'.[1]

Homeless and nearly destitute, Martin and Catherine Davitt resigned themselves to the final humiliation of seeking admission to the local workhouse, at Swinford. But it turned out that a workhouse regulation required male children above three years of age to be separated from their mothers; on hearing of this Catherine seized her four-and-a-half year old son in her arms, and declaring that she would rather die by the roadside than submit to such a condition marched her family out of the workhouse where they had stayed only one hour.[2] To have been in a workhouse was looked upon by self-respecting Irish families as such a badge of shame that Martin Davitt ever afterwards avoided all reference to the Swinford incident in reminiscences of his eviction. But his son took a different view: 'I know of nothing', he wrote in Portland prison in 1881, 'which I should be ashamed to acknowledge in connection with my life save an action that would leave behind it a stain of moral obloquy upon my character'.[3] In this he followed the example of his mother, who, in recalling her family's early struggles, referred frankly to their having entered Swinford workhouse; and, wrote Michael, 'I love truth and the memory of *her* action . . . on that occasion too much to conceal the fact of our having once reached the zero of adversity'.[4]

At this point the fortunes of the Davitts took a turn for the better. Martin and Catherine decided to join the emigrant stream that had already carried off many thousands of Mayo people to Lancashire and Yorkshire by way of Dublin and Liverpool. They fell in with an emigrating family from near Straide, who were making the journey to Dublin with the help of a horse and cart. The two families joined forces, and Martin contracted for seats in the cart for Catherine and her children in return for a promise to pay an agreed sum when he should have found a job in England. This amicable arrangement worked well enough. 'Among the few incidents of my early childhood in

[1] DA/1, p. 4.

[2] DA/1, pp 5-7; *S.C.P.*, ix, 352, x, 557; *Defence*, p. 202.

[3] DA/1, p. 7.

[4] Ibid. A hagiographical and inaccurate sketch of Davitt's early life, written by his youngest sister, Sabina, after his death (May 1906) is the source of a story that the evicted family was given temporary housing by the parish priest, Fr John McHugh, in his new barn, and that the mother and children lived there for eighteen months while the father was in England looking for work (M.M. O'Hara, *Chief and tribune: Parnell and Davitt* (1919), p. 19; DP/T). The story finds no support in Davitt's own account of the eviction and its sequel, written in 1881. One wonders what John Davitt was doing when his brother was evicted.

Ireland', Davitt recalled in 1881, 'riding in that particular cart is about the one I remember best'.

It was as innocent of springs as the watch which Brian O'Lynn 'fashioned out square' from a turnip; and as for the animal which drew it, he manifested his patriotic displeasure at facing a journey to England by breaking the traces a half dozen times ere reaching Dublin and bolting towards pastures green, in preference to dragging a heavy load towards pastures new. He one day upset the whole of us in the middle of the highway and made such a run for 'Ireland' as took his owner and my father near the whole of that day to catch him again.[1]

However they eventually reached Dublin, and landed at Liverpool on 1 November 1850.[2]

Their destination was the small textile town of Haslingden, in east Lancashire, about seventeen miles north of Manchester.[3] It was pleasantly situated on the slopes of Cribden Hill which separates it from the valley of the River Irwell, at the edge of the rugged mountain region of Rossendale Forest—a setting incomparably more impressive than the surroundings of Straide. The choice of Haslingden was due to the fact that former neighbours of the Davitts had found work in it and had reported favourably on the prospects for Irish immigrants.[4] Haslingden's principal industries were cotton and woollen manufactures and stone-quarrying, the former giving employment to women as well as men. Of its population of 9,000 in 1851, about 430 were Irish-born, and nearly all of these clustered thickly in particular streets in the poorer and more insanitary parts of the town. While most of them were employed in cotton mills and quarries, a substantial number earned their living as cap-makers, milliners, rush-chair bottomers, farm labourers, and hawkers. The position of Haslingden at the centre of a ring of larger towns—Blackburn, Burnley, Rochdale, Bury, and Bolton—within a radius of ten miles favoured the hawker's trade, which by 1851 was sufficiently developed for the census enumerator to classify the goods it dealt in as fruit, salt, hardware, caps, and 'smallware'. The Haslingden hawkers had mostly been Scots; now they were as distinctively Irish, and hawking was the occupation into which the latest impoverished arrivals from Ireland were apt to move.[5]

After staying a few days with friends in Liverpool, the Davitts

[1] DA/1, pp 8-9.

[2] Ibid., p. 9. The year given in the MS is 1851, but this is untenable; see above, p. 8, and below, p. 11.

[3] See map IV.

[4] DA/1, pp 7-8; DA/2, pp 3-4.

[5] Census returns, township of Haslingden, Lancs., 1851, in P.R.O., H.O. 107/2250/477/4a; *Slator's Commercial Directory and Topography of Lancashire* (1856), pp 132-6; *Victoria history of the county of Lancaster*, ii (1908), pp 337, 454, vi (1911), pp 427-33; Christopher Aspin, *Haslingden, 1800-1900: a history* (1962), p. 68; information kindly supplied by Mr John Dunleavy, of Haslingden.

covered the last stage of their journey, some fifty miles, on foot, scowled at by the local people who looked on the immigrant Irish as intruders, obnoxious alike on economic, religious, and political grounds. Arrived in Haslingden (November 1850), Martin quickly found temporary lodging for his family in the house of an acquaintance. From this, however, they were summarily expelled after two days, on the discovery that Michael had measles. Snow was falling when they were thus again evicted, and Michael's career might have ended under the improvised tent that his father rigged up against a sheltering wall. But word of their plight had gone round, and a good Samaritan appeared in the person of James Bonner, a tin-plate worker from County Armagh, who took the sick child in his arms and warmly invited the Davitts to share his home. He had a wife (a hardware-hawker) and four children ranging in age from five to three,[1] but his humanity overbore any fears of infection he may have had. Under his hospitable roof Michael recovered from his illness.[2]

On 30 March 1851, the Davitts were recorded in the census returns for Haslingden as lodgers in the house of Owen Eagan in Wilkinson Street[3]—a typical working-class street of small, two-storey, terrace houses, teeming with people mostly Irish. Martin Davitt and his wife described themselves as fruit-hawkers. Owen Eagan was a cap-hawker, his wife a cap-maker, and of their six children four were cotton-mill workers. There were altogether eight Eagans, six Davitts, and one visitor, John McGlaine, in the house, all fifteen Irish-born.[4] They were living under conditions of almost maximum congestion; only one other house in Wilkinson Street had so many occupants—that of a widow, Mary Higgins, with three young sons and eleven lodgers, all Irish-born.[5]

The Davitts did not remain long in Wilkinson Street. Martin and Catherine soon succeeded in earning enough to rent a house of their own. It was one of an isolated row of ten small houses at a place called Rock Hall, high up on the north-east edge of Haslingden, where the

[1] Census returns, Haslingden, 1851, as above, f. 38.

[2] DA/1, pp 9-12; DA/2, pp 4-6.

[3] See plate I.

[4] Census returns, Haslingden, 1851, as above, f. 47. This is the earliest contemporary reference to Michael Davitt and his family. It establishes that they were in Haslingden at least nine months before the day (Nov. 51) indicated by Davitt himself (DA/1, pp 9-10, and above, pp 8, 10). 1852 is the date hitherto generally accepted (e.g. *Haslingden Guardian*, 1 June 1906). A memorial stone in Wilkinson Street, Haslingden which claims to mark 'the site of the home of Michael Davitt', says that he resided in Haslingden 'from 1853'. This is wide of the mark. The Davitts lived in Haslingden from November 1850 to March 1870 and during most of that time their home was at Rock Hall. They lived in Wilkinson Street for a short time after their arrival in Haslingden and again during their last three years there.

[5] Census returns, Haslingden, 1851, as above, f. 42.

town ended (and still ends) on a green hillside against which they crouched.[1] They were two-storey labourers' houses, solidly built of local stone, and all were occupied by families from the west of Ireland—Gallaghers, Kellys, McHales, Maddens, Morans, Timlins. In nearly all of them there were lodgers as well as the householder and his family: the census of 1861 shows that the Davitts then had four lodgers, three of them mason's labourers and one a millworker.[2] The Davitts' home thus had ten occupants, which was above the average for Rock Hall, with its total population of about 90 in 1861.[3] Here Michael's only brother, James, was born on 30 June 1853. He was the last of Catherine Davitt's children, and he did not survive infancy: all that is known of him is that he died at Rock Hall on 12 March 1855, after three days in convulsions without medical attention.[4]

At Rock Hall the Davitts became part of a miniature Irish colony, known locally as 'little Ireland', knit together not only by kinship in language, religion, and traditions, but also by the necessity of mutual protection. Among the English working classes in the industrial towns and villages of the north, animosity towards the Irish newcomers was widespread. It was the outcome of fear that they would reduce the price of labour to starvation point, of religious prejudice as catholic churches sprang up wherever the Irish settled in numbers, and of political prejudice against them as nationalists. These very conditions impelled the Irish to live together in small self-conscious groups, which intensified English hostility. Popular assaults on Irish quarters in the north of England were a common occurrence in the fifties, and Rock Hall was prepared at all times to defend itself. It was well situated for defence, as the enemy could not approach unobserved; and whenever the alarm was sounded, as on a Saturday night when quarrymen from a neighbouring village were in the habit of going into Haslingden for a drink and a bout of Irish-baiting, the men from the ten houses were ready to give a good account of themselves with picks and shovels and other implements of their trade. In Michael's enthusiastic recollection the assailants were always repulsed on these occasions. Such communal conflict was paralleled by personal encounters between English and Irish in mills, factories and on the streets, and young Michael soon earned a reputation for being a tough opponent.[5]

By 1853 Martin Davitt had graduated from hawker to farm labourer and was earning fifteen shillings a week. His wife, with the baby James

[1] DA/1, pp 11-12; DA/2, pp 5, 11.

[2] Census returns, Haslingden, 1861, in P.R.O. R.G. 9/3061/477/4B, f. 21^{v}.

[3] Ibid., ff 21-2^{v}.

[4] Records of the birth and death of James Davitt (described as Devitt), in Haslingden Register Office.

[5] DA/1, pp 12-13; DA/2, pp 5-6.

to look after, had ceased to be a hawker, but their eldest child, Mary, aged twelve, was now employed in a cotton-mill. Michael followed her example in the spring of 1855, at the age of nine.[1] In 1857 his mother resumed her former occupation as a hawker, possibly because Michael, as the result of an accident, was no longer a wage earner.[2] By 1861 Anne and Sabina (aged thirteen and eleven respectively) had also become cotton operatives. Their father was now a mason's labourer.[3] There is some indication that he was unable to stick at any one job for long, and that his health was uncertain; probably the two things were connected. The Davitts had thus succeeded in reestablishing themselves. Their life was hard and infinitely laborious; they had few comforts and little privacy; and it is some measure of their standard of living that, though Martin Davitt made a hobby of helping his neighbours to read and write, his two elder daughters grew up illiterate. But the family income was rising; and, poor though they still were, the Davitts enjoyed at Rock Hall a rich community life.

Martin and Catherine Davitt and their neighbours, Shemus and Molly Madden,[4] were leading figures in this 'little Ireland' society, as Michael recalled it years afterwards. Martin was the general letter-writer for most of the Irish in Haslingden, and after a hard day's work would spend hours of his time in this way. In the same spirit of helping others he started an evening school in his house, where by the light of two farthing candles he would patiently struggle with the illiteracy of his huge quarrymen pupils. To stimulate scholastic ambition he offered a prize, usually a clay pipe, to the best pupil of the evening. But the highest trophy of the school, a copy of Archbishop MacHale's Irish catechism, was never won, and Michael was confident that his father never intended this treasure to be taken from his library of six books except for some supreme intellectual feat. While Martin Davitt taught his pupils to read and write English, the domestic speech of the Rock Hall community was Irish, and some of them, like Shemus Madden, never spoke a word of English. Their principal entertainment was the *céilí*, the social evening of Irish story-telling, music, and dancing, of which in winter there were one or two sessions a week, held in the Davitts' house or in Molly Madden's. Gathered about

[1] DA/2, pp 26-7.

[2] Distributors' register of licences, Haslingden, 1849-64 (the property of Mr John Driver). Catherine Davitt held a hawker's licence till at least 1864, when the register ends. For Michael's accident see below, pp 17-18.

[3] Census returns, Haslingden, 1861, in P.R.O., R.G. 9/3061/477/4B, f. 21^{v}.

[4] Mary Madden appears in the Haslingden census returns for 1861 (P.R.O., R.G. 9/3061/477/4B, f. 22) as a widow, occupying with her son and daughter and four lodgers a house next to the Davitts.

a blazing coal fire, friends and neighbours of all ages would listen spellbound to performances by rival story-tellers, preeminent among them Martin Davitt, Michael More Timlin,[1] and Dick Halloran. Their repertoire was a luxuriant patchwork of ancient sagas and myths, lives of saints and tales of the 'good people' (fairies), heroic legends of Patrick Sarsfield, 'Dan' (O'Connell), and 'Boney' (Bonaparte), narratives of the French landing at Killala in 1798 and Humbert's defeat of the British at Castlebar (familiar ground to many of the listeners), traditions of poteen-making and the outwitting of excise officers along the shores of Lough Conn (no less familar), bitter memories of the great famine and evicting landlords. When this last subject arose, the gaiety would cease, faces grew pale and tense, and eyes flash in the firelight as personal experiences of the horrors of the great starvation were retold.[2]

It was accepted without question that the famine was inseparable from the land system, and that the landlords were the natural enemies of the peasantry. There would be savage satisfaction in recalling

> how wild justice overtook some of the worst of the tyrants, and curses hearty and deep would be heaped upon the head of every landlord, in words barbed with the memories of happier days in Mayo, and by the thought that at five the following morning all the adults present would have to rise for a hard day's toil... to earn the barest necessaries of existence among... strangers.[3]

To Catherine Davitt in particular all this had a terrible actuality; and her son could never forget hearing her describe how three hundred poor people who had died of starvation near Straide had been thrown into one pit in the yard of Swinford workhouse 'without coffin, without sermon, without anything which denotes respect for the dead'. 'So great an impression did this make upon me in my youthful days in Lancashire that when I visited Swinford, twenty-five years afterwards, I went to the very spot where these bodies had been so buried without asking anyone to direct me to the place.'[4]

But the lighter side of the Rock Hall *céilí* was no less characteristic. Molly Madden had a sweet voice and was adept in singing the peasant love-songs of Connacht, with their playful commentary on courtship and marriage. 'The man who came courting my father's grey mare' and 'The red-haired man's wife' were examples of the genre. Patriotic songs

[1] In the Haslingden census returns for 1861 Michael Timlin is recorded as the occupant of a house in Rock Hall with his wife, four children and six lodgers (P.R.O., R.G. 9/3061/477/4B, f. 21).

[2] DA/2, pp 7A-8, 11-20, 22-4; DA/1, pp 1-2, 3.

[3] DA/2, p. 23.

[4] *S.C.P.*, x, 557-8 (29 Oct. 89); *Defence*, p. 202. A plaque in the grounds of what was formerly the workhouse of Swinford, Co. Mayo, marks the site of a mass grave in which 564 victims of the famine are stated to have been buried.

were less in demand, but '*Roisín dubh*', that sublime expression of romantic devotion to Ireland,[1] was a favourite with young and old. Dick Halloran was a fiddler as well as a *seanchaí* and loved to get the company on its feet to dance the strenuous jigs and reels with which an evening's *céili* usually ended. However much the exiles might lament their separation from Ireland, they had succeeded remarkably well in transplanting a bit of Mayo into Lancashire.[2]

In the spring of 1855 Michael Davitt was a pupil at an infant school conducted by Dan Burke when he decided that it was time for him to contribute to the family income. He was now aged nine. It was unusual in Haslingden for children to be employed in the mills as young as this but it was not unknown: in 1851, Honor Eagan, youngest of the six children of Owen Eagan, with whom the Davitts lodged in Wilkinson Street, was a cotton doffer at the age of eight,[3] and John Kildun, son of a neighbour with seven children, was a woollen carding piecer at nine.[4] Michael Davitt committed his first act of rebellion when he turned his back on 'Burke's spelling purgatory' and found a job in Parkinson's cotton mill at Ewood Bridge, about two miles south of Haslingden. Under the factory acts the working day of children under thirteen was limited to eight hours, and such child workers were permitted to be 'half-timers', that is, to alternate factory work with school attendance. Michael passed himself off as thirteen and was engaged by Parkinson's as a 'full-timer': his hours were from 6 a.m. to 6 p.m. with 1½ hours off for breakfast and dinner, except on Saturday, when half an hour was allowed for breakfast and work ceased at 2 p.m. For these 60 working hours he was to receive a wage of 2*s*. 6*d*. a week. Elated by the prospect, filled with a new spirit of independence, and proud of his coveted status as a wage-earner, he resisted all his mother's efforts to send him back to school. So began two years of grinding toil and hardship as a mill-hand.[5]

Glimpses of life in a Haslingden cotton mill are afforded by the factory rules, dated September 1851, of Lawrence Whittaker and Sons, owners of Waterfoot Mill. These prescribed penalties for a long list of offences: for arriving five minutes late, 2*d*.; for dropping a bobbin on the floor, 2*d*.; for breaking a bobbin, its replacement value; for wasting oil or spilling it on the floor, 2*d*. for each offence and the

[1] This is the song rendered into English so superbly by James Clarence Mangan as 'Dark Rosaleen'.

[2] DA/2, pp 12, 20-22.

[3] Census returns, township of Haslingden, Lancs., 1851, in P.R.O., H.O. 107/2250/477/4a, f. 47.

[4] Ibid., f. 49.

[5] DA/2, pp 26-8, 30. The date given in *Who's who* for Davitt's first employment as a mill-hand is 1856 (*Who was who, 1897-1916*, p. 185), which is untenable; see below, pp 16-17.

value of the oil; for neglecting to oil at the proper time, 2*d.*; for leaving work and talking with other workers, 2*d.*; for using oaths or insolent language, 3*d.*, and, if repeated, dismissal; for smoking, instant dismissal. 'If two persons are known to be in one necessary together, they shall be fined 3*d.* each; and if any man or boy go into the women's necessary, he shall be instantly dismissed.' Whittakers recommended their workpeople to wash themselves every morning, and required them to do so at least twice a week, on Monday and Thursday; anyone found not thus washed would be fined 3*d.* for each offence. But the most telling rule was the one that required all employees to serve four weeks' notice before leaving Whittakers' employment, while stipulating that Whittakers could dismiss anyone without any notice being given.[1]

Despite the factory acts and the efforts of the factory inspectors, life in a cotton mill, harsh and dangerous as it was for adults, was a cruel ordeal for children. They were exhausted by the long hours, the unhealthy atmosphere, and the laborious nature of the work itself, for which they were often too small and too ill-fed. No one was surprised when they were kicked and beaten by their masters for mistakes and negligence that were the direct outcome of overwork or lack of sleep or simply of strength. To all this were added the hazards of exposed shafts, belts, cog-wheels, and drums. Accidents caused by machinery were a commonplace,[2] and it was impossible to walk the streets of a manufacturing town without seeing proofs of the fact in boys and young men maimed in arms and legs. Among Michael's own friends we know of three thus maimed.[3] Catherine Davitt had to drag her son from his bed each morning at five, and her eyes were often wet as she watched him trudging from the door, heavy with sleep, on his way to the mill.[4]

Michael remained only a month in his first employment, the man for whom he worked having gone on a spree and embezzled his wages. His second job was at Holden Mill, owned by Lawrence Whittaker, on the outskirts of Haslingden. Here too his stay was short. His playmate John Ginty, aged thirteen, who lived a few doors from the Davitts in Rock Hall, was employed in the same mill. On 18 October 1855 the two boys walked to their work together; that afternoon John was caught in a revolving belt, his skull was fractured, and he was killed

[1] Aspin, *Haslingden, 1800–1900: a history*, pp 37–8.

[2] See *Reports of the inspectors of factories to her majesty's principal secretary of state for the home department for the half year ending 31 October 1855* [2031], H.C. 1856, xviii, etc, for details and statistics.

[3] John Ginty, Tom Burke, and Martin Haran (below, next par., and pp 44–5).

[4] DA/2, pp 28–30.

instantly.[1] Michael found him lying on the floor, his blood spattered over machinery and walls. In the evening, at Rock Hall, he saw John's mother sitting by his dead body, rocking herself to and fro in her grief, unable to shed tears but chanting a dirge or *caoine* for him in the traditional Irish manner. Michael's parents would not allow him to return to Holden Mill, and he found his third job in Stellfoxe's Victoria Mill at Baxenden, about two miles from Haslingden on the road to Accrington, where his sister Mary was also employed. He was now a spinning-room handylad, working a twelve-hour day for five shillings a week.[2]

Michael remained at Victoria Mill for just over eighteen months. On the morning of 8 May 1857, when he was a little over eleven, the room overseer, Proctor, ordered him to take over the work of an absent machine-minder, a boy named Mitchell, aged seventeen. Michael understood the technique required, but objected that he was neither old nor tall enough to manage Mitchell's machine (a 'doffing' or carding engine). Proctor's reply, reinforced with his boot, was to threaten Michael with dismissal, and he at once gave way. He was only half an hour on his new job when it became necessary, without stopping the engine, to remove an obstruction that had got into the teeth of the 'doffing comb', through which the film of untwisted cotton had to pass. To do this the minder had to stretch his right arm across cog-wheels at the front of the engine. Not being tall enough, Michael tried to make up for lack of inches by standing on tip-toe, but lost his balance. The folds of his shirt-sleeve, which was rolled above the elbow, were caught by the cog-wheels. He made a desperate attempt to free himself, failed, and his upper arm was mangled between the cogs.[3]

Crudely bandaged and accompanied by his sister, Michael was driven home in a cart, leaving a trail of blood on the road. With John Ginty's fate fresh in his mind he felt death to be near. But at one point in his two-mile journey a stranger, seeing the trickle of blood, stopped the cart, and tieing the bandage more carefully above the gaping wound said reassuringly: 'Keep up your spirit, my lad. You won't die. You'll give a good account of yourself with one arm, never fear.' His mother

[1] Record of the death of John Ginty (described as Genty), in Haslingden Register Office; *Blackburn Weekly Times*, 20 Oct. 55; *Blackburn Standard*, 24 Oct. His was one of eleven fatal accidents reported for the period Apr.–Oct. 55 by the factory inspector for Lancashire (*Reports of the factory inspectors . . . for the half-year ending 31 October 1855*, p. 9 [2031], H.C. 1856, xviii).

[2] DA/2, pp 30–33; D to John Thornton, 10 Feb. 92, in *Accrington Observer and Times*, 18 July 1925; see plate II.

[3] DA/2, pp 33–4; D. to his father, mother, and sisters, 11 July 70 (DPC); D to John Thornton, as above; DN/38, 8 May 97. In DA/2, Davitt gives the date of the accident as 8 May 58, but this is incompatible with the other evidence.

received him in speechless agony, believing that he had almost bled to death. The local doctor was undecided whether to try to save the arm or to amputate. After a week's delay, Dr Taylor of Rawtenstall, who was far-famed for his limb-setting and surgical skill, was called in. He declared that immediate amputation alone could save Michael's life, mortification having already begun.[1]

News of the intended amputation was privately conveyed to Michael by his friend Molly Madden, who, in her most beguiling Irish, ministered this advice (as he recalled it) to the injured boy:

> The doctors are going to butcher your arm, acushla. Don't let them. Your poor mother is crying outside the door. What will you be with only one arm?—a cripple for life. Every Sassenach boy will insult and beat you. You cannot defend yourself when attacked. You won't be able to work for your mother or yourself; how can you with your right arm cut off? What will become of you? Think of all this and then think of what I am going to say to you. Your little brother James is in heaven. He is an angel, with wings. He is in a beautiful place with all the saints, and you will go up there too, where there will be no pain or hunger, suffering or tears, but all joy and singing and happiness. You will be an angel too, bright and glorious; and sure, asthore, it will only be a few short years until your mother joins you, and there will only be a wee bit of a separation. Don't let them cut your arm off. They will put a handkerchief to your mouth, and you will be forced into a sleep, and when you wake again you will be a cripple.[2]

This appeal, rich in revelation of the Irish peasant mind with its horror of physical deformity in men, was conclusive for Michael. 'I resolved to join the angels and became quite enthusiastic over the heavenly prospects pictured to my enraptured mental vision.'[3] But Catherine Davitt's maternal feelings were stronger than her response to Molly Madden's pleading. The attempt to recruit her son for a premature 'angelic vocation' was frustrated, and Michael, fiercely resisting, had in the end to be forcibly chloroformed. When he awoke he was minus his right arm from just below the shoulder.[4]

Michael's accident received no notice in the press, and in the factory inspector's report for Lancashire covering the six months in which it occurred it is presumably one item in the total of 164 accidents classified as causing amputations of hand or arms.[5] But it was a turning-point in Michael's life. It identified him permanently with the suffering

[1] DA/2, pp 34-7. Davitt describes the doctor who decided for amputation as 'Dr Haworth, the neighbour and friend of the Brontës'. I have been unable to identify this Dr Haworth; the name is that of the village in Yorkshire, about 25 miles E.N.E. from Haslingden, where the Brontës lived. According to A. J. Chappell ('Briar'), who was a journalist in Haslingden for nearly sixty years and a unique repository of local information, Dr Taylor of Rawtenstall was the man in question (*Accrington Observer and Times*, 18 July 1925; *Haslingden Observer*, 2 Mar. 1946). [2] DA/2, pp 37-8. [3] Ibid., p. 38. [4] Ibid., p. 38-9.

[5] *Reports of the inspectors of factories . . . for the half year ending 31 October 1857* [2314], H.C. 1857-8, xxiv.

and danger inseparable from the lot of industrial workers at that time. He was still a child in years, but in depth of experience he was well-developed. He had shown some of the qualities that were to distinguish all his adult life—sense of duty, self-reliance, courage, endurance. He was now more intensely aware of industrial servitude in England than of the agrarian servitude in Ireland with the thought of which his whole upbringing was so much imbued. He was never to forget his kinship with working men, even though, as a competitor in the struggle for employment, he had been all too conscious of the enmity of English workers, and even though his accident put an end to his short but sharp experience of factory life. When he had recovered from his operation, his parents, helped by John Dean, a local cotton-manufacturer and prominent Wesleyan,[1] decided to send him back to school. The local Wesleyan school, conducted by George Poskett, a gifted teacher, was recommended by the parish priest, Rev. Thomas Martin, as the best to be had in Haslingden; and here, for the next four years, Michael proved an apt and rewarding pupil.[2] He won the lasting respect and affection of his schoolmaster,[3] from whom, as he said in a speech in Haslingden many years later,[4] he never heard a single word that could hurt his feelings as a catholic.[5] The disaster that cost him his arm thus led to the blessings of an education that fostered his mental powers, and taught him to accept religious diversity as a social fact and not a source of estrangement among men. The influence of his parish priest reinforced this attitude. Fr Martin was a man of liberal views, who believed strongly in 'different denominations all mingling together in social harmony and brotherly love—no distinction between protestants and catholics, English and Irish, but all blending together in one social brotherhood'.[6]

About August 1861 Michael again became a wage-earner, this time under much more favourable conditions. He was employed as errand boy by Henry Cockcroft, who combined the office of postmaster of

[1] 'Briar' (see opp. page, n. 1) in *Accrington Observer*, 25 July 1925, and in *Haslingden Observer*, 27 July 1935. 'Briar' learnt about John Dean from Rev. James Ancliffe Cooper, of the Methodist Church of Canada, who had been a pupil-teacher at the Wesleyan School, Haslingden, when Davitt was attending it, and who revisited Haslingden in 1913 (*Accrington Observer*, 18 July 1925).

[2] Sabina Davitt, Sketch of Davitt's early life (MS version in DP/T; another version in M. M. O'Hara, *Chief and tribune: Parnell and Davitt* (1919), p. 21); *Post Office Directory of Lancashire* (1858), p. 180.

[3] *Preston Herald*, 3 Nov. 82; George Poskett to D, 2 July 89 (DP/V).

[4] DN/10, 15 Jan. 83.

[5] *Accrington Times*, 20 Jan. 83, p. 6. Obituary of George Poskett (1819-1907) in *Haslingden Gazette*, 24 Aug. 1907, p. 5.

[6] Speech at St Mary's Catholic School soiree, Bacup, reported in *Bacup Times*, 4 May 67, p. 5.

Haslingden with a printing and stationery business.[1] Cockcroft found him a willing, resourceful, intelligent, and reliable employee, competent, in spite of his disability, to take on a variety of jobs including typesetting. He soon promoted him assistant letter-carrier, and book-keeper in the printing-house. The hours were nearly as long as at the mill—7 a.m. to 7 p.m. except on Saturday, when he left at 2 p.m. and on Monday, when he began at 9—but they were less rigid and the work more agreeable and interesting. He had no fixed holidays but could always get a day off if he wanted it. For some years he carried the mail bags to the railway station twice a day, and whenever the postman was away he took his place and delivered letters.[2] On one occasion (2 February 1863) he deputised for an absent printer, to the astonishment of Cockcroft, who was so favourably impressed that he recorded the incident in a letter which was published in a local newspaper:

About eighteen months ago I took into my employment a poor lad of the name of Michael Davitt, who had lost his right arm in the mill. My wish was to furnish him with the means of getting his living as a letter-carrier, since which time he has done odd jobs in the office, as well as being errand boy. Yesterday (February 2) being fair day here, my printer was not at work, and a posting bill having been ordered this boy commenced the task himself with his left hand, and in three hours and a half he fully completed a very neat bill. . . . The boy put the chase and furniture round the type, drove in the quoins, and when I entered the office he was alongside the imposing stone with the forme standing on its edge, concocting a plan to get it on to the press, which was in an adjoining room. Not a letter dropped out, and when the bills were worked off and the forme lifted, only a single letter remained on the press. Some apprentices would feel grateful if they could with two hands perform a piece of work like it in the same time. I do not think there was an equal to it in my day, and I entered the buisiness at Burnley in February 1820.[3]

In the following year (14 September 1864) Michael performed another feat of dexterity when with his one hand he printed 500 pulls of an advertisement in one hour and a quarter, the same time exactly as was afterwards taken by Cockcroft's printer to do the same job using both his hands.[4] Throughout his life Michael was to show phenomenal skill and resource in making up for the loss of his right arm.

Michael thus seemed to be heading for a secure and respectable future. Since 1858 he had been attending evening classes at the

[1] *Post Office Directory of Lancashire* (1858), p. 179; —(1864), p. 219.

[2] *C.C.C. minutes*, lxxii, 326-7, 344 (evidence of Thomas Cockcroft, son of Henry Cockcroft); *Kimberley comm. rep.*, iii, 529.

[3] 'A persevering printer's devil' in *Burnley Free Press*, 14 Mar. 63. This is the earliest public reference to Michael Davitt known to me.

[4] Copy of posting bill signed by 'H. C.' (Henry Cockcroft), 14 Sept. 64, from N.L.I. (DP/A43).

Mechanics' Institute, where he also had the benefit of a library and of a newsroom in which the leading newspapers and periodicals of Britain were available. He began to study Irish history. 'The Mechanics', he recalled years later, was the regular meeting-place of men from factories and workshops who had the ambition and the stamina to improve themselves. There were, he reckoned, over 200 Irish families in Haslingden, but he and one companion were the only Irish to attend the institute. Other Irish used to call at his house at night to draw on the knowledge of current affairs he acquired at the newsroom.[1] He had met many former Irish acquaintances of Haslingden scattered over England, Scotland, and the U.S.A.

> and found them just as they were fifteen or twenty years previously . . . 'hewers of wood and drawers of water' like the majority of our race, while my English associates of the Mechanics' Institute evening classes have probably all become either skilled artizans or superintendents in workshops or employers of labour on their own.[2]

It was now that his thoughts began to turn seriously to politics. He came into touch with Ernest Jones, the veteran chartist leader who had been sent to prison for two years in 1848 for seditious speeches, and who, in the fifties, was still an irrepressible and undaunted preacher of a working-class radicalism that included land nationalisation.[3] Among his most successful writings were his political songs, notably 'The song of the lower classes',[4] and 'The song of the factory slave', which almost certainly found a responsive reader in Michael. Jones settled at Manchester in 1861 to practise at the northern bar, and for the next five or six years was 'the most influential political leader of the Lancashire working-class movement'.[5] He was a dynamic and ubiquitous lecturer, and Michael attended a meeting, probably in Haslingden, at which he spoke on the land question: 'the first man after my father whom I ever heard denouncing landlordism, not only in Ireland but in England, was Ernest Jones'.[6] Jones was in full sympathy with Irish claims to national independence, and insisted that

1 Haslingden Institute, Members' subscription book, 1846-67 (Haslingden Public Library, reference department, local collection); Davitt's name is entered in the subscription book for Sept. and Oct. 58, Aug. 64, Mar.-Dec. 66, Jan.-May 67. *C.C.C. minutes*, lxxii, 325, 328 (evidence of Martin Haran and Patrick Fearon, 16 July 70); DA/1, f. 122v; *Accrington Times*, 20 Jan. 83.

2 DA/1, f. 122v.

3 *D.N.B.*; *Ernest Jones, chartist: selections from the writings and speeches of Ernest Jones*, ed. with introd. by John Saville (1952). For his views on land nationalisation see ibid., pp 152-7.

4 Reprinted in *The Oxford book of Victorian verse* (1925), pp 323-4.

5 G. D. H. Cole, *Chartist portraits* (1941), p. 353, cited in *Ernest Jones, chartist*, as above, p. 77.

6 *S.C.P.*, x, 437; *Defence*, p. 30.

the interests of Irish nationalism and British democracy were identical:

> Men of Ireland! *Our* rulers, who oppressed us oppressed you. . . . Those who robbed you of your lands robbed us as well. Those who ejected the cottar in Ireland created the pauper in Great Britain . . . Brothers in suffering, fellow soldiers in resistance, your foes are our foes, . . . your hopes are our hopes. . . . *You* have no parliament in College Green—*we* have no parliament anywhere. . . . Let us each be masters in our own land.[1]

Such views reinforced the other influences that were impelling Michael into revolutionary politics. Towards the end of 1865, the year in which Parnell entered Magdalen College, Cambridge, Michael took the fateful step of joining the fenian organisation.[2] Thus began an involvement in public affairs that was to last for forty strenuous years.

By this time the Davitt family had begun to branch out. Michael's eldest sister Mary had married, on 16 May 1863, an Irishman from her native Mayo, Neil Padden. They were both twenty-two. He had been born in the parish of Coolkarney, in Mayo, and had first come to England as a 'harvester' or migratory labourer. He had then become a bricklayer's labourer in Haslingden, where his marriage to Mary Davitt took place in St Mary's Church, Michael being one of the witnesses. The first child born to Neil and Mary, John, died in infancy, probably in 1864.[3] Between that date and June 1865 Neil emigrated to America, going first to Albany, in New York state, where he had friends.[4] Soon afterwards he moved south to Scranton, a new and rapidly growing industrial town in north-eastern Pennsylvania, 135 miles from New York and 160 from Philadelphia.[5] It stands on the River Lackawanna, a tributary of the Susquehanna, in a fine setting of massive blue hills, not unlike the Galtees in Tipperary. It owed its industrial growth largely to the energy and enterprise of George Whitfield Scranton, who since 1840 had pioneered the exploitation of extensive anthracite deposits in the Lackawanna valley for iron smelting.[6]

1 Jones in *People's Paper*, 8 Mar. 56, reprinted in *Ernest Jones, chartist*, as above, pp 216, 217, 218.

2 *S.C.P.*, ix, 352.

3 Record of the marriage of Neil Padden and Mary Davitt, in Haslingden Register Office, and in St Mary's R.C. Church; personal information supplied by Mrs Kathleen Burns, of New York, a granddaughter of Neil and Mary Padden.

4 Information supplied by Mrs Kathleen Burns (see preceding note) and confirmed by letters of Davitt to his mother, 1 Mar., 31 May, *c.* May, and 30 Aug., 75 (DP/C2); Sabina Davitt in M. M. O'Hara, *Chief and tribune: Parnell and Davitt*, p. 19.

5 See map V.

6 David Craft and others, *History of Scranton* (Dayton, Ohio, 1891); B. H. Throop, *A half century in Scranton* (Scranton, 1895); *Portrait and biographical record of Lackawanna county, Pennsylvania* (New York and Chicago, 1897); F. L. Hitchcock, *History of Scranton and its people* (New York, 1914); *Dictionary of American biography*, George Whitfield Scranton.

Many Welsh and Irish[1] had been attracted to Scranton by the opportunities of employment in the mines, and Neil Padden found work as a miner with the Lackawanna Iron and Coal Company.

Mary joined Neil in Scranton in 1865, sailing from Liverpool and arriving at New York on 17 June. A son, James, was born to them on 17 April 1866 and a daughter, Catherine, on 3 December 1867. Though both Mary and Neil were illiterate, they were capable, hard-working, and enterprising. While Mary had a sound business head, Neil was ingenious and could turn his hand to anything, though he remained a miner to his death. Both were kind-hearted, patient, and good-humoured. Their life in Scranton was an incessant struggle, but it soon proved more rewarding than life in Haslingden: they contrived to build a house of their own, which they occupied on Christmas day 1867, and of their nine children all except two (John, the first-born, and Michael, who also died in infancy) thrived and did well for themselves.[2] The Davitt exodus from Straide had thus been carried a stage further. The venture of Mary and Neil had created a Davitt connection with America which was to become permanent, and to have far-reaching effects on the Davitts who remained in Haslingden and not least on Michael himself.

[1] The R.C. Cathedral Cemetery at Scranton is a microcosm of Irish family names. The census returns of 1870 for Scranton (typescript summary in Scranton, Lackawanna Historical Society) and the Scranton city directories from the late sixties show many Irish householders.

[2] Passenger list of the *Resolute*, Captain N. C. Harris master, 17 June 65 (Washington, D.C., National Archives, Passenger arrival lists, Port of New York); *Scranton City Directory*, 1867-95; Davitt to Mary Padden, 24 Apr. 82 (DP/A3); art. on James Padden in *Portrait and biographical record of Lackawanna county, Pennsylvania* (1897), p. 342; personal testimony of Mrs Kathleen Burns (see above), and of the late Michael Davitt Crowley and Mary Ellen Crowley, of Scranton, nephew and niece respectively of Mary Padden.

II

In the Irish republican movement, 1865–70

THE fenian organisation, also known as the Irish Republican Brotherhood (I.R.B.)[1] was the secret military body founded in 1858 to achieve Irish independence by physical force. It was one expression of a complex movement to undo the union, which, in 1801, in the interests of Britain's security, had put an end to Ireland's existence as a separate kingdom, with a parliament of her own, and made her juridically part of the United Kingdom of Great Britain and Ireland. The architect of the union, William Pitt, intended it to be a beneficial arrangement for Ireland as well as for Britain. National self-consciousness had not yet permeated the mass of the Irish people, and there was 'a vacuum in Irish politics'[2] at this time that Britain might have used to turn the union of the two kingdoms into a union of hearts. Instead, the government of Ireland continued to be conducted on a basis of protestant ascendancy. The relief measure that Pitt had encouraged the catholics to expect as a reward for their support of the union was denied till 1829, and was only conceded then before a tidal wave of agitation inspired and organised by the greatest popular leader Ireland had ever produced, Daniel O'Connell. In the process of winning catholic emancipation, catholics of all classes were awakened to a sense of their common interests and their collective strength, at the same time that they were taught by experience to identify the union with denial of their rights. Conversely Irish protestants, and especially those in Ulster, were drawn together under the common fear that protestant ascendancy might be replaced by a catholic ascendancy and the growing certainty that only through the union could such a disaster be averted.

Though the union did eventually bring advantages that were widely shared, such as reformed administration, central and local, expanding social services, and state-supported education at primary, secondary, and university level, it was more characteristic of the union regime not to understand, or to misunderstand, or to ignore, Ireland's distinctive problems. In a classic age of parliamentary blue-books, copious

[1] *S.C.P.*, ix, 400.
[2] J. C. Beckett, *The making of modern Ireland*, p. 285.

information about Irish population, poverty, land, and other problems was available in the reports of innumerable committees and commissions of inquiry; but they made remarkably little impact on the statesmen for whom they were prepared. With her one-hundred representatives in the parliament of the United Kingdom, Ireland was in theory involved in the political life of the most liberal state in Europe, yet in fact she was ruled from Dublin Castle as a province by a government which, though often well-meaning, was not responsible to Irish interests or opinion. Social reforms were wrung from parliament after long delays and in response to mass agitation, whereas coercion acts were a commonplace of British legislation for Ireland. After half a century of union with Great Britain, Ireland was a byword for poverty, backwardness, discontent, and disturbance. In the eyes of a majority of Irishmen the union stood condemned, identified as it was with hopes disappointed, promises unfulfilled, grievances unremedied, liberties denied, with industrial stagnation and, above all, with the agony of the great famine (1845-9).

The economic depression that characterised pre-famine Ireland, by contrast with the general economic expansion of the preceding century, was due to the undermining of Ireland's small-scale industries by the highly-developed and advancing industries of Britain under the improved conditions of transport within the British Isles brought about by the railways and the steamship; and to the consequent dependence of the great bulk of the population on agriculture for their livelihood in an age when the conditions of the English market imposed on Irish agriculture the necessity of a far-reaching change from tillage to grazing. The union did not create these conditions, though it probably hastened their rise; parts of rural England shared in the same decline. But nationalists did not hesitate, both then and since, to attribute Irish depression and poverty to British neglect. The great famine, when the potato crop on which the rural masses depended for survival failed disastrously, seemed to exemplify the evil in a peculiarly terrible way. Great Britain was not responsible for the famine, and at that time no government could have coped satisfactorily with so vast a calamity, but government relief-measures (excepting Peel's during the first nine months of the emergency) were slow, cautious, unimaginative, and ineffective. Detached from the tragic realities of Irish suffering, government was dominated by the prevailing *laissez-faire* economics and influenced by the pressures and tensions of British party-politics. Most Irishmen believed that the suffering and loss from the famine would have been incomparably less if Ireland had had her own parliament; and it is doubtless true that relief measures would have been initiated far more rapidly and realistically by a responsible government in Dublin. As it was, Ireland in her desperate extremity was treated not as an integral part of the United Kingdom but as a separate and inferior entity, on which the British taxpayers' money must not be spent uneconomically. How different it would have been, Irishmen bitterly reflected, if a comparable calamity had occurred in England. From the famine onwards, hostility to Britain and determination to undo the union were fed by one of the most significant consequences of the famine, the vast migration of embittered catholic Irish to Britain, and still more to America, and the catastrophic reduction and continuing decline in Ireland's population, which made her unique in the demographic history of Europe. Moreover, despite the widespread and active sympathy felt in Britain for the victims of the famine, the British attitude to Ireland changed for the worse, especially after the Young Ireland rising of 1848 had offered its hopeless gesture of defiance. In British eyes the majority of Irishmen were seen to be not only backward and incapable but irresponsible, ungrateful, and rebellious.

Nationalist action assumed two forms which corresponded to two distinguishable, if never wholly separable, traditions. O'Connell had established a constitutional tradition by the use he made of Ireland's representation in the British parliament, and by generating mass agitation outside parliament. His methods earned immense prestige by the success of his agitation for catholic emancipation (1829), and by the benefits—tithe reform (1838), a poor law (1838), the reform of municipal corporations (1840), and sympathetic administration at Dublin Castle—that he secured by cooperating with the whig party in parliament. But when he attempted by mass agitation to bring about the repeal of the union, he quickly exhausted the possibilities of moral force. A section of the Young Ireland group, who had been his auxiliaries, driven to desperation by the famine eventually accepted the logic of this defeat: by the rising of July 1848, fiasco though it was, they revived the tradition of physical force dormant since the days of Tone and Emmet. From this time onwards there were two schools or traditions of nationalism: the one constitutional, the other revolutionary; both sought self-government for Ireland, but while the constitutional tradition tended to regard self-government primarily as a means to good government the revolutionary tradition saw it primarily as the inherent right of a nation; and whereas the one was prepared to settle for domestic self-government within the union, the other was essentially separatist and aimed at complete national independence through the destruction of the union. From 1848 to the end of the union the two traditions coexisted; and though, until the Anglo-Irish war of 1919-21, revolutionary nationalism made only two attempts—in 1867 and 1916—to fight it out with Britain, during most of those seventy years the revolutionary and the constitutional movements were reacting on each other, and each exerted its maximum impact on Britain when both took part under the inspiration of Davitt in the 'land war' of 1879-82.

By the middle of the century, not only were the majority of Irishmen alienated from the union on practical grounds, but the undoing of the union was increasingly demanded as the inalienable right of an awakened nation. Irish nationalism was now a fully developed creed, to which Thomas Davis, the leader and prophet of Young Ireland, had just given classic formulation. The nation, he taught, is a community engendered by devotion to a common country, by a common inheritance of tradition, values, and patterns of living, and by the conscious will of its members to share a common future. It is the duty as well as the right of such a community to strive for its own fulfilment, to develop its own genius, and so to contribute to the common stock of humanity. This it can do only if it has the power of self-government. Good government imposed by an alien power can never recompense a nation for the denial of self-government. All this was in tune with the liberal concept of nationality current at the time in continental Europe, but Davis drew his inspiration from Irish sources and his statement of the doctrine became canonical for Ireland. It combined three streams: the liberal, rationalist, and democratic tradition of Wolfe Tone and the United Irishmen; the Gaelic and catholic tradition of the common people, awakened to a sense of their rights and their power by the tremendous leadership of O'Connell; and the romantic nationalism of contemporary Europe. This combination gave to the idea of an Irish nation the distinctive character it has borne ever since. While recognising the unique importance of the Gaelic past and of the catholic faith in the national inheritance, Davis claimed the whole of Irish history for that inheritance; and in the spirit of the United Irishmen he affirmed that the Irish nation was not based on any exclusive principle of blood or religion or culture, but sought the allegiance of all Irishmen, whatever their antecedents. While welcoming every ameliorative measure that could be won for Ireland under the conditions of the union he insisted that Ireland could never be at peace with Britain until the union was dissolved and an independent Ireland established.[1]

Struggles for national self-determination were characteristic of the

[1] T. W. Moody, *Thomas Davis, 1815-45* (1945), and 'Thomas Davis and the Irish nation' in *Hermathena: a Dublin university review*, no. ciii (1966), pp 5-31.

age, and public opinion in Britain responded sympathetically to the national aspirations of Greeks, Serbs, Poles, Hungarians, Italians, and Latin Americans. But the Irish claim to self-government encountered massive resistance. The maintenance of the union was believed to be a vital interest of Britain, though the nature of that interest was seldom defined. British people denied that the Irish possessed the attributes of nationality, and argued that Ireland was merely part of a larger whole, no more entitled to self-government than Wales or Scotland or Yorkshire. This view found some support in the divisions that disrupted Irish society. For the Irish nation of Tone and Davis remained an unrealised ideal.

The most significant lines of cleavage were religious. Religious differences were important not only in themselves but as the expression of other deep-seated conflicts. Protestants, who were only 22 per cent of the whole population in 1861, owned the bulk of the country's wealth. The landowning class was overwhelmingly protestant, the tenant-farmer class as distinctively catholic, and political power was no less unevenly distributed than economic power. Irish nationalism as an idea was non-sectarian, but catholics formed the bulk of the nationalists as protestants did of the unionists. Although nationalism was not a class doctrine, its strength lay among the catholic middle and lower classes, whereas the landowners as a class were unionists. But the Irish opposition to self-government did not come only from the landowning class, mainly protestant and thinly spread as it was over the country as a whole. In Ulster, the most prosperous of the four provinces, where half the population was protestant, and descended from English and Scottish colonists of the seventeenth century, unionism was concentrated in a protestant community that comprised all social classes. Here the landlord-tenant relationship tended to be more equitable and humane than anywhere else in Ireland, and in some areas the tenants were recognised by the 'Ulster custom' to have a sustainable interest in their holdings that included a saleable property in their improvements. And, unlike all the rest of Ireland, east Ulster experienced during the first half of the century an industrial revolution that gave new prosperity to the region and transformed Belfast into a great centre of linen and shipbuilding, whose vital connections were with industrial Britain rather than with Dublin and the south. This Ulster industry, though it employed many catholics, was controlled by protestants, whose energy and capital had created it, and was a powerful vested interest on the side of unionism.[1]

[1] See T. W. Moody and J. C. Beckett (ed.), *Ulster since 1800* (2 series, 1955, 1957).

The estrangement of the majority of Irishmen from the British government of Ireland had its roots not only in political alienation but still more in the alienation of the tenant farmers from the landlords. The greatest of Ireland's social problems was the land system, a fact fully and formally recognised in the monumental report (1845) of the Devon commission of inquiry into the occupation of land in Ireland, the first of a long line of special inquiries covering every aspect of the problem. Nearly all the land was owned by a small number of large landowners who let it on yearly tenancies to a very large number of small tenant farmers. In 1870 3,761 owners of estates of 1000 acres and upwards owned 81 per cent of all the land, whereas 267,017 tenants, or 50 per cent of all tenants, occupied holdings of under 15 acres, and 391,528, or 73 per cent of the total, occupied holdings of under 30 acres.[1] The concentration of ownership in comparatively few hands reproduced the landlord pattern of Britain, which in this respect differed from most of the Continent where, since the French revolution, occupying ownership had become the prevailing pattern.[2] The land law of Ireland before 1870, when a radical change was introduced by the first Gladstone land act, was substantially the same as that of England, and many of the great landowners of England also owned estates in Ireland. But whereas in England the majority of farmers were capitalists with holdings of some 50 acres and upwards, and the farms they rented included buildings and other improvements supplied by their landlords, in Ireland the majority were occupiers of under 30 acres whose capital consisted mainly of their buildings and stock, and whose landlords supplied them with nothing but the bare land. The multiplicity of small and impoverished tenants, which made the pattern of landholding in Ireland so different from that of England, had been brought to a critical point by the rise in population before the great famine, when economists pointed to Ireland as a classic instance of the disastrous effect of excessive pressure of population upon natural resources. The famine, among other catastrophic changes, acted as a surgical operation on the population problem, eliminating 1½ out of 8 million people through death and emigration in five years, and permanently reversing the upward trend of the preceding half-century. This decline, which affected the poorest elements in the population—very small tenants and agricultural labourers—most, was accompanied by a gradual increase in the average size of holdings and by rising incomes and rising expectations among the farmers. But their grievances remained the great problem of Irish life.

[1] Appendices A and B.

[2] See *Reports from her majesty's representatives respecting the tenure of land in the several countries of Europe*, pt I 1869 [C66], pt II 1869-70 [C75], H.C. 1870, lxvii, 1-548, 549-930.

The overwhelming majority of Irish farmers were tenants from year to year: 526,539 agricultural holdings in 1870, or 77 per cent of the total, were occupied by such tenants, while 135,392, or 20 per cent, were in the hands of leaseholders and only 20,217, or 3 per cent, in those of owners.[1] The landlords were legally entitled to alter the rents of the yearly tenants as they pleased. Till 1870 such tenants could be ejected[2] by legal process, initiated by their landlords at any time, without compensation for their improvements. If the ejectment was for non-payment of rent, the tenant, after judgment had been given against him by the court concerned, was allowed six months within which he might redeem his interest by paying the rent due, together with full legal costs. The landlord could also eject a yearly tenant whose rent was not in arrears by giving him six months' notice to quit, and by taking proceedings against him in the courts for overholding, if the tenant did not surrender possession at the end of the six months.[3] The legal power of the landlords over their tenants was immense. But law and practice diverged: the tenants had an ineradicable belief in their right to continuous occupancy so long as they paid their rents, and the landlords generally took the line of least resistance, aiming at steady incomes from their estates through the punctual collection of a multitude of moderate rents. Rack-renting was in fact exceptional, and rents in many estates remained unchanged for long periods. During the 25 years from 1854 to 1878, which on the whole, and apart from a serious depression in 1860-63, was a period of rising agricultural production, the tenants' income from the land increased at a much greater rate than that of the landlords, and in the seventies a tendency to extravagant spending by farmers was observed. Eviction was rare except for non-payment of rent, and the rate of eviction was low in relation to the number of agricultural holdings. The number of evictions ranged from 311 in 1869 to 1,825 in 1854 and averaged 754 a year over the 25 years, which represented a rate of only 1.36 per 1000 holdings over one acre. Thus though legally the mass of the farmers had no security in their holdings, in fact most farms all over Ireland remained indefinitely in the possession of the same families.[4]

Rural conditions showed wide regional variation—most marked in

[1] Appendix B2.

[2] In popular usage 'evicted', which was also the term used by the police in their statistics of ejectments.

[3] T. de Moleyns, *The landlord's and agent's practical guide* (1860), ch. III, IV.

[4] *Report from her majesty's commissioners of inquiry into the state of the law and practice in respect of the occupation of land in Ireland*, H.C. 1845 (605), xix, 1-56 (Devon comm. rep.); *Bessborough comm. rep.*, pp 2-3. W. E. Vaughan, 'A study of landlord and tenant relations in Ireland . . .. 1850-78' (Ph.D. thesis, University of Dublin, 1973), especially pp. 34, 137-48, 155, 159, 225-31. And see below, appendices D1 and G1.

the contrast between the fertile east and north-east, where there were many prosperous farmers, small and large, and the rocky western seaboard, where a high proportion of holdings were uneconomic and where poverty was general. A rough measure of these extremes is the fact that the average valuation of agricultural holdings in Leinster in 1871 was £39 and in Connacht £12, the corresponding figures for Munster and Ulster being £29 and £20. A still sharper contrast is between Meath, where the average valuation of holdings was £52, and Mayo, where it was £9.[1] But there were significant variations within each province and even within the same county, and in every county tenants comprised a wide variety of social classes. Probably about half the rural population was prospering during most years between the famine and the late seventies, while the other half, widely scattered but largely concentrated in Donegal, Connacht, and Kerry, was struggling for survival. The treatment of the tenantry by the landlords also varied greatly both between estates and even between holdings on the same estate. While there were many benevolent and beneficent landlords, who carried out improvements themselves and helped their tenants to do so, the great majority of landlords did not regard themselves as in any sense partners with their tenants in improving the land. But their worst faults were not so much heartlessness or heavy-handedness as apathy and neglect, habits of extravagance, and on large estates the impossibility of taking a constructive interest in a myriad of very small holdings. They tended to be absentees mentally even when they were resident geographically, and many were never resident at all: in 1870 only 41 per cent of all owners of above 100 acres usually lived on their estates and 12 per cent were seldom or never resident in Ireland.[2]

With important exceptions in Ulster, the land system was characterised by tensions between landlords and tenants, reflected in the annual list of offences classified by the police as 'agrarian outrages' under three heads—(a) homicide, assault, and other 'offences against the person', (b) injury to property, chiefly incendiarism and the killing and maiming of animals, and (c) threatening letters and notices, and other 'offences against the public peace'. The Irish government claimed that ordinary legal procedures were ineffective against such crimes, especially as organised by secret societies, and repeatedly applied to parliament for special powers to deal with it. In consequence, throughout the nineteenth century it was seldom that Ireland was not subject

[1] *Agricultural statistics, 1871.*

[2] *Return for the year 1870 of the number of landed proprietors in each county classed according to residence . . .*, H.C. 1872 (167), xlvii, 775-84.

to coercion acts which, apart from intervals of threatened or actual rebellion, were largely directed against agrarian crime.[1] But such crime, far from being wholly the work of tenants against landlords, was often the outcome of conflict among tenants. And it included many petty offences not necessarily connected with land. Even so, the number of agrarian outrages during 1854-78 averaged only 305 a year, the equivalent of 0.55 per 1000 holdings above one acre, though this includes artificially inflated totals for 1869 and 1870. The annual total of agrarian homicides never exceeded 11, and in most years did not exceed 5. Perhaps the most telling measure of agrarian outrages, as reported by the police, is that, apart from 1869-71, they never amounted to more than 12 per cent of total crime, and in most years were under 10 per cent.[2]

It has been commonly said that agrarian outrages were a response to, or a defence against, evictions. The statistics of agrarian outrages and evictions show some correlation between the two during the years 1849-53 and 1879-83, but not during the 25 intervening years. In 1854-78 Connacht had by far the highest average rate of evictions (2.12 per 1000 agricultural holdings), but Leinster of agrarian outrages (0.82). Connacht had the highest rate of evictions in 16 of the 25 years but the highest rate of agrarian outrages in only one year (1870). Leinster had the highest rate of evictions in only 4 of the 25 years but of agrarian outrages in 18. Munster had the highest rate of evictions in 4 of the 25 years and of agrarian outrages in 5. Ulster had the lowest rate of evictions in 23 of the 25 years and of agrarian outrages in 17.[2]

Within the provinces both evictions and agrarian outrages were relatively heavy in very few counties. The number of evictions exceeded 50 a year more than twice in only 9 counties. Four of these were in Connacht—Galway, Mayo, Roscommon, and Leitrim, four were in Munster—Kerry, Tipperary, Clare, and Cork, and one was in Ulster—Donegal. Agrarian outrages exceeded 20 a year more than twice in 9 counties: four in Connacht—Leitrim, Mayo, Roscommon, and Galway, three in Leinster—King's County, Westmeath, and Longford, one in Ulster—Donegal, and one in Munster—Tipperary. Galway and Mayo were by far the worst counties for evictions, and Donegal, Tipperary, Leitrim, and Mayo were the worst for agrarian outrages. But it has to be emphasised that the most numerous category of agrarian outrages consisted simply of threatening letters and notices. For 1869 and 1870 the police adopted a new method of computing such offences, and also the administering of unlawful oaths, which the

[1] See I. S. Leadam, *Coercive measures in Ireland, 1830–1880* (1880).
[2] Appendices D1 and E1.

inspector general explained by the following examples. In Mayo on the night of 13 January 1870, notices were posted on the houses of 22 tenants in one townland threatening them with death if they paid rent above the government valuation. This would previously have counted as one outrage but was recorded in 1870 as 22. Again, on 27 December 1869 a party of some 20 men visited the homes of 30 persons in Mayo and 'swore them all on a book' not to pay more than the government valuation for their land. This was recorded as 30 cases of administering unlawful oaths.[1] There was undoubtedly a flare-up of agrarian disorder in 1869 and 1870 in Mayo, Sligo, and Westmeath, but the unprecedented totals of agrarian outrages in Ireland for those two years depends largely on the inflated figures for administering unlawful oaths and intimidation in the three counties. Statistically Sligo was one of the least disturbed counties in Ireland, and Mayo was not a specially turbulent county. If Mayo's sensational total (665) of outrages for 1870 is excluded, its outrage rate per 1000 agrarian holdings above one acre is below the average rate for Connacht and below the national average.[2]

This is in many ways a very different picture of the rural scene from the one indelibly imprinted on Davitt's youthful mind by his parents and the Irish exiles among whom he grew up in Haslingden. His picture was dominated by conditions in west Connacht, and especially in Mayo. Lord Dufferin, a large and enlightened landowner of County Down, described west Connacht as 'a broad riband of hopeless misery' and 'perennial destitution',[3] and James Hack Tuke, a shrewd English quaker, with a deep knowledge of the west, wrote:

> To nine-tenths of the population of Connaught the possession of a bit of land is the sole means of existence. . . . Take away from the tenant his little holding and nothing is left to him but the workhouse. . . . They [the tenants] are like ship-wrecked sailors on a plank in the ocean; deprive them of the few inches by which they 'hold on', and you deprive them of life.[4]

These statements were made in 1880, at a time of exceptional distress, but they have a general application to west Connacht over a long period. There is nothing surprising in the bitter indignation that the poverty of Mayo, contrasted with the rentals of great landowners of the county, inspired in Davitt, nor in his tendency to exaggerate the militancy of the Mayo people in resisting 'landlordism'.[5] But Davitt

[1] P.R.O., CAB 37/4/72, p. 13.
[2] Appendices D and E, and sources there cited.
[3] *Lord Dufferin on the Three Fs* (Irish Land Committee, 1881), p. 22.
[4] J. H. Tuke, *Irish distress and its remedies* (1880), p. 95.
[5] See *Fall*, pp 144–5.

inherited a peasant tradition that saw landlords in general as ruthless predators, against whom the tenant farmers were engaged in a chronic war for survival; and this shaped his view of the land system as a monstrous and alien 'feudalism'. The peasant tradition received support from contemporary inquirers and observers, Irish and English, the latter including such eminent Victorians as John Bright and John Stuart Mill. The case for the landlords was presented with great ability but with incomparably less popular appeal. In the long run the landlords proved to be on the losing side, and the tenant tradition became incorporated into a conventional historiography that presents Irish rural society in the nineteenth century as convulsed by agrarian conflict and attributes Irish poverty mainly to the farmers' lack of security in their holdings. But the story thus embalmed is one-sided and uncritical, and is being transformed by new research, especially on estate records, the only archival evidence of the land system as it actually worked.

Tenant tradition, however, though highly distorted, was a distortion of realities. Evictions were generally infrequent after 1853, but there had been evictions on a catastrophic scale immediately before: in the 'great clearances' of 1849-53 nearly 47,000 impoverished families, mostly occupants of very small holdings, were evicted. They represented 69 per cent of all families evicted between 1849 and 1880. These mass evictions were partly the backlash of arrears of rent accumulated during the famine years, and partly the work of new proprietors who had bought bankrupt and encumbered estates from old owners through the encumbered estates court established in 1849. The memory of the 'great clearances' was a continuing reality to country people, and all the more so to those who, like Davitt's parents, were among the victims. There was no recurrence of mass evictions on the scale of the 'great clearances', but there were sensational incidents, such as the Partry evictions of 1860 and the Derryveagh evictions of 1861, to remind the peasantry that the legal powers of the landlords remained unimpaired. The threat of eviction and the sense of uncertainty that it bred cast a long shadow, even though the rate of eviction was generally low. It was common practice on many estates to shower notices to quit on the tenants without any intention of acting on these reminders of their legal subjection. Such conditions were all the more resented just because the real incomes of many tenants were increasing: they had more to lose and more to defend; their expectations and their will to resist were alike rising. The rate of eviction was probably no higher than the insolvency rate in urban business, but an eviction, which might be accompanied by the levelling of the house of the evicted family,[1] was a uniquely terrible event and a potential source of dangerous excitement in the countryside: it meant that one more family was rendered homeless, and, in the absence of alternative employment, forced to choose between the workhouse and going into exile. While the flow of emigration during and after the great famine was fed largely by agricultural labourers and farm servants, it is significant that the peak years for emigration–1851-4, 1863-5, 1883–coincided with, or immediately followed, years when evictions were also at their highest.[2]

The condition of the agricultural labourers was a problem in itself, which tended to be obscured by that of the tenant farmers. Labourers as a class suffered the heaviest casualties of the great famine. The steep reduction in their numbers through death and emigration created a scarcity of labour in some parts of the country, mainly Munster, and this helped to improve wages. But the labourers continued to be the most depressed class in rural society–badly paid, wretchedly housed, harshly treated by farmers even more than by landlords, and highly vulnerable to failures of the potato crop. Despite their diminished numbers they still constituted a large part of the rural population in 1871. Ireland as a whole had an average of 136 labourers to every 100 occupiers of land above one acre, but this average was very unevenly spread: in Munster it was 184; in Leinster 170, in Connacht 110, and in Ulster 107.[3]

The land problem of the nineteenth century had its own distinctive character, but it was also in part an inheritance from a distant past. The landlords as a class were the successors of the protestant ascendancy of the eighteenth century, whose privileges and property were founded upon the defeat and expropriation of catholic Ireland during the seventeenth century, while the tenants (with important exceptions in Ulster) were the descendants of the catholics who had been defeated and expropriated. The landlords were preponderantly of British origin, identified themselves with the culture of England, regarded the union as the only ultimate security for their privileged position, and were themselves regarded as the 'English garrison', in Ireland. The tenants, on the other hand, except in the colonised areas of Ulster, were largely descended from the indigenous Gaelic population, whose cultural traditions had survived the destruction of their

[1] In the 21 years between 1849 and 1869 over one quarter of the houses of evicted tenants were thus levelled (*Evictions, Ireland, 1849-69* (20 Jan. 70) in S.P.O., R.P. 1874/685).

[2] Appendix D1; Vaughan and Fitzpatrick, *Irish historical statistics, population 1821-1971*, pp. 261-2.

[3] Appendix C; J. S. Donnelly, *The land and the people of nineteenth century Cork* (1975), pp 227-30, 234-42.

political and social institutions by the English in the sixteenth and seventeenth centuries. In these traditions the English feudal principle of land-holding was seen as an intrusion into a Gaelic world in which the social structure was based on family ownership of land. The tenants' claim to an indefeasible interest in their holdings was increasingly presented by their spokesmen as a claim to restitution of rights of which their ancestors had been wrongfully deprived.

This view was formulated in 1848 with revolutionary fervour by one of the Young Ireland group, James Fintan Lalor. His thinking expresses the overwhelming importance of the land question, the bitterness and desperation of the famine era, and his own passionate conviction that the landlords were no part of the nation. Repeal of the union he regarded as in itself a paltry issue, which the mass of the people would not fight for.

> A mightier question moves Ireland today. . . . The soil of Ireland for the people of Ireland, to have and to hold from God alone who gave it. . . . From a worse bondage than the bondage of any foreign government, from a dominion more grievous and grinding than the dominion of England in its worst days, from the cruellest tyranny that ever yet laid its vulture clutch on the body and soul of a country, from the robber rights and robber rule that have turned us into slaves and beggars in the land that God gave us for ours—deliverance, oh Lord, deliverance or death![1]

Ireland's most vital need, Lalor went on, was 'not to repeal the union, but to repeal the conquest, . . . to found a new nation, and raise up a free people . . . based on a peasantry rooted like rocks in the soil'. He believed that national independence could be won only through the emancipation of the peasantry by the method of a general strike against rent. The tenants, he urged, ought 'to refuse all rent to the present usurping proprietors until the people, the true proprietors . . ., have in national congress or convention decided what rents they are to pay and to whom'.[2] The question of independence would thus be joined to the land question like a railway train coupled to an engine powerful enough to draw it to its destination.[3] This tremendous challenge to both the social and political system evoked no response from a people exhausted and dispirited by the famine. The combination of the land question with the question of national independence, of tenant right with nationality, which Lalor urged, was only to be fully realised in the land war of 1879-82. But his seminal idea was transmitted by John Mitchel to Irish nationalist thinking in America,

[1] Lalor in *Irish Felon*, 24 June 48, quoted in *James Fintan Lalor: patriot and political essayist,* ed. L. Fogarty (1918), pp 57-8.

[2] Lalor in *Irish Felon*, 8 July 48, quoted as above, p. 95.

[3] Lalor in *Irish Felon*, 1 July 48, quoted as above, p. 83.

which was to have a decisive influence on Davitt in 1878[1] and through Davitt on the land war.

A contemporary in whom Lalor's words kindled a flame, Thomas William Croke, the dynamic young catholic curate of Charleville, County Cork, was to be a direct link with the land war. In January 1850 he founded the Charleville Reading Society, for the immediate purpose of fostering popular education but with the ulterior motive of helping on the 'great national struggle' for tenant right which then seemed to be looming up, but which did not materialise. He proposed the formation of local tenant societies on lines that could have been a pattern for the branches of the future Land League.[2]

> Every tenant farmer in the district gives his name to the secretary of the society, who enters it in a book. . . . Together with his name, he mentions his place of residence, the extent of his holding, his acreable rent, and his landlord's address. These things being duly registered, the assembled farmers pledge themselves in words of the following import: 'We promise God, our country, and each other never to bid for any farm of land from which any industrious farmer in this district has been ejected'.

Here Croke enunciated the basic principle that was to be applied with sensational success by the Land League nearly thirty years later: tenant farmers exposed to the chronic threat of eviction have it in their power to eliminate the evil, and with it the 'land-grabber', by collective action among themselves.[3]

The concept of tenant right as a historic claim of the dispossessed Irish against alien and usurping landlords was voiced in the fifties and sixties by such moderate nationalists as Charles Gavan Duffy, John Blake Dillon, and Sir John Gray,[4] and drew strength from a revival of scholarly interest in early Gaelic society exemplified by the publication of the first two volumes of the *Ancient laws of Ireland* in 1865 and 1869.[5] The historicist approach was supported by English social thinkers, especially the philosopher and economist, John Stuart Mill, one of the great intellectual forces of the age and the most damaging critic of the economic orthodoxy that dominated English policy towards Irish land down to 1870. His authority could be quoted with telling effect against the landlords by selective citations from the

[1] See below, pp 233-4.
[2] Cf. below, pp 344-5.
[3] Mark Tierney, *Croke of Cashel* (1976), pp 21-4.
[4] E. D. Steele, *Irish land and British politics: tenant-right and nationality, 1865-70* (1974), pp 19-20.
[5] *Ancient laws of Ireland: Senchus Mor.* Vol. i, preface by W. Neilson Hancock; vol. ii, preface by W. Neilson Hancock and Thaddeus O'Mahony. Dublin, 1865, 1869. See also Clive Dewey 'Celtic agrarian legislation and the Celtic revival: historicist implications of Gladstone's Irish and Scottish land acts, 1870-1886' in *Past and Present*, no. 64 (Aug. 1974), pp 30-70.

successive editions of his *Principles of political economy* (1848-65);[1] and in his pamphlet, *England and Ireland* (1868), Mill has a classic statement of the historicist case for Irish tenant right.

> Before the conquest, the Irish people knew nothing of absolute property in land. The land virtually belonged to the entire sept [extended family]; the chief was little more than the managing member of the association. The feudal idea, which views all rights as emanating from a head landlord, came in with the conquest, was associated with foreign dominion, and has never to this day been recognised by the moral sentiments of the people. Originally the offspring not of industry but of spoliation, the right has not been allowed to purify itself by protracted possession but has passed from the original spoliators to others by a series of fresh spoliations, so as to be always connected with the latest and most odious oppressions of foreign invaders. In the moral feelings of the Irish people, the right to hold the land goes, as it did in the beginning, with the right to till it. Since the last confiscations nearly all the land has been owned from generation to generation with a more absolute ownership than exists in almost any other country (except England) by landlords (mostly foreigners and nearly all of a foreign religion) who had less to do with tilling it, who had less connection with it of any useful kind—or indeed of any kind, for a large proportion did not even reside on it—than the landowners of any other country.[2]

And Mill went on to argue that the only real solution to the Irish land problem was the conversion of the tenants into peasant proprietors. Mill's writings were to become the bible of Irish land-reformers, though till 1879 the tenants' spokesmen generally demanded only changes in the land law to give recognition to tenant right.

The Young Ireland rising of July 1848 failed both through deficiencies of leadership and because this middle-class movement had little contact with the mass of the people and had little to offer them. The 1848 leaders had rejected Lalor's plan of agrarian revolution as too defiant, but they had done nothing to implement a more moderate and statesmanlike plan drafted by Gavan Duffy and approved by the Irish Confederation (the official organisation of Young Ireland) in February 1848, five months before the rising. Duffy advocated an aggressive Irish parliamentary party which should be the authentic voice of the nation and which, acting independently of all other parties, should obstruct the business of the house of commons till either an Irish parliament was conceded or the Irish members were forcibly expelled. In the latter event, the expelled members should turn their backs on the British parliament for ever, return home, and set up a 'great council of the nation' to provide for the restoration of a parliament in Dublin.[3] This imaginative scheme contained in essence

[1] Steele, op. cit., pp 48-55.

[2] *England and Ireland*, pp 12-13.

[3] C. Gavan Duffy, *Four years of Irish history, 1845-9* (1883), pp 486-90; *My life in two hemispheres* (1898), i, 248-51.

the policy of independent opposition first attempted in the fifties and applied with dramatic success by Parnell twenty-five years later. But the real sting in the tail of it—the policy of collective withdrawal of the Irish members from Westminster—was to remain an untried though frequently ventilated theory till, adapted and developed by Arthur Griffith, it was put into effect with momentous results in January 1919 by Sinn Féin.

It was inevitable that, in the reaction against 1848, the next attempt at national effort should be made on a strictly constitutional basis and with a limited objective. In August 1850 the Irish Tenant League was formed to protect tenant farmers threatened by the 'great clearances' of the post-famine era. The league combined catholic and protestant farmers all over Ireland in defence of a programme of tenant right that came to be known as the '3 Fs'—(1) a fair rent, to be determined by an impartial valuation, (2) fixity of tenure, subject to the payment of this rent, and (3) freedom for the tenant to sell his interest in his holding.[1] Under the leadership of Frederick Lucas, Gavan Duffy, and George Henry Moore, steps were taken to create a parliamentary party on the lines suggested by Duffy in 1848, pledged to oppose all governments that did not accept the league's demands. In the general election of July 1852, forty-eight Irish members professing to support the league's programme and the policy of independent opposition were returned to parliament out of a total representation of 103. This party held the balance between the two British parties, and was able to put its policy into effect in the following December when it combined with the liberal opposition to defeat the conservative government of Lord Derby. The new movement had thus been a rapid and remarkable success; but from this point onwards the fortunes of the party declined as the combined result of internal dissension, the defection of a number of its members, conflicts with Paul Cullen, archbishop of Dublin (1852-78), and many of the catholic clergy, and difficulties arising out of an electoral system dominated by landowners. Among these composite causes of failure what most struck the public at the time was the conduct of William Keogh and John Sadleir, who accepted office in the liberal-coalition government formed in December 1852; they had made themselves egregious as champions of catholic interests and they were now exposed as pledge-breakers and careerists.[2]

[1] Duffy, *The league of north and south* (1885), ch. III; J. H. Whyte, *The independent Irish party, 1850-9* (1958), pp 4-5, 12. The resolutions of the tenant-right conference (6-8 Aug. 1850) are reprinted in E. Curtis and R. B. McDowell (ed.), *Irish historical documents* (1943), pp 250-52.

[2] Duffy, op. cit. Whyte, op. cit., and *The Tenant League and Irish politics in the eighteen-fifties* (Dublin Historical Association pamphlet, 1963); 'Political problems, 1850-60', in P. J. Corish (ed.), *A history of Irish catholicism*, V, ch. 2 (1967), pp 12-24.

The parliamentary tradition was thus discredited among Irish nationalists, and was rejected by the spirited men who, on 17 March 1858, initiated a new revolutionary effort, the fenian movement. The founders of this movement—James Stephens, John O'Mahony, and Thomas Clarke Luby—had been connected with the rising of 1848 and inherited the Young Ireland tradition. But they began at the point that Young Ireland had reached only after six years of fruitless endeavour to achieve their purpose by peaceful means. They and the other moving spirits in fenianism during its early years—Jeremiah O'Donovan Rossa, Charles James Kickham, and John O'Leary—committed themselves and their movement to the dogma that Great Britain would never surrender sovereignty to the force of argument and that Ireland's claim to national independence would be conceded only to the argument of force. They taught that to prepare for a military struggle with Britain was the only 'true path'. They regarded nationalists who hoped to win independence by parliamentary action with a mixture of contempt and hatred. The British parliament was a 'talking-shop', membership of which was injurious to the military virtues and consumed energies that could be more usefully employed. Parliamentary agitation was futile, since on all questions where Irish interests clashed with imperial policy the Irish members were always outvoted. In any case Irish nationalists who took part in the British parliament were acknowledging the legitimacy of Ireland's servitude, and thus stultifying themselves. The founders of fenianism had no illusions about the strength of the enemy, but they hoped to offset it by secret organisation, by the high morale of their followers, and by choosing the moment to strike when circumstances, and especially the international situation, would be adverse to Great Britain. They concentrated on the single aim of independence, insisting that all other questions were a secondary consideration. To pursue particular national objectives before self-government had been won would be a dangerous deviation. This applied even to the land question, for which, in the spirit of Fintan Lalor, they saw the only remedy in the transformation of the tenant-farmers into peasant proprietors. But unlike Lalor they had no positive plan for bringing this about: 'the only way for us to settle the land question satisfactorily is to win national independence. Then the people could establish a peasant proprietary. This is the true and only remedy for our agricultural population.'[1] And yet fenianism, unlike previous revolutionary movements, made its own converts almost entirely among the working classes—small farmers and agricultural labourers, clerks, shop assistants, railwaymen,

[1] *Irish People*, 28 Nov. 63.

seamen and soldiers, and urban workers generally. That it included a small middle-class element—schoolmasters, commercial travellers, business and professional men—made its distinctively working-class character all the more striking. The fenian leaders, themselves nearly all middle-class, held firmly that nationalism was of no one class or creed, but they wrote off the landed aristocracy as a whole, were suspicious of the well-to-do middle classes, and pinned their faith to the common man.

The response of the common man justified this faith: by 1865 there were many thousands of enrolled fenians not merely in Ireland but also among the Irish in Great Britain, prepared to go into action. The social composition of the movement, combined with its secret organisation, was the basis of the charge frequently made against the fenians that they were communists. But a crucial fact about this largely working-class movement was that its thinking was simply nationalist. It had no specific social programme for the democratic Irish republic of its dreams; from a Marxist standpoint it was painfully naive. It had no distinctive doctrine of nationalism, but accepted the national creed of Wolfe Tone and the United Irishmen, of Thomas Davis and Young Ireland. It was essentially a separatist, but not a doctrinaire republican, movement. As the name fenian[1] implies, it had a tinge of Gaelic revivalism, notably exemplified in O'Mahony, an Irish scholar and translator of Keating's *Foras feasa ar Éirinn*, who 'looked forward to the restoration of Gaelic as one of the certain results of the achievement of national independence'. Many of the local fenian leaders in Connacht and Munster were Irish-speakers and enthusiasts for the revival of the language. But the fenian movement was preoccupied with politics and had no official attitude towards Irish.[2] Nearly all fenians were catholics, but the movement was strictly non-sectarian and welcomed all Irishmen to its ranks. It was fiercely condemned by Archbishop Cullen and a majority of the catholic clergy, partly on the ground of its secret and oath-bound character, still more for its extremism and the absolute claims it made on its members: for every fenian had to take an oath of allegiance to the Irish republic 'now virtually established'. In face of clerical condemnation the fenians showed unparalleled intransigence, insisting that a line could be drawn between faith and morals on the one hand and politics on the other, and that, while the catholic clergy were the final authority for catholics in the former sphere, they had no authority whatever in the latter. On the contrary, their political judgment was often sadly at fault.

[1] *Fianna Eireann*, legendary warrior-bands of Ireland.
[2] Devoy, *Recollections*, pp 262-3.

From this position the fenians refused absolutely to budge (even when fenianism was explicitly condemned by Rome in 1870), and in consequence large numbers of fenians went excommunicate. Finally the movement differed from all previous national movements in that it drew its support not only from the Irish at home but also from the new Ireland that the famine emigration had created in Britain and America. It was, indeed, among Young Ireland refugees in New York, headed by John O'Mahony, that the initial steps in the founding of the movement were taken. The fenians in Britain formed an integral part of the home organisation, while those in America constituted a separate body whose special function was to aid the home organisation with arms and money.

The leaders of fenianism were in various ways quite unfitted to conduct a rebellion. They were writers, thinkers, and scholars rather than men of action. Kickham, 'the gentle Charles', the personification of the fenian spirit at its highest, had been deaf and nearly blind since the age of thirteen; he was a gifted poet and novelist whose writings, and especially *Sally Cavanagh, or the untenanted graves*[1] and *Knocknagow, or the homes of Tipperary,*[2] show unrivalled insight into the realities of life in rural Ireland. The great man of action among the fenian chiefs, James Stephens, who at the outset was entrusted with autocratic powers, had a genius for organising and for inspiring loyalty, but few of the other qualifications of a successful military leader. The secret organisation that he devised seems initially to have served its purpose, giving the movement a widely extended but coherent character and incorporating a numerous fifth-column among Irish soldiers in British garrisons in Ireland. To direct the fighting that he promised for 1865 he enlisted as prospective officers many Irish-Americans serving in the federal armies in the American civil war. On the other hand, with sublime inconsistency he founded in 1863 a newspaper, the *Irish People*, under the editorship of O'Leary, Kickham, and Luby, to be the mouthpiece of the movement; and in this it succeeded so well that the government was greatly assisted in acquiring information about the conspiracy. Yet if, as Stephens originally intended, rebellion had been launched in 1865 when the American civil war ended with plenty of bad blood between Britain and the United States, the fenians might well have given a good account of themselves. By the summer of 1865 there were several hundred trained American officers in Ireland, but the American arms on which Stephens relied were not

[1] First published serially in *Hibernian Magazine*, 3rd series, i, nos 1-6 (July-Dec. 64); and as a separate book in Mar. 69.

[2] Ch. I-XXXVI published serially in the *Emerald* (New York) and the *Shamrock* (Dublin), Mar.-Sept. 70; first complete edition in book form, Dublin 1873; innumerable later reprints.

forthcoming, because the fenian movement in America became paralysed by a split. Stephens decided on postponement; soon afterwards the *Irish People* was suppressed and three of his principal colleagues—Luby, Rossa, and O'Leary—were arrested (15 September). Other arrests followed, including those of Kickham and of Stephens himself (11 November). Rescued from Richmond prison, Dublin, on 24 November, Stephens again postponed a rising. The situation became hopeless when, in the spring, the spread of fenianism in the British army was discovered and effectively dealt with. At the end of 1866, having failed to fulfil yet another promise of action, Stephens was deposed. The decision of his Irish-American successors to fight early in 1867 was taken by desperate men unable to endure further inaction. So the 'rising' of March 1867 was no more than a gesture.

After the rising the I.R.B. was faced with the task of rallying its broken ranks and resuming preparations for insurrection without the hope of coming to grips with the enemy in the foreseeable future. That the movement succeeded in reorganising itself under a representative government, the supreme council, and in remaining faithful to its original purpose is a tribute to the strength of its principles and the devotion of its members. It was to continue in being, in varying degrees of animation, for over fifty years. In its chosen sphere of activity it encountered nothing but failure and disappointment till the Easter rising of 1916. It was always an underground and a minority movement, and continued inactivity inevitably produced frustration, demoralisation, and disruption. An extremist and irresponsible wing resorted to a barren policy of dynamite and sporadic terrorism; and the larger, opportunist, element that joined forces with constitutional nationalism in the 'land war' had the ironical experience of assisting in a victory that ensured the dominance of the constitutional movement in Irish politics for many years. Yet fenianism as an ideal proved to be the most militant, pervasive, and undeviating influence in Irish politics down to 1916. To supporters of the union, fenianism was a particularly vicious form of nationalism, infecting the rabble of Ireland like an insidious disease; but to those who believed in it and those who respected it, fenianism was a pure flame that summoned Irishmen to sacrifice everything to the cause of national regeneration.

Given the time and place, and given the temperament and family background of Michael Davitt, it would have been surprising if he had not become a fenian. Industrial Lancashire was a stronghold of fenianism in Britain;[1] and it was natural for high-spirited young Irishmen of

[1] P.R.O., H.O. 45/O.S.7799/62, 124, 135, 221 (Jan. 66-Sept. 67).

the class to which Davitt belonged to join the movement.[1] He became a fenian in 1865,[2] at the age of nineteen, with the encouragement of his parents, and was clearly a welcome recruit, for he was soon elected 'centre' of the Rossendale 'circle' of the I.R.B. A fenian circle by this time was a group or cell of from 10 to 100 men, under the command of its 'centre'. There were about 50 members of the Rossendale centre, distributed over four or five small towns in the valley. The post of centre was a localised responsibility, and Michael contrived to combine it with his duties in Cockcroft's business.[3]

Michael's closest associate in the Rossendale circle was Martin Haran, who was a trusted friend of the Davitt family.[4] Born in Ireland about 1832, he had come to Haslingden—probably as a famine emigrant—a few years before the Davitts, and he had known Michael since he was a small boy. The difference in their ages—about fourteen years—did not prevent them from enjoying one another's company, and both were good walkers.[5] It may well have been he who initiated Michael into fenianism. Haran was a drapery hawker, living with his four children (his wife being dead) in George Street, next to Wilkinson Street, where the Davitts had formerly lived and to which they were to return, in March 1867, after about fourteen years at Rock Hall.[6] His second son, Frank, aged twelve, had had a similar experience to Michael's: he had lost his right hand in a mill accident and in consequence had been sent by his father to the Wesleyan school that Michael had attended a few years before. Here he was laying the foundation of a career as a schoolmaster. Frank's elder brother, Martin, aged fourteen, was an apprentice in the printing office of Henry Cockcroft; he had got the job on Michael's recommendation, and he and Michael were to be fellow-workers for several years.[7] It is probable that Martin and Frank Haran both became fenians: 'every smart respectable young fellow' among the Irish of Haslingden, Frank Haran recalled years later, was a sworn member.[8]

[1] *S.C.P.*, ix, 417.

[2] There is, of course, no contemporary evidence for this dating, which depends on statements of Davitt's to the *Times*-Parnell commission in 1889 (see next note) and on circumstantial evidence.

[3] *S.C.P.*, ix, 352, 399, 402-3; *Kimberley comm. rep.*, ii, 529.

[4] See below, pp 164-5, 173.

[5] H.-C. Joseph Murphy to I.G.P. 22 Feb. 70 (S.P.O., 5817R); H.-C. Murphy to H.-C. Bodley, 11 Apr. (S.P.O., 6223R/6246R); *The Times*, 18 July, p. 11 col. 3.

[6] Census returns, Haslingden, 1861, in P.R.O., R.G./9/3061/477/4B. f. 8; Haslingden Institute Members' subscription book 1846-67 (Haslingden Public Library, reference department, local collection); Francis Haran to Mrs Mary Davitt, 7 Nov. 1907 (DP/P).

[7] Francis Haran to Mrs Mary Davitt, 15 Oct., 7 Nov. 1907 (DP/P); Martin Haran to Mrs Mary Davitt, 23 Dec. (DP/P); 'Briar' (see above, p. 18 n. 1) in *Haslingden Observer*, 27 July 1935. Francis Haran was assistant master at St Alban's School, Blackburn, for 44 years; he died in 1935 ('Briar', as above).

[8] Francis Haran to Mrs Mary Davitt, 7 Nov. 1907 (DP/P).

In the I.R.B. at this time were many young Irishmen or sons of Irish parents, mostly from Connacht, who had settled in Lancashire. Typical of these were Tom and Martin Burke, Mark Ryan, John and Bernard Denvir, John O'Connor Power, and Arthur Forrester. Tom Burke and his brother Martin were both factory workers in the village of Stacksteads, five miles east of Haslingden. Tom had been born in Michael's native village of Straide. He resembled Michael physically, and like him lost an arm in a factory accident from which he seems never to have fully recovered. He was sent back by his friends to Mayo, but died there in 1869. Martin remained in Lancashire and was to prove a staunch personal friend to Michael.[1]

Mark Francis Ryan was the eldest son of John Ryan, of Kilconly parish, County Galway, who, after being evicted from three separate farms in the same parish, had emigrated to Lancashire in 1860 and opened a small provision shop at Stacksteads. Mark first learnt of fenianism from the Burkes, and was initiated into the movement by Davitt in 1865, at the age of 21. He served in the Lancashire Volunteers for two periods in 1865-6 to acquire military training in preparation for the expected fenian rising, and went to Tuam, County Galway, early in 1867, to take part in it. But finding no rising there, he turned to education: by way of the Christian Brothers' School at Tuam he entered St Jarlath's College, a residential secondary school under the direction of the archbishop of Tuam, which prepared ecclesiastical students for Maynooth and other seminaries and lay students for secular professions or public office. Though one of the oldest institutions of its kind in Ireland—it was founded in 1800—it was unconventional in two ways that appealed to Ryan: the Irish language had an honoured place in its course of studies and there was a fenian connection among its students. Its president, Fr Ulick Bourke—like the patriarchal archbishop, John MacHale, who lived next door to the college—was devoted to Irish and was far from unsympathetic to the fenians. Its student body included a distinguished nucleus of fenians—two sons of the exiled fenian leader, O'Donovan Rossa, two sons of John O'Donovan, the famous Celtic scholar, and a son of Michael Larkin, one of the 'Manchester martyrs'.[2] Ryan appears to have spent the summer term of 1867 at St Jarlath's, and then, after a year with the Christian Brothers, was continuously at the college from September 1868 to July 1871. He showed promise as a scholar but his efforts were divided between his studies and fenian activities that were all the more disturbing to his fellow-students because he was considerably

[1] Ryan, *Fenian memories*, pp 12-13; *C.C.C. minutes*, lxxii, 323-6, 328; and see below, pp 96, 97, 164, 170.

[2] See below, pp 51-2.

older than they. Even Fr Bourke began to show embarrassment, and Ryan took the hint. He ceased to be a member of St Jarlath's but continued to promote fenianism among its students, and, operating both from County Galway and his home in Lancashire, to organise the purchase and secret transmission of arms to fenians in the west of Ireland. After a short time as assistant in a chemist shop in Tuam, he went on to Queen's College, Galway, where he laid the basis of a career in medicine, which, combined with continued and unwavering devotion to fenianism, was to last nearly fifty years, forty-two (1882-1924) spent in London.[1]

An older man than Davitt and Ryan, and more deeply rooted in Lancashire, was John Denvir, whose father, a native of County Down, had settled in Liverpool early in the century. He was employed in the building trade, and about 1833 went with his family to Bushmills, on the north coast of County Antrim, to act as clerk of works for the building of a castle for Sir Francis Macnaghten. It was thus that his son John was born in Ireland. The family returned to Liverpool after a few years, and John was to spend almost the whole of his long life there and in London, actively involved in Irish affairs and accumulating an unrivalled personal knowledge of the Irish in Britain.[2] He served his apprenticeship as a joiner, and for some years after 1855 carried on a joinery and building business of his own. He then became secretary of the Boy's Refuge, an organisation for destitute and homeless boys conducted by Father James Nugent, the catholic chaplain of Liverpool borough jail. Later he conducted Fr Nugent's newspaper, *The Catholic Times*, for several years. It was while in Fr Nugent's service that, in 1866, apparently without any sense of conflicting loyalties, he joined the I.R.B. Soon afterwards he came into touch with Davitt.

> He was little more than a boy when I first met him at a small gathering to which none but the initiated were admitted. From the first I was strongly drawn towards that tall, dark-complexioned, bright-eyed, modest youth, with his typical Celtic face and figure. He was in company with Arthur Forrester, who was a fluent speaker and writer, and who on this occasion did most of the talking, Davitt only throwing in some shrewd remarks from time to time.[3]

In the I.R.B., Denvir's distinctive role was that of contact man, and as such he came to know many of the leading personalities of the

[1] Ryan, *Fenian memories*, pp 7, 12-13, 17-19, 20, 25-30, 31-2, 47-57, and passim. *Iarlaith: St Jarlath's College, Tuam, past pupils' magazine* (1955), pp 83, 209. St Jarlath's College, Tuam, Fee-payment book, 1838-67, session 1866-7, p. 8; 1867-80, pp 11, 17, 27, 36, 60, 65. S.P.O., A files, nos 526, 527, 567, 584, 585.

[2] See his book, *The Irish in Britain from the earliest times to the fall and death of Parnell* (1892).

[3] Denvir, *Life story*, p. 204.

fenian movement as they visited or passed through Liverpool. About 1870 he started a small printing and publishing business, and began to realise a long-cherished ambition with a series of penny booklets of biography, history, stories and songs designed to sustain Irish national morale and known as 'Denvir's Irish Library'.[1] John Denvir's fenianism was not of the militant kind. But he had a brother, Bernard, who, behind the facade of his newsagent's and stationer's shop in the Tithebarn Road, Liverpool, was a fenian activist, and stood high in the fenian organisation. He was reported by a police spy in January 1870 to be closely associated with Davitt at a time when Michael was expecting to be arrested and preparing to resist arrest by force.[2]

Two other friends of Davitt's in his early fenian days were O'Connor Power and Forrester, of whom the first was soon to be one of the foremost personalities in Irish politics and the latter to have a disastrous impact on Davitt's career.

John O'Connor Power, known to the police as '*alias* John Fleming, *alias* John Webster, *alias* Charles Ferguson',[3] by his own statement was the third son of 'Patrick Power of Ballinasloe, gent.',[4] but was alleged by Fr Patrick Lavelle, P.P. of Partry, County Mayo, to be the illegitimate son of a policeman named Fleming from County Cavan.[5] He was born in Ballinasloe in 1846, and spent part of his childhood in the local workhouse. About 1861 he went to Lancashire to live with relatives in Rochdale, where he learnt the trade of house-painter. He joined the I.R.B., and spent some years as a fenian organiser in Lancashire. He appears to have become acquainted with Davitt soon after his arrival in Lancashire. 'O'Connor Power I knew when I was a boy', Davitt told the *Times*-Parnell commission.[6] Mark Ryan met them both about 1865.[7] Power was medium-sized and heavily built, with large, rather coarse, features and pock-marked face.[8] William O'Brien describes him as 'a man of great resolution, with a merciless under-jaw,

[1] Ibid., pp 2, 27-40, 54-5, 65-72, 74-6, 91, 137-8, 153-9, and passim; Ryan, *Fenian memories*, pp 182-3; S.P.O., Fenianism, index of names, 1866-71, p. 210.

[2] Ibid., p. 209; H.-C. Murphy to I.G.P., 5 Jan. 70 (S.P.O., 5438R); informant to H.-C. Murphy, 10 Jan. (S.P.O., 5478R).

[3] S.P.O., Abstracts of cases of persons arrested under habeas corpus suspension act, iii, 28-9.

[4] *Register of admissions to the Honourable Society of the Middle Temple* (3 vols, London, [1950]), ii, 609. Power was admitted to the Middle Temple on 14 Feb. 78 and called to the bar on 17 Nov. 81.

[5] Lavelle to Isaac Butt, 12 Mar. 74, quoted in Thornley, *Butt*, p. 184, n. 17. Lavelle detested Power but could scarcely have invented the Fleming paternity, which is consistent with what is otherwise known of this enigmatic man, whom Davitt once refers to as 'Jack Fleming *alias* O'Connor Power' (DN/9, 28 June 82).

[6] *S.C.P.*, ix, 357.

[7] *Fenian memories*, p. 13.

[8] S.P.O., Description of fenian suspects, p. 1 (1868); see plate V.

a furious temper governed by a carefully studied urbanity of manner and a calm strong voice, that made the most commonplace observation impressive'.[1] Tim Healy speaks of him as 'reeking of the common clay'.[2] He already had a reputation as an orator. He was intelligent, ambitious, and full of restless energy.[3]

Arthur Forrester, four years younger than Davitt and Power, was born at Salford in 1850, the son of an Irish mother, Ellen Magennis, who had left her native Clones about 1845, at the age of seventeen, to earn her living as a nursery governess in Liverpool. She moved to Manchester where, about 1847, she married Michael Forrester, a stone mason. He was a hard drinker and died young, leaving her to provide for five children of whom the eldest was only ten. Her life became a grinding struggle against poverty and her own weak health, but she had a buoyant temperament and a genius for making the best of things. She had shown precocious literary facility, and from an early age was a contributor of popular verse to several weekly papers, Irish and English. Her flow of verse, published in the *Weekly Budget* and elsewhere, now helped to keep her family alive. A gentle and affectionate woman, she was none the less an ardent nationalist and identified herself with the fenian movement in the Manchester area. Davitt came to know her well, and thought very highly of her character and talents. Her son, Arthur, and two daughters, Fanny and Mary, all inherited her gift for versifying. Arthur Forrester at fifteen was giving voice to a militant nationalism in verse and prose, published under the pseudonyms 'Angus' and 'William Tell' in the *Irish People*. After the suppression of that paper and the arrest of the fenian chiefs in September 1865, he visited Dublin under the name of Thomas Brown to make personal contact with the revolutionary movement there. He associated with Thomas Baines, notorious for his activities in making converts to fenianism among soldiers. He returned to Lancashire early in 1866, just before the habeas corpus act was suspended (18 February).[4]

Davitt, Power, and Forrester all took part in the fenian attempt on Chester castle which was to have been a preliminary to the 1867 rising in Dublin, initially fixed for 11 February. The plan, devised by John

[1] W. O'Brien, *Recollections*, p. 140. [2] Healy, *Letters and leaders*, i, 65.

[3] DN/15, 25 Apr. 84; W. O'Brien, *Recollections*, pp 139-40; O'Connor, *Memoirs* (1929), i, 83-7; Healy, *Letters and leaders*, passim; MacDonagh, *Home rule*, pp 30, 32; *D.P.B.*, i, 74-5.

[4] M. McDonagh, *Irish graves in England* ('Evening Telegraph' reprints, vi (1888)), pp 141-4; D. J. O'Donoghue, *The poets of Ireland* (2nd ed., 1912), p. 151; Denvir, *Life story*, pp 130-4; Ryan, *Fenian memories*, p. 14; *Irish People*, 19 Aug. 65 (p. 616), 26 Aug. (p. 637), 2 Sept. (p. 652), 9 Sept. (p. 668), 16 Sept. (p. 683); Supt Daniel Ryan to C.P., 9 Mar. 67 (S.P.O., 2483R); *Irishman*, 16 Mar. 1867, p. 595; *Irish Weekly Independent*, 4 Aug. 94, p. 4.

McCafferty, the fire-eating Irish-American who had been a guerilla captain in the confederate army during the civil war, was this: a strong body of armed fenians, drawn from Irish groups in Lancashire and other parts of the north of England and led by American officers, were to converge secretly on Chester in ones and twos on 11 February; that night they would be admitted to the lightly-guarded castle by soldiers of the garrison who were fenians, and would seize the arms stored there; they would commandeer the mail train on its way from London to Holyhead; having torn up the railway lines behind them and cut the telegraph wires, they would transport themselves and their booty to Holyhead; here they would capture the mail boat and cross in her to Ireland. No opportunity was afforded the author of this spectacular design to learn at how many points it was certain to go wrong, for the Liverpool police received warning of it from a fenian informer, Corydon, late the night before, and troops were rushed to Chester by special trains. When the would-be raiders, numbering about 1,000, arrived at Chester in the early morning of 11 February in obedience to their orders, they found that there was nothing they could do except extricate themselves from a dangerous position.[1]

Davitt led a detachment of fenians from the Haslingden area to Chester on the morning of the intended raid. It was his first—and was to be his only—fenian military operation. Many fenians retreating from Chester did not return home but crossed to Dublin by steamer from Liverpool and Holyhead, hoping to take part in the rising, which, unknown to them, had been postponed to 5 March. Most of them on landing were arrested under the habeas corpus suspension act. Forrester and the Manchester men who were under his command at Chester were among these. Davitt, in withdrawing his men and directing their return to their homes, showed a cooler head and better judgment, and a sense of responsibility that Forrester notably lacked; and he eluded the attention of the police.[2]

Like Davitt, O'Connor Power did not go to Ireland after the Chester affair. He had some connection with the fenian rescue operation at Manchester in the autumn; and later went as a fenian agent to America to discuss the reorganisation of the I.R.B. with American fenians. He returned in January 1868 to play an active part in the setting up of a representative governing body for the I.R.B., the supreme council. He was arrested in Dublin, under the habeas corpus suspension act,

[1] Liverpool Central Library, Head constable's reports to the watch committee, 352 POL/2/4, no. 107, pp 139-40 (11 Feb. 67), no. 111, pp 147-9 (14 Feb.); P.R.O., H.O. 45/0. S. 7799/153, 157, 177-82, 187-90, 209, 222 (Dec. 66-Apr. 67); *Annual Register*, 1867, pt II, pp 23-7.

[2] Cashman, pp 19-20; S.C.P., ix, 353; Denvir, *Life story*, pp 81-5; A. M. Sullivan, *New Ireland* pp 275-6; Devoy, *Recollections*, pp 65-6, 137-9. See below, pp 84-5.

on 17 February 1868, and spent the next five months in Kilmainham and Mountjoy jails. From his release in July 1868 he was in the inner ring of the I.R.B., an influential member of its supreme council and one of its most aspiring politicians.[1]

Forrester had been arrested in Dublin on 16 February 1867 but was quickly released on account of his youth: he was just turned seventeen, was under-sized (5′ 1″ in height), and slight in build. He was in Dublin at the time of the rising (5–6 March) and was rearrested on 9 March in circumstances that cast a strong light on his character. The police were searching for arms and had come upon ten suspects in a public house at 92 Camden Street. Four of the men drew revolvers, and their leader, who was subsequently proved to be Forrester, swore that he would kill the first policeman who laid hands on him. He was overpowered after a scuffle in which two armed constables knocked him down and disarmed him, whereupon he declared that his only regret was not to have shot one of his captors. He was charged with being in possession of a revolver in a proclaimed district, pleaded guilty, and was sentenced to six months' imprisonment. At this point he described himself as a letterpress printer and bookkeeper. He was committed to Kilmainham jail on 25 March. Two months later his mother petitioned the lord lieutenant for his release: he was extremely young and delicate, and imprisonment was ruining his health; he was very sorry for his misconduct; he promised to be 'a good boy' in future and to make amends for the great affliction his 'indiscretion' had brought on his sorrowing mother; his punishment, already adequate, would be a salutary lesson to him for the rest of his life; he was firmly resolved to have nothing more to do with secret political societies. This does not sound like the Forrester known to the police. The chief superintendent of the 'G' (detective) division of the Dublin Metropolitan Police, Daniel Ryan, described him as 'a most determined vagabond',[2] and it is not surprising that the Irish government did not accede to Mrs Forrester's petition. Forrester remained in Kilmainham till 8 October, when he was discharged.[3] He returned to Lancashire, and far from renouncing fenianism he accepted an appointment as organiser and arms agent of the I.R.B. in the north of England. The police kept an eye on him, and when on 31 October two constables were shot in Dublin Superintendent Ryan at once suspected him of being the assassin. The Manchester police were telegraphed for information of his whereabouts and seem to have accounted for him

[1] S.P.O., Abstracts of cases of persons arrested under habeas corpus suspension act, iii, 28–9; MacDonagh, *Home rule*, pp 30–31; *D.P.B.*, i, 74–5. See plate V.

[2] Supt Daniel Ryan to C.P., 9 Mar. 67 (S.P.O., F2483).

[3] See plate IV.

satisfactorily. They had him under close observation and knew from letters intercepted under post office warrant that he was trafficking in arms for fenian purposes, but they seem to have been interested in his movements as a source of information rather than as grounds for a prosecution.[1]

Forrester combined his secret activities with writing and public speaking. From January 1869 he was a regular correspondent of the *Irishman*, a weekly owned and edited by Richard Pigott which, since the suppression of the *Irish People*, had become the principal organ of fenianism.[2] A collection of his verse appeared in 1869 in a small volume entitled *Songs of the rising nation*, to which his mother and his sister Fanny were also contributors. It was published by the Glasgow firm of Cameron and Ferguson, which specialised in cheap, popular books on Ireland of a nationalist hue. The whole volume is painfully sentimental and much of it, including 'Temperance lays' by Arthur (doubtless inspired by childhood memories of a drunken father), is moralising and domesticated; but the title has its justification in a group of 'Battle ballads', which Arthur, as he is at pains to tell his readers, had composed to express the indignation of a martial spirit on fire with the memory of his country's wrongs. These 'ballads', set to popular airs, gained some celebrity, and Forrester became well known to Irish audiences in England as an itinerant lecturer and verse-speaker.[3]

With the failure of the rising in March 1867 the outlook for fenianism seemed hopeless. All its leading men were in jail, the Irish government was in a stronger position than before, and British opinion was incensed against fenianism by two violent incidents that occurred later in 1867. The first was the dramatic rescue of two fenian prisoners, Thomas J. Kelly and Timothy Deasy, from a police van on its way through Manchester to Salford jail, which had the incidental result of killing a police sergeant, Charles Brett (18 September); the second was

[1] S.P.O., Abstracts of cases of persons arrested under habeas corpus suspension act, i, 416B; police reports on Forrester, Mar. 67-Apr. 68 (S.P.O., F2483); return of prisoners committed to Kilmainham, 6 Mar.-30 June 67, no. 256 (S.P.O., R.P. 1862/13521); Ellen Forrester to lord lieutenant, 23 May (S.P.O., F2483); photograph and description of Forrester on discharge from Kilmainham, 8 Oct. (S.P.O., Photographs of fenians; see plate IV); Supt Daniel Ryan to chief constable of Manchester, 31 Oct. (S.P.O., R.P. 1867/19274); chief constable of Manchester to home office, 26 Nov. (P.R.O., H.O. 45/O.S. 7799/291); *Irishman*, 16 Mar., p. 595; *F.J.*, 2 Nov. 67, 28 Jan. 95; *Irish Weekly Independent*, 4, 11 Aug., 15 Sept. 94.

[2] Supt Daniel Ryan to C.P., 4 Dec. 69 (S.P.O., Fenian papers, 5169 R); cf. Richard Pigott, *Personal recollections of an Irish national journalist* (1883), pp 276-8; *S.C.P.*, v, 444 (20 Feb. 89).

[3] *Irishman*, 27 Mar. 69 (p. 611), 21 May 70 (p. 749, col. 2; p. 752, cols 2-3); *The Times*, 19 July, p. 11, col. 2; Denvir, *Life story*, pp 130, 204; Healy, *Letters and leaders*, i, 117.

an explosion outside the wall of Clerkenwell prison, in the City of London, intended to effect the escape of the fenian, Ricard O'Sullivan Burke, but resulting instead in the death of twelve innocent people and injury to many more (13 December).[1] It was peculiarly hazardous, as well as dispiriting, to be engaged in fenian activity in England at such a time. But this is what Davitt persisted in doing, and with greater self-abandonment than before. He disapproved of the Clerkenwell attempt, but the Manchester rescue was an operation that he might easily have been involved in himself: 'if I had been ordered . . . I would have gone there'.[2] The killing of Sergeant Brett—a 'brave policeman' who 'lost his life in doing his duty'—he sincerely deplored, but he was quite sure, from what he learned at the time and later, that no killing was intended. He believed that if he had been in charge of the rescue himself there would have been no killing. He considered that the three young men, William Philip Allen, Michael Larkin, and Michael O'Brien, who were executed in consequence of Brett's death, were sacrificed to anti-Irish clamour in England. In this view of the 'Manchester martyrs' he was at one with large numbers of his countrymen who were not fenians and with some eminent Englishmen, including John Bright. His sympathy with the Manchester men took a practical form, and in October and November 1867 he twice appeared in the press as a subscriber to their defence fund.[3]

With an irony that was often to be paralleled in his later life Davitt became involved at this time in the defence of his parish church, St Mary's, which the Irish of Haslingden had helped to build with their own hands. It had been opened in 1859 and was a focal point of their social life. At the first confirmation service in St Mary's, conducted by the catholic bishop of Salford, Dr William Turner, on 22 September 1861, Michael and his three sisters had been among those confirmed (Michael under the name Joseph).[4] In 1868 it was threatened by an upsurge of protestant bigotry in Lancashire inspired by an Irish demagogue, William Murphy. The 'Murphy riots' were specially directed against catholic churches, and Michael, the more indignant because he was himself so free from catholic bigotry, organised a body of young men of Irish origin to protect catholic churches in Haslingden and its neighbourhood. They served as a flying-squad, prepared to

[1] *Annual Register, 1867*, pt II, pp 131-4, 171-6; Devoy, *Recollections*, pp 237-43, 248-50.
[2] *S.C.P.*, ix, 416.
[3] *S.C.P.*, ix, 416-17, x, 439; *Defence*, pp 33-5; *Irishman*, 26 Oct., 9 Nov. 67; *Bacup Times*, 2, 16 Nov.
[4] Record of confirmations in St Mary's R.C. Church, Haslingden. Mary took the confirmation name of Agnes and Anne that of Teresa, but no confirmation name is entered for Sabina.

confront hostile mobs wherever necessary. Through their efforts, and the reputation they earned for toughness, many a church in the Haslingden-Bacup, Rochdale region was saved from damage and desecration. In June 1868 the visit of an anti-popish lecturer, Flynn, caused rioting in Haslingden, in the course of which, according to the recollections of Sabina Davitt and another contemporary, Michael and one companion confronted a wrecking mob advancing along a street of Irish houses to attack St Mary's Church. With cool determination and armed with heavy Colt revolvers, they dispersed the attackers by firing over their heads and giving the impression of being merely an advance-guard. It is probable that most of Davitt's young followers in this defence of catholic churches were fenians and as such officially proscribed by the catholic clergy.[1]

Later in 1868, when he was only twenty-two Davitt was appointed organising secretary and—in succession to the imprisoned Ricard O'Sullivan Burke—arms agent of the I.R.B. for England and Scotland. This was a key position, the holder of which was the link between all the fenian circles in Britain (over 100) and the supreme council of the I.R.B. He communicated with the council through his own particular member, that is, the member for the division of the I.R.B. in which he lived. In Davitt's case this was James Fox, of Leeds, member for the north of England; apart from him and the secretary of the council, James O'Kelly, Davitt did not know the identity of its members. The new post was a full-time commitment, and in accepting it he had no option but to resign from Cockcroft's employment. They parted about July 1868 with goodwill and regret on both sides, and probably some mystification on Cockcroft's part. For the next two years, under the guise of a hawker, Michael led a furtive, precarious, and unsettled life, moving about among the fenian circles, seeking to restore their morale and repair damage to their organisation, and procuring arms.[2]

A glimpse of one aspect of Davitt's personality at this time is afforded by the publication of four poems—his first known writing—in a London weekly, the *Universal News*, which described itself as 'the only organ of Irish catholic opinion in England'.[3] They had small merit as poetry (which Davitt in later life fully recognised[4]), but they have a special

[1] *Annual Register, 1868*, pt II, pp 55–8 (May 68); Cashman, pp 18–19; Sabina Davitt, Sketch of Davitt's early life, *c.* 1906 (DP/T); Francis Haran to Mrs Mary Davitt, 15 Oct. 1907 (DP/P); C. Aspin, *Haslingden, 1800–1900: a history* (1962), pp 104, 132–4.

[2] Evidence of Martin Haran and of Henry Cockcroft's son, Thomas, in *The Times*, 18 July 70, p. 11, col. 3; *Kimberley comm. rep.*, ii, 529; *S.C.P.*, ix, 400, 403, 407; DN/29A, 28 Jan. 95, in *I.H.S.*, iv, no. 15, p. 250; Denvir, *Life story*, p. 240; Sir Robert Anderson, *Sidelights on the home rule movement* (1906), pp 81, 85; Devoy, I.

[3] *Universal News*, 26 Dec. 68, 16 Jan., 13 Feb., 15 May 69.

[4] See below, p. 182.

value as expressing the romantic and revolutionary nationalism which he shared with Forrester, four years his junior and a more gifted versifier, from whom in character he differed profoundly. The first of these poems depicts the despair and the violent end of one who sold 'the boys' for the 'bloody Saxon gold': 'he lived a base informer's life and died as traitors should', that is, by an assassin's hand. The second poem tells how Biddy Hines becomes reconciled to her lover, Tim Delaney, on learning that his apparent neglect of her is due to his preoccupation with drilling 'fifty or sixty tall fellows' by the light of the moon. The third poem looks forward to the 'long-expected day' when 'the stalwart sons of Ireland' take up arms 'their country's rights to gain', and sounds a note that was to be characteristic of the mature Davitt:

> Now scattered sons of Innisfail
> Who *can* but *won't* unite,
> Why will ye still at variance be,
> When Ireland needs your might?
> Put all your childish feuds aside
> And cause no more delay
> In the preparations making for
> The long-expected day.

The final poem, 'A soldier's life for me', is the most personal and starry-eyed. His 'soldier' is engaged in a cause 'where victory is to be the harbinger of equal laws', the instrument of retribution for all the wrongs England's 'cursed laws' have inflicted on 'outraged man'.

> A soldier's life! to freely shed my heart's blood for the cause
> Made holy by the martyr'd dead, who braved the despot's laws
> That Ireland might a nation be, and proudly rank as one,
> Who strove to make her great and free by triumphs nobly won.

Davitt's activities as a fenian agent became all the more risky after March 1869 when the new prime minister, Gladstone, who had already embarked on his programme of 'justice to Ireland', released forty-nine of the imprisoned fenians in response to popular pressure for amnesty.[1] For it was obvious, from the government's point of view, that fenians who, in face of this gesture, persisted in preparations for fresh rebellion were irreconcilable and could expect no mercy if they were caught. It was, indeed, part of the case of the Irish Amnesty Association for the release of all the fenians still in prison that it would impress all persons with the conviction that any further attempts would be most severely punished, in consequence of the clemency extended to

[1] *The Times*, 13 Mar. 69, p. 19; *Irishman*, 13 Mar. pp 579–80 and passim. See below, pp 120–21.

the past'.[1] There is nothing to suggest that Davitt was impressed either by Gladstone's act of clemency or by his dramatic commitment to the task of pacifying Ireland.

Though Davitt went about his fenian business with some discretion, and unlike Forrester attracted no special publicity, his name appeared in the press as that of the honorary secretary of a committee in Haslingden that ran a 'ball and miscellaneous entertainment' on St Patrick's day 1869 for the benefit of the wives and children of Irish political prisoners. The correspondent who reported the occasion to the *Irishman* concluded proudly: 'in point of respectability it far surpassed anything of the sort ever before attempted in this locality'.[2] The organisation behind these festivities was fenian. Three of the four members of the committee—Martin Haran, Thomas Lyons, and John Timlin—were close friends of the Davitts.[3] Haran and Lyons were fenians[4] and it is safe to assume that Timlin was a fenian or a fenian-sympathiser. Haran was very active in the movement and was probably giving most of his time to it: a police detective described him as 'fierce-looking' and 'like an officer',[4] but he was regarded by the police as 'one of the cautious ones', better known for getting up fenian balls and concerts than as a conspirator.[5] Lyons was a stone contractor, of Horncliff Stone Quarries, Rawtenstall.[6] John Timlin, a mill worker, was a son of Michael Timlin, who had been a neighbour of the Davitts in Rock Hall.[7]

Davitt believed at the time, and continued to believe for the rest of his life, that his fenian activities were unknown to the police till after 16 December 1869.[8] In this he was mistaken. Before that date he attracted nothing like the same attention from the police as Forrester, who was pretty constantly under observation from February 1867. But about November of that year Chief Superintendent Ryan, of the Dublin Metropolitan Police, who was a highly intelligent and knowledgeable officer, received confidential information from Lancashire that Davitt was a fenian 'centre'.[9] In January 1869 'Devitt, Michael, of Haslington' had become the subject of a police file in Dublin Castle.[10] In February, Superintendent Ryan mentioned him along with Forrester in a report

[1] Isaac Butt, *Ireland's appeal for amnesty* (1870), p. 77.
[2] *Accrington Times*, 20, 27 Mar. 69; *Irishman*, 27 Mar. p. 612.
[3] *Irishman*, 13 Mar., pp 580–81; see below, pp 164–5, 173.
[4] H.-C. Joseph Murphy to I.G.P., 22 Feb. 70 (S.P.O., 5803R/5817R).
[5] H.-C. Thomas Welby to I.G.P., 28 Nov. 70 (S.P.O., 7000R/7016R).
[6] D to 'dear Bismarck' [Martin Haran], 1 Nov. 76 (DP/A5).
[7] Census returns, Haslingden, 1861, in P.R.O., R.G. 9/3061/477/4B, f. 21; see above p. 14.
[8] D to Forrester, 3 Aug. 94, in *I.H.S.*, iv, no. 15, p. 248; DN/29A, 28 Jan. 95, ibid., p. 249.
[9] Supt Daniel Ryan to C.P., 9 Feb. 69 (S.P.O., 3647R/4584R).
[10] S.P.O., Fenianism, index of names, 1866–71, p. 205, no. 2. The papers referred to, F3553–3606R, are missing.

on leading fenians made to the commissioners of police in Dublin.[1] From June 1869 onwards his name occurs intermittently in police correspondence. In July, Superintendent Ryan noted that since the passing of the Irish church act (the first of Gladstone's great remedial measures for Ireland) the fenians appeared to be dejected, but that persons of more than ordinary intelligence and fair education were still engaged in keeping the movement alive. He instanced O'Connor Power,[2] the 'agent' of the supreme council, who, with Edmund O'Donovan (son of John O'Donovan[3]), had lately made a tour of England and Scotland, and he went on to say that Davitt and Forrester were in the service of these two.[4] More detailed information is afforded in reports from two head constables of the Royal Irish Constabulary, Joseph Murphy and Thomas Welby, who, by arrangement between the R.I.C., the home office and the local chiefs of police, were stationed on detective duty at Liverpool and Manchester respectively.

The function of these two detectives was to watch the fenians in the critical area of south Lancashire and to keep the inspector general of the R.I.C. in Dublin Castle informed of fenian activities and plans. They were part of an early-warning system in England in face of the continuing danger of a fenian rising in Ireland. The inspector general decided what, if any, action was called for, and submitted recommendations to the Irish government. The latter usually referred all the most important documents to Samuel Lee Anderson, a crown solicitor, who specialised in fenian matters, and to his brother, Robert, the confidential adviser to the home office on Irish political crime, who, in his office at Whitehall, combined and coordinated all the secret information about the fenian conspiracy that flowed in to him not only from the Irish, but also from the British, police, and from British consuls and secret agents in America.[5] The system depended on the [illegible]ties of the intelligence men on the spot, and both Murphy and Welby were shrewd, alert, courageous, energetic policemen, not easily ruffled, and intent on preventing political crime by anticipating it rather than on the punishment of political criminals. Each of them employed as a spy a fenian in good standing, who was a regular attender at the private meetings of the local fenians. These, often under the guise of working-men's clubs, tontine societies, and the like, were usually held

[1] Supt Ryan to C.P., as above.
[2] See above, pp 47–8.
[3] See above, p. 45.
[4] Supt Daniel Ryan to C.P., 29 July 69 (S.P.O., 4446R/4470R).
[5] Anderson, *Sidelights on the home rule movement* (1906), pp 36, 80, and *The lighter side of my official life* (1910), pp 17–24, 32; T. W. Moody '*The Times* versus Parnell and Co., 1887–90' in *Historical Studies*, vi, ed. T. W. Moody, (1968), pp 159–61; Breandán Mac Giolla Choille, 'Fenian documents in the State Paper Office' in *I.H.S.*, xvi, no. 63, pp 270–77.

in 'beerhouses' well-known to the police as the 'fenian haunts', where the landlords were fenians themselves or fenian-sympathisers or merely keen tradesmen, and where the premises included an upstairs room with something in the nature of an emergency exist. As a rule, however, the police did not interfere with these meetings; it was much easier to keep the fenians under observation when they used the same beer-houses than if they were compelled to find new meeting-places.[1] The police also kept a close eye on the public functions—the balls, concerts, recitations, popular lectures and raffles—with which the working-class Irish of Lancashire, as elsewhere in Britain, entertained themselves and expressed their solidarity, especially on St Patrick's Day or the anniversary of the 'Manchester martyrs'. These occasions were often organised by fenians and used by them as a means of raising funds to augment the weekly and monthly contributions the circles levied on their members.

As 1869 advanced, Murphy and Welby reported increasing activity in the collection of money, the procuring and transmission of arms, and other preparations for a rising which was believed to be imminent, and especially in November, when the return of O'Donovan Rossa as M.P. for Tipperary gave a boost to fenian morale throughout Ireland and Britain.[2] During the latter half of the year Forrester figured prominently in all this activity and undoubtedly was the most colourful, as he was the most admired, personality in the fenian underworld of Lancashire. Davitt, 'the travelling organiser',[3] 'the itinerant fenian agent',[4] who operated over a much wider area, was more shadowy, elusive, and remote. His success in keeping in the shadows deceived the spies who reported on his movements into thinking that he was subordinate to Forrester, whereas in the fenian organisation of Britain as a whole he was Forrester's superior officer.[5] Though Forrester is described by Murphy's spy (known as 'C') as 'a poor little fellow' and Davitt as 'a first-class looking man only for the arm',[6] it was Forrester who mainly occupied C's attention. Forrester was known to be buying arms in large quantities from Birmingham and assembling them in a secret depot in Manchester, from which they were distributed to members of the organisation in Lancashire or secretly shipped to Ireland through Liverpool.[7] He was taken very seriously by Robert Anderson,

1 Detective-inspector Carlisle to head constable of Liverpool, 3 Aug. 69 (S.P.O., 4457R/4470R).

2 H.-C. Murphy to I.G.P., 22, 28 Nov. (S.P.O. 4986R, 5076R); Dublin Metropolitan Police report to C.P., 27 Nov. (S.P.O., 5065R).

3 H.-C. Murphy to I.G.P., 8 Nov. (S.P.O., 4857R).

4 H.-C. Murphy to I.G.P., 22 Feb. 70 (S.P.O., 5803R/5817R).

5 *S.C.P.*, ix, 405.

6 H.-C. Murphy to I.G.P., 10 Dec. 69 (S.P.O., 5226R).

7 H.-C. Murphy to I.G.P., 16 Sept., 28 Nov. (S.P.O., 4870R, 5076R).

who believed that 'no agent of the conspiracy is doing more to further its interests than this man',[1] an opinion that was shared by the chief constable of Manchester, Captain W. H. Palin, who regarded Forrester as 'the undoubted leader, as he is by far the cleverest, of all the fenians in this part of the country'.[2] Nevertheless Forrester was a man of incomparably less capacity than Davitt. Though he was clever and fluent, and had no lack of nerve, he was a vain, rash, light-headed, shallow youth, deficient in judgment and in moral courage, incurably immature.[3]

In November 1869 Forrester was clamouring for an immediate raid on Liverpool gunshops and was only prevented from making the attempt by steady opposition from Davitt, who condemned the plan as premature and insisted that such an arms-raid must be synchronised with a rising in Ireland.[4] This difference over strategy was followed by a much more dangerous difference, over the question of dealing with traitors within the camp. The right to kill traitors was an accepted principle within the I.R.B. The fenian oath pledged the taker to bear true allegiance to the Irish republic 'now virtually established', and the supreme council of the I.R.B. was therefore in logic entitled to inflict the death penalty on those who, having solemnly accepted its authority were found guilty of treason to that virtual republic. The constitution of the supreme council of the I.R.B., adopted on 18 August 1869, declared that 'every act or attempted act to subvert the authority of the supreme council . . . shall be deemed treason, and punishable with death'. An addendum to this constitution reserved the awarding of capital punishment to the council, and rejected the claim of certain local bodies within the organisation to do so.[5] In the underworld of the I.R.B. the line between the infliction of a death penalty and mere murder was hard to draw; and the I.R.B. was commonly accused of countenancing murder. Killing for alleged treason did in fact occur within the movement; but, Davitt insisted on oath before the *Times*-Parnell commission many years later, it was the work of individuals, never of the supreme council. There is no reason to doubt that the killing of anyone in cold blood, was in fact, as distinct from poetic fantasy, as repugnant to him at this time as it undoubtedly was in his later life. Forrester, on the other hand, seems to have been hyper-conscious of

[1] Minute by Robert Anderson, 18 Oct., on H.-C. Murphy to I.G.P., 12 Oct. (S.P.O., 4751R).

[2] Memorandum by Robert Anderson, 7 Feb. 70 (S.P.O., 5700R).

[3] See for example a poster he designed for a lecture in Carpenters' Hall, Manchester, on 8 Feb. 70 (H.-C. Welby to I.G.P., 2, 6 Feb. 70; S.P.O., 5783R).

[4] H.-C. Murphy to I.G.P., 12, 15 Nov. 69 (P.R.O., 4918R, 4934R).

[5] T. W. Moody and Leon Ó Broin, 'The I.R.B. supreme council, 1868-78' in *I.H.S.*, xix, no. 75 (Mar. 1975), pp 303-7.

danger from traitors and ready to advocate 'exemplary measures' against anyone whom he suspected of treachery.[1]

The presence of traitors within the organisation was a reality. As we have seen, it was on fenian informers that the police largely depended for their knowledge of what was going on inside the movement. In the last quarter of 1869 the fenian circles in Liverpool and Manchester were painfully aware of this situation and on the alert for the culprits.[2] Hugh Dolan, one of the Liverpool centres, came under suspicion in October because a printed booklet, *Laws . . . of the I.R.B.*, was found on him by Head-constable Murphy, and he was thought to have given it up too easily. Dolan had been arrested by Murphy on 22 October and remanded on a charge of treason-felony; but, five days later, the magistrates dismissed the charge owing to lack of evidence, and Dolan was released. This was seen as a sinister circumstance, confirming the belief that he was a 'stag'. On 9 December the Liverpool head-centre, Frank Kerr, received orders from London and Dublin that Dolan was to be immediately expelled from the I.R.B.[3] Shortly afterwards Peter Malley, a drill-instructor of fenians in Manchester, was condemned to death by a 'fenian court' for disclosing to a girl he was courting where it was he drilled 'the boys'. She gave him away after learning that he was married. His life was saved only through the intervention of the Manchester head-centre, Connor—and of Head-constable Murphy's informer, who helped to organise the trial.[4] Neither Dolan nor Malley was an informer, but since the real informer went undetected the fears and suspicions of fenians in Liverpool continued unabated. A similar situation existed in Manchester, where, in December 1869, in an atmosphere of considerable tension, Forrester denounced as a traitor a young fenian of Salford named Burke, whom he had seen speaking to a detective. Davitt insisted that this was no proof of treachery, and Forrester gave way. But soon afterwards, in Davitt's absence, he renewed his charge, informing Davitt by letter that he had overwhelming proof against Burke and that if the north of England executive of the I.R.B. did not take action, he would shoot Burke himself.[5]

Davitt had left Liverpool soon after 10 December[6] for an organising

[1] *S.C.P.*, ix, 402, x, 171-7; DN/29A, in *I.H.S.*, iv, no. 15, p. 249; Pigott, *Personal recollections*, pp 364-76; O'Leary, *Recollections*, i, 94-5; Sullivan, *Recollections*, pp 108-13; Devoy, *Recollections*, pp 38, 183-4.

[2] Minute by Robert Anderson, 11 Nov. 69 (S.P.O., 4854R).

[3] H.-C. Murphy to I.G.P., 22, 26 Aug., 27 Oct., 2, 21 Nov., 9 Dec. (S.P.O., 4527R, 4535R, 4854R, 4871R, 4969R, 5051R, 5214R, 5270R).

[4] H.-C. Welby to I.G.P., 16 Dec. (S.P.O., 5286R).

[5] H.-C. Welby to I.G.P., 21 Dec. (S.P.O., 5329R); *S.C.P.*, ix, 405; D to Forrester, 3 Aug. 94, in *I.H.S.*, iv, no. 15, p. 247; DN/29A, 28 Jan. 95, ibid., p. 249.

[6] H.-C. Murphy to I.G.P., 10 Dec. 69 (S.P.O., 5226R).

tour in Scotland. He was at Dundee on 14 December and a day later at Glasgow;[1] here he received Forrester's letter. Alarmed that Forrester might carry out his threat, he decided that the only way to stop him was not by direct prohibition but by subterfuge: he would appear to acquiesce in Forrester's murderous intention, flatter his vanity, but persuade him not to go ahead until he had obtained the approval of Fox and O'Kelly, the members of the supreme council with whom Davitt was in communication. This was the object of the following letter (known as the 'pen letter').[2]

Glasgow, Wednesday [15 December 1869]

[Dear] Friend

I have just returned from Dundee, which place I have left all right.

Your letter of Monday I have just read. I've no doubt but what the a/c is correct.

In reference to the other affair, I hope you won't take *any part* in it whatever —I mean in the *carrying of it out*. If it is decided upon and you receive *Jim's*[3] and, thro him, *Fitz's*[4] consent, let it be done by all means, but one thing you must remember, and that is that you are of far too much importance to our family[5] to be spared—even at the risk of allowing a rotten sheep[6] to exist among the flock. You must know that if anything happened you, the toil and trouble of the past twelve months will have been almost in vain. Whoever is employed, *don't let him use the pen*[7] *we are & have been selling.* Get another for the purpose—a common one.

I hope & trust that when I return to *Man*[8] I may not hear that every man, *woman, and child* knew all about it ere it occurred.

John O'Neil[9]

[1] Note by Robert Anderson, 21 Dec., on H.-C. Murphy to I.G.P., 16 Dec. (S.P.O., R.P. 1869/8461 (1877/9309)). Davitt was in error in dating this Scottish tour to November (D to Forrester, 3 Aug. 94, in *I.H.S.*, iv, no. 15, p. 247).

[2] I am accepting Davitt's own later explanation of this letter, which I have examined in 'Michael Davitt and the "pen" letter' in *I.H.S.*, iv, no. 15 (Mar. 1945), pp 224-53.

[3] James Fox of Leeds (DN/29A, 28 Jan. 95, in *I.H.S.*, iv, no. 15, p. 250); Supt Daniel Ryan to C.P., 20 Jan. 70 (S.P.O., 5562R); *D.P.B.*, i, 350 (as above, p. 53).

[4] James O'Kelly (DN/29A, 28 Jan. 95, as above). The circumstantial evidence all points to his being James J. O'Kelly, the celebrated fenian who was at this time a member of the I.R.B. supreme council (above, p. 53; below, pp 138-9), but left the I.R.B. in 1870 and became a Parnellite M.P. in 1880. He was a witness before the *Times*-Parnell commission (*S.C.P.*, x, 145-71), to which Davitt testified that he did not know where 'Jim' and 'Fitz' now were but believed them to be in America (*S.C.P.*, ix, 408).

[5] The I.R.B. [6] A traitor. [7] Revolver. [8] Manchester.

[9] The letter is here transcribed from a faded photograph of the original in S.P.O., R.P. 1877/9309, which has not hitherto been printed, though various printed versions, none of them absolutely correct, have appeared. The earliest of these is in *Daily Courier* (Liverpool), 25 Dec. 69 (p. 8, col. 6), in *Liverpool Mercury*, 25 Dec. (p. 8, col. 5), and in *Manchester Guardian*, 27 Dec. (p. 4, col. 1). An almost identical text is in *C.C.C. minutes*, lxxii, 322 (16 July 70); this is the same as the text submitted by Davitt to the *Times*-Parnell commission (*S.C.P.*, ix, 406), except that in Davitt's text (1) 'the last twelve months' becomes 'the last six months', and (2) 'that' is omitted before 'when I return to *Man*'. There are contracted versions in *The Times*, 3 June 70, p. 7, col. 3, and 19 July, p. 11, col. 3, of which the former has 'the last three months' and the latter 'the last twelve months'.

At the same time that he wrote this letter Davitt alerted Fox and O'Kelly. The scheme achieved its purpose, Davitt believed, for Forrester did not carry out this threat to kill Burke.[1] That may not have been due to Davitt's action. Forrester, as will be seen, was not in a position to kill anyone for three weeks after receiving Davitt's letter, being in jail from 16 December to 6 January. At his release he had renewed reason for suspecting Burke, but since he was bound over to good behaviour he may well have thought better of his contemplated killing, apart altogether from Davitt's effort to deter him. Whether or not the 'pen' letter was the means of preventing a murder, as Davitt was repeatedly to claim in later years, it was to have a traumatic effect on his career.[2]

The 'pen' letter—ironically the earliest surviving letter of Davitt's—was as great a potential danger to its writer as to his correspondent. For if it should fall into the hands of the police it would be construed to mean that both were criminal conspirators with no compunction about committing murder. And this was what happened almost immediately. On 16 December, Forrester arrived at Liverpool from Birmingham, and booked a bed for the night in Smith's eating-house, William Brown Street. About midnight he was in a snug there, reading the letter, which he had apparently just received, when he was suddenly confronted by Chief Superintendent Ride, Head-constable Murphy, and other police officers. Before a word had been spoken he began to tear up the letter, but his hands were quickly seized and the torn pieces collected by Inspector Horne. He was arrested and found to be in possession of revolvers. Davitt, reviewing the matter many years afterwards, asserts that Forrester, instead of taking the elementary precaution of destroying the letter as soon as he had read it, had had it in his possession for nearly a month when the police swooped on him—in consequence, it was believed at the time, of his having informed them anonymously that a fenian agent with a bagful of revolvers was to be found at a certain address. His object was simply to show how he could bamboozle the police and to be the boy-hero of an abortive prosecution; as he had a licence for selling arms his possession of revolvers was no offence.[3] But this explanation is contradicted by contemporary evidence. Far from keeping the letter a month Forrester could have had it only a matter of hours at the most, since it was seized by the police in Liverpool the day after Davitt wrote it. Forrester was arrested not through any contrivance of his own but because the Liverpool police had been warned by Head-constable Murphy on 15 December that he was

[1] *S.C.P.*, ix, 406; D to Forrester, 3 Aug. 94 (DP/Q) in *I.H.S.*, iv, no. 15, pp 247–8; DN/29A, 28 Jan. 95, ibid., pp 249–50.

[2] See 'Michael Davitt and the "pen" letter', cited above.

[3] DN/29A, 28 Jan. 95, in *I.H.S.*, iv. no. 15, p. 249.

intending to bring revolvers to Liverpool next day. Murphy had expected that he would be coming from Manchester, and would be accompanied by Davitt, of whose Scottish tour Murphy was unaware. The Liverpool police prepared to seize both men red-handed on their arrival, but in fact Forrester came from Birmingham and came alone.[1]

Manchester fenians were convinced that he was the victim of an informer, and they suspected three men, two in Liverpool and one in Salford. The Salford suspect was Burke—the fenian whom Forrester had been denouncing to Davitt as a traitor. Forrester's friends in Manchester feared that one of the suspected fenians might be produced as a police witness. They were watching Burke day and night, and Head-constable Welby felt quite sure that if he went to Liverpool to give evidence his life would be in danger.[2] Burke appears to have been identified with an anti-Forrester faction in Manchester fenianism known as the 'Molly Myfacks', and it was to them that Forrester attributed an anonymous letter he received about the end of January 1870, accusing him of having concocted his own arrest with the Liverpool police and describing him as a Corydon or a Massey (notorious fenian informers). Head-constable Welby's spy, who claimed to be intimate with Forrester, scouted the charge: Forrester (the spy declared, with commendable detachment) was the last man in the world to turn informer; he was heart and soul in the cause; his own men had complete confidence in his integrity.[3] This seems a just estimate of the man, whose qualities were not of the kind of which traitors are made. Inspector Horne's object in arresting him may have been to pull him up short: the spy C had reported him to Head-constable Murphy on 10 December as saying that 'the rising' would take place in the week after Christmas.[4] The truth seems to be that the arrest took Forrester by surprise, and that the attempt he made to destroy Davitt's letter by tearing it up before the police could seize it was no pretence, as Davitt afterwards supposed it might have been.[5]

Forrester was charged at Dale Street police court, Liverpool, on 17 December, before the deputy-stipendiary, H. Mansfield, with being in possession of firearms for which he could not satisfactorily account.

[1] S.P.O., Fenianism, index of names, 1866-71, app., p. 1, no. 2; H.-C. Murphy to I.G.P., 16 Dec. 69 (S.P.O., R.P. 1877/9309); Constable Bryan English to H.-C. Murphy, 17 Dec. (S.P.O., 5313R); H.-C. Welby to I.G.P., 19 Dec. (S.P.O., 5329R (8457R); *Liverpool Mercury*, 18, 25 Dec.

[2] H.-C. Welby to I.G.P., 21 Dec. (S.P.O., 5329R); H.-C. Murphy to I.G.P., 27 Dec. (S.P.O., R.P. 1877/9309).

[3] H.-C. Welby to I.G.P., 16 Dec. 69, 2, 6, Feb. 70 (S.P.O., 5286R, 5664R/5783R, 5684R/6292R).

[4] H.-C. Murphy to I.G.P. 10 Dec. 69 (S.P.O., 5226R).

[5] DN/29A, 28 Jan. 95, in *I.H.S.*, iv, no. 15, p. 250.

It was proved that on his arrest he had a loaded six-chambered revolver in his pocket and four similar weapons in a portmanteau. He said he had a very simple explanation of the revolvers: he had bought them in Birmingham for cash from a gunmaker whose name, Robert Minningham, he had given to the police: he had a hawker's licence and could produce witnesses—Englishmen—who could prove that they were in the habit of buying revolvers from him. As to the loaded revolver, he had had the misfortune to be robbed, and having been given a bed in a double-bedded room he had loaded the revolver as a precaution against a repetition of the experience. He was remanded in custody, pending inquiries, to 24 December. [1]

When the hearing was resumed, the deputy-stipendiary was accompanied on the bench by the mayor of Liverpool and two other magistrates. Prosecuting counsel said that the police had arrested Forrester on strong suspicion—indeed, on certain information—that he was a fenian agent. In such cases the police, of course, had more information than it was desirable to make public, and in this case the prosecution would produce no more than would justify the bench in applying to Forrester a statute of 1360 (34 Edward III, c. 1) that empowered magistrates to bind over to good behaviour persons whom they had good cause to believe dangerous or quarrelsome. As evidence of Forrester's dangerous character counsel read the letter that Forrester had failed to destroy and that had easily been pieced together.[2] It showed, counsel alleged, that the prisoner was a party to, or was in correspondence with a person intimate with, a conspiracy to assassinate someone obnoxious to the fenian organisation. Evidence of the circumstances of Forrester's arrest was given by Horne and Murphy, and the deputy-governor of Kilmainham jail testified to his conviction in Dublin in 1867.[3] Otherwise the prosecution made no attempt to establish Forrester's connection with fenianism, but asked the court to bind him over for two years. Forrester, described as 'a short, wiry-looking young man of almost boyish appearance',[4] conducted his own defence with characteristic cleverness and self-assurance. Cross-examining Horne he elicited the admission that when he was brought to the police station one of the officers who had arrested him had accused

[1] H.-C. Murphy to H.-C. Welby, 18 Dec. 69 (S.P.O., 5313R); *Daily Courier* (Liverpool), 18 Dec., p. 5, col. 6; *Liverpool Mercury*, 18 Dec., p. 8, col. 6; *Manchester Courier & Lancashire General Advertiser*, 18 Dec., p. 5, col. 1; *Manchester Guardian*, 18 Dec., p. 5, col. 5; *Irishman*, 24 Dec., p. 416, col. 1.

[2] It is evident from the photograph of the original that the letter had been torn into only three or four pieces.

[3] See above, p. 50.

[4] *Liverpool Mercury*, 18 Dec. 69, p. 8, col. 6.

him of resisting arrest and had been contradicted by Horne himself. He concluded:

I have nothing to say against being bound over to keep the peace, but I have a decided objection to the inference which is drawn that I am a dangerous person and to everything which reflects injuriously upon my character. There is no evidence before the court to show that I am not what I represented myself to be—a hawker. I referred the police to the maker of the pistols; they have means of communication with him and can learn that I have them legally in my possession for sale. As to the letter, the learned gentleman who read it forgot to mention that it was not addressed to me, and there is no proof that it was intended for me; therefore the inference drawn from the letter is unfair. In my ignorance of the law I thought justice dealt with facts and not with suppositions. The learned gentleman has supposed that I am connected with the fenian conspiracy; he has supposed that I am a dangerous person; he has supposed many other things, but no evidence has been given that his suppositions are correct. I don't object to being bound over to keep the peace, but to quietly submit would be to acknowledge that I am engaged in an unlawful occupation.[1]

The deputy-stipendiary conceded that the prisoner had satisfactorily accounted for the revolvers found on him, but held that his claim to be a hawker of pistols was very improbable. His attempt to destroy the letter implied that he was aware of its incriminating nature. The court ordered Forrester to be bound over to good behaviour for one year (not two, as sought by the prosecution), in two sureties of £100 each and his own security for £200.[2]

Although Forrester had to spend Christmas in jail and although he could obtain release only on pretty stiff terms and would be highly vulnerable for a year at least, he was technically acquitted of the charge against him. The surprising fact is that more was not made by the prosecution of his fenian connection, and especially of the assassination letter. The fenian aspect of the case was high-lighted by the press, and one newspaper alleged that at least a dozen prominent local fenians were present in the court during the hearing.[3] A number of Manchester fenians armed with revolvers arrived the night before, with the intention of attempting a rescue, but they were dissuaded by the Liverpool men. The Liverpool centres prudently insisted that only a select few should enter the court and that they must hand over their revolvers before doing so. Head-constable Welby's spy was one of several fenians employed to shuttle in and out of the court reporting what was going on to those waiting outside.[4] The Liverpool police who brought the

[1] *Daily Courier*, 25 Dec., p. 6, cols 6-7.

[2] Ibid.; *Liverpool Mercury*, 25 Dec., p. 6 (col. 1), p. 8 (col. 5); *Manchester Courier & Lancashire General Advertiser*, 27 Dec., p. 3, col. 7; *Manchester Guardian*, 27 Dec., p. 4, col. 1; *Irishman*, 1 Jan. 70, p. 435; *Nation*, 1 Jan., p. 311.

[3] *Manchester Guardian*, 28 Dec. 69.

[4] H.-C. Welby to I.G.P., 26, 28 Dec. (S.P.O., 5361R, 5381R).

prosecution seem to have been content to have Forrester bound over; had they been prepared to disclose all they knew about him they could probably have supported a charge of treason-felony, such as was shortly to be brought against Davitt.[1] But that would have meant exposing their spies whose continued activity they evidently valued more highly than a term of penal servitude for Forrester. The Manchester spy thought the Liverpool police had acted prematurely. They had arrested Forrester before they knew, what Head-constable Welby had ascertained, that he held a current hawker's licence to trade in hardware, which entitled him legally to buy and sell fire-arms in any part of Great Britain. The police ought, in the opinion of Welby's spy, to have waited and allowed Forrester to take arms to Ireland, when he could have been followed and his procedures discovered. As it was, new routes and new schemes would at once be devised by Liverpool fenians for transporting to Ireland the large supplies of arms they had accumulated. Welby entirely agreed with this and remained convinced that the arrest had been a mistake.[2]

Till the required sureties were forthcoming Forrester had to remain in Kirkdale jail. His friends in Manchester and Liverpool were generally not of the financial standing to go bail in such a large sum as £100. Davitt had returned to Liverpool from Scotland on learning from Mrs Forrester that her adored son was in trouble. The police, who had supposed, erroneously, that he had gone to Ireland traced him on the 29th to a Mrs Chalk's hotel, an 'orange resort', where he met Mrs Forrester on the day her son's trial ended. He spent several days approaching likely Irishmen in Liverpool, and succeeded in getting Arthur Doran, a wholesale newsagent (guaranteed by Pigott, of the Dublin *Irishman*, who was hand in glove with Liverpool fenians[3]), and a tailor named William Russell, to go bail for Forrester. Application to accept them as bailsmen was made by Dr Andrew Commins, barrister, on 6 January 1870, the deputy-stipendiary agreed, and Forrester was released the same day.[4] His friends believed that he would not attend fenian meetings, except occasional meetings of officers, for the next year. He ceased to be arms agent (and to draw his salary as such), while resuming other fenian activities. He was soon attracting attention again—and earning money that he urgently needed, for he was in debt to the fenian

[1] Below, ch. III.

[2] H.-C. Welby to I.G.P., 16, 21, 26 Dec. (S.P.O., 5286R, 5329R, 5361R).

[3] Above, p. 51; Supt Ryan to C.P., 12 Sept. (S.P.O., 4564R/4584R); H.-C. Murphy to I.G.P., 12, 19 Nov. (S.P.O., 4918R, 4961R).

[4] *Daily Courier* (Liverpool), 7 Jan. 70, p. 3, cols 3-4; *Liverpool Mercury*, 7 Jan., p. 6, col. 7; Denvir, *Life story*, pp 132-5; D to Forrester, 3 Aug. 94, in *I.H.S.*, iv, no. 15, p. 248; DN/29A, 28 Jan. 95; ibid., p. 250.

treasurers—by public lectures on contemporary politics. In private he was thirsting for revenge for his arrest, which had become a subject of angry recrimination among Lancashire fenians. There was a scene at a fenian conclave in Liverpool about 4 January, when a sub-centre declared that some of the centres must be in the habit of giving information to the police; another sub-centre retorted that the traitor was known and he was neither a centre nor a sub-centre. Murphy's spy, who was present, and beginning to fear discovery, felt sure that Forrester was bent on having blood spilt. The police continued to watch him, but they now seemed to be taking less interest in him than in Davitt.[1]

Davitt supposed that it was his efforts to find bail for Forrester that first brought him under police observation. He was, in fact, nearly a year in error, but he was right in the sense that his importance in the eyes of the police was enhanced as a result of Forrester's arrest. They had no doubt that he was the writer of the letter found on Forrester, which was duly transmitted to Robert Anderson;[2] and they now regarded him for the first time as the more dangerous of the two men. He was closely watched as he went about Liverpool with Mrs Forrester, and at one point there was a strong rumour among fenians that Murphy was going to arrest him.[3] He and Forrester were present at a meeting of fenian centres, sub-centres, and treasurers held in Manchester on 24 January. (One of the treasurers was Welby's spy.) Davitt announced that everything was going well, and Forrester gave some recitations. At a resumed session the following evening from which Forrester was absent Davitt told the members that he was now their organiser, and as such presided over the trial of one Quinlen, who was accused of embezzlement.[4] It is evident that Davitt had now taken Forrester's place as organiser and arms agent for the north of England in addition to his own wider responsibilities. Murphy, who was quick to realise this, learnt that Davitt had written 'from 50 to 100 letters' at Mrs Chalk's on 28 December—'he writes with fluency and dispatch with the left hand'.[5] Murphy's patient watch on Mrs Chalk's was rewarded on 31 December when he saw Davitt for the first time and took this 'mental photograph' of him:

Has lost the right arm; black, small moustache; black stunted whiskers not meeting

[1] H.-C. Murphy to I.G.P., 27, 30 Dec. 69 (S.P.O., R.P. 1877/9309; H.-C. Welby to I.G.P., 5, 18, 26, 27 Jan., 2, 6, 9, 20 Feb., 70 (S.P.O., 5439R, 5543R/5700R, 5598R/5700R, 5606R, 5664R/5783R, 5685R/5783R, 5716R/5783R, 5783R); informant to H.-C. Murphy, 10, 17 Jan. (S.P.O., 5478R, 5542R/5566R); H.-C. Murphy to I.G.P., 11, 16, 18, 21 Jan. (S.P.O., 5478R, 5606R, 5544R/5566R, 5566R).

[2] S.P.O., R.P. 1877/9309; above, p. 56.

[3] H.-C. Murphy to I.G.P., 1, 3, 5 Jan. 70 (S.P.O., 5410R, 5414R, 5438R).

[4] H.-C, Welby to I.G.P., 5, 18, 26 Jan. (S.P.O., 5439R, 5543R/5700R, 5598R/5700R).

[5] H.-C. Murphy to I.G.P., 30 Dec. 69, 28 Jan. 70 (S.P.O., R.P. 1877/9309).

under the chin but inclining to grow backwards towards the ears; regular nose; handsome face, inclined to be long; well formed chin; cheek bones a little prominent; cheeks of a vermilion tinge; hair on face delicately fair; when walking he swaggers a little and swings the left arm, he has the slightest inclination to stoop, but is straight, smart, active and gentlemanly-looking; his age is about 30 years[1]: . . . his hair is black and inclined to curl . . .[2]

Two other glimpses of him are afforded in reports of police spies a few weeks later. At the Quinlen trial in Manchester he told the accused, who was claiming it as a merit that he had returned from New York to answer the charges against him, that he had done so 'because you knew we would find you out no matter what part of the world you might be in'.[3] A week afterwards in Liverpool, where Davitt was reported to be moving about with the utmost caution, he called at several fenian resorts, and C, having failed to keep up with him, noted: 'Davitt is a quick pedestrian; he walked from Farrell's to McCann's, about 2½ miles, in half an hour'.[4] Inspector Horne, who had arrested Forrester on 16 December, was at this point cooperating with Head-constable Murphy in watching Davitt.[5]

For the first time Davitt's home and family came under police observation, following a visit by him to Haslingden on 19 February. Murphy reported that his father, an agent to a loan society, and his two unmarried sisters lived in Wilkinson Street; Michael was never seen at home except at intervals of a month or six weeks; when at Haslingden he was usually with Martin Haran and sometimes the two went off together; both had hawker's licences, and were said to be selling cloth, but whereas Haran carried a pack, Davitt never did. When Davitt was aware that the police were watching him he showed extraordinary skill in eluding their vigilance, slipping into a house by the front door and out by the back so quickly and nimbly that he seemed to disappear before their eyes. Murphy added descriptions of Haran and of two other fenian associates of Davitt's in Haslingden, Thomas Lyons and Patrick Fearon.[6]

Davitt was now making large purchases of rifles, revolvers and ammunition and organising their despatch to concealed destinations in Britain and Ireland. All this was paid for in cash, with money that Davitt received from the local treasurers of the organisation. Some of his consignments of rifles were sent by the Newport-Cork steamer to

[1] He was not quite 24.
[2] H.-C. Murphy to I.G.P., 31 Dec. 69 (ibid.).
[3] H.-C. Welby to I.G.P., 26 Jan. 70. (S.P.O., 5598R/5700R).
[4] H.-C. Murphy to I.G.P., 1 Feb. (S.P.O., 5647R).
[5] Same to same, 27 Jan., 1 Feb. (S.P.O. 5647R, R.P. 1877/9309).
[6] H.-C. Murphy to I.G.P., 22 Feb. 70 (S.P.O., 5803R/5817R); to H.-C. Welby, 22 Feb. (S.P.O., 5817R).

Cork, where their receiver, unknown to Davitt until many years later, was James Nagle O'Brien, eldest brother of the celebrated William, who on one frightening occasion took a hand in James's perilous work.[1] Another fenian at the receiving end of Davitt's arms-traffic was Mark Ryan. He describes how, while a student at St Jarlath's College, Tuam, he helped to handle consignments of arms from England disguised as ordinary merchandise addressed to a local merchant. Martin McDonnell, who unwittingly served as the consignee as far as Tuam railway station; there, with the cooperation of the stationmaster, the goods were taken over by local fenians, who included McDonnell's assistant.[2] Ryan was unaware that the other end of this smuggling system was a secret depot in Leeds operated by Davitt. A third member of the I.R.B. involved in Davitt's arms-traffic whose identity only came to light long afterwards was John Barry, soon to be a prominent figure in Irish politics. He was then a commercial traveller, living in Newcastle-upon-Tyne. Two cases of arms sent by Davitt from Birmingham were addressed to him under the alias of James M. Kershaw, a well-known north-country name. They duly arrived at Newcastle on 16 April 1870, but Barry, warned just in time that they were being watched by the police, took care not to collect them.[3]

Davitt's source of supply was a trio of working men in Birmingham, Minningham,[4] Wilson, and Gill. Among its great variety of industries Birmingham had long been famous for its manufacture of small arms. By the middle of the century the industry was the greatest source of guns in the world.[5] Of its innumerable gunmakers, many of them worked in an atmosphere of secrecy for customers about whom no questions were asked except as to the colour of their money. Birmingham, with a large Irish population among which fenianism was rife, had special advantages for the arms agents of the I.R.B. The I.R.B. had been obtaining arms from Birmingham since before the 1867 rising. The police from time to time seized suspicious collections of arms, but it was extremely difficult for them to identify those intended for illegal purposes from among the immense quantities always to be found lying at railway stations and canal wharves or in transit daily through the streets.[6]

[1] W. O'Brien, *Recollections*, pp 116–17; *Contemporary Review*, lxxi (May 97).

[2] Ryan, *Fenian memories*, pp 37–9; and see above, pp 45–6.

[3] Denvir, *Life story*, pp 127–8; *The Times*, 16 July 70, p. 11, col. 4; see below, pp 00–0.

[4] This is the spelling given in *The Times* report of Davitt's trial (see below, ch. III). The name also appears variously in the present context as Meeninham, Meaningham, Meeningham, Meenigher. Meenaghan (in Irish, Ó Muimhneacháin) is a Mayo name (Edward MacLysaght, *A guide to Irish surnames* (Dublin, 2nd ed., 1965, p. 149).

[5] Keith Dunham, *The gun trade in Birmingham* (City of Birmingham Museum and Art Gallery, 1955; corrected reprint, 1968).

[6] H.-C. Richard McHale (Liverpool) to home office, 18 Oct. 66 (P.R.O., H.O. 45/

Minningham, Wilson, and Gill had been working together for over a year. They had only a very loose partnership, and no name appeared on the two workshops, connected by an internal stairway, that they occupied in Harper's Buildings, Weaman Street, in the heart of the Birmingham gun industry. Robert Minningham was a gun-finisher, John Wilson and action-fitter, and James Gill a stocker. Like all Birmingham gunmakers they built up complete weapons from material parts supplied by specialist producers, and they put out to other specialists such final operations as rifling and sighting. They also reconditioned and converted old rifles and revolvers, and they added the finishing stages to revolvers imported in the rough from Belgium. Minningham and Gill were Irish, Wilson English. Minningham, the leader of the group, was a fenian, and so was Gill. Their customers were almost entirely fenians. The business, conducted with the utmost discretion, was probably quite lucrative. Goods were delivered in return for cash, and documents were avoided as far as possible. It was from this group that the arms Forrester had been buying for the I.R.B. had come, and Davitt continued the connection, though with extreme caution.[1]

Davitt dealt mainly with Wilson, a simple, uneducated workman, trustworthy according to his lights, and innocent of any personal involvement in fenianism. He was in the arms business solely for money, and was technically ignorant of the purpose for which the arms he supplied to Davitt were intended. It is conceivable that he did not know Davitt to be an Irishman: Davitt did not speak with an Irish accent and he used an assumed name, W. R. Jackson, in his business relations with Wilson. But nearly everyone else connected with Davitt's arms-traffic was unmistakably Irish, and though Wilson did not send arms directly to Ireland he could not have failed to guess the ultimate destination of some of the goods he sold to Jackson. He could not have been in daily contact with Minningham and Gill for over a year without at least suspecting that they were fenians and that customers of the firm were fenians. He could not have been unaware that one of these customers, Forrester, was a notorious fenian who had just ceased to be a customer as the direct result of being found in possession of revolvers supplied by Minningham and partners.

So secretly did Davitt conduct his smuggling system that the detective at Liverpool most closely watching him, Head-constable Murphy,

O.S. 7799/135; mayor of Birmingham to home office, 19 Oct. 67 (ibid., no. 263); H.-C. John Bodley to I.G.P., 17 Mar. 70 (S.P.O., 5972/6016R).

[1] H.-C. Murphy to I.G.P., 3 Dec. 69 (S.P.O., 5145R/5216R); H.-C. John Bodley to I.G.P., 3 Mar., 20 Apr., 24 May, 70 (S.P.O., 5880R; R.P. 1870/9340, 9527 (1877/9309)); Supt Glossop, Birmingham, to Robert Anderson, 17 Mar. (S.P.O., 5977R/6016R); *The Times*, 16 July (p. 11, cols 3–4), 18 July (p. 11, col. 3); *C.C.C. minutes*, lxxii, 308; above, p. 63.

was unaware of it. The clue that led the police to the discovery, first of the system itself, and then of Davitt as the brain behind it, was picked up not in England but in Ireland, where the police were familiar with the general pattern of importing arms addressed to unwitting consignees;[1] and, with an irony typical of Davitt's career, it was a clue provided by consignments of arms arriving in Ireland, probably on the order of Forrester, before Davitt had organised his system. Early in January 1870 the R.I.C. at Ballyshannon, County Donegal, seized a case containing arms but bearing the label of 'J. Reeves, Sauce and Pickle Maker, Birmingham'. A similar case, from 'R. and I. Keatinge, General Dealers, Birmingham', fell into the hands of the police at the port of Dublin on 22 January. The arms were in an unfinished condition externally, though serviceable. The second case was addressed to 'Mrs Kennedy, Sheriff Street, Dublin', a grocer who, Superintendent Ryan believed, was being used as a front for a fenian circle that met at her house on Sundays under the guise of a tontine society of which her son was treasurer. The members of this circle were nearly all sawyers and carpenters, well able to polish up the stocks and smooth the metal parts of the rifles which they bought unfinished to save expense. The Birmingham police found that 'R. and I. Keatinge' was a fiction, and that, though 'J. Reeves' had been in the sauce and pickle business, he had left Birmingham for America nine months before. Yet between 6 August 1869 and 6 January 1870 seven boxes bearing his label had been despatched from Birmingham to addresses in Ireland. Ryan had no doubt that all this pointed to systematic smuggling of arms by the I.R.B. from Birmingham, through the port of Dublin. To stop this traffic by seizing the arms on arrival was out of the question: the police would need to search every bale and case of goods unloaded at the quays, and not only would this be impracticable but if attempted would dangerously antagonise legitimate traders. What was needed was to trace the smuggling back to its source in Birmingham. For this purpose the home office (advised by Robert Anderson) suggested that a detective officer of the R.I.C. should be stationed in Birmingham, on the same footing as Head-constable Murphy in Liverpool, to investigate the whole matter in cooperation with the local police. The inspector general appointed Head-constable John Bodley, then in Belfast, to this service. Bodley arrived at Birmingham on 11 February, after a day's briefing by Murphy at Liverpool in the course of which he received a full description of 'three prominent fenian leaders who frequently visit Birmingham'—Forrester, Davitt, and William Hogan. Hogan, a shoemaker, was secretary of the St Patrick's Burial Society, Birmingham,

[1] Memorandum of Dublin Metropolitan Police, 8 Dec. 66 (P.R.O., H.O.45/O.S.7799/158).

and an active agent of the I.R.B. in the arms business there;[1] he had been reported to Murphy in December as an associate of Davitt's and as accompanying him on a supposed visit to Ireland.[2]

Bodley's investigation of the smuggling system that turned out to be Davitt's was accomplished in just over two months and in three stages. The first stage was the discovery, early in March, that the source of the arms recently seized in Dublin was the workshop of Minningham, Wilson, and Gill. At Bodley's request one of the rifles and one of the revolvers (both being without maker's names or marks) were sent to him at Birmingham where they were identified by Messrs Webley, the well-known gunmakers, of Weaman Row, as the work of Robert Minningham. Another gunmaker, Williamson, who employed about sixty men and for whom Minningham, Wilson, and Gill had formerly worked, recognised the rifling on the barrels of the two samples as the work of Thomas Bembridge, who did rifling for other gunsmiths, Williamson and Minningham among them. Bembridge confirmed this and, taken into Bodley's confidence, said he was prepared to swear that he had rifled the weapons in question for Minningham. He also gave Bodley inside information about Minningham's business, of which he had become suspicious, and offered his services as a spy in Weaman Street. Bodley, conscious of the futility of pursuing inquiries himself in a street inhabited only by gunmakers sensitive about strangers, accepted Bembridge's offer.[3]

It was one thing to know that Minningham and partners had made arms that had been smuggled into Ireland for fenian purposes, but quite another to discover whether they were continuing to do so, how the arms were conveyed from their workshop out of Birmingham, by what route they were transmitted to Ireland, who were the intended recipients in Ireland and who the fenian agents directing the traffic in England. These were the questions that Bodley set himself to answer, with the help of Bembridge and Detective-sergeant John Seal, of the Birmingham police, and with the cooperation of railway officials.

[1] H.-C. Murphy to I.G.P., 10 Dec. 69. 27 Jan., 11 Feb. 70 (S.P.O., 5226R, 5609R/5808R, 5729R/6016R; Supt Ryan to C.P., 24 Jan., 23 Feb. (S.P.O., 5578R/5694R, 5808R); head constable of Birmingham to home office, 26 Jan., 4 Feb. (S.P.O., 5601R); home office to head constable of Birmingham, 27 Jan. (S.P.O., 5601R); memorandum by Robert Anderson, 5 Feb. (S.P.O. 5689R); I.G.P. to H.-C. Murphy, 8 Feb. (S.P.O., 5601R); H.-C. John Bodley to I.G.P., 12 Feb. (S.P.O., 5733R/6016R).

[2] H.-C. Murphy to I.G.P., 27 Dec. 69 (S.P.O., R.P. 1877/9309); minute of T. H. Burke, 29 Dec. 69 (ibid.).

[3] H.-C. Bodley to I.G.P., 15 Feb., 3, 22 Mar., 24 May 70 (S.P.O., 5750R/6016R, 5880R/6016R, 6016R; R.P. 1870/9527 (1877/9309)); Supt Ryan to C.P., 23 Feb. (S.P.O., 5750R/6016R); Supt Glossop (Birmingham) to Robert Anderson, 17 Mar. (S.P.O., 5977R/6016R).

Answering the first and second questions occupied the next stage of his inquiry.

To trace the movements of weapons from any particular workshop in Birmingham was far more difficult than might appear. The Weaman Street area was swarming with small gunmakers whose activities were interconnected, who bought from and sold to one another, who were in and out of one another's workshops but were accustomed to turning blind eyes, and who were adept at concealing revolvers and components of rifles in their pockets or in innocent-looking parcels. Twice Bodley learnt from Bembridge that quantities of arms had been conveyed from Minningham's to another gunmaker in Weaman Street, Hillebrandt, a Prussian, and twice he traced consignments of rifles and revolvers from Hillebrandt's to Dunkerley and Steinmann, shippers, of Liverpool, only to find that they were destined for bona fide export abroad. The core of the problem was that Minningham, Wilson, and Gill continued to produce large quantities of weapons and continued to get rid of them invisibly. Bodley felt hopeful that one of the three could be persuaded to give information 'in return for a substantial consideration', but this proved unnecessary, for on 25 March Bembridge produced the essential clue to the solution of Bodley's problem: rifles had been taken in a handcart by Minningham's young brother from the workshop in Weaman Street to an obscure cottage about a mile away, at the end of an alley off Caroline Street occupied by a still more obscure Irishman, J. Rafferty, a suspected fenian, who worked as a 'dipper and silverer' in the jewellery trade.[1]

Accompanied by Bembridge and Sergeant Seal, Bodley watched Rafferty's cottage from 5 p.m. on the 25th to 7 p.m. the following evening, when their vigilance was rewarded; young Minningham and Wilson arrived with a handcart, and soon afterwards wheeled away a packing case. Followed by the watchers, they delivered the case to a goods receiving office of the Midland Railway in George Street Sandpits, half a mile from Rafferty's cottage. They departed, and Bodley and his companions examined their prize. It was addressed to 'John Wilson, Midland Goods Station, Leeds, from John Wilson—to be called for', and on being opened was found to contain twenty rifles and bayonets, all (except one rifle) in a very rough state, the barrels not 'browned', the stocks not smoothed or stained, the mountings crudely

[1] Constable John Doran, Liverpool, to I.G.P., 9 Mar. (S.P.O., 5916R/6016R); H.-C. Bodley to I.G.P., 10, 12, 17, 22, 26 Mar. (S.P.O., 5924R/6016R, 5943R/6016R, 5972R/6016R, 6016R, 6058R); H.-C. Murphy to H.-C. Bodley, 14, 23 Mar. (S.P.O., 5943R/6016R, 6034R/6138R); Supt Glossop (Birmingham) to Robert Anderson, 17 Mar. (S.P.O., 5977R/6016R); H.-C. Murphy to I.G.R., 24, 28 Mar. (S.P.O., 6034R/6138R, 6067R/6138R); *C.C.C. minutes*, lxxii, 296.

filed, and all maker's marks removed. There were no bills, invoices, or other documents in the packing-case. The police had it refastened and sent on its way to Leeds, Bodley following by the first train next morning.[1]

The third stage in Bodley's inquiry took place in Leeds. Wilson's case of arms arrived at the Midland Railway Station there on 28 March and, watched by detectives, was collected by Wilson and a man calling himself Henderson who, accompanied for a short distance by Wilson, conveyed it on a handcart to a capacious but well-concealed warehouse in a small court off Swinegate—a low locality, Bodley observed. Next morning there appeared on the scene the man who was about to be revealed as the brain behind the whole operation—Jackson *alias* Davitt. He spent some time in the warehouse, to which Henderson, who acted as his warehouseman, brought a number of empty barrels. Later he helped Henderson to lift two loaded barrels on to a handcart, which Henderson wheeled away to the railway station. The operation was repeated with two more barrels. The four barrels were examined secretly at the railway station by the police, and Bodley telegraphed the inspector general in Dublin that two of them, consigned by 'J. Henderson, commission agent, Leeds' were addressed to John Flannery, Ballaghadereen, County Mayo, and Martin McDonnell, Tuam, County Galway, and that the other two, consigned by 'L. and W. Rawlinson, general dealers, Leeds' were addressed to John James White, Athlone, and Margaret Delmeyre, Castlerea, County Roscommon. These barrels, together with two others—from 'L. and W. Rawlinson' to Cecilia Higgins, Newport, County Mayo, and from 'J. Henderson' to Richard Cunningham, Boyle, County Roscommon—were seized by police officers of Superintendent Ryan's when they arrived at the North Wall, Dublin, by the steamer *Windsor* on 31 March from Liverpool and by the *Stanley* and *Countess of Erne* on 1 April from Holyhead.[2]

All six barrels contained arms, and the total haul amounted to 24 breech-loading rifles with 100 cartridges, 19 muzzle-loading rifles, and 13 revolvers with 600 rounds of ammunition. All the rifles had bayonets. The weapons, though rudely finished, were all in first-class working order, and fit for immediate use. The breech-loaders and revolvers were 'of superior style'; the muzzle-loaders appeared to be old weapons renovated. The stocks of the rifles had been cut in two to reduce their length, which enabled them to be packed in what appeared to be

[1] H.-C. Bodley to I.G.P., 26 Mar. (S.P.O., 6058R); *C.C.C. minutes,* lxxii, 296-7 (15 July, John Seal), 302 (John Bodley).

[2] H.-C. Bodley to I.G.P., 29 Mar., 3, 4 Apr. (S.P.O., 6076R, 6115R/6246R, 6114R/6246R); Supt Ryan to C.P., 31 Mar., 1 Apr. (S.P.O., 6090R/6095R, 6095R); *C.C.C. minutes,* lxxii, 300 (15 July, Eugene Hyde).

American flour-barrels; but one part of the cut stock was fitted with a brass band, so that it could easily be reunited to the other part with screws. The packing in barrels was, of course, done as a disguise; firearms in the legitimate course of trade were transported in deal packing-cases without any concealment. Ryan suggested that the barrels, which had been removed to the police stores in Lower Castle Yard, should be allowed to proceed to their destination under the eyes of detectives. He was overborne by the assistant inspector-general on the ground that the consignees almost certainly knew nothing about the consignments, which, if released, might be seized by fenian agents in transit. The assumption that the consignees were innocent parties was soon proved to be correct, and police attention was directed back to Leeds. The names and addresses on all six barrels were observed to be in the same handwriting; and it was not long before the police decided, on the evidence of the 'pen' letter, produced by Robert Anderson for the purpose,[1] that the hand was Davitt's. They found that, under the name W. R. Jackson, he had rented the warehouse off Swinegate on 28 January ostensibly as a store for soap, soda, and other dry goods but really as a fenian arms-depot. From 29 March police were watching every movement he made. He stayed for some days in Leeds, at 22 Oak Road, where Henderson also lodged; and on 4 April, before leaving for Birmingham, he cashed at the local branch of the Bank of England a draft for the large sum of £60, issued at the Newcastle branch of the bank in favour of William Roberts and endorsed by him with that name. At this point the cautious Bodley committed himself to the view that 'this man is a leading spirit in all the business'.[2]

It was the eleventh hour for Davitt though he did not realise it. News of the arms seizure at Dublin port got into the press, despite the efforts of the police to keep it quiet;[3] and in any case Davitt was bound to hear of what had happened through the fenian bush-telegraph. Moreover a second consignment of arms, despatched on the same day as the barrels that had been seized in Dublin, had similarly miscarried. This was a barrel of revolvers, sent via Rafferty's cottage on 29 March to 'Matthew Ward, 68 Rutherglen-loon, Glasgow, from J. Johnson'. Followed by the police, it was eventually seized in Glasgow on 2 April in the house of an Irishman, John McNamara, an old-clothes dealer, whom the police knew to be a 'fenian-sympathiser'. This second disaster,

[1] Above, p. 60: minute of Robert Anderson, 8 Apr. (S.P.O., R.P. 1877/9309).

[2] Supt Ryan to C.P., 31 Mar., 1 Apr. (S.P.O., 6090R/6095R, 6095R); H.-C. Bodley to I.G.P., 3, 4 Apr. (S.P.O., 6115R/6246R, 6114R/6246R); *C.C.C. minutes*, lxii, 299 (15 July, John Smith, Henry Woodthorpe), 300 (Eugene Hyde), 302 (John Bodley), 308 (James Castle).

[3] *Irish Times*, 1 Apr. (p. 5, col. 4), 2 Apr. (p. 5, col. 6); *The Times*, 2 Apr. (p. 12, col. 2), 4 Apr. (p. 5, col. 3).

also reported in the press,[1] should, one would suppose, have been sufficient warning to Davitt that the game was up. Certainly all traffic to and from his depot in Leeds ceased, though he and his warehouseman visited it several times, and when the police effected a stealthy entrance to it they found only a quantity of barrels. He made some attempt to bluff the police into thinking that he had gone to America by the R.M.S. *Cuba*, which sailed from Liverpool on 2 April with his parents on board.[2] Then he paused a few days, and on 8 April put out a feeler—a case containing four revolvers and six packages of ammunition, conveyed from Rafferty's cottage to the Globe Parcels Office, Birmingham (where it was privately examined by Bodley and Seal), for despatch to a parcel office in Leeds. Next day at Leeds it was collected by Davitt's warehouseman and taken to a private house, unobtrusively watched by Bodley. The fact that this consignment reached its destination without being visibly interfered with by the police was taken as a favourable sign by Davitt, who had returned to Leeds to see what happened. On 14 April three substantial cases of revolvers were despatched from Rafferty's cottage by the Midland Railway to Newcastle-upon-Tyne, two addressed to 'J. M. Kershaw, Glassmakers' Arms Inn, Bailiff Gate' and one to 'C. H. Williams, Globe Express Office, Pilgrim Street'; and on 18 April two further consignments followed, one to 'C. H. Williams' at Newcastle, the other to 'Benjamin Richards, Globe Parcels Express Office, Market Street, Manchester'. Kershaw, Williams, and Richards were fictitious names; the Glassmakers' Arms was a beerhouse kept by an Irishman, George Mullins, and frequented by Irish labourers. All five consignments were watched by the police at both ends of their journey, and all were seized by them at the delivery end, not without further publicity. The labels on all of them, as with the Dublin and Glasgow consignments, had been written by Davitt. Still unaware of the hot breath of the police, he had the nerve, on 18 April, to call at the Globe Parcels Office, Manchester, to claim the case consigned to 'Benjamin Richards'. Informed that it had not arrived, he next day sent two Irishmen, Patrick Carthy and another, with a written order, signed by him as Benjamin Richards, to collect it. They came with a horse and cart and, followed by Detective-inspector William Henderson in a cab, took the case to the house of a man called Geoghegan, a joiner, who refused to accept it. They then went to a beerhouse kept by Carthy, and known to the police as a fenian drilling-place. At that point they became aware that they were being shadowed. The unnamed man ran away while Carthy took the case into his house, where it was seized by

[1] *F.J.*, 4 Apr., p. [3], col. 5; *Irish Times*, 4 Apr., p. 5, col. 2.
[2] See below, p. 79.

Henderson. It was found to contain 1,100 rounds of revolver cartridges and 400 rounds of Snider's rifle cartridges.[1]

The police had now identified sixteen separate cases or barrels originating with Davitt in less than three weeks—the fourteen already mentioned and two barrels that had arrived at Waterford and Portlaw (County Waterford) from 'J. Henderson' but, being unclaimed, had been returned to Leeds and there quietly seized.[2] How much longer would the traffic continue? Minningham and his partners had been alarmed but not deterred by the news of the arms seizures. Their position, however, became more dangerous when, towards the end of April, reports appeared in the press of a fenian plot to blow up the offices of *The Times* and the *Pall Mall Gazette*, and reference was made to the accumulation of arms in the hands of fenians in London and to 'a fenian agent' who had been or was engaged in purchasing arms in Birmingham.[3] Minningham and partners, Bembridge reported, had a large stock of revolvers waiting to be disposed of, and as late as 26 April fenians in Ashton-under-Lyne and Oldham were expecting rifles for which the money had already been paid by Davitt. But it was now decided that to continue the traffic through Rafferty's cottage was as risky as to use the Leeds depot. Rafferty himself had disappeared. The partners agreed that Minningham and Gill would for the present lie as low as possible, and that all the external contacts of the firm should be conducted by Wilson, who, being English, was 'the best man to put to the front'. He had plenty of nerve, for he challenged the agent of the Globe Parcels Office to explain why goods he had recently forwarded to Newcastle had not been delivered. The agent referred him to the police, whereupon Wilson threatened legal proceedings—with the sole object, Head-constable Bodley considered, of trying to discover the source of

[1] Supt Ryan to C.P., 31 Mar. (S.P.O., 6090R/6095R); H.-C. Patrick Harvey to I.G.P., 1, 3 Apr. (S.P.O., 6125R); H.-C. Bodley to I.G.P., 3, 4, 8, 11, 13, 17, 21, 22 Apr. (S.P.O., 6114R/6246R, 6115R/6246R, 6177R/6246R, 6193R/6246R, 6246R, 6269R; same to same 20 Apr. (S.P.O., R.P. 1877/9309); H.-C. Murphy to H.-C. Bodley, 11 Apr. 70 (S.P.O. 6223R/6246R); Constable Thomas Skuce to H.-C. Murphy, 12 Apr. (S.P.O., R.P. 1877/9309); H.-C. Bodley to H.-C. Welby, 17, 18, 22 Apr. (S.P.O. 6269R); minute by Robert Anderson, 26 Apr. (S.P.O., 6343R); *C.C.C. minutes*, lxxii, 298–9 (15 July, Henry Taylor), 304 (William Sinclair), 304–5 (John Lockhart), 305 (Audley Thompson), 306 (Mark Thorburn), 307 (William Henderson).

[2] The 16 were made up as follows:

Birmingham to Leeds (26 Mar., 8 Apr.)	2	
Leeds to Dublin (29 Mar.)	6	
Leeds to Waterford and Portlaw (*c.* 29 Mar.)	2	
Birmingham to Glasgow (29 Mar.)	1	
Birmingham to Newcastle-upon-Tyne (14, 18 Apr.)	4	
Birmingham to Manchester (18 Apr.)	1	16

[3] *Manchester Courier and Lancashire General Advertiser,* 22 Apr., p. 3, col. 4; *The Times,* 25 Apr., p. 5, col. 6; *Irishman*, 30 Apr., p. 706, cols 1–2.

the information that had led to the seizures. He obviously did not realise that his connection with Davitt was fully known to the police. On the contrary he was prepared to cooperate with Davitt in further movements of arms, but on a different plan.[1]

This was the situation in which Davitt took lodgings in London on 29 April, renting a second-floor back room at six shillings a week from Mrs Jane Robson, of 35 Milman Street, Bloomsbury, under the name of J. D. Matthews. Discarding the elaborate concealments of his previous trafficking, he arranged that Wilson should bring revolvers to London by passenger train as hand luggage—ostensibly for sale in the ordinary course of business, actually for delivery to Davitt in return for cash. He should have known that this was to take too serious a risk. *The Times* of 25 April, in a paragraph on fenian activity in London, had announced that the police intended, so far as practicable, to examine all packages arriving in London by rail from Birmingham and other places from which arms might be sent in quantity.[2] The statement referred to traffic by goods train, but to assume on that account, as Davitt seems to have done, that passenger traffic from Birmingham to London was immune from police vigilance, was quite unwarranted. On the evening of 14 May, Wilson, accompanied by a stranger, boarded a train for London at the Great Western Railway station, Snow Hill, Birmingham. Sergeant Seal, Head-constable Bodley, and Bembridge saw young Minningham and a boy handing Wilson three heavy parcels covered in black oil-cloth, which they had carried from the workshop in Weaman Street. Seal at once informed the chief of police in Birmingham, who telegraphed police superintendants at Paddington station and Scotland Yard. As the train arrived at Paddington station at 10.40, Davitt was waiting for it, and he and Wilson were separately arrested.[3] Nothing more was heard of the stranger whom Seal had seen entering the train with Wilson. But a story derived from Frank Haran[4] makes it likely that he was an accomplice of Davitt's from Haslingden, Tom Lakin, who, having travelled in another part of the train, alighted unnoticed at Paddington to witness Wilson's arrest, and immediately rushed by cab to Davitt's lodgings where he anticipated the police by seizing all documents. A few days later he visited Davitt in prison, and conveyed in Irish the welcome news that evidence which would have

[1] H.-C. Bodley to I.G.P., 13, 22, 29 Apr., 6, 13 May (S.P.O., 6223R/6246R, 6271R, 6327R, 6369R, 6409R); H.-C. Welby to H.-C. Bodley, 26 Apr. (S.P.O., 6327R).

[2] *The Times*, 25 Apr., p. 5, col. 6.

[3] H.-C. Bodley to I.G.P., 16 May (S.P.O., R.P. 1870/9491-2 (1877/9309)); *The Times*, 16 May (p. 7, col. 5), 21 May (p. 11, col. 4); *C.C.C. minutes*, lxxii, 298 (15 July, John Seal), 309 (Mrs Jane Robson).

[4] See above, p. 44.

led to the arrest of dozens of London fenians had been destroyed.[1]

The arrest, which was the work of the London Metropolitan Police, was made, it may safely be assumed, on the advice of Robert Anderson, who had evidently decided that the pear was ripe. He had waited for nearly seven weeks, during which evidence of the arms traffic was piling up, before reaching a decision, and he must have reached it now because, for the first time since the discovery of the arms depot at Leeds, the opportunity was offered of catching Davitt and Wilson together in possession of arms. The R.I.C. detectives at Liverpool and Manchester who had kept police headquarters so well informed about Lancashire fenians were not consulted about the arrest. Murphy, at Liverpool, deplored it as 'premature' and put his finger on a serious blunder the London police had made: it was a pity, he remarked, that Davitt was not allowed to come in contact with Wilson and the revolvers, 'so as to perfect a tangible case against him'.[2] Welby wrote from Manchester that he considered it 'too abrupt', and that the chief constable of Manchester, Captain Palin, was of the same opinion, 'but I did not then know that Corydon knew anything of him [Davitt]'.[3] Corydon was an informer who had been produced as a crown witness at many fenian trials since 1867; and the point of Welby's statement must be that, until he learnt of Corydon's appearance (27 May) at Davitt's preliminary examination before a police magistrate,[4] he had supposed that there was no witness whom the police could afford to use to prove Davitt's connection with the I.R.B.

Davitt's arrest was a heavy blow to the fenian movement. The recent seizures of arms by the police had caused commotion among Manchester fenians, and a centre, Murphy, had resigned on 13 May, insisting that some of the fenian officials must have given information to the police. Nerves were rather strained when Davitt's plight came up for discussion at a well-attended meeting of fenian officials in Manchester on Sunday evening, 22 May. Though many of them were friends of Davitt's, many contended that he was unfit for the work he had been engaged in, being a marked man with his one arm. All were concerned about the large amount of money (£153)—their money—he had on him, and some felt that he had not shown sufficient caution. Their depression was temporarily dispelled by news of the American fenian 'invasion' of Canada (25-6 May), and Welby wrote that it would be impossible to describe the mad feelings of the Irish in every part of

[1] Francis Haran to Mrs Mary Davitt, 15 Oct. 1907 (DP/P; 'Briar' (see above, p 18 n. 1) in *Haslingden Observer*, 27 July 1935.

[2] H.-C. Murphy to I.G.P., 17 May (S.P.O., R.P. 1870/9503 (1877/9309)). See below, p. 81.

[3] H.-C. Welby to I.G.P., 30 May 70 (S.P.O., 6469R).

[4] See below, p. 91.

his district. They did not believe one word of the reported repulse of the invaders, and there was nightly drilling in upstairs rooms in the beerhouses frequented by fenians. But the more sensible of them were, he believed, less elated over the raid on Canada, than sorry about Davitt's arrest.[1] They blamed Forrester, who was then on a lecturing trip in Ireland,[2] for recommending so conspicuous a man for the business, but agreed that Davitt must be supported.[3]

The increasing hazards of his position since the beginning of 1870 had made Davitt uncomfortable about the presence of his parents and sisters in England. He persuaded himself that it would be best for them to follow Mary to America, where they would incur no discredit because of his revolutionary activities, and that it would be best for him to be left to serve the cause unfettered by family responsibilities. With some premonition of what was in store for him, he enlisted Mary's help in urging her parents and sisters to join her in Scranton where there was a small colony of Irish from Haslingden. Both Anne and Sabina had been wage-earners for some years, so that the Davitts were probably in a better financial position than they had been hitherto. Head-constable Murphy was told that they had absconded to avoid paying rent and other debts, but there is no evidence to support this and it is quite out of character.[4] Davitt's parents had no wish to leave England except to return to Ireland, and it was only under strong pressure from Michael that they yielded. Preceded by the two girls, they left Liverpool by the R.M.S. *Cuba* on 2 April, arrived at New York on 13 April, and reached their destination at Scranton almost exactly one month before Michael's arrest.[5]

[1] H.-C. Welby to I.G.P. 2, 14, 25, 30 May 70 (S.P.O., 6352R/6474R, 6417R/6474R, 6474R, 6494R).

[2] *Irishman*, 14 May, p. 733; 21 May, p. 749, col. 2; p. 752, cols 2-3.

[3] H.-C. Welby to I.G.P., 18, 30 May (S.P.O., R.P. 1870/9507 (1877/9309); 6494R).

[4] H.-C. Murphy to H.-C. Bodley, 11 Apr. 70 (S.P.O., 6223R/6246R); to Constable M. Skuce, 12 Apr. (S.P.O., R.P. 1870/9293 (1877/9309)).

[5] Passenger list of R.M.S. *Cuba*, Captain E.R. Moodie master, 13 Apr. (Washington D.C., National Archives, Passenger arrival lists, Port of New York); D to his father and mother, 18 June; to his father, mother, and sisters, 11 July 70, 17 July 71; to his mother, 29 Jan. 72 (DP/A); Sabina Davitt, Sketch of Davitt's early life (DP/T); DN/7. 18-20 July 80.

III

Trial for treason-felony, July 1870

THE London police, alerted by Birmingham, were prepared for trouble from fenians when the 10.40 train from Birmingham arrived at the Great Western Railway terminus, Paddington, on the night of Saturday, 14 May 1870. About twenty members of the 'X' division of the Metropolitan Police were in readiness, but nothing unusual happened as the train pulled in. Chief-inspector George Clark, of Scotland Yard, was on the arrival platform with several other detective officers. He had come by underground to Praed Street where, as he emerged from the staircase leading to the street, he had seen Davitt standing in the station entrance under the gaslight. He had followed him across Praed Street into the Great Western terminus, and on the arrival platform had instructed Detective-sergeant William Henry Campbell to keep him under close observation and to arrest him if he attempted to make off. Davitt was still on the platform when passengers began to pour out of the Birmingham train. Wilson, conspicuous with his three heavy parcels, was stopped by Detective-sergeant John Foley and asked what he was carrying. He replied 'only revolvers'. Asked where he got them from he said that he made them himself and he handed the sergeant a card inscribed 'John Wilson, gun and pistol maker, Harper's Buildings, Weaman Street, Birmingham'. He had brought the revolvers to London for sale, but knew no one there. Foley took him under arrest to Paddington Green police station, where his luggage was found to contain fifty revolvers bearing a Belgian maker's name, 'La Fourchure (brevetė)'. A slip of paper was in his pocket bearing the name 'Mr Matthews, 35 Milman Street, Guildford St, London W.C.'. He was charged with being in possession of revolvers of which he did not give a satisfactory account. Simultaneously Sergeant Campbell had been dealing with Davitt, who, either because he saw Wilson being arrested or because he had otherwise become alive to the danger he was in, began to move away from the arrival platform in the direction of Praed Street underground station. At that point Campbell accosted him. Asked what he was doing, Davitt said he was waiting for a friend, but declined to give his own or his friend's name except to the proper authority. Asked where the friend was coming from, he said 'Manchester'. He was taken to Paddington Green police station and searched: £150 in notes together with three sovereigns and two keys, but no arms or papers, were found on him. Asked his name, he said he was Michael Davitt. He had come from Manchester that morning and had no fixed address in London; later he said that he had been in London five days. He had been a printer in Haslingden, then a hawker of drapery and hardware, and since last November 'a speculator' who attended races and speculated on public events. He gave his address as Wilkinson Street, Haslingden.[1] He was charged with loitering. He and Wilson were held in custody at the police station during the week-end. They pretended not to know each other, but the keys found on Davitt proved to be those of a carpet bag belonging to 'J. D. Matthews' at the address found on Wilson.[2] The police, however, had blundered in not giving the two men an opportunity to meet before arresting them. The arrest of Wilson almost as soon as he stepped off the train made that impossible even if Campbell had not arrested Davitt when he did. Had Davitt and Wilson met, as of course they intended to do, that would have afforded direct evidence of a connection between them, which, in the sequel, the police were never able to prove except by circumstantial evidence.[3]

Davitt's appearance attracted some attention. A reporter from *The Times* described him as 'a remarkably tall, powerful-looking man, neat in his dress, and with a military bearing . . . His hair, short whiskers and closely-trimmed moustache are dark; his eyes are dark-blue, and his nose, mouth and chin indicate great readiness and decision of character.' The loss of his right arm had made it easy for the police to follow his movements. He gave his age as twenty-five but appeared to be from three to five years older. He was in fact only twenty-four; and his eyes were brown, not blue. Wilson gave his age as forty-three.[4]

On Monday, 16 May, the two prisoners were brought before the Marylebone police court for examination. The magistrate, D'Eyncourt, thought the evidence against them very slight but agreed to remand them till Friday, in response to a request from Superintendent Adolphus Frederick Williamson, chief of the detective department at Scotland Yard, who was watching the case on behalf of the commissioners of

[1] Cf. above, p. 67.

[2] *The Times*, 16 May 70, p. 7, col. 5; 17 May, p. 5. col. 2; p. 7, col. 5; 18 July, p. 11, col. 1; *Birmingham Daily Gazette*, 18 May, p. 6, col. 6; *C.C.C. minutes*, lxxii, 309–10, 311–12.

[3] Cf. above, p. 78.

[4] *The Times*, 18 May, p. 7, col. 5; 16 July, p. 11, col. 3.

police. Williamson called Inspector Clark and Sergeant Foley to give evidence of the arrest, and declared under oath that he believed Davitt to have been for some months engaged in travelling through the north of England for the purpose of buying arms for the fenian organisation. The magistrate was willing to accept bail of £100 for each prisoner, but as they had no friends in London they were remanded to the House of Detention, Clerkenwell. Davitt asked that the money taken from him should be returned to enable him to provide for his defence. Superintendent Williamson objected, and D'Eyncourt said that Davitt might have the three sovereigns.[1]

On Friday, 20 May, the prisoners were again brought before the Marylebone police court, the police, warned by the Manchester rescue, providing an escort of a sergeant and eight constables of the 'X' division, armed with revolvers. The prisoners were placed on the floor of the court in front of the dock, against which Davitt leaned 'watching the proceedings with apparent nonchalance'.[2] H. B. Poland, counsel to the treasury at the central criminal court and adviser to the home office in criminal matters, now appeared for the prosecution, while W. H. B. Pain, solicitor, represented the prisoners. Poland asked for a further remand: an important witness who could prove that the prisoners had met before was on his way to London; though the police had no doubt of Davitt's connection with the fenian movement, more time was needed to substantiate the very serious charges the state would have to bring against the prisoners. Davitt had told the police at his arrest that he had just come from Manchester, but evidence was now given that he had been lodging at 35 Milman Street, Bloomsbury, since 29 April, under the name of J. D. Matthews, and that in the previous October or November he had stayed at the Bell Restaurant, Euston Road, under the name of W. R. Jackson. His landlady at the former address, Mrs Jane Robson, had found him 'a very gentlemanly man'.[3] Detective-sergeant Andrew Lansdowne, who testified to having seen him at the latter address, said that he knew Davitt 'through having had to watch him in connection with the fenian movement'.[4] The magistrate said that, so far as the evidence went, it was favourable to Wilson, who was at Birmingham collecting evidence for the prosecution, had sent world that he had just received information proving Wilson's connection with Davitt, whom the police knew to be connected with the tion with Davitt, whom the police knew to be connected with the fenian movement. D'Eyncourt therefore granted the remand. He again

[1] *The Times,* 17 May, p. 5, col. 2; *Birmingham Daily Gazette,* 18 May, p. 6, col. 6.
[2] *The Times,* 21 May, p. 11, col. 4. [3] *The Times,* 16 July, p. 11, col. 5.
[4] *Birmingham Daily Gazette,* 21 May, p. 5, col. 3.

agreed to accept bail, but no bailsmen were forthcoming. He also ordered £10 to be returned to Davitt. Behind the scenes police officers at Birmingham, Liverpool, Manchester, and other places, and also in Ireland, were now busily engaged in providing information relating to the case and preparing witnesses.[2]

When the prisoners appeared before the court for the third time, on Friday, 27 May, Wilson was separately represented–by R. H. Collins, barrister. Poland announced that the evidence now warranted a charge of treason-felony against both men. It would be proved that Davitt's object in waiting at Paddington station was to meet Wilson, that Davitt was a member of the Fenian Brotherhood, and that both men were involved in supplying arms to the fenian movement. At this point the prisoners were removed from the floor of the court and placed in the dock. As proof of Davitt's connection with fenianism a notorious ex-fenian informer, J. J. Corydon, swore that he knew Davitt and had seen him at Liverpool immediately after the Chester castle attempt (11 February 1867) in the company of prominent fenians. Questioned by the magistrate on how long he had lived in Ireland Corydon replied enigmatically that he had done so as long as the law would let him, whereupon Davitt interjected: '*you* could not live in Ireland–reptiles cannot live there'.[3] Detailed evidence of the prisoners' traffic in arms during the previous March, April, and May was given by police officers and others from Birmingham, Manchester, Leeds, Newcastle-upon-Tyne, Glasgow, Dublin, and London, in proceedings extending over four days (27 May, 2, 7, 14 June).[4] On 2 June a handwriting expert, Charles Chabot, identified Davitt as the writer of the names and addresses on consignments of arms seized by the police and also of the letter found on Forrester on 16 December.[5] It had been mentioned by Corydon in his evidence and was now read to the court. On 7 June, when Davitt and Wilson were formally charged with treason-felony, the law officers of the crown suggested that the prisoners would probably be tried at the Leeds assizes, both because most of the felonious acts alleged against them had taken place in the north of England and also because Leeds would be a convenient meeting-place for witnesses from the north, the midlands, and London. But at the final examination before the Marylebone magistrate, on 14 June, when the prosecution

[1] Ibid.; *The Times,* 21 May, p. 11, col. 4; H. C. Bodley to I.G.P., 18 May (S.P.O., R.P. 1870/9507 (1877/9309)).

[2] S.P.O., R.P. 1870/9507, 1909, 9525, 9527, 9539, 9549, 9561, 9574, 9579, 9592, 9601, 9612, 9616, 9633, 9634 (1877/9309), 18 May-7 July.

[3] *The Times,* 28 May, p. 12, col. 4.

[4] Nearly all of this evidence was repeated at the trial in the central criminal court in July (below, pp 88-9).

[5] Above, pp 60-63, 72-3.

concluded its case, the depositions of the witnesses were read over, and the prisoners reserved their defence, Davitt and Wilson were committed for trial at the central criminal court (the Old Bailey). Two further sums of £10 had been returned to Davitt on 27 May and 2 June; to this was now added £20 making a total of £53 returned out of the £153 found on him at his arrest. He was removed to Newgate, the prison to which the central criminal court was attached.[1]

While at Clerkenwell Davitt had been in touch with his solicitor about his defence. Convinced that the weakest link in the prosecution's case was its attempt to prove his connection with fenianism, he attached primary importance to evidence which, he believed, existed in Cockcroft's office-records providing an alibi for the period when Corydon claimed to have seen him in fenian company at Liverpool. The solicitor learnt from Cockcroft's son, Thomas, that one of two time-keeping books covering February 1867 contained entries in Davitt's hand showing him to have been at work on 12 and 16 February, but that the other book was missing. This was known as the 'tillet book' because it recorded only printing done on 'tillet' or coarse cloth used in packing woollens for export. Davitt had worked largely on tillet printing;[2] he believed that he been so engaged on 13, 14 and 15 February, and that the fact had been recorded in the tillet book. He put the point urgently in a letter to Cockroft, evidently hoping that the missing book could be found. If it did not include the expected entries 'as I am confident that I was working for your father all that week . . . I believe the record of said work must be entered somewhere'. If the record could be found it might, Davitt thought, help Cockcroft to recall other circumstances that would strengthen his present belief that Davitt was at Haslingden during the critical week. The fact that the entries for the 12th and 16th in the extant office-book were in his own handwriting 'does not go to prove that I was *not* working on the respective dates alluded to—neither is it, as you say, very strong evidence in my favour'.[3]

Both the content and the earnest tone of this letter to Cockcroft, taken along with all that is otherwise known of Davitt's involvement in the Chester castle affair, warrant two conclusions: (a) the alibi Davitt sought to establish related not to Monday, 11 February, the day of the raid, but to the ensuing days 12-16 February; (b) it was not a concoction but a genuine alibi and this is what explains his vehemence

[1] *The Times,* 28 May, p. 12, col. 4; 3 June, p. 7, col. 2; 8 June, p. 5, col. 4; 15 June, p. 11, col. 5. *Birmingham Daily Gazette*, 28 May, p. 5, col. 5; 3 June, p. 4. col. 3; 15 June, p. 5, col. 3.

[2] *C.C.C. minutes,* lxxii, 326-7 (Thomas Cockcroft).

[3] D in House of Detention, to Thomas Cockcroft, *c.* 4 June (DP/A 43). This letter was acquired by the National Library of Ireland in 1968 from the grandson of Henry Cockcroft.

about the missing record. The tillet book did not turn up, but it is safe to assume that Davitt was in fact at work in Cockcroft's business on 12 February and for the rest of the week. He must have got back from Chester to Haslingden late on 11 February, or early the following morning. Throughout the proceedings against him no crown witness ever claimed to have seen him on 11 February, at Chester or Liverpool or elsewhere, and it was therefore unnecessary to account for his absence on that day.[1]

The case had now received considerable attention in the press. Full reports of each day's proceedings appeared in *The Times*; and the press generally, in London and throughout the country, covering the police-court examination in varying degrees of detail, accuracy, and hostile comment. In Davitt's home town, the *Haslingden Chronicle* of 21 May made it the subject of an editorial 'Revival of fenianism', which, having described fenians as 'designing knaves or ignorant, credulous unthinking men', implied that Davitt's real object had been to put money in his purse.[2] On Monday, 30 May, *The Times* carried news of a fenian plot to reenact the Clerkenwell explosion of 1867. On the preceding Saturday, Scotland Yard had received an anonymous letter threatening that, if Davitt and Wilson were not immediately released from the House of Detention, instead of a wall being blown down as in 1867 the greater part of the prison would be blown up. A strong force of armed police was at once sent to Clerkenwell which cordoned off the prison and patrolled all the neighbouring streets throughout the night. Every place known to be frequented by fenians in London was visited by police and all reported fenians were carefully watched.[3] A few days later, on 2 June, Woolwich Arsenal was reported to be expecting a fenian attack: special guards were stationed at the powder magazine, boats manned by armed Thames police were cruising in front of the arsenal, and vessels navigating the river were being watched.[4] On 7 June there was news of a fenian threat to Tynemouth castle, where the arms and ammunition for the military district between the Tweed and the Humber were stored. The garrison was hastily reinforced and the castle put into a strong state of defence. Among the Irish employed in the shipbuilding and iron industries on Tyneside it was believed that there were many fenians, and that arms recently seized by the police —apparently arms despatched by Davitt—were intended for them.[5]

[1] F. Sheehy-Skeffington (*Michael Davitt*, ed. F. S. L. Lyons, 1967, pp 37, 38-9) is in error on these points.

[2] *Haslingden Chronicle and Ramsbottom Times*, 21 May 70, p. 2, col. 4.

[3] *The Times*, 30 May, p. 14, col. 2. *Birmingham Daily Gazette*, 31 May, p. 5, col. 4.

[4] *Birmingham Daily Gazette*, 2 June, p. 8, col. 2.

[5] *Birmingham Daily Gazette*, 7 June, p. 4, col. 2.

None of these alarms seems to have been substantiated; but *The Times*, in a lengthy resumé of Davitt and Wilson's examination under the caption 'The newest phase of fenianism', declared on 6 June: 'there is . . . abundant evidence to show the continued activity of the Fenian Brotherhood'.[1]

On 18 June Davitt wrote from Newgate prison to his father and mother informing them of the state of the case:

> At first sight, and in the total absence of any part of my defence, it appears very serious; but when examined into carefully it is but a loose composition of vague suppositions and distorted facts, most of which can easily be set on one side by substantial evidence which will be forthcoming on my behalf . . . I will, if I can, be defenced by the best counsel at the London bar. I am nearly certain to get off as my witnesses will be all respectable and therefore contrasting favourably with the only witness against me—the infamous Corydon.[2]

At this point he evidently was in some uncertainty about money for his defence. But eventually the balance of the money found on him at his arrest—which, of course, had come from the I.R.B.—seems to have been returned. In addition a loan was hastily raised by fenians in Manchester, and a defence fund for both prisoners was initiated by Forrester.[3] With the money thus provided, George Summers Griffiths, John Baker Stafford Greene, and George Moody were engaged to defend Davitt, while the defence of Wilson was entrusted to Richard Henn Collins (who had represented him at the police court examination) and Henry Thorowgood Hunt. These barristers were overshadowed in legal eminence by counsel for the prosecution, who included the two principal law officers of the crown, Sir Robert Collier (attorney general) and Sir John Coleridge (solicitor general). Associated with them were Harry Bodkin Poland (who had appeared for the prosecution at the police court examination), Francis Thorne Cole, and Thomas Dickson Archibald.[4]

The trial began at the Old Bailey on Friday, 15 July, before the lord chief justice, Sir Alexander Cockburn, a distinguished judge with fourteen years experience on the bench.[5] The proceedings, which received a good deal of publicity, continued throughout Friday and Saturday, and concluded on Monday, 18 July.[6] The prisoners were indicted

[1] *The Times,* 6 June, p. 10, col. 1.

[2] D to his father and mother, 18 June (DP/A).

[3] S.P.O., Fenianism, index of names, 1866-71, app., p. 2, no. 11; *Irishman,* 17 Dec. 70, p. 397.

[4] D to Sabina Davitt, 15 Apr. 77 (DP/A; smuggled); DN/29A, 28 Jan. 95, in *I.H.S.,* iv, no. 15, p. 250. Joseph Foster, *Men-at-the-bar* (1885); *D.N.B.,* P. R. Collier, J. D. Coleridge, T. D. Archibald; *D.N.B., 1901-11,* R. H. Collins; *D.N.B., 1922-30,* H. B. Poland.

[5] *D.N.B.*

[6] The proceedings were reported in considerable detail in *The Times* (16 July 70, p. 11,

under the treason-felony act[1] on two counts: the first alleged that they feloniously intended to deprive the queen of her style and title as queen of the United Kingdom of Great Britain and Ireland, the second that they feloniously conspired to levy war against the queen in Ireland in order by force to compel her to change her measures and counsels. The indictment specified under each count thirty-four 'overt acts' by which these felonious intentions were 'uttered, expressed and declared', contrary to the treason-felony act. These consisted partly of conspiring—both with each other and with 'other evil-disposed persons'—to commit, and partly of actually committing, various felonies, including: insurrection; subverting the constitution; inciting citizens of the United States to invade Ireland; becoming members, and inciting others to become members, of an organisation, the Fenian Brotherhood, having for its object the establishment of a republic in Ireland; attending fenian meetings; making and procuring large quantities of arms and ammunition with which to levy war against the queen within the realm; causing arms and ammunition to be conveyed into Ireland to aid the fenian association there; attempting to seize arms at Chester in February 1867 and to remove them to Ireland there to be used against the queen; aiding the Fenian Brotherhood to make war against the queen at various places in Ireland on 5 March 1867; sending large quantities of arms from Birmingham to Ireland, Leeds, Glasgow, Newcastle-upon-Tyne, and Manchester; conveying arms to Paddington railway station, in the county of Middlesex (within the jurisdiction of the central criminal court) to be used against the queen; endeavouring to meet at Paddington station in pursuance of their felonious intentions.[2] In the long catalogue of overt acts the prosecution was to rely mainly, as against Davitt, on those that concerned his being a member of the fenian organisation and his procuring and transporting of arms and

cols 3-5; 18 July, p. 11, cols 1-3; 19 July, p. 11, cols 2-3) and in the principal London and provincial newspapers. Their general coverage is much less full and consistent than that of *The Times,* but on particular points they occasionally supply detail not in *The Times* (for a critical instance see below, p. 90, n. 1). No press report attempts to record the evidence verbatim, as elicited from the witnesses by examination and cross-examination; but this, fortunately, is done in the sessions papers of the court: *Central criminal court, sessions paper, . . . seventh session . . . minutes of evidence,* lxxii (London, [1870]), pp 296-335. The case was also the subject of a law report, by the chief legal reporter for *The Times,* W. F. Finlason: *Reports of cases in criminal law, argued and determined in all the courts in England and Wales,* ed. E. W. Cox, xi, 1867-71 (London, 1871), pp 676-83; this includes an abstract of the indictment and an extensive resumé of the judge's summing-up. The original indictment is in the archives of the central criminal court; the abstract in Cox has numerous errors of detail and is not self-consistent.

[1] 11 & 12 Vict., c. 12 (1848).

[2] Central Criminal Court, Old Bailey, London: Indictments, 11 July 1870, Reg. *v.* Wilson and Davitt (107); *Reports of cases in criminal law,* ed. E. W. Cox, xi (1871), pp 676-8.

ammunition for fenian purposes; and as against Wilson on the second category only.

The section of the treason-felony act (section 3) under which Davitt and Wilson were indicted provided that anyone who should 'compass, imagine, devise or intend' to deprive the queen of her royal style and title, or to levy war against her in order by force to compel her to change her measures or counsels, and should express, utter or declare such compassings, imaginings, devices, or intentions by printing, writing, speaking or by any overt act or deed, should be guilty of treason-felony. The offence was not the actual commission of the crimes specified, but the intention to commit them as manifested by overt acts; and the effect of the statute was to convert an offence that was previously high treason into one for which, on conviction, the punish-was less severe.[1]

In opening the case for the prosecution the attorney general claimed that it was one of great public importance. Although the fenian attempt in 1867 to plunge the United Kingdom into anarchy and bloodshed had been frustrated, the fenian conspiracy still existed, and it was only through the constant vigilance of the police that renewed violence had been prevented. At the beginning of 1870 the state of Ireland was so unsettled that parliament had felt it necessary to pass a new coercion act, which prohibited the possession of arms in Ireland, especially revolvers, except under stringent conditions.[2] Early in the year information from the Irish police caused the police of Birmingham to watch an arms manufactory in that city carried on in Weaman Street by three working men, the prisoner John Wilson (an Englishman), and two Irishmen, Minningham and Gill. The attorney general went on to sketch the story, narrated above, of Davitt's secret despatches of arms from this source, beginning with the police discovery on 26 March of the role of Rafferty's cottage in the system and ending with the arrest of Davitt and Wilson on 14 May.[3] Though he did not disclose the whole inside story, he recounted all the salient facts and called many witnesses to support his statements. Most of them had already given evidence at the police examination, but they were reinforced by many others. It was a well-organised array, forty strong, drawn from a wide area: from Birmingham Detective-sergeant Seal, and Head-constable Bodley of the R.I.C., the rifler Bembridge and a craftsman who had worked for him, the maker of the packing cases used by Wilson, and

[1] I am indebted to Judge Cahir Davitt, son of Michael Davitt and formerly president of the high court of Ireland, for a valuable memorandum on legal points in the case.

[2] Peace Preservation (Ireland) Act 1870, 33 Vict., c. 9, 4 Apr. 70; see *Hansard 3*, cc, 81–127, 328–1051.

[3] *The Times*, 16 July, p. 3, col. 5; *Daily Telegraph*, 16 July, p. 5, col. 6.

four employees of the Midland Railway; from Leeds the chief of police and two detective officers, the agent who had let the warehouse to Davitt, the cashier of the Bank of England who had cashed his draft for £60, the manager of the Midland Railway goods station, and the inspector of the Leeds joint station of the London and North Western Railway and the Lancashire and Yorkshire Railway; from Ireland the two detectives of the Dublin Metropolitan Police who had seized the arms discharged at the port of Dublin on 31 March and 1 April, John Flannery of Ballaghadereen, Arthur McDonnell of Tuam (proprietor of Martin McDonnell & Co.), Richard Cunningham of Boyle, Cecilia Higgins of Newport, and Charles Haugh of Portlaw, to all of whom unsought supplies of arms had been consigned by Davitt; from Glasgow a detective officer, the goods manager of the Glasgow and South Western Railway, and a carter; from Newcastle-upon-Tyne the superintendent of the detective police and one of his officers; from Manchester Detective-inspector Henderson and an employee of the Globe Parcels Office; from London Inspector Clark, Detective-sergeants Foley, Campbell, and Lansdowne, two officers on duty at Paddington Green police station when Davitt and Wilson were charged, a warder from the Clerkenwell House of Detention to whom Davitt had made a written complaint, the head viewer of small arms at the Tower of London, Davitt's landlady in Milman Street (Mrs Jane Robson), and the handwriting expert Chabot.[1]

All this evidence left no doubt that Davitt and Wilson had been engaged in a widely-ramified and secret traffic in arms of which Davitt, described by the attorney general as a labouring man of no occupation, was the organising genius. The attorney general had no difficulty in showing that it was not 'in the way of legitimate trade'. He instanced the unfinished condition of the rifles, the fact that some of them were packed in barrels with their stocks cut in two, the absence of invoices, the use of fictitious or misleading names both for consignors and consignees, Davitt's impersonation of one of the consignees, and his possession of an amount of money inconsistent with his being a labouring man. But clandestine traffic in arms was not necessarily criminal; and the onus was not on the accused to prove that it was innocent traffic but on the prosecution to prove that it was criminal by connecting Davitt with the fenian conspiracy. Here the attorney general was at a loss for evidence. Davitt, he said, had frequently been seen at Liverpool in February 1867 in the company of leading fenians, many of them Irish-American officers, who were the chief instigators of the fenian

[1] *C.C.C. minutes*, lxxii, 296–314, 321–2; *The Times*, 16 July, p. 11, cols 3–5; 18 July, p. 11, col. 1.

attempt on Chester castle and the ensuing rising in Ireland. Liverpool was their assembly point for the purpose of these designs, and Davitt had attended meetings there about the time of the Chester castle attempt. From this point onwards his activities could not be traced (though he was more than once seen at Wilson's workshop in Birmingham) till he was found to be engaged in the arms traffic that led to his arrest. But he was known to have been at Liverpool early in January finding bailsmen for Forrester, and the letter seized from Forrester would be proved to be in his handwriting. The attorney general read the letter, but did not place much emphasis on it, though it was to prove the most damaging document produced against Davitt.[1]

The terms of the indictment made it necessary for the attorney general to show that there had been, and still was, a fenian conspiracy; and accordingly a number of police officers gave evidence of the attempt on Chester castle, the rising in Ireland, and the current situation. Detective-sergeant William Bray, of Chester, said that about 2,000 strangers arrived in the city on 11 February 1867 only to find that they had been forestalled. The danger thus averted had been very serious, for there were 30,000 stand of arms and a large quantity of ammunition in the castle, and until reinforcements arrived these were guarded by only 100 men.[2] Officers of the Royal Irish Constabulary testified to attacks on police barracks in Ireland on the night of 5-6 March. A sergeant of the Dublin Metropolitan Police, Francis Sheridan, who was on duty with three constables at Milltown village, near Dublin, on 5 March, described how, about midnight, they were surrounded by a party of 700-800 fenians in military formation, armed with pikes, rifles, and revolvers, and forced to accompany them on a march into the Dublin hills that resulted in the capture of police barracks at Stepaside and Glencullen. Constable John Brown gave evidence of an attack on his barracks at Ballyknockane, near Cork, in which 150 fenians led by William Mackey Lomasney and J. F. X. O'Brien set the building on fire.[3] Head-constable Richard Adams, in charge of the police barracks at Kilmallock, County Limerick, described how, about 6 a.m. on 6 March, the place was attacked by about 500 men who attempted to set it on fire and called on Adams and his fourteen constables to surrender 'in the name of the Irish Republic and of Colonel Dunn'. The defenders returned the insurgents' fire and fighting went

[1] *The Times*, 16 July, p. 11, col. 3; *Daily Telegraph*, 16 July, p. 5, col. 6; *C.C.C. minutes*, lxxii, 322. The only press report that refers to this reading of the 'pen' letter is that in the *Daily Telegraph*. From the reports in the other papers we should have to suppose that the letter was put in later by the defence.

[2] *The Times*, 18 July, p. 11, col. 2; *C.C.C. minutes*, lxxii, 319; above, pp 48-9.

[3] *C.C.C. minutes*, lxxii, 320; cf. Devoy, *Recollections*, pp 199-200, 207-9.

on for three hours till some troops came in sight, whereupon the police sallied forth and the insurgents ran away, leaving two of their number dead on the field.[1]

William Horne, senior inspector of the detective department in Liverpool, who had arrested Forrester in December 1869, said that he had been keeping watch on the fenians, that there were still a great many of them in Liverpool, and that they continued to hold meetings. He described the arrest of Forrester and produced the 'pen' letter, which Forrester had tried to destroy. He saw Davitt in Liverpool soon afterwards with Forrester's mother, and had seen him several times previously, but merely in the street and alone. Davitt did not appear to be in any regular employment, though he was said to be a hawker.[2]

The handwriting expert, Chabot, swore that he believed the 'pen' letter to be in Davitt's handwriting.[3]

The evidence on which the attorney general principally relied to prove Davitt's complicity with fenianism was that of the informer Corydon, whom he introduced apologetically: his evidence was 'the only kind that could reasonably be expected' in such a case, and 'it would be received with a certain amount of caution'.[4] John Joseph Corydon (also spelt Corrydon and Corridon), *alias* Carr, had called himself a medical student from New York when he approached the Liverpool police in September 1866 with a view to giving information, but the head constable of Liverpool thought he looked an 'Irish yankee' of a low type. In a confidential statement Corydon said he had been born in Washington (he subsequently claimed Ireland as his birthplace[5]) about 1838. At the opening of the civil war he joined the 63rd New York Volunteers as a medical cadet, and was attached to the Army of the Potomac, where he remained till the end of the war. He came into contact with fenianism in the army, and about 1862 was enrolled as a member of the organisation. In 1865, after the war, he was one of a number of American fenians sent to Ireland by John O'Mahony to be in readiness for the intended rising. He went to Dublin and had several interviews with James Stephens; on the suspension of habeas corpus in February 1866 he and many other American officers were withdrawn to England. He took lodgings in Liverpool and awaited orders, frequently attending meetings of fenian leaders. He was

[1] *The Times*, 18 July, p. 11, col. 2; *C.C.C. minutes*, lxxii, 320; cf. the rather different account of the Kilmallock attempt in Devoy, *Recollections*, pp 223-8.

[2] *The Times*, 18 July, p. 11, col. 2; *C.C.C. minutes*, lxxii, 320-21. The 'pen' letter is not mentioned in any press report of Horne's evidence.

[3] *C.C.C. minutes*, lxxii, 313 (no reference to this in press reports).

[4] *The Times*, 16 July, p. 11 col. 3.

[5] *The Times*, 28 May, p. 12, col. 4; *C.C.C. minutes*, lxxii, 317.

promised £5 a week by the paymaster of the American fenians in Liverpool, but never received more than half that sum and then very irregularly. This no doubt helps to explain why he decided to turn traitor. He was told that if he gave useful and reliable information to the police, money would be no object.[1] On the night of 10 February 1867 he learnt of the Chester castle design and gave the warning that completely frustrated the conspirators next day. Soon afterwards, when large numbers of fenians crossed from Liverpool to Dublin, he was instrumental in having sixty of them arrested on arrival. He then took the irrevocable step of appearing publicly as an informer, earning unrivalled notoriety as chief witness for the prosecution in the trials of his former associates.[2]

Corydon said (16 July) that he had seen Davitt at three meetings of fenians held in Mullens's beerhouse, Birchfield Street, Liverpool, after the Chester castle attempt. He could not swear that he saw him the day after, but it was very soon after: McCafferty, Flood, Deasy, Dohany, O'Sullivan Burke and other fenian leaders—'about thirty altogether, all American officers'[3]—were present along with many fenian 'centres' from the Liverpool and neighbouring areas. Mullens's beerhouse was swarming with them, upstairs and down. They discussed the Chester fiasco and made preparations for a rising in Ireland on 5 March. They met every day until they left for Ireland to lead the rising, Davitt was well known to some of the leading centres who attended these meetings—to which no 'privates' were admitted. He had lost his right hand. He wore a moustache, but Corydon was uncertain whether he had a beard. Asked why he had not reported Davitt to the police, he contradicted himself by explaining that he had much bigger fish to fry, and that Davitt held no rank in the I.R.B. He did not claim to know Davitt well, as, for example, he knew Arthur Forrester, whom he had seen more often at fenian meetings, and of whose arrest at Liverpool in December 1869 he was aware. Under cross-examination he said that the business of informer was far less profitable than was generally supposed. He received only his expenses from the government and considered that he was owed £300. He had nothing else to do 'but to look after these people'. He had become a social outcast and went in danger of his life. But he intended to punish as many of the fenians as possible: 'they have ruined Ireland and many respectable young men'.[4]

Corroborative evidence was given by a Liverpool police-constable,

[1] P.R.O., H.O.45/O.S.7799/121, 124.

[2] Ibid., 177–9, 182, 187, 209; *The Times*, 28 May, p. 12, col. 4; *C.C.C. minutes*, lxxii, 314–16.

[3] Ibid., lxxii, 315.

[4] *The Times*, 18 July, p. 11, cols 1–2; *C.C.C. minutes*, lxxii, 314–18.

Thomas Skuce, who, in February 1867, had been specially employed in watching the movements of fenians in Liverpool. He had seen Davitt in the street with Flood and other fenians a few days before the Chester castle attempt, and at Watson's public house in Marybone, a place frequented by American fenian officers, on the two days (12 and 13 February) following the raid. Davitt had lost one arm. He had a moustache, whiskers, and a beard. Skuce confirmed that Mullens's was one of several fenian meeting-places in Liverpool, and this was corroborated by a sub-inspector of the R.I.C., Martin Meagher, who had been in charge of members of the Irish force watching the fenians in Liverpool at the time of the Chester affair.[1]

Inspector Clark of Scotland Yard, who had been making inquiries into Davitt's whereabouts around 11 February 1867, said that he had visited Haslingden and had ascertained from Henry Cockcroft, the postmaster, that Davitt had been in his employment for some years, but otherwise Clark could make little of what he told him, as Cockcroft—'a gentleman of great respectability'—was so mentally confused. He had examined Cockcroft's time-keeping books but found that the entries were not continuous for any one employee: 'no doubt to show the cost of some particular work being done, . . . if a man was engaged four hours one day he was charged four hours that day, and it might go on for a week before he was charged so again'.[2]

The crown's case for Davitt's complicity in fenianism did not amount to much. Even if Corydon had been a satisfactory witness—and the rambling, egotistical, and evasive character of his answers did not inspire confidence—his evidence related only to February 1867. A Liverpool policeman did add some precision to Corydon's dating but his description of Davitt did not agree with Corydon's. The other Liverpool policeman called as a witness, Inspector Horne, though he had known Davitt as an active fenian in January 1870,[3] had nothing incriminating to say, and was not questioned about the 'pen' letter, which he put in as part of his evidence. Inspector Clark's contribution was simply that Cockcroft's office-records were inadequate as evidence of Davitt's whereabouts during the week of the Chester castle attempt. But what of the overwhelming evidence of Davitt's fenian activities accumulated since February 1869 by Head-constables Murphy and Welby in Liverpool and Manchester?[4] Either it had not been brought to the notice of the attorney general or it was deliberately not used by him. In either case the explanation must be that, as at Forrester's

[1] *The Times*, 18 July, p. 11, col. 2; *C.C.C. minutes*, lxxii, 318–19.
[2] *C.C.C. minutes*, lxxii, 310–11; *The Times*, 18 July, p. 11, col. 1.
[3] Above, p. 67. [4] See above, pp 56–79.

trial in Liverpool, the police were not prepared to expose their secret agents by bringing them into court.

Whatever view is taken of the evidence produced by the prosecution to connect Davitt with fenianism, there was none at all to connect Wilson. It was not even proved that Wilson had ever met Davitt before the two were arrested. The attorney general admitted the difficulty, but it was not, he contended, in the nature of things that Davitt's conspiracy with Wilson should be proved by direct evidence. He quoted Mr Justice Coleridge's dictum in a similar case:

> it was unnecessary to prove that two persons came together and actually agreed in terms to a common design, for if by their acts they pursued the same object, one performing one part and the other another part of the same act so as to complete it with a view to the attainment of the common object, it would be concluded that they conspired to effect that object.

If the jury were satisfied that the prisoners had the common aim of supplying arms to the fenian movement, they would be discharging an important public duty by finding them guilty.[1]

When the evidence for the prosecution had been presented Griffiths submitted that there was no case to go to the jury, as it had not been proved that any overt act had been committed within the jurisdiction of the court, there being no evidence that Davitt had caused the revolvers to be brought to London. The judge overruled the objection: if the jury believed the evidence as to what had occurred at Birmingham, Leeds, and other places, they would be justified in drawing the inference that Wilson had brought the revolvers to London for the purpose of delivering them to Davitt.[2]

The defence of the prisoners was opened on 16 July by Collins, counsel for Wilson, who pointed out as one of several features of the case that it was not being tried in that part of England in which most of the alleged overt acts had been committed. There was no question that his client had supplied the arms and ammunition referred to in the evidence, 'but was there', he asked, 'a single gunsmith in the town of Birmingham or any other part of the United Kingdom who would have refused any such orders?' There was no evidence that Wilson had ever been a fenian or that he had ever been in the company of reputed fenians; Corydon had disclaimed all knowledge of him. He knew Davitt only as Jackson, a merchant of Leeds and a tolerably good customer. No one could prove that he was aware of Davitt's real or reputed profession or that he had done anything foreign to the usual course of trade. He had never been seen dealing with the arms except on one

[1] *The Times*, 16 July, p. 11, col. 2.

[2] *C.C.C. minutes*, lxxii, 322; *Birmingham Daily Gazette*, 18 July, p. 7, col. 3.

occasion, at Leeds, when he had received a box at the railway station and taken it to Davitt's warehouse, and even then it was not shown that he had met Davitt at the warehouse. He had not used false names or in other ways acted furtively. When arrested he had given his name and address and admitted that he was in possession of revolvers for sale. There was no proof that he knew Davitt was waiting for him at Paddington railway station, but, if he did, what more natural than that he was expecting to be paid for the revolvers? If the fenian organisation were really behind Davitt's purchases of arms what would have been the advantage of letting a small Birmingham gunsmith into the secret? He was much more likely to have been an innocent dupe.[1]

The lord chief justice here interposed to ask the attorney general whether, supposing Wilson had had nothing to do with fenianism but was willing to supply with arms men whom he knew to be fenians, it was to be contended that he was involved in their felony? Was he, knowing the character of his customers but free from any intention of aiding in their designs, to be charged with complicity in their crime? The attorney general replied that if the prisoner knew the illegal purpose for which the arms were intended, without any complicity on his part other than their mere sale, he would be guilty of felony. But in this case the prisoner had done more than merely sell the arms; he had gone to Leeds to cooperate with Davitt in handling them. 'It may be so', the lord chief justice admitted.[2]

Collins concluded with the point that it was not for the prisoner to prove the innocent nature of his dealings but for the prosecution to establish his guilt. He emphatically denied the attorney general's assertion that his client had cooperated with Davitt in dealing with the arms: on his one visit to Leeds he had called at the railway station for a consignment of rifles that he had directed to himself and had signed the receipt for them in his own name. He was merely a small dealer anxious for business. Collins called no witnesses as to the facts but called two as to Wilson's good character. Samuel James Harper, a gunmaker, of Weaman Street, Birmingham, had known him for seven years as an honest, respectable man. Wilson had been his tenant for the past four years and had carried on business for himself for eighteen months. Another gunmaker, David Gardiner, similarly swore to the good character of Wilson, whom he had known for forty years.[3]

Collins's defence of Wilson was very able but not calculated to help Davitt, whose counsel, Griffiths, hopefully announced his intention of

[1] *The Times*, 18 July, p. 11, col. 2.
[2] *The Times*, 18 July, p. 11, cols 2-3; *Reports of cases in criminal law*, ed. E. W. Cox, xi, 681.
[3] *The Times*, 18 July, p. 11, col. 3; *C.C.C. minutes*, lxxii, 323.

satisfying the jury that the case against his client was entirely unfounded. The only overt act to which their attention must be directed was that of receiving the revolvers at the railway station—the only overt act committed within the jurisdiction of the central criminal court—and on that there was no evidence to connect the prisoner with any illegal organisation. He had bought arms from Wilson to send them to Paris and Madrid, from which he had received orders. Witnesses would have been called to prove this but for the unsettled state of the Continent. (Counsel was here referring to the mounting tension between France and Prussia that had now reached an explosive stage and was to result in war being declared between the two states on 19 July.) Corydon's evidence, lacking corroboration on any material point, was not worthy of credence: his statements were conflicting and lacked precise dates; and it was unlikely that an informer who had violated his fenian oath for private gain would have any more respect for the oath under which he had given his evidence. Counsel was instructed to say that Corydon had confused the prisoner with a man named Burke, now dead, who bore a strong resemblance to Davitt and like him had lost an arm. This was Michael's late friend, Tom Burke, formerly of Stacksteads.[1] Even if Corydon's statements were true, there was no evidence to connect Davitt with fenianism since 1867, and fenianism was now a spent force. Counsel did not deny that casks of arms had been addressed by the prisoner, but the mere sending of arms was no offence. He was directed, he said, to explain that his client, while travelling about Lancashire as a drapery hawker, had realised that agrarian outrages were frequent in Ireland, and that there was profit to be made in supplying arms for the protection of the Irish gentry. He obtained arms for the purpose from Wilson in the ordinary course of business and without the slightest concealment. Neither the cheapness of the arms nor the fact of the prisoner's having a considerable sum of money in his possession was evidence of guilt. Griffiths concluded by disclaiming on behalf of his client all participation in the fenian organisation, reiterating his entire innocence, and protesting his perfect loyalty.[2]

It was an indifferent performance if not worse. To ask the jury to ignore all the evidence of the prisoners' traffic in arms except that of Wilson's arrival at Paddington with the revolvers was unrealistic. To speak of Davitt's 'receiving' the revolvers was gross carelessness, seeing that the two men had not been given the opportunity even to meet when they were arrested. It was not credible that these weapons were

[1] Above, p. 45.
[2] *The Times*, 18 July, p. 11, col. 3.

really intended for export to continental buyers, and it was quite incredible that Irish landlords would obtain arms for self-defence from an obscure drapery hawker in Lancashire, and under the conditions in which Davitt had been transmitting arms to Ireland. The only part of Griffiths' argument that had substance was his criticism of Corydon —whom he had vigorously cross-examined—and his use of the Burke alibi.

For Davitt ten witnesses were called, of whom six were from Haslingden and its vicinity. They were old friends of Davitt's and the burden of their evidence was to confute Corydon's statements about having seen him at fenian meetings in Liverpool shortly after the Chester castle attempt. Martin Haran, who said he had known him fourteen or fifteen years, recollected seeing him in Cockcroft's employment in Haslingden at the time of the Chester raid. He also swore that he had been with Davitt at his own house every night during the week preceding the raid and every night after the raid until the end of June. Davitt then wore a moustache. Haran had known Tom Burke: he was very like Davitt in appearance, having lost an arm (his left), and was probably a fenian. Haran's story was in substance repeated by Matthew Shearin, a drapery hawker, and Patrick Fearon, a weaver. Shearin, who said he had been a schoolfellow of Davitt's, was the subject of an unflattering sketch by Head-constable Bodley, who was attending the trial and taking notes: 'consumptive appearance [Shearin said he had suffered from bronchitis]; pale sickly complexion, round face, gray sunken eyes, nose slightly cocked; five feet six inches; about twenty-six; full black beard, whiskers, and moustache; squeaky voice; dark tweed suit'.[1] Shearin and Fearon both agreed with Haran that Davitt had condemned the Chester raid as foolish and futile. All three declared that they and Davitt reprobated fenianism. Further confirmation of Tom Burke's resemblance to Davitt was supplied by Burke's brother, Martin, a woollen-carpet printer of Stacksteads, and his sister Anna.[2] The complete unanimity of these witnesses—all of them fenians[3] except Anna Burke—probably owed much to the fact, elicited from Martin Burke by the attorney general, that they had all been living together since they came up to London for the trial.[4] More convincing was the evidence of Thomas Cockcroft, son of the postmaster of Haslingden, who was himself too ill to appear. Thomas Cockcroft was relieving officer for the Haslingden district. He no longer lived with

[1] H.-C. Bodley to I.G.P., 22 Nov. (S.P.O.,6986R/7016R).

[2] *The Times*, 18 July, p. 11, col. 3; 19 July, p. 11, col. 2; *C.C.C. minutes*, lxxii, 323-9.

[3] H.-C. Murphy to I.G.P., 22 Feb. (S.P.O., 5803R/5817R); H.-C. Bodley to I.G.P., 22 Nov. (S.P.O., 6986R/7016 R).

[4] *C.C.C. minutes*, lxxii, 329.

his father but was familiar with the routine of his father's business. He produced an office book showing that Davitt had worked for his father on 12 and 16 February and had made entries in the book on those days; this was the book that Inspector Clark had seen. If Davitt had been engaged on tillet work[1] during the intervening days a record would have been entered in a book kept for that purpose, but Cockcroft had not seen this tillet book for the past two years. Davitt was a very respectable, steady, honest young man who had very seldom been absent from his work, though Cockcroft admitted that he would not have remembered an absence of a day or less. He did not remember the Chester castle raid—'I have nothing to remember it for'. If this was true, as it probably was, Cockcroft cannot have known that Davitt was at Chester on 11 February. But his lapse of memory may have been due to a wish to shield Davitt.[2]

Two witnesses were produced to show that Davitt was a bona fide dealer in arms. James Broderick was the former lodger in Eliza Geoghegan's house, 41 George Leigh Street, Manchester, to whom the revolvers and cartridges found there by the police on 19 April were alleged to belong. He said he was the son of Irish parents, and that Davitt had been introduced to him as a hawker of fire-arms. He was then intending to go to Philadelphia, where his father and sister lived, and understood that it was the general practice in America to carry a revolver. Believing that he could buy revolvers more cheaply here than there, he bought three from Davitt at 27*s*. each, together with 100 cartridges. He left them in Eliza Geoghegan's house because he owed her £2 3*s*. rent. Mrs Eliza Geoghegan, who had been Broderick's landlady, gave evidence in corroboration of his statement. Another witness, James Clark, a copper extractor, of Willington-on-Tyne, said he had bought revolvers from Davitt eighteen months previously for Fr Sharples, his parish priest, who wanted them for protection because houses of catholic priests in the neighbourhood had been robbed.[3]

The remaining witness for the defence was Arthur Forrester, who described himself as a correspondent of Pigott's *Irishman* and a lecturer, living at 18 Brighton Street, Salford. He appeared, he said, to contradict the evidence given by Corydon on 27 May during Davitt's examination before the Marylebone magistrate. He swore repeatedly that he had never attended fenian meetings. He first saw Corydon in March 1867 when he was in Kilmainham jail;[4] Corydon had been brought in to identify him and had failed to do so. He had known Davitt for

[1] See above, p. 84.

[2] *The Times*, 18 July, p. 11, col. 3; *C.C.C. minutes*, lxxii, 326–7, 334–5.

[3] *The Times*, 19 July, p. 11, col. 2; *C.C.C. minutes*, lxxii, 333–4.

[4] See above, p. 50.

eighteen months or two years and had seen him pretty frequently at Manchester and, he thought, at Leeds. He understood him to be a travelling draper. He himself was hawking revolvers at the time of his arrest in Liverpool (16 December 1869), but not since. He had bought the revolvers from Minningham, of Weaman Street, Birmingham. The letter that he had tried to tear up, as the Liverpool police were about to arrest him, was a copy in Davitt's hand of an original received from an unknown source. Davitt had sent him the copy, accompanied by a note that the letter looked like a police trap and asking for his opinion on it. Forrester realised that the letter was a dangerous document to have on him; he supposed that it had reference to a traitor to the fenian or some other secret society and that 'pen' as used in it meant 'revolver'. He destroyed Davitt's covering letter at once, but unaccountably kept the copy letter. Much of all this came out under a cross-examination by the attorney general far more prolonged and exacting than that of any other witness in the case.[1]

The case for the defence was then (18 July) summed up by Griffiths, who reviewed the evidence at some length. The question for the jury to consider was whether Davitt was a fenian, and that rested entirely on the evidence of Corydon, who was unworthy of credence and was not corroborated. If they disbelieved his testimony there was no case against Davitt. His statement about the Liverpool meetings really applied to Thomas Burke, who resembled Davitt and was known to be a fenian. At the worst the case against Davitt was only one of suspicion. Collins summed up his previous argument on behalf of Wilson.[2]

Replying to the case for the defence the attorney general insisted that no 'fair explanation had been given of the pinch of the charge against Davitt'—the clandestine traffic in arms. Davitt knew to whom he consigned the arms and yet had not called a single one of these consignees to establish the alleged innocence of his transactions. The suggestion that they were sent for the use of Irish landlords against fenians or agrarian terrorists was merely ridiculous. Nor had any attempt been made to show the source of the £60 bank bill that Davitt—ostensibly a travelling draper—had cashed at Leeds, or of the very large sum he was carrying at his arrest. No excuse had been invented by the defence for not calling the persons from whom Davitt derived that money. The defence indeed had thrown new light on the whole business by revealing that the witness Forrester had also been trafficking in arms obtained from the same source in Birmingham upon which Davitt drew

[1] *The Times*, 19 July, p. 11, col. 2; *C.C.C. minutes*, lxxii, 329–33.

[2] *Daily Telegraph*, 19 July, p. 3, col. 1; *Morning Post*, 19 July, p. 7, col. 3; *The Times*, 19 July, p. 11, col. 2; *Haslingden Chronicle and Ramsbottom Times*, 23 July, p. 2, col. 6.

his supplies.[1] No one who had heard Forrester's evidence could doubt that he was a fenian.[2] The attorney general now attached great importance to the 'pen' letter, not as explained by Forrester but as establishing Davitt's connection with a criminal conspiracy. He also urged that the secret consignments of arms all emanating from the shop of the prisoner Wilson and all transmitted by the other prisoner were proof of the complicity of both prisoners.[3]

The lord chief justice, summing up, asked the jury to consider, first whether the arms in question were provided in Britain for the purpose of being sent to Ireland to be used for rebellious purposes, and second, whether they were sent by the prisoners with the intention of being so used. The procuring and sending of the arms by the accused was not in doubt; the vital question was, had they been sent to further the objects of the fenian conspiracy? The answer to this depended partly on Davitt's connection with the fenian movement and partly on the nature of the arms traffic in which both prisoners had been engaged. There was no evidence that Davitt had been involved in the Chester castle attempt, and it was just possible that Corydon, in testifying to his presence at fenian meetings in Liverpool shortly afterwards, had confused him with Burke. But whether or not the jury accepted the evidence of the informer, they had that of the letter found on Forrester to consider. He had admitted that it referred to a secret society, and the inference seemed irresistible that it implicated Davitt in 'a fenian scheme of the deepest atrocity'. Even if they rejected Corydon's testimony and accepted Forrester's explanation of the letter, there remained the evidence of the overt acts alleged in the indictment and proved by the prosecution: the sending of repeated consignments of arms to a disaffected country, the contrivances and subterfuges used in sending them, and the rough and unfinished state of many of the arms, which made them unfit for sale though perfectly usable. In the absence of any reasonable explanation of all this, the jury would not find it difficult to draw their own conclusion. It was, of course, for the crown to make out the case against the accused, but often it was impossible to give direct evidence of a man's motives in a particular matter. A jury must often look at the act itself and judge the motive from the nature of the act.[4]

Defending counsel, the judge went on, had said that the fenian conspiracy was at an end. 'Would to God they could believe that it was.'

[1] *The Times*, 19 July, p. 11, col. 2.
[2] *Yorkshire Post and Leeds Intelligencer*, 19 July, p. 8, col. 3.
[3] *Reports of cases in criminal law*, ed. E. W. Cox, xi, 681.
[4] Ibid., xi, 681–3; *The Times*, 19 July, p. 11, col. 3.

Of all the insane projects in history . . . there was never, perhaps, one equal to this, of persons being induced to join a few obscure and comparatively unknown men, with little or no funds at their disposal, who fancied they could cope with the power of this great country, and wrest from the queen one of the best and brightest parts of her dominions—as if England could, under the circumstances, have submitted to what would be a dire catastrophe alike to this country and to Ireland herself. How people could have been induced to join such a movement, set on foot by individuals so obscure and comparatively powerless, passed comprehension; but however that might be, that there still lingered an amount of disaffection which, if not carefully watched, might again break out, there could be no question.[1]

Whether it would not have been better for the state to have been satisfied with the seizure of the arms and not to have instituted these proceedings was not a matter for the jury or for him. If the jury believed that the arms were sent to Ireland for the purpose of levying war against the authority of the crown, the case against the prisoners was established.[2]

All this, the judge went on, applied more particularly to Davitt. Wilson's case was rather different. There was no doubt that the arms were made by him, and if he did no more than make and supply them, shutting his eyes to their destination, that would not be sufficient to convict him.

But if you believe that, on supplying the arms, he had a knowledge that they were about to be used for a traitorous purpose, and with the intention that they should be so used, then he is involved with the other prisoner in a common guilt. If he was indeed ignorant of their destination, then it would be otherwise; of this you must form your own judgement.

If the jury were satisfied that the arms were sent for a traitorous purpose and if both prisoners knew of it, then both were guilty; if only one of them knew, then that one was guilty.[3]

The jury, after an absence of twenty minutes, returned a verdict of guilty against both prisoners on both counts of the indictment.[4] In answer to the question whether they had anything to say why sentence should not be passed on them, Wilson replied that he had never sent a firearm to Ireland, that he knew Davitt only as Jackson and did not know that he was an Irishman. He had been led to believe that the arms were for volunteers and never had any idea of doing wrong. He was an Englishman and had never been out of England. Davitt followed with a vehement appeal on behalf of Wilson—'as good an Englishman as anyone on the jury'. If Wilson was guilty he, Davitt, alone was to blame. He was not admitting that the arms were for an illegal purpose but he insisted that Wilson never knew till he was arrested that Davitt

[1] *The Times*, 19 July, p. 11, col. 3. [2] Ibid. [3] *Reports*, ed. E. W. Cox, xi, 683.
[4] *Copies of the record of the conviction of William O'Mara Allen, . . . Michael Davitt and John Wilson*, p. 3, H.C. 1877 (424), lxix, 363.

was an Irishman or that his name was other than Jackson. Davitt would cheerfully undergo any punishment rather than that Wilson and his wife and family should be made to suffer. He begged that Wilson be exonerated and Wilson's sentence added to his own.[1] He ended on a note of reckless defiance not reported in *The Times*:

He denied point blank that he was in Liverpool at the time stated by Corydon. He was not going to say what the arms were intended for, but when persons heard the sentence that would be passed upon him they would be thankful they were not in London with money in their pockets. They would perhaps find as much difficulty in proving their innocence as he had done. Take away the evidence of Corydon, and there was nothing to show that he had been connected with fenianism. He did not deny that he was an Irishman, with Irish sympathies, and a long term of imprisonment would not alter his sympathies. He believed he should only be made a better Irishman, and if he ever regained his liberty and his services should be required, they would be placed at the disposal of his country.[2]

The lord chief justice, addressing Davitt, said he had been convicted on evidence that could not leave the slightest shadow of doubt in the mind of any reasonable man that he had bought arms and sent them to Ireland to be used in the event of a fenian rising there. It was melancholy to think that misguided men like him, possibly from some erroneous motive of patriotism, should be able to induce others to enter into a conspiracy that could only lead to bloodshed without the slightest possible chance of obtaining the end they had in view. Davitt had done himself much credit by the way he had spoken of Wilson, but he, the judge, was compelled to pass a severe sentence upon him to deter others from following similar disastrous courses. He viewed with the utmost horror the letter of Davitt's, about which Forrester had told a story that no sensible man could believe, and which clearly implied a readiness to resort to assassination if it were found expedient. The judge sentenced Davitt to penal servitude for fifteen years. As to Wilson, though he appeared to be a mere tool in the hands of others—very likely of Minningham and Davitt—the judge could not believe him to have been ignorant of the use to which the arms might be put. He therefore sentenced him to penal servitude for seven years, but promised to have further inquiries made, and if the advisors of the crown should think Wilson to have been duped they would take his case into their merciful consideration.[3]

These heavy sentences should be seen in perspective. In 1865 O'Donovan Rossa had been sentenced to penal servitude for life, Luby

[1] *The Times*, 19 July 70, p. 11, col. 3; *Morning Post*, 19 July, p. 7, col 4; *Standard*, 19 July, p. 5, cols 6 – 7.

[2] *Morning Post*, 19 July, p. 7, col. 4; *Standard*, 19 July, p. 5, col. 7.

[3] *The Times*, 19 July, p. 11, col. 3; *Morning Post*, 19 July, p. 7, col. 4.

and O'Leary to twenty years each, Kickham to fourteen years, and Devoy in 1866 to fifteen years, for their involvement in fenianism. And at the same session of the Old Bailey at which Davitt and Wilson were tried, an Englishman who pleaded guilty to stealing three pounds of bacon was sentenced to seven years' penal servitude.[1]

The hopefulness with which Davitt had viewed his prospects on the eve of the trial had evaporated in the course of it. Though his sentence was much worse than he had feared,[2] he was indignant rather than shattered by the outcome of the trial. 'A more biassed or onesided affair', he wrote to his parents on 22 July, 'never disgraced the annals of justice'.

Imagine the two witnesses, Corydon and a policeman, swearing that they recognised me 'because I had my arm off at the *wrist*'. And again the policeman swearing I had a beard and Corydon swearing I had none—yet Corydon's evidence was believed altho' six witnesses, Thomas Cockcroft among them, swore to my being in Haslingden at the time Corydon swore he saw me in Liverpool. All that true friends and money could effect was done, but of no avail. It was a battle against perjury but the odds were against truth because prejudice was appealed to by the prosecution. They could not prove that the arms I sold were intended for any illegal purpose, but what they knew not to be true they assumed to be facts and the jury accepted them as such. There were no papers found upon me nor was there any attempt made to prove that I had belonged to fenianism since 1867, all their efforts being to show that the arms I sent to Ireland were intended to be used against the government. Where all the legal ability at the command of the government was employed to show a prejudiced jury the necessity of convicting me upon the evidence of a salaried perjurer, you will not be surprised at truth being at a discount. How can *I* complain when an *Englishman* got seven years merely for selling me arms?[3]

Press comment on the verdict and sentence was much less, in view of the attention the case had received, than might have been expected. This was because the war that had just broken out between France and Prussia now dominated the news. *The Times*, in a lengthy editorial, set the general tone by expressing satisfaction at the outcome of the trial. There could be no doubt of the prisoners' guilt, though Wilson was less to blame than Davitt. Davitt's appeal for Wilson showed a generosity that did him honour, but amounted to an admission of his own guilt. The lord chief justice's doubt whether the prosecution ought to have been brought would not be shared by the public. The sentences were severe but salutary. 'We owe it to the well-disposed inhabitants of Ireland and our much-injured fellow-subjects of Canada to repress with the utmost sternness every attempt to revive . . . [the fenian] . . . conspiracy.'[4]

[1] *C.C.C. minutes*, lxxii, 335; cf. below, p. 161. [2] *Leaves*, i, 149.
[3] D to his father, mother, and sisters, 22 July (DP/A). [4] *The Times*, 19 July, p. 9, col. 4.

The *Daily Telegraph*, of Newcastle-upon-Tyne, thought the story of Davitt and Wilson to be 'another illustration of how futile this wretched conspiracy has been':

Were it not that the movement is guided by men who will shrink at nothing, and is regarded by thousands in the sister isle as the all-in-all for the redress and revenge of wrongs, real or imaginary, we might be inclined to feel compassion for two men who are sent off to waste so long a portion of their best days in prison. But on the other hand, it is such plotters working in secret at materials for the avowed purpose of destroying life, and sending them amongst the gullible peasantry of Tipperary with that object, who keep the passion alive, and the sooner their contaminating presence is removed the better.[1]

The London *Standard* argued that the trial showed the failure of Gladstone's policy of pacifying Ireland 'for which we have sacrificed so much'.

England, like France, has her irreconcileables, and England, no less than her nearest neighbour, is compelled to acknowledge that, after all her efforts to subdue them by severity or to mollify them with kindness, they remain irreconcileable still. On no other hypothesis can we justify the institution of a state prosecution against two persons of no particular importance, whose only claim to notoriety is based upon the fact that they have been engaged in a clandestine traffic in small arms of inferior quality and dispatched in quantities sufficient, when taken in conjunction with surrounding circumstances, to indicate their evil intentions, but which are simply ludicrous as a means of effectively arming a body of would-be insurgents.

The heavy sentences were 'dictated by a spirit of the truest mercy to the misguided men who share the prisoners' infatuated attachment to a worthless cause'.[2]

The catholic *Universe* appeared to share the judge's feeling that it might have been better if the prosecution had not been brought at all. 'Certainly so long as Corydon is the leading witness, no faith ought to be placed in the evidence.'[3] The liberal *Glasgow Herald*, contrasting the almost comical insignificance of the Davitt-Wilson story with the vastness and tragedy of the death-struggle just opening on the Continent, remarked:

Yet Davitt and Wilson are heroes after a fashion. Fenianism had for its object the dismemberment of the British Empire, and the establishment in Ireland of a republic. Profoundly impressed by the wrongs Ireland had long suffered, and was still suffering, under the tyrannic domination of Great Britain, the Fenian Brotherhood did not shrink from the idea of vengeance on the most extensive scale . . . The offence of which Davitt and Wilson have just been convicted shows that they were faithful instruments of the brotherhood.[4]

In Dublin the principal dailies—the *Freeman's Journal*, the *Irish*

[1] *Daily Telegraph* (Newcastle-upon-Tyne), 19 July, p. 2, col. 6.

[2] *Standard*, 19 July, p. 4, col. 7.

[3] *Universe* (London), 23 July, p. 1, col. 2.

[4] *Glasgow Herald*, 21 July, p. 4, cols 2–3.

Times, *Saunders News Letter*, the *Dublin Evening Mail*, the *Daily Express*—made no comment on the outcome of the trial. Two weeklies, the *Nation* and the *Irishman*, referred editorially to it. The *Nation*, which catered for moderate nationalist opinion, called attention to Davitt's appeal for Wilson: 'this was surely the language of an honourable, high-souled, chivalrous man'.[1] In the *Irishman*, Pigott's fenian organ, a second leader discussed the trial at some length and made some interesting points. One of the prisoners, Wilson, had been convicted on the evidence of his clandestine sending of arms to Ireland, which was assumed to be proof of fenianism. This involved the notion that every man who wanted to possess arms in Ireland intended to use them against the government, a notion consistent with the long series of arms acts that had at last reduced the people of Ireland to abject slavery. A disarmed people were an enslaved people, as the framers of the English Declaration of Rights recognised when they affirmed the inalienable right of every English freeman to bear arms.[2] Wilson's conviction had evidently raised a doubt in the judge's mind, and he might yet be pardoned. If so, he would owe it to the noble intervention of Davitt, whose highmindedness had extorted the judge's admiration. Davitt was in the same position as Wilson apart from the evidence of Corydon, who swore to his being implicated in the Chester castle raid. But even if Corydon were a reliable witness, and even if he had been corroborated, his evidence would have proved only that Davitt had been engaged in fenian activity in February 1867. Not a particle of evidence had been produced to give a treasonable character to his actions of three years later. The attorney general had boasted of the relative leniency of the treason-felony act, but had Davitt been prosecuted under the treasons act of 1696, two witnesses would have been necessary and in any case the lapse of three years would have made the alleged treason a thing of the past.[3] The *Irishman* went on to 'presume' that the government would not think of carrying out the sentences on either Davitt or Wilson: it would probably not wish at that moment to establish the doctrine that every man who sent a box of arms, even clandestinely, must be responsible for the intentions of those who purchased them. For if this doctrine were admitted 'what becomes of England's neutrality while Birmingham gunsmiths are sending boxes of arms to the Rhine'?[4]

[1] *Nation*, 23 July, p. 784, col. 1.

[2] Clause 7 of the Declaration of Rights (1 Wm and Mary, sess. 2, c. 2) reads: 'that the subjects which are protestants may have arms for their defence suitable to their conditions, and as allowed by law'.

[3] This statement is in accordance with 7 & 8 Wm III, c. 3, cl. II, V.

[4] *Irishman*, 23 July, p. 56, col. 3; p. 57, col. 1.

From Dartmoor, seven years later, Davitt formally petitioned the home secretary for an impartial inquiry into his case, claiming that he had been unjustly convicted on the uncorroborated evidence of a common informer. As in his letter of July 1870 to his parents he stressed the weaknesses of Corydon's evidence and the absence of proof that he himself had supplied arms to fenians or that arms he supplied were used or intended to be used for illegal purposes. Surreptitious dealing in arms was a long-established practice of the English gun-trade: it was well known that arms were thus supplied to nations at war with, and subjects in revolt from, the queen, as during the Chinese and African wars and the Indian mutiny. Davitt went on to allege misconduct on the part of the police. They were aware in March of his storing arms in a rented warehouse in Leeds. If they had known him to be a fenian at that time, or had regarded his traffic in arms as illegal, they could have taken him *in flagrante delicto*. Either they had no grounds for arresting him or they allowed him to continue in transactions they knew to be illegal in order to procure his arrest in circumstances more favourable to a conviction. At his arrest, though no incriminating documents were found on him, he was remanded in custody because an inspector from Scotland Yard assured the magistrate that a witness would be forthcoming to prove the prisoner's complicity in the Chester castle raid.[1] No such evidence was produced, but in the interval between the police court proceedings and the trial a detective visited Haslingden and inspected Cockcroft's office records.[2] He found an entry showing that Davitt was present in the printing-house on 11 February, the day of the raid, but that there were no entries for his attendance there from 12 to 15 February inclusive, with the result that Corydon selected those as the days on which he claimed to have seen Davitt at fenian meetings in Liverpool. Yet 'a highly respectable Englishman' [Thomas Cockcroft] had deposed that he remembered conversing with Davitt at the printing-house not only on the day of the raid but also on each of the four following days. Davitt also complained that while he was awaiting trial sensational paragraphs appeared in the press calculated to prejudice the public against him: he was connected with a design for private assassination; he had succeeded a convicted fenian (Ricard O'Sullivan Burke) as arms agent of the I.R.B.; he was the object of another fenian plot to blow up the Clerkenwell House of Detention.[3] Finally he complained that during his trial repeated allusions were made by prosecuting counsel to the fenian rising in Ireland, the Manchester rescue, and the Clerkenwell explosion, though

[1] Cf. above, pp 48–9. [2] Cf. above, p. 93. [3] Cf. above, p. 52.

no evidence could be produced to connect him with any of these events.[1]

Soon after his release from Dartmoor, speaking at a public meeting in London on 9 March 1878, Davitt added two items to these charges. First, his identification by Corydon in the House of Detention was a fraud. The informer was supposed to find him by looking through the inspection hole of each cell in the ward where he was located. Corydon did so, but only after he had seen his man being marched from one cell to another. Second, after an interview with his solicitor's clerk, a warder reported to the prison governor that he had seen Davitt hand over to the clerk a plan of the prison along with instructions to his legal adviser. On the strength of this fiction, the instructions were seized by the governor and only allowed to be transmitted after being read by him. Davitt's line of defence was thus communicated to the prosecution.[2]

Did Davitt receive a fair trial? The instances of unfairness that he cites have little substance, apart from the use of Corydon as a witness. In all probability Corydon had never set eyes on Davitt before he 'identfied' him. But though the 'identification' may, as Davitt alleged, have been fraudulent, it does not appear to have served any purpose. If the testimony of Corydon, an informer, had been the only evidence that Davitt was a fenian, there would have been substance in Davitt's claim to have been convicted unjustly. But the judge held that the case against Davitt did not ultimately rest on Corydon's evidence, and he attached much less weight to it than to the 'pen' letter as proof of Davitt's guilty connection with fenianism.

As to the date of Davitt's arrest, the police were surely not at fault in waiting till they judged the time to be ripe. Nor does Inspector Clark appear to have acted in the sinister way Davitt imputed to him. Nothing in the reported proceedings suggests that he claimed to have proof of Davitt's participation in the Chester castle raid, the prosecution made no attempt to substantiate this item in the indictment, and the judge pointed out that no evidence was forthcoming to connect Davitt with Chester. Clark's inspection, after 5 July, of Cockcroft's office book made no difference to Corydon's evidence, for neither in the police court on 27 May nor at the Old Bailey on 16 July did Corydon specify the dates on which he claimed to have seen Davitt at fenian conclaves in Liverpool. Davitt's assertion that Cockcroft's office book provided an alibi for 11 February was irrelevant and inconsistent with the argument in his own letter of *c*. 4 June 1870 to Thomas Cockcroft and

[1] P.R.O., H.O. 144/5/17869 (25 June 77); and see below.

[2] Cashman, pp 24-5.

with Cockcroft's evidence for the defence at the trial. And it was not true that Cockcroft had vouched for his presence in Haslingden on 11-15 February.

Is it credible that the press reports of fenian activities were all fabricated for the purpose of predisposing the jury against Davitt? Is there any good reason for supposing that they were unduly influenced by the natural prejudice of Englishmen against fenianism? The jurymen were a mixed bag—two corn dealers, a hairdresser, a draper, a tailor, a coffee-house keeper, a brassfounder, a piano-maker, a builder, a lodging-house keeper, a leather-seller, and a publican; none of the jury panel had been challenged by the defence, whereas two had been asked to stand aside by the prosecution.[1] The verdict in the case was entirely in accordance with the judge's summing-up.

Were the prosecution's references to the fenian rising of 1867 made in order to injure Davitt? There is no reason for supposing so; the attorney general was technically bound to produce evidence of the rising,[2] but he made no attempt to connect Davitt with it. And if he referred to the Manchester rescue and the Clerkenwell explosion he did not lay emphasis on either. Was Davitt's line of defence disclosed improperly to the prosecution? His complaint could not have referred to the fiction that he had been engaged in supplying arms to Irish landlords, for his counsel put this forward without his authorisation.[3] As to the theory that the arms were intended for Paris and Madrid, it would have made no difference to the case if the prosecution had been informed of it in advance. If the prosecution knew beforehand of the plea of mistaken identity or of the intended alibi they made no apparent use of the knowledge, and the judge conceded that Davitt might have been confused with Burke. Inspector Clark's visit to Haslingden may have been due to the interception of Davitt's instructions to his solicitor, but it needs no such explanation and, as we have seen, it did not affect the prosecution's case.

The particular grounds on which Davitt protested against the conduct of his trial do not stand up to close examination. But there were technical grounds that seem to have escaped him for holding that he —and Wilson—were not tried in strict accordance with the rules of English justice.

The attorney general appears to have been inaccurate in some of his references to the evidence, as, for example, when he said, on the question of Davitt's alibi for the fenian meetings at Liverpool, that Davitt had lost his right *hand* just above the wrist whereas Burke's left *arm*

[1] *Daily Telegraph*, 16 July 70, p. 5, col. 6; *C.C.C. minutes*, lxxii, 296.
[2] Above, pp 90-91.
[3] *S.C.P.*, ix, 408 (2 July 89).

had been torn from its socket at the shoulder; in fact both men had lost an arm, as the evidence showed, and the judge made the point in his summing-up. Such inaccuracies were probably not intentional and the example cited did Davitt no harm. But the attorney general also stated as a fact that Davitt had been seen more than once at Wilson's workshop in Birmingham. His only evidence was that of a witness who said he had seen Davitt twice—once by himself in Harper's Buildings (where Minningham and Wilson worked) and once (in April) with Minningham in the workshop he occupied below Wilson's; he knew it was Davitt because 'he had one arm off, just above the wrist'. This was a material point since it bore upon the question of conspiracy between the prisoners. Again, the attorney general, in stressing the failure of the defence to produce as witnesses any of the ostensible consignees of the arms despatched by Davitt, seemed to imply that there was some onus on him to prove his innocence, whereas it was a basic principle of criminal law that the onus was on the prosecution to establish the guilt of the accused beyond all reasonable doubt and that the accused was under no obligation to prove anything.

The judge himself did remark in his charge to the jury that it was for the crown to prove its case, but, as reported, he did not adequately instruct them on the question of the onus of proof, or on the closely related question of circumstantial evidence, on which the crown's case largely depended. Nor did he warn them about the danger of accepting the evidence of an informer, nor explain the legal conception of conspiracy, nor comment on the absence of legal proof that the alleged conspirators, Davitt and Wilson, had ever met before their arrest.[1] But it has to be remembered that the standards applicable to the conduct of criminal trials were less exacting at that time than they have become since the institution of the court of criminal appeal. And if an appeal against Davitt's conviction, on the ground that the judge did not properly instruct the jury on certain points, were being considered by an appeal court today, it would probably hold that, despite some failure on the part of the judge, no miscarriage of justice had occurred. On the other hand it is conceivable that an appeal against Wilson's conviction on the same ground would succeed.[2] This view of the matter is consistent with Cockburn's own reservations about Wilson and the distinction he drew between Wilson's guilt and Davitt's. It is not, of course, meant to suggest that Wilson was not in fact guilty but only that he was not proved beyond all reasonable doubt to be guilty.

Whatever shortcomings there may have been in the judge's conduct

[1] Cf. above, p. 94.

[2] This is the opinion of Judge Cahir Davitt, after full consideration of the case.

of the trial there is nothing to suggest that he was prejudiced against the accused, however much he reprobated fenianism. And he was not one to show any indulgence to the police. He severely rebuked Detective-sergeant Foley for putting questions to Wilson when he had the intention of arresting him:

If you ask a man questions with an honest intention to elicit the truth and to ascertain whether there are grounds for apprehending him, that is a totally different thing; but with a foregone intention to arrest him, to ask questions for the main purpose of getting anything out of him that may be afterwards used against him is a very improper proceeding.

Detective-sergeant Campbell was similarly castigated for questioning Davitt in the course of arresting him; and Sergeant Joseph Wunton, the officer on duty at Paddington Green police station when the prisoners were brought in, who also questioned Davitt, was roundly told that his only duty was 'to take the charge'.[1] Moreover the judge expressed doubt whether the proceedings should have been brought at all against the prisoners—influenced, probably, by the fact that however treasonable their intentions, no one appeared to have been injured by them. Finally Cockburn was obviously well impressed by Davitt's appeal on behalf of Wilson, and seems to have taken account of it in making the distinction he did between Davitt's sentence and Wilson's.[2]

The worst feature of Davitt's trial from a legal standpoint, and the one he complained about least, remains to be considered: the conduct of his leading counsel, Griffiths. He was a senior barrister, having been called in 1852; he conducted the defence almost entirely alone, and he did not spare himself. On two points—his theory that Davitt's business was selling arms to Irish landlords and his protestations of loyalty on Davitt's behalf—he acted egregiously without his client's instructions.[3] In general he was specious and unconvincing. But in calling Forrester to give evidence he was guilty of a blunder so rudimentary and disastrous to his client that it suggests either gross stupidity or gross negligence. He could not have been unaware that Forrester was notorious for his fenian connections and that he and Davitt had been closely associated. He must have known that, apart altogether from the 'pen' letter, Forrester as a witness would be as dangerous to the defence as Davitt himself if—as was not then possible—he were to be called as a witness. But with the 'pen' letter produced as evidence against Davitt it was absolutely vital for the defence to keep Forrester out of the case; for, once in the witness-box, he was certain to be cross-examined about the letter. Davitt himself expressly instructed his solicitor not to let

[1] *The Times*, 18 July 70, p. 11, col. 1.
[2] Ibid., p. 11, col. 1; 19 July, p. 11, col. 3.
[3] *S.C.P.*, ix, 408.

Forrester appear.[1] But Forrester insisted, and Griffiths did not prevent him, as he could and should have done. Davitt's own later explanation—that Forrester controlled the money provided by the I.R.B. for his defence and that 'this gave him power to override the counsels of my friends'—does not explain away Griffiths' conduct in calling such a witness as Forrester. Both the truth and the lies Forrester told for the defence damned Davitt in the eyes of judge and jury far more effectively than the lies told by Corydon for the prosecution. They clinched the charge against Davitt and ensured the exceptionally heavy sentence the judge felt it necessary to inflict.[2]

Forrester's conduct seems so irrational that we are tempted to rationalise it by supposing that he was really acting in collusion with the police, as he had been accused of doing in December 1869.[3] How otherwise can we account for the fact that the police did not, after hearing his evidence, bring a charge of treason-felony against him? To suppose him a traitor would neatly resolve the problem of his giving evidence; but it would raise greater problems, and must be rejected. The extensive information about Forrester in the confidential reports of the detectives who were watching him is incompatible with any theory of an understanding between him and the police. Moreover he could not have been a traitor without raising suspicions in the minds of Davitt and his friends. But though the 'pen' letter was to be a cause of intermittent disturbance to Davitt for the rest of his life, and though in retrospect he took an increasingly severe view of Forrester's conduct, he never questioned Forrester's loyalty. And though Forrester lost the confidence of Lancashire fenians through his action at the trial, they did not suggest that he was a traitor.[4]

When the trial was over, Forrester was charged by some of Davitt's friends from Haslingden and Manchester with the responsibility for Davitt's sentence, and blows were exchanged. Next day, he and a few others were permitted to say goodbye to Davitt at Newgate prison; he broke down, protesting his good intentions towards Davitt, who responded generously, without disguising his opinion that Forrester ought to have respected his wishes. Soon afterwards Forrester felt it necessary to publish a letter (dated 26 July), in the *Irishman* 'to set myself right . . . with the friends of Michael Davitt who, from the garbled and mutilated reports of my evidence which appeared in the daily press, might think I had done the brave convict more injury than benefit by appearing as a witness in his defence'. He had come forward

[1] Ibid., ix, 411.
[2] Cf. DN/29A, 28 Jan. 95, in *I.H.S.*, iv, no. 15, pp 250–51.
[3] Above, p. 62.
[4] H.-C. Murphy to I.G.P. 18, 23 Nov. 70 (S.P.O., 6980R, 699[8]R).

both to contradict Corydon's evidence and to explain the incriminating letter. But his explanation differed from the report of his evidence in *The Times* only in emphasising that he and Davitt both believed the letter to have been concocted by the police.[1]

Davitt did not doubt Forrester's good intentions even after seven years of imprisonment. In April 1877, hearing that friends in the I.R.B. had accused Forrester not only of injuring him at the trial but also of embezzling money raised for his defence, he wrote from Dartmoor to his sister Sabina and to Ellen Forrester strongly expressing his belief in Forrester's integrity. 'If his evidence did go against me, it was not his intention that it should do so, and I attach no blame whatever to what was done or said unintentionally'.[2] But Davitt came to take up a much more critical attitude to Forrester's conduct when, after his release from prison, he found himself subjected to intermittent persecution by political enemies on the strength of the 'pen' letter. He disclosed the truth about the letter, but without disclosing Forrester's connection with it, before *The Times*–Parnell commission in 1889, and he appealed to Forrester, without mentioning his name, to substantiate his statement. Forrester, then in America, did not respond. He died in January 1895 without making the only reparation he had it in his power to make. In the course of a long review of the whole story in his diary for 28 January, Davitt wrote:

> He insisted upon giving evidence in order to clear himself (!) with reference to the letter . . . His evidence, though meant, I am sure, to serve me, simply damned my case beyond the hope of redemption. The letter . . . was so 'explained' and interpreted by his hopeless vanity and imbecility in the witness box that the judge . . . was convinced it related to some diabolical plot to murder some informer.[3]

In retrospect Davitt considered that the letter would not have injured his case if Forrester, having got himself into the witness box, 'had only told the facts simply as they occurred'.[4] But the truth about the 'pen' letter would have established Davitt's and Forrester's criminal connection with the I.R.B. even more certainly than Forrester's lies. When Davitt was under cross-examination before *The Times*–Parnell commission in 1889, the president, a high-court judge, suggested that he ought himself to have revealed the truth about the letter at his trial, to which Davitt replied that to have done so would have incriminated the man to whom it was directed.[5] The true explanation could have been put before the court by Davitt's counsel, or by Davitt himself in

[1] *Irishman*, 30 July, p. 57; cf. above, p. 99.
[2] D to Sabina Davitt, 15 Apr. 77 (DP/A; smuggled).
[3] DN/29A, 28 Jan. 95, in *I.H.S.*, iv, no. 15, pp 250–57.
[4] D to Forrester, 3 Aug. 94, ibid., p. 247.
[5] *S.C.P.*, ix, 407–8 (2 July 89).

an unsworn statement from the dock, but it could not have been given by him in evidence, for in 1870 English law did not permit an accused person to be heard as a witness in his own case.[1] This, however, was no disadvantage to Davitt, as his counsel could not have taken the risk of putting him into the witness-box. For counsel's case, apart from the denial that Davitt had been at Liverpool when Corydon swore to have seen him at fenian meetings there, rested entirely on lies.

For defence counsel to say that Davitt's business was exporting arms to the Continent or supplying them to Irish landlords, that he had had no part in the fenian conspiracy but—he must have squirmed to hear it—was a loyal subject of the queen, and that fenianism was a spent force—all this was a pack of lies. The Haslingden witnesses were lying when they sought to prove an alibi for the day of the Chester castle raid, and in all that they said about their own and Davitt's attitude to fenianism. All this was known to Davitt and it reflects the moral dilemma inseparable from conspiracy against an established government: a high-spirited, high-minded, conscientious, and honest young man, Michael's very idealism had placed him in a situation where subterfuge, dissimulation, and lying were inevitable. His complaint about his trial was not that he was innocent but that he had not been proved guilty. And yet he seems at times to have lost sight of the distinction between fact and law, as when, on the eve of his trial, he speaks of establishing his 'innocence',[2] or when, in the cell in Newgate under the court-room where he awaited the jury's verdict, he added one more to the melancholy inscriptions that crowded the walls: 'M. D. expects ten years for the crime of being an Irish nationalist and the victim of an informer's perjury'.[3]

Yet it is not difficult to understand Michael's state of mind. He believed himself to have been exceptionally successful for five years in concealing his fenian activities from the police; he had organised an elaborate and effective system of gun-running; and in the end he had the mortification of being found guilty of treason-felony on evidence that was essentially presumptive. On the other hand the weapons he supplied had never been used and many of them had been seized by the police. He had never personally been involved in violent action against the state. His actual treason was no greater than that of Forrester, O'Connor Power, Mark Ryan, and many other fenian contemporary whose arms-trafficking was known to the police and who never had to undergo penal servitude. The severity of his sentence was due largely to the letter he had written to save a man from being murdered. It is

[1] This restriction was removed by the criminal evidence act, 12 & 13 Vict., c. 77, 12 Aug. 98.

[2] D to his father, mother, and sisters, 11 July 70 (DP/A).

[3] *Leaves*, i, 147–9.

no wonder that in his more despairing moods he felt himself to be a victim. He *was* a victim; not of injustice, not of an informer's perjury, but of his own commitment to fenianism.

Wilson, who had no such commitment, was perhaps even more unfortunate. Technically the case against him was slight, and the judge in pronouncing sentence had held out some hope that it might be mitigated by the home secretary. But if the further inquiries he contemplated were made, they must have confirmed Wilson's guilt, for he had served his full sentence, less the period of remission to which he was entitled, when, in January 1876, he was released on ticket of leave.[1] He returned to Birmingham hoping to resume his former occupation. But his home, his workshop, and his livelihood were gone, and he was penniless. He tried to contact his former partners with a view to recovering his share of the assets of the firm, but without success. Minningham, who had disappeared as soon as he heard of Wilson's arrest, had decamped with his brother to America some months later, and steadily ignored Wilson's entreaties. Nor could Wilson get anything out of Gill who, unknown to him, had sold the firm's stock of arms to the gunmaker Williamson for about £300.[2] It was probably Gill who also disposed of the plant, which Minningham reckoned to be worth about £700. Wilson was in great poverty and distress when, in January 1878, Davitt, just released from prison, came to his help with £5.[3] Part of the collections raised at public lectures given by Davitt during the next year went to Wilson, and Davitt helped him with applications to the home secretary for the recovery of the revolvers which the police had seized in 1870; 50 out of the 150 revolvers he claimed—the 50 found on him when arrested at Paddington—were in fact returned. But his efforts to rehabilitate himself all seemed to go wrong. Reduced to pushing a truck through the streets in all weathers, he was repeatedly soaked to the skin and had no change of clothes. He was still struggling desperately to make a living in March 1879, when he drops out of Davitt's surviving correspondence.[4]

Wilson regarded himself as having a moral claim on the I.R.B. no less than that of Davitt and other fenians whose imprisonment he had shared. After Davitt's release this came to be acknowledged in fenian circles: one of the most prominent of American fenians described him

[1] P.R.O., H.O.45/9329/19461/91.

[2] H.-C. Bodley to I.G.P., 24, 31 May, 21 June (S.P.O., R.P. 1877/9309); same to same, 20 Nov. (S.P.O., 6985R). See above, p. 71.

[3] John Ryan to Mrs Mary Davitt, 28 July 1908 (DP/04).

[4] John Wilson to home secretary, 13 June 77, and related papers (S.P.O., R.P. 1877/9309); Wilson to D, 15, 18, 19 Feb., 2, 25 Mar., 21 Apr., 1 Oct. 78, 21 Mar. 79 (DP/R); D to Thomas Chambers, 15 Aug. 78 (Cashman, pp 54-5).

in August 1878 as 'the English gunsmith who so faithfully kept the secrets of the I.R.B. during his trial and incarceration and for whom or his family nothing has yet been done';[1] and a collection was raised for him at a public meeting addressed by Davitt at Newark, New Jersey, on 30 September 1878.[2] Whether or not the I.R.B. took its obligations seriously, Davitt never forgot him, and there were other individual Irishmen who rallied to his support. It is probable that he eventually made good, for he lived to be nearly eighty. In January 1905 Davitt learnt of his death in Birmingham from James Doherty, one of a group of Birmingham Irish who for years had made it their business to care for him in his old age and had latterly kept Davitt informed of his condition. Davitt paid all the expenses of the funeral (£7 2*s*.) and had a modest tombstone placed on the grave.[3]

Davitt's trial for treason-felony was the second great crisis of his life; and it is not surprising that now, at the age of twenty-four, he began to see himself as a man prone to misfortune. This was never to become his settled state of mind, for at the heart of him there was unquenchable optimism, unshakeable conviction that life was worth living, and unbending will to fight the good fight. But he had reason to reflect during the long years of his imprisonment that he had had an undue share of bad luck. Misfortune had overshadowed his birth and his childhood in Ireland; yet, on the other hand, he had always been blessed with good and affectionate parents and a stable home. The loss of his right arm when he was eleven was a major misfortune; yet in a sense he had been lucky not to have lost his life, and the accident that had cost him so dear had had its compensations—four years of unexpected schooling leading to employment that offered scope for his abilities. But he had sacrificed a promising future to the increasing demands of fenianism—and all to no purpose, as it now seemed. His secret traffic in arms for the fenian organisation was exposed in consequence of a seizure by the police in Ireland of consignments that had not originated with him. His fenian activity had resulted in his disastrous association with Forrester, who, though no less guilty of offences against the state than Davitt and better known to the police, went unscathed. Perhaps his worst piece of bad luck had been Forrester's appearance as a witness for the defence, which had done Davitt far more harm than the informer Corydon's appearance for the prosecution. Finally there was the loss of Cockcroft's tillet book, which deprived the defence of evidence that would probably have substantiated Davitt's claim to have been in Haslingden on the days immediately following the Chester

[1] William Carroll to John Devoy, 10 Aug. (*D.P.B.*, i, 341). [2] Below, p. 235.

[3] D to James Doherty, 22 Jan., 23 Mar. 1905 (DP/04).

Castle raid when Corydon swore that he saw him at fenian meetings in Liverpool.

In a larger sense Davitt was unlucky in the timing of his arrest. Five days afterwards Isaac Butt launched his brave new effort in constitutional nationalism, the home rule movement, with the support of leading fenians, including an old acquaintance of Davitt's, John O'Connor Power, who also had taken part in the Chester castle attempt and who, as a member of the fenian supreme council, had been in a position of authority over Davitt.[1] Into this new movement much fenian energy and hope were drawn; and in a few years there emerged the fenian-dominated Home Rule Confederation of Great Britain, with its headquarters at Manchester and with John Barry, who had been involved in Davitt's arms-traffic, as its secretary. Is it fanciful to suppose that, if Davitt had not fallen into the net of the police when he did, he too might have been deflected from hard-line fenianism into cooperation with the home rule movement?

The crises of 1857 and 1870 both had a decisive effect on Davitt's whole life. Without the accident and its sequel he would no doubt have gravitated into feniansm but would hardly have become the key-man that he was in 1870. Without his conviction for treason-felony and his imprisonment, it is improbable that he would have won the unique reputation he enjoyed among his countrymen when he returned to Ireland in 1878 or that he would have been the highly-tempered instrument of popular revolt he then was.

[1] Above, pp 47–8, 49–50, 56.

IV

The home rule movement and the first fenian 'new departure', 1870–77

DAVITT'S imprisonment lasted from 14 May 1870, the day of his arrest, to 19 December 1877, when he was conditionally released. These seven and a half years of isolation were a time of important new developments in Irish politics, which both helped to expedite his release and shaped the new political situation that awaited him on his return to public life. The central figures in these new developments were W. E. Gladstone, Isaac Butt, and Charles Stewart Parnell.

In the early 1860s Gladstone was recognised to be the coming leader of the British liberal party, and from 1868, when he formed his first administration, to his final retirement in 1894 he was the dominating personality in British politics. For quarter of a century, during fourteen years of which he was in office as prime minister, Gladstone's impact on the Irish question was immeasurably greater than that of any other British statesman.[1] His conscience was first troubled on the subject of Ireland in 1845 through contacts with public men on the Continent, but it was not till 1867 that he was fully awakened to the nature of the Irish question.[2] He reached this point in response to two quite opposite influences. The first was that of the National Association (founded in Dublin in December 1864), in which, under the auspices of Archbishop Cullen, bishops and priests combined with liberal politicians to agitate for a number of specific reforms: the disestablishment of the protestant episcopal church, land reform on the basis of tenant right, and state-supported denominational education.[3] This moderate

[1] J. L. Hammond's *Gladstone and the Irish nation* (1938; new impression, 1964) is the great book on its subject; Lord Eversley's *Gladstone and Ireland* (1912) is also valuable; a recent short study, learned, critical, and sympathetic, is David Steele's 'Gladstone and Ireland' in *I.H.S.*, xvii, no. 65 (Mar. 1970), pp 58–88.

[2] Hammond, op. cit., pp 51, 68–81.

[3] E. R. Norman, *The catholic church and Ireland in the age of rebellion, 1859–73* (1965), ch. IV and passim; *The catholic church and Irish politics in the eighteen sixties* (Dublin Historical Association pamphlet, 1965), passim. P. J. Corish, 'Political problems, 1860–78', in P. J. Corish (ed.), *A history of Irish catholicism*, v, ch. 3 (1967), pp 23–36.

constitutional alternative to fenianism defined for Gladstone the vital areas in which reform was needed. The second influence that moved him was that of the fenian disturbances of 1867, which convinced him that the time for remedial action had come. While expressing extreme detestation of 'these horrible outrages', he insisted that they did not in any way release England from the duty of removing the causes of Irish disaffection. When that had been done—and only then—'instead of hearing in every corner of Europe the most painful commentaries on the policy of England towards Ireland, we may be able to look our fellow Europeans in the face'.[1] Fenian violence, he came to believe, had presented Englishmen with a challenge to which they had reacted not merely with angry indignation but, more significantly, with an 'attitude of attention and preparedness . . . which qualified them to embrace, in a manner foreign to their habits in other times, the vast importance of the Irish controversy'.[2] He could no longer doubt that he was called upon to grapple with the Irish problem. In the general election of 1868, which brought him to power as prime minister for the first time, he announced his determination to 'do justice' to Ireland, and to 'open a future of happiness, prosperity, and contentment which shall stand in joyful contrast with the past of that unhappy land'.[3] Till 1885 he believed that the Irish problem was essentially a problem in misgovernment, which could be solved by a policy of bold and imaginative reforms. His church act of 1869 and his land act of 1870 were the first instalment of his programme.

The former measure[4] disestablished and disendowed the Anglican church in Ireland and abolished all connection between the state and the several churches. For the first time the church of the large majority of Ireland's population was placed on a footing of legal equality with the churches of the protestant minority. Catholic emancipation in the ecclesiastical field was thus at last completed; and with the setting up of an independent Anglican church in Ireland the united church of England and Ireland was partitioned, and the first institutional breach in the union of Great Britain and Ireland accomplished. The land act[5] gave legal recognition to the tenant's interest in his holding by entitling him, if evicted from it, to claim compensation for disturbance (unless the ejectment was for non-payment of rent) and for improvements made by him with his landlord's consent. Although the landlord retained his legal right to evict as he pleased, his exercise of it in future

[1] Speech at Southport, 19 Dec. 67, in *The Times*, 20 Dec., pp 5–6.
[2] *Hansard 3*, cxcvi, 1062 (31 May 69).
[3] Speech at St Helen's, 5 Aug. 68, in *The Times*, 6 Aug., p. 6, col. 4.
[4] 32 & 33 Vict., c. 42.
[5] 33 & 34 Vict., c. 46.

would render him liable to financial penalties.[1] But the act did not give the tenant what he wanted most, continued occupancy of his farm at a fair rent; for he had first to surrender his farm before he could claim the benefit of the act, and with one exception the act gave the courts no power to propose or determine a fair rent. The exception was the case of a tenant of a holding not exceeding £15 rental ejected for non-payment of a rent adjudged by the court to be 'exorbitant', a provision of great importance in principle but attracting little attention at the time. The act could be set aside by the granting of a lease for at least thirty-one years, and some landlords in fact compelled tenants to contract themselves out of the act by imposing such leases on them. In general, the subtlety and complexity of the act severely diminished its value for those whom it was specially intended to help. Yet it opened a new era in the history of the Irish land question. It marked a radical departure from the principle of free contract, on which the existing law of landlord-tenant relations was based, in favour of the historicist claims urged by the advocates of the tenants;[2] and it thus effected a fundamental divergence between the land law of England and that of Ireland. It meant that, for the first time, parliament had in principle interfered with the rights of private property in land. Gladstone's achievement was even greater than it seemed: the cabinet that he induced to accept so unprecedented an invasion of vested interests in land was composed largely of great whig landowners; and they yielded only because he persuaded them that no milder measure would avert an agrarian crisis in Ireland that would have dangerous repercussions in Britain itself.[3] Gladstone's Irish measures of 1869–70 also set an important new precedent in another way. Both his church act and his land act included clauses providing for the conversion of occupying tenants into owners through state-aided land-purchase. Under the church act the state was to advance a sum not exceeding three-quarters of the purchase price, to be repaid by annuities at the rate of 4 per cent for 32 years; under the land act the sum advanced was not to exceed two-thirds of the purchase price, to be repaid by annuities of 5 per cent for 35 years. The number of tenants thus affected was very small, and there was no intention of extending the scheme to the tenantry as a whole. But the principle that the state should assist tenants in buying out their holdings from their landlords was capable of unlimited application.

If fenianism served as a catalyst to Gladstone's thinking about Ireland

[1] See A. G. Richey, *The Irish land laws* (London, 1880), ch. IX. [2] See above, pp 37–8.

[3] This theme has been worked out in detail by David Steele in his *Irish land and British politics: tenant right and nationality, 1865–1870* (Cambridge, 1974).

it completed a process long germinating in Isaac Butt. An Ulster protestant, who had succeeded to O'Connell's preeminence at the Irish bar, Butt was the classic example of a conservative unionist finally converted to nationalism by the courage and self-abandonment of the fenians. His experience of Irish suffering in the great famine had shaken his belief in the value of the union. As defending counsel for O'Brien, Meagher, and other Young Irelanders on trial for treason in 1848, he had been moved by their sincerity, their fortitude, and their self-sacrificing patriotism to ask himself whether the whole system was not unhinged that condemned such men to a traitor's doom. In 1865–7 he stood in the same relationship to the fenian leaders, and he asked himself again: 'Is there no way to arrest this? Are our best and bravest spirits ever to be carried away under this system of constantly resisted oppression and constantly defeated revolt?'[1] He eventually found an answer in a new effort to achieve self-government by parliamentary action—the home rule movement.

Butt had already made his name as an authority on the land question and as an earnest and eloquent champion of land reform. It was he above all who rescued the tenant right movement from the collapse of the Irish Tenant League of the fifties. Tenant farmer clubs and associations all over Ireland, such as they were, looked to him as the best exponent of their claims.[2] No one was more profoundly aware of the evils of the land system, or more vividly felt the human misery that the landlord's power of eviction could lawfully inflict. His advocacy of their claims helped to convince Gladstone of the need to intervene in the land question. After 1870 he incessantly urged parliament to remedy the deficiencies in Gladstone's land act. He was certain that, if the expatriation of the Irish peasantry was not arrested by an act of parliament, it would be arrested by a violent upheaval of the whole people.[3]

It was one of the ironies of Irish history that, while Gladstone was battling for 'justice to Ireland' in the hope of winning Irish loyalty for the union, Butt was preparing to launch a new movement for Irish self-government. He shared the popular revulsion in Ireland against the heavy sentences passed on convicted fenians in and after 1865. He was the leading spirit in the amnesty movement, which began in 1868 and took shape in the Amnesty Association, founded in Dublin on 28 June 1869 to agitate for the release of the fenian prisoners.[4] It was typical

[1] *D.N.B.*; T. de V. White, *The road of excess* (1946; a biography of Butt). The late D. A. Thornley's *Isaac Butt and home rule* (1964) is a learned and perceptive study. D has a well-informed and sensitive chapter on Butt in his *Fall*, pp 79–99.

[2] *Fall*, pp 91, 94; above, p. 39.

[3] *Fall*, pp 94–5; Thornley, *Butt*, pp 247–50, 259–61, 272–5, 280, 287.

[4] Butt, *Ireland's appeal for amnesty* (1870), pp 28–34; Thornley, *Butt*, pp 53–4, 65–7.

of this movement that, while Butt was its president, its secretary was a fenian—John (known as 'Amnesty') Nolan, a young man of great organising ability, resourcefulness, and audacity, who was employed in a Dublin drapery store.[1] He and Davitt had been known to each other as fenians in the days before Davitt's arrest.[2] Under Butt's invigorating leadership and Nolan's skilful organisation, men of all shades of nationalism were drawn into an agitation unparalleled in magnitude and exuberance since the days of O'Connell.[3] 'There never was a political object', Butt claimed, 'on which the whole heart of Ireland was so earnestly and passionately set'.[4] The release of 49 of the prisoners, including Kickham, by Gladstone's government in March 1869, was the first victory of the amnesty movement, but it was regarded as a miserable half-measure by the friends of amnesty, who demanded the release—and, pending that, the more humane treatment—of all the remaining prisoners. A second exodus of prisoners, numbering 33 and including Luby, Rossa, O'Leary, and Devoy, rewarded their efforts in January 1871. The remaining prisoners for whose release the Amnesty Association continued to clamour included Davitt and Wilson; they alone had been convicted for offences commited since the amnesty agitation began.[5]

The amnesty agitation kindled a new nationalist ardour throughout Ireland, which combined with the reaction against Gladstone from those whom his reforms had disappointed or antagonised to precipitate the 'home rule' movement.[6] Initiated by Butt at a private meeting in Dublin on 19 May 1870 (five days after Davitt's arrest at Paddington), and organised on a nation-wide footing in November 1873, this movement reasserted 'the inalienable right of the Irish people to self-government' and declared that the restoration of an Irish parliament was essential to the peace and prosperity of Ireland. But instead of demanding repeal

[1] *Fall*, pp 86, 97-9; W. O'Brien, *Recollections*, p. 135; Ryan, *Fenian memories*, p. 30. The shop where Nolan was employed was Peter Paul McSwiney's, in Sackville Street, now Clery's, in O'Connell Street (ibid.).

[2] D to John O'Leary, 11 Mar. 88 (DP/ZZ).

[3] Figures for attendance at amnesty meetings in 1869 are given in Butt's *Ireland's appeal for amnesty*, app., pp 81-2, and in 1873 in the *Irishman*, 29 Nov. 73, p. 344.

[4] *Irishman*, 11 Oct., p. 230.

[5] *Irishman*, 1868-73; Butt, *Ireland's appeal for amnesty; Return of the names and sentences of the fenian convicts now proposed to be released*, pp 1-2, H.C. 1868-9 (72), li, 531-2; *Return of the names of the fenian convicts recently released . . .*, H.C. 1871 (144), lviii, 461; H.S. Winterbotham to Hartington, 7 Oct. 73 (Gladstone papers, B. L. Add. MS 44144, ff 131-2); *Return of the names of persons suffering imprisonment on account of their conviction for the murder of Sergeant Brett, for treason-felony, etc.*, H.C. 1874 (119), liv, 493.

[6] On Butt's home rule movement generally see: A. M. Sullivan, *New Ireland* (1877), ch. XXVIII-XXXII; MacDonagh, *Home rule*, ch. I-VIII; McCaffrey, 'Irish federalism; and especially Thornley, *Butt*.

of the union as O'Connell had done, Butt proposed a federal arrangement, which would secure to the Irish parliament the right of legislating for and regulating the internal affairs of Ireland, while leaving to the imperial parliament, in which Ireland would continue to be repesented, the power of dealing with all questions affecting the imperial crown and government, legislation for the colonies and other dependencies of the crown, the relations of the empire with foreign states, and all matters appertaining to the defence and stability of the empire at large. This scheme, to be established by act of parliament, was designed to give a substantial measure of self-government without disrupting the United Kingdom or impairing the prerogatives of the crown.[1]

The home rule movement was initiated largely by protestants, but after the opening years drew its main strength from the catholic middle classes, which had responded with enthusiasm to Gladstone's call for justice to Ireland and had voted solidly for the liberals in the general election of 1868. But they had quickly become disenchanted: the inadequacies of Gladstone's land act of 1870 disappointed the whole tenant farmer interest, and his university scheme of 1873, with its refusal to endow denominational education, actively antagonised the whole catholic clergy, and led to the defeat of the government. The right wing of the home rule movement, distinctively protestant and land-owning, was motivated by resentment against Gladstone on quite different grounds—his disestablishment of the Anglican church and his interference with the rights of landed property; they were unstable allies and they soon fell away. The left wing, drawn largely from the catholic lower-middle and working classes, was very different.

From an orthodox fenian standpoint the home rule movement, relying as it did on parliamentary action and explicitly repudiating separation, was self-condemned. Nevertheless Butt commanded respect among the fenians, and there were opportunists in the I.R.B. who were impressed by his movement as a revival of the national spirit which they sought to support and if possible to direct. They knew that they might wait a long time before the I.R.B. could put an army into the field to fight England, whereas, by taking part now in the constitutional movement, they could hope to mould it to their own ends.[2] The principal exponents of this point of view in Ireland were John O'Connor Power and Patrick Egan, both of them members of the supreme council of the I.R.B. and both prominent in the amnesty movement. It was due largely to their influence that the fenians adopted

[1] *Proceedings of the home rule conference held at the Rotunda, Dublin, on the 18th, 19th, 20th and 21st November 1873* (1874), pp 6, 33; see also Butt's *Irish federalism: its meaning, its objects and its hopes* (1870).

[2] R. B. O'Brien, *Parnell*, i, 65.

an attitude of friendly neutrality towards the genesis of the home rule movement in 1870; and that strong fenian support was forthcoming for Butt at the critical conference held at the Rotunda, Dublin, on 18-21 November 1873, under the chairmanship of William Shaw (a protestant merchant of Cork and liberal M.P. for Bandon), from which emerged the Home Rule League, the national organisation of the new movement. This support for the home rule movement was the first of three 'new departures' or deviations from fenian orthodoxy that occurred in the 1870s. The way was prepared for it by an amended constitution adopted at an I.R.B. convention in Dublin on St Patrick's day 1873, of which the third clause introduced a new principle:

The I.R.B. shall await the decision of the Irish nation as expressed by a majority of the Irish people as to the fit hour of inaugurating a war against England, and shall, pending such an emergency, lend its support to every movement calculated to advance the cause of Irish independence consistently with the preservation of its own integrity.

It was in the spirit of this new rule that, on the eve of the Rotunda conference, a number of leading fenians (Power, Egan, Nolan, Charles Guilfoyle Doran (of Queenstown), Matthew Harris (of Ballinasloe), and others) together with Joseph P. Ronayne, M.P. for Cork and John Ferguson of Glasgow, agreed at a secret meeting in Dublin to support Butt's movement for a trial period of, it would appear, three years.[1]

O'Connor Power had held a commanding place in the fenian organisation since his release from prison in July 1868.[2] The Irish police kept him under observation, and knew that, till 1874, he was active in fenian business, including the transmission of arms to Ireland.[3] But during these years he seems to have been moving away from his earlier, intransigent fenianism. He afterwards claimed to have pioneered, in 1868-9, a policy of combining revolutionary and constitutional elements in a new national movement, and to have persuaded George Henry Moore, of Moore Hall, County Mayo, who was M.P. for the county, to assume the leadership of it. While this claim is not supported by contemporary evidence,[4] it agrees with Davitt's later view that Power, whom he knew well since his early days, was 'the first "old

[1] *Proceedings of the home rule conference . . . 1873*; T. W. Moody and Leon Ó Broin, 'The I.R.B. supreme council, 1868-78' in *I.H.S.*, xix, no. 75 (Mar. 1975), pp 289-90, 314; *D.P.B.*, i, 374; W. O'Brien, *Recollections*, pp 139-41; White, *The road of excess*, pp 239-41, 262, 272-82; Thornley, *Butt*, ch. IV.

[2] Above, pp 47-8, 49-50, 56.

[3] S.P.O., Abstracts of cases of persons arrested under habeas corpus suspension act, iii, 28-9; Fenianism, index of names, 1866-71, p. 752, app. p. 5, no. 25; Fenian papers, A files, no. 567.

[4] His papers were used by Michael MacDonagh for his *Home rule movement* (1920), but seem not to have survived.

fenian" to work on a policy of parallel action between the revolutionary and constitutional parties'.[1] There is no doubt of Moore's high reputation among serious nationalists and of his readiness to lead a new national effort on the basis indicated by Power. But Moore died suddenly in April 1870, and this left the way open for Butt. Power, it is clear, used his great abilities to swing many fenians over to support of Butt's movement.[2]

A surprising aberration in Power's hitherto harsh and rugged career began in January 1871, when, at the age of 24, following in the wake of Mark Ryan,[3] he entered St Jarlath's College, Tuam, to acquire a belated secondary education, without giving up his fenian activity. During his first half-year he was a fellow-student of Ryan's; and, a collaborator in arms-trafficking throughout his period at St Jarlath's, he remained on the books of the college till the summer of 1874.[4] These years witnessed a decisive change in him: not only were his powers as a speaker and writer perfected, but his political outlook became pragmatic rather than dogmatic. He was later to speak of his 'college days' as marking an epoch in his career. His expenses while he was at St Jarlath's appear to have been met from the proceeds of lectures organised for his benefit in England and Ireland by fenians; and this made the strict observants among them the more resentful when, as it seemed to them, he turned his back on fenianism in identifying himself with the home rule movement.[5]

Patrick Egan, no less active in backing home rule, was a prosperous business-man, the managing director of the North Dublin City Milling Company (one of the largest of its kind in Ireland) and co-proprietor, with James Rourke, of the City Bakery. He combined great executive ability, shrewd judgment, and inexhaustible energy, with integrity, charm, and generous sympathies. He was clear-sighted and cool-headed, but his mild and quiet manner concealed a fighting spirit. He was intensely nationalist, with a flexible attitude to politics and advanced views on the land question. A politician of extreme sagacity, dexterity, and prudence, he preferred to work behind the scenes and was seldom known to make a speech. He had helped to found the Amnesty Association, and he brought a fund of sophisticated fenian opportunism to the help of home rule.[6]

[1] D to R. B. O'Brien, 6 Dec. 93 (DP/ZZ).

[2] MacDonagh, *Home rule*, pp 114–16; Ryan, *Fenian memories*, p. 46; *D.P.B.*, i, 74–6; Thornley, *Butt*, pp 89–91; *D.N.B.*, G. H. Moore; see also above, p. 39. [3] Above, pp 45–6.

[4] Tuam, St Jarlath's College; Fee-payment book, 1867–80, pp 64, 76, 92, 120, 147; S.P.O., Fenian papers, A files, no. 567.

[5] S.P.O., Description of fenian suspects, p. 6; Devoy, VII.

[6] *D.A.B.*; A. M. Sullivan, *New Ireland* (15th ed. [1882]), p. 439; Denvir, *Life story,*

In the Irish national movement in Britain, two men, John Barry and John Ferguson occupied a place similar to that of Power and Egan in Ireland. Barry, who was born in Wexford in 1845, the son of a coast-guard, had lived in the north of England since his early years. From very small beginnings at Newcastle-upon-Tyne[1] he had risen to be chief commercial traveller for a large Scottish firm of linoleum manufacturers; in the seventies he was settled in Manchester, with a prosperous business of his own. His business capacity was equalled by his consuming interest in Irish politics. Like Power and Egan he was a fenian and a member of the supreme council of the I.R.B.; and like them he was quick to see the possibilities of fenian infiltration into the home rule movement. He and Ferguson were very active in promoting the formation of local home rule associations; and by the end of 1872 such bodies had emerged in most of the greater industrial towns of Britain. Barry, as secretary of the Manchester Home Rule Association, occupied a key position in the movement.[2] Tim Healy, who was related to him and first came to England to stay with him at Manchester, speaks of his affable manner, his wit, and his buoyancy. He liked the English and the Scots no less than the Irish, and was 'comically quizzical' about all three.[3] Davitt describes him as 'of conspicuous ability, open-handed and generous to a fault, and very popular among all sections of Irishmen in England and Scotland'.[4]

Barry's position in the home rule movement in England was paralleled in Scotland by that of John Ferguson. He was an Ulster presbyterian, born in 1834 or 1835 in Belfast, where he had learnt the stationery and printing business. In 1860 he had moved to Glasgow to become partner in the firm of Cameron and Ferguson, printers and publishers, whose publications included a substantial list of popular books relating to Ireland. A strong and striking personality, widely and deeply read in the social sciences, an intellectual radical steeped in John Stuart Mill and Herbert Spencer, he was an advanced land-reformer, and a fervent admirer of Gladstone and Bright.[5] He was one of the earliest champions in Scotland of Butt's new movement.

By the end of 1872, home-rulers in Britain were conscious of the

pp 219–26; W. O'Brien, *Recollections,* pp 135–7; Healy, *Letters and leaders,* i, 77; Ryan, *Fenian memories*, p. 35.

[1] Cf. above, p. 68.

[2] Denvir, *The Irish in Britain*, pp 264–5; O'Donnell, *Irish parl. party*, i, 161–3; O'Connor, *Memoirs*, i, 101–2; Thornley, *Butt*, p. 141. Barry is the 'X' quoted extensively by R. B. O'Brien in his *Parnell* (see i, 121–2).

[3] Healy, *Letters and leaders*, i, 30.

[4] *Fall*, pp 227–8.

[5] *S.C.P.*, vii, 141–2, viii, 268–71, 368; *Glasgow Observer*, 28 Apr. 1906; Denvir, *Life story*, p. 176; W. O'Brien, *Recollections*, p. 140; *Fall*, p. 714; MacDonagh, *Home rule movement*, p. 29.

need for a national organisation to direct the Irish vote in British constituencies in the home rule interest. It was due to the political acumen and the initiative of Barry that such an organisation was successfully established. With fenian support the Home Rule Confederation of Great Britain, which integrated the local home rule associations under a representative government, was founded at Manchester in February 1873. The functions of the confederation were to ensure that Irish voters were duly registered and strongly persuaded to vote only for candidates from whom pledges of support for home rule had been extracted. The home rule movement in Britain was thus provided with an efficient electioneering machine, loosely linked with the Home Rule League in Dublin by the expedient of coopting two members of the council of the league to the executive of the confederation.[1]

The confederation differed from the league (which in point of time it preceded) in several respects that made it a more effective instrument of advanced nationalist opinion. It was a genuine party machine, with a strong executive elected by an annual convention of delegates, a network of branches, and well-defined practical objectives, whereas the league was simply a central body of subscribers and enrolled supporters. 'There are no branches of the league. The state of the law in Ireland is such that branches are illegal and would bring all members into danger. There are many local associations and clubs working in harmony with the league.'[2] The league had no other organisation than an annual general meeting and a council of one hundred, meeting once a month, whose main functions were to admit new members and make policy statements.[3] The confederation was largely managed by fenians, as the league was not; and whereas the league was preponderantly middle-class in social composition the confederation was as characteristically working-class, because that was the stratum to which most of the Irish in Britain (like Michael Davitt himself) belonged.[4]

The home rule movement, like the fenian movement, had its overseas dimension. Steps were being taken to form a home rule association at Montreal as early as October 1873, and in August 1875 M. W. Kirwan, secretary of the Home Rule Confederation, was sent on an organising tour of Canada at the expense of the confederation and with the blessing of the council of the Home Rule League. The council asked Kirwan

[1] Home Rule League letter-book, 1873–8 (P.R.O.N.I., D213), pp 64–5, 181–2, 242; Denvir, *The Irish in Britain*, pp 264–5; R. B. O'Brien, *Parnell*, i, 121–5; McCaffrey, 'Irish federalism', pp 36–7; Thornley, *Butt*, pp 291–2.

[2] J. P. McAlister, asst. sec., H.R.L., to James McAleese, 12 Jan. 76 (Home Rule League letter-book, pp 161–3).

[3] C. C. O'Brien, *Parnell*, pp 122–6; Thornley, *Butt*, pp 169–72.

[4] Ibid., pp 141, 291.

to take care to harmonise his arrangements with those of O'Connor Power, 'one of the ablest and most trusted of their number',[1] who would be in Canada at the same time on a lecture tour for his own benefit but also to publicise the home rule movement. By 1875 the league was receiving financial support not only from Canada but also from the U.S.A., South America, New Zealand, and Cape Colony.[2]

The general election of 1874, the first since the introduction of the secret ballot (1872), though it took the Home Rule League by surprise, recorded a spectacular success for Butt's new movement. More Irish seats were contested (52 out of 64) than in any previous election under the union, and 60 professing home-rulers were returned out of a total representation in the house of commons of 103, the remaining members consisting of 33 conservatives and 10 liberals. At the preceding general election, in 1868, the total membership of 105 had been divided between 39 conservatives and 66 liberals.[3] The general election of 1874 was thus a turning-point: for even though only about one-third of the 60 so-called home-rulers of 1874 were really committed to home rule, the new movement had 'destroyed liberal unionism as a political force in Ireland'.[4] From 1874 onwards the most significant line of division among the Irish representatives was between supporters and opponents of home rule.[5] Under Butt's leadership the home-rulers resolved to constitute themselves a separate and distinct party, holding aloof from, and independent of, conservatives and liberals alike, and united in their endeavour to obtain self-government as already defined (3 March 1874).[6]

During the next few years the case for home rule was argued by Butt in parliament with the utmost tact, eloquence, reasonableness, and pertinacity, but without any success. Nor did he make any headway with other measures—principally to improve on the land act of 1870 and to reform the municipal franchise and the grand jury system of local government—that he repeatedly brought before the house of commons. His land bill of 1876 gave detailed expression to the '3 Fs'—which Gladstone had rejected in 1870 as a general principle of settlement and which were still the measure of tenant right generally demanded by farmers' organisations, now combined under the Central Tenants' Defence Association.[7]

[1] Home Rule League letter-book, 1873–8, p. 127. [2] Ibid., pp 62–205, passim.

[3] B. M. Walker, 'Parliamentary elections, 1801–1980' in *A new history of Ireland*, ed. T. W. Moody, F. X. Martin, and F. J. Byrne, ix. [4] Thornley, *Butt*, p. 179.

[5] L. J. McCaffrey, 'Home rule and the general election of 1874' in *I.H.S.*, ix, no. 34 (Sept. 1954); Thornley, *Butt*, pp 195–204. [6] Ibid., pp 212–14.

[7] Ibid., pp 260, 273–4; *Defence*, p. 190; Kettle, *The material for victory: being the memoirs of Andrew J. Kettle*, ed. L. J. Kettle (1958), pp 13–14; H.C. 1876 (10), 415–42.

The problem of landlord-tenant relations, which the act of 1870 had failed to solve, was not acute during the six years of relative prosperity that followed. The total value of agricultural production—crops (exclusive of potatoes, turnips, and hay), livestock, and livestock products—was rising steadily—from £39.2 millions in 1871 to the unprecedented peak of £43.7 millions in 1876. Evictions were relatively few, ranging from 368 to 596 a year and averaging 481, or 0.9 per 1000 holdings above one acre, which was well below the general average for 1854–78. The rate of agrarian crime was also low, ranging from 136 to 373 a year and averaging 241, or 0.45 per 1000 holdings over one acre. The homicide rate averaged only 6.[1] But 1877 proved to be the first of three calamitous years for Irish agriculture that were to culminate in the greatest crisis of post-famine Ireland.

The home rule programme was essentially moderate and conservative, but it involved the transformation of the union and encountered scarcely less resistance in Britain than O'Connell's demand for the total repeal of the union had done. Disraeli, prime minister in the conservative administration that replaced Gladstone's after the general election of 1874, did not take seriously Butt's claim to separate nationhood for Ireland. This was the attitude that generally prevailed among both conservatives and liberals, though it was significant that Gladstone made no public statement against the principle of home rule, and had not done so since 1871.[2] If Butt's movement was to succeed, he had to win the support of one of the two great British parties, but far from doing so, he made remarkably little impression on the house of commons. This, apart from his own deficiencies as a leader, was almost inevitable because of the nature of the forces he led.

Butt's 'party' was a very mixed bag, ranging from committed home-rulers to mere place-hunters, and including a good many members who were really liberals and had professed conversion to home rule merely to gain admission to parliament or to retain their seats. The home-rulers were committed on a single issue only; on all other issues they had no obligations to one another. Thus the conditions of party solidarity and party discipline did not exist. Moreover the social composition of the party made it quite unfit to play a radical role. Elected on a very restricted franchise by under five per cent of the population it was heavily weighted on the side of property: nearly one third of its members were landowners, nearly one-third of whom owned over 1000 acres, and all the rest except two were of the upper middle class.[3] Such

[1] Appendices D1, E1, G1, and cf. above, pp 30–32.

[2] Hammond, *Gladstone and the Irish nation*, pp 114–17.

[3] O'Connor, *Parnell movement*, pp 140–41, 144–5; W. O'Brien, *Recollections*, pp 146–7; C. C. O'Brien, *Parnell*, p. 18; McCaffrey, 'Irish federalism', pp 22, 24–5; Thornley, *Butt*, ch. VI.

a party could not be the effective voice of a people consisting preponderantly of small tenant farmers.

On the denominational level the home rule party was in a stronger position. The Irish electoral system was still so little representative of numbers that, although three-quarters of the population were catholics, protestants were in the majority among Irish M.P.s until 1880. But of the 60 members of the home rule party, 47 were catholics, and these, together with 2 catholic liberals, came near to equalling the number of Irish protestant members (54).[1] This helps to explain why it was that, during the lifetime of the parliament in 1874, the only important Irish measures conceded by Disraeli's ministry were the intermediate education act of 1878 and the university education act of 1879, with both of which the catholic clergy were deeply concerned. But the issues that stirred the mass of Irishmen most profoundly were the land question and home rule.

Butt was seriously handicapped as leader of the home rule party not only by financial embarrassment and failing health but also by his own too pliant, too jovial, too impressionable and self-indulgent temperament. Moreover, radical critics within the party held that his parliamentary tactics were quite wrong: he tried to conciliate and convince the house of commons, whose forms and traditions he venerated, and the house responded with indifference and contempt. The right policy was to attack and exasperate both British parties by all means available, and thus compel their attention to Irish claims. This was the policy pioneered by Joseph Gillis Biggar, who had been returned as M.P. for County Cavan in the general election of 1874. He was a wealthy provision-merchant of Belfast, a member of the city council and other public bodies. He came of strong presbyterian stock, but joined the catholic church in 1875 apparently to show his solidarity with nationalist Ireland. A diminutive hunchback, he was a man of unbounded courage and determination, whose bluntness of speech, uncouth manner, and rasping voice concealed great kindliness and generosity. He was shrewd and relentlessly honest; and the whole force of his rock-like character was directed against British rule in Ireland. He had no respect for the house of commons, but saw it as a field for offensive action against Britain. He respected the fenians but regarded their reliance on physical force as unrealistic; after his election to parliament he joined the I.R.B., and later accepted a seat on its supreme council, but only with a view to winning fenian support for parliamentary politics.[2]

[1] McCaffrey, 'Irish federalism', p. 22.

[2] *D.N.B.*; *S.C.P.*, vii, 5, viii, 371–2, 375–6; O'Connor, *Parnell movement*, pp 145–9, 155–7; W. O'Brien, *Recollections*, pp 259–65; Healy, *Letters and leaders*, i, 39–44; MacDonagh, *Home rule*, pp 117, 119–20.

Biggar initiated his offensive tactics in the house of commons in 1874. Parliamentary obstruction was an established weapon of the opposition against the government, subject in its exercise to restraints imposed by tradition and the knowledge that the next general election might reverse the position of the contending parties. But Biggar as an obstructionist was an alien force, deliberately exploiting the procedure of the house, without any traditional restraint, for the purpose of delaying or disorganising or blocking not simply the government's but the house's business. This was his way of harrassing the enemy, and the anger and hatred it drew upon him showed how effective it was. Biggar, with none of the gifts that made Butt superb as a parliamentary orator, was soon exerting a greater impact on the house of commons than his leader.[1] He became the nucleus of a handful of 'active' home-rulers, chief among them a newcomer to Irish politics, Charles Stewart Parnell.[2]

Parnell was a protestant landowner of County Wicklow, who had spent most of his early life in England, at school and at the University of Cambridge. But he inherited the seeds of Irish nationalism from two generations of Irish ancestors on his father's side; and local influences that affected him deeply as a young man in his native Wicklow combined with the anglophobia inculcated by his American-Irish mother to foster in him an invincible antipathy to British domination. Behind his cold and aloof manner and his outward self-restraint, there lurked a dynamic and passionate nature of exceptional intensity and strength of purpose. Conservative by temperament and social outlook, with the concrete approach of a pragmatist and a clear eye for possibilities, he limited his objectives as a politician to the minimum of change that he judged to be necessary to solve Ireland's vital problems, while conveying an impression of dangerous and exciting extremism. He proved to have incomparable gifts for leading a constitutional movement in a combative and revolutionary spirit.

As a student at Cambridge (1865-9) he had followed the fenian movement during its critical years with some interest, but it was Gladstone's ballot act of 1872 that first attracted his attention seriously to politics. He had read about the independent Irish party of the fifties, and was quick to see that the introduction of the secret ballot, by freeing the

[1] R. B. O'Brien, *Parnell*, i, 81-4, 89-91, 92-4, 102-3, 109; Thornley, *Butt*, pp 235-8, 255-9, 300-29; W. O'Brien, *Recollections*, pp 214-15.

[2] Till recently the one indispensable book on Parnell was the *Life* by R. B. O'Brien (2 vols, 1898). Though it remains of great value, the study of its subject has been raised to a new level by C. Cruise O'Brien's *Parnell and his party, 1880-90* (1957), F. S. L. Lyons's *The fall of Parnell, 1890-91* (1960), R. F. Forster's *Charles Stewart Parnell: the man and his family* (1976), and by Dr Lyons's magisterial biography, *Charles Stewart Parnell* (1977).

electors from control by their landlords, created a situation favourable to a fresh essay in independent opposition.[1] Returned to parliament in April 1875 in a by-election for County Meath, Parnell quickly earned notoriety as Biggar's most distinguished pupil in the art of parliamentary obstruction. He was a poor speaker and disliked speech-making, but he developed a technique of obstruction more refined and more devastating than Biggar's, and even more detestable to English opinion. He made a point of addressing himself not so much to the house itself as to Irish opinion, and especially extremist opinion, outside.[2] During 1877 he made his position perfectly clear in speeches at a series of public meetings in Britain and Ireland. Was the correct policy for the home rule party (within the parliamentary field of forces) to be one of peace or of war? 'I am satisfied', he said at Glasgow on 29 May 1877, 'to abide by the decision of the Irish people. Are they for peace and conciliation, or for hostility and war?' If the former, he would bow to their decision, but his constituents would in that case have to get someone else to represent them.[3] Obstruction, he pointed out, was important not in itself but as an expression of the energy and determination with which the enemy ought to be assailed.[4]

Parnell's ablest colleagues in obstruction were John O'Connor Power and Frank Hugh O'Donnell. Both men, though fenians, sought a seat in parliament at the general election of 1874 (January-February). Power stood for County Mayo, but, to the indignation of his supporters, was induced by clerical disapproval to withdraw. The two successful candidates, both home-rulers, were then unseated on petition, and Power reentered the contest. He was returned (May 1874) by a narrow majority after a fierce struggle in which local fenians, including Matthew Harris, Thomas Brennan, and P. W. Nally (all to become famous in the land war) worked hard for him against solid opposition from the clergy, headed by Archbishop John MacHale of Tuam—at whose college of St Jarlath's Power was still a student.[5] With his great gifts as an orator, his stubbornness, and his courage, he became a formidable member of the obstructionist group.[6] Frank Hugh O'Donnell was a later adherent. Born at Devonport in 1848, he was the son of a soldier from Donegal, a captain in the Northumberland Fusiliers. He distinguished himself as a student of Queen's College, Galway,[7] and

[1] *S.C.P.*, vii, 1-2. [2] R. B. O'Brien, *Parnell*, i, 86-7, 97-8, 107-14; Thornley, *Butt*, pp 276, 278, 300-29. [3] R. B. O'Brien, *Parnell*, i, 128. [4] Ibid., i, 150.

[5] He paid a year's fees (£24) for the session 1873-4 on 28 Aug. 73 (Tuam, St Jarlath's College: Fee-payment book, 1867-80, p. 147).

[6] *S.C.P.*, vii, 4, 5, x, 178-9; Ryan, *Fenian memories*, pp 44-6; MacDonagh, *Home rule*, p. 89; Thornley, *Butt*, pp 183-4, 246-7, 256, 308-29.

[7] B.A. 1865 (2nd class honours in English, logic, and metaphysics); M.A. 1868 (*The*

had begun a career in London journalism when, in 1874, he was elected M.P. for Galway city after the elevation to the peerage of a successful rival for the seat. He was in turn unseated on a charge of clerical intimidation. He had been initiated into the I.R.B. by Mark Ryan, and in August 1876 was elected a vice-president of the Home Rule Confederation of Great Britain and its honorary secretary in succession to John Barry. He was returned to parliament in January 1877 in a by-election for the town of Dungarvan, and at once brought a large accession of strength to the obstructionists. O'Donnell later claimed, and wrote his *History of the Irish parliamentary party*[1] partly to prove, that he had been the inventor and chief practitioner of the obstructionist policy. It was characteristic of the man, in whom great intellectual powers and a distinguished presence were rendered completely ineffective by an egotism and an eccentricity amounting to a disease.[2] Power and O'Donnell had this in common that they were both ambitious, and both appear to have aspired to the leadership of the Irish party, but whereas Power had strong qualifications for such a role O'Donnell had fatal disqualifications. T. M. Healy described him as 'Crank Hugh O'Donnell', and W. E. Forster said of him in the house of commons: 'I cannot imagine any sane body of men for any good or evil purpose taking the hon. member into their confidence'.[3]

The behaviour of the obstructionists was as obnoxious to the party leader and to the majority of the party as it was gratifying to advanced nationalists. On 12 April 1877, during the uproar produced by Parnell's obstruction of the mutiny bill, Butt openly rebuked him before the house. This only improved Parnell's standing with advanced nationalists.[4] He and his supporters excelled all their previous records by their performance on the committee stage of the South Africa bill, when they kept an infuriated house of commons in continuous session for almost twenty-one hours (from 5.15 p.m. on 31 July to 2.10 p.m. on 1 August 1877).[5] Parnell won a decisive victory over Butt when, at the convention of the Home Rule Confederation of Great Britain at Liverpool, on 27 August 1877, he was elected president in Butt's place.[6] Butt was still president of the Home Rule League and chairman of the

Queen's University calendar, 1882: a supplement to the preceding series of calendars (1882), pp 257, 321).

[1] 2 vols, London, 1910.

[2] DN/11, Feb.-June 1883, p. 102; *Fall*, p. 109; Healy, *Letters and leaders*, i, 54–6, and passim; Ryan, *Fenian memories*, pp 62–3; MacDonagh, *Home rule*, pp 90–99; Thornley, *Butt*, pp 190–91, 294, 308–29.

[3] W. O'Brien, *Recollections*, pp 247–8.

[4] R. B. O'Brien, *Parnell*, i, 111–13, 114–20.

[5] Ibid., i, 134–6; Thornley, *Butt*, p. 313.

[6] R. B. O'Brien, *Parnell*, i, 143–4; W. O'Brien, *Recollections*, p. 212; O'Donnell, *Irish parl. party*, i, 248–51; Denvir, *Life story*, pp 191–4; Healy, *Letters and leaders*, i, 54; McCaffrey, 'Irish federalism', p. 42; Thornley, *Butt*, p. 331; Lyons, *Parnell*, p. 67.

parliamentary party, but it was as apparent that his power was in decline as that Parnell's star was rapidly rising. On 26 September, in a speech in Belfast, Parnell contended that an Irish party in earnest about home rule must be impatient to force on parliament the alternatives of conceding their demand or suffering the consequences. They should never allow themselves to feel at home at Westminster, and should recognise that parliamentary methods, however aggressively employed, might in the end prove fruitless.[1]

Participation in the home rule movement had now caused deep division among the fenians. It had been consistently opposed by those who believed, with Kickham and O'Leary and the rest of the fenian Old Guard—all the more critical because, though again at large, they were condemned to endless inaction—that parliamentary politics were futile and demoralising, and that fenianism was in danger of being undermined. But in 1876, when over two years had elapsed without any tangible result,[2] a strong fenian reaction against the home-rulers set in. An attempt, led by John Daly and a band of young militants armed with blackthorns, to prevent a home rule meeting from being held in Limerick on 17 April 1876, failed, and Butt duly addressed his constituents, but not before open fighting had resulted in many casualties. Similar strong-arm methods were directed against home rule meetings in Ireland, Scotland, and England during the next two years Some of the fenian leaders who had originally supported the Home Rule League, including C. G. Doran, secretary of the supreme council, turned against Butt and still more against fenians who continued to support him. At a meeting of the supreme council of the I.R.B. on 20 August 1876 it was proposed and carried by a majority of one

> that the countenance which we have hitherto shown to the home rule movement be from this date, and is hereby, withdrawn, as three years' experience of the working of the movement has proved to us that the revolutionary principles which we profess can be better served by our organisation existing on its own basis pure and simple; and we hereby request that all members of our organisation who may have any connection with the home rule movement will definitely withdraw from it their active cooperation within six months from this date.[3]

The position of Egan and Barry, both active home-rulers while members of the supreme council of the I.R.B., was anomalous enough; but that of O'Connor Power and Biggar was infinitely more so, for they had taken conflicting oaths of allegiance, to the Irish republic and to

[1] *Ulster Examiner*, 27 Sept. 77, p. [3]; McCaffrey, 'Irish federalism; pp 43–4.

[2] Above, p. 123.

[3] On two flimsy sheets in C. G. Doran's hand; undated, but the date is supplied by an entry in Doran's minute book of the supreme council (T. W. Moody and Leon Ó Broin, 'The I.R.B. supreme council, 1868–78' in *I.H.S.*, xix, no. 75 (Mar. 1975), p. 294).

Queen Victoria. Power was an object of special animosity among strict fenians; for unlike Biggar, who had not been a fenian at the time of his election as M.P., he was a leading member of the organisation when he secured a seat in parliament. Fenians as unlike as the intellectually fastidious John O'Leary and the brawny and impetuous John Daly of Limerick regarded him as an unscrupulous careerist and turncoat, who had initiated the new policy for selfish ends and was using his position in the I.R.B. to further his own ambitions. Father Patrick Lavelle, the pro-fenian parish priest of Partry, spoke of him venemously in 1874 as having 'managed to live on his wits and the gullibility of others and myself for years'.[1] The fact that Power was the ablest orator in the home rule party after Butt made him all the more odious to his fenian critics; in 1876 and 1877 meetings in Britain at which he was to speak were broken up by gangs of militant fenians. A tough and courageous man, Power was not intimidated, and retained his popularity among fenian home-rulers in Ireland and Britain, while continuing to inspire loathing among the strict observants.[2]

The anomaly of active home-rulers sitting on the supreme council was removed in March 1877, when the council decided to enforce its resolution of 20 August 1876. Egan (then treasurer) and Barry thereupon resigned from the council. Parnell advised Biggar to resign but Biggar refused. Power took the same line, and both men were expelled. Fenian orthodoxy was thus unequivocally asserted. Nevertheless the opportunist policy continued to make headway, and therefore to create dissension among fenians.[3] The authority of the supreme council itself was challenged: the north of England division of the I.R.B. withdrew its allegiance from the council, and James Stephens attempted to recover his former headship of the entire fenian movement.[4] The movement was thus in disarray, and by the end of 1877 counted for far less in Irish politics than the new constitutional movement it had helped to rear. But it remained a force to be reckoned with by home-rulers.

The rise of Parnell and the conduct of his fenian supporters in Ireland and Britain had begun to attract attention among the Irish in America. There the revolutionary movement had shown an early tendency to fission. The original Fenian Brotherhood, founded by John O'Mahony

[1] Fr P. Lavelle to Butt, 12 Nov. 74, quoted in Thornley, *Butt*, p. 184, n. 17.

[2] MacDonagh, *Home rule*, pp 112-14, 117-20, 122-5; *D.P.B.*, i, 75-6, 121, 160-61, 164, 192-3. 282, 312, 374.

[3] S.P.O., Government files memoranda of 1876-80, no. 47 (see C. J. Woods in *I.H.S.*, xviii, no. 70 (Sept. 1972), p. 276); A files no. 589. *S.C.P.*, vi, 372, 373-4, vii, 5, viii, 365, 372-3; D to R. B. O'Brien, 6 Dec. 93 (DP/ZZ); R. B. O'Brien, *Parnell*, i, 156-7; MacDonagh, *Home rule*, p. 125; Healy, *Letters and leaders*, i, 44.

[4] *S.C.P.*, iv, 506-7; and see below, p. 312.

in New York in 1858, had split in 1865 into two main groups over personalities, organisation, and whether it was more important to strike at Britain in Ireland or through an invasion of Canada. In June 1867 a new body, Clan na Gael or the United Brotherhood, was formed to bring the divided fenians together, and in the seventies this became by far the most effective body of its kind in Irish America. Its leading spirits were Dr William Carroll and John Devoy.[1]

William Carroll, a prosperous physician of Philadelphia, had been brought to America from his native Donegal at the age of three by his Ulster presbyterian parents. He served as surgeon-major in the federal armies during the civil war, and afterwards settled in Philadelphia where he remained for the rest of a very long life. He joined the Fenian Brotherhood during the civil war and Clan na Gael soon after its foundation. In 1875 he was elected chairman of the Clan executive, an office in which he continued for five critical years. Tall, handsome, and charming, of quick intelligence and cultivated tastes, he combined a successful medical practice with ardent devotion to the cause of Irish independence; and being unmarried he was the better able to indulge his passion both to serve Ireland and to injure Britain. He was untypical of Irish-American nationalists in being a member of the presbyterian church. His reputation stood high in Clan na Gael, but he was not very formidable as a revolutionary.[2]

The same could not be said of John Devoy. Born at Kill, County Kildare, in 1842, he spent his earliest years in rural Ireland under the influence of a remarkable father. The elder Devoy who, like Martin Davitt, was a 'scholar', contrived to bring up and educate his family on the produce of half an acre and miscellaneous earnings as a labourer. He was one of O'Connell's 'repeal wardens' and an ardent reader of the *Nation* in the exciting days of its beginnings. One of Devoy's earliest recollections was of a crowd of men in corduroy knee breeches, with pipes in their mouths, sitting round the fire while his father read the *Nation* for them—every word of it.[3] In 1849, in the depression resulting from the famine, he moved with his family to Dublin and eventually obtained employment as gate clerk in Watkins's Brewery. In Dublin, John Devoy received a tough but effective schooling and his initiation into politics. He joined the I.R.B. in 1861, ran away from home to the

[1] W. D'Arcy, *The fenian movement in the United States, 1858-1886* (1947), pp 13, 102-3, 372-4, 385-6; T. N. Brown, *Irish-American nationalism* (1966), pp 38-41, 64-5; *D.P.B.*, i, 8-9, 46-7, 52-3; S.P.O., A files, nos 501, 615, 616.

[2] Devoy, IX; *D.P.B.*, i, 125-6 and passim; O'Donnell, *Irish parl. party*, i, 272-9; S.P.O., A files, no. 510.

[3] Devoy, *Recollections*, p. 378; cf. C. Gavan Duffy, *Young Ireland* (final revision, 1896), ii, frontispiece.

French Foreign Legion, and after an intensive year's experience of soldiering in Algeria, returned to Dublin to take an active part in preparations for a rising. From October 1865 he served under Stephens as chief propagandist and organiser of fenianism among Irish soldiers in the British army. Arrested in February 1866, he was tried and sentenced to penal servitude for fifteen years. He was among the fenians amnestied in January 1871. With O'Donovan Rossa and three other released prisoners[1] he went to New York, where he found work as a reporter on the staff of Gordon Bennett's *Herald*, of which he soon became foreign editor. For fifty-seven years he earned his living in journalism in New York, identifying his personal life completely (like Carroll he was unmarried) with the cause to which he had committed himself. He was highly intelligent, a correct and fluent writer, and an omnivorous reader. He was the most clear-headed, realistic, implacable, and incorruptible of all the fenian leaders, and he pursued the ideal of Irish independence throughout his long life with unflagging vigour, indomitable perseverence, and ruthless devotion.[2]

Under the intelligent direction of Devoy and Carroll, Clan na Gael combined thousands of working-class Irish-Americans in a secret organisation which promised effective action against Britain and did achieve some tangible results, most notably the rescue (April 1876) of six fenians imprisoned at Fremantle, Western Australia, by the *Catalpa* expedition from Boston, Massachusetts.[3] The Clan also gained control of the 'skirmishing fund', initiated in December 1875 by another of the fenian exiles, O'Donovan Rossa, for the purpose of conducting uninhibited guerilla warfare against the British Empire. A substantial sum was raised, but Rossa, who succeeded O'Mahony as head centre of the Fenian Brotherhood in February 1877, was incapable of carrying out any serious purpose, however bloodthirsty his announced intentions; and he gave way to Clan na Gael when in March 1877 the board of trustees (Rossa, Carroll, John J. Breslin, and James Reynolds) of the fund (renamed the 'national fund') was augmented by the addition of Devoy and two other Clan members, T. C. Luby and T. F. Bourke. The fund was not at this time used for terrorist activities, but its lurid reputation even among nationalists was a measure of the extremism to which the Clan was in theory at least committed. The orthodox fenian policy of preparing to attack Britain when involved in war seemed now more realistic than ever because of the tension between

[1] They sailed on the S.S. *Cuba*, and were known as the 'Cuba five'; see plate VI.

[2] *D.A.B.*; Devoy, *Recollections*; Desmond Ryan, *The phoenix flame: a study of fenianism and John Devoy* (1937); *D.P.B.*, i, 10, and passim.

[3] Davitt has a lively account of the *Catalpa* rescue in his *Life and progress in Australasia* (1898), pp 464–70.

Britain and Russia in the Balkans from 1875 to 1878. Devoy and his colleagues hoped that Britain would become embroiled with Russia, and to prepare for the eventuality the annual convention of Clan na Gael, meeting at Philadelphia in August 1876, decided to form a joint revolutionary directory, intended to consolidate the Irish revolutionary movement throughout the world under a single effective head. Of its seven members three were to be nominated by the executive committee of Clan na Gael, three by the supreme council of the I.R.B., and one by the executive of the movement in Australia and New Zealand. This decision was ratified by the Clan na Gael camps (branches) in March 1877, and the directory was set up, its Clan members being Carroll, Devoy, and Patrick Mahon.[1] By this time a Clan na Gael delegation, consisting of Carroll, Devoy, General F. F. Millen, and two other Clan leaders, had had an interview at Washington (1 November 1876) with the Russian ambassador, Shiskin, who promised to transmit to St Petersburg their memorial urging that it was to Russia's interest to help Ireland. But he pointed out that there was no public demand in Ireland for separation from Britain, that the Irish appeared to want only a limited measure of self-government within the United Kingdom, and that every public body in Ireland was ready to welcome any visiting representative of the British crown. This view of the Irish situation made a lasting impression on Devoy.

It is thus not surprising that Clan na Gael, though it watched with interest the new activist policy of the Parnellite group, was highly sceptical of its value. Many American fenians were prejudiced against the Parnellites through antipathy to O'Connor Power, who made two visits to the United States (August 1875-March 1876 and October 1876-March 1877) as I.R.B. envoy, despite indignant protests from O'Leary and Kickham. In America he was at the same time engaged in discussions with Clan na Gael about the projected joint revolutionary directory and in propaganda for the home rule movement. The ambiguity of his position was highlighted by a lecture tour he made in America, extending from October to December 1875. Though the tour was organised for him by American fenians, his treatment of Irish politics in his lectures, beginning with that in the Cooper Institute, New York, on 26 October, was construed by Devoy and others as an insidious attack on fenianism. Power was denounced as a renegade by leading fenians at a public meeting in the Cooper Institute on 23 November, and the ensuing recriminations in the *Irish World* were continued by

[1] Brown, *Irish-American nationalism*, pp 65-74; D'Arcy, *Fenian movement*, p. 394. *D.P.B.*, i, 10-12, 105-6, 141-2, 172-82, 198-9, 219-20, 245-6, 270-71; ii, 556-8; Devoy, *Recollections*, pp 251-60, 399-400. P.R.O., H.O. 45/9330/19461B/1-5; S.P.O., A files, 500-07.

a fierce debate in the Dublin *Irishman* (January–March 1876) between Power on the one hand and Rossa and Devoy on the other.[1]

Till the end of 1877 Devoy and Carroll shared the orthodox I.R.B. view of the Power–Biggar deviation and regarded parliamentary obstruction as ridiculous or worse. 'Is the policy of obstruction', wrote Devoy in a letter published in the *Irishman*, 'the highest effort that such men as Mr Parnell are capable of, and do they really believe that the battle of Ireland's rights is to be fought out on the floor of the house of commons?'[2] Carroll, in a private letter to Devoy, was more pointed: 'Mr Parnell is doubtless a man of nerve and spirit as I suppose also is Mr Biggar, but what as reasonable men can they hope for in the end without a military force to back them?'[3] He went on to suggest an appropriate course of action for the home rule party:

> If they will demand in a dignified manner repeal of the union, as you suggest, and abstain from voting at all for or against anything else, as Mitchel suggested, there would be something manly in their attitude which would command the world's respect and would deserve all the support we could give them. Of course they would fail, but it would be with credit and in a dignified manner, and at a proper time they could retire in a body declining thenceforth and forever to attend a British parliament at all.

This was in essence the policy that Gavan Duffy had proposed to the Irish Confederation in February 1848, and it was implicit in the speech Parnell had made at Belfast in September 1877.[4] But Carroll had no hope that it would be acted upon by 'a body of home-rulers sent there [to parliament] by Cardinal Cullen and marshalled by Butt and Co.'[5]

In Clan na Gael, however, as in the I.R.B., the idea of cooperation with Parnell had made its converts, most notable among them James J. O'Kelly, a colleague of Devoy's on the New York *Herald*. He was the son of a blacksmith, and he and Devoy had been boys together in Dublin. They had been sworn into the I.R.B. early in 1861 while attending an Irish class that met in the editorial offices of the *Nation*. Soon afterwards, at the age of sixteen, O'Kelly went to live with an uncle in London, and two years later, following Devoy's example, enlisted in the French Foreign Legion. In 1867 he returned to London just in time to be consulted about the fenian rising, which he argued strongly against, because of the lack of arms. He had much to do with

[1] *D.P.B.*, i, 71-6, 118, 121-2, 128, 149-50, 152-3, 158-61, 164, 192-3, 197, 198, 208, 213; T. W. Moody and Leon Ó Broin, 'The I.R.B. supreme council, 1868-78' in *I.H.S.*, xix, no. 75 (Mar. 1975), p. 319; *I.W.*, 30 Oct., 6 Nov., 4 Dec. 75; *Irishman*, 1, 29 Jan., 12 Feb., 4, 11, 25 Mar. 76; Devoy, VII.

[2] Devoy to editor of *Irishman*, 24 Dec. 77, (*Irishman*, 12 Jan. 78, p. 444); see also Carroll to Devoy, 16 Nov. 77 (dated 1879 in error), *D.P.B.*, i, 280.

[3] Ibid.

[4] Above, pp 38–9, 133.

[5] Carroll to Devoy, as above. Cf. Lyons, *Dillon*, p. 23.

the reorganisation of the I.R.B. in England after the rising, and as a member of the newly formed supreme council was in charge of the arms collecting in which Davitt was so disastrously involved. In 1870 he rejoined the French army to fight against the Prussians. In 1871 he moved to New York to begin a career in journalism that proved no less eventful than his life as a soldier.[1] An old friend of O'Connor Power's,[2] he had seen the advantages, since the beginning of the home rule movement, of a combination between constitutional and revolutionary nationalists. In August 1877, while in Europe as a war correspondent, he had two interviews with Parnell. Writing to Devoy after the first, he described Parnell as a man of promise, who ought to be supported:

He has the idea I held at the starting of the home rule organisation—that is, the creation of a political link between the conservative and radical nationalists. He has many of the qualities of leadership—and time will give him more. He is cool —extremely so, and resolute. With the right kind of support behind him and a band of real nationalists in the house of commons, he would so remould Irish opinion as to clear away many of the stumbling blocks in the way of progressive action.[3]

Devoy was not convinced, nor was Carroll, who was sent to Europe in November 1877 at the expense of the 'national fund' as envoy to the home organisation and to fish in troubled waters against Britain. There was a feeling of great expectancy among American fenians because it seemed that war between Britain and Russia might at any moment be precipitated by the victorious Russian advance on Constantinople, and that, if so, Spain might take a hand against Britain for the purpose of seizing Gibraltar, and Afghanistan be encouraged to revolt against British rule. Carroll, accompanied by O'Kelly, had an interview in Madrid and the Spanish prime minster, who firmly rejected their efforts to embroil Spain in war with Britain (January 1878). This rebuff no doubt caused him to regard Parnell more favourably, and it reinforced the argument for the greatest possible measure of unity among honest nationalists. A meeting with Parnell in January 1878 left Carroll no longer in any doubt that the leader of the obstructionists was an honest nationalist, with whom Clan na Gael could safely do business.[4]

The national feeling among Irish-Americans of which fenianism was an extreme expression was not simply an importation from Ireland. Among the fenian exiles typified by John O'Mahony and John Devoy the 'phoenix flame' never ceased to burn; for them the pursuit of a

[1] *Who was who, 1916–28*; O'Connor, *Parnell movement*, pp 188–93; *S.C.P.*, ix, 421–2, x, 145–71; Devoy, I; Devoy, *Recollections*, pp 275, 333–46; *D.P.B.*, passim; W. O'Brien, *Recollections*, pp 245–7, 296, 397.

[2] Devoy, *Recollections*, p. 283.

[3] O'Kelly to Devoy, 5 Aug. 77 (*D.P.B.*, i, 267–8).

[4] *D.P.B.*, i, 271–99.

free and self-respecting Ireland was a self-justifying end. But for the mass of Irish-Americans, Irish nationalism was a response not so much to the needs of the homeland from which they had come as to their own needs as immigrants in a land in which they were one of the lowest of the economic and social strata. They brought few possessions and few skills with them as they flooded into the industrial cities and towns of America but they brought their catholicism and a wealth of bitter memories rooted in eviction, poverty, and famine. Their nationalism inherited the political doctrines of Tone and Young Ireland, 'but it was from life in America that it derived its most distinctive attitudes: a pervasive sense of inferiority, intense longing for acceptance and respectability, and an acute sensitivity to criticism'.[1] It was a source of solidarity, of pride, and of strength to them in face of the harsh realities of their lives. In taking up the cause of Ireland they were building up their own morale in the most effective way they knew. This element in Irish-American nationalism was not rooted in nostalgia for Ireland, for it flourished no less among second- and third-generation Irishmen than among the immigrants themselves.[2]

Irish-American nationalism assumed a variety of institutional forms of which in the seventies Clan na Gael was only one. Confronted with violent popular prejudice as aliens and catholics—in the fifties there were pitched battles between Irish and nativists in the streets of many an American city—the Irish in America had combined for mutual protection either in open associations such as the Irish Catholic Benevolent Union, or in secret societies, such as the Ancient Order of Hibernians (A.O.H.), that partly served benevolent purposes and partly were inspired by the militant tradition of agrarian secret societies in Ireland. The A.O.H., established in the thirties and the largest of these secret societies, was a catholic freemasonry of the Irish working classes. In the great depression of the seventies, when industrial America was ravaged by unemployment, strikes, and rioting, the A.O.H. was implicated in a ferocious labour struggle in one of the most depressed areas, the anthracite coalfields of Schuylkill county, north-eastern Pennsylvania. A group of Irish miners within the local lodges of the A.O.H., known as 'Molly Maguires', earned a blood-curdling notoriety for themselves and the A.O.H.—and the excommunication of the catholic church—by a campaign of outrage and murder directed against mine bosses and their officials. For several years they terrorised Schuylkill county until they were finally broken up in a series of sensational murder-trials in 1876-7. The Molly Maguires were an example of militant

[1] Brown, *Irish-American nationalism*, p. 23. This book is at once a pioneer work and a classic on its subject.

[2] Ibid., ch. II, passim.

trade-unionism rather than of nationalism, but they help to explain the social conditions in which Irish-American nationalism grew. Clan na Gael, though on friendly terms with the A.O.H., not only held aloof from the Molly Maguires but undertook missionary work in their area.[1] 'We are very glad', Carroll wrote to Devoy on 12 January 1876, 'to get a footing in the coal region, where hitherto all kinds of *so-called* Irish societies have held ground to the exclusion of the only *really Irish* society of which I have any knowledge'.[2] From the Clan's point of view it was better for the morale of victimised Irish workers to contribute to the winning of political independence for Ireland than to throw their energies into class conflict in America.[3]

The Irish-American commitment to Irish independence was not, of course, motivated merely by the immigrants' sense of grievance. Irish-American nationalism had a positive, humanitarian, idealistic aspect derived from consciousness of being American and of sharing American traditions and values. In working for Irish independence the Irish immigrant could feel that he was living up to the ideals of the Declaration of Independence, valid not only for Americans but for all men.[4] 'The cause of America in 1776', the *Irish World* declared, 'is the cause of Ireland in 1876'.[5] The career of Patrick Ford, the editor and proprietor of this paper, illustrates, and was an indispensable part of, the Irish-American situation in the seventies.

Ford's parents had emigrated from Galway to Boston in 1841 when Patrick was only four, and they died young. His youth was a fight against poverty and the anti-Irish and anti-catholic prejudice sweeping over America in the fifties. As he walked the streets of Boston in search of work he was confronted with notices that read: 'no Irish need apply'. He came to see himself as the victim of the 'conditions of poverty and enslavement' that blighted Ireland, and he decided that 'it was necessary for everyone of Irish blood to do all in his power to change that state of things'.[6] He served his apprenticeship as a printer, and began to write for the press in 1855. He worked his way up as a journalist in Boston and Charleston (S.C.) till in 1870 he was able to found in New York a weekly, the *Irish World*, to serve as a medium of communication among the Irish in America. The venture was a remarkable success: the *Irish World* was soon the most widely-read and influential newspaper among Irish-Americans. Catering primarily for the working-classes, it was a pioneer in the techniques of 'yellow journalism', and

[1] W. G. Broehl, *The Molly Maguires* (1965), p. 323. [2] *D.P.B.*, i, 127.
[3] Brown, *Irish-American nationalism*, ch. III, passim; Broehl, *The Molly Maguires*, passim.
[4] Brown, *Irish-American nationalism*, p. 24.
[5] Quoted ibid., p. 31.
[6] Ibid., p. 22.

exuberantly exploited the sensational headline and the lurid illustradition. Ford was an unbridled critic of capitalist society, a champion of the common man, a radical reformer, and a controversialist whose explosive style was combined with the phraseology of the Old Testament. Though a strict catholic his democratic dogmatism and his hostility to the 'priest in politics' brought him frequently into conflict with the clergy: for example he defended the A.O.H. against clerical condemnation at the height of the Molly Maguire crisis. Without being a member of the fenian organisation, he shared the fenian ideal of complete independence for Ireland to be achieved by military action. In his unflagging championship of this and other Irish causes he was a classic instance of the longing in the Irish immigrant to free himself from the stigma of his origin by freeing Ireland from poverty and British domination. Many thousands of working men and women contributed generously to the successive appeals for Irish causes, including the notorious 'skirmishing fund', that he made a feature of the *Irish World*. But his Messianic vision extended far beyond Ireland.[1]

To Ford the sufferings of Ireland and those of the common man in America and everywhere were inseparable. Slave-emancipation, temperance, monetary reform, and above all the abolition of private monopoly of land were causes on which he lavished his overflowing energies. American speculators in western land, railroad companies, and mineowners were incessantly denounced in the *Irish World* in no less extravagant terms than Irish landlords. Land, created only by God, belonged to the whole people and could never justly be appropriated by individuals. The Irish landlords as a class were robbers, with no moral right to the land they misused. They must be expropriated, and their estates divided into small farms among the occupying peasantry. The most effective way of bringing this about was a general strike of the tenant farmers against payment of rent. Just as the great depression had shown that American democracy was a sham unless grounded in economic and social justice, so in Ireland political independence would be illusory if not linked to a just settlement of the land problem. Such doctrine, which Lalor had preached to deaf ears in Ireland thirty years before, had become a commonplace of the *Irish World* by 1877.[2]

Second in influence to the *Irish World* among Irish-Americans, oldest and most respected of Irish-American newspapers, was the *Pilot*, of Boston, edited by John Boyle O'Reilly. Born at Dowth, on the River

[1] *D.N.B.* and *D.A.B.*, Patrick Ford. Brown, 'The origins and character of Irish-American nationalism' in *Review of Politics*, xviii, no. 3 (July 1956), at pp 331-2, 349-50; *Irish-American nationalism*, pp xv-xvi, 22-4. Broehl, *The Molly Maguires*, pp 294-5.

[2] Brown, *Irish-American nationalism*, pp xv-xvi, 49-52, 57-60.

Boyne, in 1844, O'Reilly had worked as a printer and afterwards as a reporter when in 1863 he enlisted in the Tenth Hussars, then stationed in Drogheda. He had already joined the I.R.B., but it was two years before he engaged in making recruits for fenianism among his fellow soldiers, an activity which brought him into contact with John Devoy[1] and earned him a death sentence from a court martial in 1866. The sentence was commuted to penal servitude for twenty years, of which he served a year in England—partly in Dartmoor prison— and another year in Western Australia. He escaped from Bunbury prison, a hundred miles south of Fremantle, on 18 February 1869,[2] and made his way to Boston, Massachusetts. He was only 25 and knew no one in the United States, but quickly made friends and obtained work on the *Pilot*; in July 1876 he had become its editor and later, with John J. Williams, the catholic archbishop of Boston, its joint owner.

As a public figure in Boston O'Reilly fulfilled all that the immigrant Irish most aspired to be—admired, respected, accepted in the American community—while remaining unmistakably Irish-American. 'We can do Ireland more good by our Americanism than by our Irishism', he assured his Irish readers.[3] He combined the roles of poet, editor, publicist, and man of action. He published the first of four volumes of poetry, *Songs from the southern seas*, in 1873; and he also wrote a best-selling novel, *Moondyne* (1880), based on his prison life in Australia. He ceased to be a member of the fenian organisation in 1870, but continued to be actively associated with the Irish revolutionary movement. He was a trusted friend of John Devoy, and was consulted by him and other Clan na Gael leaders on all their major undertakings. He took part in the final fenian raid on Canada in May 1870, criticising it severely as a correspondent for the *Pilot*; and he was deeply involved in the Clan na Gael expedition to Western Australia in 1876 which succeeded in rescuing his former comrades from Fremantle. But it was through his control of the *Pilot* that he made his greatest impact on Irish-America. Like Ford, he not only addressed himself to the immigrant Irish but made his paper the champion of the unprivileged as such, demanding social justice in the name of American liberal and democratic values.

> What is the good of having a republic unless the mass of the people are better off than in a monarchy? Does not a real republic mean that all men have an equal chance and not millions born to suffering and poverty?[4]

[1] Above, p. 000.

[2] D has a chapter on O'Reilly and his escape from Bunbury in *Life and progress in Australasia*, pp 455–63.

[3] Quoted in W. V. Shannon, *The American Irish* (1963), p. 135.

[4] Quoted in Brown, *Irish-American nationalism*, p. 53.

But in spirit and style the editor of the *Pilot* was very different from the editor of the *Irish World*—O'Reilly measured and realistic, Ford reckless and visionary; O'Reilly pragmatic and tolerant, Ford doctrinaire and evangelising. While both men were catholics, Ford's attitude to the clergy was uninhibited by comparison with that of O'Reilly, with an archbishop as partner in the ownership of his paper. Both men were sincere and earnest reformers and both, on the question of Irish independence, were also revolutionaries, but whereas Ford preached violence and revenge against England, O'Reilly's attitude to the national enemy was that of the professional soldier. If Ford reached a wider public, O'Reilly appealed to the more thoughtful and respectable among Irish-Americans, and was read by American, as well as Irish, Bostonians.[1]

So when Davitt was released from prison at the end of 1877 the political situation was altogether different from that of 1870. The foundation and growth of the home rule movement offered to nationalists of various persuasions the opportunity of working for a measure of self-government on the only level on which action was feasible. To revolutionary nationalists, weary of the endless frustration of preparing to fight Britain in a future indefinitely postponed, this new venture in constitutional nationalism made a strong appeal. For a time it had enjoyed at least the friendly neutrality of the I.R.B. supreme council, and continued to receive fenian support after this official attitude was reversed in protest against the failure of Butt's policy to achieve results. The rise of Parnell and his challenge to Butt's leadership opened up exciting possibilities of a new combination of nationalist energies. Parnell's parliamentary style and strategy gave constitutional action a revolutionary look, and earned him a following among fenians, especially in Britain. In Irish-America the sense of commitment to Irish independence was stronger than it had ever been, and revolutionary nationalists, reorganised and reactivated, were keenly aware of the new political developments at home. Eager for military action but baffled by unfavourable circumstances, they were hotly debating whether they could come to some kind of working arrangement with Parnell.

While home rule was the issue that made most noise, what mattered most to most people in Ireland was the land question, which was entering a critical phase when Davitt found himself again at large.

[1] Ibid., pp xiv, 52-3, 55, 56; *D.N.B.* and *D.A.B.*, John Boyle O'Reilly; *D.P.B.*, i, 14-15, 41, 43-4, and passim.

V

Penal servitude, 1870–77

BEFORE his trial began on 15 July 1870, Davitt had already spent over two months in prison—a week-end in Paddington police station (14–16 May),[1] a month in the Clerkenwell House of Detention (16 May–14 June),[2] and a month in Newgate prison.[3] After his trial, he was removed from Newgate to Millbank Penitentiary on 29 July, and from Millbank to Dartmoor prison on 25 May 1871.[4] There he remained, with a month's interval at Portsmouth prison (14 June–15 July 1872),[5] till 19 December 1877, when he was released on ticket of leave.[6] He was thus continuously a prisoner for seven years and seven months—one-eighth of his entire life.

The penal servitude system, as regulated by acts of 1853, 1857, and 1864,[7] divided a convict's sentence into three stages: (i) a period of solitary confinement, in Millbank or Pentonville, supposed to last nine months; (ii) the main part of the sentence, spent in a 'public works prison'—Borstal, Chatham, Dartmoor, Portland, or Portsmouth—in which the convicts slept and had their meals in separate cells but worked in association; (iii) a period of release on licence or ticket of leave. During the first stage the convicts only met one another at the daily exercise-hour and when attending chapel, and then under a rule of strict silence. For the rest, they worked in their cells all day on bag-making, weaving, oakum-picking and the like, with intervals for eating and for reading what was officially described as 'religious and educational books, ... with a limited number of works of general literature' known as 'library books'. In the public-works prison the convicts were employed in gangs, chiefly on heavy outdoor labour such as building,

[1] *The Times*, 17 May 70, p. 5.
[2] Ibid., 18 May, p. 7, 21 May, p. 11, 30 May, p. 12, 3 June, p. 7, 8 June, p. 5, 15 June, p. 11.
[3] Ibid., 15 June, p. 11; P.R.O., H.O. 24/11/6721.
[4] Ibid.
[5] *F.J.*, 3 Sept. 72, p. 6.
[6] P.R.O., H.O. 144/5/17869/31; Cashman, p. 43.
[7] 16 & 17 Vict., c. 99; 20 & 21 Vict., c. 3; 27 & 28 Vict., c. 47.

excavating, stone-cutting, brick-making, and farming; also, indoors, at such trades as tailoring, shoe-making, carpentering, and smithing. There were arrangements for exercise (for those engaged on indoor work and, on Sundays, for all convicts), church attendance, and reading, as in the solitary confinement stage. All communication between convicts, except what was indispensable to their work, was strictly forbidden. Convicts were classified not according to the nature of their crimes but according to the time they had served and their conduct in prison. They were graded into five classes—probation, third, second, first, and special—promotion from one class to another depending on marks earned for good conduct and industry, qualified by the rule that the minimum period for probation, third class, and second class was one year each, and that the special class could only be entered after exemplary conduct in the first class and within one year of discharge from prison. No marks could be earned during solitary confinement, and prisoners on light labour were penalised by not being allowed to earn marks at the full rate. A convict who daily obtained the maximum mark would reach the first class in three years and would become entitled to the maximum period of remission of his sentence, i.e. one-fourth of the term due to be spent on public works; a convict whose average daily mark did not exceed seventy-five per cent of the maximum earned no remission and had to serve the full sentence in prison. Promotion entitled the prisoner to increasing privileges: more frequent letters, more frequent and longer visits from relatives and friends, an improved rate of earning a gratuity, and more Sunday exercise. Convicts were allowed to write one letter on reception at Millbank or Pentonville and another on reception at a public-works prison. They might receive and write one letter after six months in the probation class, another on reaching the third class, and one thereafter at intervals of six, four, three, and two months according to class; a visit of twenty minutes' duration (increased to thirty minutes in the first and special classes) was allowed at similar intervals. The maximum gratuity that first-class convicts might earn was £3, and those who attained the special class might earn an additional sum of £3, the whole being payable in instalments on and after their discharge.[1]

Prison life inevitably presents different and often contradictory aspects to the prisoner and the prison authorities. Of Davitt's prison treatment as seen by himself there is contemporary evidence in his letters, especially those smuggled out of Dartmoor in 1872 and in 1875-7,[2] but

[1] *Kimberley comm. rep.*, i, pp vii-xx; iii, 1138-40.

[2] All his surviving prison letters are in DP/A, except two, for which see below, pp 152, 157 n. 7.

the fullest information is retrospective: an account of his prison experiences given in a speech to an amnesty demonstration in St James's Hall, London, on 9 March 1878,[1] and in expanded form in a pamphlet published before 6 May;[2] the testimony that he gave under oath on 20 June before a commission of inquiry, under the chairmanship of Earl Kimberley, into the working of the penal servitude acts;[3] and incidental references in a book resulting from his second term in penal servitude, published in 1885.[4] On the side of the government and of the prison authorities there are home office records,[5] contemporary statements made in the house of commons, and the testimony of prison officials before the Kimberley commission.[6] Partly these two types of evidence complement, and partly they contradict, each other.

Davitt's story as told by himself begins with his initiation into the rigours of solitary confinement during the two months that preceded his trial. Though legally presumed to be innocent prior to his conviction on 18 July, his punishment in fact began from the day of his arrest.[7] At the outset he spent a sleepless week-end in the semi-darkness of a cell at Paddington that had neither bed nor bedding. At Clerkenwell he was given a bed—'a dirty blanket and rug on a bare unmattressed hammock'—and was permitted to buy his own food. Solitary confinement was relieved only by one hour of exercise daily and by interviews with his solicitor's clerk. He found conditions more tolerable at Newgate, then used as a prison only during the sessions of the central criminal court;[8] four days after his removal there on 14 June he assured his parents that he was being very considerately treated and had nothing to complain of.[9]

Millbank prison, in which Davitt began the probation stage of his sentence on 29 July, stood on the north bank of the Thames, close to Westminster Abbey and the Houses of Parliament. It had been founded by parliament in 1811-16 as a model prison where criminals would be reformed by constant work in solitude and by religious instruction.[10] Its tomb-like silence, the loneliness and bleakness of the cells, and the grinding monotony of the prisoners' existence were the more terrible

[1] DP/U. [2] Reprinted with omissions in Cashman, pp 23-43. See below, pp 199-200.

[3] *Kimberley comm. rep.*, ii, 515-45. [4] *Leaves from a prison diary.*

[5] There are records in Dartmoor prison itself from 1852, but nothing appears to have survived for the period of Davitt's imprisonment.

[6] *Kimberley comm. rep.*, ii, 243-4, 676-87; iii, 712, 747-8, 754-6, 761, 882-3.

[7] Cf. Wilfrid Macartney, *Walls have mouths* (1936), pp 31-2.

[8] Arthur Griffiths, *The chronicles of Newgate* (1884), ii, 502-3.

[9] D to his father and mother, 18 June 70. Speech in St James's Hall, London, 9 Mar. 78 (DP/U); Cashman, pp 23-6.

[10] Arthur Griffiths, *Memorials of Millbank* (new ed., 1884), ch. I-II.

to Davitt by contrast with the many-voiced roar of London surging unseen outside the prison walls. Time seemed to pass all the more slowly as he listened to the strokes of Big Ben reverberating every fifteen minutes through the prison. 'The chant of Westminster clock will ever haunt my memory, and recall that period of my imprisonment when I first had to implore divine providence to preserve my reason.'[1] Once as he sought to kill the deadly monotony of his life he found the name 'John Devoy' on the back of his cell-door, where it had been scratched by a fenian predecessor who was yet to play an important part in the history of fenianism and of Davitt's own later career.[2] His cell at Millbank was relatively large—nine or ten feet long by about eight wide—and was furnished with a plank bed, bucket, wooden platter and spoon, pint tin and chamber pot. The bucket, fitted with a lid, served the dual purpose of water-holder and seat, fourteen inches high, on which he sat for ten hours a day, picking oakum as best he might with his solitary left hand. The stone-floored cell was so cold in winter that prisoners became numb as they sat at work, and pacing the cells was prohibited. Bedding was dirty and quite inadequate in winter. A bath was allowed once a fortnight, but the same water had often to serve for several prisoners. Davitt complained of insufficient exercise, and after eight months the prison doctor ordered him an extra half-hour each day. An application for extra food, on the ground that he was losing weight, was refused. The standard rations for a convict were as follows: for breakfast, eight ounces of bread and three-quarters of a pint of cocoa; for dinner, on weekdays, four ounces of meat on four days, one pint of soup on one day, and one pound of suet pudding on one other day, together with six ounces of bread and one pound of potatoes; for Sunday dinner, twelve ounces of bread, four ounces of cheese, and one pint of water; for supper, six ounces of bread and one pint of gruel. On such a stodgy diet, and compelled to lead so sedentary a life, Davitt was not likely to lose weight, and according to the prison records he was 3½ pounds heavier on leaving Millbank (150½ lb) than on entering it (147 lb).[3]

For reading matter Davitt was expected to content himself with four small religious books suitable for children, two elementary school books, and 'library books' with such titles as *Naughty Fanny* and *Grandmother Betty* only one of which was allowed every fortnight. This puerile fare he owed to his being a catholic: solid Victorian serials

[1] Cashman, p. 29.

[2] *Defence*, p. 96; see above, pp 135–6.

[3] Cashman, pp 26–30; *Return of the various diets . . . which have been in use at Millbank . . . since 1870 inclusive,* H.C. 1877 (204), lxix, 719; *Kimberley comm. rep.*, ii, 515–20.

such as *Good Words*, *Leisure Hours*, and *Sunday at Home*, which were the stand-by of protestant prisoners, were forbidden to catholics by their chaplains—and this, Davitt believed, was a reason why it often happened that men who were catholics during a first term of imprisonment became protestants during a second. He twice complained to the priest at Millbank about the unsuitability of the books issued to him, but to no effect. Both at Millbank and Dartmoor he had the impression that the catholic chaplain avoided him as a fenian; and he sent for the chaplain only four or five times during his entire imprisonment. His conversation during ten months at Millbank—with warders, chaplains and, surreptiously, with other prisoners— would not, he asserts, have taken twenty minutes to repeat. Twice he applied for a visit, first from Martin Haran of Haslingden, his 'most intimate friend', and then from Mrs Ellen Forrester. Both applications were refused without any reason being given, though, on the second occasion, the governor read to Davitt an order from the home secretary forbidding Mrs Forrester to see him.[1] When his old school-teacher at Haslingden, Miss Mary Gorman, wrote to the governor asking 'whether there is any chance of a visit or a letter from Michael Davitt', the governor replied that Davitt was entitled to a visit but that all visits were then disallowed 'on account of the smallpox'.[2]

Davitt's departure from Millbank was marked by what he felt to be a refinement of cruelty. On 25 May 1871, a warder came to his cell with the electrifying news that his discharge had arrived from the home office and that he was to be released the same evening or the following morning. Davitt never thought of doubting that he had been amnestied. Some time later he was conducted to the prison entrance, to find that he was to be discharged—to Dartmoor.[3]

Dartmoor, a wild, granite upland in south Devon, is a region of great natural beauty, with its green hills and heathery bogs, its rocky tors, leafy glens, and tumbling streams, but what counted most with the inmates of its great prison was the severity of the climate during most of the year. The prison originated in 1806 as a prisoner-of-war camp for French, American, and other soldiers and sailors captured by Britain in the Napoleonic wars. At Princetown, about fifteen miles from Plymouth and nearly 1400 feet above sea level, some 10,000 prisoners of war were at one time confined in a cluster of three-storey stone buildings constructed for the purpose and surrounded by a double line of high walls. This war-prison was closed down at the peace in 1815, having

[1] *Kimberley comm. rep.*, ii, 517-18, 519, 520-21, 535-6, 590-91; Cashman, p. 29.
[2] Mary Gorman to governor of Millbank, 6 Mar. 71, (DP/D5); governor to Mary Gorman, 8 Mar. (DP/D5).
[3] Speech in St James's Hall, 9 Mar. 78 (DP/U); *Prison life*, pp 12-13.

earned an evil reputation for the treatment of the prisoners, who had twice risen in open revolt. The buildings were largely disused till 1850, when they were restored and adapted to the purpose of a convict settlement: in each block the floors were removed and a free-standing stack of back-to-back cells was erected in the middle of the hall thus formed. In Davitt's time these reconstructed buildings housed about 1000 convicts. The site was regarded as exceptionally suitable for a large prison because of its isolation and its invigorating climate. It was usual to send convicts to Dartmoor who, on account of disease or injury, were looked upon as unfit for the heavier labour required at other public-works prisons. But the theory that Dartmoor was suitable for convicts suffering from pulmonary ailments was contradicted by the medical officer of the prison in his report for 1871: while it was true, he wrote, that its highly ozonised air might have a curative effect on consumptive or bronchitic prisoners during a warm summer, this was completely nullified by the cold and damp that prevailed during eight months of the year. The fact was that the greatest single cause of death among prisoners was tuberculosis.[1]

Davitt began his life in 'The Moor' by being located in the punishment cells ('chokey'). This was a security measure, for there was no charge of misconduct against him. The punishment cells were larger and better ventilated than the ordinary cells, but he found it nearly impossible to sleep owing to the howling of refractory convicts undergoing punishment on bread and water. After a week he obtained a transfer to the block known as 'No. 2 Prison', which remained his base for the next five years. Here the cells were corrugated-iron cages, seven feet long, four feet wide, and about seven feet high, with floors and roofs of slate. They were arranged on four landings each containing forty-two cells placed back-to-back. As the cells had no direct access to daylight or the open air, the light in them was bad and the ventilation worse. Light was admitted to each cell from the adjoining hall through two plates of thick glass, eighteen inches long by six inches wide, and air by an opening of two or three inches at the bottom of the door and by small holes at the top of the cell. Under favourable conditions reading was difficult, and on the two upper landings it became impossible in foggy weather, which was all too common in winter. When the convicts were in their cells—as they were continuously from 7.45 p.m. to 6.45 a.m. and at other times—the atmosphere,

[1] W. F. V. Harris, *Dartmoor prison, past and present* (Plymouth, [c. 1876]), pp 1-45. (Harris had been deputy governor of Dartmoor and was governor during the last year and a half of Davitt's imprisonment there.) Extracts from the medical officer's report on Dartmoor prison, in *Report of the directors of convict prisons . . . for the year 1871,* pp 307-9 [C 449], H.C. 1871, xxxi, 725-7.

in contrast with that of the wind-swept moor outside, soon became very foul, and was made far worse by the stench from tubs in which the excrement of 168 men was accumulated on each landing for use as manure—at weekends these tubs were not emptied from Saturday night to Monday morning. On the fourth landing there were no air holes at the top of the cells, and here the air became so stifling that men could only breathe with difficulty: Davitt often found it necessary to kneel with his mouth to the opening under the door to suck in a little air. In being assigned to No. 2 Prison, he was unfortunate: a new block, 'No. 5 Prison', in which conditions were much better, was built by convict labour soon after his arrival, but he was located there for only the few weeks prior to his discharge.[1]

The work at Dartmoor was incomparably more strenuous than at Millbank, but the food-ration differed only in the addition of four ounces of bread a day, which was partly offset by a deduction of one ounce of meat a week. The inadequacy of this ration was illustrated by the prevalence of candle-eating, which was a punishable offence. The quality of the food was the worst and the cooking the filthiest that Davitt had known since his arrest. It was not uncommon to find cockroaches in soup or bread; but men ravenous with hunger soon learnt not to be squeamish.[2]

Davitt's first employment was on stone-breaking, a week of which made his one hand too blistered to continue. He was then attached to one of the gangs engaged in hauling carts about the prison, but after a few months the harness which he wore injured the stump of his right arm, so he was put back to stone-breaking (October 1871). This was his occupation during his first winter at Dartmoor (1871–2). In April 1872 he was given indoor work—pounding bones for manure—a task he loathed on account of the stench of the putrifying bones, aggravated by the proximity of the bone-shed to the prison cess-pool, where the human soil of the entire prison was collected before being used as a fertiliser on the surrounding fields. The stench was at its worst in hot weather, as he had reason to know. He was kept at bone-breaking from April to the following September, with an interval of just over a month (14 June–15 July) at Portsmouth prison. The Portsmouth episode is inexplicable. Davitt had apparently no inkling of why he was transferred to Portsmouth, and the only reason he could think of for his early return to Dartmoor was that, in a letter to his mother,[3] he spoke of Portsmouth as being an improvement on the prison he had left. He

[1] *Prison life*, p. 17; Cashman, pp 31–3; *Kimberley comm. rep.*, ii, 521–4, 676–7; Harris, *Dartmoor prison*, p. 45.

[2] Cashman, p. 33; *Kimberley comm. rep.*, ii, 524–7, 677–80.

[3] D to his mother, 12 July 72.

travelled to Portsmouth in a party of 30 convicts chained together by the wrist, and no concession was made to his being one-armed; on the return journey he was handcuffed to a madman. It was soon after this that he succeeded in conveying the first news of his condition to the public: a letter addressed to 'My dear M.', and dated 1 August 1872, was smuggled out of Dartmoor by a discharged prisoner and published in several Irish and English newspapers, for which it was evidently intended.[1] Though no formal action was taken against Davitt for this breach of discipline, he was made to smart for it by being forcibly deprived of the one privilege allowed to treason-felony convicts, that of retaining their beards.[2]

From July 1872 he was successively employed at bone-breaking, cart-hauling, work as a mason's labourer, and stone-breaking. He continued at stone-breaking till August 1876. For three long Dartmoor winters he suffered intensely from the icy north-east winds that swept through the prison yard where he worked. He repeatedly applied to the governor for indoor occupation during the winter, but in vain. Then, quite unexpectedly, in August 1876 he was transferred to the prison wash-house. This was done not as a concession but as a precaution against an attempt which, it was believed, might be made by Davitt's friends to repeat the recent exploit of Clan na Gael in rescuing six fenian convicts from Fremantle prison, Western Australia (April 1876).[3] The wash-house was in a secure place in the centre of the prison; there Davitt was under close surveillance as he worked interminably at the wringing-machine. This was the hardest labour of all, but at least he was saved from the rigours of another Dartmoor winter out of doors. And because of the excessive sweating caused by work in the wash-house he also gained the advantage of a bath once a week, instead of only once a fortnight. But, as hitherto, he more often than not had to bath in water already used by other prisoners. At the same time he and another fenian, Thomas Chambers, were moved from the ordinary to the punishment cells, where they remained from 16 August 1876 to 9 November 1877. On the door of one of these cells Davitt found the legend—'J. B. O'R., 20 yrs'—written nine years before by the fenian, John Boyle O'Reilly.[4] While located in the punishment cells, Davitt seldom had an unbroken night's sleep. Every hour a warder shone a lamp on him through an iron trap-door, which he noisely threw open and slammed-to again with no more regard for the prisoner inside than

[1] *F.J.*, 3 Sept., p. 6; *Nation*, 7 Sept., pp 563-4; *Irishman*, 7 Sept., pp 147, 154; *Universe*, 7 Sept.; *Accrington Times*, 7 Sept., p. 5. 'M.' was probably Martin Haran.

[2] Cashman, pp 33-5, 40-42; *Kimberley comm. rep.*, ii, 522, 527-8, 539, 676-7.

[3] Above, p. 136. [4] Davitt, *Life and progress in Australasia*, p. 457; above pp 142-5.

if he had been a wild beast. And all this on top of the intermittent uproar from maniacs and prisoners on bread-and-water diet. Every twelve days Davitt was shifted to a new cell and in consequence had to clean up the mess his predecessor usually left behind.[1]

It was not only during his last sixteen months in Dartmoor that Davitt felt himself to be under exceptionally close surveillance; he was always more strictly watched than anyone else. Every prisoner was searched four times a day, and was liable, at the discretion of a warder, to be stripped from time to time and have his entire body and his clothes minutely examined. Davitt alleged that he was never exempt from this latter kind of searching, which he fiercely resented, especially at the hands of a malicious warder. During his first winter in Dartmoor, on returning dripping wet to his cell for dinner he frequently found that the cell had been rummaged and his bed-clothes strewn over the damp floor, so that he had to spend his dinner hour in restoring order. And throughout his imprisonment, at Dartmoor as at Millbank, he experienced an isolation more extreme than that of ordinary convicts. One of the rewards of good conduct most coveted by prisoners was the right to receive visits from friends at prescribed intervals. Davitt was generally rated as a good-conduct prisoner, yet repeated applications for permission to visit him, made by himself and by friends outside, were all refused. Again, whereas ordinary convicts were allowed to choose a companion from the same ward to exercise with on Sundays, he was forbidden to choose the one man whose company would have been congenial—Thomas Chambers, a fellow Irishman and fenian. Yet another continuing grievance was that whereas transfers from one form of work to another at the request of prisoners were a matter of routine, all Davitt's applications for more suitable employment were refused: either he was given work that called for the use of both arms, or work such as bone-breaking indoors in summer and stone-breaking outdoors in winter that seemed calculated to strain his physical endurance to the limit.[2]

Reviewing his prison experience as a whole, Davitt had no doubt that his physical health had been permanently injured. He considered the diet at Dartmoor to be quite inadequate for any man of his size, doing the work he was required to do; and he claimed that he lost over two stone in weight (from 151½ to 122 lb) during his last sixteen months, owing to the exertions he had to make in the wash-house. He also believed that the cumulative effect of too hard and unsuitable

[1] Cashman, pp 35–7; *Prison life,* pp 30–32; *Kimberley comm. rep.*, ii, 528–9, 532, 543, 676–7.

[2] Cashman, pp 37–8, 39–40, 42–3; *Kimberley comm. rep.*, ii, 520–21, 530–32, 535, 541–3.

work, of insufficient food, of exposure out of doors and lack of ventilation indoors, was to bring on a bronchial and heart condition. While at Portsmouth prison in 1872 he had an attack of what he took to be bronchitis or quinsy, but the assistant doctor who examined him, while admitting that there was some inflammation in his throat, reported him for 'falling out' without sufficient reason. In the winter of 1872–3, when engaged in stone-breaking, he felt symptoms of bronchitis and heart disease, but the doctor could find no trace of either. There seems to be no independent evidence of heart disease, but Davitt had had bronchitis before his imprisonment and some pulmonary weakness was undoubtedly present when he emerged from Dartmoor.[1]

The prison doctor played a critical role in the prison system: he had the power of deciding whether prisoners were malingering or were genuinely ill, whether they should be admitted to the infirmary or merely given medicine in their cells, whether they should be recognised as fit only for light labour, whether they were fit to undergo punishment on bread and water diet, and whether and at what point, when on this diet, they were unable to endure further punishment. It was inevitable that prisoners should complain of his professional conduct and competence, and Davitt shared the prevalent view. He instanced the case of a prisoner whom he often noticed 'falling out' to see the doctor but who was never admitted to the infirmary; one morning he saw this man drop dead at work, apparently from heart failure. Another prisoner whose disease similarly went undetected had often complained to the doctor of some internal trouble, without obtaining any relief, when he too died suddenly, from 'ossification of the lungs'. A third prisoner, apparently in the best of health, died under an operation for stricture, because, it was generally believed, of the unskilful manner in which he was treated. The work of examining convicts reporting sick devolved mainly on the assistant-surgeon, who was usually inexperienced and had the reputation of doing his work perfunctorily. When convicts died through disease or accident (and there were four fatal accidents during the building of the new block), inquests were held before what was called 'the standing jury', consisting of tradesmen and others dependent on the prison, and, so far as Davitt could learn, no intelligent convict was ever called on to give evidence.[2]

Davitt believed that he was treated worse than ordinary criminals, whereas, being a political prisoner, he felt entitled to be treated better. The distinction between political and ordinary crime, though unknown

[1] Cashman, pp 34–7; *Kimberley comm. rep.*, ii, 526–7, 538–9; below, pp 469, 476, 478.
[2] *Kimberley comm. rep.*, ii. 536–9, 540–41; Cashman, pp 35–6.

to the law, was in principle recognised by public opinion in Britain no less than in Ireland, but in practice Irish political prisoners who had been found guilty of attempting to overthrow British authority were, naturally, not regarded by the British public with the sympathy it was prepared to extend to rebels against oppressive foreign governments. Irish allegations of exceptional severity towards fenians in English convict prisons became so insistent that in May 1867 the home secretary appointed a commission of inquiry. The report of the commissioners dismissed these charges as 'simple falsehoods', the invention of a few of the most turbulent of the fenian prisoners aided by their friends outside; the prisoners were better fed, better housed and cared for, and had lighter work, than the bulk of the labouring classes in the three kingdoms. Penal servitude, the commissioners admitted, was a terrible punishment, but it was intended to be so.[1] This did not silence the charges of ill-treatment of fenian prisoners. A second commission of inquiry, appointed by the home secretary in May 1870 with the earl of Devon as chairman, reported favourably on the general administration of convict prisoners and confirmed its predecessor's conclusion that there was no justification for charges of exceptional harshness towards political prisoners as a class, but made a number of important reservations. On the treatment of prisoners generally the report expressed some criticism of the prison diet, the qualifications of prison medical officers, the medical care of prisoners, the lighting and ventilation of cells, sanitary arrangements, the nature of the work required from prisoners, and the system of discipline—criticism that all helps to substantiate Davitt's own account of life in prison. As to political prisoners the tone of the report was remarkably liberal: they were prisoners convicted of offences that in their own view implied no moral stigma, and it was inevitable that they should resent the degrading though ordinary incidents of convict life with peculiar impatience. But the commissioners did find and condemn particular cases of ill-treatment, especially that of O'Donovan Rossa.[2] They observed that, in some convict prisons (not Dartmoor), the authorities did relax the rules in favour of political prisoners, and they concluded by recommending that such prisoners should be segregated from the general body of convicts and located in a detached part of some convict prison.[3] This proposal was not adopted, but from 1870 onwards the Devon commission's report could be quoted in favour of preferential

[1] *Report of the commissioners on the treatment of the treason-felony convicts in the English convict prisons,* pp 1-26 [3880], H.C. 1867, xxv, 673-98. [2] See below, pp 176, 178.

[3] *Report of the commissioners appointed to inquire into the treatment of treason-felony convicts in English prisons*, pp 1-60 [C 319], H.C. 1871, xxxii.

treatment for political prisoners. Gladstone, who twenty years before had stirred the conscience of Europe by his exposure of the sufferings of political prisoners in Naples,[1] now spoke, with reference to fenian prisoners, of 'the distinction we found it our duty to draw between criminality of a general character and those political offences which, according to modern sentiment, were justly treated with comparative leniency'.[2] It was in virtue of this distinction that he amnestied most of the fenian prisoners in March 1869 and January 1871.[3] These he admitted to be 'political prisoners', while firmly denying that the remainder who were not released could be so regarded.[4]

Whereas Davitt believed that he was victimised for being a political prisoner, the official view was that he was neither a political prisoner nor victimised. Internal evidence shows that the attitude of the home office towards Davitt and Wilson was clearly defined at the outset. In April 1871 the directors of convict prisons asked the home office whether these two prisoners, having now completed their nine months in solitary confinement, were to be kept apart from ordinary convicts and to receive special treatment on being transferred to public-works prisons. The home office decided that they were to be treated in the same way as any other convicts.[5] This ruling appears to have been consistently applied with the qualification that, being regarded by the home office as a particularly dangerous conspirator, Davitt was subjected to special precautions to prevent him from escaping or having any communications with former confederates. It is easy to understand, in the light of this, why he was not allowed to exercise with Chambers. His transfer to the prison wash-house and the punishment cells in August 1876 was, as he was aware at the time, a security measure.[6] And the prohibition on visits was due to the reputation of the proposed visitors.

Ellen Forrester was refused permission to visit him in Millbank because the home office was advised by the director of convict prisons that she was 'a notorious fenian-sympathiser'.[7] It was probably for the same reason that Martin Haran was turned down.[8] Applications to visit Davitt in Dartmoor, made by John O'Connor Power in October 1871 and September 1874, were refused by the home office because Power

[1] Gladstone, *Letters to Lord Aberdeen* (1851); John Morley, *Life of Gladstone* (1903), i, 389-401.

[2] Gladstone to J. F. Maguire M.P., 12 Oct. 72, in *Nation,* 19 Oct., p. 660.

[3] Above, p. 121.

[4] *Nation,* 31 Aug., pp 545, 547; 7 Sept., p. 561; 21 Sept., pp 593, 597; P.R.O., H.O. 45/9331D/6.

[5] P.R.O., H.O. 144/5/17869/2.

[6] *Kimberley comm. rep.,* ii, 520, 541-3, 676, 681-2.

[7] P.R.O., H.O. 144/5/17869/1; above, pp 48, 149. [8] Above, pp 44, 149.

was suspected of holding an important position in the fenian organisation.[1] 'Convicts are not allowed', the director of convict prisons primly reminded the home office, 'to receive visits and keep up communications with those who are suspected of being connected with them in crime'.[2] This was no denial of Davitt's right to receive visits from qualified persons, but all his immediate relatives were in America, and it was he himself who dissuaded his mother from making the Atlantic crossing to see him. It is, however, surprising that O'Connor Power was refused permission to visit him in 1874, for Power was now M.P. and he was allowed to visit a fenian prisoner, James Clancy, at Portsmouth.[3] He renewed his efforts to see Davitt, and in June 1876, thanks probably to the pressure for amnesty then being exerted by himself and other home rule members in the house of commons, he was informed that he might visit Davitt and other fenians at the regulation times if they wished to be visited by him.[4] From this point onwards nearly all the fenian prisoners received visits from political friends.[5] That Davitt did not do so appears to have been his own choice. Referring in April 1877 to other fenian prisoners who were expecting visits he wrote in one of his smuggled letters: 'I don't care for a visit myself'.[6] Seven months later he had changed his mind, and his last letter from Dartmoor was to John Ryan, of Chelsea, from whom he requested a visit. Ryan was active in the fenian movement, and Davitt refers to him as an old and intimate friend.[7] The necessary visiting order appears to have been issued, for Davitt thought that Ryan had arrived when on 19 December 1877 he was summoned from the prison wash-house to the governor's office to learn that he was to be released.[8]

The publicity given to Davitt's letter of 1 August 1872 led to an inquiry by H. A. Bruce, then home secretary, into Davitt's allegation of harshness and cruelty. On the basis of reports from the governors of Millbank and Dartmoor, Bruce came to the conclusion that some of Davitt's statements either exaggerated or distorted the occurrences of which he complained, while others related 'to incidents which are only the ordinary lot of prisoners who have been convicted of grave crimes against the laws of their country'. Furthermore, Bruce brought before the cabinet the question whether Davitt's offence was such as to justify any more lenient treatment than that of ordinary convicts. The cabinet decided in the negative, on the ground that the offence was of 'the gravest character' and was aggravated by the fact that Davitt

[1] P.R.O., H.O. 144/5/17869/3, 4, 8. [2] P.R.O., H.O. 144/5/17869/4 (3 Jan.).
[3] P.R.O., H.O. 144/5/17869/8; *Irishman*, 3 Oct. 74, p. 215; 20 Mar. 75, p. 599.
[4] P.R.O., H.O. 45/9329/19461/168, 171, 173. [5] *Irishman*, 3 June 76–29 Dec. 77.
[6] D to Sabina Davitt, 15 Apr. [7] D to John Ryan, 23 Nov. (DP/04). [8] Cashman, p. 43.

and Wilson were caught distributing arms for insurrectionary purposes after an amnesty had been granted to many of the fenians imprisoned for complicity in the late insurrection.[1] In brief, Davitt was treated no worse than ordinary convicts and had no reasonable claim to be treated better.

These decisions found their way into the press in October 1872. A month later the *Flag of Ireland* published allegations of continued ill-treatment of Davitt and other prisoners,[2] which the home office referred to the governor of Dartmoor. His confidential report, dated 20 December, elucidates a number of particular points. Davitt had been assigned to stone-breaking because, having only one arm, he was classed with the 'light labour' prisoners. It was at his own request that he was transferred to one of the haulage gangs, as he preferred this work to sitting still breaking stones. There was no truth in the allegation that he had protested against being so employed and that in consequence he had been punished by solitary confinement. There was no shadow of foundation for the statement that his single arm had been heavily ironed and fastened to his leg for several days. On the contrary, since his admission to Dartmoor the worst punishment he had had was solitary confinement on two occasions, of one day each—first, for writing in his cell with a pencil and eating the paper when discovered (1 January 1872), and, second, for refusing to have his beard clipped and for insolence (26 August 1872). Apart from this, he had been merely cautioned for offences that, in another prisoner, would have been severely dealt with—having a piece of looking-glass concealed in his cell, leaving the ranks without permission, seeing the assistant surgeon off parade unnecessarily, giving bread to another prisoner (these last two offences committed at Portsmouth), refusing to have his whiskers and moustache clipped, having a piece of white paper concealed on his person. He had not been deprived of any privileges. He had written all the letters to which he was entitled. He was not searched more rigorously than other prisoners and he had never made any complaint on this score.[3]

All this is in general agreement with the references to Davitt in the quarterly returns from the governor of Dartmoor of the condition and behaviour of convicts from 30 June 1871 to 31 March 1876, when the series ends.[4] In 13 out of 20 quarters he is rated as 'invalid' or 'crippled', and for only seven as 'healthy'. His conduct is rated as 'good' or 'very good', except for the quarter ending 30 September 1872, when it ap-

[1] *Nation,* 19 Oct. 72, p. 660; *Irishman,* 19 Oct. p. 245; cf. *Hansard 3,* ccxvii, 997-8 (25 July 73).

[2] *Flag of Ireland,* 30 Nov. 72.

[3] P.R.O., H.O. 144/5/17869/5-6.

[4] P.R.O., H.O.8/188-207.

pears as 'indifferent'. The official record for three-quarters of Davitt's time in Dartmoor thus shows that he was regarded as a well-behaved prisoner except when he was in trouble with authority over the publicity he secured in the press. It also shows that, except in the June quarter of 1872 and from June 1873 to September 1874, he was not regarded as physically equal to the ordinary work of convicts. As such he was entitled to be employed only on 'light labour'; and technically stone-breaking, bone-breaking, and cart-work belonged to that category. That he found this work so hard was certainly not due to any reluctance, or (despite the constant handicap of his being one-armed) inability, to exert himself. It may well have been due to the policy of the prison authorities to give 'light-labour' men of his type work in which their rate of earning marks was reduced as little as possible.[1] And it may have been his very disablement that had caused Davitt to be assigned to Dartmoor.[2]

If the evidence of official action towards Davitt is set against his own statements, it would appear certain that, so far as the government, the home office, and prison administration were concerned, there was no intention of treating him with exceptional severity. The official intention was to treat him according to the ordinary rules of the prison system, and broadly speaking that was how he was in fact treated. It was really the system itself, with all its built-in cruelty and indignity, and its indiscriminate herding together of all types of law-breakers—from first offenders to habitual and hardened criminals—that he was in revolt against. That he underwent suffering in prison unknown to the ordinary convict was inevitable just because, far from being an ordinary convict, he was a proud, sensitive, and dedicated young man who had broken the law of the land in obedience to what he believed to be a higher law. For him, as for many another political prisoner, there was no choice between resistance and submission to the prison system. He was convinced that to succeed best in prison one had to be a habitual criminal, dead to feelings of honour and the sense of shame.[3] Had he not been temperamentally incapable of acquiring the prison-technique of habitual criminals, he would have avoided much of that petty tyranny that galled him so deeply.

It was the tyranny of the petty official, not of the higher authorities of the prison, from which such men as Davitt smarted most. Against arbitrary action on the part of a jailor the convict's remedy was a complaint to the prison governor, or to one of the directors of convict

[1] Above, p. 146; below, p. 215. [2] Above, p. 150.

[3] *Inquiry as to the alleged ill-treatment of the convict Charles McCarthy in Chatham convict prison*, p. 16 [C 1978], H.C. 1878, lxiii, 784.

prisons who visited the prisons monthly, or, in the last resort, a petition to the home secretary.[1] But in hearing such appeals the higher authority was always predisposed to accept the jailor's version of what had happened and would not admit the testimony of another convict. Moreover, in the enclosed conditions of a prison it was easy for the jailor to get his own back on the complainant: 'prisoners who complain of . . . prison officials', as Davitt said, 'are looked upon as "troublesome men" and are subjected to petty annoyances in consequence'.[2] Most of the instances of discrimination against him which Davitt relates prove nothing more than that he was very much at the mercy of his jailors and that he was not popular with some of them. He did on several occasions complain to the prison governor and at least once to the visiting director of prisons, without success.[3] When he eventually exercised his right of petitioning the home secretary, in June 1877, it was not against his prison treatment but against his conviction for treason-felony seven years before that he appealed.[4]

At about the time Davitt was admitted to Dartmoor a convict ('X') was discharged who, in 1867, had been convicted of embezzlement and sentenced to five years' penal servitude. Some years later he published an anonymous account of his three years' experience of Dartmoor, which serves as a control for Davitt's story.[5] X was in several ways quite different from Davitt—he was a middle-class Englishman, educated and urbane, with a wife and family, and before his conviction had been doing well in the City. His passage through Dartmoor was much less painful than Davitt's: for his first two years he was employed in the tailors' shop, and, during his last year, in the office of the clerk of works for the new block then being built (No. 5 Prison).[6] He was able to take a more detached view of the prison system than Davitt. He considered that in many ways the discipline, far from being too strict, was not strict enough, nor the work hard enough. Every man did as little as he possibly could, and his day's work (of six to seven hours)

[1] *Report of the commissioners appointed to inquire into the treatment of treason-felony convicts . . .*, pp 9–10 [C 319], H.C. 1871, xxxii; *Kimberley comm. rep.*, ii, 682–5.

[2] *Inquiry as to the alleged ill-treatment of the convict Charles MacCarthy*, as above; *Hansard 3*, ccxxxiv (5 June 77); *Irishman*, 9 June.

[3] D to Mary Gorman, 2 Dec. 73; *Kimberley comm. rep.*, ii, 530–1, 533.

[4] Petition dated 25 June 77 in P.R.O., H.O.144/5/17869/14; D to his mother, 28 Feb., 11 Mar. (smuggled), 29 May, 22 Aug.; see above, pp 106–7.

[5] *Five years' penal servitude*, by 'One who has endured it' (1877; new edition, 1878). The book was referred to from time to time in the proceedings of the Kimberley commission on penal servitude (see below, pp 211 ff). Its author was Edward Callow, of East Finchley (Samuel Halkett and John Laing, *Dictionary of anonymous and pseudonymous authors*, ix (ed. D. E. Rhodes and A. E. C. Simon, 1962), p. 107); the identification in vi, 350, is self-evidently wrong.

[6] Ibid., pp 181–90, 319, 332; above, p. 151.

was equivalent to only half or two-thirds that of a tradesman outside.[1] He had no complaints about the food; he had more bread than he wanted and used to give it away secretly to other prisoners.[2] The hammocks in which prisoners slept he found warm and comfortable.[3] He describes a poor farm-labourer, serving a sentence of seven years for stealing a dozen eggs from under a duck, who often told him that he worked far harder for his eleven shillings a week when he was free than he ever did at stone-quarrying as a prisoner; that at home he could scarcely ever afford meat and his bed was far inferior to his prison hammock.[4] X made a friend of the head schoolmaster, and gained full benefit from the prison library: in his cell during the dinner hour and before bedtime he read a good deal of history—Macaulay, Froude, Napier, Strickland, Morley, Prescott, and others—taught himself the rudiments of Spanish, and passed many an hour with Euclid.[5] Davitt says nothing about the books available in Dartmoor but his silence, compared with his strictures on the inanities he was served with at Millbank, can only mean that his insatiable appetite for serious reading was not starved. It would be impossible otherwise to account for the evidence of wide general reading he showed as soon as he was at large again. He probably also acquired the knowledge of French and the rudiments of other modern languages that he was to use to advantage a few years later.[6] But it is mainly on the dark side of the story that X's experience of Dartmoor agrees with Davitt's, and X's testimony is the more impressive just because he has so much to say on the other side.

X lived in a different block, No. 4 Prison, but it was similar in design to No. 2; and, like Davitt, X had reason to hate its ill-lighted and ill-ventilated iron cells, from which every sound, from the slamming of a door to the clanking of the chains of a prisoner in irons, resounded throughout the entire structure.[7] Though he himself had enough to eat, he was well aware of prisoners who could never get enough and would steal anything eatable, especially candles, they could lay hands on.[8] He suffered from such indignities of the system as the repeated stripping and searching of prisoners and the cropping of their hair;[9] from the 'brutal farce' of the medical treatment dished out during the dinner hour to men in their cells who had asked to see the doctor;[10] and from the tyranny of individual warders.[11] Though he speaks with

[1] Ibid., pp 315, 348, 376, 377. [2] Ibid., pp 298–9.

[3] Ibid., p. 169.

[4] Ibid., pp 299–301.

[5] Ibid., pp 195–6, 213–14. [6] Cf. *Leaves*, i, 185–6, and below, pp 503–4.

[7] *Five years' penal servitude*, pp 160–64, 165–6, 168. [8] Ibid., pp 298–9.

[9] Ibid., pp 156, 159, 174–5, 226, 288–9, 321, 325–6. [10] Ibid., pp 196–8, 225–30.

[11] Ibid., pp 24–5, 179–81, 225–34, 289–91, 309–14, 349–50.

appreciation of a few,[1] most of the warders, he considered, were of a very poor type, who took the job as a last resort—men who never had had the slightest authority over others and suddenly found themselves in a position of almost autocratic power. Very few became efficient officers, but most of them were 'perfect tyrants', who soon learnt that any accusation they made against a prisoner would be listened to, and the prisoner's word would never be believed.[2] The regular visits of a director of convict prisons from London were no security against the abuses and corruptions of the prison system, for the director's intention to visit was known beforehand and everything was prepared accordingly.[3] X proved the truth of the advice given him by the chaplain at Newgate immediately after his sentence:

> You must just consider yourself as a slave till your time is out. Every action of your life will have to be just what your taskmasters may command you to do. Try and bear up meekly and submissively. Avoid giving offence to any of the officials, and remember that, though your body is condemned to slavery, your thoughts, your mind and heart are free.[4]

Many years afterwards an Irishman, Jim Phelan, who as a youthful member of the I.R.A. had been convicted of a bank robbery in England and sentenced to fifteen years' penal servitude, developed a variation on this theme in a prison autobiography that records and analyses his experiences of prison life in Dartmoor and elsewhere. He found conditions in the Dartmoor of the 1920s and 1930s scarcely less savage, and the treatment of prisoners no less cruel, than Davitt had done fifty years before: 'the men of The Moor were dealt with as that most dangerous of beasts, the human outlaw'.[5] Phelan divides the convict population into two classes, described in prison slang as 'wides' and 'mugs'. The 'wides' are the professional criminals, who adapt themselves readily to prison conditions.

> It is a regrettable fact, but an interesting and ineluctable one, that only the professional thief has sufficient mental alertness and resource to avoid the cumbrous clutchings and crushings of the English jail-machine . . . For him the evasion, the furtiveness, the suspicious alert circumspection are part of his equipment in the ordinary business of earning his living.[6]

The 'mugs' are novices who expect that normal standards of conduct and the rules of logic obtain in prison. To such

> the jail-controllers say in effect, whatever they may intend to say: 'we will put you in our jail-machine. You will be squeezed of all initiative and resource till you become like a mummy or an automaton; or you will be driven into neurosis, perhaps insanity; or you will become violent and dangerous; or again, you will be a

[1] Ibid., pp 166–8, 177, 182. [2] Ibid., pp 314–15, 350–51. [3] Ibid., pp 388–91.
[4] Ibid., p. 47. [5] *Jail journey* (1940), p. 101. [6] Ibid., p. 22.

good prisoner while retaining your sanity and initiative—if you can learn to behave like a professional pick-pocket'.[1]

Phelan's definition of 'mug' fits Davitt's case exactly. For example Davitt cites as evidence of exceptionally harsh treatment his confinement to the punishment cells for a week and deprivation of privileges during two months for refusing to substitute 'sir' for 'here' in answering his name to an assistant warder. The prison rules, he said, required prisoners to be respectful at all times, but did not specify the terms to be used in addressing warders. He had always been respectful in his language towards the official in question, and no objection had previously been made to his answering 'here'. Therefore, he concludes, the punishment 'was nothing more than a gratuitous piece of petty tyranny'.[2] This is the logic of the 'mug'; a 'wide' would never have thought of contesting a prison official's ruling on what constituted respectful language. The incident is the more revealing because it occurred at Easter 1876, after Davitt had six years' experience of imprisonment.

Davitt's attitude to the prison system was not, however, entirely self-consistent. He was ready to assert his rights under the rules while at the same time secretly breaking them. Even before he succeeded in smuggling his letter of 1 August 1872[3] out of Dartmoor, he was suspected of being in secret communication with friends in Lancashire. The authorities were alerted from Manchester by the vigilant Head-constable Welby, who reported on 29 July 1872 that money was being raised by the local fenian treasurers to buy expensive books for Davitt. The governor of Dartmoor ascertained that no such books were reaching him, but failed to discover the identity of the 'delinquent warder' with whom Davitt was presumed to be in collusion.[4] He was no doubt closely watched, for it was not till about May 1875 that he succeeded in establishing a secret channel of communication with his family and friends. The smuggled letters that have survived are written in pencil, on odd scraps of paper, and some are signed 'Joseph', his confirmation name, which he used for private references to himself in the open correspondence. The smuggling was worked at the Dartmoor end through a friendly warder or through discharged prisoners on their way out. Letters were conveyed—whether through the post office or not is uncertain—in the first instance to Haslingden, where his faithful friend, Martin Haran, acted as a forwarding agent, receiving letters from Davitt

[1] Ibid., pp 22-3.

[2] *Hansard 3*, ccxxxiv (5 June 77); *Irishman*, 9 June, p. 788; Cashman, p. 42; *Kimberley comm. rep.*, ii, 522.

[3] Above, p. 152.

[4] H.-C. Welby to I.G.P., 29 July, 30 Aug., 28 Oct., 72; Robert Anderson to T. H. Burke, 8 Oct. (S.P.O., R.P. 1877/9309).

and directing them to their destinations according to his instructions. Many years later one of Martin's sons, Frank, recalled how letters from Davitt used to arrive at their home in Hindle Street—'written in pencil on bits of brown paper'—and how he used to walk to Bacup or Ramsbottom (about five miles away) to post some of them there, for greater security, instead of in Haslingden.[1] Letters for Davitt's mother were addressed to her as 'Mrs Bryant', at an hotel in Port Richmond, Philadelphia, run by an old friend, Martin Burke.[2] Davitt tried writing direct to her at this address so as 'not to bother the life out of old Bismarck' [Martin Haran], but the experiment was not a success.[3] Some part was also played in the forwarding of letters by another Irish friend, Thomas Lyons, of Rawtenstall.[4] In-letters seem to have followed the same route in reverse, except that, at the receiving end, Davitt was entirely dependent on the cooperation of a warder. In addition to these systematic breaches of prison rules Davitt on at least two occasions—May 1876 and February 1877—laid plans for an escape, which did not mature.[5]

Nearly all Davitt's letters from prison that have survived were addressed to his parents or, after his father's death, to his mother. The regular letters, written at prescribed intervals on official blue forms were censored and despatched by the prison authorities. Their rather stilted and pedantic style was intended partly to conceal the paucity of matter—for no mention of public affairs was permitted—and partly to disarm the censor. The smuggled letters are vigorous, unaffected, and outspoken, and sometimes refer to external events. But the spirit and tendency of both series of letters are the same. They reveal an affectionate son and brother, bent on sparing his family grief on his account and eager to maintain the fullest possible contact with them. Though only one side of the correspondence has survived, the loyal response of his family is reflected in his running commentary on the contents of letters from home. After the death of Martin Davitt in 1871 all these letters were written, as all his letters were read, by Michael's youngest and only literate sister, Sabina. She was a strong-minded, militant young woman, whose fervent and unshakeable devotion to her revolutionary brother did not prevent her from taking him to task on occasions: he refers to her good-humouredly as 'your accomplished secretary' and also as 'your exact and fault-finding secretary'.[6] It is to her scrupulous care that the survival of Michael's prison-letters to his family is primarily due.

[1] Francis Haran to Mrs Mary Davitt, 15 Oct. 1907 (DP/P); 'Briar' (above, p. 18 n. 1) in *Haslingden Observer*, 27 July 1935.

[2] See below, p. 170.

[3] D to his mother, 7 Feb., and Easter, 76 (smuggled).

[4] D to 'Dear Bismarck', 1 Nov.

[5] D to his mother, 13 May, 76, 4 Feb. 77 (smuggled); *Fall*, pp 566, 589.

[6] D to his mother, 31 May, 29 Nov., 75.

His first letter, written in Newgate prison while he was awaiting trial, is full of confidence that

before the September sun gilds the black hills of Scranton, you will see me walk into your shanty or whatever abode you may by that time have. . . . I am, thank God, in as good health and as lively in spirit as ever I was in my life . . . I earnestly request of you to be of good heart and look forward with hope and not to be cast down on my account. Even if the worst should happen and . . . I should be debar[r]ed from seeing you for a few years, you must not despair . . . Remember I am accused of no heinous or dishonest crime which could cause you to blush for your son.[1]

A few weeks later, still in the same strain, he speaks of the interest his many friends, and especially Haslingden friends, have shown in his case. He is immensely relieved to know that his parents are taking a sensible view of his position, and he again tries to prepare them for the possibility of a disappointment:

What is a few years more or less when the mind is still the same? . . . Let it be imprisonment or freedom . . . I feel confident in my own strength and belief in God's merciful providence to sustain me no matter what the future may have in store for me. Remember that thirteen years ago I was almost on the threshold of death,[2] yet am I today as strong and as good a man . . . as any Davitt who ever drank poteen at the fair of Straide . . . If I were satisfied that my mother would not give way to useless sorrow or regrets I would not care one pin for whatever term of imprisonment I might receive. I hope however that the same fortitude and resignation which always characterised her under severe trials will also sustain her now. You are, thank heaven, among dear friends and sympathetic neighbours from dear old Haslingden who will not be backward in lending you assistance should you ever stand in need of it, and I have full confidence in Neil's[3] affection, [and] that he will prove a better son to you than ever I was.[4]

After receiving his sentence he remains undismayed: 'I shall never abandon the hope of once more seeing you all . . . I was never in better health in my life and am quite reconciled to my fate. The only fear I have is that you, my dear father and mother, may give way to unnecessary grief on my account.'[5] On his arrival at Dartmoor ten months later he believes that the change from the close and unhealthy conditions of Millbank to 'this alpine-like abode' will benefit his health, even though, at the time of writing, he is more closely confined than when in London.[6] During his years in Dartmoor he sometimes confesses to temporary ill-health and occasionally (in the smuggled letters) refers to the harshness of his treatment, but always with assurances that he

[1] D to his father and mother, 18 June 70. This is the earliest of Davitt's letters to survive in the original. The original of the 'pen' letter, 15 Dec. 69 (above, pp 60–61) has not survived.
[2] See above, pp 17–18. [3] Neil Padden was Davitt's brother-in-law; see above, pp 22–3.
[4] D to his father, mother, and sisters, 11 July.
[5] D to his father, mother, and sisters, 22 July.
[6] D to his father and mother 31 May 71.

does not and will not despair, and admonitions to his family not to worry about him. 'You ought not to conclude that I must necessarily be ill when I mention some trifling indisposition, and that my habitual cheerfulness is but assumed with the view to quieting your fears, and conjectures as to my health and treatment.'[1] He awaits the periodic letter from home with a mixture of eagerness and apprehension;

and when it brings your news I am then prepared to battle for the next three months with anything calculated to disturb the repose of my monotonous existence. You probably share in the belief of those unenlightened people who have never had the advantage of prison experience that time must be dreadfully slow when it forms the barrier between the unfortunate mortal and his liberty; but I assure you it has not appeared so to me as yet. Our correspondence I make my calendar, and four letters knock down a twelvemonth. The past five years have been satisfactorily accounted for by some twenty of my precious epistles, and something like three dozen more will 'backward turn the iron screw of fate'.[2]

On the occasions when he refers, in the secret letters, to ill-treatment, his general outlook is the same. 'They have done their worst', he writes in 1876, 'and continue to deny me even the privileges accorded to the common herd, . . . but I am sustained by the consciousness of my imputed 'crime' being an honourable one . . . My only anxiety is that you fret yourself too much on my account.'[3] Three months later he tells his mother that he has lost the privilege of writing till August, but she is not to let the non-arrival of official letters trouble her now that he has a secret channel of communication. 'Their cowardly inhuman conduct can never break my spirit. I feel certain I shall with God's help escape the end they would like to bring me to.'[4] But references to ill-treatment are few and these are the two strongest. More typical is his account of the security measures applied to him in August 1876:[5]

The good people who are taking such particular care of me are [so] very much afraid lest anyone should hear from me or speak to me or attempt to run away with me that I am more strictly guarded now than at any former period of my imprisonment. I have been removed from my occupation of stone-breaking to work which you will be astonished to hear I am capable of performing. Could you ever imagine me becoming a washerwoman?[6]

Helping to maintain the morale of his family was probably the best way for Davitt to maintain his own. While his habitual mood was optimistic and good-humoured, moments of deep despondency show themselves in his letters. In March 1875 he dismisses the possibility of not outliving the term of his sentence because, as death 'could not

1 D to his mother, 2 June 74.
2 D to his mother, 1 Mar. 75.
3 D to his mother, 7 Feb. 76 (smuggled).
4 D to his mother, 13 May (smuggled).
5 See above, p. 152.
6 D to his mother, Oct. (smuggled).

appear in any other capacity than that of a friend, I have good reason to believe he will not pay me a visit'.[1] In February 1877 he wonders whether he will 'live to emerge from my inferno and . . . mingle in the world's commotion again'.

I fear, however, that if I continue growing 'gradually small and unmistakably less' . . . as I have done in the past, I shall soon be a living embodiment of a physiological discovery—that the vital principle can exist in skin and bone independent of . . . bodily development. Should this refined state of being prove an obstacle to the success of my future plans of life, why a post of honour in Barnum's Museum as the most attenuated living specimen of the genus homo must satisfy my accommodating ambition.[2]

The severest test of his morale, however, was not caused by prison conditions but by the death of his father.

The first letter Michael received in Dartmoor, in March 1871, brought news that his father was unwell, but no suggestion of serious illness.[3] The next letter from home, three months later, caused Michael great anxiety,[4] and in December 1871 Martin Davitt died at Scranton, aged about 57.[5] Nothing that happened during his imprisonment seems to have shaken Michael's composure so much as this:

The sad tidings of my father's death . . . found me entirely unprepared for such a calamity. I find it impossible to describe to you the sorrow . . . with which the news struck me and the feeling of remorse at the thought of being in part the cause of his demise. He would never have quitted England but for me, and might still be alive had I not compelled him to an unwilling exile. Yet I can conscientiously call heaven to witness that I did it fully believing it would be better for him and you all to be among friends and in a land where the country of his birth would be no reproach to him. Still, his dying calls for me will never cease to sound in my ears as so many reproaches for my absence at the last moments of his life. He believed that no one else loved him as I did; but what must have been his thoughts of me when I was not present to comfort him at his last hour? I pray God he did not then upbraid me for my absence. You tell me that he died peacefully, but you omitted to mention whether he left this world fortified with the consolations of religion or not. May God give eternal rest to his soul.[6]

His father's death, Michael wrote in his next letter, was the only occasion since his imprisonment on which he had given way to grief and lamented for his parents' sake that he was a convict.[7]

From this point onwards Davitt's mother occupies a key position in his letters home. Attached to each other as they were by deep and tender affection, mother and son were both strong personalities. Even before his father's death she had expressed an intention to visit him,

[1] D to his mother, 1 Mar. 75.
[2] D to his mother, 21 Feb. 77.
[3] D to his father and mother, 31 May 71.
[4] D to his father, mother, and sisters, 17 July.
[5] He is buried in the Cathedral Cemetery, Scranton.
[6] D to his mother, 29 Jan. 72; see above, p. 79.
[7] D to his mother, 12 July.

and his response was to obtain permission for a special letter to dissuade her. It would, he insists, be the height of folly for her to travel 6,000 miles to see him for twenty minutes; he is not hankering after visitors and is wholly resigned to his present lot.

> But when my mother talks of coming all the way from Scranton to see me—and when I . . . think of . . . the trouble and sorrow I have caused you all, it is too much for me to bear. . . . Write immediately and assure me that she will never undertake such an absurd journey.[1]

He had his way, but within a year Catherine Davitt was again talking of visiting her son; and again, by special letter, he induced her not to do so. There was not, he wrote, the slightest need for such an undertaking. He had recovered from the dispiriting effect of his father's death, and having been transferred from Dartmoor to Portsmouth 'I have left a great deal of annoyance behind me. I like this place much better on account of the climate.'[2] Two years later he again found it necessary to insist that she must not come to see him.[3] Finally, in May 1875, he writes: 'I hope you have abandoned the idea of coming to see me. There is no necessity for it and it would do neither of us any good'.[4]

Knowing how passionately his mother would have reacted against Dartmoor, Michael was determined to save her and himself the anguish of a twenty-minute meeting in such an environment. He feared the hardships of the journey for her, and he knew that she could not afford it. She on her side felt it her duty to visit her only son, whatever the difficulties; after her husband's death, she even seems to have thought of returning to England permanently.[5] In resisting her intention to visit him Michael frequently appeals to her accustomed resignation to the will of God, and protests that this is his own sustaining principle. But resignation did not come easily to him, and was scarcely compatible with planning an escape and petitioning against his sentence. What Catherine Davitt thought of his schemes of escape or, indeed, whether she was aware of them, is not known, but she was sceptical of his decision to petition the home secretary and warned him not to build any hopes of a favourable outcome.[6] He replied that he expected nothing except the satisfaction of placing on record that, as he had said at his trial, he had been convicted unjustly.[7] But when his petition was dismissed he wrote: 'Better to bear the ills we have . . . than to seek redress and, instead of receiving it, experience the mortification of being told "there are not sufficient grounds for inquiring into your case"'.[8]

When Davitt's imprisonment began his parents and his two un-

[1] D to his father and mother, 17 July 71.
[2] D to his mother, 12 July 72.
[3] D to his mother, 2 June 74.
[4] D to his mother, [May 75] (smuggled).
[5] D to his mother, 4 Dec. 72.
[6] D to his mother, 29 May 77.
[7] D to his mother, 11 Mar. (smuggled).
[8] D to his mother, 22 Aug.

married sisters, Anne and Sib (Sabina), were living with Neil and Mary Padden at Scranton. Mary already had two children, James and Catherine, and five others were born to her while Michael was in Dartmoor. The Paddens thus had a crowded home as well as a heavy burden of work and responsibility, and it needed all their strength of character and their practical abilities to carry them through this difficult time. Neil cheerfully assumed the place in the family that Michael had left empty, and to this Michael frequently refers with gratitude and appreciation. Neil's faithfulness, all the more important after Martin Davitt's death, did not cease when, in 1873, Catherine Davitt moved with Anne and Sib from Scranton to Manayunk, a small industrial suburb of Philadelphia, on the Schuylkill River, about 160 miles from Scranton.[1] Like Scranton it already had an Irish colony,[2] and it is probable that the move from Scranton, a town much subject to industrial trouble, was caused by lack of employment for Anne and Sib and news from friends in Manayunk that suitable work was to be had in the mills there. Neil and Mary kept in close touch with Catherine and her daughters, and Neil went to see them as often as possible.

Other relatives who showed a continuing interest in the Davitt women at Manayunk were Michael's Uncle Harry and Cousin John. They had emigrated from Straide to Haslingden,[3] and later to Albany, New York, where they had done well for themselves. Uncle Harry, presumably Henry Davitt,[4] a brother of Martin, seems to have preceded his nephew John to Albany and may have been already there when Neil Padden emigrated via Albany to Scranton.[5] He was regarded as a steady bachelor, and Michael was astonished to learn in 1876 that he had succumbed to marriage: 'I cannot help admiring his desperate courage to take a wife at his time of life. However, may he live to see his great grandchildren.'[6] Cousin John was the son of John Davitt, another brother of Martin's, who died at Straide in 1873.[7] Three years later another of his sons, Michael, followed his brother John to Albany. Michael in Dartmoor refers with pride to the 'brilliant career' before John, who, he prophesies, will end up in Congress;[8] and he hopes that Michael 'is a better Irishman than his unfortunate namesake'.[9]

[1] See maps V, VI.

[2] The gravestones in the graveyard of St John the Baptist Church, Manayunk, bear innumerable Irish names.

[3] This is an irresistible inference drawn from a reference to John and Harry respectively in letters from Davitt to his mother of 30 Nov. 74 and 30 Aug. 75.

[4] See above, p. 7. [5] See above, pp 22–3. [6] D to his mother, 22 Nov. 76.

[7] John Davitt and his wife Mary are buried at Straide beside Michael Davitt; their gravestone, erected by their son Michael, of Albany, records that he died in Mar. 73, aged 76, and she in Dec. 82, aged 70.

[8] D to his mother, 30 Nov. 74, 1 Mar. 75. [9] D to his mother, 22 Nov. 76.

Visits from Harry and John were evidently a source of great pleasure to the Davitts of Manayunk. But their most frequent visitor was Martin Burke, an old friend of Michael's,[1] who had emigrated from Lancashire to Philadelphia soon after 1870. An enterprising, breezy character, with a prodigious voice and a passion for recitation, he became the flourishing proprietor of a hotel at Port Richmond—which, Michael understood, would give him a rank equivalent to that of 'kurnel'. 'I always thought he had a soul above the common proletariate'[2] (he had been a millworker). Michael smiles to think that he will now have a captive audience for his eloquence, and recalls the happy days 'at home', when he used to hold forth and 'when poor Tom (God rest his soul), John, and myself joined him to our heart's content'.[3]

Michael's first niece to be born after he went to Dartmoor Mary Anne, was specially endeared to her grandmother, and was allowed by her parents to stay with Catherine for a time at Manayunk. 'I am well pleased that she prays for me every night', Michael writes in 1874.[4] 'If she has not outgrown the age of dolls by the end of my sentence, she may count on the choicest on Broadway—if my £3 [gratuity on discharge] can purchase it.'[5] Next year: 'Mary Anne acts in the spirit of a future advocate of women's rights in claiming all that would be mine if I were at home'.[6] In the first of his smuggled letters (*c.* May 1875), he asks for a photograph of his mother with Anne and Sib on either side and Mary Anne in front.[7] Photographs as requested soon reached him through the secret post, and he comments to his mother:

> You can little imagine what a source of pleasure I find in them. I try to persuade myself that you do not show the traces of sorrow and grief my misfortunes must have caused you, and that you appear no older than when we parted nigh six years ago. But you always had a stout Irish heart and, God knows, enough of trouble to daunt it, though I console myself in thinking you have become resigned to all and will wait patiently until it pleases providence to bring us all together again. I fail to see any remarkable change in Anne's appearance to account for a statement to that effect in one of Sibby's letters. She seems to me the least changed of any. Sib herself looks as if she were the recognised champion of women's rights, so determinedly American does she appear. The little stranger, I suppose is M[ary] Anne, though Martin [Haran] told me in a letter you sent her home on account of some sickness in your neighbourhood. You will feel the loss of her noisy innocent prattle and I hope she will soon be back again. She has a very intelligent face, wearing quite a saucy look.[8]

By this time three more children, Sabina, Margaret, and Michael had

[1] Above, p. 45.
[2] D to his mother, 30 Aug. 75.
[3] D to his mother, 30 Nov. 74. 'Poor Tom' was Martin Burke's brother (see above, p. 45). It is made clear by the context that 'John' is Michael's cousin.
[4] D to his mother, 3 Mar.
[5] D to his mother, 2 June.
[6] D to his mother, 1 Mar. 75.
[7] D to his mother, [May 75] (smuggled).
[8] D to his mother, Sept. (smuggled).

been added to Mary's family; and their uncle in Dartmoor rejoices both that there are 'three more innocent little voices praying for me' and 'to see the Scranton folk intent on fulfilling the divine precept, to increase and multiply'.[1] In October 1876, however, he is seeking to console Mary on the death of her little boy—his first namesake.[2] Six months later he sends his *céad míle fáilte* to a new niece, Bridget, and asks James, the eldest of the Padden children (now aged eleven), to write a few lines to him.[3] James evidently did so, for on 22 August Michael writes:

As you have brought Mary Anne back from Scranton I desire her to write her name at the end of her brother's portion of your answer to this. Of course I cannot doubt but that among the many accomplishments of an American lady of the advanced age of six years the art of writing will be conspicuous. In what James writes he will be careful not to mention political affairs, as no such demoralising subject is permitted to disturb this serene seclusion from your noisy world.[4]

That young James Padden was able to write to his Uncle Michael was itself a significant fact. Davitt's father was literate but not his mother, and of their children only Michael and Sabina could read and write. But all the Padden children who survived infancy were given a good primary education. Life was hard for the Paddens in the seventies, but thanks to the unflagging efforts of Neil and Mary their standard of living was improving and the prospects for the children of rising out of the manual-worker class were good. Scranton was badly hit by the economic depression that swept over the United States in 1876–7 and was particularly severe in Pennsylvania.[5] This was the critical time for the 'Molly Maguire' troubles, of which the Paddens must have felt some repercussions, Neil being a miner and Scranton being in a coalfield near the one most affected.[6] But no trace of this appears in Michael's letters, though he read in an extract from the *Scranton Republican* that 500 families were preparing to move out further west.[7] The Paddens seem to have fared much better in this crisis than Catherine Davitt and her two daughters in Manayunk.

The three women, of whom two were wage-earners, seem in general to have lived in modest comfort, but in May 1876 they were unable to raise 20 dollars that Michael wanted for a scheme of escape.[8] Michael had unusual delicacy in money matters, and when, months later, he learnt that his mother had been in financial difficulties he was filled with remorse:

I cannot tell you how grieved I was to hear of the straightened circumstances in which you were placed . . . To think that I should have acted so selfishly as to write

[1] D to his mother, 31 May.
[2] D to his mother, Oct. 76 (smuggled), 22 Nov.
[3] D to his mother, 15 Apr. 77 (smuggled), 29 May.
[4] D to his mother, 22 Aug.
[5] D to his mother, 11 Mar., 15 Apr. (smuggled).
[6] Above, p. 140.
[7] D to his mother, 15 Apr. (smuggled).
[8] D to his mother, 13 May 76 (smuggled).

to you for what I could do without and what you could not spare is punishing me justly for my unfeeling conduct . . . Were I fully aware of your distress I would have never thought of asking a cent.[1]

Conditions had improved when he wrote, but he was determined never to risk embarrassing his mother again. When he next wanted money he characteristically tried to earn it by writing verses for publication.[2] Part, and perhaps the whole, of the 20 dollars he had asked for had apparently been supplied by his relatives in Albany, who had also come to the assistance of his mother:

It will be impossible for me ever to repay Cousin John and Uncle Harry for their generous behaviour to you and myself. Such acts as theirs are not to be measured by the common rule . . . As for U[ncle] H[arry] saying he was under an obligation *to me*, it is but his kindly feelings going in advance of his generosity and enhances all the more the act which prompted his making such a remark. Unfortunately it is with him as with all my other friends, I am always the receiver, and can only lay claim to the hope that he believes I would act in like manner to himself if fate had reversed our careers.[3]

Having learnt of a fund for the relief of the families of Irish political prisoners, he inquires whether his mother has received anything from it, and on hearing that she has not, writes: 'I suppose no money is advanced except to those who apply for it, and I am well pleased . . . that no such application has been made by any of mine'.[4]

The first centenary of the American revolution was celebrated in 1876 by a great exhibition held at Philadelphia in Fairmount Park near Manayunk, and this was the occasion for many visits to Catherine and her two daughters from relatives and friends in Scranton and Albany.[5] It also proved to be the only topic of public interest permitted to appear in the censored correspondence. Davitt stretched this latitude pretty far:

It is consoling to remember that the men whose glorious deeds a great people are now commemorating were stigmatised at the outset of their labours as 'rebels', 'traitors', and 'incendiaries', but having carried their impious principles to that magical point of transition where wrong is changed into right, these 'rebels' were at once recognised as the benefactors of the human race. But as 'successful crime' alone is justified, unfortunate 'criminals' must bear the penalty, which 'right divine to govern wrong' inflicts upon its unlucky adversaries.[6]

Though Davitt at this time knew nothing of America at first hand, he was already thinking of Pennsylvania as a second home, and looking

[1] D to his mother, 4 Feb. 77 (smuggled).
[2] See below, p. 174.
[3] D to his mother, 4 Feb. (smuggled).
[4] Ibid.; D to [Sabina Davitt], 15 Apr. (smuggled).
[5] D to his mother, 7 Feb., 13 May 76 (smuggled); 23 Aug., 22 Nov. See map VI.
[6] D to his mother, 23 Aug. See plate VII.

forward to the day when he could turn his back on England.[1] Yet he shared the nostalgia that his parents felt for Haslingden—'that dear old place to which our memories must always cling, from the many dear associations it will ever awaken'.[2] In his official letters he repeatedly asks to be remembered to old Haslingden friends—Martin Haran and his family, Mary Gorman and her mother, a Miss Johnson ('my fair schoolfellow'),[3] a Mrs Grady and her daughter, and the Timlins. One or two of his letters he sent in the first instance to Miss Gorman, who passed them on to his mother.[4] He was grieved to learn of the death of his old employer, Henry Cockcroft, who died in March 1871, aged sixty-five, after forty years in business at Haslingden. Michael was unaware that his death was due to 'suicide while of unsound mind'; at the inquest there was a suggestion that Michael's arrest and conviction had contributed to his mental depression.[5]

When St Patrick's day comes round Michael remembers the balls and entertainments they used to enjoy so much in the public hall of Haslingden.[6] He hopes that this custom is maintained, reflecting that to celebrate the day 'in a sober, respectable manner' is more in keeping with the occasion than to make it 'a drunken festival and tap-room saturnalia'. But Lancashire seems more remote than America in Michael's letters, and the only relative in Ireland that he mentions is Uncle John Davitt, of Straide, from whom he had had news of the departure of more Davitts to America. How many other kinsmen, he wonders, have left the old place for that insatiable Yankee-land to which so many friends of his Lancashire days have emigrated?[7]

Near the end of his imprisonment, Michael acquired another kinsman in America. On 7 October 1877 his second sister, Anne, was married to Edward Crowley in St John the Baptist Church, Manayunk, the witnesses being Cousin John and Mary McHale. Crowley was a labourer, the son of Irish emigrants from County Cork. The young couple made their home with Catherine Davitt and Sib in Manayunk.[8]

Davitt's smuggling system enabled him not only to supplement his regular correspondence with his family but also to maintain some contacts with the world of politics. His first smuggled letter (1 August 1872), with the disclosures of his sufferings, produced a stir in Ireland

[1] D to his mother, 3 Mar. 74; see also 'Christmas musings in prison, 1875' below, p. 174.
[2] D to his mother, 28 Feb. 76. [3] D to his mother, 1 Mar. 75.
[4] D to Miss Gorman, 2 Dec. 73.
[5] D to his mother, 12 July 72; *Accrington Times,* 1 Apr. 71, p. 5, col. 5.
[6] D to his mother, 1 Mar. 75, 28 Feb. 76; cf. above, p. 55.
[7] D to his mother, 2 June 74, 22 Nov. 76.
[8] Certificate of marriage of Edward Crowley and Anne Davitt ('Devit'), 7 Oct. 77 (Manayunk, Philadelphia, Records of St John the Baptist Church); *Philadelphia City Directory,* 1879, p. 398; personal testimony of Mrs Kathleen Burns.

and to a lesser extent in England. 'A disgusted Irishman' writing from Haslingden to the Manchester *Examiner and Times*, denounced it as a forgery, concocted in a public house by factory hands and hawkers. This elicited two indignant rejoinders; one was from Mathew Shearin,[1] on behalf of Irish people in Haslingden, the other from 'one of the released Manchester men', the ex-convict who had brought the letter out of Dartmoor and delivered it to the press.[2] Several years later Davitt described further ill-treatment in letters conveyed by discharged prisoners to O'Connor Power, who made effective use of them in the house of commons on 5 June 1877.[3]

Davitt also sought to communicate with the outside world—and incidentally to earn a little money with a view to escaping—by writing patriotic verse and smuggling it out of prison. He was in touch in January 1877 with Richard Pigott, editor and proprietor of the *Irishman*, the *Flag of Ireland*, and the *Shamrock*, who made his living out of peddling extreme nationalism and was the most strenuous advocate of the prisoners' cause. Davitt sent Pigott a poem in five parts entitled 'Christmas musings in prison, 1875',[4] with a note to say that a few pounds were needed 'for a particular purpose'. Pigott neither sent the author any money nor published the poem at the time. But he kept both poem and note; the poem he published in the *Irishman* four years later,[5] when Davitt was at the height of his fame, and he used the note in 1886 as the exemplar of one of the celebrated forgeries that he sold to *The Times*.[6] Another of Davitt's prison-pieces, the 'Irish felon's song', was sent to Martin Haran, who had it secretly printed and circulated in Haslingden in March 1877. This unsigned production, on a single small sheet, earned Davitt £2.[7] At the same time he was exerting himself on behalf of fellow-prisoners who, he thought, had been forgotten— e.g. Thomas Chambers and Thomas Ahearn in Dartmoor and James Clancy in Portsmouth. He suggested the formation of a political prisoners visiting committee, to arrange for regular visits to the prisons and to give publicity to the prisoners' treatment and complaints.[8] Such a committee was actually formed in London, in April 1877, and included

[1] See above, p. 97.

[2] *Examiner and Times* (Manchester), 11 Sept. 72 ff; *Accrington Times,* 7, 14, 28 Sept.; *Irishman,* 7, 14, 28 Sept.

[3] *Hansard 3*, ccxxxiv, 1309–28 (5 June 77); *Irishman,* 9 June. See below, p. 179.

[4] D to his mother, *c.* 24 Feb. (smuggled).

[5] 'Michael Davitt as a poet' in *Irishman,* 12 Feb. 81, p. 524, cols 2–4; 19 Feb., p. 540, cols 3–4; 26 Feb., p. 556, col. 4.

[6] D to T. D. Sullivan, 13 Dec. 1901 (DP/02); *Fall,* pp 566, 589.

[7] [Martin Haran] to Catherine Davitt, 16 Mar. 77 (DP/C); 'The Irish felon's song' is reprinted in Cashman, pp 15–16 and in J. B. O'Reilly (ed.), *The poetry and song of Ireland* (New York, 2nd ed. [1889]), p. 1025.

[8] D to Sabina Davitt, 15 Apr. 77 (smuggled).

among its members Butt, Parnell, Biggar, O'Connor Power, and F. H. O'Donnell, with Davitt's friend, John Ryan of Chelsea, and Maurice Collins as joint treasurers.[1] Davitt also wrote to Isaac Butt, requesting him, as leader of the home rule party, to bring the amnesty question before the house of commons, and making a special appeal for 'my prison-chum Tom Chambers and the other life-sentenced men. The few remaining years of my term will soon slip by, but they have no fixed time to which they may look forward to restore them to friends and liberty.'[2] He was now able to follow the course of the amnesty agitation and the rise of Parnell to an ascendant position in Irish politics: during 1876 Irish and American newspapers occasionally reached him, and from November 1876 till at least April 1877 (when the evidence ceases) the *Irishman*, of Dublin, was being despatched to him frequently—perhaps weekly—and the *Irish World*, of New York, at longer intervals, by Thomas Lyons, from Rawtenstall.

Agitation for the release of the remaining fenian prisoners, still headed with characteristic ardour by Butt, had continued after the amnesty of January 1871 with unabated passion and pertinacity. The prisoners, all of them previously unknown to the public, numbered about twenty, of whom the large majority were soldiers, convicted before courts martial in Ireland in 1866–7 for mutiny and similar offences. All the soldiers except three, Thomas Chambers, Charles McCarthy, and John Patrick O'Brien, had been transported to Western Australia in October 1867. Chambers was in Dartmoor, McCarthy and O'Brien in Chatham. Besides the soldiers there were two small groups of civilians, one consisting of men convicted for complicity in the Manchester rescue (September 1867), the other of Davitt and Wilson, whose arrest three years after the fenian 'rising' was an isolated incident.[3] Till 1874 the amnesty agitation took the form mainly of great popular demonstrations, organised by the Amnesty Association, at which speeches were made and resolutions passed calling on the government to release the prisoners; from 1874 the cause of amnesty was largely sustained by the home rule party in the house of commons. In both phases, no single case was so prominently ventilated as Davitt's; this was partly due to the publicity he secured in the press in September 1872, and partly to the efforts of 'Amnesty' Nolan,[4] John O'Connor Power, and other personal friends on his behalf. Butt himself, though he had never met Davitt, showed a kindly interest in his case.[5]

The Amnesty Association contended that there was no essential

[1] *Irishman*, 21 Mar. p. 685; 12 May, p. 732.
[2] D to Sabina Davitt, 15 Apr. (smuggled).
[3] Above, p. 121.
[4] D to John O'Leary, 11 Mar. 88 (DP/ZZ).
[5] *Fall*, p. 93.

difference between the offences of the fenians still imprisoned and of those who had been amnestied, and that it was unjust to deny to the followers the clemency shown to the leaders.[1] The government's attitude to Davitt's charges of ill-treatment in 1872 was challenged by the association on two grounds. (a) It was based on statements of prison officials, who were the parties complained of.[2] In the notorious case of O'Donovan Rossa the home secretary in the house of commons had denied the prisoner's allegations, but was proved to have been misinformed when a commission of inquiry[3] established the fact that Ross's hands were kept continuously manacled behind his back, except at meal-times, for five weeks (17 June–20 July 1868). In Davitt's case therefore the Amnesty Association demanded a public inquiry before an impartial tribunal.[4] (b) The government's refusal to recognise Davitt as a political prisoner was unreasonable. How could the gravity of his offence alter the fact that it was political in its nature just as certainly as that of Luby, O'Leary, and O'Donovan Rossa, or of the Neapolitan prisoners on whose behalf Gladstone had thundered so memorably?[5] And if the gravity of the offence were a relevant consideration, how could Davitt, sentenced to fifteen years, be regarded as more criminal than Luby and O'Leary, sentenced to twenty years, and O'Donovan Rossa, sentenced to penal servitude for life, all four being convicted of treason-felony?

The amnesty agitation reached a climax during the autumn of 1873, when a campaign opened by a monster meeting at Clontarf on Sunday, 7 September at which Butt was a principal speaker, was continued for nine successive Sundays from 28 September to 23 November—at Drogheda, Dundalk, Bray and Cork, Newry, Blackheath (S.E. London), Limerick and Arklow, Maryborough, Hannahstown (near Belfast) and Waterford, and finally at Glasnevin.[6] It was estimated that 250,000 people were present at Clontarf, 10,000 at Blackheath, 50,000 at Limerick and 300,000 at Glasnevin;[7] and though these figures were no doubt an exaggeration, the campaign was a demonstration of Irish opinion that was not lost on Gladstone. At his request the chief secretary for Ireland, Lord Hartington, inquired into the cases of all the

[1] *Nation,* 9 Sept. 71, pp 903–5. [2] Ibid., 26 Oct. 72, p. 679. [3] Above, p. 155.

[4] *Hansard 3,* cxcvi, 1238–42 (4 June 69), cxcviii, 1422–33 (6 Aug.); *Report of the commissioners appointed to inquire into the treatment of treason-felony convicts in English prisons* pp 14–16 [C 319], H.C. 1871, xxxii, 14–16; *Irishman,* 26 Oct. 72, p. 679; *Nation,* 2 Nov. p. 705.

[5] *Nation,* 9 Sept. 71, pp 903–5; 31 Aug. 72, p. 540; 7 Sept., p. 561; 14 Sept., p. 579; 21 Sept., p. 593; 2 Nov., p. 705. *Irishman,* 21 Sept., p. 182. And see above, p. 156.

[6] *Irishman,* 13 Sept. 73, pp 165–8; 4 Oct., pp 214–15; 11 Oct., p. 230; 18 Oct., pp 246–7; 25 Oct., p. 262; 1 Nov., pp 277–8; 8 Nov., pp 294–5; 15 Nov., p. 307; 22 Nov., p. 327; 29 Nov., pp 342–3. [7] Ibid., 29 Nov., p. 344.

prisoners. Supplied with full information by the home office and advised that the only cases which might possibly call for reconsideration were those of Davitt and Wilson, Hartington reported that, in the existing state of Ireland, there was no political reason for reducing the sentences of any of the prisoners.[1] Gladstone accepted this judgment and published his decision even though it was made clear that he would forfeit Irish support in British constituencies at the next general election.[2] That election came in February 1874, brought the conservatives under Disraeli back to power, and gave the newly formed Home Rule League a parliamentary party of 59 members led by Butt.[3] Disgusted with Gladstone, the amnesty leaders allowed themselves to hope that his rival, in the flush of his electoral victory, would release the prisoners. But in fact the conservatives thought that Ireland had been petted and spoiled by Gladstone and that not one of the fenians ought to have been released. When Butt presented Disraeli with an amnesty petition, signed by nearly 80 M.P.s, he received an evasive reply.[4] On the same day, 27 March, the new home secretary, R. A. Cross, announced in the house that the government did not intend to interfere with the course of the law.[5]

From this point onwards the Amnesty Association falls into the background, confining itself largely to the provision of relief for the prisoners' families; 'Amnesty Nolan' himself retired to the U.S.A. in July 1875;[6] and though Butt never abandoned his advocacy of the prisoners' cause, the lead in the amnesty agitation was taken by O'Connor Power, now M.P. for Mayo. His foremost supporter on the amnesty question was Parnell, who entered parliament in April 1875. Power launched the parliamentary campaign on 13 July 1874 by moving for an address to the queen requesting a return of the names of all persons who, within the previous ten years, had died or become insane or permanently disabled while suffering imprisonment for political offences. The motion was lost by 92 votes to 21.[7] In the following March, he attacked the contention that the prisoners' offences were not political by demanding how a conviction for treason-felony could be held to imply felony only, and not treason. He went on:

> If I consider for a moment the character of Mr Davitt, I must exclude from my mind everything of a sordid or selfish nature. He is the only one of those on whose behalf I now plead with whom I have had any personal acquaintance. He was one

[1] Gladstone Papers, B.L., Add. MS 44144, ff 129–33v (7–18 Oct. 73).

[2] *Irishman* 30 Aug., p. 131; 6 Sept., p. 157; 20 Sept., p. 187; 27 Dec., p. 409.

[3] Above, p. 127.

[4] *Irishman*, 21 Mar. 74, pp 598, 600; 28 Mar., p. 613; 4 Apr., pp 629, 630; 30 May, p. 757.

[5] *Hansard 3*, ccxvii, 347 (27 Mar.).

[6] *Irishman*, 10 July 75, p. 19.

[7] *Hansard 3*, ccxx, 1609–11.

of the most disinterested men I ever met—upright and honourable in every relation of life. I say he was, for the tomb could not more effectually separate him from life . . . than the prison in which he has been confined for the last five years; and I say it is monstrous for a government that professes to be based on the people's will and to be supported, too, by the public opinion of a great empire, to condemn such a man to waste away the flower of his ripening manhood in the company of the burglars and garotters and wife-murderers of England.

He had been refused permission to visit Davitt; and being thus prevented from judging for himself the truth or falsehood of statements in the press regarding Davitt's cruel treatment,[1] he must presume them to be true. What confidence could be placed in official denials after the O'Donovan Rossa scandal?[2] A few months later, Mitchell Henry, M.P. for County Galway, developed this line of attack by moving—without success—for reports on the treatment of political prisoners in foreign states.[3]

Amnesty and home rule were linked in a resolution carried at a public meeting of the Home Rule League at the Rotunda, Dublin, on 14 September 1875; the mover was Butt and the seconder Rev. Joseph Galbraith, Fellow of Trinity College.[4] In November, when John Wilson was almost due for conditional release, A. M. Sullivan, M.P., editor of the *Nation*, appealed privately to the home secretary for Davitt's release at the same time: Davitt's parents, old and in need of support, were in America; Davitt, a good and affectionate son, would willingly leave the United Kingdom permanently and devote himself to caring for them. Sullivan obviously knew little of Davitt, but his sincerity was undoubted and his reputation as a moderate nationalist stood high. The government, however, rejected his appeal. Wilson had served his full sentence (less the period of remission to which he was entitled), when he was released on ticket of leave in January 1876, and the government could see no reason for releasing Davitt, considering the distinction the trial judge had made between his sentence and Wilson's.[5]

The amnesty question was raised by Parnell in the debate on the address following the opening of parliament in February 1876; and the case of one of the prisoners, Edward O'Meagher Condon, who was an American subject, was aired not only at Westminster but also in the U.S. house of representatives. It was announced that the proclamation of Queen Victoria as 'empress of India' (1 May) would be followed by

[1] The reference is to D's letter of 1 Aug. 72.

[2] *Hansard 3*, ccxxii, 1759-64 (12 Mar. 75); *Irishman*, 20 Mar. pp 598-9. The quoted passage is not included in *Hansard*.

[3] *Hansard 3*, cxxv, 1198-1205 (8 July).

[4] *Irishman*, 18 Sept., pp 180-81.

[5] A. M. Sullivan to R. A. Cross, 27 Nov. 75, 10 Jan. 76; R. A. Cross to A. M. Sullivan, 12, 26 Jan. (DP/02). P.R.O., H.O.45/9329/19461/91; H.O.144/5/17869/9, 10, 23.

the release of all the prisoners.[1] The amnesty leaders pressed forward with a new petition, signed by 136 M.P.s. including all the home-rulers and many English liberals and radicals.[2] Again Disraeli disappointed Irish expectations. With reference to Davitt, he asked the house to remember that the judge who sentenced him to double Wilson's term must have considered that 'there were very aggravating circumstances' about his offence; to which Parnell made the rejoinder that Wilson was an Englishman, Davitt an Irishman.[3] After this rebuff the news of the *Catalpa* rescue (April 1876) gave enormous delight to Irish nationalists everywhere, including Davitt when he learnt of it several months later.[4]

The amnesty question was reopened in the house of commons by Power on 1 August. The number of the prisoners was now reduced to nine, and the feeling—strongly voiced on this occasion by John Bright—that more than enough vengeance had already been taken for all fenian offences, was growing among English members. In defending the government's policy, Cross mentioned that, when he became home secretary in 1874, he had been troubled about Davitt's case, and had carefully examined the facts. He was satisfied that the difference between Davitt's sentence and Wilson's was a just one; and he quoted from the judge's summing up at the trial to the effect that Wilson had been a tool in the hands of others, whereas Davitt was a principal and one who was prepared to resort to assassination if he found it convenient.[5] The amnesty motion was lost by 117 votes to 51, the minority including such distinguished Englishmen as John Bright, Sir Charles Dilke, and John Morley.[6] The fight was renewed in the spring of 1877, during the debates on the English prisons' bill, when Parnell and Power, in a masterly display of obstructionist tactics, forced on the government a number of amendments mitigating the barbarism of the jail-code, with special reference to political prisoners. It was at one of these debates that Power read letters from Davitt to illustrate the savage conditions under which the fenian prisoners were still living, and the helplessness of the convict before cruel and arbitrary conduct on the part of jail officials.[7] The final scene in the house of commons came on 20 July, when Power once again moved for the release of the prisoners. The secretary for war, G. Gathorne Hardy, in a heated outburst, indiscreetly declared that an amnesty would be regarded by Ireland not

[1] *Irishman*, 12 Feb., pp 516-17; 26 Feb., pp 551, 555; 18 Mar., p. 597; 29 Apr., p. 693; 6 May, pp 711, 712. *Hansard 3*, ccxxvii, 113-14 (9 Feb.), 1025-6 (28 Feb.), 1718 (9 Mar.).

[2] *Irishman*, 13 May, p. 727; 20 May, p. 745.

[3] *Hansard 3*, ccxxix, 1039-52 (22 May).

[4] Above, p. 136; *Irishman*, 10 June, p. 790; 24 June, p. 319.

[5] See above, p. 102.

[6] *Irishman*, 5 Aug., pp 84-5; *Hansard 3*, ccxxxi, 285-318 (1 Aug.).

[7] Ibid., ccxxxiv, 1309-28 (5 June 77); *Irishman*, 9 June 77.

as an act of mercy but an act of contrition on behalf of the government. Gladstone, for whose support Power had privately appealed,[1] now at last came down on the side of complete amnesty, thereby incurring an obvious taunt from Cross, the home secretary, who had already decided to release Davitt.[2]

A minute by Cross dated 11 July reads: 'Davitt might be released at the expiration of two years from the conditional release of Wilson. Not to go into the office or be made public till the time arrives.'[3] He privately conveyed some hint of this to O'Connor Power, who in consequence did not proceed with a question regarding Davitt that he had put on the order paper.[4] Five months later, on 19 December, the government released Davitt without making any reference to the amnesty agitation and without any admission that he was a political prisoner. Early in January 1878 three other fenians, Chambers, McCarthy, and O'Brien were similarly released.[5] Unlike the fenians previously amnestied, who were granted a free pardon, these four were released on ticket of leave, that is, on the same footing as ordinary convicts who had earned remission of their sentence by good conduct. The licence or ticket of leave granted to Davitt on 18 December authorised him to be at large during the remaining portion of his term of penal servitude unless in the meantime he should be convicted of some indictable offence within the United Kingdom, in which case the licence was at once to be forfeited, or unless the queen should previously revoke or alter it. The licence was issued subject to a number of stated conditions: (1) the holder was to produce it when called upon to do so by a magistrate or police officer; (2) he was to abstain from any violation of the law; (3) he was not habitually to associate with bad characters such as reputed thieves and prostitutes; and (4) he was not to lead an idle and dissolute life, without visible means of earning an honest livelihood. There were also provisions to ensure the observance of these conditions, the most significant being that the licence-holder must report himself to the police once a month and notify the police of any change of residence within forty-eight hours.[6]

The timing of Davitt's release was decisive for his place in history. If the law had taken its course he would not have emerged from Dartmoor (assuming that he did not forfeit any marks for misconduct)

[1] Power to Gladstone, 18 July (N.L.I., MS 11445).

[2] *Hansard 3*, ccxxxv, 1587-1626 (20 July).

[3] P.R.O., H.O.144/5/17869/19A.

[4] Ibid.

[5] P.R.O., H.O.45/9329/19461/91.

[6] P.R.O., H.O.144/5/17869/31. A not entirely accurate copy of the licence is in Cashman, pp 150-53. For a reproduction of the original see plate VIII.

till December 1881.[1] In that case there would have been no Davitt in Ireland to organise the farmers in the crisis of 1879–80.

The seven years of penal servitude thus ended form an era in Davitt's life. Like his youth they were years stamped with suffering, and with sustained refusal to accept defeat. Penal servitude was an ordeal that demanded great reserves of moral and intellectual strength; he lived up to his own splendid boast to his mother: 'don't fret about me at all; all the prisons in Europe would not break my spirit'.[2]

Davitt's prison experience was not unique in the history of fenianism, but, except Tom Clarke, none of the fenians who survived imprisonment to play an effective part in politics was imprisoned for so long or was so isolated in prison as Davitt. He emerged from Dartmoor weakened in health but with his mind unimpaired, his spirit unembittered, his steadfastness and courage magnificently vindicated. He was not, of course, unscathed by penal servitude: the introspectiveness, the tendency to play a lone hand, the readiness to be over-critical of other men's motives, that were thenceforth to be characteristic of him, were probably accentuated by prison conditions. But he remained an incurable idealist, impervious alike to cynicism and pessimism.

Of his sex life we know nothing. He had grown up in a society in which there was no segregation of boys and girls, and to judge from the evidence of his later life he seems always to have found relations with women as little of a problem as relations with people of a different religion. He had been attracted by a girl ('Miss S. S.') about 1868,[3] but, perhaps because of his commitment to the I.R.B., he had evidently formed no lasting attachment when, at twenty-four, he was removed to an all-male world of convicts and jailors. In this unnatural situation it is safe to assume that he was not lacking in self-discipline. As to his religious life, of which we know almost nothing, there is no reason to doubt that he held firmly to the catholic piety in which he had been reared, while casting a cold eye on the unsympathetic catholic clergy whom he encountered as a prisoner.

Ironically, it is in his letters from prison that we have the first self-revelation of Davitt's personality; and through this restricting medium he appears as the strong, decisive character his previous career would lead us to expect. His prose style, though inclined to be laboured and diffuse, was clear and rounded, with good vocabulary and an eye for the telling phrase; for someone whose formal education had been

[1] H. S. Winterbotham to Hartington, 7 Oct. 73 (Gladstone papers, B.L., Add. MS 44144, f.131), [2] D to his mother, [May 75] (smuggled).

[3] Known only from a reference in his diary for 22 June 80; see below, p. 396.

interrupted at the age of nine, resumed at eleven, and terminated at fifteen, it was remarkable. It was the style of a man with some literary ambition, who had not allowed his education to stop when he left school, and who in prison continued the work of self-education. The literary ambition is still more evident in the poetry Davitt produced in Dartmoor, which shows versatility without any poetic quality. Of this Davitt was well aware, and many years later, in reply to an inquiry from T. D. Sullivan, wrote of these and earlier[1] verses:

in the name of all the poets who ever sang in Erin, don't disinter from a kindly oblivion the effusions to which you refer. In all my political and party differences with opponents and friends these past transgressions against the 'Mooses' were not flung at me, and I feel sure that you will be equally charitable.[2]

For his political career the Dartmoor years were decisive. The amnesty agitation not only shortened his imprisonment but transformed him from an unknown conspirator into a public figure. Years before his release his name was established in the imagination of his countrymen as the symbol of invincible and self-immolating resistance to British rule. He emerged from prison, as he had predicted before he went in,[3] a far more dangerous enemy to Britain than before. He went to prison a romantic conspirator of twenty-four, an unquestioning disciple of fenianism. He came out a mature man of thirty-one, tried and tempered by suffering; an unrepentant fenian, determined to renew the fight, but by methods more appropriate and effective than those he had used to no purpose and at such cost to himself. On this aspect of Davitt's life John Devoy, though he had already become a bitter opponent, made a perceptive comment in 1882:

A weak man is ruined mentally and physically by imprisonment, but a man of strong fibre sent to prison for standing by his native land, although injured physically by the confinement, comes out more resolute, more self-contained, and with a clearer view of things than if he had spent his years in the heat and strife of the outside world. It was so with Davitt. He acquired a habit of thinking out a subject while sitting at his silent task or pacing his lonely cell during seven long years, and he emerged from the prison with a truer conception of the needs of the movement, in the success of which his heart was set, than he could have realised had he escaped imprisonment.[4]

No contemporary evidence of Davitt's political thinking while in prison exists: his smuggled communications are as silent on the subject as his official letters. We depend for our knowledge of it on explanations that he himself supplied at later stages of his career, notably in November 1878, in 1882, and in 1889. That he had begun to work out a new approach to Irish politics in the light of his own experience

[1] See above, pp 53–4.
[2] D to T. D. Sullivan, 13 Dec. 1901 (DP/02).
[3] See above, p. 102.
[4] Devoy, *The land of Eire*, p. 39.

and of the political news reaching him towards the end of his imprisonment is, however, so inherently probable that there is no reason to question his accuracy when in November 1878 he wrote:

. . . I found myself in prison for sending a few rifles to Ireland, without the consolation of knowing that one of them was ever shouldered to smite an enemy of my country. I was in prison only for *resolve*, not for an act whereby a single link of Ireland's chain was broken . . . The years I had laboured in the national cause . . . were therefore, barren of practical results . . . , and I resolved that no other period of my life should be so . . . if I ever . . . regained my liberty.[1]

In 1878, and again in 1882, he explained why he had become critical of fenian methods and attitudes. To rely wholly on secret conspiracy in an age when public opinion counted for so much was to ignore the principal weapon of the weak in a fight for justice against the strong; and to treat all Irishmen who were not fenians as unionists was to make enemies of potential supporters and fatally divide the national ranks.[2] So much may be accepted as reflecting Davitt's thought by 1877.

His retrospective statements, however, carry the story very much further than this, and with varying emphasis and detail claim that the idea of cooperation between revolutionary and constitutional nationalists on the land question, which, in 1879, was to take shape in the Land League, was conceived by him in Dartmoor. For example in 1882 he wrote:

I have worked at breaking stone when the cold was such that the birds would drop dead around me, and [I] was unconscious of it, so intently was I thinking out the true solution of Ireland's difficulties. When I came out I was armed with a plan of which the Land League is the result.[3]

And again, in another place:

When I was in prison I spent my time thinking of what plan could be proposed which would unite all Irishmen upon some common ground . . . I made up my mind that the only issue upon which home rulers, nationalists, obstructionists, and each and every shade of opinion existing in Ireland could be united was the land question.[4]

In 1889, before the *Times*-Parnell commission, he said:

The Land League, which is here on its trial, was largely, though not entirely, the offspring of thoughts and resolutions which whiled away many a dreary and tedious hour in political captivity. It lightened the burden of penal servitude, and brought compensating solace to some extent for the loss of liberty, of home, and of friends, to think, and reason, and plan, how, when freedom should once again restore me to the rights and privileges of society, I should devote to the good of

[1] *Irishman*, 14 Dec. 78, p. 379.
[2] *Daily World* (New York), 9 July 82, in Cashman, pp 210-11.
[3] *Pilot* (Boston), 8 July, quoted in Brown, *Irish-American nationalism*, p. 84.
[4] *Daily World* (New York), 9 July, in Cashman, pp 210-11.

Ireland what strength of purpose or ability of service long years of patient study and yearning aspirations should equip me with in a just cause.[1]

On the strength of these persuasive claims it has been generally accepted that Davitt came out of Dartmoor 'with the Land League in his brain'.[2] This view, however, is not tenable.[3] Close analysis of his subsequent political behaviour shows that the state of mind he attributes to himself while still in Dartmoor did not begin to take shape in him till late in 1878, and was not fully developed till 1879. Even if he could have foreseen the situation that was to arise in 1878-9, which is highly unlikely, it is quite certain that he had no new plan for a settlement of the land question to offer until, in the autumn of 1878, he came into direct contact with American fenians.[4] This fact has been obscured by a legend that he himself created. That he did so reflects an aspect of his personality that runs right through the story of his life.

One of Davitt's distinguishing characteristics, which increasingly came to be recognised by contemporaries, was his deep concern for the truth. Lying was repugnant to him—as it was not, for example, to Parnell if the occasion seemed to demand it. Yet, paradoxically, from the age of nineteen his sense of political obligation had involved him in activities from which furtiveness, deception, and evasion were inseparable. He had reaped the bitter harvest of these activities in a trial in which lies were freely employed in his defence as well as by the prosecution, and about which, in his protestations of unjust treatment, he seemed to confuse legal innocence with real innocence. While he had unbounded courage, moral and physical, and great power of decision, he lacked self-assurance and had a tendency to self-questioning encouraged, no doubt, by prison conditions. And not only was he ready to learn from his own errors, but as soon as he regained his liberty he showed himself quick to absorb new ideas and to respond to new situations. All this was reflected in changes of political outlook and action that were not inconsistent with his fundamental political thinking, but do raise problems of causation and continuity. Passionately anxious to see his past and present conduct as a self-consistent whole, he was to interpret and reinterpret his career on a number of critical occasions in relation to the needs then uppermost in his mind. This was to have the result of providing retrospective explanations that on certain issues owed more to wishful thinking than to the facts. It was one aspect of the contrast between Davitt and Parnell that the former repeatedly

[1] *S.C.P.*, x, 422; *Defence*, p. 2.
[2] Desmond Ryan, *The Phoenix flame*, p. 249.
[3] It is subjected to rigorous criticism in Brown, *Irish-American nationalism*, ch. V.
[4] See below, ch. VII

sought to justify himself, whereas the latter, except under compulsion, never attempted to explain his conduct (and under compulsion did not hesitate to lie).

In another way the years that Davitt spent in prison were a preparation for future activity. Just as his early experience of factory life gave him a lasting sympathy with working men, so life in prison left him with a permanent concern for men in captivity. His right to be heard on the problem of penal servitude gained public recognition. He gave evidence before the Kimberley commission on the working of the penal servitude acts in 1878. He became well known as an advocate of prison reform. His first book, *Leaves from a prison diary* (1885), partly written during a second period of penal servitude (1881–2), has much to say on criminal life and character, and on the problem of crime and punishment. On 9 April 1898, ex-convict W822,[1] now Michael Davitt M.P., a member of the committee on the prisons bill, returned to Dartmoor with a special order from the home office authorising the governor to permit him 'to view the prison and to afford him every facility for seeing the system of discipline and treatment of prisoners in all its branches'.[2] The wheel thus came round full circle.

[1] His number when he left Dartmoor and during his imprisonment in Millbank and Portland (1881–2).

[2] E. Ruggles-Brise, chairman of the prison commission, to D, 6 Apr. 98 (DA/3A, p. 63); home office to governor of Dartmoor prison, 6 Apr. (DPA).

VI

A fresh start, December 1877–July 1878

ARRIVING in London on Wednesday night, 19 December 1877, Davitt was welcomed by Isaac Butt and other members of the political prisoners visiting committee. The chairman, Richard O'Shaughnessy, M.P., felicitated him on his release and expressed hope that the remaining political prisoners would soon be liberated. F. H. O'Donnell, who now met him for the first time, describes him as a 'tall, dark, romantic-looking man, . . . more like a starved poet than a revolutionist'.[1] At O'Donnell's, suggestion it was decided to hold a public meeting soon, at which Davitt would give some account of his experiences in prison. There were none of Davitt's own family to greet him, all of them being in America; he had no relatives in England, and he was out of touch with his relatives in Ireland, on which he had not set foot since he was four. It was all the more fortunate that he had a good friend in London, John Ryan,[2] a former associate in fenianism, who was joint treasurer of the prisoners visiting committee. He was a bootmaker by trade, living at 14 Shawfield Street, Chelsea, and Davitt stayed with him over Christmas, exulting in the delight of being restored to the world of real people after seven years of exclusive contact with cells and prisoners and warders; it was, he felt, like coming up into the sunshine after a lifetime in the depths of a coal mine.[3] It was in this mood that, two or three days after reaching London, he sought out Parnell, O'Connor Power, and a few others, to thank them in person for the interest they had shown in him while in prison and for their efforts to effect his release.[4]

The meeting with Parnell, the first between the two men, made a lasting impression on Davitt, which, in 1903, he thus recalled:

He struck me at once with the power and directness of his personality. There was the proud, resolute bearing of a man of conscious strength, with a mission, wearing

[1] O'Donnell, *Irish parl. party*, i, 253. [2] See above, p. 157.

[3] *Universe*, 22 Dec. 77; *Irishman*, 12 May, p. 732; 22 Dec., p. 389. *Inquiry as to the alleged ill-treatment of the convict Charles McCarthy in Chatham convict prison*, p. 15 [C 1978], H.C. 1878, lxii, 783. Cashman, p. 44. *Fall*, pp 93, 110. O'Donnell, *Irish parl. party*, i, 365–6.

[4] *S.C.P.*, ix, 356.

no affectation, but without a hint of Celtic character or a trait of its racial enthusiasm. 'An Englishman of the strongest type, moulded for an Irish purpose' was my thought, as he spoke of imprisonment, of the prevailing state of affairs in the home rule movement, and of the work which 'a few of us' were carrying on in the house of commons. There was not a suspicion of boastfulness in anything he said, nor of confident promise for the future. He expressed, as I am sure he felt, a genuine sympathy for those who had undergone the ordeal of penal servitude, with its nameless indignities and privations. 'I would not face it', I recollect him saying. 'It would drive me mad. Solitude and silence are too horrible to think of. I would kill a warder and get hanged rather than have to endure years of such agony and of possible insanity.'

Parnell spoke of Butt in fair and generous terms while conveying a highly favourable estimate of Biggar, O'Connor Power, and O'Donnell as exponents of the obstructionist policy. He said nothing about his own part in the new movement, or of his plans for the future, but showed a kindly curiosity about Davitt's intentions. 'I shall rejoin the revolutionary movement, of course', was Davitt's reply, on which, characteristically, Parnell made no comment.[1] But he formed a very high opinion of Davitt—for his judgment, his decision of character, and his courage. 'I believe', he told the *Times*-Parnell commission in 1889, 'I looked forward at that time to his taking a very distinguished part in the future political and social history of Ireland'.[2]

Despite the obvious danger for a ticket of leave man, inevitably under police observation, Davitt did not hesitate to renew his connection with the I.R.B., and his standing in the movement was recognised by his election to the supreme council as member for the north of England. By his own explanation to the *Times*-Parnell commission, he 'rejoined the movement for the purpose of trying to convert it into a movement of open and constitutional action'.[3] Contemporary evidence, especially his correspondence with Devoy,[4] during the three years following his release, and his own later account of discussion with Parnell,[5] indicate that no such simple and clear-cut plan was in his mind at this time. Certainly he took care to dissociate himself from fenian intolerance of other nationalists. His head was full of projects for the national movement, and he was impatient for action[6] but still had much to learn and was feeling his way in Irish politics during most of 1878.

Early in January he was joined in London by the three other released prisoners, Thomas Chambers, Charles Heapy McCarthy, and John Patrick O'Brien. All three were ex-soldiers who had been court-martialled in Dublin in 1866-7 and sentenced to penal servitude for life,

[1] *Fall*, pp 110-11.
[2] *S.C.P.*, vii, 5 (30 Apr. 89).
[3] Ibid., ix, 354 (2 July).
[4] See *D.P.B.*, i-ii, letters for 1878-80.
[5] See below, pp 206-7.
[6] Devoy, *The land of Eire*, p. 39.

for breach of the articles of war. A fenian group in Dublin, headed by Patrick Egan, made arrangements with Davitt for the four men to come to Ireland together and be welcomed as national heroes. Plans were worked out in detail by Egan, who made it his business to see that the occasion should have a broadly-based nationalist character and not be exploited by any political clique. He was determined that nothing should be done to compromise the ex-prisoners (whose intention to visit Dublin was a subject of communication between the Irish government and the home office) or interfere with the chance of release for the fenians still imprisoned.[1] A reception committee was set up consisting of Parnell, John Ferguson, John Dillon, and many fenians, including men already well known in Irish politics—Barry, Biggar, and Egan himself—and a larger number of unknown men, of whom Thomas Brennan, James Carey, and Daniel Curley were soon to make news, Brennan as a land agitator, the other two for their part in the Phoenix Park murders. If fenians thus preponderated on the committee, the range of political outlook that they represented was considerable.

The released prisoners left London for Holyhead on Saturday night, 12 January, accompanied by John Ryan and Maurice Collins, representing the political prisoners visiting committee. They slept at Holyhead, left for Kingstown on Sunday, 13 January, at 2.5 p.m. by the mail steamer, *Ulster*, and arrived punctually at 6 p.m. to find the harbour illuminated and dense crowds, headed by Parnell and others, awaiting them. The *Ulster* berthed at Carlisle Pier amid uproarious cheering and jubilation, which the four men acknowledged from a conspicuous position in front of the port paddle-box. As they stepped ashore, brass bands played rousing music, rockets streaked the sky, and bonfires blazed on Howth and on Dalkey Hill. Apart from O'Brien, who seemed in excellent condition, they showed signs of weakness and privation, and seemed prematurely old. McCarthy especially, with his worn face, sunken eyes, and broken voice, struck everyone as a very sick man, unequal to the strain of the occasion. When the tumult on the landing-stage had been reduced to comparative calm, Brennan read an address (of which Egan had had copies printed for the press) on behalf of the people of Dublin:

Fellow-countrymen! We approach you to offer you our warmest congratulations, to bid you, with all the fervour and affection of our hearts, welcome home to Ireland, and to thank you for your courageous and uncompromising devotion to the national cause.

Roman history reveres the tradition which tells of the heroic self-sacrifice of the patriot Marcus Curtius, who saved the city by casting himself into the yawning abyss opened in the forum. With a self-denying patriotism equal to his, you have

[1] Egan to D, 9, 11 Jan. 78 (DP/RR); S.P.O., R.P. 1878/583, 696, 905 (1882/26234).

made an offering of life, fortune, and liberty on the altar of your country; and if by such sacrifices as yours her freedom has not been achieved, her honour has been saved, her manhood has been vindicated, and a fund of public virtue has been created amongst us which will yet redeem and regenerate the land . . .

To this Davitt—described by the *Freeman's Journal* reporter as 'a comparatively young-looking man with a heavy black moustache'[1]—responded on behalf of himself and his three colleagues in a prepared speech of thanks the text of which Egan had also had printed. The four men then boarded the boat-train, accompanied by Parnell, Egan, Ferguson, O'Connor Power, Major Purcell O'Gorman M.P. (famous for his wit and humour no less than for his corpulence), Richard Pigott (proprietor of the *Irishman*), and other public figures. At Westland Row station, Dublin, there were larger crowds and greater enthusiasm than ever. With difficulty a bodyguard of young men forced a way for the returning heroes to a waiting wagonette, around which a monster procession (including many of the Dublin trade bodies) eventually formed itself. To the strains of eighteen brass and reed bands and lighted by thousands of torches, it moved triumphantly through the central streets of the city, taking nearly three hours to reach the European Hotel, in Bolton Street, where the ex-prisoners were to stay. The roadway in front of the hotel was so densely packed that two of them had to be hoisted from the waggonette into the hotel through a window, Davitt alone making his entry by the main door.[2] It was a strenuous homecoming, but to men who had endured isolation and humiliation for so long it was infinitely gratifying to receive such spectacular demonstrations of popular appreciation and affection. To Davitt it was the more heart-filling, because he was an almost total stranger in Dublin, which he had seen only once before, in 1850, when as a child of four he had passed through the city with his parents and sisters on their way into exile.

For McCarthy the strain proved too great. He had shown signs of extreme exhaustion during the reception ceremonies, but had rallied sufficiently to go with Davitt on Monday night to see Boucicault's *The shaughraun* at the Gaiety Theatre.[3] Next morning (15 January) he and his three colleagues were at Morrison's Hotel,[4] where they had been invited by Parnell to breakfast. The party, including Dillon, Biggar, Power, Egan, Brennan, T. D. Sullivan, and Pigott, had just gathered

[1] See plate IX.

[2] Cashman, pp 44–9 (dating wrong); *F.J.*, 14 Jan.; *Irishman*, 5, 12, 19 Jan.; *S.C.P.*, v, 165, 220–21, ix, 417; *Gaelic American*, 9 June 1906.

[3] First performance, New York, 1875; first performed at the Gaiety, 27 Dec. 76 (S. J. Brown, *A guide to books on Ireland*, pt I (1912), p. 195).

[4] At the angle formed by Nassau Street and the east side of Dawson Street.

when McCarthy suddenly collapsed and died. At the inquest held on 16 January by the city coroner the jury returned a verdict of death from heart disease, accelerated by ill-treatment in prison. Evidence was given by Davitt, Chambers, and O'Brien, of whom the last had been a fellow-prisoner with McCarthy at Chatham and was able to testify to the severities inflicted upon him. McCarthy's funeral was the occasion for renewed public demonstrations: his body lay in state in the Confraternity Room of the Carmelite church in Clarendon Street (the only church that would receive it, since McCarthy was a fenian), and the procession to Glasnevin cemetery on 20 January was claimed to be the largest since the funeral of O'Connell.[1]

Davitt shouldered responsibility for much of the business inevitably arising out of McCarthy's death, and it was not till Saturday, 26 January, that he was able to leave Dublin for a visit to Mayo, O'Brien and Chambers also setting out at the same time for their native counties. He was welcomed by enthusiastic crowds awaiting the arrival of his train at Ballyhaunis and other stations in Mayo on his route to Castlebar. At Claremorris he was met by two well-known nationalists from Balla, about ten miles away, John W. Walshe and John W. Nally. Walshe, a cousin of Davitt's and the son of a substantial farmer, was a commercial traveller with a wide and intimate knowledge of local conditions. Nally (known as 'Scrab'), the eldest son of a large farmer who was also a landowner, was Walshe's brother-in-law. 'A rollicking good-natured poor devil', he was hail-fellow-well-met with everybody and taken seriously by nobody.[2] His trouble was drink. He kept a public house in Balla, having several years previously been evicted from a farm with his wife and twelve children.[3] His attentions must have been embarrassing to Davitt, with his strong temperance views. He was accompanied by Walshe and Nally to Balla, where a deputation, supported by a host of 'patriotic young ladies', induced him to make an unscheduled stop of two hours (5-7 p.m.), in the course of which he was entertained at 'Nally's hotel'. Afterwards Nally, Walshe, and other nationalists went on with him to Castlebar. As they drove by horse car through the darkness the party was greeted at many points along the road by cheering groups carrying torches.

At Castlebar Davitt was the guest of James Daly, editor of the weekly *Connaught Telegraph*, a town commissioner, and a poor law guardian. The two men had become acquainted in Dublin, on 15 January, when

[1] *F.J.*, 16, 17, 21 Jan. 78; *Irishman*, 19 Jan.; *Universe*, 28 Jan.; *Inquiry as to the alleged ill-treatment of the convict Charles McCarthy in Chatham convict prison*, pp 15-16 [C 1978], H.C. 1878, lxiii, 783-4; [C 1978-I], H.C. 1878, lxiii, 797.

[2] *Defence*, p. 211.

[3] Personal histories, pp 19-21; *S.C.P.*, i, 541, vii, 6, ix, 441, 443; *Defence*, p. 210.

Daly had invited Davitt to visit Mayo as his guest. A strong and colourful personality, described by an acute observer in 1879 as a 'rough-spoken giant, with an inexhaustible fund of knowledge of the people and the quaintest mother-wit',[1] Daly had distinguished himself as the champion of the small farmers of Mayo and had made his paper a trumpet of tenant grievances in Connacht generally. Along with Matthew Harris and Michael Malachy O'Sullivan, both of Ballinasloe, and others, he had for several years been promoting an agitation among the tenants in Mayo, Galway, and Roscommon. Harris, a farmer's son, was a building contractor whose business brought him into contact with a large area of the west. In 1876 he had founded the Ballinasloe Tenants' Defence Association. He was a prominent fenian, who had been engaged in importing and distributing rifles to members of the I.R.B. in Connacht, and it is quite possible that some of the arms transmitted by Davitt from England in 1870 may have passed through his hands.[2] O'Sullivan, also a fenian, was a national teacher at a catholic college in Ballinasloe.[3] At meetings in 1876–7 at which the reported attendance ranged from 2000 to 5000 these three were foremost in denouncing rack-renting and evicting landlords, large graziers, and home rule politicians such as the O'Conor Don and the Hon. Charles French, M.P.s for County Roscommon, who failed to support Butt's land and grand jury bills in the house of commons. The measure of land reform generally demanded as an immediate need was the 3 Fs, with peasant proprietorship as the ultimate aim. From November 1876 Daly was endeavouring to rouse the Mayo farmers into forming a defence association. He declared to a protest meeting held at Headford, County Galway, that landlords had no right to trade in land as though it were like any other commodity. He advised tenants to pay no more than a fair rent and to show solidarity with one another by refusing to take a farm from which a tenant had been evicted, by raising a fund to support evicted tenants, and by setting up a committee to publicise every case of landlord oppression in the area. The tenants, he declared, in an editorial of 5 May 1877, had so often been denied justice that, if England were to be at war tomorrow and an invader were to land in Ireland, no one save the landlords and a few thousand orangemen would resist them. Some of the local clergy, including Bishop Duggan of Clonfert, supported the agitation, which its leaders were careful to insist was strictly within the law. The parish priest of Louisburgh, Rev. William Joyce, warned of an impending crisis in an open letter

[1] W. O'Brien, *Recollections*, p. 224.
[2] *S.C.P.*, xx, 177–8; see above, pp 67–8.
[3] Personal histories, p. 14.

of 10 November 1877 to E. Dwyer Gray, M.P., editor of the *Freeman*: the potato crop of that year had failed so badly in Connacht that he feared they were on the eve of another famine; tenants were heavily in debt, and he wondered how they could pay next year's rents, which, he said, had been nearly doubled since 1846.[1]

Davitt must have learnt something of all this during his three days as Daly's guest. On Sunday evening (27 January) Daly presided at a great open-air meeting in Davitt's honour on the green opposite the court house, which was preceded by a torchlight procession through the town. He took up a suggestion from one of the crowd that Davitt and the other liberated fenians owed their release to the emperor of Russia, with whom, it seemed, Britain was now on the point of going to war over the Russian invasion of Turkey;[2] never, he said was the aphorism that England's difficulty was Ireland's opportunity more appropriate than in the present crisis. The British government wanted the Irish people to help them against the Russians, but the Irish people should not waste their blood for 'a government that allowed their race to be exterminated wholesale'.

What he would suggest to them would be to tell them to get the lords of the soil, who evicted their friends and replaced them with the short-horn and the black-face, to go and fight the Russians, aided by their short-horns and black-faces. (Cheers and laughter.)

Davitt followed with a short speech of thanks, in which he said that the reception he met with everywhere made up for all he had suffered in prison. Thanks might be due to the emperor of Russia but the ex-prisoners themselves attributed their release to the unceasing exertions of the worthy member for Mayo, John O'Connor Power, who, Davitt felt certain, would continue to exert himself on behalf of the remaining political prisoners.[3]

On Monday, 28 January, Davitt visited Straide, his birthplace, where, as reported in the *Connaught Telegraph*, 'he was received with all the tenderness and affection his two uncles and several cousins could bestow'. He himself, in his only surviving letter referring to the occasion, told his mother: 'I saw Mary Davitt, John's sister, who was out in America some time ago; also uncle Pat and Tony'.[4] Mary Davitt was a cousin, a daughter of Michael's uncle John. Uncle Pat must have been a Kielty; for, of Michael's two paternal uncles, John Davitt was dead and Henry was in America.[5] Tony was probably uncle Pat's son. These were the first relatives Michael had met in nearly eight years. As for

[1] *Connaught Telegraph*, 1876–7, 16 June 1906.

[2] Cf. above, p. 139.

[3] DN/1, p. 2; *F.J.*, 29 Jan. 78; *Connaught Telegraph*, 2 Feb.

[4] D to his mother, 7 Feb. (DP/D5).

[5] Above, p. 169.

Straide, he had not set eyes on the place since his departure as a child, twenty-seven years before. Not a vestige of his former home remained: its very stones and those of houses once occupied by neighbours had, according to the *Connaught Telegraph*, been used by the present landlord, Henry Joynt, to build boundary walls round the farms he had created by consolidating the small holdings of such as the Davitts. Only an old poplar tree and 'a slight unevenness' in the ground marked the spot where Michael was born. But the ruins of the abbey were little changed, and he lingered over the once familiar ground before returning to Castlebar.[1]

Next morning (29 January) Michael visited the site of the 'Castlebar races' and paid tribute to the bravery of the French troops under General Humbert who, in their memorable epilogue to the United Irish rising, had routed a superior British force on 27 August 1798. He left Castlebar by train in the afternoon, to receive a second and vociferous welcome at Balla, where he was introduced by John Walshe as 'Mayo's noble and patriotic son and martyr'. In his reply Davitt expressed his concern for the fenians still imprisoned. That evening there was a torchlight procession and a bonfire, followed by a party at Nally's, where singing, dancing, and recitations went on till 3 a.m. Next day, Wednesday, 30 January, accompanied by Walshe, Davitt drove to Swinford and then to Ballyhaunis, at both of which he was welcomed with no less warmth and jubilation. At Swinford he visited the district bridewell and contrasted its 'comparative luxury' with the savage conditions he had experienced in Dartmoor. He spent some time with a Conn Davitt (probably a relative), from a window of whose house he addressed a large and enthusiastic crowd. Ballyhaunis, which he reached late on Wednesday evening, was illuminated, and about 2000 people gathered to hear him speak, followed by Walshe. From Ballyhaunis Davitt went on to Athlone (31 January) and there turned back west to Ballinasloe and Galway before returning to Dublin on 2 February. At Ballinasloe he had a meeting with Matthew Harris.[2]

In one strenuous but invigorating week he had renewed his long-interrupted contact with his native Mayo, where, he told his mother, he was 'received like a prince'. He had made the aquaintance of, and favourably impressed, the militant editor of the *Connaught Telegraph*, James Daly, the 'storm centre'[3] of the tenant right agitation in Mayo. He had met another Connacht celebrity, Matthew Harris, who combined land agitation with fenianism. He had also made contact with other

[1] *Connaught Telegraph*, 2 Feb. Cf. above, p. 4.
[2] DN/1, p. 2; *Connaught Telegraph*, 2 Feb.; *S.C.P.*, x, 178.
[3] W. O'Brien *Recollections*, p. 224.

local leaders, mostly fenians. Such men must have had much to say of the growing agricultural distress that was soon to bring about a major crisis in rural Ireland.

By his visit to the west Davitt had broken one of the conditions of his ticket of leave. Convicts released on licence were required, among other conditions, to report themselves to the police once a month and to notify the police, within 48 hours, of any change of residence. Davitt had duly reported himself to the detective office on 15 January two days after his arrival in Dublin, when he told the police that he intended to go to America to join his mother and sisters. He did not notify the police before leaving for the west on 26 January, but on his return he again reported himself to the detective office, explaining that he had intended to be absent only about 48 hours and to go *incognito* but had found it impossible to do either. The home secretary, R. A. Cross, informed of this breach of regulations, decided (4 February) that there was no need to be as strict with Davitt and the two other released fenians as with 'criminals of the ordinary, habitual type'; and Dublin Castle was advised that no notice should be taken of their failure to report themselves. It was the first official admission (and it was entirely private) that Davitt was not an ordinary criminal. He was not directly informed of Cross's decision, but it seems to have been conveyed to him through Parnell or O'Connor Power, both of whom had pressed the government to dispense with the humiliating restriction. At all events he ceased to report to the police, and they, while keeping him under surveillance, did not interfere with him. R.I.C. men were present at the Castlebar meeting on 27 January, and the acting county inspector reported to the inspector general of police that the account of the meeting in the *Freeman's Journal* was 'very much exaggerated', and that Davitt had not said that his release had been largely due to the emperor of Russia. The R.I.C. inspector for the west riding of Galway considered that Davitt's main object in the west was to become acquainted with local fenians and to propagate fenianism.[1]

He left Dublin on 4 February for Haslingden,[2] and by the 7th was back in London on business connected with McCarthy's death. He was thinking of settling down in Ireland after that, having some prospect of employment as a commercial traveller for a wine and spirit merchant in Dublin, where, he wrote to his mother, he hoped to provide a comfortable home for her and his unmarried sister, Sib.[3] If he seriously entertained the idea of such a career he must soon have abandoned it.

[1] S.P.O., R.P. 1878/1033, 1746, 1925, 2498, 2909 (1882/26234); R.P. 1878/2889; *F.J.*, 29 Jan.; P.R.O., H.O. 144/5/17869/19, 20, 22B, 31.

[2] Ibid., 20.

[3] DN/1, p. 1; D to his mother, 7 Feb. (DP/D5).

For he was learning to make his living by writing and public speaking, as incidental to political commitments. It is hard to imagine Davitt comfortably established in the wholesale liquor business, but understandable that the employment he had in mind was on the road, and not at a desk. From now onwards he was seldom to remain long in any one place; was it that an itch to be moving had got into his blood during his years as a fenian arms-agent, or was it that prolonged reaction against being cooped up in Dartmoor incessantly drove him on?

The question of the late Charles McCarthy's treatment in prison had been raised in the house of commons by O'Connor Power on 29 January. Cross, the home secretary, had conceded Power's demand for an inquiry, and had appointed Sir James Ingham, chief magistrate of Bow Street metropolitan police court, assisted by Dr Henry Pitman as medical assessor, to conduct it. Ingham was given no power to administer an oath to those from whom he obtained evidence, and his inquiry at Chatham prison on 4 and 11 February was conducted in private. O'Connor Power strongly objected to both conditions and insisted that, if the inquiry were to command respect, (a) it must be conducted in public, (b) every statement received should be given an oath, and (c) the relatives or next-of-kin of the deceased should be present or represented by counsel. His claim was not accepted. The report of the inquiry, dated 5 March 1878, declared (i) that McCarthy's treatment in prison had not hastened his death, and (ii) that it had been as lenient as was consistent with penal discipline and the precautions that became necessary to prevent his escape. This conclusion settled nothing. The inquiry was denounced by O'Connor Power and others as a device to whitewash the Chatham authorities, and its findings were generally rejected by national opinion which regarded McCarthy as a martyr.[1]

The three ex-prisoners had no doubt that McCarthy's health had been undermined by the rigours of Chatham, and they submitted written statements of their views, with supporting detail, through O'Connor Power to the Ingham inquiry. Davitt's statement (14 February) criticised the whole existing system of penal servitude. Its tendency was to induce heart disease and pulmonary tuberculosis in prisoners. His own imprisonment had induced heart disease, as he had learnt from 'competent medical authority' since his release. He was convinced that he could not have survived in prison another two years. The men appointed as medical officers in prisons were generally deficient in qualifications and experience, and prisoners with the most serious complaints

[1] *Hansard 3*, ccxxxvii, 622, 726, 1051–2 (29, 31 Jan., 5 Feb.); *Inquiry as to the alleged ill-treatment of the convict Charles McCarthy* . . . [C 1978], H.C. 1878, lxiii; Thomas Chambers to J. B. O'Reilly, 18 Feb., in *D.P.B.*, i, 304–5; *Nation*, 30 Mar.

were the most neglected. As to political prisoners, he made the charge which he was often to reiterate that they had 'beyond doubt been treated with greater severity, subjected to more indignities, and suffered more neglect from prison doctors, than any other class of prisoners'. No effort was spared by jailors to show such prisoners that they were in exactly the same category as convicts guilty of murder and other revolting crimes.[1] The statements of Chambers and O'Brien corroborated these charges and showed that they, like Davitt and McCarthy, had suffered in prison from hunger and cold, the foul air in their cells, nightly disturbance by jailors, repeated searchings, exceptional surveillance from August 1876 onwards, and numberless indignities.[2]

A campaign of public meetings to demand the release of all the fenians still in prison and to raise funds for those who had been released and for McCarthy's family was launched in London on Saturday, 9 March, in St James's Hall, Piccadilly. O'Connor Power, who seems to have been a moving spirit behind the campaign, presided, and a responsive audience of about 2,500 ticket-holders, nearly all London Irish, filled the hall. The district home rule associations attended with bands and banners, and there were deputations from the Manhood Suffrage League and the Labourers' Union. The platform party comprised Davitt, Chambers, and O'Brien; ten home rule M.P.s, six of them supporters of Butt—E. Dwyer Gray, Mitchell Henry, Chevalier Keyes O'Clery, R. D. O'Shaughnessy, W. A. Redmond, and Dr M. F. Ward, and four obstructionists—Parnell, O'Donnell, O'Connor Power, and Richard Power; two English liberals—C. H. Hopwood, Q.C., M.P. for Stockport, and J. D. Hutchinson, M.P. for Halifax; Dr Andrew Commins, barrister, of Liverpool, who had been president of the Home Rule Confederation of Great Britain;[3] William Tallack, secretary of the Howard Association, and more than a dozen other sympathisers, Irish and English. Two home rule M.P.s. A. M. Sullivan and Lord Francis Conyngham, and the radical leader, Joseph Chamberlain, sent their apologies, and there were good-will messages from the home-rulers of Liverpool and other Irish centres in Britain.[4]

Three resolutions, all of which were carried unanimously, were before the meeting. The first, calling for unconditional amnesty for the remaining Irish political prisoners, was moved by Gray, seconded by Hutchinson, and supported by Parnell and Hopwood. Gray reminded the prime minister (Beaconsfield) of his words in 1844 when he had

[1] *Inquiry*, as above, pp 15–16 [C 1978], H.C. 1878, lxiii, 783–4; cf above, pp 154–9. Chambers to O'Reilly, 18 Feb., as above.

[2] *Inquiry*, as above, pp 13–15, 16–17 [C 1978], H.C. 1878, lxiii, 781–3, 784–5.

[3] In 1874–6 (Thornley, *Butt*, pp 292, 294), see above, p. 65.

[4] *F.J.*, 11 Mar. 78.

described the Irish question as that of 'a starving population, an absentee aristocracy, and an alien church, and in addition, the weakest executive in the world'. The only offence of the men for whom they were demanding amnesty was that they had taken such words too literally. Hutchinson, who pleaded for amnesty in the context of 'justice to Ireland', declared that undoubtedly the prisoners had done wrong and had suffered for it—'but they were not so ignobly wrong as to merit the treatment they had received'. The point was seized upon by Parnell in a characteristically short and trenchant speech:

Englishmen may think—and Mr Hutchinson, as an Englishman, had perhaps an excuse for thinking—that the Irish political prisoners have been wrong; but we Irishmen have every excuse for thinking that they have been right. We have seen that the only shreds of beneficial legislation that we have had for Ireland since the union have been due to the sacrifices of such men as they.

Hopwood urged that Britain should follow the example of clemency set by the United States government after the civil war.

The second resolution protested against the cruel punishments inflicted on the political prisoners, who had been subjected to greater severity than ordinary criminals, whereas policy, justice, and humanity demanded that they should be treated as first-class misdemeanants. Before this resolution was proposed the chairman called on Davitt to speak. As Davitt came forward the whole audience rose and cheered him, waving their hats and handkerchiefs. He began with an apology for reading his speech:[1] as he had serious charges to make against the prison authorities he wanted to make sure that he was correctly reported. He then described his experiences in prison, with detailed examples of his ill-treatment.[2] He disclaimed any wish to parade his punishment before the public; his object was to expose a monstrous system in the interests of the eight Irish political prisoners still its victims—Thomas Ahearn, James Clancy, Edward O'Meagher Condon, John Dillon, Robert Kelly, Patrick Meledy, Edward O'Connor, Edward O'Kelly.

Like my own their offence is denied to have been political—and while thus unjustly maligned in public they are treated as fenians in prison, placed in penal cells and made to feel that penal discipline is not sufficient to punish them. If we were not political prisoners why treat us in prison as such. . . . Would Ireland send forth a unanimous demand for the liberation of men whose encounter with the law had stained them with a brand of moral obloquy? Would *you* assemble here tonight and tolerate me for a single moment if I were what ministers have declared me to be—an accomplice of assassins? Would you, in your thousands, come to demand

[1] The text, in Davitt's own hand, is in DP/U (12 pp foolscap).
[2] See above, pp 146–54.

the release of those eight men and condemn their long and inhuman punishment if they were common malefactors?

Far from being that, their only offence was their connection with a movement which, at a time when the resources of constitutional action for the remedying of Ireland's wrongs had been exhausted, had turned to revolutionary action. Was that something that should horrify Englishmen, of all people?

While in prison, 'classed with the lowest scum of society' he could justly say to his jailors:

I have read the history of England and learned that revolution has made her what she is, great and powerful. I have seen the sympathies of Englishmen extended to struggling Poland, to Italy, to Switzerland, and to Spain, and have known them to have inculcated revolutionary ideas the world over. I have read of English statesmen admitting that Ireland was justified at periods of her history in rebelling against England–I have heard Mr Gladstone admit a justification for fenianism in tory misgovernment of Ireland. I have seen 'peaceful agitation' in England obtain reform in 1832, repeal of the corn law, borough franchise, and the ballot, but the same kind of agitation in Ireland obtain nothing except eventually a suspension of the habeas corpus act. I have never seen a concession made to Ireland that had not to be extorted either by actual insurrection or a threatened one. I have noted the one predominant characteristic of Englishmen to be this: to have their country free from all and every foreign power, temporal and spiritual–and I have satisfied myself that if I was classed among thieves and murderers in an English prison it was for learning English history well, for understanding English statesmen and writers logically, and for cherishing that feeling for my own country which is the proudest boast of an Englishman for his.

From this characteristic reading of English history Davitt went on to describe England as foremost in the world in denouncing vindictive and cruel punishment of political prisoners. One of her greatest statesmen had used his eloquence and his generous enthusiasm to focus the indignation of Europe on the treatment of the Neapolitan prisoners.[1] How different England's conduct towards Irish nationalists who had struggled for their country just as unselfishly as the victims of the Neapolitan tyrant had done for Italy!

In its obvious sincerity, its convincing detail, and its realism combined with its restraint, this speech had a powerful effect on Davitt's listeners: they responded indignantly to the more harrowing passages and when he had finished they gave him a second standing ovation, lasting several minutes. Then Mitchell Henry, who moved the resolution, spoke with feeling on the sufferings of the political prisoners and deplored the damage their ill-treatment had done to England's reputation in the world. The final resolution, moved by Richard Power and seconded by Dr Commins, authorised the chairman to convey the two

[1] See above, p. 156.

preceding resolutions to the home secretary and to the chief secretary for Ireland as the opinion of the meeting.[1]

The meeting drew attention from the press both in England and Ireland. It was reported at length by the *Freeman's Journal* (of which E. Dwyer Gray was editor and proprietor), and it is a measure of the national status Davitt had attained that this oracle of constitutional nationalism and middle-class catholicism devoted an editorial largely to him. The terrible details he had disclosed bore the stamp of truth. No one could doubt his story 'who looked on the worn and prematurely aged features of the three survivors—who saw the hectic flush which, alternating with a deathly pallow over Davitt's face, too surely tells of the disease which fastened upon him in consequence of his treatment'. It would have been more merciful to have executed the prisoners than to have subjected them to the years of horrible torture and unspeakable degradation they had endured. The result was that these men, of obscure origin, who had not even occupied the position of leaders in the fenian movement, were now 'honoured by the Irish people as never minister was honoured'. Their reception at St James's Hall was one of which a prince might be proud. Was it wise of British statesmen to bring about such a situation? Did they think that this was the way to stamp out Irish nationalism? The story of the barbarities practised on Michael Davitt would be circulated to every corner of Europe. Would it add to Britain's prestige? How long was this compound of ferocity and folly to be permitted to continue under the name of British statesmanship?[2]

The St James's Hall meeting was a landmark in Davitt's life not only as the occasion of his first conspicuous appearance on a public platform but also because it was associated with his first significant publication. The speech he delivered represented an abridged version of an account of his imprisonment that he was preparing to issue in pamphlet form. This he intended as a contribution to two good causes: amnesty for the eight fenians still in prison and reform of the penal servitude system itself, a subject that had recently become a live public issue through the appointment on 12 February of a royal commission on the working of the penal servitude acts under the chairmanship of Lord Kimberley.[3] *The prison life of Michael Davitt, related by himself* was completed before the end of March and was in print before 6 May.[4] It took up wider ground than the St James's Hall speech and ended with suggestions for reform to the Kimberley commission signed 'Michael Davitt,

[1] *F.J.*, 11 Mar. [2] *F.J.*, 17 Mar. [3] *Kimberley comm. rep.*, i, pp iii–v.

[4] It is mentioned in a report of Davitt's speech at Newcastle-upon-Tyne on 6 May (*Newcastle Examiner*, 10 May). See also *Kimberley comm. rep.*, ii, 527, 543–5, 685. For a note on this pamphlet see bibliography, III 2.

ex-treason-felony convict W822'. Despite its woodenness, this first pamphlet is lucid, well-arranged, and compact, conveying much information in very short space; and though poignant and harrowing, it is free from egotism and hyperbole. Perhaps its chief literary fault is that it is so solemn and humourless, comparing unfavourably in that respect with other prison narratives by fenians, for example O'Donovan Rossa's *Prison life*[1] and Tom Clarke's *Glimpses of an Irish felon's prison life.*[2] It has the advantages as well as the disadvantages of being written almost immediately after its author's release, while the experience it describes was hot in his mind, whereas Rossa and Clarke were several years at large before writing. Both in spirit and content it has much more in common with Clarke's brief and trenchant sketches than with Rossa's expansive and exuberant narrative. All three books are alike in their testimony to the squalid brutalities of the English penal-servitude system and to their authors' conviction that it was loaded against them as Irish political prisoners.

From London, Davitt carried the amnesty campaign into the provinces. On 16 March, he spoke in Sheffield at a meeting presided over by James Delahunty, home rule M.P. for Waterford, at which he described Delahunty and himself as representatives of two different ways of working for the welfare of Ireland. Delahunty and those who thought like him were sincere but mistaken. The only way, Davitt believed, of securing Ireland's well-being was through national independence. The meeting was followed by a concert in Davitt's honour and the next day (St Patrick's) by a social.[3] On 18 March he was the guest of honour at a banquet and ball in Preston; on 22 March at a ball in Burnley where he was presented with a gold watch; and on 23 March at a ball in Haslingden, his old home.[4] After that he spent nearly a month in London, working on a statement for the Kimberley commission.[5] On 28 April he spoke at the Adelphi Theatre, Liverpool, after a lecture on Irish independence by O'Connor Power. He described himself as a working man with nothing to give for Ireland except his liberty, which he was ready to sacrifice again. Was it coincidence that the chairman of the meeting, Dr Andrew Commins, the mover of the amnesty resolution,

[1] Jeremiah O'Donovan Rossa, *O'Donovan Rossa's prison life: six years in English prisons* (New York, 1874); later editions entitled *Irish rebels in English prisons: a record of prison life* (New York, ?1882).

[2] First published as articles in *Irish Freedom*, 1912–13. Issued as a pamphlet, with introduction by P. S. O'Hegarty, Dublin, 1922; reprinted, Cork, 1970.

[3] *Sheffield Telegraph*, 18 Mar. 78.

[4] DN/1, p. 3; *Accrington Times*, 30 Mar.; *Irishman*, 30 Mar. The watch, which Davitt wore for the rest of his life, was presented by his son, Judge Cahir Davitt, to the National Museum of Ireland in Oct. 1972.

[5] DN/1, p. 3; *Kimberley comm. rep.*, ii, 545.

John Denvir, and Power himself each had some association with Davitt's fenian life in Lancashire.[1]

From Liverpool, accompanied by Chambers and O'Brien, Davitt went on to Scotland. On 20 April, before a large audience at the City Hall, Glasgow, he referred to his determination to promote harmony among his countrymen wherever he found them. Still strongly identified with nationalist principles, he was prepared to suffer again in the national cause but it must be the cause of a united Ireland, not a section of the Irish people. The meeting was presided over by John Torley, a leading fenian in Scotland, and the concluding speaker was John Ferguson, who was deeply impressed by Davitt, and who from now onwards was a constant admirer and friend.[2] On 1 May at Govan, near Glasgow, Davitt said he believed that many of his audience shared his ambition to see Ireland with a flag of her own. This was followed by a reckless speech from Chambers in which, announcing that he was still a soldier in spirit, he said that the time would come when all would see that there was only one way to serve Ireland—with a bayonet.[3] These statements were duly noted by police observers, one of them being Head-constable Joseph Murphy, who had a professional interest in Davitt going back to 1869–70.[4] On 1 May Davitt and Chambers had reported themselves at the central police office in Glasgow, and when Davitt left the area on the 4th without notifying his change of address the Glasgow police informed the R.I.C. and suggested that his licence might now be revoked, being evidently unaware of the dispensation of 4 February.[5] The question was referred to the home secretary who replied that he thought it undesirable to take any action 'at present'.[6] After visiting Dumbarton castle and Edinburgh, Davitt spoke on 6 May at Newcastle-upon-Tyne, where he received an illuminated address of welcome.[7] Having returned to London, he went north again on 12 May for a meeting at the Theatre Royal, St Helens, Lancashire, at which Parnell was the first speaker and the amnesty resolution was seconded by John Denvir. On the following evening he spoke at the Cooperative Hall, Oldham. John Barry moved the amnesty resolution, and Davitt said that the object of the fenian organisation, the recovering of Irish independence, might be a crime in the eyes of the British government but not in the eyes of the

[1] *Liverpool Daily Post*, 30 Apr. 78; Denvir, *Life Story*, pp 199–200; above, pp 46, 47, 65.
[2] See above, p. 125; *S.C.P.*, viii, 270, ix, 357.
[3] DN/1, p. 4; *Glasgow Weekly Herald*, 4 May; *Irishman*, 4 May.
[4] Above, p. 56 ff.
[5] Above, p. 194.
[6] S.P.O., R.P. 1878/8204, 8572 (1882/26234).
[7] DN/1, p. 4; *Newcastle Examiner*, 10 May.

world.[1] About a week later he crossed to Dublin, and on the 23rd went by train to Belfast, with Chambers, to wind up the campaign.

It was Davitt's first visit to Belfast, and he was warmly received by nationalists of various hues. Cheering crowds awaited his arrival on 24 May at St Mary's Hall, the great catholic meeting-place recently built in a back-street within a stone's throw of the centre of Belfast. Here he addressed an audience of nearly 2,000, mostly working men with some publicans and six red-coated soldiers, all of whom had paid an admission charge of 6*d.* or 1*s.* The chairman was Peter Rooney, a flax-dresser, who spoke of himself as 'a man of no property' and 'not afraid of the sword'. Davitt took care to describe Belfast as the 'Athens of the north' and paid tribute to the memory of William Orr and Henry Joy McCracken, executed as United Irishmen in 1797–8. He did not, he told his hearers, feel it necessary to defend either his own past career or the political principles of the men whose release they had met to advocate. He gave some examples of his own ill-treatment in prison, and claimed that Gladstone's attitude towards such prisoners as himself was inconsistent with his recent denunciation of Turkish atrocities. Chambers also spoke. Twice there seemed a danger that the meeting would be disrupted—first by some audible discord between home-rulers and advanced nationalists and later by a demand for the ejection of someone suspected of being a policeman in plain clothes. On both occasions Davitt successfully intervened to prevent any disturbance. In fact, the suspicion of police surveillance was well-founded: Davitt had been constantly shadowed since he left Dublin and his movements reported to the inspector general of police. But the information thus obtained did not add much to what appeared in the local press: a drive through Belfast with two local nationalists in the afternoon before the meeting, on the next day a visit to a convent on Crumlin Road, and on the 26th an all-day excursion into the country, in the direction of Carrickfergus, with Chambers and a local man. Throughout his four-days visit (23–7 May) the local police could find nothing incriminating in his conduct. His associates—James Henry (clerk), Edward Gilmore (plumber and gasfitter), Edward McEntee (stationer), Bartholomew McManus (shoemaker), and Peter Rooney—were described by the police watcher as 'obscure persons' of 'no influence even with the working class', and as 'strong fenian sympathisers' but not 'connected with fenianism'[2] But John Mallon, now superintendent of the Dublin Metropolitan Police, expressed the opinion to his chief commissioner

[1] *St Helens Newspaper and Advertiser*, 18 May; *Oldham Express*, 14 May.

[2] S.P.O., R.P. 1878/11304. *Ulster Examiner*, 25 May; *Morning News* (Belfast), 25 May

that Davitt was 'a mischievous tool' in the hands of agitators.[1]

From Belfast Davitt returned by way of Dublin to London. In the four months since he first set out on his travels he had covered several thousand miles in Ireland, England, and Scotland, and had spoken on some fifteen public occasions.[2] In the north of England and Scotland he was back again on familiar ground; in Ireland he was seeing his native land with adult eyes for the first time; but wherever he went it was in the new role of public speaker. His latent powers as an orator were suddenly brought to the surface. He had almost no previous experience of the platform: his five years as a conspirator had imposed a silence upon him scarcely less unbroken than that of his seven years in penal servitude. Now for the first time he found that he could make effective use of what was then the principal medium of mass-communication. He was never in the first flight as an orator: he lacked qualities of imagination, command of language, and felicities of phrase characteristic of oratory at its highest. He was handicapped here, as in his writing, by inadequate general education and lack of special training. His style was inclined to be turgid and repetitive, with laboured constructions and stilted vocabulary; and though both his literary and his oratorical powers improved with practice, he never entirely overcame these faults. Nevertheless he was immensely impressive on the platform. His tall, lean figure, large, expressive brown eyes, jet-black hair and beard, the ascetic lines of his face, his alert, soldierly bearing, his empty sleeve, his air of courage and self-reliance—all these appealed strongly to an audience; and with his distinguished presence he combined a deep, resonant voice, clear-cut utterance, transparent sincerity, and passionate seriousness of purpose. None of his contemporaries surpassed him in the power to move a mass audience over some question in which his sense of justice or his compassion was roused, or to hold the attention of an audience out of sympathy with the views he was expounding. He had not yet attained his full stature as an orator, but it was evident in the spring of 1878 that a strong new personality, capable of drawing men in large numbers to hear him, had been added to the Irish political scene. He estimated that since January he had addressed over 17,000 people, at meetings ranging in numbers from 2500 in London to 300 in Govan.[3]

Davitt's speeches at these meetings had two prevailing themes: the major theme was the cruel and degrading treatment of Irish political prisoners and the demand for the release of the fenians still enduring it; the minor theme was the need for more understanding among honest

[1] Mallon to C.P., 27 May (S.P.O., A files, no. 561).

[2] DN/1, pp 3-7.

[3] DN/1, p. 8.

home-rulers and nationalists divided by deep differences of approach and method. His lecturing tour brought him into personal contact with large numbers of his countrymen at home and in Britain, and gave him an insight into the state of the national movement. On the amnesty issue there was a large body of favourable opinion not only among Irishmen but also among Englishmen and Scotsmen; and between August and November, all the fenian prisoners whose cause Davitt so dramatically helped to publicise were released. On the other issue he was pleased to find that a new spirit was at work within fenianism and that it was very much in harmony with his own outlook.[1] At the same time he was made sharply aware of the hostility of orthodox fenianism. Richard Pigott, of the *Irishman*, who was wide awake to any deviationist tendency, censured Davitt for innocently playing into the hands of constitutional agitators and thereby helping to give parliamentary action a new lease of life. His only concrete charge against Davitt, however, was of 'frequent dissertations on the evils of disunion and dissension, and on the virtues of toleration'.[2] Davitt in reply denied any connection with parliamentary politics and declared that since his return to the outer world he had been trying to arouse public sympathy on behalf of the remaining political prisoners, and in doing so had appealed to Irishmen of all shades of politics. If he did not join in the hue and cry against Irishmen who did not share his separatist views, he was none the less a nationalist for that.

> I cannot ignore the fact that there are Irishmen holding opinions less advanced than my own who have that claim upon my toleration . . . which I have upon theirs. . . . If they do not deem my separatist views feasible I will not thrust them further from the national ranks . . . nor will I act in any way calculated to perpetuate discord . . . among Irishmen. With Thomas Francis Meagher I am of opinion that 'from the divisions of Irish society the chief obstacles to Irish freedom arise'.

Commenting editorially on this statement Pigott drew a sharp distinction between the separatism of the nationalists and the federalism of the home-rulers, the one designed to overthrow the union, the other to make it perpetual. When Davitt 'speaks favourably of an alliance between two such political organisations . . . he really asks the sincere and earnest advocates of Irish independence to unite with its most subtle enemies'.[3]

This antithesis did not impress Davitt. He saw in Parnell and his handful of 'activists' in the house of commons potential allies in broadening the basis of nationalist action without impairing the integrity of

[1] Devoy, *The land of Eire*, pp 39-40.
[2] *Flag of Ireland*, 1 June; cf. above, p. 174.
[3] *Flag of Ireland*, 8 June.

fenianism. He was thus moving on parallel lines with the fenians at home who were supporting Parnell and with Dr Carroll, the envoy from Clan na Gael, who had been in Dublin in January, had met Davitt and had been well impressed by him.[1] Carroll had some frank exchange of view with Parnell, who convinced him that he believed in complete independence for Ireland and that as soon as the Irish people were prepared to go the whole way he would go with them. Carroll told him that Clan na Gael would support him and would ask the I.R.B. to support him in all his efforts towards complete independence.[2]

About the same time, a national conference of the home rule movement, held in Dublin on 14–15 January 1878, marked a further victory for Parnell over Butt. Though Butt was retained as leader, the conference endorsed Parnell's demand that the home rule party should act with more energy and solidarity in parliament. The conflicting attitudes of the two men were pin-pointed by Butt's reprobation, and Parnell's defence of obstruction. Butt continued to believe that if only the party could persuade liberal-minded Englishmen fairly to consider remedies for Irish misgovernment, they would come to the conclusion that there was only one way of giving Ireland good government, and that was by allowing Irishmen to govern themselves. Parnell, with relentless precision, admitted the possibility, and even the probability, that Butt could persuade a fair-minded Englishman in the direction he had indicated, but did not think that the house of commons was mainly composed of fair-minded Englishmen.[3]

> If we had to deal with men who were capable of listening to fair arguments there would be every hope of success for the policy of Mr Butt as carried out in past sessions; but we are dealing with political parties who really consider the interests of their political organisations as paramount, beyond every other consideration.[4]

Davitt may have been present at this conference and he certainly knew all about it. As a member of the I.R.B. supreme council he probably also knew of a secret meeting held in March at the hotel in London where Carroll was then staying. The meeting was called by Carroll with a view to bringing about a working arrangement between Parnell and the I.R.B., and it was attended by three groups: (a) Parnell and two other 'activist' M.P.s, F. H. O'Donnell and W. H. O'Sullivan, (b) James J. O'Kelly and Carroll, representing the fenian opportunist policy of support for the Parnellites, and (c) John O'Leary and John O'Connor, secretary of the supreme council of the I.R.B., spokesmen

[1] Devoy, I; *S.C.P.*, ix, 439; above, p. 139.
[2] Carroll to Devoy, 24 July 1906 (*Gaelic American*, 4 Aug. 1906); *D.P.B.*, i, 296–9.
[3] R. B. O'Brien, *Parnell*, i, 153–4.
[4] Ibid., p. 154.

of high fenian orthodoxy. By Carroll's account all present were in complete agreement as to absolute separation as the end in view, but controversy raged over the extent of the support to be given to the public, by the secret, movement. According to Devoy (who presumably derived his information from Carroll or O'Kelly), there was heated debate between O'Kelly and O'Leary on the subject of O'Connor Power, the one defending, the other denouncing him, and this prevented any formal agreement being reached with Parnell. O'Donnell, with characteristic egotism, writes of the meeting as if it had been dominated by a verbal combat between himself and O'Leary. From this incongruent testimony, one thing alone seems certain—the one thing inherently probable—that Parnell was a listener rather than a talker and that he committed himself to nothing. At all events Carroll was satisfied that Parnell was well disposed to the fenians and that the fenians could rely on him to advance the common interests of fenianism and the activists in parliament. This was a main theme of his letters to Devoy at the time.[1]

Parnell was now obviously a key figure in Irish politics, and Davitt, having gauged the situation, tried to reach an understanding with him. Carroll speaks of 'a meeting we had near Manchester at which Davitt, Chambers, and other fenians met the parliamentarians and I.R.B. men', and at which 'a *modus vivendi* was agreed upon which enabled both to go on with their work without clashing'.[2] This vague statement, which relates to the spring or early summer of 1878, at least indicates that by that time Davitt was known to be directly involved in negotiations between fenians and Parnellites. He himself, in 1903, describes a private conversation he had with Parnell on 12 May 1878, when the two men were travelling by train from London to Liverpool to speak at an amnesty meeting at St Helens Davitt pressed Parnell to join an I.R.B. reformed, in accordance with his diagnosis of its weaknesses worked out in Dartmoor, as a small efficient body of picked men working in secret to accumulate arms for an eventual appeal to force. But this would not be enough: 'the first line of defence ought to be an open movement on constitutional lines'.

This should be made to invite all men of separatist principles, and not to exclude honest moral-force advocates. Such a movement should embrace similar

[1] Carroll to Devoy, 30 Mar. 78, in *D.P.B.*, i, 323–5; ibid., i, 298–9, 209, 310, 323–4; Carroll to Devoy, 24 July 1906 in *Gaelic American*, 4 Aug. ; Devoy, 'Parnell and the fenians' in *Chicago Journal*, 29 Mar. 99; Devoy, *Recollections*, p. 283; O'Donnell, *Irish parl. party*, i, 271–83. R. B. O'Brien's account of the meeting in his *Parnell*, i, 159–60 was presumably derived from John Barry (ibid., p. 160 n. and pp 65, 121–5), not from J. J. O'Kelly as stated in *D.P.B.*, i, 324.

[2] *D.P.B.*, i, 298.

parliamentary action to that which the obstructionists were pursuing, but there must be more immediate issues put before the people, such as a war against landlordism for a root settlement of the land question, the better housing of labourers, doing away with the need for workhouses, and capturing the municipalities for nationalism; the parliamentary representation to be, as far as possible, recruited from men of separatist convictions, but who had not been openly identified with the Fenian Brotherhood. An Irish party of this calibre, at an opportune time—that is, when the country was sufficiently organised—to make a reasoned demand in parliament for a repeal of the act of union, and in the event of the ultimatum being refused to leave the house of commons in a body, return to Ireland, summon a national convention, and let the members of the party go into session as an informal legislative assembly.[1]

Parnell, Davitt says, listened to all this in silence, and then firmly refused to join the I.R.B. or any other secret political society:

It would hinder and not assist me in my work for Ireland. Others can act as seems best for themselves. My belief is that useful things for our cause can be done in the British parliament in proportion as we can get reliable men to join us and follow a resolute policy of party independence. We must endeavour to reestablish faith in parliamentary work of an earnest and honest kind, and try in this way to secure the good will of men like yourself who are justified in doubting from past experience whether any real service can be rendered to the Irish people by electing representatives to go to Westminster. I agree with a good deal of what you suggest about putting a stronger programme before the public, especially in relation to the land question, and I see no reason why men who take opposing views as to the best way of liberating Ireland cannot work in harmony for minor reforms. Possibly the result of our present line of conduct in parliament will be that we will be turned out of the house of commons, in which event we could then give your informal Irish parliament a chance.[2]

There is no other evidence for this critical conversation than Davitt's own statement, written twenty-five years afterwards, but written, he tells us, 'from notes made at the time'. No such notes survive among his papers, but his statement is to some extent confirmed by the fact that the two men did speak at an amnesty meeting at St Helens on the evening of 12 May.[3] It may be accepted that they travelled to Liverpool in the same carriage, and that they exchanged views on the general lines indicated by Davitt. That Davitt tried to recruit Parnell for a reformed I.R.B. is as inherently probable as that Parnell would have none of it.[4] The idea of withdrawing from parliament and setting up a national convention in Ireland was not new. It had been formulated by Gavan Duffy in 1848 and was in the minds of Clan na Gael leaders at this time.[5] Davitt may well have derived the idea from Carroll. Moreover Parnell, who knew about the independent Irish party of the fifties,

[1] *Fall*, pp 111-12. [2] Ibid., pp 112-13. [3] See above, p. 201; below, p. 210.

[4] Cf. John Denvir's account of a conversation he had with Parnell in the train between Liverpool and St Helens later the same day (*Life story*, pp 201-2). [5] Above, pp 38-9, 138.

had already hinted publicly at a policy of withdrawal for the home rule party.[1] On this topic, therefore, the two men probably had much in common and would be likely to converse as Davitt says they did. They probably also discussed the land question, in which Parnell had shown himself deeply interested ever since he entered public life. What is open to doubt is Davitt's proposal to Parnell regarding 'a war against landlordism for a root settlement of the land question'. For there is no contemporary evidence that Davitt's thinking had advanced so far by May 1878. Hatred of the land system was in Davitt's blood and was part of his fenian tradition, but a plan for the abolition of the system was quite a different matter.[2] Davitt did not read Lalor's revolutionary doctrine till 1880,[3] and his speeches at this time are silent on the land question. If the plan for a combined political and agrarian movement that he was to expound in America towards the end of 1878 had already crystallised in his mind it is not credible that he would have given no hint of it in public. In default of other evidence Davitt's claim in 1903 that he proposed 'a war against landlordism' to Parnell in May 1878 cannot be accepted,[4] and was probably due to antedating by a year the proposition he was to make to Parnell in April 1879.[5] Other points that he says were in the plan he put before Parnell in May 1878—better housing for labourers and 'nationalising' the municipalities—were, like his radical settlement of the land question, only to become part of his public programme in the following autumn.[6]

Nevertheless the land question was assuming a new urgency by May 1878. In the winter of 1877-8 it had been high-lighted by events in Tipperary on an estate that comprised many small hillside farms on the stony slopes of the Galtee Mountains. The estate had recently been acquired as a speculation by a wealthy English manufacturer, Nathaniel Buckley, whose agent, Patten Smith Bridge, gained an evil reputation for his rent-raising severities towards the hillside tenants. Two attempts were made on his life in 1876, the second of which succeeded in wounding him and unintentionally killing his driver. A local fenian, John Sarsfield Casey, continued the offensive by letters to the press in April 1876 accusing Bridge of inhuman treatment of his tenants and vividly describing their miserable condition. Bridge sued Casey in the court of queen's bench for criminal libel. After an eight-days' trial (27

[1] *S.C.P.*, vii, 2; C. Gavan Duffy, *My life in two hemispheres*, i, 248-51; see above, p. 133.

[2] See above, pp 8-9, 14, 183-4.

[3] *S.C.P.*, ix, 419 (3 July 1889); see above, pp 36-7.

[4] This view modifies what I wrote on the matter in 'The new departure in Irish politics, 1898-9', in *Essays in British and Irish history in honour of James Eadie Todd*, ed. H. A. Cronne, T. W. Moody, and D. B. Quinn (1949), pp 316-17. See my article. 'Irish-American nationalism' in *I.H.S.*, xv, no. 60 (Sept. 1967), pp 438-45.

[5] Below, p. 288.

[6] Below, pp 236-7.

November–5 December, 1877), in which Butt, as counsel for the defence, made the most of his opportunities to expose the sufferings of the Galtee tenants, Bridge lost his case through the disagreement of the jury. This result was followed by preparations to evict nearly fifty of the tenants. At that point the proprietor of the *Freeman's Journal*, Dwyer Gray, commissioned the rising young national journalist from Mallow, County Cork, William O'Brien, to make an intensive inquiry into the Galtee situation on the spot. O'Brien went to Tipperary, and made a case-study covering 226 households, which he published in a series of letters to the *Freeman's Journal*, in December 1877 and January 1878, entitled 'Christmas on the Galtees'. The letters made a sensation and were reprinted as a pamphlet in March 1878.[1] Soon afterwards the murder of a notorious landlord of County Donegal, Lord Leitrim, on the shore of Mulroy Bay (2 April), cast a grisly light on landlord-tenant relations in another region.[2]

Independently of the landlord system, Irish agriculture was suffering an economic decline. The total value of agricultural output, which had risen to a peak of £43.7 millions in 1876, had taken a downward turn in 1877 to £40 millions. In that year the series of wet summers and bad harvests that was to culminate in the disaster year of 1879 began. The value of all the principal crops, exclusive of potatoes, turnips, and hay, fell from £6.1 millions in 1876 to £5.6 millions in 1877, and that of the potato crop from £14.7 millions to £10.8 millions. Livestock and livestock products declined from £37.6 millions to £34.4 millions. The depression was reflected in the eviction of insolvent tenants. The number of evictions rose sharply—from 406 in 1877 to 843 in 1878—and the number of agrarian outrages also rose, but less sharply—from 236 in 1877 to 301 in 1878.[3]

Quite apart, then, from his own direct observations during his recent visit to Mayo, Davitt must have been made aware that the land question was again in an acute phase. He must have known of Butt's efforts to obtain new legislation on the basis of the '3 Fs'. And he must also have known that the radical solution of the land question, the conversion of the small farmers as a body into owner-occupiers—in principle Lalor's solution[4]—was again in the air.[5] A committee of the house of

[1] *F.J.*, 28 Nov.–1 Dec., 3–6 Dec. 77; 27 Dec. 77–5 Jan. 78. O'Brien, *Christmas on the Galtees: an inquiry into the condition of the tenantry of Mr Nathaniel Buckley* (1878). *Fall*, pp 141–2; O'Brien, *Recollections*, pp 188–97; Healy, *Letters and leaders*, i, 58–60.

[2] *F.J.*, 3 Apr.; *Hansard 3*, ccxxxix, 665–6 (5 Apr.), 1095 (11 Apr.), 1195–1219 (12 Apr.), 1259–63 (12 Apr.).

[3] Appendices E1, G1, and G2.

[4] See above, pp 36–7.

[5] G. J. Shaw-Lefevre (Lord Eversley), *English and Irish questions* (1881), pp 115–16.

commons had been appointed on 1 May 1877 under the chairmanship of G. J. Shaw-Lefevre to inquire into the failure of the land-purchase provisions of the land act of 1870. It reported, on 27 June 1878, that there was a strong desire among tenants to buy out their farms and that they should be given greater facilities for doing so by the state.[1] One of the witnesses was Matthew Harris, of Ballinasloe, whom Davitt had met for the first time in January 1878.[2] He argued strongly that, unless the small farmers in the west were enabled to buy out their holdings, as many could do if assured of advances of three-quarters or four-fifths of the purchase price, then small tillage farmers would be replaced by large grass farms, which gave almost no employment and were very detrimental to the community.[3] Parnell himself had said in the house of commons, in connection with the appointment of the Shaw-Lefevre committee, that he 'firmly and strongly believed' that the land question 'would never be settled on any other basis than that of giving to the Irish people the right and liberty of living on their own farms as owners'.[4] There is nothing to show that Davitt's position on the land question in May 1878 was any more advanced than this.

At the St Helens meeting on 12 May neither Davitt nor Parnell said anything about the land question. Davitt declared that if people would only support the action of Parnell, O'Connor Power, and others in parliament, it would not be long before the remaining political prisoners were liberated. Parnell offered some interesting reflections on the obstructionist policy. He had often, he said, felt it a disadvantage to appear in the character of a member of parliament, and he admitted that those who had no confidence in parliamentary action had ample justification. But since the constituencies could not be prevented from sending representatives to parliament, nationalists should study how to make the Irish representation as little demoralising, as combative, and as beneficial as possible. If the obstructionist policy were pressed home, one of two alternatives must result: either ameliorative measures for Ireland would be conceded, or the Irish members would be expelled from the house of commons in a body. That would be equivalent to sending them back to Ireland to set up their own parliament and thus to repealing the union.[5] This comes very close to what Davitt says he suggested to Parnell during their conversation in the train.

[1] *Report from the select committee on Irish land act 1870 . . .*, H.C. 1877 (328), xii, 1878 (249), xv. [2] Above, pp 191, 193.

[3] *Report from the select committee on Irish land act 1870 . . .*, pp 270–73, H.C. 1877 (249), xv, 312–15 (11 Apr. 1878).

[4] *Hansard 3*, ccxxxiv, 178 (1 May 1877); F. S. L. Lyons, 'The economic ideas of Parnell' in *Historical Studies*, ii (1959), p. 62.

[5] *St Helens Newspaper and Advertiser*, 18 May 78; quoted in part in *Fall*, p. 113.

As he came to the end of his lecture tour, tired but elated, Davitt was undecided whether to settle down in London or in Dublin. O'Connor Power strongly advised the former and Davitt was inclined to agree, especially as Power and other friends were looking out for some occupation for him there. In conveying this news to an impatient Sib he said nothing more about bringing her and his mother back to Ireland, but expected soon to be able to fix a date for visiting them in America.[1] His idea of settling down in London or anywhere else soon proved illusory. He seems not to have had any immediate worry over money: he probably received something from the I.R.B. on his release, he shared in the proceeds of his lecturing, and he could expect help from a fund started in Dublin in April, under a representative national committee, to enable the released prisoners to reestablish themselves.[2] From January till his departure for America in July, he spent his time, in the intervals between lecturing and preparations for lecturing, in reading, writing, and discussion. He had drawn up and submitted to the Kimberley commission in April a statement of his intended evidence, and he took pains to prepare himself for his oral examination before the commission, which was held in London on 20 June.[3]

On the basis of his written submission and of his *Prison life* he was examined[4] not only about his own case and the problem of the political prisoner but also about charges he had made of ill-treatment of individual prisoners and of prisoners in general. He was closely questioned by several of the commissioners, and his answers on a number of critical points were later referred for comment to some of the prison officers involved who appeared before the commission—Captain W. V. F. Harris, governor of Dartmoor from May 1876 and deputy governor several years previously; William Fagan and William Morrish, directors of convict prisons; R. E. Power, medical officer at Dartmoor; Rev. James Francis, Anglican chaplain. There was no reconciling Davitt's charges of personal victimisation with Captain Harris's disclaimers, and it has been shown that the evidence in favour of the official view is stronger than Davitt's evidence to the contrary.[5] Harris summed up his own attitude when he said that anything exceptional in Davitt's treatment was due solely to the need for special precautions for his safe custody, 'but the greatest care was taken that no privilege should be denied him to which he was justly entitled by his class and conduct'.[6] This was not inconsistent with Harris's admission that he had Davitt's beard removed despite the fact that his predecessor, in

[1] D to Sabina Davitt, 24 May (DP/D5); cf. above, p. 194. [2] *Irishman*, 6 Apr.
[3] *Kimberley comm. proc.*, ii, 45; DN/1, p. 6; E. R. Wodehouse to D, 9 Apr. (DP/A 11 (i)).
[4] *Kimberley comm. rep.*, ii, 515–45. [5] Above, pp 156–7. [6] *Kimberley comm. rep.*, ii, 681.

accordance with a practice resulting from the Devon commission's report,[1] had allowed treason-felony convicts to retain their beards. There was no legal ground for the privilege, and it seemed to Harris that he was in duty bound to withdraw it; Davitt must be treated exactly like any other prisoner.[2] In the main that was how he was treated, and his testimony is all the more telling an exposure of the barbarities of penal servitude.

On nearly all matters within his own direct experience Davitt's charges (other than his charge of victimisation) were confirmed. True he corrected a statement that he had seen ravenous men eat old poultices found buried in heaps of rubbish: he had seen only one man doing so, but he had seen several men eat remnants of candles, one of whom had retrieved them from the prison cesspool. Pressed to say how often he had found cockroaches in his food he replied that he had done so twenty to thirty times. Had he ever complained to the governor about the food? He had not done so, because as a rule there were a score or more prisoners complaining every week, and their complaints had no effect.[3] Questioned closely on certain charges relating to medical treatment and to inquests on prisoners, he admitted that they were not based on direct observation but on information he had acquired from other prisoners and believed to be true.[4]

Power, the medical officer at Dartmoor, said he considered that the dietary was quite insufficient for men engaged in outdoor work under the weather conditions that prevailed. They needed more nourishment at Dartmoor than at other prisons, as was shown by the fact that nearly all of them, especially the tall ones, continually lost weight.[5] On the other hand Governor Harris asserted that the food was adequate in quality and quantity, though he conceded that candle-eating was common. This was due not to hunger, but to the belief among prisoners that candles melted into cocoa or gruel made it more palatable. Nor was hunger the cause of poultice-eating and other such aberrations; these he attributed to the itch of some prisoners to attract attention: 'I remember a man who was in the habit of filling his pockets with young frogs, which he placed in his hand and swallowed in rapid succession on the appearance of a stranger'.[6] He admitted that the bakehouse swarmed with cockroaches, but, asked whether it would be desirable to get rid of them, he said that that had never occurred to him.[7]

Harris agreed in general with Davitt's strictures on the older prison

[1] Above, pp 155-6.
[2] Above, pp 152, 158; *Kimberley comm. rep.*, ii, 522, 676-7.
[3] Ibid., ii, 525-7.
[4] Ibid., ii, 541.
[5] Ibid., iii, 749.
[6] Ibid., ii, 680.
[7] Ibid., ii, 677-80; iii, 749.

buildings: the cells were too small, the ventilation and lighting were bad, and the water-closets could become offensive on Sundays. Director Morrish told the commission that all cell windows ought to open on to the outer air; but Dr Power, confirming that the atmosphere in the iron cells was very bad, pointed out that convicts generally came from a class that preferred closeness to fresh air. On the subject of bathing, Harris admitted that, though prisoners were supposed to bath once a week, 'from inefficient accommodation' they were able to do so only once a fortnight.[1] The water was supposed to be changed for each man by the prisoner-orderly on duty, but Davitt alleged that this was seldom done and that it was common for prisoners to have their fortnightly bath in dirty water. Harris thought it possible that an orderly might be negligent in this way but not that the responsible warder would tolerate his neglect. As to excessive surveillance, he admitted that Davitt was hourly inspected in his cell at night by a warder with a lamp. But, he explained, constant inspection of all prisoners—though not necessarily every hour—during the night was a duty that he insisted upon as the best precaution against attempts to escape; and the men became so used to it that it did not disturb their sleep in the least.[2]

If Governor Harris seemed happy enough about his Dartmoor, it was very different with a witness who had been Anglican chaplain several years before Harris's governorship, Rev. James Francis. Davitt had learnt from other prisoners that he had been removed from his post for intervening between the prison authorities and prisoners whom he considered to be cruelly treated. Questioned before the commission Francis explained that he had not been removed but had resigned from the service, because his relations with the then governor, Major R. F. Hickey, had become so strained and because the governor was solidly backed by the visiting director, Captain W. J. Stopford. The source of the tension was the excessively harsh regime introduced by Hickey. A half-witted or hot-tempered prisoner, in an outbreak of fury would commit half a dozen breaches of discipline in quick succession —most commonly abusing or threatening a warder—and instead of being punished for one offence would be subjected to three days bread and water for each item of indiscipline separately, with an interval, as required by the regulations, of one day between each punishment. The succession of punishments often became more than a man could physically bear and he would then be removed to the infirmary, but as soon as the medical officer decided that he was sufficiently recovered his interrupted punishment would begin again. At any stage in the process the prisoner might lose control and commit a fresh series of offences,

[1] Ibid., ii, 680. [2] Ibid., ii, 666, 669, 676, 677, 680-82.

so that the chain of punishments went on lengthening; Francis knew of a man thus kept on bread and water for twelve months, and of punishment being inflicted in December for an offence committed in the previous August. Having frequently protested to the governor against such punishments in vain, Francis referred to the matter in his annual report for 1869 but when the general report on Dartmoor was in due course printed he found that the passage in question had been expunged. The same thing happened the following year with this difference that the form of the general report was altered and the chaplain's statement appeared under the heading 'Extracts from the report of the chaplain'.[1] Besides his charges of excessive punishments, Francis pointed out that warders would impose unofficial punishment on prisoners whom they disliked by locating them on the top landings where the light in the cells was exceptionally bad and the air exceptionally foul. For example, a prisoner known to be fond of reading would be put in such a cell, where he could not see to read, and this would sometimes so infuriate him that he would beg the chaplain to remove his books to save him from tearing them to pieces.[2]

Director Stopford, while questioning some details in Francis's statements, confirmed their general accuracy but claimed that they related only to certain extreme cases. He admitted that the directors of convict prisons had censored the chaplain's report and argued that it was necessary to do so in fairness to Governor Hickey. Stopford regarded Francis as unwarrantably interfering between governor and prisoners in matters of discipline, and was supported by the chairman of the directors, Sir Edmund Du Cane, the presiding genius of the penal servitude system. Questioned about the suppression of parts of Francis's report, Du Cane said that if it was the chaplain's duty to report on the prison discipline as he had done, it was no part of the director's duty to publish his unbalanced statements. But, as Lord Kimberley pointed out, the knowledge that any part of a report that did not please the prison authorities might be suppressed tended to deprive that report of any value whatever.[3]

Being physically handicapped Davitt felt it a peculiar injustice that prisoners, employed on light labour owing to some physical disability, were subjected to a reduced diet and a reduced rate of earning marks for the remission of their sentences. He himself experienced the first condition only during his month at Portsmouth prison and seems not

[1] The *Report of the directors of convict prisons . . . for the year 1870* [C 449], H.C. 1871, xxxi, includes reports for each prison from its governor, chaplain, and medical officer, but in succeeding *Reports* these are replaced by extracts.

[2] *Kimberley comm. rep.*, ii, 536; iii, 882–6, 889–91.

[3] Ibid., iii, 972–9, 1055–8.

to have experienced the second at all, but he was none the less concerned about both.[1] Director Morrish explained that there were different scales for hard-labour and light-labour men, and claimed that prisoners were given the rations suitable to the work they had to do. He referred to Davitt himself as 'a man able to work pretty well'.[2] Sir Edmund Du Cane was questioned about the rule that penalised convicts on light labour by reducing their rate of earning marks. The chairman asked him whether it was consistent with justice that a man convicted of a very serious crime who was of great bodily strength should be allowed to earn the maximum remission of sentence, while another man, convicted of a lesser offence but of poor health or physically disabled, was debarred from earning remission at the full rate. Du Cane defended the rule, first, by analogy from ordinary civil life, where a man able to work hard earned more than one unable to do so, and second, as a necessary insurance against the malingering and idleness to which prisoners were notoriously prone. He went on to explain that the authorities sought always to mitigate the unfair effect of the rule by employing disabled men in skilled occupations or finding suitable work for them in hard-labour parties.[3]

Davitt was questioned about three cases of prisoners whom he alleged to have been cruelly treated, Ruotta, Bidwell, Murphy and five associates. Ruotta was an Italian, orginally sentenced in 1865 to five years penal servitude for demanding money with menaces. He had a shocking record of violent conduct in prison, including an attempt on the life of the governor of Woking for which he had been tried and given a second sentence, of twenty years, in 1870. Davitt encountered him first in Millbank, where scarcely a week passed that he was not under punishment. When Davitt next saw him, in Dartmoor, he had lost his right arm—it had been amputated because of a disease in the elbow joint, which, Davitt was told, had been induced by constant leaning against the damp walls of the punishment cells. His health had always been bad and he was now very weak. About January 1875 Davitt saw him on parade dragging himself feebly along in the wake of a work party to which he was attached. Apparently because he was not keeping up with the party a warder struck him with a staff on the shoulder where his arm had been amputated, and he fell to the ground. Principal-warder Coffey, who was present, went across to the officer who had struck Ruotta and appeared to reprimand him. Davitt did not see Ruotta again for several months and he died suddenly on 3 April 1875. A post-mortem showed extensive tuberculosis and heart disease.

[1] *Prison life*, pp 28, 39.
[2] *Kimberley comm. rep.*, ii, 243-4.
[3] Ibid., ii, 38-41.

Coffey, questioned about the alleged assault, absolutely denied all knowledge of it. He had never seen Ruotta struck at any time. Director Fagan said that the alleged assault had not been brought to his notice, and that if the warder really had struck Ruotta and had been reprimanded, as Davitt supposed, he would in all probability have been dismissed.[1] But neither Coffey nor Fagan attempted to explain how, if their statements were correct, Davitt came to make the charge he did.

Bidwell, serving a life sentence for forgery, was the exact reverse of Ruotta in that he was almost entirely passive. His legs appeared to be completely paralysed and for nearly three years he had been immobile 'with his legs cramped up'.[2] Davitt was told by other prisoners that he was removed to the punishment cells once a year to test whether or not he really was paralysed. Davitt twice saw him in these cells and heard him being dragged along the floor from the governor's office. On Good Friday 1877, while the deputy governor was making the rounds of the punishment cells, Davitt heard Bidwell appealing to him for a drink of water and the deputy governor replying: 'you have water inside your cell door; if you want it you can get up for it'.[3] Governor Harris, questioned about Bidwell, was inclined to think him a malingerer and admitted that he had been punished from time to time with three days bread and water for dirty behaviour, idleness, and insolence. The medical officer, Power, denied that Bidwell was periodically removed to the punishment cells. During Davitt's time in Dartmoor, Bidwell was taken to the punishment cells only once, and that was because, being then able to sit up in a chair, he refused to knit stockings. All he wanted was to avoid work; and he succeeded in spending a good part of his time in the infirmary, 'reading books and enjoying himself'. Yet Power, who had vainly tried by screw splints and electric-shock treatment to straighten Bidwell's legs, was unable to decide whether his condition was caused by disease or by his constantly feigning paralysis.[4]

Murphy, an excitable youth of 18–20 years,[5] while engaged in making hay on 14 August 1877, was, according to Davitt, accused of slacking by the officer in charge, Principal-warder Westlake, and warned that he would be reported. Attempting to strike Westlake in the legs with a wooden rake, he was felled by a blow on the head from the butt-end of the officer's rifle. Five prisoners in the same party cried 'shame'. They and Murphy were tried by Directors Fagan and Morrish and were each punished by three dozen lashes, twenty-eight days bread and water, and six months in cross-irons. Davitt, who was never allowed

[1] Ibid., ii, 533–4; iii, 712, 760–61.
[2] Ibid., iii, 754.
[3] Ibid., ii, 544; *Prison life*, p. 34.
[4] *Kimberley comm. rep.*, ii, 544–5; iii, 754–6.
[5] *Prison life*, p. 35.

outside the prison walls, was asked how he came to know all this. He replied that he learnt it from prisoners who worked in the same party as Murphy, that he saw Murphy on the evening of the incident with a gash in his forehead, and that he read the sentences of the six men over their doors in the punishment block. Governor Harris gave a quite different explanation of the incident: it was a case of quasi-mutiny on the part of a group of prisoners who normally worked in the prison quarry, where they were sheltered from the weather and relatively free from supervision, and who resented being transferred to harvest work in the fields. Murphy was put forward by the rest of the gang to create a disturbance. He was not struck but thrown by Westlake, whom he attacked, and as the two men struggled on the ground his confederates advanced with uplifted rakes, demanding his release. They gave way when Westlake ordered two other officers to load their rifles.[1]

Davitt may have been misinformed about the Murphy affair, but so also may Harris, who derived his information from Westlake and the other two officers present. This conflict of testimony reflects an aspect of convict life that Davitt regarded as peculiarly degrading: no credence was placed by the prison authorities in any statement a prisoner might make against an officer.[2] 'Prisoners are not allowed', Governor Harris explained, 'to call upon each other as witnesses against a warder, but any statement made has to be substantiated by circumstances to which they can point as proof of their complaint'. In that case, asked the chairman, what chance of redress has a prisoner ill-treated by an officer? 'The facts of the case and circumstantial evidence are all that we have to guide us' was Harris's answer.[3] But why not, Kimberley asked, take the prisoner's evidence for what it was worth? It would be inadvisable to do so, Harris replied, because prisoners were so ready to make frivolous complaints that if they were not required to substantiate their statements by circumstantial evidence they would bring charges of all kinds against any warder who was unpopular. Under further pressure Harris said that, while not accepting 'direct evidence' from prisoners, he usually made private inquiries from those who were present when the action complained of occurred, or who could give what amounted to testimony as to the facts, and he found that information thus elicited was more reliable than anything a prisoner might say at a formal inquiry; for 'any man questioned as to facts has no means of knowing what weight his account will have in a case the particulars of which he is ignorant from not being present at the investigation'.[4] This did not dispose of Davitt's charge that an elementary

1 *Kimberley comm. rep.*, ii, 543–4; iii, 685–6; *Prison life,* pp 34–5.

2 *Kimberley comm. rep.*, ii, 543.

3 Ibid., ii, 682–3.

4 Ibid., ii, 683.

principle of justice was denied to prisoners ill-treated by officers. Evidence given by another prison governor, Major J. C. Farquharson, governor of Chatham prison, confirmed Davitt's contention. In no circumstances, Farquharson said, would he accept evidence, formal or informal, from prisoners against a warder, and in his experience of the convict service this was the invariable practice.[1]

The Ruottas, Bidwells, and Murphys were all part of that 'scum of society', with which Davitt loathed being associated, but it was typical of him that his compassion and his sense of justice were none the less roused on their behalf. So we have the paradox that, while he was constantly distinguishing between political and other prisoners, it was the problem of imprisonment as such that emerges most strongly in his testimony about prison life—the squalor, the degradation, the brutality, and the futility of it all. Writing a few years later, with wider and deeper experience of life both outside and inside jail, he described penal servitude as

> a huge punishing machine, destitute . . . of discrimination, feeling, or sensitiveness; and its non-success as a deterrent from crime and complete failure in reformative effect upon criminal character are owing to its obvious essential tendency to deal with erring human beings—who are still men despite their crimes—in a manner which mechanically reduces them to a uniform level of disciplined brutes.[2]

The report of the Kimberley commission (14 July 1879) found the penal servitude system to be on the whole satisfactory, but in need of reform at a number of particular points.[3] Without referring by name to Davitt, and only occasionally citing his evidence, it vindicated many of his charges, and its proposed reforms either confirmed suggestions he had made or were in general agreement with his views.

On a few points the commissioners' conclusions directly clashed with Davitt's testimony. The frequent and undignified searching he had found so objectionable as a prisoner they held to be necessary for the discovery of prohibited articles and for the personal safety of prison officers; in this matter they considered that the prison authorities should be left perfectly free to use their discretion, even in the searching of prisoners naked, provided that it was not done in the presence of other prisoners. Davitt had found that army and navy pensioners, who formed the bulk of the warders at Dartmoor, were more authoritarian, less intelligent, and less concerned about the reformation of prisoners than civilians of the artisan type; he had challenged the commissioners to inquire into the suitability of ex-soldiers for the prison service and into their moral and mental training for their

[1] Ibid., ii, 630-31, 684.
[2] *Leaves*, i, 249; cf. above, pp 162-3.
[3] *Kimberley comm. rep.*, i, pp xxvi-lxiv.

duties.[1] But the commissioners decided that the existing warders, whether ex-servicemen or civilians, performed their difficult and irksome duties satisfactorily, and that there was no need to institute special training for warders such as was provided in Belgium and elsewhere. The food that Davitt had complained of so strongly the commissioners found to be generally adequate in quantity, quality, and preparation. Prisoners were naturally disgruntled with a diet limited to the minimum necessary to maintain them in health and enable them to do the work required of them. The commissioners believed that candle-eating was due to the craving 'of a few individuals' for 'more fat than the dietary affords', and not to 'any deficiency in the quantity and quality of the diet'.[2]

On the other hand the commissioners condemned the corrugated iron cells from which Davitt had suffered so much, the discrimination against convicts on light labour in the earning of marks, and any absolute rejection of a prisoner's testimony, however obtained, in cases of complaints against prison officers. They were not disposed to question Director Stopford's judgment in the particular instances complained of by Rev. James Francis, but they disapproved of the practice that left prisoners with charges hanging over their heads for months. As to the censoring of reports from chaplains and others, the commissioners thought that, as with the publication of other official documents, discretion must be allowed to the directors of convict prisons, but unless this were exercised sparingly the reports would lose much of their value. While pronouncing the medical staff to be efficient they proposed two changes in the medical service very much in line with Davitt's criticism. First, a physician or surgeon of high standing and wide experience should be appointed as superintending medical officer, to supervise and inspect the medical arrangements in all the convict prisons, consult with the resident medical officers on cases of special difficulty, and investigate all allegations made by prisoners of medical neglect. Second, the post of assistant surgeon should be opened to public competition, a medical or surgical qualification and some previous experience should be prerequisites for candidature, and appointments should in the first place be made for a probationary period. As to inquests, the commissioners declared that no person should be summoned to the jury who had any connection with the prison, for example as tradesmen or contractors; and the names of all prisoners tendering evidence should be supplied to the coroner so that he might call them before him if he wished.

The most important recommendation of the commission, and the

[1] Ibid., ii, 534; *Prison life*, p. 40. [2] *Kimberley comm. rep.*, i, p. xxxviii.

only one of its kind to be adopted, was that prisoners against whom no previous conviction was known to have been recorded should be formed into a distinct class (which came to be designated the 'star class') and segregated from the general body of prisoners. The separation of first offenders from habitual criminals was a cardinal reform advocated by Davitt: he had no doubt that one of the greatest evils of the penal servitude system was the contamination resulting from the indiscriminate association of criminals of all kinds in the public works prisons.[1] It is only fair to add that Governor Harris (in common with many other prison officials) was of the same opinion.[2] On the question of political prisoners the commissioners did not adopt Davitt's suggestion of examining the eight fenians still in that category,[3] but they confirmed the recommendation of the Devon commission[4] that treason-felony convicts should be segregated, and located in a detached part of some convict prison. The argument they used made no concession to Davitt's charges:

> we see no reason to believe that increased deterrent effect is given to the sentence of treason-felony by associating prisoners convicted of this crime with other convicts, whilst the grant to them of exceptional indulgence tends to disturb the minds of the other prisoners and to interfere with the orderly administration of the prison.[5]

On the perennial problem of abuse of power by prison officers the commissioners made a radical recommendation: it would, they believed, conduce to public confidence in the system and be a valuable safeguard against abuse if provision were made for the inspection of convict prisons by persons appointed by the government but independent of the prison administration and unpaid. This enlightened suggestion was opposed by one of the six commissioners, by Sir Edmund Du Cane, and by other prison administrators, and it was not implemented till 1898, after Du Cane's retirement.[6] It was not one of Davitt's proposals but it was completely in harmony with his thinking about penal servitude.

His concern about penal servitude as a social and human problem and not simply as an incident in his career as a revolutionary was profoundly characteristic of the man. Many of his contemporaries in the republican movement—all the fenian leaders except Stephens and many of the fenian rank and file—endured penal servitude; and from John Mitchel to Eamon de Valera a host of other Irish nationalists had experience of prison life. Not one of them after his release showed anything of Davitt's continuing compassion for the plight of prisoners as such.

[1] Ibid., ii, 534. [2] Ibid., 669–70. [3] *Prison life*, p. 38; see above, p. 197.
[4] Above, pp 155–6. [5] *Kimberley comm. rep.*, i, p. xxxi.
[6] Sir Evelyn Ruggles-Brise, *The English prison system* (1921), pp 37–81, 46–7, 75–7.

VII

In America, July–December 1878: the second fenian 'new departure'

Davitt's long-intended visit to his mother and sisters had been delayed partly by his appearance before the Kimberley commission and partly by the need to accumulate money for the trip to America. A share in the 'testimonial fund' for the released prisoners[1] met immediate demands, and he hoped to make enough money in America by lecturing to be able to return with his mother and Sib in a matter of weeks. As he went with an official recommendation from the I.R.B. to Clan na Gael, and was in any case assured of a welcome from the chairman of the Clan, Dr William Carroll, he could count on help from American fenians in getting lecture engagements.[2] On this rather speculative footing he booked a passage, cabin class, on the White Star liner *Britannic*, due to sail from Liverpool to New York via Queenstown on 25 July. He travelled by train from Dublin to Cork on 23 July. The following day he attended a meeting of the Cork committee for the relief of the families of political prisoners, at which arrangements were made to help the dependants of several imprisoned fenians. On the 25th he went to see Blarney castle, where he kissed the Blarney stone ('but not in orthodox style') and spent three hours absorbing the natural beauty of the place. Having returned to Cork he went on to Queenstown, spent the night there, and on the afternoon of the 26th was taken out by tender to the *Britannic*.[3]

The *Britannic* was one of the largest and most up-to-date passenger liners in service on the North Atlantic and one of the pioneer ships of the White Star fleet built at Belfast by Harland and Wolff from 1870 onwards. Launched in 1874, she was a four-masted, single-screw, iron ship of 5000 gross tonnage, combining steam propulsion with sails, and she held the Atlantic speed-record by a passage from

[1] Above, p. 211.
[2] Devoy, I, above, pp 135, 139, 205; *I.W.*, 24 Aug. 78.
[3] D to Sabina Davitt, 24 May (DP/D5); DN/2, pp 1-3; Devoy, *The land of Eire*, p. 40.

Queenstown to New York in August 1877 in 7 days, 10 hours and 53 minutes.[1] Davitt, who had never travelled outside the British Isles before, was determined to make the most of his first Atlantic voyage, and he succeeded admirably. Apart from a spell of sea-sickness on the first night, and sleeplessness on the seventh night caused by the closeness of the air in his cabin and the incessant sounding of the ship's fog-horn, he thoroughly enjoyed his eight days on the *Britannic*. He was well pleased with the accommodation and the food, the waiters were polite and attentive, the passengers generally were agreeable, and he made a number of interesting contacts. Above all he enjoyed his daily 'promenading' on the hurricane deck, and the many hours spent, especially at night, watching the sea and sky and the motion of the ship as it glided along 'like a huge restless monster'. The diary that he kept on the voyage has frequent descriptions of these experiences which show an alert, appreciative eye and an ambitious pen.[2] One lovely morning he saw a school of dolphins pursuing the ship: 'two [of them] appeared to be running a race with the object of catching the vessel first; they would leap out of the water about two feet and go a distance of six or seven, then dive and come up again in another leap. They kept pace with us for about five minutes.'[3] He was eager to see a whale and an iceberg, and on the last day but one did see a whale, spouting away at only about 150 yards distance.[4] Minor sensations that he records were ships passing at close quarters, usually in full sail, the *Britannic's* passengers all agog.

Among his companions in the saloon were a strong-minded elderly American woman, who had spent eighteen months travelling with her daughter in Europe;[5] a Yankee lawyer, returning from the Paris Exhibition, which he pronounced to be inferior to that of Philadelphia;[6] a Scot who, having classified religions into Catholic and Christian, and being asked what a Christian was, replied 'Why, a presbyterian';[7] an old Irish priest, Rev. Patrick Murry, who had been 34 years among the Chippewa Indians and spoke their language;[8] four young priests of Irish parentage going home after three years at Louvain;[9] a Canadian who had been a captain of volunteers during the fenian invasion of Canada and held derogatory views about fenianism;[10] and a Mr Power, brother of a Father Power of Manchester.[11] Father Murry, with whom he often talked, claimed that there was a structural affinity between

[1] *Lloyd's Register of British and Foreign Shipping*, 1878-9; *Encyclopaedia Britannica* (11th ed., 1910-11), xxiv, 886; xxv, 859-60.
[2] DN/2.
[3] Ibid., p. 20.
[4] Ibid., pp 13, 21.
[5] Ibid., p. 20.
[6] Ibid., pp 6, 11. The reference is to the Paris Exhibition of 1878 and to the Philadelphia Centennial Exposition of 1876.
[7] DN/2, p. 9.
[8] Ibid., p. 7.
[9] Ibid., pp 7, 17.
[10] Ibid., p. 13.
[11] Ibid., p. 10.

the Celtic, Hebrew, and Chippewa languages. He was opposed to Irish independence, holding that it would be calamitous for Ireland, owing to her insularity, and that there were affinities between English, Scotch and Irish which necessitated their being united under one government. He regarded fenianism as similar to communism but disliked aristocracy.[1] The 'Yank' took the opposite side to Father Murry on the Irish question, to Davitt's amusement, though it turned out that he knew little enough about Ireland.[2] When the discussion turned to education, Davitt was in favour of some element of religious instruction, but the 'Yank' and an Irish-American held that that was impossible in America owing to the number of rival denominations.[3] The 'Yank', who claimed to have lost only one case in two years, declared that there were honest lawyers; Father Murry went further and believed that if Diogenes were alive he would find his honest men in America.[4] Davitt talked to Father Murry about the beauties and harmonies of nature, and Father Murry described the wild romantic scenery of the western prairies, where he had once officiated at mass sung by native Red Indians.[5] The four young priests, who were clever, well educated, and spoke with an Irish accent, proved no less congenial. They talked of their experiences in Belgium, where liberalism (which they considered as but another name for infidelity) was making rapid progress in the cities at the expense of catholicism, and where mock processions were held to bring religion into contempt.[6] Davitt drew them out on the subject of Irish politics, speaking about the state of the country, landlordism, the opposition of the clergy to advanced political views, and his own imprisonment. They were very guarded in their response, but Davitt concluded that they were as national in outlook as the discipline of their order could permit.[7]

The passengers seem generally to have been quiet and well-behaved. There was a group of 'young swells' who spent a good deal of their time gambling (except on Sunday) and drinking punch. On the sixth day out from Cork, it was discovered that a couple of New York cardsharpers were on board and had pocketed £60–£70 from other passengers, especially the young swells.[8] When he saw the cardsharpers Davitt wondered why they had not been spotted earlier, for they recalled faces all too familiar to him in 'Auld Lang Syne'.[9] Most of the women passengers, Davitt learnt, were actresses, and he noted that several of them had 'that abandon characteristic of the stage'.[10] In the steerage end of the ship there were many German and Irish emigrants,

[1] Ibid., pp 6–8. [2] Ibid., pp 7, 15. [3] Ibid., p. 8.
[4] Ibid., p. 11. [5] Ibid., p. 16. [6] Ibid., p. 17. [7] Ibid., p. 12.
[8] Ibid., pp 9, 10, 11, 13, 16, 22. [9] Ibid., p. 17. [10] Ibid., p. 16.

who, when the weather permitted, danced on the deck in the evening, the Germans their waltzes and the Irish their jigs and reels. Davitt found that steerage passengers were very poorly accommodated, which he considered unjust as they had paid nearly half the cabin rate. While among these passengers he was recognised by a young man from Haslingden, who knew some of his personal friends and introduced him to three young Irish girls from Hollymount, County Mayo, on their way to Massachusetts.[1]

On the last night at sea national flags were displayed among the decorations of the dinner tables. Davitt struck a green leaf in an orange to represent the Irish tricolour, which at once attracted unfavourable attention from some English passengers at a neighbouring table.[2] Next evening the *Britannic* entered the Hudson and anchored in the Narrows, off Staten Island, at 9 p.m. Davitt was enchanted by his first sunset in America. 'Nothing could exceed the beauty of the variegated colours which the sky presented, . . . the sea glimmering in the rays of the setting sun, and our ship gliding along in a warm pleasant breeze.'[3] Next morning, Sunday (4 August), he awoke to a lovely sunrise that disclosed the wooded slopes of Staten Island and Brooklyn, with charming villas perched upon every little hill and gardens 'exquisitely laid out' down to the water's edge. He landed at the White Star Line wharf in Manhattan, and drove to Sweeney's Hotel. Then he sallied forth to see New York.[4]

Davitt's arrival in New York for the first time was a major event in his life. For one thing it was a dramatic symbol of emancipation (however temporary) not only from penal servitude but also from British authority. His family were now all in America, and he had come primarily to renew home contacts that had been broken for over eight years. The thought of setting foot on America, with all its novelties, its boundless possibilities, and its democratic spirit, elated him, as it had done Charles Kickham fifteen years before.[5] America as the refuge of the oppressed and afflicted of Europe, especially his own countrymen, inspired him. America with its large Irish population and its extensive fenian element (including nearly all the fenian Old Guard except Kickham and O'Leary) was a stronghold of that militant Irish nationalism to which he was still devoted. American fenianism had become an important factor in his political calculations as a result of the changing attitude of O'Kelly, Carroll, and others towards Parnell and the obstructionists in parliament.[6] He had come to America with

[1] Ibid., pp 4, 5, 13, 14, 15.
[2] Ibid., p. 19.
[3] Ibid., p. 21.
[4] Ibid., pp 22-3; see map V.
[5] *Irish People*, 26 Dec. 63.
[6] Above, pp 138-9, 205-6.

no commission from the home organisation or any other body, and with no definite political plan.[1] Apart from his own family he knew no one in America except James J. O'Kelly in New York, Dr William Carroll in Philadelphia, and a few dozen old associates from the north of England now scattered over the States. But he was assured of a welcome both for himself and his views in Clan na Gael circles.[2] What happened exceeded his expectations; and the next four months were to prove an indispensable stage in his political evolution.

In high spirits he stepped out into downtown Manhattan, observing, as he walked along Broadway, Fifth Avenue, and The Bowery, how bad the pavements were (they still are). He crossed the East River to Brooklyn by ferry, close to the new suspension bridge—the longest in the world—then under construction,[3] and watched enormous riverboats passing, with bands playing and gay crowds dancing on their decks (although it was Sunday). Returning to Manhattan he went to the office of the New York *Herald* to call on the one man he knew in the city, James J. O'Kelly.[4] O'Kelly, with whom he had probably renewed contact in London in the spring,[5] introduced him to that key figure in American fenianism, John Devoy, whose views on Irish politics had changed considerably, as a result of Carroll's mission to the home organisation, since the preceding December.[6] He and Davitt took to each other at once, and when Davitt left for Philadelphia at 4 a.m. the following morning, he was accompanied by Devoy.[7]

Catherine Davitt's raptures over her son's homecoming after eight years' absence must have been a little damped when he arrived with Devoy in tow and she found that he was already committed to a political engagement. For on 5 August, his first day at home, Devoy took him to a meeting of the Clan na Gael executive at Carroll's house, 617 South Sixteenth Street,[8] Philadelphia. There he was introduced to the leading men of the Clan and persuaded, with some difficulty, to agree to a much more extended lecture-tour that he had contemplated. It

[1] In a letter to R. Barry O'Brien of 6 Dec. 93 (DP/ZZ) Davitt says that before he left Dublin he had reached agreement with Egan and Brennan on a policy of 'parallel action' between constitutionalists and revolutionists. In the absence of contemporary evidence this statement has to be treated in the same way as Davitt's account of his conversation with Parnell on 12 May (above, pp 206–8). Here also I have modified the position I adopted in 'The new departure in Irish politics, 1878–9', in *Essays in British and Irish history in honour of James Eadie Todd*, p. 318 (cf. above, p. 208 n. 4). It is possible that, in the letter to O'Brien, Davitt was unconsciously attributing to July 1878 consultation he had with Brennan (and perhaps also with Egan) in January 1879 (see below, p. 277).

[2] Devoy, *The land of Eire*, p. 40; Devoy, I.

[3] Brooklyn bridge was opened on 24 May 83, having taken 13 years to build (*Dictionary of American history*).

[4] See above, pp 138–9. [5] See above, pp 205–6. [6] See above, pp 135–9.

[7] DN/2, pp 23–4; Devoy, I, II. See map V. [8] *D.P.B.*, i, 246, 339.

was to be under the auspices of the Clan, and an initial plan was at once discussed. An assignment of about two months was suggested, to begin in the latter half of September when the heat of summer—which Davitt found 'something hellish'—had abated. It would probably take him as far west as Colorado, and he might go on from there to San Francisco. The holding of public meetings was unprecedented for American fenianism, and it spoke well for the good impression Davitt made on the Clan executive and their confidence in his political views that they undertook to provide him with a platform. Without such backing he could not have made contact with the only effective Irish political element in America. On the other hand the Clan leaders were not backing Davitt in his own interests merely. They saw in him a new and impressive exponent of fenianism, with all the prestige that seven years in an English jail conferred, whose realistic outlook and undoubted gifts as a public lecturer could be turned to good account in a pioneering effort to rally and reanimate American fenians and disheartened ex-fenians.[1] And they probably found him ready enough to undertake an assignment that required extensive travel not only in the eastern states, where the Irish were most numerous, but also in the middle west, where, though much more thinly spread, they were settled in significant numbers. There is no evidence to suggest, and no reason to suppose, that Davitt was tied to any political programme more specific than the promotion of fenianism on realistic lines.

Having committed himself to a strenuous political campaign, Davitt was able to relax for nearly three weeks. The first ten days he spent at Manayunk with his mother, who was in much better health than he had expected after her long years of trouble and anxiety. He promised to take her back to Ireland, and after that she seemed to him twenty years younger.[2] Manayunk, where she was living with Anne and her husband and Sib, at 4139 Main Street,[3] was six and a half miles from the centre of Philadelphia, on the east bank of the broad Schuylkill River.[4] Main Street, drab and industrial, skirts the river, but behind it the ground rises steeply in a series of terraces which, though now covered with houses, are not unattractive, while the opposite slopes of the Schuylkill are still largely open and green. Davitt describes the situation as a pleasant wooded valley, and no doubt the whole district was much more sylvan then than it is now. He stayed there from 5 to 15 August, spending much of his time calling on friends and sightseeing

[1] D to John Walshe, 9 Aug. 78 (National Museum of Ireland); *Defence*, pp 95–6; *D.P.B.*, i, 341, 342–3; Devoy, *The land of Eire*, pp 40–41; Devoy, I. III.

[2] D to Thomas Chambers, 15 Aug. (Cashman, pp 54–5).

[3] Above, pp 169, 173; *D.P.B.*, i, 349; *Philadelphia City Directory, 1879*, p. 398.

[4] See map VI.

in and around Philadelphia. The city itself he considered to be handsomer than New York, its public buildings finer, its houses better; some of the streets, he wrote to a friend in Mayo, were ten miles long. He sensed its significance in the history of the United States: he visited Independence Hall and saw the liberty bell, the room in which the declaration of Independence was signed, and the window from which it was read. He visited Christ Church, the Centennial Buildings, the U.S. Mint, the prison, and the Free Library. At Benjamin Franklin's grave in the burial ground of Christ Church, he felt proud that he, like Franklin, was a printer: 'I wish I could do as much for Ireland and humanity as he did for America and mankind', he wrote, recalling the occasion several years later.[1] He was suitably impressed by Fairmount Park, the largest municipal park in the world, stretching for thirteen miles south along the Wissahickon Creek and the Schuylkill to near the heart of Philadelphia, with its fountains, lakes, and walks, and its river scenery. One day he went for a drive with Carroll around the park and by a tree-lined way along the Wissahickon Creek to Indian Rock, where he viewed the 'wooded cliffs and promontories [and the] verdant precipices overhanging the singing river below'.[2]

On 15 August he set out by steamer for Cape May, a trip that gave him welcome opportunities for enjoying the scenery of the Delaware and its storied shores, including the historic town of Wilmington, where the steamer called to pick up passengers. Cape May, the southernmost tip of New Jersey, with four miles of excellent sandy beach washed by the Atlantic, and a large landlocked harbour, was the oldest seaside resort in the state. Popular with holiday-making Philadelphians since colonial times, it had been recommended to Davitt in preference to the much larger, newer, and more showy Atlantic City. He wrote to Devoy after his arrival:

> I think it will be more suitable for a few weeks' quiet than the other. Many of my 'friends and relations' from Manayunk and Port Richmond 'excur' to Atlantic City very often, and my time would be occupied in useless confab with every blatherumskite I would thus come across. I'll get on very well here as nobody knows me.[3]

Bathing in the great Atlantic rollers, walking, meeting and making friends, writing every day, sometimes attending dances and other entertainments in the evening, and all the time free from political

[1] Notes made in Portland prison in the margin of his copy of Alfred Webb's *Compendium of Irish biography* (Dublin, 1878), p. 214. They include a copy of the famous epitaph beginning 'The body of Benjamin Franklin, printer' written by himself many years before his death but not inscribed on his tombstone.

[2] DN/2, pp 24–6; D to John Walshe, as above.

[3] D to Devoy, 16 Aug. (*D.P.B.*, i, 348).

contacts, he passed his time at Cape May very pleasantly. In his diary he remarks, with implicit approval, on the fact that men and women bathed together and that the same type of bathing suit—a loose-fitting robe from the neck to below the knees, caught in by a girdle round the waist—was worn by both sexes. But the women also wore fancy stockings and showed their legs—if they were shapely. At dances he saw 'beautiful women, exquisitely dressed', and he admired the skill and grace of the dancing. On Sunday, 18 August, he went to mass in a crowded chapel, and thought the sermon poor. He bathed as usual, bathing being as general on Sunday as on other days at Cape May.[1]

Eight unprecedented days thus passed, his health was steadily improving and he was expecting to stay for a week or so longer when he received a telegram, from New York, inviting him to attend the annual excursion of the Irish Volunteers (the military branch of Clan na Gael) of the city on Sunday, 25 August.[2] Sighing at his usual bad luck, he packed his bag, and turned his back regretfully on Cape May. He left by steam car on the 24th at 7 a.m. (noting how much more convenient rail travel was in America than in England), arrived at Philadelphia at 9 a.m., stayed several hours with his mother at Manayunk, and left Philadelphia by the 4 p.m. train for New York. Next morning he joined the excursionists, 2500 strong, on three large boats. He was introduced to many of them, including some beautiful Irish girls. There was music and dancing as they sailed up the magnificent valley of the Hudson to Excelsior Grove, a park area on the high west bank of the river at Alpine, in Bergin county, New Jersey.[3] Here the whole party had a picnic—the word was used of pleasure parties of any size at which all had refreshments out of doors. An address of welcome to Davitt, signed by T. C. Luby, John Devoy, J. J. O'Kelly, J. J. Breslin, and others on behalf of the nationalists of New York, was read by the veteran fenian, Luby. Davitt was deeply touched. In expressing his thanks he recalled how, some thirteen years before, his boyish heart had been fired by admiration for the men who confronted Ireland's enemy. He had become a humble disciple, and he still adhered to the principles he then imbibed. A public expression of his opinions as a nationalist would be injudicious, but he declared that imprisonment had neither changed his political convictions nor lessened his faith in the ultimate triumph of the cause of Irish independence. Such speech-making did not interfere with the conviviality of the occasion. Davitt was pleased with

[1] DN/2, pp 27–30; Carroll to Devoy, 10, 14, 19 Aug. (*D.P.B.*, i, 341, 344, 348).

[2] Announcement in *I.W.*, 24 Aug., p. 8.

[3] *Hudson by Daylight map from New York Bay to the head of tidewater* (New York, 1878). I am grateful to my former student, Dr W. J. Lowe, of Lake Erie College, for the identification of Excelsior Grove and also of Alpine Grove (below, p. 398). See map VII.

the trip, though not with the drunkenness of some of the men who took part in it: on the return journey two men fell overboard but were rescued. Next day he was the guest of honour at a picnic at Newark, New Jersey, where good order prevailed, though large numbers attended. On the 29th he took part in yet a third picnic, at Brooklyn, where, so he records in his diary, some 5000 or 6000 people were present. He returned to Philadelphia the following day.[1]

Since the meeting of the Clan na Gael executive on 5 August, Carroll had been working out a detailed programme of lectures for Davitt, and in conjunction with Devoy in New York had been making practical arrangements. Carroll was confident that the forthcoming tour would be a success both financially and politically. For the opening lecture he had sold $105 worth of tickets to delegates from the fenian clubs in Philadelphia before the tickets themselves were printed, and he felt assured of being able to hand over at least $500 to Davitt as the net proceeds. While the organisation of the lecture-tour was carried out entirely by fenians, Carroll took care to seek the support of representative Irish-Americans outside the fenian body. Among these the most important were Patrick Ford, of the *Irish World*, and John Boyle O'Reilly, of the Boston *Pilot*.[2] Carroll, probably helped by Devoy, persuaded Ford to take a friendly interest in Davitt, and one result was that the first reports of Davitt's activities in America appeared in the *Irish World*.[3]

During the first half of September Davitt stayed at Manayunk, preparing his lectures and improving his acquaintance with the Philadelphia area. He bought a new suit and did himself proud, paying $15.65 for the cloth, besides $3 for a hat.[4] He was the guest of honour at a dinner of the Sheares Club of Philadelphia on 9 September, at which the members attended in force. After dinner he proposed the toast, 'Washington and America, the home of the exile and the outcast', which was one of many, and it was 2 a.m. before the club adjourned.[5] On 12 September he visited Laurel Hill Cemetery, near Manayunk, and commented in glowing terms on the tombstones, the sculpture, the obelisks, and the splendid situation of this famous necropolis on the eastern slopes of the Schuylkill. It would, he notes in his diary, almost make him wish to die, to be assured of burial in such a place[6]—a sentiment curiously untypical of his general outlook.

1 DN/2, pp 27-31; Carroll to Devoy, 10, 14 Aug. (*D.P.B.*, i, 341, 344); *I.W.*, 14 Sept., pp 5, 6; Devoy, *The land of Eire*, p. 41.

2 Above, pp 141-4.

3 *D.P.B.*, i, 341-3, 344-6, 353; *I.W.*, 24 Aug., pp 5, 6, 8; 31 Aug., pp 3, 8; Devoy, I, III.

4 DN/2, pp 31-3.

5 *I.W.*, 14 Sept., p. 8.

6 DN/2, p. 32. See map VI.

Two days afterwards, his sister Anne gave birth to her first child, a son, who was christened Michael Davitt in honour of his uncle.[1]

Davitt's lecture-tour began, appropriately, in Philadelphia, where, in the Concert Hall, on 16 September, he addressed an enthusiastic audience of over 1000 on 'The Ireland of the present'. The stage of the hall was decorated with the green flag of Ireland flanked on the right by the American flag and on the left by the Russian. In front of these were drawn up the bands of the Galloglasses and the Sheares Rifles (formations within the military organisation of Clan na Gael in Philadelphia),[2] which entertained the audience with Irish music until the arrival of the lecturer. Davitt was received with rapturous applause and a glowing address of welcome:

> On behalf of the thousands of the exiled children of Ireland who have made this city and its suburbs a place of refuge we bid you *cead míle failthe* amongst us. As a martyr in your efforts to raise the people of Ireland from a state of serfdom to the enjoyment of freedom we greet you, [and] tender you our highest esteem and most grateful thanks.

Davitt responded to all this warmth with one of his best oratorical performances. He declared himself an unrepentant and uncompromising fenian—'my . . . imprisonment has not caused me to deviate one iota from my original ideas or from the track I have previously pursued for the salvation of my country'—which made Carroll apprehensive on the score of Davitt's ticket of leave. Davitt claimed that British rule in Ireland was maintained only by coercion, and described the country as packed with soldiers, police, and spies. He counselled unity among Irishmen, defended himself and fenians generally against clerical charges of communism and infidelity, sounded a warning that Beaconsfield's government was seeking to exert diplomatic pressure at the Vatican against Ireland, censured the anti-national politics of the catholic hierarchy in Ireland while praising Archbishop McHale of Tuam for his efforts to preserve the Irish language, paid tribute to Parnell for his 'manly, honest, and indefatigable' conduct in the house of commons, and denounced F. H. O'Donnell for identifying himself with sectarian education and with British policy against Russia in the near-eastern crisis.[3] He felt that he had been a success,[4] and Carroll, who had presided at the meeting, wrote jubilantly to Devoy:

> The audience . . . were charmed from first to last with matter, manner, and man; as well they might, for a more clear, concise, logical, and unanswerable statement

[1] Certificate of baptism of Michael Davitt Crowley, 22 Sept. (Manayunk, Philadelphia, Records of St John the Baptist Church). He died at Scranton, Pa, on 9 Sept. 1968.
[2] S.P.O., Fenian papers, A files, no. 508.
[3] *D.P.B.*, i, 345–5 (17 Sept. 78); *The Record* (Philadelphia), 17 Sept.; *I.W.*, 28 Sept.
[4] DN/2, p. 33.

of their case has never been given here. Then there was through all the manly eloquence of earnest conviction of its truth and an entire freedom from all the set phrases and tricks of platform so characteristic of O'C. Power and a good many others I know.[1]

The only jarring note in the press reports of the lecture was struck by the *I.C.B.U. Journal*, of Philadelphia. This organ of the Irish Catholic Benevolent Union, an association formed to promote the interest of Irishmen in America on a Catholic basis, took Davitt to task editorially for his reference to the Irish hierarchy and the Vatican. When he read the editorial weeks later Davitt published a vigorous rejoinder: he was surprised that an Irish-American editor would so closely identify politics and religion as to construe criticism of the political behaviour of the clergy into an attack upon the church; 'I have never uttered a word in public in my life against our priesthood in its religious capacity'. No religious issue was involved in the struggle for Irish national independence that would hurt the conscientious scruples of an Irish catholic.[2]

Devoy had suggested to Carroll that Davitt should be invited to attend private meetings of Clan na Gael in New York and Brooklyn. Carroll's advice was that Devoy should consult Davitt himself, though, he added, Davitt was not a cool counsellor where his personal interests were concerned, 'danger being something he never thinks of'. There would certainly be danger in his attending Clan meetings, but perhaps no more than he had already incurred elsewhere since his release.

It would do immense good, and if he thinks best himself I should say yes, under the precaution that it be confined to such men as you deem safe, and that they swear, on assembling, never to allude to the meeting to others. I am greatly concerned about his course and its consequences to himself, and think on his return home he should at once retire into the background *apparently*. His lecture last night was full of the old treason, but I suppose he considers her majesty's government knows him, and the people may as well also.[3]

Davitt did say yes and not only attended secret meetings of Clan na Gael at New York but at many other places throughout his lecture tour.

The next phase of the tour was planned for New England. Davitt travelled by train on 17 September to New York, from there by night boat to Fall River, Massachusetts, on an inlet of Narragansett Bay, and from there by train to Boston.[4] He greatly enjoyed the sea trip through Long Island Sound, which, with a stateroom and supper, cost him only $2.50. At Boston, on 18 September, he called on John Boyle O'Reilly, editor of the *Pilot*, and made a good impression on him but

[1] *D.P.B.*, i, 354-5 (17 Sept.).
[2] *I.C.B.U. Journal*, Oct., Nov.
[3] *D.P.B.*, i, 354 (17 Sept.).
[4] See map VII.

found his political outlook disappointingly tame. He spoke that evening at Lawrence, in north-east Massachusetts,[1] and on 21 September at New Britain, in central Connecticut, successfully, he judged, at the former, only barely so at the latter. At Lawrence, one of the principal textile towns in America, with a large foreign-born population in which the preponderant element was Irish, he was given a great welcome. He met 'lots of old friends' (Irish from the north of England), and shook hands with everybody after the lecture. 'Crowds of beautiful young girls' acted as collectors for the national fund and their 'patriotic importunities' were irresistible. Davitt also had a private meeting with fifty of the local fenians. The trip from Lawrence via Hartford to New Britain took him through a charming landscape of wooded hills and quiet river valleys. He spent Sunday, the 22nd, at New Britain, then a small town of 12,000 people of whom 5000 were catholics, presumably of Irish origin. He returned to New York on 23 September; his first experience of New England had been relaxed and enjoyable, and he had made at least one important political contact, with O'Reilly.[2]

At New York, on 23 September, Davitt lectured at the Cooper Institute, T. C. Luby in the chair, to an audience of about 1000 on the ironical theme 'England's magnanimity to her enemies'. He spoke at some length, contrary to his usual practice, on his own prison experiences, and denounced the atrocities inflicted in prison on Daniel Reddin, Charles McCarthy, and Edward O'Meagher Condon. He described the policy of home rule as impracticable and chimerical, and as at Philadelphia attacked F. H. O'Donnell, but concluded by appealing for solidarity among Irishmen throughout the world. After the lecture two resolutions were proposed by Devoy and passed unanimously. The first asserted Ireland's right to an independent national existence: 'as Ireland has never forfeited her right to independence, and as no action on the part of England has given any justification for the acceptance of the union, we hereby protest against all attempts at compromise and renew our resolve to work for the complete overthrow of British domination'. The second declared that the landlord system, forced on Ireland by British legislation, was a disgrace to humanity and to the civilisation of the nineteenth century; that it was the direct cause of the expatriation of millions of Irishmen and of the miserable condition of the Irish peasantry; and that 'as the land of Ireland belongs to the people of Ireland, the abolition of the foreign landlord system and the substitution of one by which the tiller of the soil will be fixed permanently upon it, and holding directly of the

[1] *I.W.*, 12 Oct., p. 8.
[2] DN/2, pp 33-5; *D.P.B.*, i, 355-6, 381; Devoy, IV.

state, is the only true solution of the Irish land question, which an Irish republic can alone effect'.[1]

In a remarkable essay in contemporary history, forming the first part of his book, *The land of Eire*, published in 1882, Devoy disclosed that these resolutions had been discussed and approved at a secret conference of Clan na Gael leaders at Sweeney's Hotel immediately before the Cooper Institute meeting.[2] This is inherently probable and may be accepted as correct. In 1884 Devoy asserted that the resolutions had been drafted by himself.[3] Further disclosures appeared in 1906, on the occasion of Davitt's death, when Devoy published a long series of articles in his newspaper, the *Gaelic American*, on Davitt's career during the twelve months that followed his arrival at New York.[4] Derived from personal experience substantiated by much documentary material, these articles are a major source for Davitt's political conduct during this period. In one of them Devoy claimed that the Cooper Institute resolutions were accepted without demur by the Clan na Gael men at Sweeney's Hotel as expressing what they all believed, but that Davitt had objected to them as imprudent, and had only with great difficulty been convinced to the contrary by Devoy and Breslin. The first resolution was orthodox fenian doctrine, and it was apparently Devoy's object to show that the second, which he says was a revival of the 'Mitchel and Lalor programme'—the coupling of independence to agrarian revolution—had also good fenian ancestry.[5] It was true that Lalor's revolutionary spirit, transmitted through Mitchel, was among the origins of fenianism, and that the original fenians believed in principle in peasant proprietorship. But agrarian revolution was no part of the fenian programme.[6] The resolution was careful to avoid any conflict with fenian doctrine by declaring that only after national independence had been won could a real solution of the land question be forthcoming.

Davitt's public statements on both sides of the Atlantic had as yet proposed no innovation in fenian thinking except readiness to appreciate and encourage honest effort in the national interest by men who were not fenians. At the Cooper Institute meeting he told his audience that he would say nothing 'that has not already been stated by me in England and Scotland and Ireland'. If he referred to the land question

[1] *I.W.*, 21 Sept., 5 Oct.; New York *Weekly Union*, 5 Oct.; DN/1, p. 8; DN/2, p. 35; R. B. O'Brien, *Parnell*, i, 166–7.

[2] *The land of Eire*, p. 42.

[3] Devoy in *Irish Nation*, quoted in *United Ireland*, 28 June 84.

[4] 'Davitt's career' in *Gaelic American*, June-Nov. 1906.

[5] Devoy, II; see above, pp 36–7.

[6] Cf. Devoy, *Recollections*, p. 17; above, p. 40.

at all it must have been only incidentally. What gave historical significance to the Cooper Institute meeting was the enunciation by Devoy, after Davitt's lecture, of the 'land for the people' doctrine, and in its most extreme form, state ownership. From this point onwards Davitt's political thinking advanced rapidly, and Devoy collaborated with him in working out and launching a new policy for the national movement in which a radical treatment of the land question was an essential factor, Devoy, reviewing in 1906 the beginnings of this new policy, was anxious to establish that the 'new plank in the fenian platform' was first suggested by himself and not by Davitt, and that the idea of it originated neither with Davitt nor Clan na Gael but was derived from Lalor. Devoy's outlook was coloured by the fact that, from having been Davitt's collaborator, he had by 1882 become his bitter enemy.[1] Nevertheless Devoy was probably correct in claiming the credit for initiating the Cooper Institute resolutions.[2] He and several other Clan na Gael leaders had read Lalor,[3] but they had no need to look back to him as the source of the 'land for the people' doctrine, for it had been a theme of the *Irish People* (1863-5) and it was familiar to readers of the *Irish World*, with its recurrent philippics against the abomination of land monopoly.[4] His silence on the contribution of Ford and his paper to the radical climate of opinion among Irish-Americans may have been unintentional; but it probably reflects the animosity with which he had come to regard Ford no less than Davitt.

Two days after the Cooper Institute meeting Davitt left New York for Scranton.[5] His route lay west across New Jersey to the Delaware at Easton, and from there north by the Lehigh river over the watershed into the valley of the Susquehanna. He observed it all with great interest, and was enchanted by the alpine scenery of the Lehigh valley, where the railway followed the windings of the river through magnificent pine-clad mountains. He visited Wilkesbarre, Wyoming, and Pittston, on the Susquehanna, and on the 27th arrived at Scranton to meet Mary and Neil whom he had not seen for over thirteen years. They now had a family of six,[6] of whom the eldest, James, was now twelve, and the youngest, Bridget, not yet two. They had recently moved into a house, in what was then a pleasant open neighbourhood, at the corner of Washington Avenue and Phelps Street which, with

[1] *S.C.P.*, ix, 433; *Defence*, p. 120; Devoy in *Irish Nation*, quoted in *United Ireland*, 28 June 84.

[2] *S.C.P.*, ix, 428-30.

[3] Devoy, reviewing R. Barry O'Brien's *Life of Charles Stewart Parnell*, in *Chicago Journal*, 24 Mar. 99.

[4] Above, p. 142.

[5] See map V.

[6] James J., Catherine, Mary Anne, Sabina, Margaret, and Bridget. John, the first child, and Michael, the seventh, had died in infancy. See above, pp 22-3, 168-9, 170-71.

later extensions, was to remain in Padden occupation for nearly ninety years.[1] He returned to New York on 28 September in time to assist at the reception ceremonies for Edward O'Meagher Condon and Patrick Meledy, the recently released fenian prisoners who arrived on the 29th. On the following evening he was the principal speaker at a crowded meeting in Library Hall, Newark (New Jersey), organised for the joint benefit of the ex-prisoners Daniel Reddin and John Wilson. He was accompanied by Condon and Meledy, who spoke after him; and two fenian celebrities, John J. Breslin and O'Donovan Rossa, also took part, the former as chairman, the latter as concluding speaker. Davitt's subject, as at Philadelphia, was the present condition of Ireland, and his lecture was largely a repeat performance. But he appears to have struck a new note in references to the 'horrible barbarities' of the land system. His object, he explained, in undertaking his lecture-tour was 'to aid in bringing about a better understanding and more united action between our countrymen across the water and here, for national purposes in Ireland'.[2]

The next day (1 October) he left New York for a second trip to New England.[3] He visited New Haven and Meriden in Connecticut, Providence and Pawtucket in Rhode Island, lecturing at each place except Providence. There were good audiences at Meriden and Pawtucket, but at New Haven, on 2 October, he spoke (as he wrote to Devoy) 'with *threminjous* effect to . . . upwards of eight hundred empty seats! Hurrah! Down with the bloody Sassanach!' The local fenians who had organised the meeting were more disappointed than Davitt: 'spouting is becoming dry and distasteful, and I am not surprised at our people having the good sense to stay at home rather than pay 25 cents to hear England knocked to smithereens and Ireland freed on a public platform'. He felt compensated for the fiasco of his lecture by the success of a private meeting held afterwards with the Clan na Gael club: 'its members reflect credit on our movement for their sobriety, intelligence, and respectability'.[4] As on his previous trip to New England he found much to attract him, especially along the Connecticut coast with its many picturesque inlets, and at New Haven—'city of elms'—where he visited Yale College: 'miserable-looking exterior—row of brick buildings— . . . splendid library of over 100,000 vols— . . . no discipline imposed upon students save to be present at certain recitations

[1] *Scranton City Directory*, 1867 ff. Margaret Padden, sixth and last surviving child of Neil and Mary, was resident in this house when she died on 29 May 1964.

[2] DN/2, pp 35–36B; *Newark Morning Register*, 1 Oct. 78; *Irish American*, 12 Oct.; *I.W.*, 12 Oct., p. 8.

[3] D to Devoy, *c.* 30 Sept. (*D.P.B.*, i, 357).

[4] D to Devoy, 3 Oct. (*D.P.B.*, i, 358); *I.W.*, 19 Oct., p. 8.

during the day—over 1000 students on list now'.[1] At New London the train was shipped aboard a ferry-boat and carried across the river in ten minutes. He watched this operation with delighted interest, and made the return journey from Pawtucket to New York by the same route, arriving on 6 October.[2]

There followed an interval of six days at home, in Manayunk, spent mainly in writing. On 11 October he gave a public lecture at Chester, near Philadelphia, the mayor of Chester presiding over a thinly attended house.[3] This was the prelude to a lecture at the New Park Theatre, Brooklyn, on 13 October,[4] that proved to be the most critical of the series. The subject, which had been specially prepared for the occasion, was 'Ireland in parliament from a nationalist's point of view'. Congressman William E. Robinson was in the chair, Carroll, Devoy, Breslin, and Meledy were among the platform party, and the large audience included Patrick Ford, whom Davitt now met for the first time.[5] Davitt's starting point was that the home rule party grossly misrepresented Ireland at Westminster, and that nationalists (that is, fenians) must bear a large share of responsibility for this. Irish members would be returned to parliament whether nationalists liked it or not,[6] and by holding aloof from parliamentary politics nationalists had given the home rule party a free hand to propagate a false image of Ireland. The party's aim, O'Connor Power had declared in America, was to place Ireland in the same relationship to the British Empire as the state of New York to the American union; but the will of the Irish people was for a separate national existence. The British government's policy was to West Britainise Ireland; the present prime minister (Beaconsfield) was trying to cajole the Irish people by concessions to Irish catholics, and hoped to use the priesthood as an instrument for crushing the national spirit. It was necessary to meet the threat by 'a tangible national policy'. The home rule party was useless for this purpose. Most of its members were corrupt, or mercenary, or half-hearted. Butt himself had failed as the party leader, and was doing all he could to imperialise Ireland. There was not one member of the party, unless it was Parnell, who fitly represented the Irish people. If the national will were not to go on being misrepresented before the eyes of the world, nationalists must take an active interest in elections, however much against the grain it might be to do so. They should make it their business to ensure the return of men imbued with nationalist spirit to all public bodies, from parliament to boards of poor-law

[1] DN/2, p. 38.
[2] Ibid., pp 36B–40.
[3] DN/2 p. 40; *I.W.*, 12 Oct., p. 8.
[4] DN/2, pp 40–41.
[5] *S.C.P.*, ix, 383, 432.
[6] Cf above, p. 210.

guardians. The introduction of the secret ballot had released the rural voters from subservience to the landlords and thus opened the way for the return of genuine representatives. Parnell's popularity showed that he did express the national sentiment; and the 'honest men' such as Biggar whom he led, all young and talented, were doing all they could for Ireland with courage and persistency. To increase their number by twenty or thirty would have great advantages from a nationalist standpoint, both in educating world opinion on the Irish question and displacing charlatans and tricksters.[1]

Davitt concluded his lecture by suggesting five principles to which parliamentary candidates must pledge themselves in order to secure the electoral support of nationalists:

(1) that self-government is the chief want of Ireland;

(2) that Irish representatives in parliament should oppose the government, tooth and nail, in every effort to coerce Ireland;

(3) that there should be an agitation for a settlement of the land question on the basis of security against eviction (except for non-payment of a just rent) and the gradual growth of a peasant proprietary, holding title from the state;

(4) that Irish industries should be developed, labourers' dwellings improved, and an educational system that is not anti-national provided;

(5) that every Irishman has the right to carry arms.[2]

After a short speech from Meledy, there were loud calls from the audience for Devoy, who reluctantly came forward in response to the chairman's invitation. He endorsed the views expressed by Davitt and the public policy he proposed for the nationalists but felt that some points required elaboration and plainer speaking. It was high time that nationalists should step to the front and push aside the men who misrepresented Ireland in parliament and in the local public bodies. 'Every public body in the country, from the little boards of poor-law guardians and town commissioners to the city corporations and members of parliament should be controlled by the nationalist party.' Until they controlled all these bodies they would be regarded by foreigners as a powerless and insignificant faction, and this would be fatal to their hope of foreign intervention if Britain should become involved in war, which it then seemed might blow up with Russia over Afghanistan.[3] In

[1] *I.W.*, 26 Oct., p. 6; *Irish American*, 26 Oct.
[2] Ibid.
[3] Cf above, pp 136-7.

the event of such a war the nationalist leaders would be bound to appeal to Russia for help, only to be answered:

We have no doubt of your sincerity, but you are only a small party; you don't represent Ireland and we can't affort to make alliances with small parties without power or standing in their country. All your M.P.s are loyal to England, and your local public bodies present addresses of loyalty to every little representative of English power who comes among them. These are the only tests we know and they show that you have no weight in the country.

This was the opinion that prevailed in Russia, France, Germany, Spain, and even in America itself, and it would continue to prevail so long as Ireland sent only two sets of men to parliament, one to support the present state of things, the other to proclaim to the world that she would be satisfied with the bastard federal connection proposed by Butt.

As to the land question—'the question of questions for Ireland'—Devoy declared that he was, of course, in favour of stopping evictions and encouraging measures making for peasant proprietorship, but he went further than this:

I think the only true solution of the land question is the abolition of landlordism. The landlord system is the greatest curse inflicted by England on Ireland, and Ireland will never be prosperous or happy until it is rooted out. The land of Ireland belongs to the people of Ireland and to them alone, and we must not be afraid to say so.

The system, he went on, in terms that were almost pure Mill,[1] was imposed on Ireland by the English conquest. Before that the land belonged to the clan, which represented the state, and each man had his portion. The chief of a clan was not a landlord but the elected ruler of a free community. English law assumed that the land belonged to the chief, and that the clansmen stood in the same relationship to him as feudal tenants to their overlords. The land was thus robbed from the people who owned it and either given to adventurers from England, if the chief was a rebel, or conferred by an English title on the chief himself if he were a traitor to Ireland. Devoy concluded:

I believe in Irish independence, but I don't believe it would be worthwhile to free Ireland if that foreign landlord system were to be left standing. I am in favour of sweeping away every vestige of the English connection and this accursed landlord system above and before all. But while I think it is right to proclaim this, and that the national party should proclaim that nothing less than this would satisfy it, I know it is a solution that cannot be reached in a day, and therefore I think we should, in the meantime, accept all measures looking to the prevention of arbitrary eviction and the creation of a peasant proprietary as a step in the right direction.[2]

[1] Above, pp 37-8.
[2] *I.W.*, 26 Oct., p. 6; *D.P.B.*, i, 362.

The Brooklyn meeting as compared with the meeting in New York three weeks previously, marked a distinct advance in the formulation of the new policy. For the first time Davitt advocated participation by fenians in constitutional politics and a combination of parliamentary action with agrarian agitation. Devoy, whose impromptu statement was the speech of the evening, was more outspoken and explicit on the land question than Davitt and showed much more awareness of the international situation and its potentialities for fenian strategy. He underlined the proposal Davitt had made—which had been official I.R.B. policy in 1870[1]—that the local public bodies should be infiltrated by nationalists. But Devoy also claims, at first in 1884, and more fully in his account of Davitt's career published in 1906, that the Brooklyn meeting had undertones not apparent in the printed reports.

Davitt had carefully prepared his speech, Devoy says, and had read his first draft of it to him and a few others. They criticised his proposed remedies for the land question, which went no further than Butt's '3 Fs', and in consequence he amended his draft. But when he came to the meeting he found, too late, that he had brought the wrong draft, and in his irritation did less than justice to himself. He cut down his speech and ended abruptly. It was now only about 9 p.m. and the audience, mainly old fenians, wanted more. It was in these circumstances that Devoy was called upon to speak. He was taken by surprise, and was not a practised public speaker, but realised, on catching sight of Patrick Ford's clouded face in the front row of the auditorium, that Davitt had made a very bad impression on the formidable editor of the *Irish World*. Knowing how dangerous Ford's disapproval could be, he hastened to make good the deficiencies in Davitt's speech. That he succeeded was evident from the tumultuous applause that greeted his remarks and from Ford's private admission that, but for his intervention, he would have felt bound to denounce Davitt in the next issue of the *Irish World*. Instead he published both Davitt's speech and Devoy's, each revised by its author.[2] This explanation, unsupported by any contemporary evidence so far available,[3] must be regarded with reserve; but it is in keeping with the fact that, as reported in the *Irish World*, without any comment from Davitt, Devoy's speech at Brooklyn was the more radical and telling of the two. There is, moreover, a ring

[1] *Address of the supreme council of the Irish republic to the people of Ireland*, Jan. 70, in T. W. Moody and Leon Ó Broin, 'The I.R.B. supreme council, 1868-78' in *I.H.S.*, xix, no. 75 (Mar. 1975), p. 310.

[2] *United Ireland*, 28 June 84; Devoy, II.

[3] It would be reasonable to expect that Patrick Ford would have left some record of what passed at the Brooklyn meeting, but repeated efforts have so far failed to discover what happened to Ford's private papers.

of truth about the details of Devoy's story. There seems more to be said for accepting than rejecting it, and if it be accepted it is further evidence that, at this critical stage in his political development, Davitt was learning more from American fenians than they were learning from him.

On 14 October, the day after the Brooklyn meeting, Davitt set out by train for Cleveland, Ohio.[1] As he sped along the Hudson in the luxury of a 'drawing-room car' he noted his impressions:

> Exquisite scenery meets the eye at every bend of the river. The left side going up stream is clothed with trees for whose leaves autumn's artist hand is now lavishing its rich and varied tints. The placid surface of the broad majestic Hudson, the colouring of the trees, the bold precipitous rocks, islands, villages, and isolated mansions that flit before the eye make up an ever-varying picture such as poets' imagination alone could do justice to. Cone-shaped hills clad with trees to the summit, promontories jutting out into the river, and breaks in the river's boundary hills, revealing valleys, villages, and landscapes, pass in panoramic view from Pickskill [Peekskill] . . . to Po[ugh]keepsie.

From there he travelled to Albany and up the Mohawk valley to Little Falls, where he spent a pleasant evening as guest of Rev. J. M. Ludden, editor of the *Catholic Telegraph*, one of the first local newspapers to announce his lecture-tour and invoke a welcome for him.[2] On the 15th he went on through rather tame country to Rochester, on Lake Ontario, where he met the local Clan na Gael club, including Patrick Mahon, treasurer of the Clan, who struck him as a man of sound judgment. Next day he visited Niagara Falls: 'impossible to describe them —I was somewhat disappointed at first sight, but the more I gazed the more awful they appear'. After some hours at Buffalo, he made a night journey along the unseen shore of Lake Erie, reaching Cleveland in the early hours of the 17th, to be met at the station by 'a poor fellow who saw me in York (England) ten years ago'. He wrote a few lines to Devoy about fenian contacts he had made at Albany, Little Falls, Rochester, and Buffalo and ended on a despondent note: 'I am heartily sick of *public* spouting and wish I had never consented to anything but *private* "oratory".' But this mood was quickly changed by the success of the lecture he gave that evening at the Globe Theatre to an appreciative audience of about 600, the mayor of Cleveland presiding.[3]

His theme was again 'The Ireland of the present', and he went over much the same ground as at Philadelphia and Newark, with emphasis on the alleged design of the British government to array the catholic

[1] See map VIII.
[2] *Catholic Telegraph* (Little Falls, N.Y.), 28 Sept. 78.
[3] DN/2, pp 41–4; *D.P.B.*, i, 360–61.

clergy against the cause of Irish independence and to stigmatise nationalists as communists and infidels, on the discreditable failure of the home rule party, and on the general impoverishment of the country through excessive taxation and lack of capital. He described the land system as 'the greatest disgrace ever imposed upon the Irish people by the British government'. On the other hand he saw promise in Parnell, and again spoke with admiration of Archbishop MacHale of Tuam, for his championship of the Irish language. Finally he appealed to the Irish in America to cooperate with their brethren at home in unceasing effort for the welfare of their native land.[1] He left Cleveland early next morning and spent the whole day travelling, through the flat pastoral landscape of Ohio and Indiana, to Chicago. All the following day (19 October) he travelled across the rich farm-lands of Illinois to the bustling river-port of St Louis, the gateway to the west, on the Mississippi. Here he stayed three and a half days, strenuously sightseeing and making contact with Irish organisations including Clan na Gael, the Ancient Order of Hibernians, and the Knights of St Patrick. The Irish were believed to account for a fifth of the city's population of half a million, but unlike New York, which Americans and Irish virtually had to themselves, St Louis struck Davitt as swarming with negroes and Germans. He counted about forty catholic churches, some named after Irish saints. He visited the famous corn exchange, the criminal courts, and the county prison—which, he observed with an experienced eye, was 'extraordinarily comfortable, splendidly ventilated and heated'.[2]

He had not expected to stay at St Louis as long as he did, but the local fenian organiser of his tour delayed him there for two and a half days and then sent him on an itinerary in the prairies of Missouri that needed twice the time allowed for it. Missouri, in the heart of the midwest corn-belt, was one of the most thriving regions of America, and a source of those cheap agricultural products whose influx into Europe was contributing to the increasing agricultural depression in Ireland. Of this Davitt seems to have been unaware during three days (23-6 October) of almost incessant railway journeys through many miles of country south and north of the Missouri river. He followed a route that took him west as far as Sedalia—'queen city of the prairies'—, near the centre of the state, and then back in a north-east direction to the Mississippi at Hannibal. At Sedalia he lectured in the catholic school, the local priest in the chair, to what he described as a 'fair audience for a small Irish population'—about 800 in a town of 15,000. In this region Germans outnumbered all other national groups put together,

[1] DN/2, p. 44; *Cleveland Leader*, 18 Oct. [2] DN/2, pp 44-54.

and Davitt admired their sound judgment 'in selecting the best and widest field for their enterprise. Would that our people had their strong practical good sense.' About thirty miles north of Sedalia he visited a new town, Marshall, when the civil court was in session: 'judge sitting with feet cocked up, lawyers ditto, chewing quids and spitting almost everywhere–singular unconcernedness of all present'. He read with surprise of the death of Cardinal Cullen in Dublin the previous day and made the characteristic fenian comment, 'blow to England and west-Britainism', but added 'de mortuo nil nisi bonum'. Marshall was the county town of Saline, whose population included 500 Irish, some of them in a new settlement nearby that was getting on well. The Emmet Club of Marshall gave a ball in Davitt's honour, at which there were some very handsome Irish girls and some new and pretty dances. The dancing went on all night, but he had to retire early to be up at 3.45 a.m.[1]

At 4.15 a.m. on the 26th he left Marshall in an open buggy, drawn by a team of good horses, for Miami Ferry, on the Missouri, to connect with a main east-west railroad north of the river. It was very dark, sleety, and bitterly cold. The young Yankee driver was unfamiliar with the route, the track was invisible, and progress was very slow. The horses, shying at trees by the roadside, lost the track, floundered into a fence, and were attacked by dogs. Being frightened, they had to be led by their driver till, groping painfully in the darkness, he at last got them back on the road. Some miles further on they lost their way again. It was not till daylight came that they were able to show their paces; from then on they galloped through snow, rain, and mud till at last they brought their weary passenger to Miami Ferry and breakfast. It had taken nearly four hours to cover the seventeen miles from Marshall. From Miami he travelled by train to Hannibal, arriving at 5 p.m. for a lecture that evening to find that it was arranged for the following evening.[2] He vented his irritation at the mismanagement of his tour in a letter to Devoy. He was the more impatient because the proceeds of his lectures were so disappointing (only $14.50 at Sedalia): 'if this isn't doing the devil of a penance for "spouting" I don't know what is'. On the other hand he felt that his private meetings had been successful. He was in touch with fenian affairs at home and was vexed to hear that John O'Connor, the secretary of the supreme council, was neglecting the north of England division of the I.R.B., which Davitt represented: 'I never intended holding that position longer than to do the work which he had failed to accomplish'.[3]

[1] DN/2, pp 54–9; *D.P.B.*, i, 362–3.
[2] DN/2, pp 59–61.
[3] D to Devoy, 26 Oct. (*D.P.B.*, i, 363).

Next morning, Sunday, 27 October, in more sanguine mood he went to mass and heard a 'splendid sermon', by Patrick John Ryan, the Tipperary-born coadjutor bishop of St Louis,[1] who propounded 'unanswerable arguments' against infidelity, paganism, and pagan morality. He visited the Sisters of St Joseph and had an interesting talk with Mother Gabriel 'from rebel Cork'; and he called on the parish priest. It was at Hannibal that Mark Twain had spent his adventurous boyhood, which, only two years before, he had immortalised in *Tom Sawyer*, a fact that Davitt was not likely to have missed as he quickly absorbed the atmosphere of this small Mississippi town. In the evening he lectured in the Mozart Hall to a 'large, intelligent, and appreciative audience' that included many Americans and Germans as well as Irish. He left Hannibal by night train for his next lecturing assignment, about 250 miles up the Mississippi at Dubuque, in Iowa, but had to make a wide detour westwards to meet a Clan na Gael club at Ottumwa the following night (28 October).[2]

When he reached Dubuque on the evening of the 29th, a large reception committee, headed by the mayor, was waiting at the station to welcome him, and after that he was the guest of honour at a reception, lasting nearly two hours, in the principal hotel. Dubuque, with a population of about 25,000 was one of the leading manufacturing centres of Iowa, and its strong foreign-born element was mostly German and Irish, the latter entrenched in the corporation and the civic administration. Davitt's lecture in Globe Hall on the following evening was fairly well attended, and though he felt that he had delivered it badly it was favourably reported by two newspapers that catered for the Irish element in Dubuque. He discovered that a disparaging remark about himself in the *Daily Herald* had been strongly resented by the *Daily Telegraph*, that there had been sharp recriminations, that the mayor and corporation (predominantly Irish-American) had sided with Davitt's defender and that each paper had then aimed at outdoing the other in its appreciation of him. He was described by the *Telegraph* as 'a man of excellent education, good powers of observation, large experience and general information', and by the *Herald* as having a ready command of language but never straining after effect; familiar with Irish history and the present condition of his country; 'but above all he is in earnest, which gives to his utterances a patriotic fervour akin to eloquence which reaches out and grasps the heart of the hearer and holds it firmly'.[3]

[1] *D.A.B.*.
[2] DN/2, pp 61-3.
[3] DN/2, pp 63-4; *Daily Telegraph* (Dubuque), 30 Oct.; *Daily Herald* (Dubuque), 31 Oct.; *D.P.B.*, i, 366.

The theme of his lecture, as at Cleveland, was contemporary Ireland, and he addressed himself not only to the Irish but also to the Americans in his audience. Despite all the vaunted ameliorations conceded by the British parliament to Ireland the will of the Irish people for total separation from England was as strong as ever. The British claim that Irish disaffection was confined to a small minority and that the great majority of Irishmen were contented and loyal subjects of the queen was incompatible with the regime of repression that Britain maintained in Ireland. If the Irish were loyal subjects why were they prohibited from carrying arms? The British government was attempting by a policy of concessions to the catholic church to separate the hierarchy from the people, and some of the bishops were cooperating with the government in the hope that they could thus bring about the restoration of England and Scotland to the catholic church. But the national question was not a question of religion, and Davitt declared that he would not sacrifice Irish independence to the conversion of England. He was confident that the Irish clergy as a whole would never be separated from the national cause. The 'greatest Irish patriot now living' was the archbishop of Tuam, that patriarch of the west whose splendid services to the revival of the Irish language were an inspiration to national self-respect. As to the land question, so long as England turned a deaf ear to the peasantry's cries for relief 'such scenes as the execution of Lord Leitrim would recur. In his native county of Mayo, he had seen near Castlebar a fertile and extensive estate, that of Lord Lucan, from which the former tenants had been driven out to live on patches of stony hillside where they looked down on the productive acres that had belonged to their fathers and now were used only to graze the cattle of an absentee landlord. What Ireland needed most was that her claims to justice and to independence should be unmistakably voiced and boldly prosecuted. The West British press devoted itself to fomenting sectarian divisions, but the 'national' newspapers, despite legal restrictions, did manage to speak for the great majority of the people and 'to enlighten the world as to the real condition of Irish affairs'. Of the Irish party at Westminster only Parnell and a few other members truly represented Ireland, but Davitt prophesied that after the next general election Parnell would supersede Butt as leader. Finally Davitt appealed to Irish-Americans for sympathy and support, on two grounds: first, because of the services rendered by Irish exiles to the cause of American liberty in the war of independence and the civil war; second, because Ireland's struggle for independence was in principle the same as that of the thirteen American colonies. He was not asking Irish-Americans for anything inconsistent with their duties as American citizens, and if they refused the help Ireland sought they were untrue to the land that bore them and unworthy of American citizenship. 'It was the best lecture', the *Telegraph* declared, 'ever given in Dubuque on the Irish question.'[1]

Davitt spent the next day (31 October) driving around Dubuque—'beautifully situated on the Mississippi, surrounded on three sides by hills'[2]—and meeting the local fenians in private. He found time to write to Devoy, as usual mainly on fenian matters. He had had meetings with Clan na Gael clubs at St Louis, Sedalia, Marshall, Hannibal, Ottumwa and Dubuque: 'I am sorry I cannot see more of these splendid western fellows. What a field there is out here for work in our movement.' He had given up his intention of going further west, to Omaha (Nebraska) and Denver (Colorado), because some of his projected lectures had been cancelled and the proceeds of the remainder had not covered his expenses.

These people out here believed that my only object was to make money, and they frankly tell me that lecturing won't do it. Had they been posted on my real desire (to see the V.C.[3]), they would have met me half-way by endeavouring to defray expenses . . . As it is they have attempted to do nothing, under the impression that more was required than they could accomplish.

He had heard from James J. O'Kelly in Boston that if the fenians there cooperated with O'Reilly and Joyce[4] he could be assured of a lecture that would be a financial success. As his expenses out west had been so 'devilish heavy' he feared that he must 'go on the damned stump in the east again to take myself and mother home'.[5]

He went on to refer to a project under discussion between Carroll, Devoy, and himself, the founding of a nationalist weekly in Dublin (with possibly a Philadelphia edition) to be run by Clan na Gael in association with the I.R.B. and to be financed initially by the Clan. It was intended to be the authentic voice of honest and intelligent nationalists, replacing the undistinguished and unreliable papers (the *Irishman*, the *Flag of Ireland*, and the *Shamrock*) of Richard Pigott.[6] Such a project had been contemplated in 1975-6 by several I.R.B. men—Biggar, Barry, Egan, and Doran—in conjunction with Butt, Parnell, and other home-rulers, but nothing had come of the negotiations except abundant evidence to those concerned of Pigott's shiftiness, plausibility, and chronic impecuniosity.[7] Carroll held that the projected weekly must

[1] *Daily Telegraph* (Dubuque), 31 Oct.; *Daily Herald* (Dubuque), 31 Oct.

[2] DN/2, p. 64. [3] United Brotherhoood or Clan na Gael. [4] See below, pp 359-60.

[5] D to Devoy, 31 Oct. (*D.P.B.*, i, 366). [6] See above, pp 174, 204.

[7] J. G. Biggar to C. G. Doran, 19 Oct. 75; P. Egan to Doran, 3, 15 Apr. 76; R. Pigott to Doran, 6, 10, 12 Apr., 6 May (Doran papers).

be 'equal to the ablest organ of the enemy',[1] and its editor must command the respect, if not the cooperation, of such writers as Lecky, Prendergast, and Allingham. He dreamed of Kickham in this role but knew that he was physically unequal to it.[2] He wished that Davitt would not return home since that might well mean a return to prison ('they, of course, know in Scotland Yard what he is doing here'), but would remain in America 'to travel and organise and push the paper'.[3] Davitt, who saw himself as playing a central part in the new venture, showed no sign of wanting to remain in America. He toyed with the idea that the paper should be edited by Devoy from Paris (since he could not legally return to Ireland or Britain till the expiration of his sentence), and believed that a man ideally qualified to act as Devoy's deputy in Dublin was James J. O'Kelly, then in Boston, who would be willing to go to Ireland if asked by Clan na Gael.

He shares our ideas in everything—excepting a more 'charitable' opinion of O'Donnell and Power. . . . I think no more suitable man could be found for the work to be done, and it ought to be our particular desire *now* to wheel every thinking and earnest man of our movement into positions where they can do most good.[4]

Nothing came of this newspaper project, and Devoy considered Davitt's idea of editorship by remote control absurd. But Pigott's conduct of the *Irishman* was to become an acute problem for nationalists.[5]

On 1 November Davitt travelled by train along the east bank of the Mississippi, enjoying the beauty of the great, broad river with its rocky bluffs rising up behind tree-lined banks and sometimes looking like a system of strong fortifications, its innumerable tiny islands of every imaginable shape, and its stern-wheel steamers one of which signalled his train to stop to pick up two passengers. From La Crosse, where he had to wait seven hours, he completed the journey to St Paul in a sleeping car which he found almost as comfortable as his cabin on the *Britannic*. About 6 a.m. he reached St Paul, a city of about 30,000. Though one third of them were Irish, his lecture that evening was very thinly attended. He learnt that this was due to a report in the Cleveland *Universe* that he had there attacked the catholic priesthood and the confessional. It was too late to counteract the lie, but he had the compensation that two young Irishmen travelled one hundred miles simply to meet him. Next day, Sunday, 3 November, he went to mass at the cathedral and heard a sermon by John Ireland, coadjutor bishop of St Paul. As a preacher he was not to be compared, Davitt thought,

[1] Carroll to Devoy, 17 Sept. 78 (*D.P.B.*, i, 354).
[2] Ibid., i, 361.
[3] Carroll to Devoy, 24 Oct. (ibid., i, 362).
[4] D to Devoy, 31 Oct. (ibid., i, 367).
[5] Devoy, IV.

with Ryan of St Louis, but like the latter was 'reputed to be patriotic'. In conversation with Davitt he produced the lying statement in the Cleveland *Universe* and showed what he thought of it by asking Davitt's leave to attend his lecture that evening in Minneapolis. Bishop Ireland, a native of County Kilkenny, was famous not only for liberal views but also as a dynamic 'frontier bishop', deeply involved in social problems. He was a champion of total abstinence ('the Father Mathew of the west') and the author of an imaginative plan to found agricultural colonies of catholics, especially poor Irish immigrants from the industrial towns of the east. His Catholic Colonization Bureau of St Paul, founded in January 1876, had already been the means of establishing many catholic settlements in western Minnesota (two of his new towns were named Clontarf and Avoca), though his colonists were generally not industrial labourers seeking a new way of life but small farmers who sold good farms to buy better.[1]

From St Paul Davitt was escorted to Minneapolis ten miles away, by a deputation from the latter place that included a detective and a policeman. Minneapolis was a handsome and rapidly expanding city of about 40,000, with a much smaller Irish element than that of St Paul. He was taken to see Minnehaha Falls, found the scenery lovely and, recalling 'Hiawatha', felt that the falling waters really had a laughing sound. Many friends came to see him at his hotel and he had an enthusiastic audience for his lecture at the Spence Opera House that night. All the Americans present waited on him afterwards to assure him that their sympathy was with Ireland. He was 'highly delighted' with Minneapolis, which he decided to make the western terminus of his trip.[2]

He set out on his return journey next morning, 4 November. As far as Winona his route ran south along the Mississippi by the way he had come, and he was able to view a stretch of the river which, three days before, he had traversed in darkness. At Chicago, where he spent two days (5–7 November), he witnessed an election for the federal house of representatives ('no excitement—awfully tame'), did a round of sight-seeing, called on the principal newspapers, met the veteran fenian, P. W. Dunne, and had an interview with General Philip Henry Sheridan, the distinguished civil-war soldier of Irish parentage who was now in command of the western and south-western military divisions of the U.S. He made the acquaintance of the Chicago lawyer, Alexander Sullivan, an able and ambitious Clan na Gael leader who, in the eighties, was to become involved in a ferocious power-struggle with Devoy in

[1] See James P. Shannon, *Catholic colonization on the western frontier* (New Haven and London, 1957).

[2] DN/2, pp 65–9.

which Davitt was to take Sullivan's side. Davitt was also seen by Major Henri Le Caron, formerly of the American army and now practising medicine at Braidwood, Illinois, who was a trusted member of Clan na Gael and whose real identity as a British government spy was successfully concealed till he himself dramatically threw off the mask before the *Times*-Parnell commission in 1889.[1] Some forty miles from Chicago Davitt visited the state prison at Joliet, and noted that prisoners slept two together, were given meat *ad lib.* for dinner, and were allowed tobacco and newspapers. From Chicago he returned to New York (7-14 November) by the route he had taken on the outward journey, stopping at Cleveland, Buffalo, Niagara, Rochester, and Albany. At Buffalo, separated from Fort Erie, in Canada, by the Niagara river, he was reminded of the fenian raid across the river in June 1866 and was told by local fenians of the excitements of that time. They recalled that a priest had refused to read the burial service over a man who had died of wounds received in the fighting at Ridgway (near Fort Erie), 'because his body was accompanied into the church by men in green uniforms'. Davitt revisited the Falls and crossed the new suspension bridge. He travelled down the Mohawk valley by moonlight, an enchanting experience. At Albany he fell ill and had to remain in his hotel a whole day (13 November). On the 14th he was back again at Sweeney's Hotel, New York.[2]

The month he had spent on tour in the middle west was a memorable time both for himself and for American fenians. He had made himself known to large numbers of Irish and Irish-Americans spread out along the southern shores of the great lakes and in the region west of the Mississippi that was little more than a generation removed from the primitive conditions of the frontier. His public meetings, though many were only thinly attended, had something of the character of a successful revivalist campaign: 'I wish', Carroll wrote to Devoy (29 October), 'we could keep him constantly on the road on this side of the sea. Our needed 100,000 members could soon be recruited and the whole country awakened.'[3] In accordance with the views announced at his New York and Brooklyn lectures Davitt's message was essentially a call to fenians to support aggressive constitutional action for self-government in association with radical change in the land system. The apprehensions that this departure from fenian orthodoxy aroused he allayed in his private meetings with Clan na Gael clubs by reiterated assurances that the public movement he proposed would be used not

[1] *S.C.P.*, iv, 489-91, 503-4, 514 (5 Feb. 89).
[2] DN/2, pp 69-75; *D.P.B.*, i, 205-6, 378; *S.C.P.*, ix, 392; *D.A.B.*, P. H. Sheridan.
[3] *D.P.B.*, i, 364.

to injure fenianism or diminish fenian ideals, but only as a means of broadening the scope of fenian activity and committing the mass of the Irish people to a more advanced programme than that of the Home Rule League.[1] The only witness to these assurances is Devoy, but the closeness of his relations with Davitt at this time is all in favour of his testimony. Devoy considered that Davitt was doing the work of the Clan na Gael executive, and on that ground persuaded Carroll that the executive ought to pay the expenses of his tour so as to leave him the receipts from his lectures to go home with; Carroll eventually authorised payment of $200 for this purpose.[2] It is a measure of Davitt's standing among the Clan na Gael chiefs that, while he was still in Chicago, Carroll arranged for the revolutionary directory and the Clan executive to meet in New York at a date (24 November) when it was certain that he would be able to attend.[3]

It would, however, be a mistake to see this first western tour of Davitt's merely in political terms. With insatiable zest for new people and places he had extended his acquaintance with America from the north-eastern seaboard to the heartland of the middle west, and he had found the experience immensely stimulating if at times too exhausting. Wherever he went he was alert to the character of the landscape as well as to the human impact upon it, to natural beauty as well as to technological progress, to the splendours of Niagara Falls as well as to the telephone system in Chicago. He had an appraising eye for law courts and prisons. While he showed a typically fenian attitude to the 'priest in politics', he went to mass on Sundays, took a discriminating interest in sermons, and talked with priests, nuns, and the most outstanding bishop of the middle west. These aspects of his tour are reflected only in his diary, which was written in a quite different style and spirit from those of his letters to Devoy. These two sources seem almost to belong to different states of mind—the Devoy letters colloquial and slangy in manner and esoteric in matter, the diary (in which neither fenianism nor any individual fenian is ever mentioned) sober, direct, and without expletives.

While Davitt was away in Missouri the New York *Herald* received from Dublin and published on 24 October a telegraph message which Devoy and other Clan na Gael men interpreted as requiring immediate action by the advocates of the new policy. What had happened was that the Home Rule Confederation of Great Britain had held a convention in Dublin on 21-2 October, against Butt's wishes, and had

[1] Devoy, *The land of Eire*, p. 43; Devoy, IV.
[2] *D.P.B.*, i, 361, 383.
[3] Ibid., i, 361, 369, 374.

re-elected Parnell as its president. Devoy concluded, erroneously, that the final break between Butt and Parnell had come. After hasty consultation with political colleagues in New York, and by telegram with leading nationalists (not including Davitt) in other parts of the United States, he concocted the following message, signed by himself, Carroll, Mahon, Breslin, and Millen and addressed to a veteran fenian in Dublin, James O'Connor, who was sub-editor of the *Irishman* and a friend of Charles Kickham, then chairman of the I.R.B. supreme council:

Show following to Kickham, and if approved present to Charles Parnell and friends:

> Nationalists here will support you on following conditions:
>
> (1) abandonment of federal demand [and] substitution [of] general declaration in favour of self-government;
>
> (2) vigorous agitation of land question on basis of peasant proprietary, while accepting concessions tending to abolish arbitrary eviction;
>
> (3) exclusion of all sectarian issues from platform;
>
> (4) [Irish] members to vote together on all imperial and home questions, adopt aggressive policy and energetically resist all coercive legislation;
>
> (5) advocacy of all struggling nationalities in British Empire and elsewhere.[1]

This message, sent by telegraph on 24 October, was published in New York the next day, but not till 11 November in Dublin.[2]

The first condition laid down in the telegram rejected Butt's so-called federalism, which aimed only at a subordinate legislature in Dublin, to be created, and therefore revocable, by act of parliament, and substituted the fenian aim of national independence.[3] The second condition linked the question of independence with agitation for a radical solution of the land question and implicitly rejected Butt's demand for the '3 Fs' as a principle of settlement. The third condition expressed the fenian refusal to identify national independence with the interests of the catholic church as such. The fourth demanded an independent and disciplined parliamentary party, such as Butt's egregiously was not, whose aggresive activity would prove to the world the reality of Irish disaffection. The final condition was intended to promote solidarity between the Irish and other oppressed nationalities, especially the Boers and the Indians, struggling against the same enemy;[4] it was a direct challenge to Butt's imperialist position.

[1] S.P.O., A files, no. 550; this is a transcript of the office copy in the G.P.O., London, of the telegram received by James O'Connor on 24 Oct. at the *Irishman* office, 33 Lower Abbey Street. The transcript was supplied to the Irish government by the postmaster general on 15 Nov. in compliance with a warrant from the lord lieutenant.

[2] New York *Herald*, 25 Oct. 78; reprinted passim, especially in Boston *Pilot*, 2 Nov., *F.J.*, 11 Nov., *Irishman*, 16 Nov., *Nation*, 16 Nov.; Devoy, *The land of Eire*, pp 43-4; Devoy, IV; *Fall*, pp 125-6 (where the telegram is wrongly dated 7 Nov.).

[3] Cf. above, pp 236-7; below, p. 264.

[4] Devoy, IV.

On Sunday, 27 October, two days after its publication of the telegram, the New York *Herald* carried a news article entitled 'An Irish new departure', which gave a full and vigorous exposition of the policy that had been taking shape since Davitt's first lecture. The preface described the telegram as being the subject of much comment among the Irish in America—'and it is thought that the next few weeks will see a veritable "new departure" in Irish national politics'.

The change, it is said by those competent to speak on the subject, will take the shape of a combination between the advocates of physical force and those who believe in constitutional agitation, such as will leave the former free to prepare for active work while, in the meantime, giving a reasonable support to a dignified and manly demand for self-government on the part of the constitutionalists.

The more thoughtful leaders of advanced nationalism were convinced that mere conspiracy would never achieve their ends. A public policy was necessary if the will of the majority in Ireland was to prevail. That will was overwhelmingly for separation from England, but the nationalist policy of abstention from public life had created the illusion that the majority favoured union with England.[1] The anonymous writer of this preamble was Devoy, and so also was the *Herald* 'reporter' whose imaginary 'interviews' with four prominent nationalists made up the body of the article. The four were T. C. Luby, J. J. Breslin, T. F. Bourke, and one unnamed but obviously intended to be Devoy himself. Devoy submitted his text of the 'interviews' to the other three before publication.[2] Their names, and the fact that the article was reprinted as a pamphlet and issued to every branch of Clan na Gael, gave it an official sanction, even though, like Devoy's telegram itself, it had not been authorised by the Clan executive. In the history of the prolonged and bitter controversy that was to follow, it was the foundation document.

The new policy enunciated in Devoy's article was the second in the series of three 'new departures', or deviations from orthodox fenianism, of the 1870s.[3] It was the most sensational and most publicised of the three and was to become the most notorious. And since it was soon to be confused with the third in the series, it is important to define it as precisely as possible. Six crucial points can be identified in Devoy's article.

(1) There was to be no abandonment of fenianism. Ireland could not be freed except by physical force, but on the other hand little insurrections that England could easily suppress were useless. The right policy was to prepare for the time when England was at war or could otherwise be taken at a disadvantage. In that situation Ireland should

[1] Devoy, V. [2] Devoy, IV. [3] Cf. above, pp 122–3.

declare her just demands and, at least for a time, maintain a state of passive resistance while nationalists outside actively assisted England's enemies and struck at England whenever and wherever they could.

(2) Constitutional agitation was one means of preparing for the decisive war of independence. The world judged Ireland by its public representatives, but Ireland must not be misrepresented any longer either at Westminster or on the local public bodies. It was futile to send men to the British parliament to beg, but men should be sent there to protest before the world against England's right to govern Ireland.

(3) When a majority of Irish M.P.s were of this kind and when the situation was ripe (especially if England were at war) the Irish M.P.s should withdraw in a body to Dublin, declare themselves an Irish legislature, and act accordingly. This would be the best way of enlisting the active sympathy of 'the whole Irish race' and giving Ireland a standing before the world that no mere insurrection would ever do. (Here Devoy wrote into the new programme the strategy of withdrawal from the British parliament which Clan na Gael had inherited from the 1848 men, which Davitt had discussed with Parnell, and which Parnell had suggested as a possible development of the obstructionist policy.)[1]

(4) Butt's leadership of the Irish parliamentary party was no longer to be taken seriously; and Parnell and the activists who had won the respect of advanced nationalists would be assured of their full support on the terms stipulated. In particular the Parnellites must discard Butt's 'mongrel federal scheme', grapple realistically with the land question, drop sectarianism, and act together on all questions. If they did this the next general election would return Parnell with a party of some fifty 'earnest representatives' and some thirty or forty other members who would vote with them in order to keep their seats.

(5) The vital question for Ireland and the one that demanded immediate attention was the land question. The feeling among Irish-Americans against landlordism in Ireland was intense, and while credit was given to certain members of the landlord class, it was 'almost universally' held that the only real solution to the land problem was the sweeping away of the whole existing system.

(6) The cause of national independence must be kept separate from the aims of the catholic church.

> We don't propose to turn over the education of the rising generation to the catholic hierarchy, many of whom are the bitterest enemies of an independent Irish nationality. We want a sound national education for all creeds and classes ... Our grievance with regard to the present so-called 'national' system of education [i.e.

[1] Above, pp 138, 206-8, 210.

primary education] is that, while the teaching is really very good, it is not national in any sense of the word, but the bishops offer us nothing better. The Catholic University wastes the people's money on illuminations for the Prince of Wales and gives its best professorships to English catholics.

Nationalists had no intention of making the national movement an engine for the conversion of England to catholicism, and were determined to leave the pope to settle his differences with Italy without Irish interference. The church could do its own work through its own machinery. 'We don't care whether English rule in Ireland is catholic or protestant, we want to put an end to it.'[1]

Davitt heard of Devoy's telegram and the *Herald* 'interviews' while on his way back from Minneapolis. Though well-impressed by Devoy's formulation of the 'new departure',[2] he considered that his sensational overture to Parnell was rash and blundering. This open offer of alliance from a group of notorious revolutionaries to a member of parliament aspiring to the leadership of a constitutional party would be certain, he thought, to impede rather than promote Parnell's accession to power. He wrote hurriedly to expostulate with Devoy, and on his return to New York the question was thrashed out between him and Devoy and other Clan na Gael men. He seems to have been brought round to their view that Parnell would not be injured by the telegram[3] and that the time had come for the fullest possible ventilation of the new policy.[4]

Reports of Davitt's Brooklyn meeting and of the telegram had now appeared in the Dublin and London press, and a heated controversy over the 'new departure' proposals had begun. John O'Leary had written privately to Devoy from his exile in Paris inquiring tartly what he meant in his statement at Brooklyn by recommending the fenian body to send 'nationalists' to the British parliament.

I care very little about Mr Davitt's speech, but yours is, of course, quite a different thing. I suppose I need not inform you that Mr Davitt, like your friend Mr Kelly (if he be still your friend) is a thick and thin friend of Mr O'C. P. [O'Connor Power]. . . . It seems to some people in Ireland that in this matter of parliament ye have been led astray now by Mr Davitt, as in the matter of Mr O'C. P. ye were formerly led astray by Mr Kelly.[5]

Kickham himself, in Dublin, disapproved of Devoy's telegram, which was therefore not presented to Parnell,[6] and, in an unsigned editorial

[1] [Devoy], 'An Irish new departure', in New York *Herald*, 27 Oct.; Devoy, V.
[2] Carroll to Devoy, 8 Nov. (*D.P.B.*, i, 372).
[3] Carroll to Devoy, 10 Nov. (ibid., i, 374–5).
[4] Devoy, V; *Defence*, p. 97; *Fall*, pp 125–6.
[5] O'Leary to Devoy, 8 Nov. (*D.P.B.*, i, 373–4).
[6] *S.C.P.*, vii, 92; ix, 355–6.

in the *Irishman*, he expressed the orthodox I.R.B. disapproval of the proposed new policy. Fenians who became parliamentarians would seem to be recognising English rule as an evil to be endured and to be content to work for its improvement within the lines of the constitution. A fenian could enter parliament only after taking an oath to Queen Victoria incompatible with his principles as a separatist. There was nothing in the Brooklyn proposals that could not be acted upon more appropriately by ordinary home-rulers than by fenians. 'We hold to the conviction, which has stood the test of lengthened experiment and has never been controverted, that the English parliament is no place for an Irish patriot.'[1] The reaction of moderate nationalists was voiced in the *Freeman's Journal* in an editorial on Devoy's telegram. Gray questioned the reality of Clan na Gael's offer: such 'conspiring in public' was either mere bombast or done by enemies of Parnell to discredit him or to use against him in parliament. Still, the nature of the new proposals was a welcome sign that the extreme nationalists were abandoning their traditional aloofness from constitutional action.[2]

Parnell himself took no notice of Devoy's telegram, but speeches that he made on the land question at Tralee on 15 and 16 November may have been meant as a veiled contribution to the new departure controversy. Nothing, he said on the 15th, could be won for Ireland by conciliation but only by energy, acitivity, and determination both inside and outside parliament. The first duty of Irish representatives was to show whatever British government might be in power that, if they refused a settlement of Ireland's vital problems, they would do so at their peril. But there were all too few M.P.s imbued with this spirit. The political air of Westminster was contaminating, and a man might be the best in the world in Tralee and yet, somehow or other, when he got to London the cutting edge of his patriotism became blunted. But a general election must come within two years at most, and the people of Ireland could then decide whether they wanted to have parliamentary energy or parliamentary sloth. Let them make up their minds and not fall between two stools. They now had the means of enforcing their wills through the ballot box denied to the people of his own county, Wicklow, when they resorted to rebellion in 1798. He called on the Irish people to return, at the next election, 'men who would not be afraid to do their work, men whom obloquy would not put down, men who would remember the suffering people they had left behind them in Ireland'. Above all he wanted the people 'to save themselves from the grasp of the landlords and to deprive those landlords of a power which turned Christians into demons'. Addressing

[1] *Irishman*, 9 Nov.

[2] *F.J.*, 11 Nov.

the Kerry Tenants' Defence Association on 16 November, he took up the question of how the landlord system could best be dealt with. Unless they went in for revolution he did not see how the radical change to peasant proprietorship could be achieved in the near future, and therefore he felt disposed to concentrate on Butt's plan of a settlement on the '3 Fs' principle,[1] and on an extension of the 'Bright clauses' (the land-purchase provisions) of the land act of 1870. He hoped for important results from the recent report of the Shaw-Lefevre committee,[2] and thought that, if the farmers were thus given increased facilities for buying out their holdings, the way might be prepared for the only real solution of the problem—the ownership of the soil by the people who cultivated it.[3] In thus leaving his options open Parnell's political realism was very evident.

The most vociferous assailant of the new proposals was Richard Pigott,[4] who, on 9 November, denounced Davitt and Devoy in the *Irishman* as political heretics. He was well aware that if fenians were to engage openly in public life the *raison d'etre* of his newspapers would disappear.[5] A wordy debate conducted mainly in the *Irishman* and the *Freeman's Journal*, ensued, in which Davitt took a prominent part. From his mother's home in Manayunk, to which he had returned from New York, he wrote a long letter to the *Irishman* on 20 November, counter-attacking Pigott and defending his own conduct and the new proposals with great vigour.[6] The opinions he had been expressing during the past ten months, Davitt asserted, were the fruit of years of reflection in prison.

> Finding myself cut off from the world . . . I naturally employed my mind upon why I found myself in prison and upon what my labours should be in the national cause if I ever again regained my liberty. In reviewing the history of Irish revolution—particularly the one with which I was identified—I found their characteristics to be . . . generous enthusiasm, self-sacrificing impulse, and . . . impatience of results, a total disregard of the strength of the power to be overcome . . . , the utmost contempt for cool judgment . . . , and the bitterest prejudice against every Irishman who should doubt the sanguine results of premature insurrection.[7]

He had made up his mind that if he ever emerged from prison he would serve Ireland in a sure, realistic, and effective way.

What was needed was 'a calm, systematic, methodical revolution, organised in thought and judgment and handled by discretion and prudence'—a revolution with the strength of purpose to strike only when circumstances offered reasonable hope of success. How and when to strike were vital questions for a people contending against

[1] Above, pp 39, 127, 209.
[2] Above, pp 209–10.
[3] *F.J.*, 18 Nov.; *Irishman*, 23 Nov.
[4] See above, p. 204.
[5] Devoy, VI.
[6] *Irishman*, 7, 14 Dec.
[7] Ibid., 14 Dec.

overwhelming odds. England would prefer to crush Irish insurrections every ten or fifteen years[1] rather than to know that separatists were resolved to husband their resources until her difficulties should give them the opportunity to attack. Wolfe Tone, 'the only real revolutionist we ever had', created his and Ireland's opportunity by winning the help of England's enemy, but he was able to do so only by convincing the French government that the disaffection in Ireland and the public spirit of the country justified the expenditure he demanded; and had not the weather taken sides decisively against Ireland, independence would have been the outcome of Hoche's expedition to Bantry Bay. The successors of the United Irishmen, the men of 1848, were little better than theoretical revolutionists, but in seeking to enlist the sympathy of other powers in Ireland's cause they were more realistic than the fenians who made the rising of 1867 on a basis of pure enthusiasm.

One of the worst blunders of fenianism was to assume that all real nationalists were included in its ranks and to oppose and despise every Irishman who refused to join them. By dividing all Irishmen into nationalists and West Britons fenians had made a host of enemies out of potential friends. Butt had had 'the skill to sow the seeds of his home rule scheme in the rich soil which we contemned'. Home rule was now played out, but Parnell had come to the front with a popular following that demanded the most serious attention from fenians. His honesty of purpose was believed in the world over. He was not a separatist but was still further from being a West Briton. By cooperating with his group fenians would crush the anti-national element in Irish politics and rescue Ireland from the reproach which her parliamentary 'representatives' had earned for her in the past. Leaving Parnell unsupported meant increasing the number of sham home-rulers in the house of commons. Parnell's conduct in the house of commons had attracted attention in the press of America, Germany, France, and Russia, and it was vital that this should continue if foreign states were to understand what Ireland's national aspirations really were, Moreover Parnell's views on the land question[2] were the nearest approach to those of the fenians, and his efforts to mitigate the wretchedness of 'our land-robbed people' deserved to be earnestly supported.

Would it be foreign to the purpose of the separatist movement for its members to resort to every means within their power—constitutional if no other be opportune—to stay the robber-hand of the landlords from crushing out the life-blood of our people? If the revolution is not to be accomplished but by physical force,

[1] Cf. Devoy in New York *Herald*, 27 Oct. (above, p. 251).
[2] See above, p. 210.

and therefore not perhaps for ten, fifteen, or twenty years to come, is there no other weapon by which in the meantime to exterminate the land system, ere our people are exterminated by it and the landlords?[1]

He yielded to no man, Davitt went on, in his devotion to the principles of fenianism, but how could he become less national by favouring a public policy founded upon common sense and in accordance with Ireland's social and political needs? Refusal to make use of parliament because to do so might be construed as admitting that parliament could fully satisfy Ireland's demands was not less unreasonable than refusing to use British currency lest the inscription on it might tarnish nationalist principles. The party that took part in public affairs had the public ear; the one that did not could never be rightly understood. The adoption of a policy of public action by separatists would not involve any abandonment of their essential aim. To go on abstaining from every line of action except one, and rejecting the help of every Irishman who did not see the feasibility of that one, was short-sighted, unreasonable, and weak. If the third estate in 1789 had refused to participate in the states general because summoned by Louis XVI, the French revolution would not have occurred when it did. If the English revolutionists had not sworn allegiance to the king and thus got themselves into parliament in 1640, they could never have dethroned Charles I. In both instances (remarkable examples of Davitt's historical perception and misconception combined), 'the end excused the means'. 'To overlook or discard the necessity of expediency in revolution is playing *Hamlet* with the principal character left out.' After talking with representative Irishmen of all parties and shades of political belief on both sides of the Atlantic, Davitt was convinced that there was 'a universal desire for a "new departure", a platform upon which the national energies . . . may be put forth and a real struggle for self-government be inaugurated'.

In the past we have all placed party above country, partizanship before patriotism. The time has arrived when this must be reversed, for if party feeling and prejudice is for ever to determine the policy of the national movement . . . , the future will be but a repetition of the failures of the past.

The next best thing to seeing one's country freed was to lighten the task of the generation that would have to make the final effort.

If we resolve to transmit . . . an earnest national sentiment, with ideas and systems of practical work for its application, while keeping the passions and dissensions of the present to our own time, then the men who will step into our places will find the revolution half accomplished.

He himself could not hope for many years of life, owing to an 'insidious

[1] *Irishman*, 14 Dec.

disease', the legacy of imprisonment, but he was determined to devote such time as remained to playing the part of peacemaker among workers in the national cause.[1]

During the second half of November, apart from five days at Manayunk Davitt was mostly at New York, where, on the 24th, he attended the meeting of the Clan na Gael executive specially timed to suit him. The 'new departure' as enunciated in Devoy's telegram and interpreted by the *Herald* 'interviews' was approved. So too was Davitt's intention of returning to Ireland to promote the new programme and his urgent request that Devoy should also cross to Europe to assist him in the difficult negotiations with the I.R.B. and Parnell that lay ahead.[2] Devoy, by his own account, was reluctant to accept this assignment: he was in the line of promotion on the *Herald*, and a long absence would mean a sacrifice of his prospects; besides Carroll's mission to the I.R.B. a year before[3] had fulfilled its purpose and a second envoy from Clan na Gael so soon afterwards seemed unnecessary. But, Devoy says, 'it was Davitt's strong pleading with me to stand by him in the bitter fight he saw before him that finally decided me'. He agreed to go, and obtained leave of absence without pay from the *Herald*.[4] This explanation, supplied by Devoy in 1906 after Davitt's death and not supported by independent evidence, must be taken with reserve: from 1882, when the two men had become estranged,[5] it was Devoy's interest to emphasise that in December 1878 he and Davitt were in complete agreement. It is highly probable that Davitt did urge Devoy to make the journey to Europe, but also quite possible that Devoy would have gone in any case. For he went as official envoy of the Clan na Gael executive to a meeting of the supreme council of the I.R.B., and the instructions he received related, not to the 'new departure', but entirely to the orthodox fenian objective of preparing for war with Britain. The place of meeting was to be Paris, as the safest and most convenient centre outside British jurisdiction; and in Devoy's instructions the meeting was stated to be summoned 'for the purpose of further consolidating the union between the V.C. [United Brotherhood or Clan na Gael] and the I.R.B. and devising some means of perfecting the work of preparation for a revolutionary struggle in Ireland'.[6]

Later the same day Davitt caught a train for Philadelphia and arrived there just in time to take part in an anniversary meeting in honour of the 'Manchester martyrs', held at the Horticultural Hall. The principal

[1] *Irishman*, 14 Dec. [2] Devoy, V, VI. [3] Above, p. 139.
[4] Devoy, VI. [5] Above, p. 234.
[6] Devoy's report to Wilkesbarre convention, 11 Aug. 79, in *S.C.P.*, iv, 505.

speaker was Patrick Meledy, who had served over ten years in prison for his part in the Manchester rescue. As he came near the end of his speech 'a tall, one-armed man, of dark complexion, and a strong Websterian head' appeared on the stage, and Meledy gracefully gave place to Davitt. In the course of a short speech Davitt deplored the fact that, unlike Meledy, he had not the satisfaction of recalling anything he had done for Ireland to deserve imprisonment. He presented Meledy with an address from Irish residents of Manchester congratulating him on his release.[1]

As the final stage of his missionary campaign in America Davitt made a third lecture-tour in New England, having prepared the way by a a quick visit to Boston a fortnight previously.[2] On 29 November he addressed a fair-sized audience at Springfield, Massachusetts, and was well pleased with the response to his lecture. Next morning, before leaving for New Haven, he visited the great federal arsenal, established by the Continental Congress during the war of independence; he climbed the central tower and had a splendid view of the city spread out on the east bank of the Connecticut. At New Haven, though his lecture on 1 December was reasonably well attended, he felt that he had been a failure—'bad subject' (Ireland at Westminster) 'and damned bad lecture'. He left by the midnight train for Boston, and there he was joined by Devoy for a conference with John Boyle O'Reilly and his friend Robert Dwyer Joyce, an Irish immigrant who, like O'Reilly, had made good in Boston, being a successful physician and a no less successful writer of songs and ballads (one of his most popular poems, *Deirdre*, had appeared in 1876). Davitt took to him at once: 'a soldier, poet, painter, doctor, and Irishman rolled into a fine specimen of the genus homo—has a Scandinavian head but a Clareman's brogue—O for a thousand of such men'. Joyce found time to read Davitt an unpublished poem, but the subject of discussion was the 'new departure', to which O'Reilly and Joyce were already well-disposed. Davitt and Devoy gained their enthusiastic support for it as approved by the Clan na Gael executive—'and that means', Devoy wrote, 'favourable consideration from the whole Boston press'. They proposed that it should be publicised over the signatures of leading Irishmen on both sides of the Atlantic, and that then a public appeal should be made in the press for 1000 men willing to subscribe $1000 each to support the new movement and provide material for the fighting that would come 'when our demand shall have been made in the name of the nation and rejected'.[3] Both O'Reilly and Joyce were eager to begin preparations

[1] *Philadelphia Times*, 25 Nov. 78. [2] DN/2, pp 75–6.
[3] Devoy to James Reynolds, 2 Dec. (*D.P.B.*, i, 381).

for active service in Ireland, and were disappointed when Devoy assured them that the fighting was still some years ahead.[1]

From Boston on 3 December Davitt doubled back on his tracks to lecture at Worcester (Mass.) on 'Irish nationality and future policy for Ireland'; he spoke 'fairly well', he thought, and was well received. He returned to Boston on the 4th for four days of sightseeing and private meetings with leading Irishmen of the city, including O'Reilly, Joyce, and P. A. Collins. On 7 December he dined with Joyce, O'Reilly, and Devoy at Joyce's house.[2] This time he was completely won over to O'Reilly:

Remarkably successful man. Immense influence as editor of *Pilot*. Nominated for state treasurership—declined. President of press and literary societies. Poet of no mean order. Forcible writer. Thinks deeply on national affairs. Vigorous speaker. Fine head, alive with genius. Compact figure.[3]

On Sunday night, 8 December, the Mechanics' Hall, Boston, was the scene of his final lecture, chaired by O'Reilly. He had an excellent audience, of about 1000, and with tickets at the high price of 25 cents the occasion answered financial expectations.[4] He felt satisfied with his performance, but glad that the 'spouting' was ended[5]; perhaps he was conscious that the style of his lecture was more than usually diffuse and inflated. Yet his message was clear and impressive. His subject was 'The past and present policy of the nationalists', and he ranged over the whole ground of the public discussion that had opened with his Philadelphia lecture of 16 September. The Irish as a people lacked moral courage: they were far more interested in eulogising Irish virtues than in recognising Irish failures and seeking to remedy them. Seven centuries of struggle against English rule had shown Irish nationality to be indestructible, but Ireland's present condition was entirely unworthy of the sacrifices Irishmen had made for her. There had been reckless waste of national strength, thanks to the nationalist party's failure in policy, prudence, and judgment. James Stephens, after turning many who might have been his allies into enemies, had fixed a date for taking the field when he had not enough war material to arm 1000 men; and so the magnificent national spirit of '65 had collapsed in the desperation of '67. Yet even so, the nationalist party had stuck to its suicidal policy of regarding all Irishmen who were not separatists as West Britons. 'Unless we change our plans and policy . . ., we will hand down to the next generation, what we received from '48, a chaos of emotions.'

[1] *D.P.B.*, i, 380-81; Devoy, III, V, VI; DN/2, pp 76-9.
[2] *Fall*, p. 130; Devoy, III.
[3] DN/2, pp 79-80.
[4] See above, p. 245. Admission card in DP/EE.
[5] DN/2, p. 81.

What then ought Irishmen to do to put the national cause on a stronger footing? His audience would not, Davitt hoped, need his assurance that his belief in the necessity of physical force remained unshaken. Whatever other forces he might wish to bring into play, he was convinced that only 'the manhood strength' of Ireland could 'give the *coup de grâce*' to British rule. But there were other ways of working for the country's social and political redemption. Above all, the nationalist party should make it their business to win over to nationalism the solid mass of the tenant farmers, hitherto politically apathetic, and to convince the outside world that the Irish people were in earnest about independence.

To show why the tenant farmers as a class were outside the nationalist ranks, Davitt asked his hearers to visualise an impoverished tenant of a small farm in the Galtees, one of Patten Bridge's victims (a reference, though not explicit, to William O'Brien's articles, 'Christmas on the Galtees', in the *Freeman's Journal* a year before).[1] Only by incessant back-breaking toil could he extract a bare subsistence for his six children from the barren mountain, while the rich pasture-land in the plain below was fattening his landlord's sheep. He had no hope of any improvement unless help came from outside. He and his like were repeatedly told that they had friends in all political parties. But the home-rulers at Westminster showed as much interest in Turkey as in Ireland, and the nationalists who promised that when independence was won the tenants would no longer be at the mercy of English landlords did nothing in the meantime to protect them.

> If the nationalists want me to believe in . . . independence, they must first show themselves desirous and strong enough to stand between me and the power which a single Englishman wields over me . . . Let them show that the social well-being of our people is the motive of their actions . . . and then the farming classes in Ireland will rally round them . . .

In the world outside, the Irish demand for independence was not taken seriously because Ireland was misrepresented in parliament, municipal councils, and other public bodies. This would never be changed so long as nationalists held aloof from public life and regarded all other Irishmen as enemies. What was needed was a common 'platform' on which, without sacrificing principle, nationalists, home-rulers, and other patriotic Irishmen could unite for the common good in such matters as the preservation of their distinctive national identity (including the revival of their ancient language), the elimination of religious and provincial antipathies, the physical, social, moral, and

[1] Above, pp 208–9.

intellectual advancement of the Irish people, and, above all, the rescuing of the peasantry from an infamous land system, together with improvements in the housing of the whole rural population and in the condition of agricultural labourers. The resulting growth of public spirit and political education would focus international interest on the Irish as a renascent people capable of affecting the destiny of a declining empire whose power was obnoxious to rival nations; and it would win sympathetic support from the vast Irish and Irish-American element in the United States that hitherto had seen no practical way of sharing in Ireland's struggle for independence.

Until a 'common public platform' was established, Castle government would continue. The new attitude taken up at Westminster by M.P.s such as Parnell—'the most popular and most trusted of Irishmen'—gave more hope than ever before that good could be got out of parliamentary action. Davitt therefore declared that, without any surrender of his principles as a nationalist, he was ready to cooperate with home-rulers on the following programme.

(1) The indispensable qualification in an Irish M.P. should be a public profession of his belief in the inalienable right of the Irish people to self-government, and recognition that self-government was Ireland's chief need.

(2) The Irish M.P.s should present Irish national aspirations to the world and uncompromisingly oppose the government on every prejudiced or coercive policy.

(3) Immediate reform of the land system should be demanded, on the principle of peasant proprietorship such as existed in France, Belgium, and Prussia, the land to be purchased or held directly from the state. This demand should be grounded on the fact that the land formerly belonged to the people (being held in trust for them by elected chiefs or heads of clans), and that it was the duty of the government to resume possession of it and compensate the landlords.

(4) Legislation should be obtained to encourage Irish industries, to develop national resources, to replace grazing by cultivation as far as possible, to reclaim waste lands, to protect fisheries and to improve the housing of the peasantry.

(5) The county franchise should be assimilated to the borough franchise, and the law relating to grand juries and to conventions should be reformed.

(6) Vigorous efforts should be made to improve education and to prevent an anti-national bias from entering into it.

(7) The right of the Irish people to carry arms should be legalised.

To nationalists who objected that, if such a programme were realised by parliamentary means, the Irish people would cease to strive for independence, Davitt replied that the danger was imaginary; and he quoted a classic nationalist dictum of T. F. Meagher: 'from the Irish mind the inspiring thought that there once was an Irish nation, self-chartered and self-ruled, can never be effaced, the burning hope that there will be one again can never be extinguished'.[1]

The seven-point Boston programme, clause 5 excepted, was a restatement, with some elaboration, of Davitt's Brooklyn proposals.[2] The reference in clause 5 to the county franchise and the grand juries was an addition, extending the idea of gaining control of local public bodies. The suggested repeal of the convention act (1793), which seems to have been an original contribution of Davitt's, showed perceptiveness and foresight: so long as the law prohibited the assembling of representative conventions in Ireland, the agrarian agitation contemplated by the 'new departure' would be subject to crippling restriction. The myth of public ownership of land in early Irish society reflected Devoy's (and, through Devoy, Mill's) influence on Davitt, just as, in the body of his speech (and in his public statements generally since the Brooklyn meeting), the concept of world opinion as a factor in Irish politics was a borrowing from Devoy. Indeed the Boston speech amounted to a final turning-over of ideas and suggestions whose authorship has to be shared between the two men. What stood out as most distinctively Davitt's thinking was the dramatic figure of the Galtee tenant appealing to nationalists for help against the relentless pressure of the land system. The speech ended on a note of passionate incitement to a struggle for the land:

> No party has a right to call itself national which neglects resorting to all and every justifiable means to end the frightful misery under which our land-crushed people groan . . . The cry has gone forth 'down with the land system that has cursed and depopulated Ireland' . . . In the name of the common good of our country, its honour [and its] interest, social and political, let the two great Irish parties agree to differ on party principles while emulating each other in service to our improverished people.

[1] Boston *Pilot*, 21 Dec.; reprinted, with omissions, in Cashman, pp 57–71. The seven-point programme is reprinted in *Defence*, pp 99–100, from the *Pilot* report, but only in a severely pruned version in *Fall*, pp 130–31. The passages from the speech quoted in *Fall*, pp 131–3, are only a small selection, freely rearranged.

[2] Above, p. 237.

As the marching-song of their united effort he suggested:

We want the land that bore us
We'll make that cry our chorus
And we'll have it yet, though hard to get
By the heavens bending o'er us.[1]

The exposition of the 'new departure' was completed by a long letter from Devoy to the editor of the *Freeman's Journal.*[2] Devoy submitted a rough draft to Davitt, Carroll, O'Reilly, Joyce, Collins, Luby, O'Kelly, Breslin, and other fenians for their comments, so that in its final form the letter should crystallise the views not only of himself but also of 'the best thinkers in the national movement in America'. In his cabin on the French liner *Canada*, on which he sailed from New York to Le Havre on 11 December, he recast the entire letter in the light of comments received. He dated it 'New York, December 11', and when he reached Paris forwarded it to the *Freeman*, taking care to conceal the fact that he was in Europe.[3] The letter exposed weaknesses in the position both of home-rulers and of orthodox fenians; it sought to clear away misunderstandings, and it flayed the misrepresentations of critics such as Pigott—'men who live by scribbling cheap treason'; above all, it argued the case for, and countered nationalist objections to, the proposed new departure.

Butt's 'federalism' conceded England's right to rule Ireland. The claim that it would place Ireland in exactly the same relationship to Britain as the state of New York to the U.S.A. was nonsense; the true American analogy would be the relationship of the city to the state of New York: 'the municipality of New York is created and its powers defined by a state legislature, and the charter is tinkered-up afresh every time there is a change of parties in the legislature'. Unless the home-rulers changed their programme on this vital point, they could never command the support of the whole country. Nor could repealers hope to do so; for though they had strong historical precedent in their favour, they were unorganised, and their programme of simple repeal involved the absurdity of restoring the Irish house of lords. Many of them, like many weak-kneed fenians, supported the home rule party for want of something better. In face of this situation the abstentionist policy of fenianism had become a policy of self-effacement.

Mere conspiracy would never save Ireland but neither would parliamentary action alone. An 'honourable compromise' between nationalists and home-rulers was needed. The nationalists had never explained

[1] Boston *Pilot*, 21 Dec. In the second line of the stanza, 'cry' was substituted by Davitt in *Fall*, p. 132, for 'want', the word given in the *Pilot* report, which must surely have been a slip.
[2] Published in *F.J.* on 27 Dec.
[3] Devoy, VI.

what kind of an Ireland they hoped to achieve, nor how they proposed to grapple with any of the burning social and political questions that would demand solution if the country were free tomorrow. It would be a necessary part of the proposed compromise to leave the form of self-government undefined until the nation was in a position to decide for itself. But on one vital issue both nationalists and home-rulers must make a commitment here and now if their combination were to have any hope of winning the support of the mass of the people. They must commit themselves to a radical reform of the land system on the principle of enabling the tenants to buy out their holdings as in France, Prussia, and Belgium. The Irish landlords should be given a last chance of settling the land question amicably on this basis. The buying-out process should begin with the absentee landlords, including the London companies in Londonderry. Evictions should be stopped at all hazards. If the British parliament refused to do these things, Ireland would have to wait till an Irish parliament could do them better; but in the meantime agrarian agitation would inculcate sound principles and rouse and organise the country. Those who were alarmed by such language should look not only at France, Prussia, and Belgium, whose prosperity was rooted in the great numbers of peasant owners, but also at England itself, where increasing commercial and manufacturing depression was certain to threaten the continued monopoly of land by the few, and where the redistribution of land might soon be seen as a means of staving off a social convulsion.

Next after landlordism the curse of Ireland for centuries had been sectarianism, an evil rooted in alien rule and fostered by the denominational system in which young Irishmen were educated. Protestants would never join any political party that devoted its principal efforts to a purely catholic object. It was fear of the catholic majority more than love of England that made 'anti-Irish Irishmen' of so many protestants. To win them over to nationalism was well worth paying for, and the price was 'the exclusion of all sectarian issues from the national platform'.

The entire people had an interest in local as well as in national administration, and to capture the local public bodies for nationalism would enable nationalists to make good their lack of training in public business, which had hitherto told heavily against them. For nationalists to seek election to these local bodies was quite a different thing from seeking to enter parliament. It was high time that 'the present abortion of county government' by grand juries of landowners was replaced by elective county councils. The elective franchise should be completely democratic, but till that could be achieved the least that should be demanded was the equalisation of the Irish franchise with that of England.

The new departure was not a device to send fenians to Westminster, but it called upon nationalists to back up all honest parliamentary representatives who, without being bound by the fenian oath, could be trusted to act, both inside and outside parliament, in the national interest. With the municipal bodies under popular control and men of spirit and determination as M.P.s and backed by the country and by millions of the Irish abroad, Ireland would have no need to go to London either to beg or obstruct.

To the objection that the announcement of such a programme was the avowal of designs that England would take good care to provide against, Devoy replied that publicity was of the essence of the new policy and that England would no longer treat Ireland as in the past.

That vast agglomeration of hostile races and conflicting interests scattered over the world called the British Empire had been held together . . . by favourable circumstances which are disappearing day by day. It is filled with inflammable material within and beset with powerful and watchful enemies without. . . . It has passed the summit of its glory and its infamy, and is now on the descent which leads inevitably to ruin. It is our turn now. Our watchwords should be—patience, prudence, courage, and sleepless vigilance.

If, as seemed likely, the eastern policy of Disraeli's government were to result in war between Britain and Russia, 'the blood and treasure of Ireland would be poured out like water for the interests of a power which has robbed us of everything and rooted out and exterminated our people'. Should Ireland not have something to say about such an expenditure of her vital resources? This was a question that both home-rulers and nationalist might at any time be called upon to answer.

The new departure did not propose anything not strictly within the law. It did not mean an 'alliance' between home-rulers and fenians (here Devoy seemed to be disowning the word 'combination' that he himself had used in his anonymous *Herald* article of 27 October),[1] but simply 'the adoption of a broad and comprehensive public policy which nationalists and men of more moderate views could alike support without sacrifice of principle'.[2]

The *Freeman's Journal* of 27 December, in which Devoy's letter appeared, carried an appreciative editorial, pinpointing his argument and admitting that there was much to be said for it. The editor believed that Devoy's ultimate objective was utopian and mischievous, and that, if every adult in Ireland were to be given the opportunity of voting

[1] Above, p. 251.

[2] *F.J.*, 27 Dec. 'A very dishonest summary' (Devoy, VI) was published in the *Irishman*, 4 Jan. 79; the letter is reprinted in *S.C.P.*, v, 175–84, and in *Gaelic American*, 14 July 1906.

on the issue of separation, a majority would not go with him. Nevertheless the entry into parliamentary politics of an influential body of Irishmen should be welcomed. Among other advantages it might teach the nationalists that constitutional methods were far more powerful than physical force. On the land question the editor was inclined to agree with Devoy, even though there might be those who would condemn his proposals as 'revolutionary and communistic'. Irish landlords might regret when too late that they had not entered into some compromise that would have ensured full compensation for their losses. But while going all the way with Devoy on the question of peasant proprietorship, the *Freeman* characteristically sounded a warning on his 'exclusion of all sectarian issues' as the price to be paid for protestant support. Did this mean that the demand of the catholic people of Ireland for religious education was to be no part of the national platform? If so, Devoy would discover that there were questions on which Irish catholics would not compromise and on which no 'American teaching' would be accepted by them.

There was no question at this stage of any difference in principle between the co-authors of the new departure. Ten years later, when their personal relations and the political situation had been transformed, Davitt before the *Times*-Parnell commission was to make a distinction between the new departure of his Boston speech, which he described as 'an effort on my part to substitute an open agitation for secret conspiracy', and Devoy's new departure, 'which sought to dictate to Mr Parnell the terms on which its advocates would consent to support him'.[1] Such a distinction is not sustainable. Davitt's momentary objection to the telegram was merely an incident: from his Brooklyn speech to Devoy's *Freeman* letter there is a clear and logical development, in which successive declarations by the two men all fall into place. Alike in the spirit and in the letter the message of Davitt's speeches in America was that both open agitation and secret preparation, both constitutional action and physical force, would be necessary to free Ireland. He had repeatedly affirmed that he remained faithful to the fenian doctrine that Britain would never concede Irish independence to the force of argument but only to the argument of force. When, however, he was to look back at his first American campaign from the standpoint of 1889 he saw it all through a distorting medium.

Returning from Boston, Davitt spent two days (9–10 December) at New York (partly, it may be assumed, in Devoy's company) before making his final visit to Manayunk. He spent a day (10–11 December)

[1] *Defence*, pp 101, 102.

at home with his mother and sisters, packing and preparing for the trip to Europe. Catherine Davitt and Sib had now 'resolved to stay till spring', and Michael left 130 dollars with his mother to pay her fare to Ireland, but that is all he tells us of a change of plan that must have caused much heartburning to all three.[1] His visit must have had its disappointments for his mother: he had come to America primarily to see her and bring her back to Ireland, but on the very day of his arrival he had been caught in a whirl of political activity, in which his personal and family life had become submerged. During August he had managed to spend three weeks at Manayunk or at Cape May, and during September sixteen days at Manayunk, but during October and November he was only five days at home each month, and in December only one day.[2]

He took farewell of his mother, Sib, Anne, and her husband and baby early on 11 December, and arrived at New York in time to join Carroll and O'Kelly in giving Devoy a send-off on board the *Canada*. It was agreed that he would meet Devoy in Paris early in January.[3] He had another meeting with Ford and was introduced by him to Henry George, who was to become a close personal friend and to have a profound influence on his thinking.[4] Next day he left New York as a cabin passenger on the White Star liner *Baltic*, bound for Queenstown and Liverpool. She was a similar ship to the *Britannic*, but smaller (3700 gross tons), older (launched at Belfast in 1871), and slower.[5] Davitt was on board at 5.30 a.m., went to bed at once and slept all day. When he awoke on the 13th the sea was rough and the ship was rolling and pitching. For four days he suffered from sea-sickness and did not stir from his cabin, which was badly ventilated and compared very unfavourably with his accommodation on the *Britannic*. On 17 December he ventured on deck and saw huge cone-shaped waves sweeping against the ship's side. The sea continued turbulent, and the storm in his stomach did not subside, till the 20th. On the 21st he awoke to a calm sea. But owing to steady head-winds throughout the voyage the *Baltic* was already well behind her schedule, and she was nearly two days late when she reached Queenstown next day. Davitt left by the night mail and arrived at Dublin in the small hours of 23 December.[6]

On the anniversay of his release from Dartmoor he was well enough to take stock of the most strenuous of his thirty-two years:

How widely different the situation today and experience of the past twelve months from that of previous years. Confined for years to within a radius of about

[1] DN/2, p. 81; DN/7, 22 July 80. [2] Above, pp 194, 211, 221, 225-8, 229-30, 236, 258.
[3] Devoy, I. [4] *S.C.P.*, ix, 432, 433.
[5] *Lloyd's Register of British and Foreign Shipping*, 1878-9.
[6] DN/2, pp 81-3; DN/6, pp 1-2.

150 yards, I have travelled in the past year over 15,000 miles. Condemned to silence in prison, I have spoken to over forty public meetings comprising over 30,000 people since my release. Resolved on my discharge to denounce the treatment of my fellow prisoners still confined and appeal to the public on behalf of their liberation. There are none now in prison. This is not of course owing to my endeavours but I flatter myself that I have assisted, and thank God my conduct has not afforded an argument or pretext to prolong the confinement of a single one who suffered in the same cause.

For the liberty I enjoy and my steadily improving health I return thanks to the giver of all gifts.[1]

Taking a more sceptical view of his first year of liberation he wondered whether anyone or anything had really benefited from all his exertions. Would it not have been more prudent and sensible to have concentrated on building up his health and finding a steady job?[2] Certainly his future was still far from secure, and apart from his three weeks' relaxation in August his American visit had been physically and mentally exhausting. Yet the 'steadily improving health' for which he thanked God seems to have been a reality, while the 'heart disease' to which he had intermittently referred throughout the year seems to have been imaginary.[3] But at the time he believed that he had not long to live,[4] and this may well have contributed to the testiness apparent in his letters to Devoy, who found him inclined to alternate between extreme hopefulness and extreme irritability in face of criticism or opposition.[5] Unquestionably during his travels in America he tended to stretch his physical endurance too far and to live on his nerves. One way of seeking to reduce tension he rejected: he showed, Devoy says, a 'prejudice' against alcohol 'that was almost morbid', and absolutely refused to touch it in any form, even when, at Boston, Dr Joyce recommended him to take some claret with his dinner.[6] According to Devoy he feared that he might become a drunkard. There seems to have been nothing in his earlier life or his family history to warrant any such fear, and it is unnecessary to postulate it to explain his total abstinence at this time: his experience of the Irish in Lancashire had long ago convinced him that Ireland had no greater enemy than drink,[7]

[1] DN/2, pp 83-4.

[2] DN/1, pp 7-11.

[3] *Inquiry as to the alleged ill-treatment of the convict Charles McCarthy in Chatham convict prison*, p. 16 (14 Feb. 78) [C1978], H.C. 1878, lxiii, 784; *Prison life*, p. 19 (Mar. 78); *F.J.*, 17 Mar.; *Liverpool Daily Post*, 30 Apr.; *Irishman*, 4 May, 14 Dec. He wrote on 14 February that he had been carefully examined by 'competent medical authority' and informed that he had heart disease (above, p. 195). The earliest documentary evidence of his state of health relates to the period of his imprisonment in Portland (Feb. 81–May 82), when he was given frequent medical examinations, and both his own doctor and prison medical officers found that his only organic weakness was in his chest (below, ch. XII).

[4] Above, pp 257-8.

[5] Devoy, II, VII.

[6] Devoy, VII.

[7] Above, p. 173.

and doubtless what he had seen of the Irish in America[1] had done nothing to alter that conviction.

1878 had been a momentous year for him on many counts. He had discovered his Ireland and his native Mayo. He had rediscovered England and Scotland. He had taken with zest to long-distance travel, by sea and land. He had discovered America, 'the great shelter-land of peoples',[2] now the home of all his immediate relatives—diminished through the death of his father, but augmented by a brother-in-law and seven nephews and nieces. The visit to America was to be the first of ten, spread over the next twenty-six years, that were to give an added dimension to his life. He had become known to large numbers of his countrymen in Ireland and Britain and America as a man with a message. He had renewed contact with many old friends and made many new friends, some of whom—Parnell, Egan, Brennan, Devoy, Ford—were soon to play a dominant role in his life. He had resumed membership of the fenian organisation and had been welcomed to its inner ring both at home and in America. But while still an unrepentant fenian he had shown phenomenal sensitivity to the changing atmosphere of Irish politics, and his political ideas had been rapidly growing in response to the new challenges and opportunities that 1878 had brought. When he returned to Ireland at the end of the year he was a highly controversial figure, unquestionably a force to be reckoned with not only by fenians but also by home-rulers, and above all by Parnell and his fellow-militants inside and outside parliament.

[1] For examples, see above, pp 228–9, and *D.P.B.*, i, 357.

[2] Speech at Boston, 8 Dec., in Cashman, p. 64.

VIII

The National Land League of Mayo, January–October 1879, and the third fenian 'new departure'

When Davitt returned to Ireland from America the rural distress that was shortly to bring on a general crisis was causing deep concern to local observers, and especially in Mayo. Since the previous spring the need for an organisation to protect tenants against rack renting and capricious eviction had been voiced with increasing urgency by Daly, John James Louden, and others. Louden, of Westport, was a barrister who, in addition to his law practice ran a large ranch, rented from the marquis of Sligo and the earl of Lucan.[1] The Mayo Tenants' Defence Association was founded at Castlebar, with Louden as chairman and Daly as secretary, at a meeting on 26 October 1878 at which O'Connor Power, M.P. for the county, addressed constituents on his annual tour of the area. Besides giving an account of his stewardship he warmly supported the new association and used a phrase that was soon to become a battle cry: 'the land of Ireland for the people of Ireland'.[2] Daly praised Power as an advanced home-ruler and advised the electors to get rid of the quasi- and the sham elements in the party. In an editorial he wrote that if the people wanted tenant right they must stop sending landlords to parliament; and Power, speaking at other centres in Mayo, called on the farmers to combine in local clubs and cooperate with their M.P.s in wringing the '3 Fs' from parliament. This identification of the activists in the home rule party with the land movement in Connacht was highlighted at a meeting of the Ballinasloe Tenants' Defence Association on 3 November, when the speakers included not only the president of the association (James Kilmartin), the vice-president (Harris), the secretary (O'Sullivan), and Daly, but also Power and Parnell. Parnell defended the record of his group in parliament, expressed approval of peasant proprietorship, and criticised Butt's moderation in seeking protection for the tenants' interests as

[1] *S.C.P.*, ix, 539–40, 545.

[2] *Connaught Telegraph*, 26 Oct., 2 Nov. 78; cf. above, pp 232–4, 238.

ineffective. Supporting letters were read at the meeting from Archbishop MacHale of Tuam, Bishop Duggan of Clonfert, and Mitchell Henry, M.P. for Galway county, a moderate home-ruler and land-reformer.[1]

Parnell's presence at the Ballinasloe meeting had an added significance because he was then visiting Connacht for the first time; and, as he explained years later, he began to take the full measure of the land question. In Mayo he was greatly struck by the wretchedness and poverty of the people, the squalor of their houses, the smallness and barren character of their holdings. He observed that the hilly and barren districts were the most congested and that the good land was relatively unpopulated.

> You could drive for miles . . . through this country, through rich, fattening, grazing land, without meeting a human being or seeing a house; and while on these drives you could see the ruins of many houses which formerly existed there—the ruined walls and the roofless houses of the former tenantry.

He now began to think that the '3 Fs' 'would not meet the case' of the small tenants of Connacht.[2]

Daly had been aware of Davitt's lecturing activities in America and of the new departure proposals as formulated by Devoy; and in a leader of 11 January 1879 he commended Devoy's argument but considered that there was nothing new about it except its source. Apart from hostility to denominational education—a vicious blot—the new departure might have been the product of 'ordinary home-rulers'. It seemed obvious to Daly that the measure of a good home-ruler was his concern for the small farmer; and he wondered whether, in this respect, 1879 would be as disappointing a year as 1878. 'Will the tenantry be doomed to drink to the dregs the cup of affliction which landlord tyranny has prepared?' The people could save themselves, but only if they put an end to the apathy, servility, and internal division which had so fatally weakened the nation for so long.[3]

By the beginning of 1879 Daly and his friends in Connacht had thus reached a stage in their thinking on the land question that had much in common with the new plan that Davitt and Devoy had hammered out in America. Daly was not a fenian, but he had no objection to working with fenians in an open movement to defend the farmers. His concept of the essential means to that end was a combination of local organisation and agitation with aggressive action in parliament by home-rulers of the stamp of Parnell and O'Connor Power. This was

[1] *Connaught Telegraph*, Mar.-Nov. 78; see above, p. 191. [2] *S.C.P.*, vii, 6 (30 Apr. 89).
[3] *Connaught Telegraph*, 14, 28 Sept., 12, 26 Oct. 78; 4, 11 Jan. 79.

an anticipation of the Land League as it took shape under Davitt and Parnell in the autumn of 1879.

The *Freeman* editorial for new year's day 1879 called attention to the general economic depression afflicting the British Isles, which was shared by the farming classes in Ireland, and was causing Englishmen to question those free-trade doctrines they had hitherto regarded as sacrosanct. An economic review of 1878 by the Dublin correspondent of *The Times* concluded that Ireland had been much less severely affected than England;[1] but this was no comfort to those, who, like Andrew J. Kettle, thought that rural Ireland was on the verge of disaster. A strong and progressive farmer of north County Dublin, Kettle was the founder and honorary secretary of the County Dublin Tenants' Defence Association, and of the Central Tenants' Defence Association of Ireland, the national organ of the local defence associations.[2] He reckoned that the crop of 1877 had been 'very inferior', and that the crop of 1878, though it had in some areas been promising, had turned out to be the least profitable of any raised in Ireland during the previous thirty years. The full effects of the depression had not as yet been felt, especially in the larger towns. It might seem alarmist now to speak of famine, but famine had looked more unlikely in 1845, yet it came.[3] A leading farmer of County Cork, Daniel Riordan, pointed out that the wealthy farmers of England were suffering nearly as much as the poor Irish farmers from the competition of cheap agricultural products from the American prairies. On top of this the Irish farmers had been hard hit by successive bad harvests, with the result that they could pay neither their rents nor their debts. In the civil-bill courts innumerable ejectment processes had been entered, and unless the landlords were to be merciful they would drive their tenants into bankruptcy or emigration.[4] At Clifden, County Galway, Mitchell Henry, of Kylemore Castle, at a meeting of his constituents, felt it necessary to point the contrast between the position of the large and well-to-do farmers of grazing lands, who were the preponderant element in the Dublin Tenants' Defence Association, and the plight of the small and struggling farmers of Connemara, many of them with less than fifteen acres.[5] Before the end of January the *Freeman* prophesied that land agitation would soon become intense through the inexorable pressure of falling prices on the farmers. Unprecedented numbers of judgments against farmers were being recorded in *Stubbs*, and if the

[1] *F.J.*, 1 Jan., p. 7.
[2] Kettle, *The material for victory*, ch. I–II; *S.C.P.*, ix, 365.
[3] *F.J.*, 8 Jan., p. 2.
[4] *F.J.*, 7 Jan., p. 5.
[5] *F.J.*, 23 Jan., p. 2; see also ibid., 27 Jan. and 4 Feb.

traders of Dublin realised their own interests they would be the most energetic tenant-righters in Ireland.[1]

Such premonitions of disaster, together with the exceptionally capricious behaviour of the weather, appropriately set the stage for the crisis year that 1879 was to be. But for several months the Dublin press was at least as much interested in the controversy over the new departure proposals that had opened in the previous November[2] and was kept going till well into January 1879 by Devoy, Davitt, Pigott, and others, Devoy appearing as the leading spokesman of the new departure, Davitt as his strongest supporter, and both of them as fiercely hostile to Pigott, who showed considerable dexterity in defending his own position.

Among others who now joined in the public debate, Mitchell Henry, a leading supporter of Butt's, declared his abhorrence of the proposals from America that asked home-rulers to be unfaithful to their trust and combine with those who sought separation from England,[3] an attitude sharply criticised by one of the Parnellite 'young tigers', F. H. O'Donnell, M.P. who complimented Devoy for putting forward broad and statesmanlike ideas.[4] The antipathy of orthodox fenianism to the new proposals was voiced by John O'Leary, who wrote from Paris repudiating any suggestion that fenians had been 'converted' to parliamentary methods. He saw nothing objectionable in principle, or inexpedient, in making parliamentary representation as serviceable, or at least as little injurious, as possible. In his opinion the most manly and effective way would be to imitate the Hungarians and refuse to elect members to sit in an alien parliament; the next best, to elect men not to go there; the third best, to elect men to refuse to take the oath of allegiance, or to take the oath and refuse to vote, or to vote and even to talk but to do either as little as possible. The worst course was 'the now well-known obstructionist policy of continual speeches and divisions–walking and talking'. He was at one with his friends as to the advisability of 'some sort of public action'; but (action of any kind being repugnant to O'Leary) 'of course we must all wait and see, and I hope confer and take counsel, as to what shape that action must assume'.[5]

A more primitive expression of fenian orthodoxy was placarded extensively through Dublin early in January in a manifesto 'to the

[1] *F.J.*, 23 Jan. *Stubbs & Co.'s Gazette* was a private periodical that listed bankruptcies.
[2] Above, pp 253–7.
[3] *F.J.*, 6 Jan., p. 2.
[4] *F.J.*, 13 Jan., p. 7; see above, pp 144–5.
[5] O'Leary to editor of *Irishman*, 6 Jan. (*Irishman*, 11 Jan.).

people of Ireland', dated 18 November 1878 and entitled 'Ireland for the Irish'. The police, who ascertained that it had been printed at the *Irishman* office, at once reported it to the Castle, where it was dismissed as 'a foolish rhodomontade . . . more inimical to Mr Parnell and his following than to H.M.'s government'.[1] The manifesto issued 'by order of the executive of the I.R.B.' (that is, the executive of the home organisation, as distinct from the supreme council) opened with the familiar dogma that 'Ireland has had one record for seven hundred years—that of a continuous struggle against English domination'. It put the issue raised by the new departure in engagingly simple terms:

On the one side you are invited to join the ranks of the constitutional agitators, the divided home-rulers, Parnell, O'C. Power & Co., and their new transatlantic allies, who, by this invitation, declare that they have abandoned all hope of recovering the freedom of our country by the only means through which it has ever been achieved by any enslaved nation, namely a resort to arms at the time when such a course might be resorted to with effect. On the other hand you are requested by the true nationalists of Ireland to be prepared to assert your principles and rights, whenever the opportunity shall arrive, by the same weapons . . . which your English enemies used when they deprived you of your national independence.

Constitutional agitation, under the specious name of home rule, by seeking a closer connection with Britain had surrendered Ireland's right to separation; and those who proposed an 'unholy alliance' between home-rulers and nationalists had no authority but their own for such national apostacy. The manifesto had been sent for approval to James Stephens in Paris and fully endorsed by him before being released to the Irish public. Stephens had transmitted a copy, with his blessing, to the Fenian Brotherhood in New York, whose council had published it in December in the New York *Irish-American*, along with Stephens's letter, as a faithful expression of their own views. All this, highlighting division in American fenianism between opponents (the Fenian Brotherhood) and supporters (Clan na Gael) of the new departure, as well as in the fenian ranks at home, was grist to Pigott's mill; and he published the relevant statements from the *Irish-American* in his *Irishman.*[2]

Vehement support for the new departure was forthcoming, as might be expected from his record in Connacht, from the veteran fenian, Matthew Harris.[3] It was, he wrote, held to be a violation of principle for nationalists to join in public or parliamentary agitation; and devotion to principle, especially the principle of national independence,

[1] S.P.O., R.P. 1879/293, 430, 1382 (5–24 Jan.).

[2] *Irishman,* 4 Jan. They were also published in the New York *Herald,* and this was reported on 28 Dec. 78 to the British foreign office by the British consul general in New York (S.P.O., A558; R.P. 1879/1382).

[3] See above, pp 191, 210.

was the strength of the Irish people. But the national propensity to make every mode of procedure a matter of principle was their greatest weakness. Everything in Ireland was under the control, for good or evil, of the British parliament, and to ignore that parliament was therefore unrealistic. Those who advocated doing so violated their principles every time they used a taxable commodity. In rejecting public action they rejected the two most powerful agents of public opinion, the press and the platform; and in condemning the representative system they were condemning the principle on which all free government in modern times rested. The Stephens policy, in short, was impracticable, self-contradictory, self-defeating, incompatible with the spirit of the age, and opposed alike to common sense and the genius of the Irish people. National independence would never be won by peaceful means alone, and Harris declared that he attached much more importance to secret organisation than to parliamentary action. But so long as Ireland's connection with England remained, was it not plain good sense for nationalists to use parliament for all it was worth?[1]

An anonymous writer from Cork, while affirming fenian orthodoxy as to abstention from parliamentary politics, welcomed the proposal that nationalists should take a more active part in town councils, boards of guardians, and other local bodies: it was shameful that here the West British minority should be allowed to act and speak in the name of the whole country and to disgrace it by 'exhibitions of fulsome flunkeyism'. The writer felt diffidence in discussing such questions with Davitt and Devoy in public; for though they professed 'nothing . . . not strictly within the law', any adequate treatment of their published views would involve matters not within the law and would therefore require a private meeting. Davitt's invective against the *Irishman* and its editor was deplorable, especially because Pigott's had been the voice that had constantly pleaded the cause of Davitt and his fellow-sufferers in English prisons. Davitt must not think that his past efforts for Ireland were forgotten by nationalists, and he could be assured of the writer's hope that the 'insidious disease' of which he had spoken[2] would not 'shorten by one hour the remainder of a life which might still render valuable services to his country'.

> Ireland needs the help of all her sons, and ours shall not be the part to quarrel with Mr Davitt, Mr Devoy, or any other of those who have lent the sanction of their names to this well-intentioned but mischievous 'departure'.[3]

Davitt spent Christmas in Dublin—for the first time—and began to

[1] Matthew Harris to editor of *Irishman*, 14 Jan. *Irishman*, 18 Jan.).
[2] Cf. above, pp 257–8.
[3] Christy and Co. to editor of *Irishman*, 31 Dec. 78 (*Irishman*, 11 Jan. 79).

prepare the ground for the forthcoming meeting of the I.R.B. supreme council in Paris.[1] His principal confidant among the Dublin fenians was Thomas Brennan. Born at Slane, County Meath, in 1854, Brennan was a self-educated young man who, in 1872, had entered the employment of the North Dublin City Milling Company as a clerk at Castlebar. There he had come in contact with James Daly and his radical thinking on the land question. He had been active in fenian politics, and became still more politically involved on being transferred, after a few years, to the Dublin headquarters of the company, of which Patrick Egan, a key man in Dublin fenianism, was managing director.[2] He was well acquainted with rural conditions in Connacht, for after several years at Castlebar he had frequently travelled in the west as inspector of the company's branch establishments. Revolted by the poverty and wretchedness in which so many small farmers lived, he was eager to use his talents in their defence.[3] In his ardent temperament, his social background, and his dedication both to national and human welfare, he had much in common with Davitt. The two men had first met in January 1878 and were to remain firm friends to the end of Davitt's life.[4] With him and probably also with Egan, Davitt talked over his plans, and was assured that at least the younger men in the fenian movement could easily be won over to the new departure.[5]

Devoy was already in Paris, and Davitt joined him there on 9 January. They stayed together at the Hotel des Missions Étrangères, 'a cheap but nice little place in the Rue du Bac, patronised mainly by priests and poor aristocrats', where Devoy had put up, in 1861, on his way to join the Foreign Legion.[6] Davitt showed signs of being worn out, and his appetite was poor. Devoy succeeded in overcoming his prejudice against alcohol by pointing to the sober, quiet French people in the hotel, lay and clerical, who drank wine moderately twice a day, but only with meals. Davitt agreed to follow their example; his appetite at once increased, and after a fortnight in Paris there was a marked improvement in his health.[7]

A few days after Davitt reached Paris the secretary of the supreme council, John O'Connor, arrived to make arrangements for the meeting, now planned to begin on Sunday, 19 January. Davitt tried to

[1] See above, p. 258.

[2] See above, pp 122-3, 124, 131, 188.

[3] Personal histories, pp 11-13.

[4] Above, p. 188; *S.C.P.*, ix, 357; *(Defence,* pp 118-20; interview with Brennan on Davitt's death, reported in *Gaelic American*, 9 June 1906.

[5] Devoy, VII.

[6] Above, pp 135-6.

[7] Devoy, VII. Devoy's is the only testimony for the matter in this and the following paragraph.

convert him to the new departure but found him a typically orthodox fenian, unshakeable in his belief that all constitutional agitators were humbugs if not worse. O'Connor suspected that Davitt had been influenced by O'Connor Power, and that the new departure proposals concealed some sinister scheme of Power's devising[1]—assumptions that Davitt hotly rejected. Tension had thus been built up between Davitt and O'Connor when the supreme council began its proceedings on the day appointed.[2]

The council consisted of seven elected members, one for each of the four provinces of Ireland, one for Scotland, one for the north of England, and one for London and the south of England, together with four coopted members. The Paris meeting was attended by all eleven members and also by Devoy, who was specially admitted as the representative of Clan na Gael. The names of eight of the eleven members are known: Kickham (president), John O'Connor (secretary), O'Leary, Davitt, Matthew Harris, John Ryan, Mark Ryan, and John Torley. Of these, Kickham, O'Connor, O'Leary, and Harris appear to have been the coopted members while Mark Ryan is known to have represented Connacht, Davitt the north of England, John Ryan the south of England, and Torley Scotland.[3] The meeting place was near the Odeon Theatre, in a small hotel where most of the members lodged. The sessions, which lasted a week (19-26 January)[4] were kept strictly private, and the party ate together in a private room. There is no reason to doubt Devoy's claim that the Paris meeting attracted no outside attention; and this indeed is a principal reason why we are almost entirely dependent on Devoy's testimony[5] for the internal history of this critical fenian conclave. Robert Anderson, at the home office, did not know of the Paris meeting till April 1880, when he received documentary evidence of it from his secret agent in America.[6]

Though the occasion derives its historical importance from the council's decision on the new departure proposals, most of its time was occupied by routine fenian business—reports on the numbers,

[1] Cf above, p. 253.

[2] Devoy, VII.

[3] Devoy, Report to Wilkesbarre convention, 11 Aug. in *S.C.P.*, iv, 505, 552, 554, D's evidence in *S.C.P.*, ix, 355-6, 418-19; Devoy, VII, VIII; Devoy, *Recollections*, p. 313; Ryan, *Fenian memories*, pp 64-5. Of the three unnamed members, two may possibly have been Robert Johnson (of Belfast) and P. N. Fitzgerald (of Cork), representing Ulster and Munster respectively. John Levy's evidence before the special commission, which purports to give the names of members of the supreme council during 1876-80, is confused and self-contradictory, and is useless for the Paris meeting (*S.C.P.*, vi, 370-80).

[4] Devoy, Report to Wilkesbarre convention, as above.

[5] Ibid., iv, 505-11; Devoy, VII, VIII.

[6] Robert Anderson's memorandum, dated 3 Apr. 80, on Devoy's report to Wilkesbarre convention, 11 Aug. 79 (S.P.O., A files, no. 612).

discipline, and morale of the organisation in its several divisions, arrangements for the procuring, transmission, and use of arms, co-operation between the I.R.B. and Clan na Gael, and the like.[1] It was agreed at Devoy's request that he should make a tour of the fenian organisation in Great Britain and Ireland, see conditions for himself, ascertain the views of the members, and so be enabled to report back to Clan na Gael on his return to America. It was a risky assignment, for Devoy's release from prison in 1871 had been made conditional on his keeping out of the United Kingdom till the expiration of his sentence (10 February 1882); but he was determined to take the risk.[2] It is in the context of such perennial fenian preparations for armed revolt that the new departure debate should be seen.

All the council members except Davitt, Devoy, and Harris came to the meeting believing that the new plan amounted to a betrayal of, or at best a retreat from, fenianism; and discussion of it at Paris was apt to degenerate into a wrangle over the alleged treachery of O'Connor Power, in whom the Old Guard saw the prototype of new departure fenianism. There were frequent clashes between Davitt and Mark Ryan on this subject.[3] The Old Guard was headed by Kickham, who presided at all sessions; and the fact that he was blind and deaf heightened the explosive possibilities of the situation. For everything that was said by others had to be conveyed to him through the fingers of his left hand by the deaf-and-dumb alphabet, and though he was extremely intelligent, alert, and perceptive, it was all to easy for communication to go wrong, especially between him and Davitt. On one occasion, mounting tension between the two men was brought to flash point by Kickham's misunderstanding of something Davitt had said. Other members joined in a heated altercation, in the midst of which 'Davitt stood up, burst into a passionate flood of tears and announced between his sobs that he would withdraw from the meeting', as he insisted on doing despite efforts to dissuade him. He was followed by Devoy and the two men spent most of the night discussing the incident. Next day, through the good offices of O'Leary,[4] they were induced to return, and the council made a fresh start. 'The thunderstorm', Devoy remarks, 'had cleared the air and a perfect calm reigned during the rest of the proceedings'.[5]

There was undoubtedly a very passionate and impulsive element in

[1] Devoy, Report to Wilkesbarre convention, as above.

[2] Devoy, IX.

[3] Devoy, *Recollections*, p. 313.

[4] Devoy does not name him in 'Davitt's career' but O'Leary is unmistakably implied; he is explicitly mentioned in Devoy's later work, *Recollections*, p. 314.

[5] Devoy, VII.

Davitt's character. Ever since his release from Dartmoor he had driven himself excessively hard and, as his letters to Devoy in America have shown, he had reacted to opposition with irritation and sometimes anger. The nervous crisis at the Paris meeting is understandable, but the flood of tears—which continued, Devoy says, as he and Davitt walked through the Rue du Luxembourg back to their hotel—is hard to credit. Davitt had been through far more gruelling situations and is not known ever to have given way to tears; on the contrary, his habitual response to such occasions had been a stoical calm. It may be that he found release from the irritation and frustration of the Paris meeting in tears, but it is much more likely that the tears are Devoy's gloss on a vociferous outbreak of hot temper. For Devoy had an interest in exaggerating the failings of his collaborator in the new departure.[1]

On the broad issue of an alliance between the I.R.B. and constitutional nationalists, which was the kernel of the new departure, the supreme council decided unequivocally against Davitt and Devoy. No one, Devoy says, 'except Davitt' was in favour of fenians taking any part in parliamentary agitation,[2] save for the purpose of demonstrations against Britain, as in the by-elections at which Rossa (1869), Kickham (1870), Martin (1870), and Mitchel (1874-5), were candidates. While individual fenians were left free to vote at parliamentary elections (though not to become M.P.s), the council firmly condemned any participation in such elections or any support of a parliamentary party, by the I.R.B. With only Davitt and Harris dissenting, the council refused to commit the I.R.B. to engaging in agrarian agitation.[2] Kickham, as was to be expected from the author of *Knocknagow*,[3] was full of sympathy with the small farmers and labourers but believed that they would gain more from the indirect effects of fenianism (he instanced the Gladstone land act of 1870) than from any direct fenian intervention in the land question. Harris, on the other hand, argued that agrarian agitation could be used as a powerful weapon on the side of political revolution. He and Davitt were almost certainly the only members of the council with any real inkling of the agrarian crisis then building up in Ireland.[4]

Against its rejection of the basic proposals of the new departure, the council's agreement that 'a public organisation' was necessary, and its approval of the policy of capturing the local public bodies for fenianism amounted to very little. The first was a vague formula, the

[1] See above, pp 232-4, 239.

[2] Devoy seems to mean that he differed from Davitt on the question both of parliamentary and of agrarian agitation. But this does not make sense. The explanation probably is that Devoy is referring only to *members* of the council, of whom he was not one.

[3] Above, p. 42.

[4] Devoy, VIII.

second merely an earlier policy of the I.R.B.[1] in reaffirming which the council felt little hope of success, first, because very few fenians had votes in local elections, and second, because it would be very difficult to find enough reliable men to fill places on the local bodies. A committee was appointed to formulate a plan of action, but, though its members spent several days in Paris discussing the matter after the council had risen, nothing definite was done.[2]

The most practical step taken by the council in relation to the public movement—and the only one on which there was absolute unanimity—was to endorse the argument of Davitt and Devoy that a new and genuinely nationalist newspaper was needed to replace Pigott's pernicious weeklies.[3] It was accepted that Pigott was dishonest and unscrupulous both politically and personally; that the extreme nationalism he professed was spurious, and his interest in it merely financial; that he peddled nationalism as shamelessly as he robbed the various funds subscribed for national purpose through his papers; and that at the same time as he was denouncing Davitt and Devoy as backsliders from fenianism he was raising money from home rule M.P.s as the price of immunity from attack. Pigott's influence for mischief was evidently rated high by the council, though Kickham had hitherto thought well of him. It was agreed that he must be got rid of, and Davitt was authorised to negotiate with Patrick Egan about buying him out. The selection of an editor for the intended new paper was discussed. Davitt, as before, thought that the best arrangement would be for Devoy to edit it from Paris, and when Devoy dismissed this as impracticable he proposed O'Kelly as editor. An alternative candidate, strongly supported by Harris, was young William O'Brien, of the *Freeman's Journal*, who was very well thought of by everyone present.[4] Harris wanted the new paper to have a mass appeal and suggested that its front page should carry 'a big splatther of a cartoon'.[5] All this was premature, but it prefigured the eventual buying-out of Pigott and the launching of *United Ireland* under William O'Brien's editorship in August 1881.

The Paris meeting marked the first major setback for the authors of the new departure. Reviewing the matter in 1889, and again in 1903, Davitt saw the supreme council's decisions as a total rejection of their programme,[6] whereas Devoy, writing in 1906, headlined one of his articles on Davitt's career: 'Fenian leaders accepted practically all of new departure'.[7] The contrast reflects the political divergence

[1] Above, p. 239.
[2] Devoy, VIII, IX.
[3] See above, pp 225-6, 264.
[4] See above, p. 209.
[5] Devoy, VII; *Fall*, pp 565-6.
[6] *S.C.P.*, ix, 356; *Fall*, pp 135-6.
[7] Devoy, VIII.

that was soon to arise between the two men. As a historical assessment Davitt's view is correct, but Devoy's headline is a better indication of how the two men felt at the time. For neither was disheartened, and both continued after the Paris meeting to act as though the supreme council had substantially endorsed their proposals. Davitt went back to England, while Devoy remained in France, with Paris as his base for the next six weeks. He could speak French fluently, and enjoyed living in Paris. With the approval of the supreme council, he applied himself to the military side of the I.R.B. business; and from Paris, by incessant correspondence with key fenians in Ireland, with Clan na Gael colleagues in America, and with Davitt, he worked hard, supported by American money, to reanimate the traffic in rifles to Ireland and the training of men in the use of them.[1] Davitt, on the other hand, was more concerned with the intended public movement, and he found an encouraging response among the fenian rank and file. He delivered a lecture in the Free Trade Hall, Manchester, on 2 February on 'Impressions of transatlantic Ireland',[2] revisited Haslingden, and returned to Dublin on 6 February to continue the offensive against Pigott. He was again short of money, through delay in the arrival of funds due to him from America; and he was again thinking of going into business or even of borrowing to start a business of his own.[3]

Davitt discussed the political situation with Parnell, who was now, beyond question, the most striking personality in the Irish parliamentary party, but the leader of only a handful of activists within it. Butt was still the party leader, though at the annual conference of the Home Rule League, in Dublin, on 4 February, it was all too evident that he was sinking fast and that the party was demoralised and disintegrating.[4] Action on the land question was urgently needed, and on the following day a land conference, convened by the Central Tenants' Defence Association, called upon the party to bring all necessary pressure to bear on parliament to adopt Butt's land bill of 1876, which embodied, a *Freeman* leader declared, 'the real claims of the Irish people' on the land question—the '3 Fs'.[5] But it was obvious—and to no one more than to Parnell—that the party was incapable of any effective action. Parnell knew that he would never be elected to succeed Butt by the existing Irish M.P.s but he looked to the next general

[1] *D.P.B.*, i, 404-7 and passim.
[2] *F.J.*, 3 Feb. 79.
[3] Devoy, IX; D to Devoy, [31 Jan.] (*D.P.B.*, i, 427), [*p.* 6 Feb.] (bid., i, 393, 396-7), 13 Feb. (ibid., i, 391-2), 20 Feb. (ibid., i. 402-3), 24 Feb. (ibid., i, 396); DN/1, p. 19; above, pp 194-5.
[4] *F.J.*, 5 Feb.; White, *The road of excess*, pp 573-5.
[5] *F.J.*, 6 Feb.; above, p. 127.

election to change all this, and in the meantime had the strongest possible interest in building up support outside parliament for his own position.[1] He had already received valuable help from fenians, and the prospect of receiving much more, especially from American fenianism, would undoubtedly appeal to him. He told Davitt that he would like to meet Devoy, and Davitt undertook to arrange a meeting.[2]

In the second week of February Davitt made a visit to the west[3] that was to have a decisive influence on his plans, and, indeed, on his whole future career. The momentous character of the second visit is not apparent in his only surviving letters of this period, written to Devoy, but was brought out in an interview he gave to the special correspondent of the New York *Daily World* in July 1882. With his base at Balla, County Mayo, where he stayed with relatives, the Walshes, he made a personal investigation of the mounting distress that now threatened the west with disaster. He was well briefed, and sometimes accompanied, by a cousin, John Walshe,[4] who, as a commercial traveller, had wide and detailed knowledge of the financial conditions of the shopkeepers. He talked with priests, farmers, and local fenian leaders, and everywhere encountered the same story: the harvests of 1877 and 1878 had failed badly, all the small farmers and cottiers were in debt to landlords and shopkeepers, and it was feared that there would be famine before 1879 was out. The great question was how the tenants would react to the danger of large-scale evictions that threatened them. There was an obvious model for organised resistance in the tenant right agitation of Daly, Harris, and their collaborators during the past three years in Connacht. But it is probable that Davitt now began to conceive of a more ambitious, aggressive, and radical plan of action, whereby nationalists of all persuasions might be mobilised on the side of the tenants in a nationwide confrontation with the landlords with the object not of reforming landlord–tenant relations (the 3 Fs) but of abolishing 'landlordism' altogether and making the tenants owners of their holdings. This social revolution was to be accomplished not by physical force but by the moral force of overwhelming numbers organised and directed within the letter of the law.[5] If this, as seems likely, was Davitt's line of thought at the time, it does not mean that he had renounced the use of physical force in principle. On the contrary, he continued to share Devoy's interest in military preparations, and was consulted about a Clan na Gael project for sending help to the Zulus, who, under their king, Cetewayo, were then at war with

[1] Above, p. 254.
[2] Devoy, IX.
[3] *D.P.B.*, i, 391–2, 396–7.
[4] See above, p. 190.
[5] Cashman, p. 213; *S.C.P.*, ix, 441–2, x, 180; *Defence*, p. 210; Devoy, XIII.

the British in Natal; 'one million cartridges placed in the hands of the Zulus', O'Kelly wrote to him from New York on 10 March, 'would help the Irish cause more than an equivalent amount of arms landed in Ireland'.[1]

Daly and other Mayo men were now engaged in preparing for a protest meeting of aggrieved farmers, to be held at Irishtown or Dry Mills, a hamlet in south-east Mayo.[2] It lay about a mile north of the boundary between that county and Galway, and being about three miles west of the meeting-point of Counties Mayo, Galway, and Roscommon was almost at the dead centre of Connacht.[3] The initiative in calling a meeting at Irishtown came from Daly. During the January quarter-sessions at Claremorris he had been approached by a deputation of frieze-coated farmers from the Irishtown locality who complained bitterly of the treatment they were receiving from their rack-renting landlords. He rejected their pleas to expose these landlords in his paper, fearing a libel action, but instead suggested a mass meeting to ventilate the plight of the farmers and to demand a reduction of their rents. He consulted two farmers of Irishtown, James Daly and Daniel O'Conner, and two shopkeepers of Claremorris, Thomas Sweeney and John O'Kane.[4] They agreed to act with him in organising a meeting, and he then obtained a promise of attendance from O'Connor Power, M.P. This was the situation when Davitt visited Mayo in February. With John Walshe and others he joined with the group around Daly of Castlebar in planning a demonstration that would highlight not only the case of the local tenants but also that of hard-pressed tenants generally, and would give a broad national character to the occasion. It was agreed that the local men would organise the meeting, which was announced in the *Connaught Telegraph* on 22 February, and that Davitt would engage visiting speakers and draft resolutions.[5]

The importance of James Daly in these beginnings of the land war has not received historical recognition till recently.[6] In the circumstantial account of the Irishtown meeting that he published in his *Connaught Telegraph* in January 1881 Daly claimed most of the credit for himself, which was not unreasonable, but he also asserted that Davitt did not join in the land agitation till the Westport meeting in

[1] *D.P.B.*, i, 391-2, 408-11. [2] *Connaught Telegraph*, 15, 22 Feb.

[3] See map II.

[4] Sam Clark, 'The social composition of the Land League' in *I.H.S.*, xvii, no. 68 (Sept. 1971), pp 458-9.

[5] *Connaught Telegraph*, 15, 22 Feb., 1 Mar., 19 Apr. 79, 1, 8, 15 Jan. 81; Cashman, p. 213; *S.C.P.*, ix, 357; *Defence*, pp 209-11; *Fall*, pp 146-7. Devoy, XIII.

[6] J.J. Lee has handsomely compensated for this neglect in his *The modernisation of Irish society, 1848-1918*, ch. 3, 4.

June, which was egregiously untrue. Davitt's own story of the Irishtown meeting, as it first appeared in July 1882, was no less faulty in that it said nothing about Daly's part in initiating the meeting and attributed its conception entirely to himself. In 1889, before the *Times*-Parnell commission, he gave a very different account of the matter. His purpose then being to establish the inevitability of the land war, he minimised his own part in it, and contended that if he had remained in Dartmoor a combination like the Land League would none the less have emerged. He spoke of Butt and the tenants' defence associations as precursors of the league and recalled meetings in 1876–9 at which O'Connor Power, Harris, Parnell, and others denounced landlordism in speeches differing little from those of landleaguers.[1] But surprisingly, neither in 1889 nor in his final version of the story in the *Fall of feudalism* (1904) did he give Daly his due either as a pioneer agitator or as the initiator of the Irishtown meeting. That meeting was a well-contrived operation in which local initiative, knowledge, and energy were effectively combined with inspiration, direction, and assistance from outside. Undoubtedly Daly was the prime mover in the whole affair, but it was Davitt's genius for a swift, imaginative response to the challenge presented by the Irishtown situation that gave distinctive shape and voice to a spontaneous local effort.[2] Superintendent Mallon, of the Dublin Metropolitan police, noted that the Irishtown meeting was promoted by 'the friends of the new departure of which Davitt was the leading advocate'.[3]

The I.R.B. as such had nothing to do with the Irishtown meeting, but, Daly of Castlebar excepted, fenians were the most active element among its promoters. Fenians headed the local organisers of the meeting: J. W. Walshe and P. W. Nally of Balla; John O'Kane and J.P. Quinn of Claremorris. Nally, a farmer and the son of a farmer, was brother of 'Scrab' Nally but very different in character.[4] He was the champion athlete of Mayo, whom Parnell admiringly described as 'a very fine, open young man, . . . a great sprint runner and a great jumper—he could jump as high as himself'.[5] He was an ardent fenian and was to pay the penalty four years later when he was sentenced to ten years penal servitude; he died in Mountjoy jail on 9 November 1891. Quinn was a young schoolteacher, and O'Kane was the county centre, or head man of the I.R.B., in Mayo.[6] These were the men on the spot

[1] *Defence*, pp 190–91.
[2] Devoy, *Land of Éire*, p. 48; Devoy, XIII; *S.C.P.*, ix, 357 (Davitt).
[3] S.P.O. A files, no. 590 (29 Apr. 79).
[4] *Defence*, p. 225; above, p. 190.
[5] *S.C.P.*, vii, 6.
[6] *S.C.P.*, iii, 316–19, 349, 352; vi, 223–5, 230–1, 245–6, 252; ix, 442–3, 485, 556–7; *Fall*, pp 146–7; Devoy, XVII; Ryan, *Fenian memories*, pp 63–4.

with whom Davitt and his fenian colleagues were most closely in touch.

Davitt was back in Dublin about the middle of February, and made two short visits to London between 24 February and early April.[1] It was during this time that the meeting he had been planning between Devoy and Parnell took place—at Boulogne, for reasons of security. Devoy, who is our only source for the meeting, was accompanied by O'Leary and Parnell by Biggar when they met there on 7 March.[2] Davitt himself thought it best not to attend. The discussion, which lasted two days, was informal, friendly, and despite Biggar's tendency to expatiate on theology, practical. Devoy, who had not previously met Parnell, found him highly congenial: he talked quietly, frankly, and directly, without any affectation, equivocation, or reserve. He admitted that he had no objection in principle to insurrection but was opposed to fighting England except under conditions that would give Ireland some chance of success. He was surprised to find that Devoy agreed with this and was able to assure him that every fenian in America whose judgment was worth considering was of the same opinion. He unreservedly approved Clan na Gael's recently announced policy of 'peace at home for the present, but vigorous attack on England abroad wherever and whenever possible', though this was regarded by O'Leary as a wildcat scheme.[3] He promised that if Clan na Gael acted energetically on such a policy he would give a good account of himself in the house of commons. This he felt, would have the same effect as the treaty of alliance that Devoy sought.[4] He made a similar point in a speech at Glasgow eleven days later when he said that, while he did not think it absolutely necessary that nationalists and home-rulers should work together, it was essential that they should not work against each other.[5]

No binding agreement or plan of united action was adopted at the Boulogne meeting, but Devoy believed that many of the obstacles to a working arrangement had been removed and that Parnell was prepared to go more than half way to meet the fenians.

> He did not say definitely, and we did not ask him to say, whether he would prefer total separation, repeal of the union, or some form of legislative independence involving some connection with England, but the impression he left on me was very distinct that he had not his mind made up as to which was the best, or the one most likely to be realised, but that he would go with the Irish people to the fullest limit in breaking up the existing form of connection with England.[6]

All this is uncorroborated Devoy, but there is nothing improbable

[1] *D.P.B.*, i, 396, 402–3, 416; DN/1, p. 18; Devoy, XIV. [2] Devoy, IX.
[3] Cf. above, p. 000. [4] Devoy, X. [5] *F.J.*, 19 Mar., p. 6. [6] Devoy, X.

about it. We may safely accept Devoy's testimony that Parnell showed no inclination to commit himself to an 'alliance', such as had been proposed in the notorious 'new departure telegram'.[1] It would seem that the political and military aspects of the new departure claimed most attention at Boulogne, the agrarian aspect counting for very little. Yet it was the agrarian crisis in the west that, within a few weeks of the Boulogne meeting, was to dwarf all other considerations in Irish national politics.[2]

About the middle of March, Davitt returned to Paris for a short consultation with Devoy, who was about to undertake a tour of inspection of the I.R.B. for which arrangements had been worked out by John O'Connor as secretary of the supreme council.[3] He was present at some of the fenian conclaves in Britain (all, of course, held in secret) attended by Devoy, including a convention of the north of England division of the I.R.B. at Newcastle-upon-Tyne and also several meetings of the executive committee of the supreme council. Only orthodox fenian business was transacted at these meetings; according to Devoy, when the new departure was mentioned at Newcastle, he and Davitt were emphatic that it was not intended 'to interfere with regular fenian work'.[4] The two men met again on 2 April in Dublin, to which, after an enforced absence of thirteen years, Devoy unobtrusively returned by a circuitous route. He spent Easter Sunday at home with his family, and Davitt had dinner with them; but on the whole, during his three and a half months in Ireland, Devoy was almost constantly occupied with the I.R.B. business for which he had come, and which took him on long and tedious journeys to all parts of the country. Davitt, on the other hand, during these same months was increasingly caught up in the agrarian crisis, as his ardent nature responded to the mounting fears of the small farmers in his native Mayo.

In his discussions with Devoy, and at I.R.B. meetings attended by Devoy, in Dublin, he increasingly stressed the agrarian crisis. The council of the home organisation was not impressed: it was too much concerned with I.R.B. business and with negotiations to get rid of Pigott; and in any case the members were mostly townsmen, who felt that the danger was being exaggerated by the press, had a very poor opinion of the farmers as a class, and saw no advantage for the national cause in a purely agrarian movement. But it was such a movement that Davitt by the beginning of April had come to see as the vital need of the hour. He had not abandoned the new departure policy, but his efforts to effect an alliance between Parnell and the fenians were now eclipsed by great eagerness to secure him as leader of the

[1] Cf 25 Oct. 78; above, p. 250. [2] Devoy, X. [3] Ibid. [4] Ibid., XI.

intended agrarian movement. Devoy was no less convinced of the value of winning Parnell, but as the leader of a national movement on new departure lines.[1]

On 6 April[2] Davitt and Devoy dined with Parnell as his guests at Morrison's Hotel.[3] Davitt urged Parnell to take the lead in a mass movement of tenant farmers against landlords, while Devoy argued for the more complex and wide-ranging programme of the new departure. Parnell was alive to the distress of the small farmers of Mayo, and he was impressed by Davitt's argument that his leadership of an agrarian movement would advance the cause of home rule. But he was reluctant to lead an agrarian movement. This was not because he was himself a landowner—his personal interest in this respect seems never to have interfered with his public action; and as if to demonstrate his commitment to a radical solution of the land question he announced a week later at a public meeting at Cavan (13 April) that he believed that the final settlement ought to be the conversion of the tenants into owners through the buying-out of the landlords.[4] His objection to leading an agrarian agitation was the danger that it might get out of hand. So no conclusion was reached either on this question or on that of an agreement between Parnell and the fenians, which Devoy still hoped to bring about. He could still speak for Clan na Gael and he believed that the council of the home organisation of the I.R.B. might be persuaded to modify the Paris decision of the supreme council.[5]

It was agreed that the three men should resume the discussion at a later date. They did so on 1 June, again at Morrison's Hotel. In the interval three things happened which decisively changed the situation for them. First, a bleak cold spring, followed by incessant rain, made it certain that the fears for the harvest of 1879 would be fulfilled and brought the threatened crisis to a head in the west. Second, the contemplated agrarian agitation was launched in Mayo on 20 April by the mass meeting at Irishtown that Davitt had helped to promote. Third, at a meeting in Dublin on 3 May, Davitt demanded official fenian support for this agitation from the council of the home organisation of the I.R.B. The council refused but agreed to allow fenians individually to take part in the agitation provided that in doing so they did not violate the principles, or injure the interests, of fenianism.[6]

[1] Devoy, XII, XIV.

[2] Devoy is not certain about this date; but if it was not 6 April it must have been 13 April (ibid., XIV), and Parnell was at Cavan on the latter date (*F.J.*, 15 Apr. 79).

[3] Above, p. 189. Davitt says (*Fall*, pp 176–7) that the meeting was at Egan's house in Synnot Place, but Devoy is positive about Morrison's Hotel and gives convincing details.

[4] *F.J.*, 15 Apr. [5] Devoy, XIV; *S.C.P.*, vii, 6, 10, 88, 95–6 (Parnell); *Fall*, pp 176–7.

[6] Devoy, XII, XIV, XV; S.P.O., A files, no. 590 (29 Apr., 3 May); *S.C.P.*, ix, 355, 356.

Consultations about the Irishtown meeting were held in Dublin between Davitt, Devoy, Egan, and Brennan, mostly at Davitt's lodgings in 83 Amiens Street, suggestions from the Mayo men were considered, and resolutions were discussed, amended, and approved. More than once Davitt returned to Mayo to maintain direct contact with the local group. It was agreed that the visiting speakers should be O'Connor Power, John Ferguson of Glasgow,[1] and Brennan, and that the local speakers should include James J. Louden, of Westport, and Matthew Harris and Malachy O'Sullivan, of Ballinasloe. Of these six all were radical land-reformers and all were fenians except Ferguson and Louden. O'Connor Power was regarded by strict fenians as an outcast, but seems not as yet to have renounced fenianism and was popular with his constituents. Ferguson and Louden were both advanced home-rulers, and both were well-to-do. Ferguson was a member of the council of the Home Rule Confederation of Great Britain, and both he and Louden were members of the council of the Home Rule League.[2] The omission of Davitt's name from the list of speakers was probably his own doing: he probably felt that the appearance of a ticket of leave man in so prominent a role at Irishtown might prejudice the meeting's chances of success.

The local organisers went vigorously to work. By 10 April the districts surrounding Irishtown were placarded with the following announcement:

THE WEST AWAKE!!!
GREAT TENANT RIGHT MEETING IN IRISHTOWN
TO COME OFF ON SUNDAY, 20TH APRIL

Charles S. Parnell Esq., M.P., John O'Connor Power Esq., M.P.,
Edwin Dwyer Gray Esq., M.P., Joseph Gyles Biggar Esq., M.P.,
John J. Louden Esq., Westport, John Barry Esq., Manchester,
John Ferguson Esq., Glasgow, Thomas Brennan Esq., Dublin,
Matthew Harris Esq., Castlebar, are expected to attend.

Stand together, brothers all
Stand together, stand together;
To live or die, to rise or fall,
Stand together, stand together.

From the China towers of Pekin to the round towers of Ireland, from the cabins of Connemara to the kraals of Kaffirland, from the wattled homes of the isles of Polynesia to the wigwams of North America the cry is: 'Down with invaders! Down with tyrants!' Every man to have his own land—every man to have his own home.

This was clearly a local production: Davitt and his colleagues in Dublin

[1] See above, p. 125.

[2] Devoy, XIII; *Fall*, p. 147; *S.C.P.*, iv, 259; vii, 141–2; viii, 268–71 (Ferguson); ix, 539–40; 545 (Louden); x, 180 (Harris).

would not have mispelled the names of Edmund Dwyer Gray and Joseph Gillis Biggar, and the expectation that four well-known M.P.s would attend the Irishtown meeting was window-dressing, as the sub-inspector of constabulary at Claremorris, J. C. Carter, informed his county inspector. Carter learnt of the intended meeting from the *Connaught Telegraph* and brought it, with the placard, to the notice of the local magistrates at their petty sessions on 12 April. After making inquiries they decided that, as there would be no opposition to the demonstrators, there was no danger of a breach of the peace and therefore no need to have any police in attendance.[1] Consequently no special report of the Irishtown meeting was made to constabulary headquarters, and for this Carter was mildly criticised by the county inspector, H. L. Owen, who thought that Carter would have done well to have had a couple of men in plain clothes at the meeting to take notes. Carter's defence was that his forecast of the orderly and non-seditious character of the meeting had been proved correct. The sub-inspector of the adjoining district of Castlerea, in County Roscommon, reacted more nervously to the news of the intended meeting, and on the 20th had a patrol posted at the extreme western edge of his district to watch the road leading to Irishtown. The constable in charge of this patrol collected information from persons who attended the meeting, and from this the sub-inspector reported that those who were prominent at Irishtown were fenians or political agitators with fenian tendencies.[2]

On Sunday, 20 April, large numbers of farmers from all over Mayo and from the counties of Galway and Roscommon, together with townspeople from Claremorris and other county towns, converged in orderly contingents on Irishtown. Many came on horseback, of whom some five hundred formed a bodyguard for the speakers. The size of the audience was variously stated to be from 4000 to 13,000 (Davitt says 7000); and certainly, alike in its numbers and its good order, the occasion was reminiscent of O'Connell's monster meetings. James Daly of Castlebar presided. He opened with some rambling remarks, but, repeating a slogan of O'Connor Power's,[3] gave a headline to the whole ensuing agitation—'the land of Ireland for the people of Ireland'—and made a pronouncement that quickly became one of its central dogmas —'those who take the land of the evicted ['land-grabbers'] are the enemies of the country, and are as culpable as the landlords'. Brennan, O'Connor Power, Ferguson, Louden, Harris, and O'Sullivan were all present as arranged and spoke, but Davitt himself did not attend. His

[1] S.P.O., R.P. 1879/8039.
[2] Ibid. R.P. 1879/8039.
[3] Above, p. 271.

absence may have been accidental,[1] but is more likely to have been due to the prudential motive that would explain the omission of his name from the announced list of speakers. Three resolutions, of which the first and second, written by Davitt, were brought from Dublin by Brennan, and the third was drafted locally, were put to the meeting and carried. The first, applying to Ireland—'our misgoverned and impoverished country'—a dictum of *The Times* that rulers who failed to govern in the interest of their subjects forfeited all claim to allegiance, declared the 'unceasing determination' of those present 'to resort to every lawful means . . . whereby our inalienable rights, political and social, can be regained from our enemies'. This rather circuitous claim to self-government was followed by a resounding challenge to the landlord system. The second resolution declared that,

> as the land of Ireland, like that of every other country, was intended by a just and all-providing God for the use and sustenance of those of his people to whom he gave inclination and energies to cultivate and improve it, any system which sanctions its monopoly by a privileged class, or assigns its ownership and control to a landlord caste, to be used as an instrument of usurious or political self-seeking, demands from every aggrieved Irishman an undying hostility, being flagrantly opposed to the first principle of their humanity—self-preservation.

The third resolution called for an immediate reduction of unjust rents pending a settlement of the land question.[2]

The speeches in support of these resolutions were in a corresponding vein, but their rousing eloquence was tempered by argument. That Ireland was misgoverned and was entitled to self-government was taken for granted. The question of the hour was the land system. 'You may get a federal parliament, perhaps repeal of the union, nay more you may establish an Irish republic on Irish soil', said Brennan, 'but as long as the tillers of the soil are forced to support a useless and indolent aristocracy your federal parliament would be but a bauble and your Irish republic but a fraud'. The only final solution of the problem was to abolish the landlord system and to make the occupying tenants the owners of the soil. Parnell's recent statement on the subject at Cavan was quoted with approval, and so was John Stuart Mill's dictum: 'when private property in land is not expedient it is unjust' (Louden). The conversion of occupiers into owners had been accomplished on the Continent both peacefully and by violence; and speakers, though

[1] Tim Healy's statement (*Letters and leaders*, i, 74) that Davitt missed the train seems to have been taken from A. M. Sullivan, *New Ireland*, p. 434, and is not otherwise corroborated; nor is the quip attributed by Healy to Daly that Davitt would have been 'father of the Land League' if he had not missed the train.

[2] *Connaught Telegraph*, and *Tuam Herald*, 26 Apr.; *S.C.P.*, ix, 357 (Davitt, 3 July 89), 544-5 (Louden, 5 July); *Defence*, pp 212, 214-15; *Fall*, pp 147-8; Devoy, XIII.

rejecting the view that the use of force on the side of social justice could never be justified, singled out the reforms of Stein and Hardenberg in Prussia rather than the violence of revolutionary France as the model to be followed in Ireland. The peaceful transformation of the Irish land system could only be achieved by sending men of the calibre of Parnell to represent Ireland at Westminster and by bringing immense popular pressure to bear on the British government and parliament; and this would call for 'the combined energy and unceasing labour of all classes of Irishman' (Brennan). Since it would be unrealistic to expect that a final settlement could thus be obtained at once, the immediate need was to make a stand against evictions.[1]

The Irishtown meeting was something quite new in the long history of agrarian troubles in Ireland. It was unprecedented for so much solidarity to be shown not only among farmers but between farmers and townspeople; for such effective cooperation to be realised between local leaders and national politicians; and for such a popular front to be wholly organised by the laity. The immediate results were also unprecedented: landlords in Mayo and Galway quickly allowed reductions and abatements of rent to their tenants, and tenants offered organised resistance to paying rents that they regarded as exorbitant.[2]

The account of the Irishtown meeting that has long been established, that of Davitt himself in his *Fall of feudalism* (1904), presents it as, in the first instance, a protest against the conduct of Rev. Geoffrey Canon Bourke P.P. He, as executor for his deceased brother's estate in the townland of Quinaltagh, near Irishtown, had threatened to evict the tenants for arrears of rent which, in common with innumerable small farmers in the west, they claimed to be unable to pay. His agent had resigned rather than carry out his instructions to proceed against the defaulting tenants. Because he was a catholic priest they could not obtain a hearing in the local press. But before 'the invasion of his quiet little village by seven thousand sturdy Mayomen' Canon Bourke capitulated, granting rent abatements of 25 per cent.[3] Sheehy-Skeffington, in his brief biography of Davitt (1908), crystallises this result in a striking sentence: 'from the flinty heart of Canon Bourke a spark had been struck which was to wrap all Ireland in conflagration'.[4] But there is in fact no evidence that Bourke's heart was flinty, and his connection with the Irishtown troubles is far from clear.

In 1879 Geoffrey James Bourke, canon of Tuam cathedral, was parish priest of Kilvine. He belonged to an old and respected family

[1] *Connaught Telegraph*, 26 Apr. 79; *Defence*, pp 212-17; *Fall*, pp 148-50.
[2] *Tuam Herald*, 17, 24 May.
[3] *Fall*, pp 146-7, 150-1.
[4] *Michael Davitt* (1967 edition), p. 80.

of catholic gentry, and lived at Oldtown Cottage, the family home in Ballinvilla townland, near Irishtown. Oldtown was the centre of a small, heavily-mortgaged estate, amounting to about 1400 acres of indifferent land mainly in the Irishtown neighbourhood, but including an outlying portion in the townland of Quinaltagh, County Galway, separated by several miles from Ballinvilla. Canon Bourke's father, Walter, was succeeded in the ownership of this estate by his elder son, Walter Joseph, a solicitor of Westport and Dublin, who was an absentee. When he died in 1873 the estate passed to his son Joseph, an army surgeon stationed at Fareham, Hampshire, who also was an absentee.[1]

No contemporary account of the Irishtown meeting or its antecedents makes any reference whatever to Canon Bourke or to his family or to the Bourke estate. But the canon was one of the platform party at the land meeting held on 13 July at nearby Claremorris and seconded a resolution moved by John Dillon.[2] When an anniversay meeting was held at Irishtown (2 May 1880), Bourke sent his apology for being unable to attend, owing to the death of a relative, but he was represented by his curate, McAlpine, whom the meeting elected as its chairman.[3] Davitt was a speaker at that meeting, but he made no reference to the canon. In his 'Story of the land war' recorded by a press-reporter in America in July 1882, he was similarly silent.[4] It was not till ten years after the first Irishtown meeting that Bourke was publicly named in connection with it. In his evidence before the *Times*-Parnell commission on 2 July 1889 Davitt described Bourke as owner of 'a very small estate' near Irishtown, and James Daly of Irishtown as chairman of the protest meeting and formerly Bourke's agent. The rents on the estate had been doubled in 1874, but as a result of the meeting the landlord immediately reduced them by 20 per cent.[5] This brought prompt and indignant public denials from both Canon Bourke and James Daly of Castlebar. Bourke, now parish priest of Cummer, near Tuam, in a short, incisive letter to the *Freeman's Journal*, denied that the rent on the Bourke estate was doubled in 1874, that he had ever been owner of the estate, and that Daly of Castlebar, the real chairman of the Irishtown meeting, had ever been his agent.[6] Daly, in his *Connaught Telegraph*, denounced Davitt for the 'crass ignorance' of men and things in Mayo revealed by his evidence to the commission.

[1] Samuel Lewis, *Topographical dictionary of Ireland* (London, 1837), ii, 218; *Thom, 1871*, pp 743, 1104, 1339; *1879*, pp 739, 959. Registry of Deeds, 1857, lib. 19, no. 7; 1859, lib. 1, no. 11; 1873, lib. 6, no. 293; 1873, lib. 34, no. 91; 1880, lib. 40, no. 107; 1881, lib. 38, no. 287. *Connaught Telegraph*, 13 July 89, 31 May 90.

[2] *F.J.*, 14 July 80; below, pp 309-10.

[3] See below, pp 377-8.

[4] Cashman, pp 213-14.

[5] *S.C.P.*, ix, 357.

[6] *F.J.*, 9 July 89; *Connaught Telegraph*, 13 July.

He quoted Bourke as saying that rents on the Bourke estate had been fixed in 1855 by leases for 31 years and so could not have been doubled in 1874, and that the calling of the meeting at Irishtown had nothing to do with the estate. Irishtown, Daly asserted, was chosen because it was central for farmers in Mayo and Galway, and the meeting was a response to grievances of tenants over a large area. Daly of Irishtown confirmed that, though he had helped to promote the meeting, it was the other James Daly who had presided at it.[1]

Davitt was shaken by these revelations. He had not been present at the Irishtown meeting, and he had not verified his information about it, received from J. J. Louden and J. P. Quinn, when he gave his evidence before the *Times*-Parnell commission. He must have overlooked a reprint of the *Connaught Telegraph* for 26 April 1879 that he had among his papers.[2] Reluctantly convinced that he was in error he asked leave of the commission on 24 October 1889 to make three corrections in his evidence: the chairman of the Irishtown meeting was Daly of Castlebar; the property in question was four miles away from Irishtown; Canon Bourke was not its owner.[3] These admissions left his essential charge against Canon Bourke unaltered. But this was obscured by the fact that he did not mention Bourke in the account of the Irishtown meeting that he gave in his speech, as distinct from his examination, before the commission. The book in which he published the speech—his *Defence of the Land League*—early in 1890 thus contained nothing to offend the canon, who died soon afterwards, on 23 May, aged 67, after a heart attack. His obituary in the *Connaught Telegraph* described him as 'most unassuming in manner and a true priest in every sense of the word', who as P.P. of Cummer for over twelve years 'devoted all his time to the advancement of religion and the interests of his flock'.[4] When Davitt made his final statement on the Irishtown meeting, in the *Fall of feudalism*, he revived, with some corrrections and additions, the story he had given in evidence before the commission. The rack-renting canon appears as his deceased brother's executor, the estate in question is described as in Quinaltagh, and instead of a 'reduction' of 20 per cent in the rents Bourke grants an 'abatement' of 25 per cent.[5]

Clearly Davitt's knowledge of the Irishtown situation was vague and confused, and continued to be so. He seems never to have understood the character and topography of the Bourke estate, and he probably

[1] *Connaught Telegraph*, 6, 13, 27 July; *Tuam Herald*, 13, 20 July; *F.J.*, 5, 8 July.

[2] DL/2.

[3] *S.C.P.*, x, 422.

[4] *Tuam Herald*, 24, 31 May 90; *F.J.*, 28 May; *Connaught Telegraph*, 31 May.

[5] *Fall*, pp 146-7, 150-51.

I The first Lancashire home of Michael Davitt, in Wilkinson Street, Haslingden (see p. 11). This and adjoining houses have long since been demolished. (Old photograph, by courtesy of Mr John Dunleavy, Haslingden)

II Stellfoxe's Victoria (later Victoria and Alliance) Mill, Baxenden, near Haslingden, where Michael Davitt was employed in 1855–7 and where he lost his right arm, 8 May 1857 (see p. 17). The buildings were demolished about 15 years ago. (Old photograph, by courtesy of Mr John Dunleavy, Haslingden)

III Michael Davitt in 1863/4 (see p. 20). From a photocopy by Markham & Johnson, 335 Washington Street, Brooklyn, of a photograph of Davitt not otherwise known, but obviously one taken in England, since he did not go to America till 1878. The photocopy is endorsed in Davitt's hand 'Michael Davitt at 17 years of age'. (Davitt papers, DPG)

V *above* John O'Connor Power, aged 22, as taken into custody in Kilmainham jail, 17 Fe 1868 (see pp 47–8, 49–50). (S.P.O., Descripti of fenian suspects, 1871–80, p. 1)

IV *left* Arthur Forrester, aged 17, on discharg from Kilmainham jail, 8 Oct. 1867 (see pp 48 50). (S.P.O., Photographs of fenians discharge from custody, 1866–70)

VI John Devoy (top left), with four other released fenians, Charles Underwood O'Connell, Harry Mulleda, Jeremiah O'Donovan Rossa, and John McClure, on arrival at New York on the S.S. *Cuba*, Jan. 1871 (see pp 135–6). (Devoy, *Recollections*, facing p. 330)

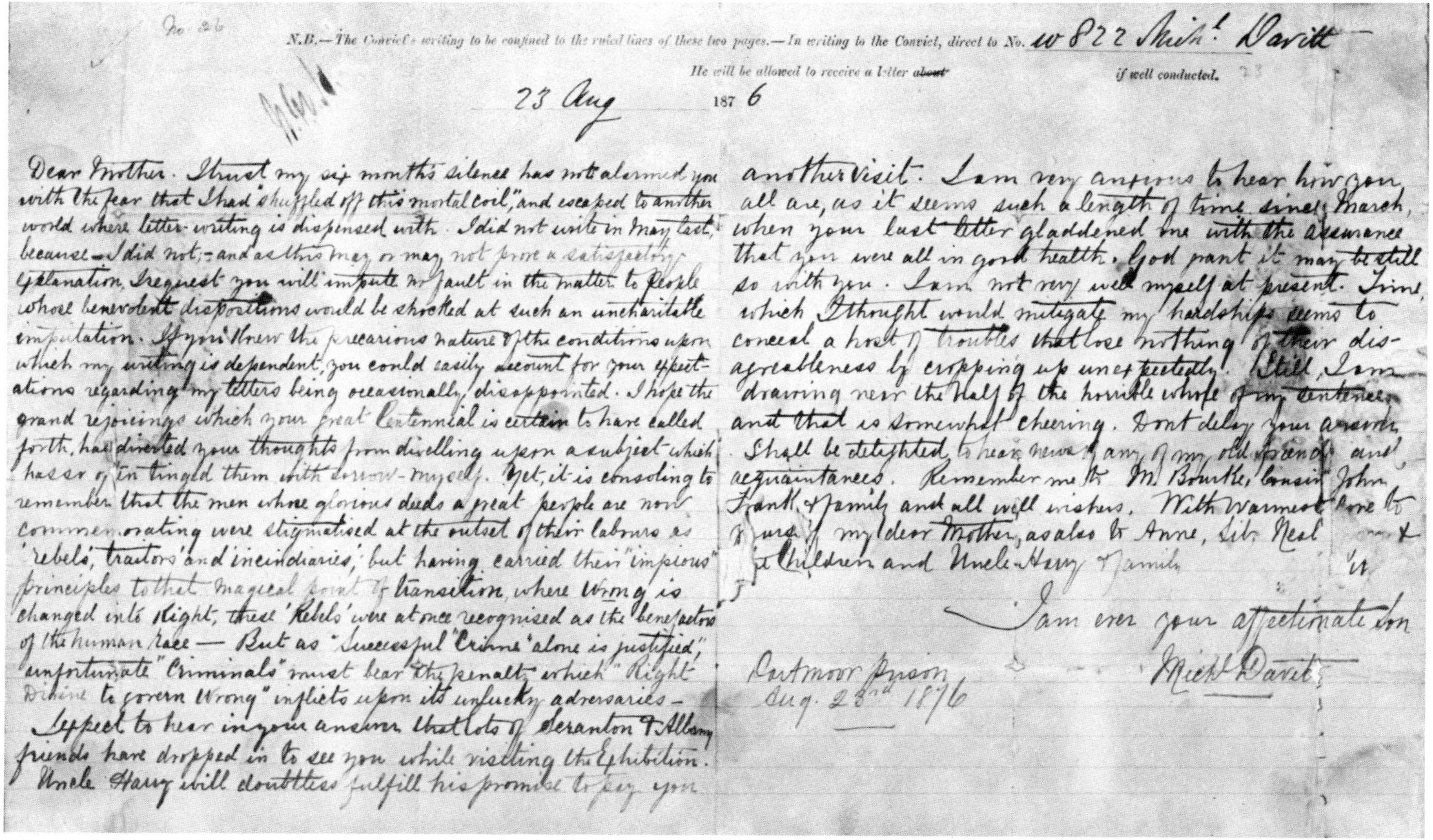

No. 26

N.B.—The Convict's writing to be confined to the ruled lines of these two pages.—In writing to the Convict, direct to No. W 822 Mich^l. Davitt

He will be allowed to receive a letter about if well conducted.

23 Aug 1876

Dear Mother. I trust my six months silence has not alarmed you with the fear that I had "shuffled off this mortal coil," and escaped to another world where letter-writing is dispensed with. I did not write in May last, because—I did not;—and as this may or may not prove a satisfactory explanation, I request you will impute no fault in the matter to people whose benevolent dispositions would be shocked at such an uncharitable imputation. If you knew the precarious nature of the conditions upon which my writing is dependent, you could easily account for your expectations regarding my letters being occasionally disappointed. I hope the grand rejoicings which your great Centennial is certain to have called forth, have diverted your thoughts from dwelling upon a subject which has so often tinged them with sorrow—myself. Yet, it is consoling to remember that the men whose glorious deeds a great people are now commemorating were stigmatised at the outset of their labours as 'rebels', 'traitors' and 'incendiaries'; but having carried their "impious" principles to that magical point of transition, where Wrong is changed into Right, these 'Rebels' were at once recognised as the benefactors of the human race— But as "Successful Crime alone is justified," unfortunate "Criminals" must bear the penalty which "Right Divine to govern Wrong" inflicts upon its unlucky adversaries—

I expect to hear in your answer that lots of Scranton & Albany friends have dropped in to see you while visiting the Exhibition. Uncle Harry will doubtless fulfill his promise to pay you another visit. I am very anxious to hear how you all are, as it seems such a length of time since March, when your last letter gladdened me with the assurance that you were all in good health. God grant it may be still so with you. I am not very well myself at present. Time, which I thought would mitigate my hardships seems to conceal a host of troubles that lose nothing of their disagreeableness by cropping up unexpectedly. Still, I am drawing near the half of the horrible whole of my sentence, and that is somewhat cheering. Dont delay your answer. Shall be delighted to hear news of any of my old friends and acquaintances. Remember me to Mr Bourke, Cousin John, Frank & family and all well wishers. With warmest love to yours my dear Mother, as also to Anne, Sis. Neal & Children and Uncle Harry & family

I am ever your affectionate son

Mich^l Davitt

Dartmoor Prison
Aug. 23rd 1876

VIIa Letter from Michael Davitt in Dartmoor prison to his mother in Manayunk, Philadelphia, 23 Aug. 1876 (see p. 172). On the inside of a folded blue form, of which the outside is reproduced overleaf. (Original in Davitt papers, DP/A5)

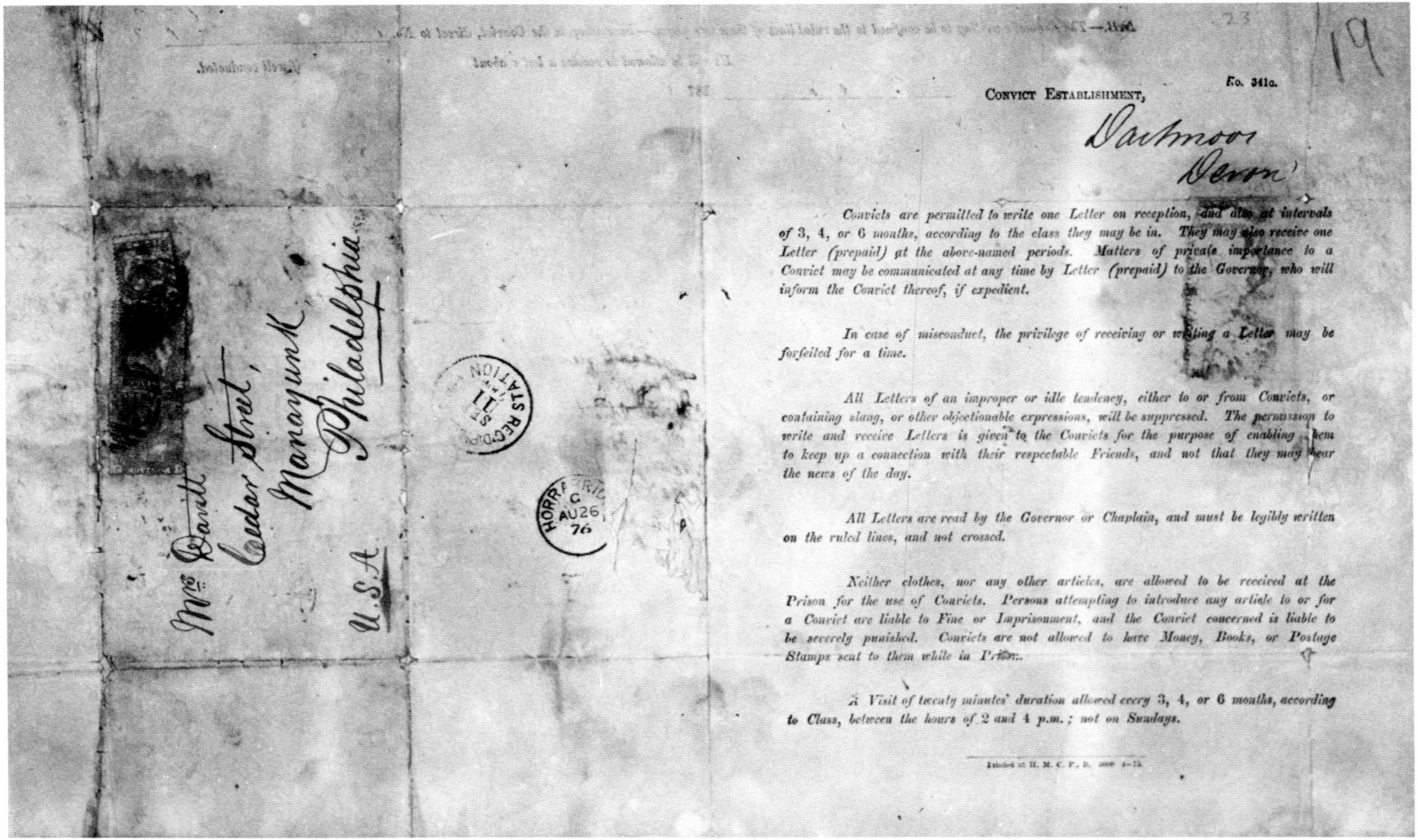
CONVICT ESTABLISHMENT, No. 341o.

Dartmoor
Devon

Convicts are permitted to write one Letter on reception, and also at intervals of 3, 4, or 6 months, according to the class they may be in. They may also receive one Letter (prepaid) at the above-named periods. Matters of private importance to a Convict may be communicated at any time by Letter (prepaid) to the Governor, who will inform the Convict thereof, if expedient.

In case of misconduct, the privilege of receiving or writing a Letter may be forfeited for a time.

All Letters of an improper or idle tendency, either to or from Convicts, or containing slang, or other objectionable expressions, will be suppressed. The permission to write and receive Letters is given to the Convicts for the purpose of enabling them to keep up a connection with their respectable Friends, and not that they may hear the news of the day.

All Letters are read by the Governor or Chaplain, and must be legibly written on the ruled lines, and not crossed.

Neither clothes, nor any other articles, are allowed to be received at the Prison for the use of Convicts. Persons attempting to introduce any article to or for a Convict are liable to Fine or Imprisonment, and the Convict concerned is liable to be severely punished. Convicts are not allowed to have Money, Books, or Postage Stamps sent to them while in Prison.

A Visit of twenty minutes' duration allowed every 3, 4, or 6 months, according to Class, between the hours of 2 and 4 p.m.; not on Sundays.

Mrs Davitt
Cedar Street,
Manayunk
Philadelphia
U.S.A

G
AU26
76

VIIb Outside of blue form, on the inside of which is the letter from Davitt reproduced overleaf.

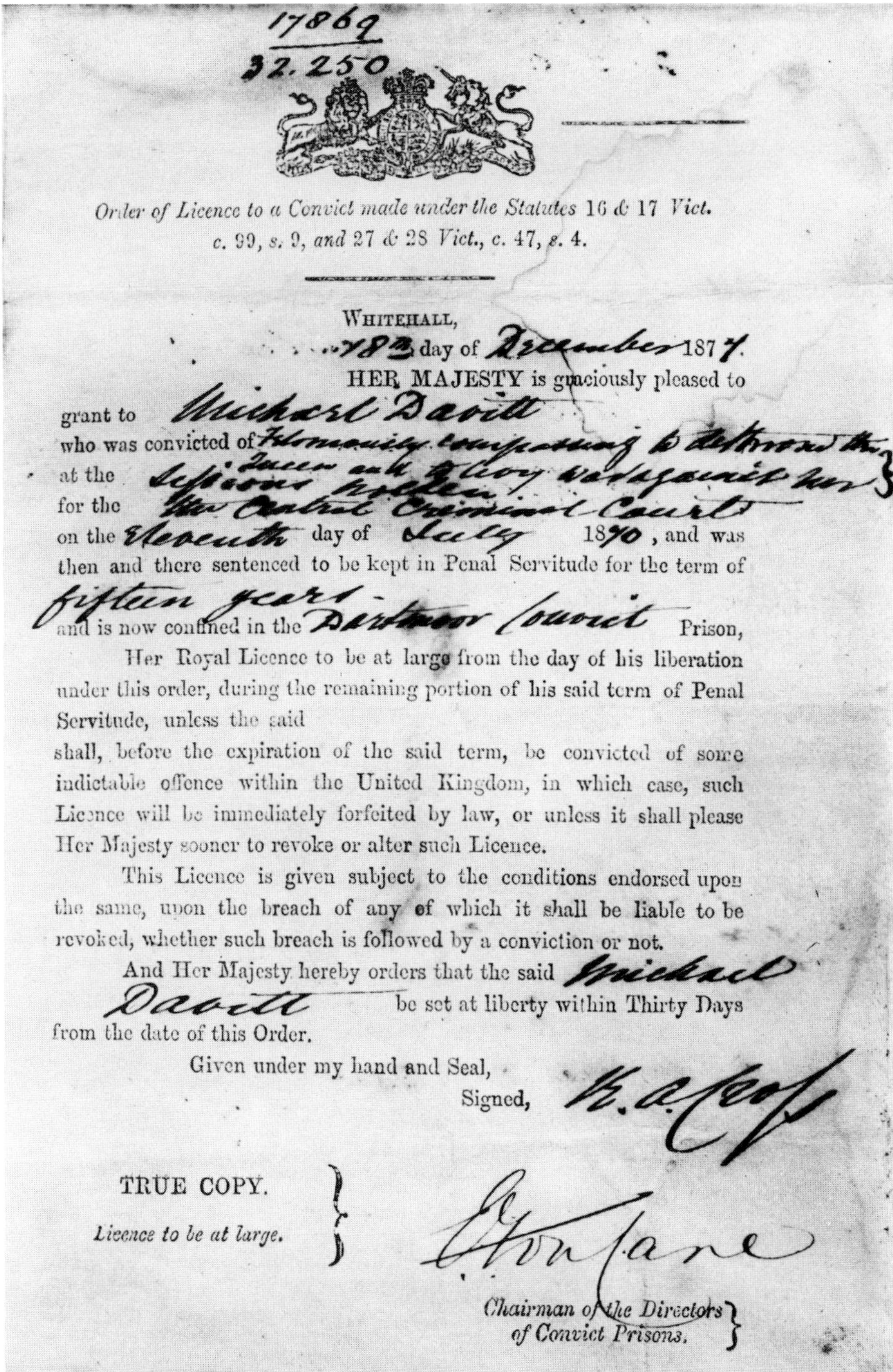

17869
32.250

Order of Licence to a Convict made under the Statutes 16 & 17 *Vict. c.* 99, *s.* 9, *and* 27 & 28 *Vict., c.* 47, *s.* 4.

WHITEHALL,

18th day of December 1877.

HER MAJESTY is graciously pleased to grant to Michael Davitt who was convicted of feloniously conspiring to dethrone the Queen and to levy war against her at the Sessions holden for the Central Criminal Court on the Eleventh day of July 1870, and was then and there sentenced to be kept in Penal Servitude for the term of fifteen years and is now confined in the Dartmoor Convict Prison,

Her Royal Licence to be at large from the day of his liberation under this order, during the remaining portion of his said term of Penal Servitude, unless the said shall, before the expiration of the said term, be convicted of some indictable offence within the United Kingdom, in which case, such Licence will be immediately forfeited by law, or unless it shall please Her Majesty sooner to revoke or alter such Licence.

This Licence is given subject to the conditions endorsed upon the same, upon the breach of any of which it shall be liable to be revoked, whether such breach is followed by a conviction or not.

And Her Majesty hereby orders that the said Michael Davitt be set at liberty within Thirty Days from the date of this Order.

Given under my hand and Seal,

Signed, R. A. Cross

TRUE COPY.

Licence to be at large.

E. Du Cane

Chairman of the Directors of Convict Prisons.

VIIIa Licence or ticket of leave issued to Michael Davitt, 18 Dec. 1877, for his release from Dartmoor prison (see p. 180). The matter on the back of the licence is reproduced overleaf. This licence was revoked on 2 Feb. 1881 (see p. 463). (Photographed from the original, by courtesy of its owner, Mrs Mairead Cahill, a granddaughter of Davitt's)

THIS LICENCE WILL BE FORFEITED IF THE HOLDER DOES NOT OBSERVE THE FOLLOWING CONDITIONS.

The Holder shall preserve his Licence, and produce it when called upon to do so by a Magistrate or Police Officer.

He shall abstain from any violation of the Law.

He shall not habitually associate with notoriously bad characters, such as reputed thieves and prostitutes.

He shall not lead an idle and dissolute life, without visible means of obtaining an honest livelihood.

If his licence is forfeited or revoked in consequence of a conviction for any Offence, he will be liable to undergo a Term of Penal Servitude equal to the portion of his term of 15 years, which remained unexpired when his Licence was granted, viz., the term of 7 years and 7 months.

The attention of the Licence holder is directed to the following provisions of "The Prevention of Crimes Act, 1871."

If it appears from the facts proved before a court of summary jurisdiction that there are reasonable grounds for believing that the convict so brought before it is getting his livelihood by dishonest means, such convict shall be deemed to be guilty of an offence against the Prevention of Crimes Act, and his licence shall be forfeited.

Every holder of a licence granted under the Penal Servitude Acts who is at large in Great Britain or Ireland, shall *notify the place of his residence* to the chief officer of police of the district in which his residence is situated, and shall, *whenever he changes such residence* within the same police district, notify such change to the chief officer of police of that district, and *whenever he changes his residence from one police district to another*, shall notify such change of residence to the chief officer of police of the police district which he is leaving, and to the chief officer of police of the police district into which he goes to reside; moreover, every male holder of such a License as aforesaid shall, *once in each month, report himself* at such time as may be prescribed by the chief officer of police of the district in which such holder may be, either to such chief officer himself or to such other person as that Officer may direct, and such report may, according as such chief officer directs, be required to be made personally or by letter.

If any holder of a licence who is at large in Great Britain or Ireland, *remains in any place for forty-eight hours without notifying the place of his residence* to the chief officer of police of the district in which such place is situated, *or fails to comply with the requisitions of this section* on the occasion of any change of residence, or with the requisitions of this section as to reporting himself once in each month, he shall in every such case, unless he proves to the satisfaction of the Court before whom he is tried that he did his best to act in conformity with the law, be guilty of an offence against the Prevention of Crimes Act, and upon conviction thereof *his licence may in the discretion of the Court be forfeited*, or if the term of Penal Servitude in respect of which his licence was granted has expired, at the date of his conviction, it shall be lawful for the court to sentence him to *imprisonment*, with or without Hard Labour, for a term not exceeding *one year*, or if the said term of Penal Servitude has not expired but the remainder unexpired thereof is a lesser period than one year, then to sentence him to imprisonment, with or without Hard Labour, to commence at the expiration of the said term of Penal Servitude, for such a term as, together with the remainder unexpired of his said term of Penal Servitude, will not exceed one year.

Where any person is convicted on indictment of a crime, and a *previous conviction of a crime* is proved against him, he shall, at any time *within seven years* immediately after the expiration of the sentence passed on him for the last of such crimes be guilty of an offence against the Prevention of Crimes Act, and be *liable to imprisonment* with or without Hard Labour, for a term not exceeding *one year*, under the following circumstances or any of them:

FIRST. If, on his being charged by a constable with getting his livelihood by dishonest means, and being brought before a court of summary jurisdiction, it appears to such court that *there are reasonable grounds for believing* that the person so charged is *getting his livelihood by dishonest means*; or,

SECONDLY. If on being charged with any offence punishable on indictment or summary conviction, and on being required by a court of summary jurisdiction to give his name and address, he refuses to do so, or *gives a false name or a false address*; or,

THIRDLY. If he is found in any place, whether public or private, under such circumstances as to satisfy the court before whom he is brought that he was *about to commit or to aid in the commission of any offence* punishable on indictment or summary conviction, or *was waiting for an opportunity to commit or aid in the commission* of any offence punishable on indictment or summary conviction; or

FOURTHLY. If he is found *in or upon any dwelling-house, or any building, yard, or premises*, being parcel of or attached to such dwelling-house, or in or upon any shop, warehouse, counting-house, or other place of business, or in any garden, orchard, pleasure-ground, or nursery-ground, or in any building or erection in any garden, orchard, pleasure-ground, or nursery-ground, *without being able to account to the satisfaction of the Court* before whom he is brought *for his being found on such premises*.

F & T 1000 9—77
[7-17-7]

VIIIb Matter on the back of the licence reproduced overleaf.

IX Michael Davitt in January 1878, aged 31, on his arrival in Dublin after his release from Dartmoor (see pp 188–9). (Photograph by A. Lesage, 40 Lower Sackville Street, Dublin, in Davitt papers, DPG)

X Eviction scene, *c.* Nov. 1880, as pictured by a correspondent of *Le Monde Illustré* (Paris). (Engraving in National Library of Ireland, from *Le Monde Illustré*, xlvii, no. 1237 (11 Dec. 1880), at p. 356; 'la police anglaise' in the caption is rendered 'la police irlandaise' in a comment on p. 355)

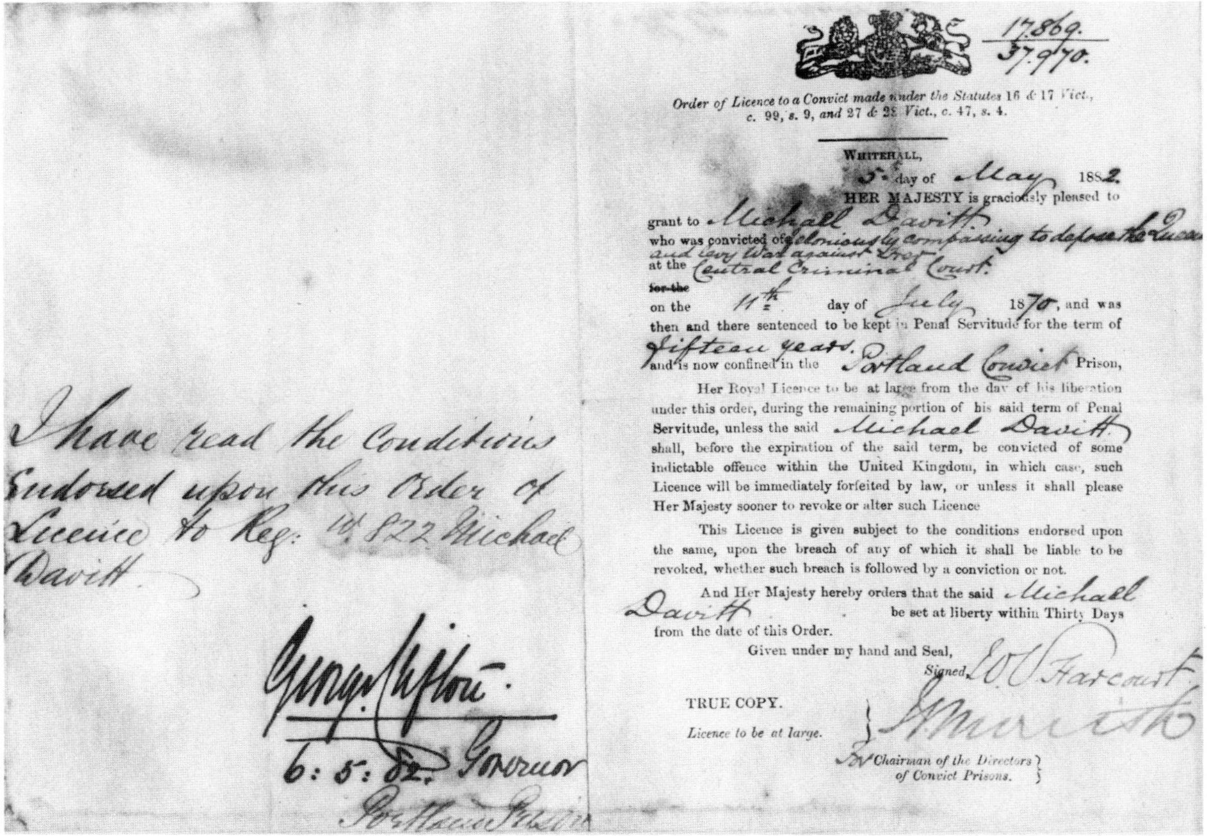

17.869.
37.970.

Order of Licence to a Convict made under the Statutes 16 & 17 Vict., c. 99, s. 9, and 27 & 28 Vict., c. 47, s. 4.

WHITEHALL,
5 day of May 1882.

HER MAJESTY is graciously pleased to grant to Michael Davitt who was convicted of feloniously compassing to depose the Queen and levy War against her at the Central Criminal Court ~~for the~~ on the 11th day of July 1870, and was then and there sentenced to be kept in Penal Servitude for the term of fifteen years and is now confined in the Portland Convict Prison,

Her Royal Licence to be at large from the day of his liberation under this order, during the remaining portion of his said term of Penal Servitude, unless the said Michael Davitt shall, before the expiration of the said term, be convicted of some indictable offence within the United Kingdom, in which case, such Licence will be immediately forfeited by law, or unless it shall please Her Majesty sooner to revoke or alter such Licence

This Licence is given subject to the conditions endorsed upon the same, upon the breach of any of which it shall be liable to be revoked, whether such breach is followed by a conviction or not.

And Her Majesty hereby orders that the said Michael Davitt be set at liberty within Thirty Days from the date of this Order.

Given under my hand and Seal,
Signed, W. V. Harcourt

TRUE COPY.
Licence to be at large.
[illegible]
Chairman of the Directors of Convict Prisons.

I have read the Conditions Endorsed upon this Order of Licence to Reg: 14.822 Michael Davitt.

George Clifton
6: 5: 82. Governor
Portland Prison

XIa Second licence or ticket of leave issued to Michael Davitt, 5 May 1882, for his release from Portland prison (see p. 531). The actual date of conviction was 18, not 11, July 1870. The matter on the back of the licence is reproduced overleaf. This licence expired on 11 July 1885. (Photographed from the original, by courtesy of its owner, Mrs Mairead Cahill)

THIS LICENCE WILL BE FORFEITED IF THE HOLDER DOES NOT OBSERVE THE FOLLOWING CONDITIONS.

The Holder shall preserve his Licence, and produce it when called upon to do so by a Magistrate or Police Officer.

He shall abstain from any violation of the Law.

He shall not habitually associate with notoriously bad characters, such as reputed thieves and prostitutes.

He shall not lead an idle and dissolute life, without visible means of obtaining an honest livelihood.

If his licence is forfeited or revoked in consequence of a conviction for any Offence, he will be liable to undergo a Term of Penal Servitude equal to the portion of his term of 10 years, which remained unexpired when his Licence was granted, viz., the term of 3 years and 2 months.

The attention of the Licence holder is directed to the following provisions of "The Prevention of Crimes Acts, 1871 and 1879."

If it appears from the facts proved before a court of summary jurisdiction that there are reasonable grounds for believing that the convict so brought before it is getting his livelihood by dishonest means, such convict shall be deemed to be guilty of an offence against the Prevention of Crimes Act, and his licence shall be forfeited.

Every holder of a licence granted under the Penal Servitude Acts who is at large in Great Britain or Ireland, shall within 48 hours of his liberation personally *notify the place of his residence to the chief officer of police of the district* in which his residence is situated, or to a constable or person appointed by him, and shall, *whenever he changes such residence* within the same police district, notify such change to the *chief officer of police of that district*, or to a constable or person appointed by him, and *whenever he changes his residence from one police district to another*, shall personally notify such change of residence to the *chief officer of police of the police district* which he is leaving, or to a constable or person appointed by him, and to the *chief officer of police of the police district* into which he goes to reside, or to a constable or person appointed by him; moreover, every male holder of such a Licence as aforesaid shall, *once in each month, report himself* personally at such time as may be prescribed by the chief officer of police of the district in which such holder may be, either to such chief officer himself or to such other person as that Officer may direct, and such report may, according as such chief officer directs, be required to be made personally or by letter.

If any holder of a licence who is at large in Great Britain or Ireland, *remains in any place for forty-eight hours without notifying the place of his residence* to the *chief officer of police of the district* in which such place is situated, or to a constable or person appointed by him, *or fails to comply with the requisitions of this section* on the occasion of any change of residence, or with the requisitions of this section as to reporting himself once in each month, he shall in every such case, unless he proves to the satisfaction of the Court before whom he is tried that he did his best to act in conformity with the law, be guilty of an offence against the Prevention of Crimes Act and upon conviction thereof *his licence may in the discretion of the Court be forfeited*, or if the term of Penal Servitude in respect of which his licence was granted has expired, at the date of his conviction, it shall be lawful for the court to sentence him to *imprisonment*, with or without Hard Labour, for a term not exceeding *one year*, or if the said term of Penal Servitude has not expired but the remainder unexpired thereof is a lesser period than one year, then to sentence him to imprisonment, with or without Hard Labour, to commence at the expiration of the said term of Penal Servitude, for such a term as, together with the remainder unexpired of his said term of Penal Servitude, will not exceed one year.

Where any person is convicted on indictment of a crime, and a *previous conviction of a crime* is proved against him, he shall, at any time *within seven years* immediately after the expiration of the sentence passed on him for the last of such crimes be guilty of an offence against the Prevention of Crimes Act, and be *liable to imprisonment* with or without Hard Labour, for a term not exceeding *one year*, under the following circumstances or any of them:

First. If, on his being charged by a constable with getting his livelihood by dishonest means, and being brought before a court of summary jurisdiction, it appears to such court that *there are reasonable grounds for believing* that the person so charged is *getting his livelihood by dishonest means*; or,

Secondly. If on being charged with any offence punishable on indictment or summary conviction, and on being required by a court of summary jurisdiction to give his name and address, he refuses to do so, or *gives a false name or a false address*; or,

Thirdly. If he is found in any place, whether public or private, under such circumstances as to satisfy the court before whom he is brought that he was *about to commit or to aid in the commission of any offence* punishable on indictment or summary conviction, or *was waiting for an opportunity to commit or aid in the commission* of any offence punishable on indictment or summary conviction; or

Fourthly. If he is found *in or upon any dwelling-house, or any building, yard, or premises*, being parcel of or attached to such dwelling-house, or in or upon any shop, warehouse, counting-house, or other place of business, or in any garden, orchard, pleasure-ground, or nursery-ground, or in any building or erection in any garden, orchard, pleasure-ground, or nursery ground, *without being able to account to the satisfaction of the Court* before whom he is brought *for his being found on such premises*.

XIb Matter on the back of the licence reproduced overleaf.

XII Michael Davitt at New York in June or July 1882, aged 36 (see p. 540). (Photograph by Napoleon Sarony, New York, 1882, in Davitt papers, DPG)

XIII Michael Davitt, *c.* Mar. 1904, aged 58. This is as his surviving children remember him. (Photograph by Prince, Washington D.C., in Davitt papers, DPG)

did not know Canon Bourke personally. Daly and Bourke were in a position to know the facts about Irishtown, and there is no reason to doubt Bourke's denials. But neither of them denied that the Bourke tenants were under threat of eviction, or that Daly of Irishtown had been the agent for the estate and had refused to proceed against the tenants. Daly of Castlebar contradicts what he had said at Irishtown when he explains why it was chosen as the place of meeting. If the Bourke estate was indeed the immediate source of the troubles that led to the meeting, Irishtown was an obvious point at which to stage a protest. Daly had a reason for taking Bourke's side against Davitt in 1889, because he and Davitt were then at loggerheads. Davitt described him to Richard Kelly, editor of the *Tuam Herald*, as 'that editorial bosthoon'.[1] But while Davitt's version of the Irishtown story is partial and inaccurate in detail, it is not substantially upset by his two critics except in the role it assigns to Bourke. There seems no reason to doubt that grievances of tenants on the Bourke estate were the immediate cause of the Irishtown meeting, but responsibility for the harsh treatment of these tenants may well have been that of the absentee owner, Joseph Bourke, not that of his resident uncle, the canon. Davitt's total silence about Canon Bourke until ten years after the event may have been deliberate reticence, but is much more likely to have been due to inadequate knowledge. In preparing his evidence for the *Times*–Parnell commission he had to fortify his memory, and he relied uncritically on information about the chairmanship of the Irishtown meeting and about the Bourke property supplied by Louden and Quinn. He was probably wrong about Canon Bourke's culpability, but if he had left the Irishtown story as it was in his *Defence of the Land League* that would have mattered little. It was his final version, in the *Fall of feudalism*, that gave Canon Bourke the odious role he has ever since held in the saga of the land war. Whether he deserved that role must be regarded as highly questionable.

The Irishtown meeting was generally ignored by the press. The only reporters present were those of the *Connaught Telegraph* and the *Tuam Herald*. The *Freeman's Journal*, which on 21 April mentioned that a great and very orderly demonstration had been held at Irishtown with the object of protecting small tenant farmers, quoted a Press Association telegram as its authority. But the *Connaught Telegraph* and the *Tuam Herald* of 26 April both carried detailed reports, and the former had an editorial hailing the meeting as a solemn protest to Ireland and the world against an iniquitous system, and emphasising that shopkeepers had an interest in the question second only to that

[1] D to Richard Kelly, 18 July 89 (DP/01).

of the tenants. An abridged account of the report in the *Connaught Telegraph* was published in the *Nation* of 3 May. As news of the meeting flew round Mayo, requests for repeat performances at other places reached the organisers. Despite clerical warnings and denunciation, they decided to go ahead. The militant temper of the farmers was demonstrated at Knock (County Mayo), where on Sunday, 1 June, a monster meeting was held to protest against the language used from the altar by Venerable Archdeacon Kavanagh P.P. the previous Sunday against farmers organising meetings to ventilate their grievances, and in particular against John O'Kane of Claremorris (one of the ringleaders of the Irishtown affair), whom he accused of preparing the country for revolution. The chairman of the meeting, a local farmer, while deprecating any disrespect to a catholic priest, warned Fr Kavanagh: 'don't stand between the people and their rights; if you do, you must . . . accept the consequences'.[1] Preparations were now well advanced locally for a land meeting at Westport on Sunday, 8 June. Parnell, fully informed about the Irishtown meeting, and urged to speak at Westport, agreed with some reluctance to do so.[2]

During May rural distress reached a dangerous level not only in the west but in other parts of the country. When the house of commons was about to adjourn, on 27 May, for the Whitsuntide recess, a number of home rule members including Parnell sounded the alarm and called for government action.[3] Thus O'Connor Power:

> If parliament did not come forward, within a reasonable time, with some measure of legislation calculated to relieve the depression of the present state of agriculture in Ireland, scenes would arise . . . that would be far more dangerous to the rights of property and to the order and tranquillity which should prevail . . . than any that Ireland had been afflicted with in her long struggle with the ignorance, if not incompetency, of the English parliament.[4]

Such warnings left the Irish chief secretary (James Lowther) unshaken: the agricultural depression in Ireland, he said, was 'neither so prevalent nor so acute as the depression in other parts of the United Kingdom'.[5]

This was the situation when on 1 June Davitt and Devoy had their second interview with Parnell at Morrison's Hotel. Davitt came to the meeting in a stronger position to put pressure on Parnell than he had been two months earlier. He could claim the Irishtown meeting as in some sense a personal triumph; for though he had neither originated it nor been present at it he had largely shaped it. The negative attitude

[1] *Connaught Telegraph*, 7 June 79, p. 5; S.P.O., R.P. 1879/9632.
[2] *Connaught Telegraph*, 26 Apr., 3 May, 7 June; *F.J.*, 7, 8 June.
[3] *Hansard 3*, ccxlvi, 1389–99.
[4] Ibid., col. 1394.
[5] Ibid.

of the government had strengthened the case for the agitation to which he was now so thoroughly committed. The need of the hour was for a leader who could control and direct the passions that would both energise, and be generated by, the agitation. Davitt characteristically did not aspire to be leader himself. Had he done so, there might well have been, as Devoy believed, 'a convulsion' ending in speedy and tragic failure. As it was, Davitt saw in Parnell the one man with the qualities, and the standing, necessary for successful leadership of the agitation. The course of events and the government's policy of drift did much to convince Parnell himself that he had no alternative but to assume the role in which Davitt was so eager to cast him. The death on 5 May of Isaac Butt (Davitt took part in the funeral procession through Dublin on the 10th) and the election of the politically insignificant William Shaw[1] ('Sensible Shaw') as Butt's successor had brought the final struggle for the leadership of the parliamentary party a stage nearer. Parnell could not be indifferent to the agrarian crisis, even if he had not been so genuinely concerned for the plight of the farmers.

Devoy also regarded Parnell as the only possible leader. Between the two meetings in Morrison's Hotel Devoy was constantly on the move, pursuing his fenian mission in all four provinces, enduring the pitiless weather, and observing the mounting distress. It was typical of the man that, during his three and a half months in Ireland (which he was not to revisit till 1924), he made almost no social contacts and saw almost none of the famous beauty-spots (except Lough Erne) he was to describe in the book that he wrote on his return to New York,[2] though his itinerary took him near many of them, from Killarney to the Giant's Causeway. He and Davitt met again in Dublin just before their second interview with Parnell, and agreed on the approach they would make to him.[3]

According to Devoy, who has left the only precise account of the meeting of 1 June, he and Davitt explained to Parnell that they had no authority to speak for the fenian organisation but that as individual fenians they were free to take part in agrarian agitation as they saw fit so long as their action was not incompatible with fenianism. They assured him that they could speak for large bodies of fenians in Ireland and America in promising to support his leadership of the land movement if he would accept four conditions:

(1) that in the conduct of the public movement, so far as Parnell and Davitt could influence it, nothing should be said or done to

[1] *F.J.*, 6, 12 May, 14 June. [2] *The land of Eire* (1882). [3] Devoy, XIV.

impair the vitality of the fenian movement or to discredit its ideal of complete national independence to be secured by the eventual use of physical force;

(2) that the demand for self-government should not for the present be publicly defined, but that nothing short of a national parliament with power over all vital national interests and an executive responsible to it should be accepted;

(3) that the settlement of the land question to be demanded should be the establishment of a peasant proprietary to be effected by compulsory purchase;

(4) that the Irish members of parliament elected through the public movement should form an absolutely independent party, asking and accepting no places, salaried or honorary, under the English government, for themselves, their constituents, or anyone else.

Parnell, Devoy says, after long discussion accepted the leadership on these conditions, and agreed to attend the meeting at Westport the following Sunday and there to commit himself formally to the land movement. In return Devoy and Davitt promised him all possible support. The compact was verbal only, but was none the less 'clear, definite, and precise';[1] and to it Parnell remained faithful to the end of his life.[2]

In Devoy's opinion the first of the four conditions was by far the most important. Without it no fenian could take part in the public movement, and without massive fenian support that movement could have no hope of success. As a corollary Devoy and Davitt promised that, while there would be no slackening in the organisation and preparation for rebellion, no attempt at insurrection would be made until the new programme had had a fair trial. They felt safe in giving this promise, knowing that the fenian leaders who differed from them had no thought of resorting to force for at least several years to come. Parnell, Devoy says, had no hesitation in accepting the first condition; and the same was true of the second, which was designed to avoid conflicts between fenians, repealers, and federalist home-rulers. Devoy did not believe that Britain would ever grant home rule in response to peaceful pressure, but he thought it possible that some kind or 'representative county government' might be conceded in the hope of allaying the demand for self-government, and he felt that it would be easier for nationalists to take advantage of such an eventuality if the definition of self-government were left open. On the land question

[1] Devoy, XV.

[2] Devoy, 'Parnell and the fenians' in *Chicago Journal*, 24 Mar. 99.

Parnell was whole-hearted for peasant proprietorship, but doubted whether compulsory purchase would be conceded and thought that many landlords would agree to sell if the funds were made available. Davitt, Devoy says, had the same doubt—he 'was only a recent convert' to peasant proprietorship and had never defined what he meant by 'the land for the people'. He had not as yet read James Fintan Lalor, or Henry George; and land nationalisation, the extreme settlement which Devoy hoped to see realised when an Irish republic had come into existence,[1] was 'not in his vocabulary'. To Parnell, land nationalisation was absolutely unacceptable;[2] and since Devoy believed in peasant proprietorship 'as an interim solution', a means 'of breaking up the big estates and destroying the power of England's landlord garrison', the three men agreed that peasant proprietorship was the thing to be demanded. The final condition, accepted by all three as a matter of course, was the policy on which Parnell was already acting. Davitt at the time was little concerned with what might be done in parliament, but he seemed to be no less strong than Devoy on a policy that carried the implication of the eventual withdrawal of the Irish party from Westminster.[3]

If the foregoing account of the Davitt–Devoy–Parnell meeting on 1 June is true, the three men made a personal treaty to act together in accordance with the new departure programme; for the four conditions defined and explained by Devoy contained the whole substance of his 'new departure' article in the New York *Herald* of 27 October 1878[4] except the repudiation of sectarianism, which could be taken for granted. But there are five objections to Devoy's story. The first is that he himself contradicts it where, assessing the changes that occurred between the two Morrison's Hotel meetings, he says that the new departure was 'jostled out of the way' by the agrarian agitation springing up spontaneously in Mayo, 'and the question confronting us was, could it be kept within rational channels'. Davitt had committed himself so completely to the land movement that 'he was ready to take Parnell without exacting any terms except a general acceptance of the Irishtown resolutions'. But, Devoy adds, 'I was in a different position and insisted on clear and definite conditions'[5]—an admission not consistent with the impression of complete solidarity with Davitt that Devoy conveys in his substantive treatment of the meeting of 1 June. The second objection to Devoy's story is that Parnell's decision to speak at Westport was taken before, and therefore independently of,

[1] Cf. above, pp 232–3, 234.
[2] *Chicago Journal*, 24 Mar. 99.
[3] Devoy, XV.
[4] Above, pp 251–3.
[5] Devoy, XIV.

his conversation with Davitt and Devoy on 1 June. For the announcement of the Westport meeting, naming Parnell and others as speakers, had been placarded throughout Mayo since before the end of April, and Parnell had confirmed his intention to be present a day or two before 1 June.[1] The third objection is that Parnell did not 'commit himself formally' at Westport to the land agitation, still less accept the leadership of it; on the contrary, he waited three months before taking that decisive step.[2] The fourth objection is that Parnell's subsequent political conduct did not conform to three of the four conditions to which, Devoy says, he remained faithful. In fact, Parnell's leadership of the parliamentary party did 'impair the vitality' of fenianism; Parnell did, in 1886, accept as a final settlement a home rule scheme that was far from offering 'a national parliament with power over all vital national interests'; and Parnell never adopted compulsory land purchase as a general principle of settlement.[3] The final objection is that Devoy's story is incompatible with the testimony of both Parnell and Davitt. Devoy did not publish his full statement of the matter till 1906,[4] when the other two men were dead, but he had made explicit reference publicly to the compact as early as 1884,[5] when they were both very much alive. In giving a quite different account of how Parnell agreed to accept the leadership of the land movement, they were therefore in no doubt that they were contradicting Devoy.

Parnell, under cross-examination before the special commission in 1889, rather tortuously denied that he saw Devoy at all, or even knew of his being in Ireland, in 1879, but admitted that, before the Westport meeting and on other occasions, he had conversations with Davitt. The denial was a brazen but politic lie; for the truth would have played into the hands of *The Times*. But his association with Davitt had never been concealed, and he spoke freely about the subject of their conversations: the desirability, urged by Davitt, of

> a combined social and political movement that would interest the tenant farmers by directing attention to their condition and proposing remedies for their relief; and a movement which at the same time would interest the Irish nation at home and abroad in the direction of the restitution of an Irish parliament.[6]

He was reluctant, as a constitutionalist, to commit himself to agrarian

[1] Archbishop MacHale's letter to the editor of the *Freeman*, 5 June 79 (*F.J.*, 7 June); Parnell's speech at Westport, 8 June (*F.J.*, 9 June).

[2] D to Devoy, 23 Aug. (*D.P.B.*, i, 453); *Fall*, pp 159–60, 164–170.

[3] See F. S. L. Lyons, 'The economic ideas of Parnell' in *Historical Studies*, ii, 64–9.

[4] In his paper, the *Gaelic American*, 9 June–3 Nov. 1906.

[5] *United Ireland*, 28 June 84; quoted in *S.C.P.*, iv, 259–60 (29 Jan. 89). In *The land of Eire*, published in 1882, Devoy speaks (p. 58) of 'repeated interviews' with Parnell and Davitt about Parnell's assumption of the leadership but says nothing of any 'compact'.

[6] *S.C.P.*, vii, 95 (1 May 89).

agitation, realising how difficult it would be to keep it under control, but 'ultimately' saw that it was necessary to take the risk. It is clear that by 'ultimately' he was referring not to the Westport meeting but to the decision he made in September to join with Davitt in founding the Land League.[1] He believed that the termination of the landlords' interest in the tenanted land would not only meet the vital need of the tenants but would 'remove a very great and formidable obstacle to the obtaining of an Irish parliament'. The connection between the 'political' and the 'social' movements thus meant for Parnell an open combination between the home rule and the land movements to save the farmers and indirectly advance the cause of home rule, not a secret combination between constitutional and revolutionary nationalists to bring about the separation of Ireland from Britain. He had never, he said in 1889, gone further either in thought or action than 'the restoration of the legislative independence of Ireland'.[2]

All this is inherently reasonable, and consistent with Parnell's character and public conduct before and after June 1879. It was part of his genius as a politician to pursue limited objectives by all possible means within the law while diffusing the aura of a revolutionary. He had convinced O'Kelly, Carroll, and finally Devoy that he respected their separatism, and their belief in physical force, but there is no evidence that he regarded either as realistic; and he would have been quite out of character to have implicated himself in a fenian scheme, as Devoy says he did on 1 June. Devoy believed that he thoroughly understood Parnell. In this he exaggerated: he had known Parnell for less than three months during which he had met him only three times. Davitt, on the other hand, had been in fairly frequent contact with Parnell for a year and a half, and something like real sympathy had sprung up between them. Behind very different exteriors they were both rather shy and lonely men, and with very different temperaments they both had proud and passionate natures. Davitt's knowledge of Parnell in 1879, partly intuitive, went deeper than Devoy's. The two men were to become bitterly alienated over the O'Shea divorce in 1890, but after, as well as before, that event Davitt's assessment of Parnell was notably fair-minded and perceptive.

On the question of the alleged compact he consistently supported Parnell's position against Devoy's. Before the special commission in 1889 he emphatically denied that there had every been any 'alliance', direct or indirect, between Parnell and any fenian element.[3] When Barry O'Brien was writing his life of Parnell in 1893 Davitt supplied

[1] *S.C.P.*, vii, 10; below, p. 325.

[2] *S.C.P.*, vii, 88.

[3] *S.C.P.*, ix, 534.

him with information about Parnell's connection with the new departure,[1] and in consequence the relevant parts of O'Brien's book[2] came in for severe criticism from Devoy, who repeated and developed his statement of 1884 about the 'compact' of 1 June 1879.[3] Davitt's last word on the subject, written in 1903, while confirming Devoy's account of the offer of fenian support he and Davitt had made to Parnell,[4] was in the main a reasoned and measured refutation of Devoy. At both the Dublin interviews, Davitt says, the conversation was general and Parnell's part was mainly that of a listener. He was interested to learn about the clerical opposition to the Mayo agitation, and about the struggle within the secret movement between 'the inflexible and [the] expedient fenians'. He thoroughly approved of 'bringing the revolutionary forces into the open' and employing them in the task of 'wringing reforms out of parliament'. But he entered into no compact of any kind; he agreed to nothing likely to involve him in treasonable proceedings. His attitude to the revolutionary movement was friendly neutrality, and nothing more. To deny the existence of a compact if it had ever been made, Davitt wrote in 1903, would serve no purpose now. This in effect corroborates Parnell's evidence before the special commission and cannot be reconciled with Devoy's insistence that there had been a 'compact'.

Each of the three men who alone knew the truth had their own reasons for giving the retrospective explanations they gave and for doing so when they did, but the weight of evidence is against Devoy. This does not mean that he deliberately invented a 'compact'. The 'conditions' that he says Parnell accepted were conditions he had been urging him to accept since the previous October, and it can be taken as certain that he made yet another effort on 1 June. What must have happened then was that he understood silence on Parnell's part to mean acceptance of his conditions. Had he not believed this to be so, the steady support he thereafter gave Parnell would be inexplicable. Yet there was no compact. After 1 June, as before, Parnell used the fenians in the interests of parliamentary action, and did not permit himself to be used in the interests of revolutionary action as they conceived it. After 1 June both Davitt and Devoy continued to be involved in the fenian and in the land movements, but whereas fenianism remained always Devoy's dominating passion, for Davitt it had become secondary to the land question in its claim on his allegiance. Yet for

[1] D to R. B. O'Brien, 6 Dec. 93 (DP/ZZ).
[2] *The life of Charles Stewart Parnell* (2 vols, London, 1898), i, 163–77.
[3] 'Parnell and the fenians' in *Chicago Journal*, 24 Mar. 99.
[4] *Fall*, pp 151–2, 176–7.

the next year and a half Davitt seemed to regard himself as committed with Devoy to the new departure, despite the I.R.B.'s rejection of their proposals and Parnell's non-acceptance of the alliance they offered.

The Westport meeting (8 June) repeated the pattern of Irishtown but on a somewhat larger scale (the *Freeman's Journal* put the number at 'over 4000', Davitt at 'some 8000'), and it had a more resounding impact. The local clergy were not consulted by the organisers of the meeting, which was held in the teeth of ecclesiastical opposition. On Saturday, 7 June, a letter was published in the *Freeman* over the name of John, archbishop of Tuam, warning the faithful against attending a meeting 'convened in a mysterious and disorderly manner' and 'organised by a few designing men'.

Of the sympathy of the catholic clergy for the rack-rented tenantry of Ireland, and of their willingness to cooperate earnestly in redressing their grievances, abundant evidence exists in historic Mayo as elsewhere. But night patrolling, acts and words of menace, with arms in hand, the profanation of what is most sacred in religion—all the result of lawless and occult association, eminently merit the solemn condemnation of the ministers of religion, as directly tending to impiety and disorder in church and society.[1]

The venerable archbishop, then in the eighty-ninth year of his age and the forty-fifth of his archiepiscopate, was perhaps the most beloved and respected public figure in Connacht; and it is a measure of the strength of the land movement that the condemnation issued over his name was quite ineffective. It was charitably believed that the real author of the letter was the archbishop's secretary and nephew, Rev. Thomas MacHale. Parnell's refusal to be deterred by it was a momentous step, which Davitt considered 'the most courageously wise act' of his whole political career'.[2]

The chairman of the meeting, the outcome of local initiative, was again James Daly of Castlebar; the principal promoter was Louden of Westport, whom Davitt had not previously met; but the most important of the speakers were Parnell and Davitt who appeared together on an Irish platform for the first time.[3] As at Irishtown there were three resolutions: (1) reasserting Ireland's right to self-government, (2) demanding the conversion of the occupying tenants into owners of the soil, and (3) declaring that, pending a final settlement, any landlord evicting a tenant for non-payment of an unfair rent was an enemy of the human race, and that his victims should be protected by every possible means.[4]

[1] *F.J.*, 7 June 79; quoted in *Fall*, p. 153.
[2] S.P.O., R.P. 1879/9571; *S.C.P.*, ix, 562-3; *Fall*, p. 154; Devoy, XVII.
[3] *S.C.P.*, ix, 357, 546; Cashman, pp 213-14.
[4] *F.J.*, 9 June; *Connaught Telegraph*, 14 June.

Davitt made the opening speech. It was his first on the land question to an Irish audience, and it began with a frank avowal that he was an unrepentant separatist. The social misery of Ireland was due to the infliction upon her of an alien system of government, of which the chief instrument and the most evil consequence was landlordism. That system, 'the bastard offspring of force and wrong', was rooted in conquest and confiscation, and every man's hand should be against it. If the tenants would organise themselves in one body and with the single purpose of becoming owners of their farms, the landlords would very soon be compelled to sell out to the government. He warned his hearers against those who, whatever the cut of their coats (he meant the clergy), were serving their own purposes in seeking to interfere in an issue of life or death for the tenants. He mentioned, only to dismiss, a suggestion that Irish farmers should make common cause with English farming interests; when, he asked, had English farmers ever shown any sympathy with anything Irish? Nor should the tenants rely on the Irish parliamentary party, in which the honest men were a mere handful. But if they relied on their own united strength, and 'if their fidelity to their country's imperishable cause' was linked with 'a firm resolve to win back the soil of Ireland from the land robbers who seized it', nothing could prevent their victory.[1]

This was strong meat, but Malachy O'Sullivan, of Ballinasloe,[2] was even less restrained: 'moral force', he said 'is truly a great power, but it becomes a greater power when backed up by physical force'. Did they expect to win autonomy from their hereditary enemies by peaceful means? Did they expect tenant right from a parliament of landlords? Coming to the immediate problem he had a clear and simple plan: let the tenants in each estate meet and agree on a fair rent, and if the landlord refused to accept this let them together refuse to pay any rent at all. Matthew Harris declared that the history of landlordism during the past thirty years was 'a terrible record of selfishness and criminality', of which the darkest chapter related to Mayo. But he rejoiced that the old attitude of slavish deference had gone; and whereas no mass meeting could hitherto be held unless it was to be presided over by his honour of the big house or 'some shoneen of a J.P.', now the people were standing on their own feet, as he had long been urging them to do. He was convinced that in Mayo the death knell of landlord domination had been sounded.

The other speakers used a more moderate tone, but all the speeches were variations on the theme—stated explicitly in several of them—'the

[1] *F.J.*, 9 June; *Connaught Telegraph*, 14 June, quoted in *Fall*, p. 155.
[2] See above, pp 191, 289.

land for the people'. Thomas Joyce, of Louisburgh, a stickler for perspective, went back to the garden of Eden, and, sketching the history of landholding from Adam through Noah and Numa Pompilius, the second king of Rome, to William the Conqueror, claimed that European society was free from landlords till the Norman conquest. John Walshe, of Balla, declared that 'the land of Ireland belongs to the people of Ireland as the soil of any country belongs to the people who occupy and cultivate it'; and that neither home rule nor repeal of the union could give peace to Ireland unless there was a radical change in the land system. Louden insisted that the tenants in Mayo could not pay the rents now demanded and that they could not survive if the present system continued. Thomas Hastings, of Louisburgh, gave some harrowing instances of landlord extortion. But the speech of the day was Parnell's.

Parnell was treated as the most honoured guest of the occasion, being escorted from his hotel to the place of meeting by a bodyguard of about five hundred young men on horseback. His speech was a characteristic mixture of realism, sincerity, political acumen, understatement, and rousing defiance. He believed, he said, that the maintenance of a landlord class was not for the greatest benefit of the greatest number. Ireland, he thought, had suffered more from the system than any other country, whereas England had succeeded better than any other country in adapting itself to it. But all over Europe the system had been found wanting and had been abolished. In France, in Belgium, in Prussia, and in Russia the land had been given to the occupying tenants; in some cases the landlords had been forcibly expropriated, in some cases they had been bought out. If, 'without injuring the landlord', the Irish tenant could be made the owner of his holding, it would be beneficial to the whole country; and he looked to this as the final settlement of the land problem. But in the meantime the tenant must be assured of the fruit of his labour so long as he paid a fair rent. What was a fair rent?

A fair rent is a rent the tenant can reasonably pay according to the times, but in bad times a tenant cannot be expected to pay as much as he did in good times three or four years ago. If such rents are insisted upon a repetition of the scenes of 1847 and 1848 will be witnessed. Now what must we do in order to induce the landlords to see the position? You must show the landlords that you intend to keep a firm grip of your homesteads and lands. You must not allow yourselves to be dispossessed as you[1] were dispossessed in 1847.

He hoped that the landlords would see reason and would make immediate reductions of rents that were 'out of all proportion to the

[1] Davitt (*Fall*, p. 154) renders this 'your fathers', here and on other points of detail departing from the press report he himself cites (*F.J.*, 9 June).

times'. But if not, 'you must help yourselves, and the public opinion of the world will stand by you'.[1]

Parnell, like Davitt, took care to connect the land question with the political question. Success in asserting the rights of the tenants, far from weakening the will for self-government, would strengthen it.

I have always noticed that the breaking down of barriers between different classes has increased their self-respect and increased the spirit of nationality amongst our people. I am convinced that nothing would more effectually promote the cause of self-government for Ireland than the breaking down of those barriers.... Nothing would be more effectual for that than the obtaining of a good land bill.... If we had the farmers the owners of the soil tomorrow, we would not be long without getting an Irish parliament.[2]

Parnell's speech at Westport ensured widespread publicity for the meeting in the press. Western papers, and especially the *Connaught Telegraph*, were enthusiastic, and in Dublin the *Nation*, and Pigott's *Irishman* and *Flag of Ireland*, were friendly; but otherwise the reaction varied from the pained reproof of the *Freeman*, no less alarmed by Davitt's reference to the clergy than by the 'wild and foolish schemes' he and others had advocated,[3] to the uninhibited denunciation by the *Dublin Evening Mail* of 'communism in Connaught'.[4] The *Belfast News Letter*, the *Limerick Recorder, The Times*, and the *Pall Mall Gazette* all shared the fear voiced in the Dublin press that law and order and the rights of property were threatened by the western agitation as never before. But the doctrine that tenants unable to pay 'unreasonable' rents had a right to hold on to their farms spread rapidly throughout Mayo. Further mass meetings, on the Westport model, were held at Milltown, in County Galway, a few miles over the Mayo border, and at Claremorris, Shrule, and Balla in Mayo. Together with those at Irishtown and Westport they established a threefold demand—for reduction of rents, for peasant proprietorship, and for national self-government. Davitt was a principal speaker at each of these meetings; Parnell did not attend any of them.

Davitt, at Milltown (15 June), proposed the second resolution, which declared the land system to be 'opposed to the moral sentiments of our race' and its continuance to be 'a criminal disregard of the social wellbeing and the best interests of our country'; and went on to demand 'the restoration of our national land system, which recognised the cultivator of the soil as the proprietor thereof'. In the meantime

he would advise the tenant farmers to feed themselves and their children, to live comfortably and decently, to keep their cabins neat and send their children to school, and, if there was sufficient left, to pay the landlords the rents they demand.

[1] Ibid. [2] *F.J.*, 9 June. [3] *Freeman* editorial, ibid. [4] *Dublin Evening Mail*, 10 June.

Let the landlords turn them out of their homes, if they would, at the point of the bayonet, and a spirit would spring up in Ireland that would be the destruction of landlords for ever.

He urged them to organise. The fenian organisation, to which he had the honour to belong, had been the means of disestablishing the anglican church in Ireland, and an organisation of the tenant farmers would disestablish the landlords.[1] The *Dublin Evening Mail* commented: 'These nihilists of Connaught . . . would reduce everthing to tumult and chaos'.[2] In the house of commons on 23 June the home rule member for Louth, Philip Callan, asked the Irish chief secretary whether the persons most prominent at the Milltown meeting were tenant farmers or in any way connected with the locality. It was a loaded question, aimed specially at Davitt and Brennan, which elicited a strictly correct and non-committal reply from Lowther,[3] and a sharp rejoinder in the *Freeman* from Davitt, who pointed out that the chairman and several of the principal speakers at the meeting were local farmers and that he and Brennan took part in the meeting by special invitation.[4] One of the local speakers, David Flannery, wrote to the *Freeman* to assure Callan that Davitt and Brennan were no strangers to the tenant farmers of Milltown; and the *Nation* commented editorially that to deny to such men as Davitt the right to intervene on behalf of the tenant farmers was on a par with sneering at Isaac Butt's efforts to reform the land system, because he was neither a landlord nor a tenant, or at Samuel Plimsoll's campaign to establish safety standards for ships because he was neither a shipowner nor a seaman.[5] O'Connor Power raised the subject again on 26 June, when Lowther referred contemptuously to the speakers at Milltown and dismissed Davitt as 'a convict at large on a ticket of leave'. This caused an uproar, headed by Power and Parnell, in which Power confronted the house with the Milltown resolutions, demolished Lowther's jibes at the speakers, and described Davitt as a man who had proved his devotion to his country by long years of suffering in penal servitude.[6]

Davitt's Milltown speech had drawn on him the renewed attention of the R.I.C., to whom he had not presented himself since 22 July 1878, shortly before his departure for America. The sub-inspector at Dunmore, County Galway, in reply to an inquiry from the inspector general of police, reported (20 June) that, apart from his violent speeches against the landlords and the politically suspect character of the people he associated with, he had done nothing to warrant forfeiture of his

[1] *F.J.*, 16 June; *Connaught Telegraph*, 21 June; *Tuam Herald*, 21 June; *Defence*, p. 219.

[2] 16 June.

[3] *F.J.*, 24 June.

[4] *F.J.*, 25 June.

[5] *Nation*, 28 June.

[6] *Hansard 3*, ccxlvii, 694–719; *F.J.*, 27 June, p. 7.

licence. He appeared to be paid for his attendance at land meetings. Superintendent Mallon, of the Dublin Metropolitan Police, reported that Davitt had not been prominent in any way in Dublin. He had no fixed address, but had stayed at the European Hotel in Bolton Street before going to America, and since his return at the Innisfallen Hotel, in Talbot Street, kept by J. W. Nally, formerly of Balla. The under-secretary (T. H. Burke) decided to take no action, but instructed the police to keep a careful watch on Davitt and to report at once if he should be guilty of any misconduct (30 June).[1]

In the interval between the Milltown and Claremorris meetings Davitt was subjected to a quite undeserved personal attack. In an open letter to the press (7 July) Archbishop MacHale declared that, next to a repeal of the union, 'beneficent legislation, defining the just rights of the landlords and tenants' was the measure dearest to the hearts of the people, but urged the farmers to act judiciously:

> Let them be guided, as of old, by their faithful allies, the priests, who, as a body, in good report and in evil report, stood in the front ranks of the combat. . . . Let no attempt at dissevering so sacred a union, fraught with blessings to the people, be tolerated.

He went on to warn them of the danger

> of finding themselves at the tail of a few unknown, strolling men, who, with affected grief, deploring the conditon of the tenantry, seek only to mount to place and preferment on the shoulders of the people.[2]

This imputation from a prelate whom he greatly respected[3] Davitt felt compelled to answer (10 July): 'I am neither a strolling nor an unknown man in the west'. The only personal advancement he was likely to obtain through his efforts for the people was a return to penal servitude.[4]

Despite MacHale's disapproval, the catholic clergy were beginning to rally to the agitation.[5] At monthly meetings of deaneries and other assemblies of the clergy in many parts of the west and south from May onwards, resolutions were adopted declaring that the tenant farmers were on the verge of ruin and appealing to the landlords to allow reasonable reductions of rent with all speed.[6] These statements were generally restrained and conciliatory, but in Clifden, on 2 July, a different note was sounded. A mass meeting of farmers, summoned for that date by the clergy and some leading laymen of the district, had

[1] S.P.O., R.P. 1879/10168, 10373 (1882/26234); A files, no. 590.
[2] *F.J.*, 10 July, Cashman, pp 94–5.
[3] Cf. above, pp 230, 241, 244.
[4] *F.J.*, 11 July p. 3; *Connaught Telegraph*, 12 July; Cashman, pp 95–7.
[5] See Matthew Harris's speech at Balla, 15 Aug. (*Connaught Telegraph*, 23 Aug.).
[6] Cashman, pp 86–7; *F.J.*, 14, 17, 19, 20 June, 4, 17, 28 July, 25 Aug.

been cancelled after the arrival of 100 armed police; and, instead, the promoters issued a fiery address, in the name of 'the clergy and people of Connemara'. No place, it was claimed, had suffered so much from the neglect of successive governments and the ill-treatment of poor industrious tenants by landlords. So long as landlord injustice continued, there would be no permanent peace, and the agitation would go on until the landlords were deprived of their legal right to commit murder by rack-rent and eviction.[1] By supporting the demand for reduction of rent the clergy incurred the charge of joining in an 'anti-rent agitation', but it was pointed out by the parish priest of Cahir that they were really the best friends of the landlords, enabling tenants to pay rents by acting as their securities with the banks.[2]

Boards of poor law guardians also joined in the swelling demand for rent-reduction.[3] The Ballinasloe guardians, while admitting that there were good landlords who had never raised rents that were 'below the valuation', asserted that, in their vicinity, whole villages had been 'swept away by the infamous Scotch'[4]—a reference to 'improving' landlords from Scotland who had invested their capital in buying estates in Galway. On the other hand resolutions of grand juries—composed of landowners and constituting, till 1898, the principal local authorities in the counties—called the attention of the government to 'the serious agitation against the payment of rents without regard to the rate or time at which the lands were let'.

> This illegal design is pursued by a system of wholesale intimidation by words and acts of menace, and by violent speeches, exciting the people to outrages against both landlords and tenants. We think these evils cannot be effectually removed without additional power being conferred on the executive by parliament.[5]

The *Freeman* described such resolutions as 'callous' and as 'placing the interests of landlords and tenants in deadly opposition'.[6] But that was just how landlords and tenants were increasingly coming to regard their interests.

Among those in whom the conviction had taken root that the only remedy for the land problem lay in peasant proprietorship was Canon Ulick Burke, parish priest of Claremorris, and formerly president of St Jarlath's College, Tuam, who had been decisively influenced by continental examples and by the teaching of John Stuart Mill.[7] He agreed to preside at the land meeting to be held at Claremorris on 13 July, which in consequence was the first in the series to be chaired

[1] *F.J.*, 3 July; Cashman, pp 91–2.
[2] Rev. John Ryan to editor of *Freeman* (*F.J.*, 24 July).
[3] *F.J.*, 18, 19, 24 June. [4] *F.J.*, 19 June. [5] *F.J.*, 21 July. [6] Ibid.
[7] Above, pp 45–6; Ulick Burke to Parnell, 18 Oct. (DP/RR2).

by a priest and to have priests on its platform. According to Devoy, he consented with great reluctance to preside after he had tried hard, but in vain, to persuade the organisers that there must be resolutions in favour of catholic education and the temporal power of the pope; they told him bluntly that sectarian resolutions were inadmissable, as they hoped to enlist protestants as well as catholics in the agitation.[1] Canon Burke opened the meeting by exhorting his hearers to show themselves worthy of the rights of freemen and warning them not to hurl defiance against either landlords or government. Davitt endorsed the first part of the admonition but blatantly ignored the second. In supporting a resolution declaring that security against eviction must be the farmers' battle cry pending 'a final settlement on the basis of a peasant proprietary', he declared 'that the farmers hitherto had been too moderate':

> They had simply asked for a reduction of rents which it was utterly impossible for them to pay. John Stuart Mill said rent was the surplus of the profits that came from the tenant's industry and outlay in tilling the soil. Where was this surplus of profits in Ireland today? In face of the depreciation of produce and large importations from America he did not say they were justified in paying no rent at all; but he did not say that a time might not come when they would have to make a protest as a nation against paying salary, in the form of rent, to a caste in Ireland that were fulfilling the duties of a landlord garrison. The old cry of 'fixity of tenure at fair rents' would do no longer. They must tell the English legislature that the concession they gave would be taken as instalments only of their just demands, and they must not be satisfied with their representatives unless they supported the full demand, that the soil of Ireland should be returned to the people of Ireland.[2]

These sentiments were warmly approved by a fiery young patriot of twenty-seven, who now for the first time identified himself with the land agitation. John Dillon, the second son of the Young Ireland leader, John Blake Dillon, was a nationalist no less ardent than Davitt; and if he was not a fenian it was because he rejected the physical force approach as inexpedient, not as morally wrong. He had joined the Home Rule League and had become a member of its council, but was sceptical of its prospects till the aggressive policy of Parnell and the obstructionists opened up new possibilities for parliamentary action. In the power-struggle between Parnell and Butt he had vehemently sided with Parnell, and his had been the hardest-hitting of the attacks the old leader had to endure at his last agonising meeting of the Home Rule League, on 4 February 1879. On the land question Dillon shared Davitt's rooted and passionate hatred of the landlord system; and his

[1] Devoy, XVII; *The land of Eire*, p. 51.
[2] *F.J.*, 14 July; *Tuam Herald*, 19 July; Cashman, pp 98–9; *Defence*, pp 220–21.

involvement in the land agitation had the self-abandoned quality so characteristic of Davitt. The paths of these two men, which now for the first time intersected, had been very different. Dillon belonged to a comfortable middle-class family of Roscommon origin. While Davitt was leading the life of a conspirator he had been studying arts in the Catholic University of Ireland, and while Davitt was enduring penal servitude in Dartmoor he had been a medical student at the Catholic University medical school in Cecilia Street. He had become a licentiate of the Royal College of Surgeons, and was demonstrating in anatomy in Cecilia Street when, in 1875, he embarked on a political career. Thereafter, thanks to his cousin, Mrs Anne Deane, and the family business ('Monica Duff') at Ballaghadereen, County Mayo, that she managed with conspicuous success, he was able to devote himself to politics without the distraction of having to earn his living.[1] But despite the contrasting patterns of their lives, and some disparities of temperament and personality, Davitt and Dillon were alike not only in their dedication to national independence and the cause of the tenant farmers but also in their integrity, their honesty, and their moral courage. The foundations were now laid of a friendship, based on mutual respect and understanding, that was never to be broken.

At Claremorris, Dillon proposed a motion calling on home rule M.P.s 'to demand with firmness, perseverance and obstructive force when necessary, the redress of those grievances which affect the agricultural classes'.

He was against physical force at present because there was too much physical force against them. They had no rifles, while the government had thousands of their fellow-countrymen [the Irish police] to oppose them. They had therefore only to look to parliament, where a man had arisen who had shown the Irish people a method by which they could win their rights, and although that man was a landlord he was not inclined to turn him out. That man was Charles Stewart Parnell.[2]

The Claremorris meeting was the only one of its kind attended by Devoy, and he was exhilarated as he watched the contingents of farmers from far and near marching into the town.

I had seen big processions in Dublin, but never a 'monster meeting' in the country, and this one was a sight never to be forgotten. Nearly every contingent had a detachment of horsemen, and all of them were marshalled by mounted men. The horses were greatly disturbed by the bands, and it was sometimes hard to keep them in line. It was very amusing to see the set faces of the mounted men as their horses reared and pranced when the banging of the big drums startled them.

The most picturesque figure at the meeting, Devoy considered, was

[1] *Fall*, p. 158; Lyons, *Dillon*, pp 1-2, 7-8, 15-18, 20-27, 148; *D.N.B., 1922-30.*

[2] *F.J.*, 14 July 79, quoted in Lyons, *Dillon*, p. 31.

'Scrab' Nally, who, dressed in light brown tweed, sat on the platform and acted as cheer-leader with marked success. Devoy was surprised to find that the chairman, whose work for the Irish language had earned him a great reputation, was not treated with any deference by the audience, and also that, though there must have been thousands of native Irish-speakers at the meeting, he did not hear a word of Irish spoken. While the public meeting was still in progress, Davitt and Devoy attended a private meeting of Mayo fenians in the upper room of the local public house. Here the perennial animosity to O'Connor Power flared up again: much to Davitt's annoyance, P. W. Nally, who was now anti-Power, was elected to represent Mayo on the provincial convention of Connacht in place of John O'Kane who was pro-Power. Power's supporters then tried, but failed, to prevent the reelection of Mark Ryan, a hard-line fenian,[1] as provincial representative on the supreme council. Davitt and Devoy accompanied Nally to the convention, held the same evening at Ballyhaunis, where, among other representatives, they met Patrick Joseph Sheridan, a hotel-keeper of Tubbercurry, who was county centre for Sligo, and soon to be one of the leading organisers of the land agitation in the west.[2]

Devoy returned to New York a few days after the Claremorris meeting.[3] During his three and a half months in Ireland his energies had been focused on fenian business; his part in the land agitation had been that of a spectator. In the report that he made on 11 August to the ninth general convention of Clan na Gael, held at Wilkesbarre, Pennsylvania,[4] he referred only to strictly fenian business—to the organisation, functioning, equipment, manpower, and morale of the I.R.B., and to the successful efforts that had been made to restore unity to the movement, which had been disrupted by the secession of the north of England division from the supreme council and by an attempt by James Stephens, supported by O'Donovan Rossa and the remnant of his Fenian Brotherhood in America, to recover his former authority. Devoy claimed that, as the outcome of his mission and that of his predecessor, Carroll, 'the national movement once more throbs with a healthy and vigorous life'.[5] Though this report had not a word to say about the land agitation, Devoy was now one of its strongest supporters in America, seeing it as the most effective means of promoting the new departure. When Davitt, finding himself in need of money to continue the agitation, thought of going on a lecture tour of the U.S. to raise funds, he wrote in August to Devoy and other American

1 Above, pp 278, 279.

2 Devoy, XVII; Personal histories, p. 17; *S.C.P.*, i, 55, 57, vi, 225; Ryan, *Fenian memories*, p. 113.

3 Devoy, XVII.

4 *S.C.P.*, iv, 505–11, 552, 554.

5 *S.C.P.*, p. 508.

friends to that effect. Devoy responded confidentially with an advance, in several instalments, of $2,000 voted by the trustees of the 'national' (formerly the 'skirmishing') fund, of whom he was one, to make it unnecessary for Davitt to go to America. Soon after the Land League was formed (21 October), rumours began to spread that it was started with money raised for terrorist purposes.[1]

Clan na Gael's undiminished interest in military preparations had been shown by the despatch of another envoy to Ireland in April 1879 to supplement Devoy's tour of inspection. This was General F. F. Millen, who was regarded as a military expert and for some years had been the most extreme advocate and projector of fenian schemes of foreign intervention in support of armed action in Ireland. He had succeeded Stephens as head of the fenian organisation in Ireland on Stephens's arrest on 11 November 1865, but had quickly lost the confidence of the military council that had appointed him and had been relieved of his office.[2] Returning to America, he had given valuable information about the fenian conspiracy to the British consul general in New York in 1866,[3] his treachery going undiscovered by his fenian associates. It remained unsuspected, even by so lynx-eyed an observer as Devoy,[4] and even though he and Davitt both distrusted Millen and cold-shouldered him during his visit to Ireland.[5] Davitt believed that his mission would not justify its cost,[6] and the pretentious report that Millen read to the Wilkesbarre convention on 9 August[7] had little of the informativeness and the realism of Devoy's. Millen was, of course, no less silent about the new departure than Devoy. But the report that the convention received on 8 August from its outgoing executive body contained explicit reference to the subject. No member of the executive, this report claimed, except Carroll, its chairman, was involved in Devoy's initiative of 24 October 1878, and no member had expressed any opinion on it, at least not officially.[8] But Clan na Gael, though it had never had anything to do with parliamentary agitation, should not be indifferent to the continued misrepresentation of Ireland at Westminster. One hundred Parnells sent there to protest 'in an

1 *D.P.B.*, i, 452, 454, 459-60, 468-9; ii, 558; Cashman, pp 217-18; *S.C.P.*, ix, 358-9; *Fall*, pp 169-70.

2 Devoy, *Recollections*, pp 73-5.

3 P.R.O., H.O.45/O.S./7799/159, 165, 210.

4 The late Desmond Ryan, who was steeped in fenian history, was evidently unaware of Millen's role as informer. The only published account of it that is known to me is in *Fenian fever* (London, 1971), pp 19-26, 47-51, 91-4, by Dr Leon O Broin, who has drawn upon the sources in the State Paper Office.

5 *D.P.B.*, i, 426-7, 430-31, 443-4, 446, 447-8.

6 D to Devoy, 13 Feb. 79 (*D.P.B.*, i. 391-2).

7 *S.C.P.*, iv, 552, 570-77.

8 Cf. above, pp 258, 264.

official and authoritative way' against 'the whole villainy of English rule' would not in itself liberate Ireland, but might favourably influence foreign governments and rouse public opinion at home to a fighting condition. Those who complained that their darling hope of dying on the battlefield of Irish independence had been ruined by the new departure should possess their souls in patience: there would yet be opportunity for those with blood to spill. But in the view both of the Clan executive and of the supreme council the immediate need was to prevent useless bloodshed in Connacht, where tenant farmers on the verge of starvation might rush into a premature local insurrection.[1]

Parnell had not as yet followed up his Westport initiative. In July he was involved in a critical by-election at Ennis, where his nominee, James Lysaght Finigan, defeated the moderate home-ruler, William O'Brien, Q.C., supported though he was by the council of the Home Rule League, the *Freeman's Journal*, and the local clergy.[2] Between the Westport meeting and 31 August he did not take any prominent part in the land agitation, and during all that time Davitt continued to be the primary inspiration and directing force behind the movement. Davitt countered MacHale's second condemnation by an orderly mass-invasion of the archbishop's cathedral town of Tuam; and on the last Sunday in July he was the principal speaker at yet another monster meeting, at Shrule, where he said that

> a reduction of rents may tide you over the present crisis . . ., but what the prosperity of your country and the social amelioration of yourselves and children demand is a . . . total eradiction of a chronic malady which has eaten into the very vitals of Ireland (27 July).[3]

The landlords, he said at Balla (15 August), were threatening through their West British press to stand on their legal rights and exact all that the law entitled them to so long as popular meetings like the present disturbed the country. Nothing could be so serviceable to the land movement as this 'headlong vindictiveness' of the landlords; for it would force the landless millions of Ireland to 'square issues with its landocracy' and settle at once and forever the question to whom the soil of their fatherland belonged. Mayo could congratulate itself on the lead it had given, especially now that the north was beginning to rally to the land-for-the-people cry. The south and east would soon follow. The sympathy of the home rule M.P.s with the farmers should be measured only by the lengths they were prepared to go to win back the soil for those who worked it; and the farmers would be false to

[1] S.P.O., A files, no. 615.

[2] *F.J.*, 28 July, pp 5, 7; R. B. O'Brien, *Parnell*, i, 101; William O'Brien, *Recollections*, p. 222.

[3] *Tuam Herald*, 2 Aug.; Cashman, pp 98-100.

their own interests if they allowed any man to call himself their representative who would not pledge himself before the world as an enemy to landlordism and an advocate of peasant proprietorship. James Daly declared that if half the Irish constituencies were represented by such men as Parnell, rents would soon be reduced; and while counselling the farmers not to commit crime, and to let the landlords evict if they dared, interpreted Parnell's war-cry at Westport to mean: 'if they turn you out by day, go in by night . . .; hold on at the point of the bayonet'.[1] This encouragement to evicted tenants to retake possession of their farms when opportunity offered was to be widely adopted.

By this time the agitation had gained two valuable new recruits, Andrew J. Kettle and Patrick Duggan, bishop of Clonfert. Kettle, an indefatigable champion of tenant right, had been a faithful supporter of Butt, had come into close contact also with Parnell, and had become acquainted with Dillon. He had been one of the first to realise the gravity of the agrarian situation, and of the agitation springing up in the west. Parnell, urged by Davitt to take part in it, had consulted Kettle, who had advised him to do so provided that it was to be an entirely open movement.[2] Kettle's own commitment to the agitation made it likely that a large body of moderate land-reformers would follow his example.

Bishop Duggan was a Galway man; like Davitt, he was the son of a small farmer evicted in the 50s and a fervent believer in 'the land for the people'. He combined extremist views with personal humility, simple living, dislike of publicity, and active concern about everything affecting his Galway diocese. He had been one of twenty catholic clergy prosecuted for using undue influence in favour of the home rule candidate in the Galway by-election of 1872, and though acquitted for lack of evidence had earned notoriety especially embarrassing to a prelate known to be a fenian-sympathiser. He had supported the Connacht tenant-right agitation of 1876–8. He entered wholeheartedly into the spirit of the new agitation, and remained a faithful though unobtrusive supporter and a trusted adviser of its leaders. Between him and Davitt, whom he greatly admired, a deep and lasting friendship grew up.[3]

Davitt was now convinced that the energies released by the agitation

[1] *Connaught Telegraph*, 23 Aug.; S.P.O., R.P. 1879/13819.

[2] Above, p. 273; Kettle, *The material for victory*, ch. I–III. Kettle's dating of his conversation with Parnell about the Westport meeting is distinctly vague.

[3] W. S. Blunt, *The land war in Ireland* (1912), passim; D to Sabina Davitt, from Richmond prison, 1883 (DP/D5); Bp Duggan to D, 20 Apr.–2 July 84, 31 Dec. 94 (DP/M); Thomas Brett, *Life of Patrick Duggan, bishop of Clonfert* (1921); E. R. Norman, *The catholic church and Ireland in the age of rebellion, 1859–73*, pp 422–8; above, p. 191.

needed to be canalised. He urged Parnell to join him in setting up a permanent organisation, but Parnell's misgivings[1] were not yet allayed, and Davitt decided that to go a stage further without him was the best way to make sure of securing him as a leader. So a convention of delegates from all parts of Mayo was summoned to meet at Castlebar for the purpose of setting up a county league of tenant farmers that would serve as the nucleus of a national body.[2]

The Castlebar convention was a historic occasion both because of its outcome and because it was the first delegate meeting since the all-Ireland catholic convention had met in Tailors' Hall, Back Lane, Dublin, in December 1792, and the Ulster protestant convention at Dungannon in February 1793. Such representative assemblies, demanding radical reform in an era of revolution, had been seen by an apprehensive government as a threat to the authority of parliament itself; consequently by the convention act of 1793[3] any assembly other than parliament chosen to represent the people as a whole, or the people of any province, county, district, or town was thenceforth prohibited. Under the union, though there was no longer a parliament in Ireland, it was unlawful to hold a delegate meeting, however small, for any purpose, however moderate, whereas other public meetings, even on the scale of O'Connell's monster gatherings, were lawful. The home rule conference of 1873 had to be summoned by the clumsy expedient of a 'national requisition'. The Home Rule League had to function without a representative assembly of its members, whereas the Home Rule Confederation of Great Britain, where the convention act did not apply, had its annual convention to which all its branches sent delegates. The Home Rule Confederation highlighted another anomaly of the act by making Dublin the venue of its annual convention of 1878 (21-2 October):[4] for the act did not prohibit the holding of a convention in Ireland if the delegates (though Irish) were from Britain. The home rule party had been demanding the repeal of the act since 1872, and in 1879, with decisive support from Joseph Cowen, liberal member for Newcastle-upon-Tyne, it won over the government, which accepted the view that the act was obsolete, there being no danger of anyone seeking to usurp the authority of parliament. In the commons no reference was made in the debate to the growing agitation in Ireland, but in the upper house Lord Oranmore and Browne alluded the meetings 'of a communistic character' lately held there.[5] The

[1] Above, pp 300-01.
[2] *Defence*, p. 222; *Fall*, pp 159-60.
[3] 33 Geo. III, c. 29 (Ire.).
[4] *F.J.*, 22-3 Oct. 78; R.B. O'Brien, *Parnell*, i, 173.
[5] *Hansard 3*, ccxliv, 1772-1821; ccxlv, 817; ccxlvi, 1428-9, 1898.

repeal bill became law on 21 July,[1] just in time to enable Davitt to follow up his three months of land meetings in Mayo with his delegate convention of farmers at Castlebar.[2]

In promoting the convention, which met at Daly's Hotel on 16 August, Davitt was helped by two local leaders, Louden and Daly,[3] and by three prominent fenians from outside the county, Egan, Brennan, and Harris. No clergy were among those reported as attending, but Rev. William Joyce, P.P. of Louisburgh, wrote regretting that he could not be present and expressing support for the objects of the convention. Under Louden's chairmanship the convention inaugurated a body called 'The National Land League of Mayo', in accordance with a statement of objects, rules, and principles, written[4] and proposed by Davitt. The objects of the league were:

(a) to use every means, 'compatible with justice, morality, and right reason, which shall not clash defiantly with the constitution', to abolish the existing land system and replace it with one that would respect 'the social rights and interests of our people' and 'the traditions and moral sentiments of our race' [in other words, peasant proprietorship];

(b) pending a final settlement of the land question, to bring the widest possible publicity to bear on the injustices and injuries inflicted on farmers in Mayo by rack-renting, eviction, and other arbitrary actions by the landlords, and to resist such actions by every means within the law;

(c) as means of affecting (b), to publish full details of landownership and landholding in the county, including rents charged in excess of the government valuation; to announce impending evictions for non-payment of excessive rent, and to make such evictions the scene of public demonstrations; to publish the names of all persons involved in evictions, and of all persons who rented or occupied farms from which others had been evicted for non-payment of 'exorbitant'[5] rent or who offered a higher rent than the previous occupier;

(d) whenever possible to render assistance to members evicted or otherwise wronged by landlords or their agents;

(e) to undertake the defence of its members or those of affiliated clubs when involved in legal actions brought by landlords or their agents in connection with their farms;

[1] 42 & 43 Vict., c. 28.

[2] O'Donnell, *Irish parl. party*, i, 327-9.

[3] See above, pp 191-2.

[4] Cashman, p. 25.

[5] Cf. above, p. 119.

(f) to organise local clubs or farmers' defence associations, hold public meetings, and issue pamphlets on the land question;

(g) finally, to act as a vigilance committee in Mayo, publicising the conduct of its grand jury, poor law guardians, town commissioners, and M.P.s, wherever the interests of its members were involved.

Membership of the league was open to anyone who endorsed its aims and paid an annual subscription of at least five shillings. Members of local defence associations elected as representatives to the league were to be *ex officio* members. Louden was elected president, James Daly vice-president, H. Feeny (town commissioner) treasurer, P. W. Nally and J. W. Walshe secretaries—all local men. Nally was not present, and subsequently declined to act.[1]

The principles of the league were set out in a manifesto on the theme: 'the land of Ireland belongs to the people of Ireland'. John Stuart Mill was cited as claiming that absolute ownership of land in Ireland only came in with the Norman conquest, and had 'never to this day been recognised by the moral sentiments of the people'. 'The right to hold the land goes as it did in the beginning with the right to till it.' Davitt went on to characterise the Irish land system as one in which the rights of the cultivators of the soil and the well-being, peace, and prosperity of the people at large were sacrificed to the interests of a small, idle, non-producing class, for whose protection Britain maintained 'a standing army of semi-military police' at the expense of the landless millions. The system must be abolished, with compensation to the landlords. 'The interests of the landlords are pecuniary and can be compensated, but the interests of the people of Ireland, dependent on the produce of the soil, are their very existence.' Privately Davitt admitted to Devoy that he would prefer to make the landlords 'disgorge', without giving them a penny of compensation, but that this was not practical politics.[2] His manifesto concluded with an appeal to the farmers to organise themselves and bring their collective strength to bear on the demand for peasant proprietorship, 'which alone can fully satisfy the Irish people'.[3]

The *Freeman*, as alert to the importance of the tenant farmers as to that of the 'time-honoured alliance' between priests and people, saw the Castlebar convention as marking a decisive stage in the land campaign. It would soon become impossible for responsible politicians to ignore any longer the necessity of dealing with the land question

[1] *Defence*, p. 225.
[2] D to Devoy, 23 Aug. 79 (*D.P.B.*, i, 453).
[3] *Connaught Telegraph*, 16, 23 Aug; *F.J.*, 18 Aug.; *Nation*, 23 Aug.; Cashman, pp 101–2; *Defence*, pp 222, 396–8; *Fall*, pp 160–64; Curtis and McDowell, *Irish historical documents*, pp 254–9.

in a broad and comprehensive spirit, and if they wanted to understand the direction the land agitation was likely to take they would do well to ponder the proceedings at Castlebar. The manifesto of the convention might have extravagances of style but it embodied 'some principles which will yet triumph'. 'We ask the landlords to examine for themselves the demands put forward and see whether they are antagonistic to any just interest.'[1]

The Land League of Mayo served its purpose admirably, lasting only two months before being absorbed by the Irish National Land League,[2] of which it proved to be the prototype. The characteristics of the Mayo league were derived from the local agitation of the preceding four months. (1) The league was an open and lawful body, which anyone willing to work for its objects could join, whatever his political or religious identity. (2) Its aims were to defend tenants against the arbitrary exercise of power by landlords—especially the exaction of unreasonable rent—and to bring about the conversion of occupiers into owners, by promoting collective action among the tenants. (3) It marked out as the enemies to be resisted not only evicting landlords but also tenants who took evicted farms or outbid other tenants: 'the land-grabber' was the buttress of the rack-renting evil and the worst foe of the struggling tenant.[3] (4) The league's prescribed methods were non-violent and technically legal, but included procedures certain to result in intimidation. (5) It was a mass movement of farmers, large and small, and of townsmen, especially shopkeepers, under middle-class leadership. (6) It combined existing farmers' clubs and defence associations whose aim had been the '3 Fs', and directed their efforts to the more radical goal of peasant propietorship. (7) It was initiated, inspired, and led by laymen, in face of open hostility from the local catholic archbishop but with growing support from the catholic parochial clergy. (8) It was in principle non-sectarian, but its members were nearly all catholics, while the landlords, against whom it was directed, were nearly all protestants. (9) It was not explicitly committed to any political object, but it was identified with the demand for self-government (nearly always the subject of one of the two or three resolutions adopted at land meetings), and its leading members were either advanced home-rulers or fenians. (10) The grounds on which it sought to justify its actions were a compound of natural rights, national claims, and English radical thought, especially that of John Stuart Mill: the landlord system was doubly condemned, both as

[1] *F.J.*, 20 Aug., p. 5; also, 14 July, p. 5.
[2] *Defence*, p. 225.
[3] See above, p. 290; *Fall*, p. 165.

contrary to social justice and as rooted in the English conquest of Ireland.

In its statement of aims the Mayo Land League accepted as the measure of a reasonable rent the 'government valuation'. This was a comprehensive valuation of holdings in Ireland for purposes of local taxation (including the poor rate), carried out between 1852 and 1865 under the direction of Sir Richard Griffith, commissioner of valuation. Generally known as 'Griffith's valuation' (also as the 'tenement valuation' and 'poor law valuation'), it was widely used as a yardstick of rent for which, on the average, holdings might reasonably be expected to let. Based on prices ruling in 1849–51, it did not represent the true value of land after 1852, when prices rose well above the 1849–51 levels.[1] When, however, as in 1877–9 the value of agricultural output slumped, 'Griffith's valuation' could be plausibly invoked as a measure of excessive rent; and in that context it became part of the vocabulary of the land war.

With the formation of the Mayo Land League the agitation acquired a solid core and began to spread to the rest of Ireland. On six Sundays from 31 August to 19 October, the land crisis was ventilated at sixteen mass meetings; four of these were in Mayo, three in County Galway, and two in County Sligo, while the remaining seven were widely scattered—one in each of the counties of Limerick, Cork, Carlow, Queen's County, Meath, and Londonderry. Davitt was the principal speaker at the western meetings, addressing one on five of the six Sundays on which they were held;[2] but Parnell, after three months of virtual silence, was just as prominent at the other meetings, and spoke at as many. While the tone in the south and east might be more moderate than that of the western meetings, the same message was delivered by Davitt, Parnell, and a host of other speakers (notably Louden, Daly, Harris, Brennan, Ferguson, Dillon, T. D. Sullivan, and a number of Parnellite M.P.s—J. G. Biggar, A. M. Sullivan, W. H. O'Sullivan) to the tenant farmers everywhere: if you stand together in refusing to pay excessive rents and in asserting your right to the ownership of your farms you can and will save yourselves from ruin and compel the state to buy out the landlords. The highly-coloured rhetoric of many of the speeches was matched by the realism with which speakers, and especially Davitt and Parnell, sought to prepare the farmers for the crisis of the coming November rent-day.

Parnell at Limerick on 31 August, and again at Navan on 12 October,

[1] W. E. Vaughan, 'Landlord and tenant relations in Ireland, 1850–78', pp 359–75.

[2] Tuam (21 Sept.), Headford (28 Sept.), Ballinrobe (5 Oct.), Annaghdown (12 Oct.), Newport (19 Oct.); he was not present at the Ballyhaunis meeting of 31 Aug.

expanded the advice he and Malachy O'Sullivan had given the farmers at Westport about not paying more than a fair rent: let the tenants in each estate combine and demand a reduction of rent; if they got no reduction let them offer the landlord what they considered to be a fair rent; if he disagreed with their estimate let them offer to submit the question to arbitration; if he refused, let them again offer a fair rent in return for a clear acquittance; if he still refused, they should put the money in their pockets and hold it until he came to his senses. If they were evicted, no one must take over their land, and there must be an end to the folly of farmers competing for such land. If the tenants acted on this plan, they could not be defeated.[1] At the Limerick meeting the condemnation of the 'land-grabber'[2] was made the subject of a resolution pledging the farmers not to take any holding from which a tenant had been evicted for failure to pay excessive rent—a pledge that was to be constantly endorsed on land platforms from then onwards.[3] At Maryborough on 5 October Dillon added the suggestion that, if tenants were evicted through acting on the plan of collective resistance proposed by Parnell, they should 'put a ban on the land'; 'if any man then takes up that land, let no man speak to him or have any business transaction with him'.[4] This appears to be the first explicit statement of the principle of boycotting, which was implicit in one of the procedures Davitt had prescribed for the Mayo Land League.[5] The agitation had already caused many landlords to yield to their tenants' demands for reductions, and Davitt privately believed that the pressure should be kept up till there was nothing left to reduce.[6] At Limerick on 31 August and at Tipperary on 21 September, Parnell made the very perceptive point that, if the current trend continued, being a landlord would become so undesirable that landlords would be glad to sell out.[7] The pressure for rent reduction at the land meetings of these months was accompanied by a growing demand for immediate government action to provide employment for farmers and labourers, through emergency schemes of 'reproductive public works' such as arterial drainage, reclamation of waste, and railway extension.[8]

Davitt was no less emphatic than Parnell in urging tenants to withhold from the November rents whatever proportion was vital to their

[1] Above, pp 304, 305–6; *F.J.*, 1 Sept., 13 Oct.

[2] See above, pp 290, 317, 319.

[3] For example, at Ballinrobe, 5 Oct.; Galway, 2 Nov.; Killanin, 16 Nov.; at Turloughmore, 16 Nov.; at Camlough, 13 Dec. (*Connaught Telegraph*, 11 Oct.; *F.J.*, 3, 17 Nov.; 15 Dec.).

[4] *F.J.*, 6 Oct.; Lyons, *Dillon*, p. 32.

[5] Above, p. 319.

[6] D to Devoy, 23 Aug. (*D.P.B.*, i, 453).

[7] *F.J.*, 1, 22 Sept.

[8] *F.J.*, 22, 29 Sept., 13 Oct.; *Connaught Telegraph*, 11 Oct.

survival. At Tuam, on 21 September he declared that, if the land did not yield sufficient profit, the tenant only had the right to withhold, but had no right to pay, rent that would ruin himself and his family—and defraud the shopkeepers of what was due to them for the credit they had allowed him.[1] A week later at Headford (County Galway), he gave a characteristic statement of the case for withholding rent:

> As rent for land can only in equity and justice be defined as the surplus profit accruing from the capital and labour expended on its use . . ., it follows that rent exists only in proportion to such surplus profits; and to claim it under conditions which admit of no profits at all, but of positive loss, would be like insisting upon income tax from a workhouse pauper. With cattle unsaleable from low prices, cereal produce reduced to half its former value by foreign competition, and the accumulative misfortune of unprecedented wet seasons, it is an insensate ignoring of terrible facts . . . to pretend that farmers can meet . . . their customary rents by November next if substantial reductions are not made. What then is to be done? Well, the question for the farmer to decide . . . is whether the supreme right of existence conferred by providence upon himself and his family is to give way to the arbitrary rights represented by the wealth and power of the landlord—whether what is required to feed himself and children during the winter should be preserved for that purpose or handed over to the lord of the soil, who never earned a penny of it. The course I would advise to be followed towards non-abating landlords would be to offer them that portion of the net profit of their farms earned during this year which would be over and above the requirements of the farmers and their families until the next rent day; and if such an offer should be 25, 50, or 99 per cent below the customary rent, but at the same time represents all they can pay without injuring themselves, starving their families, or neglecting higher claims, there is no power which in justice can compel them to pay any more. The landlord who would refuse to grant any reduction, notwithstanding the general voice of the country being in favour of the demand, should receive no rent at all.[2]

Because Davitt was so emotionally involved in the agitation, he was the more concerned to rebut the charge of incitement to violence already being cast at it. At Ballinrobe on 5 October he denied 'with scorn and contempt' that he had ever used language which had directly or indirectly encouraged or sanctioned acts of violence. The agitation had a higher aim, a nobler object than taking vengeance on individuals, and anyone engaged in it who advocated any such thing was guilty of great folly. He went on to turn the charge against the landlords themselves. Violence was built into the landlord system: agrarian outrages, far from being caused by the agitation, had long been endemic in rural Ireland. Those who charged the leaders of the agitation with responsibility for acts of violence were moral assassins; and he counter-charged the landlord system with the murder of two millions of Irish people, with the enforced exile of two millions more, and with the impoverishment of two-thirds of those whom it left alive. Such a system stood

[1] *F.J.*, 22 Sept.

[2] *F.J.*, 29 Sept.

condemned before high heaven as infamous and inhuman, and it was the duty of its surviving victims to strive continually for its abolition.[1]

Since June the R.I.C. had kept attentive eyes on Davitt, but it was not till 12 October that a speech he made at Annaghdown (County Galway) raised the question whether he should not now be required to observe the condition, waived in February 1878,[2] of regular reporting to the police. There was nothing new in the substance of the speech, but the police seem to have taken exception to rhetorical passages such as this:

> Stand firmly and self-reliantly against the brood of cormorant vampires that has sucked the life blood out of the country, that has banished our brothers and sisters, and that has made our people a nation of paupers, and ere long we will have no legalised plundering system in Ireland to sustain the most profligate horde of unmitigated land thieves that ever cursed a people and robbed them of the fruits of their industry.[3]

The Irish attorney general (Edward Gibson) considered (13 October) that Davitt might be required to comply with all the conditions of his licence, but that was a matter for the home secretary (Cross). The chief secretary (Lowther) agreed, and wondered whether a prosecution might not also be instituted against him in Ireland?[4] But for some time no action was taken.[5]

It was inevitable that at land meetings there were no spokesmen of the landlords as a class, though individual landlords were sometimes invited to attend. An invitation to a land meeting at Tullow (County Carlow) was sent to one of the great landlords of the county, the famous Art MacMurrough Kavanagh, M.P., of Borris. In his reply, which was read at the meeting on 28 September, he declared that it was a paramount duty of landlords to help their tenants in times of distress, and he believed that the landlords of Carlow would, as always, bear their reasonable share of the burden. As to a settlement of the land question, he had always supported in parliament the principle of establishing a class of peasant proprietors. But beyond that he refused to go:

> I am not prepared to take what belongs to one man to give it to another or to temporise with communism to secure a seat in parliament . . . I have the strongest objection to appear to sanction by my presence a movement which I cannot too strongly condemn, believing . . . that it is initiated solely to serve the ambitious ends of an unprincipled, unscrupulous political section, and in no sense . . . for the benefit of the tenant farmer class.[6]

Another great landlord, E. R. King-Harmon, M.P., of Rockingham,

[1] *Connaught Telegraph*, 11 Oct.

[2] Above, p. 194.

[3] *F.J.*, 13 Oct.

[4] S.P.O., R.P. 1879/13819, 16016, 17630; 10401 (1882/26234).

[5] See below, pp 350–51.

[6] *F.J.*, 29 Sept.

Boyle (County Roscommon), similarly declined to attend the land meeting held at Dromore West, County Sligo on 5 October.

Speeches have been made and sentiments enunciated which I consider to be calculated to mislead the people, to injure the cause which they profess to advocate, and to embitter the relations between classes of persons whose interests should be bound up together. The entire class of landlords has been held up to public odium, and resolutions have been passed pledging the tenants to adopt courses which, if carried out, must infallibly lead to the ruin of many. . . . Threatening letters, brutal outrages, and lately an attempt to murder in an adjoining county . . . have followed in rapid succession. It is my deliberate opinion that the cause of these terribly sad events can only be found in the speeches of reckless agitators.[1]

And at Cork on 5 October William Shaw, M.P., chairman of the home rule party, and himself a banker, showed courage and insight in arguing that the land question could not be understood in merely general terms but had to be looked at in detail. There were good and bad landlords, and good and bad tenants.

A bad landlord gives a 25% reduction when he ought, perhaps, to give 50%, having screwed the rent up to starvation point. The good landlord who has not raised his rent for generations is the man we ought to consider, and treat tenderly and generously.

There were good landlords in County Cork who, if conscious that their tenants were unable to pay, would make large reductions in their rent. There were also bad tenants who could not make a living out of their farms however moderate their rents, and it was inevitable that they should go to the wall. Resolutions calling on men not to take a farm from which such a tenant had been evicted were 'stuff and nonsense'. Unless human nature changed, there would always be farmers on the watch to add other farms to their own, and it would not surprise him if some men very eloquent on land platforms were not doing precisely this.[2]

The contrast between this and Parnell's approach to the agitation is a measure of the distance separating the official leader of the home rule party from his formidable young rival. Moderate home-rulers were alarmed by a movement inspired by the 'western incendiaries', over which they had no control; but even Parnell, though conspicuously involved in it from 31 August, was not prepared to undertake the responsibility of formally leading it[3] until he was convinced that to do so was politically necessary for him. The progress of the movement in August and September proved that necessity. By 10 September Davitt saw the agitation as destined to do more for Ireland than all previous movements since 1798: the entire countryside, he believed,

[1] *F.J.*, 6 Oct. [2] *F.J.*, 6 Oct. [3] D to Devoy, 23 Aug. (*D.P.B.*, i, 453).

had accepted the idea of abolishing landlordism, and all active nationalists would combine on this platform.[1] The agitation was now being strongly supported by the Irish-American press, headed by Ford's *Irish World* and O'Reilly's *Pilot*. Above all, the predictions of a disastrous harvest were being appallingly substantiated. Before the combined pressure of these events Parnell yielded. In discussions with Davitt and his political colleagues, he agreed to take the initiative in converting the Mayo Land League into a national organisation, under his presidency, on the understanding that its programme should be such as could be advocated in the house of commons. He also agreed that the Central Tenants' Defence Association should be merged in the new league, and that A. J. Kettle and other key men in the former should be included in the executive of the latter. On this basis Parnell issued on 29 September a letter, accompanied by an 'Appeal to the Irish race' written by Davitt, inviting a number of selected public men to join

> a committee for the purpose of appealing to our countrymen abroad and more especially in America, for assistance in forwarding the new land agitation in favour of the ownership of the soil by the occupier, and also for the purpose of upholding the tenants during this terrible crisis by the promotion of organisation. I enclose you a copy of the appeal that we have drawn up, and trust that you will permit yourself to be added to the committee, and allow your name to be appended to the appeal.[2]

With this thoroughly characteristic piece of understatement Parnell set in motion negotiations that led to the foundation in Dublin on 21 October of the Irish National Land League, a body that was shortly to challenge the very authority of the state itself.

The foundation of the Land League may be taken as the point at which the second fenian new departure, initiated and promoted by Devoy and Davitt,[3] became overshadowed by a third new departure, pioneered by Davitt and arising out of the western agitation. What was the essential distinction between these new departures? Not the concept of home rule activists and opportunist fenians making common cause. Not the concept of this community of interests being aimed immediately at a radical settlement of the land system, and ultimately at national self-government. Not the concept of Parnell's leadership of an open movement in which constitutionalists and revolutionists would cooperate for legitimate objects. These concepts were characteristic both of the second and third new departures. The essence of the distinction between the two lay in the fact that the one was a scheme,

[1] D to J.B. O'Reilly, 10 Sept. (*S.C.P.*, v, 186).

[2] *Fall*, pp 168–71.

[3] See above, pp 249–53.

designed in America and approved by the Clan na Gael executive, for a combination between the fenian body and Parnellite home-rulers to be led by Parnell on conditions prescribed by its fenian authors, whereas the other was a scheme for a popular front on the land question under Parnell's leadership, which grassroots fenians in Ireland and Clan na Gael were expected to support unconditionally. The new departure of 1878 was not carried into effect, that of 1879 was realised in the Land League. Davitt was joint-author of the new departure of 1878, but sole author of that of 1879, as founder of the Land League.

Without abandoning his fenian commitment to self-government he had plunged into agrarian agitation, and had shown incomparable genius for inspiring and organising on new lines the spirit of resistance in the hard-pressed tenant farmers of the west, to may thousands of whom he was now a familiar and greatly respected figure. No one was more uninhibited in denouncing the landlord system, or more earnest in reprobating violence. No one was more insistent that the agitation must be an open and broadly-based movement, appealing to the widest possible spectrum of the national life. For him the cause of the tenant farmers was inseparable from that of national independence, while the landlords were inseparable from the English domination of Ireland. Above all it was Davitt who constantly sought to justify the agitation on grounds of natural justice, seeing the struggle of the tenant farmers of Ireland in the perspective of humanity struggling against privilege and exploitation. The strength and sincerity of his feeling are all too often obscured for us by turgid rhetoric, but what impressed his peasant audiences was not only his matter but the intensity of his manner, the clarity of his utterance, and his striking appearance. He was the most conspicuous leader of the agitation in the west, and his reputation and influence were spreading rapidly. Until the foundation of the Land League he was not on the same footing as a national leader with Parnell, or even with O'Connor Power or Biggar or O'Donnell; but as soon as the league got under way he was almost at once to assume a unique place at the very centre of Irish politics. How great a change this was is indicated by the fact that only seven months previously Biggar was able to confuse him with Daniel Reddin, a released fenian prisoner, who died in March 1879: the secretary of a fund for Reddin's funeral received from Biggar £1, 'being a subscription of 10*s*. each from C. S. Parnell M.P. and myself towards expenses of the funeral of Michael Davitt'.[1]

Of Davitt's personal life during the ten momentous months between his return to Ireland and his founding of the Land League there is very

[1] J. G. Biggar to J. P. O'Brien, 17 Mar. (DP/V).

little trace. When he was not on the move he stayed in lodgings in Amiens Street, Dublin, or at the Innisfail Hotel, Talbot Street.[1] It was now that he came to have a close and friendly relationship with Parnell, who, in the autumn of 1879, frequently dropped in at Amiens Street for a chat with him and with Brennan, Egan, and other 'new departure' fenians. Many years later Davitt recalled these occasions with pleasure.

No man enjoying such growing popularity and political prospects could be more modest in his talk and manner, or more agreeable to those whom he met. He had a perculiar personal charm when in company where all formality was suspended. He was in complete health at the time and looked the very picture of manly strength, being strikingly handsome. . . . His laugh was most infectious, his whole countenance lighting up with merriment, and the eyes expressing a keen enjoyment of the fun or point of the story or incident. He liked to listen to stories about eccentricity of character or ridiculous situations in which some acquaintance, political or personal, might be involved. He frequently told a good story himself.[2]

Till near the end of August Davitt managed to pay his way and to meet necessary expenses of the agitation with money he had earned in America. From August to the setting up of the Land League he received timely help from the Clan na Gael 'national fund'.[3] He had begun to write for the American press with an article on the current situation in Ireland, sent to O'Reilly's *Pilot*, of Boston, on 1 May, and from October he was contributing letters to that paper and to Ford's *Irish World*.[4] Earnings from such work and from lecturing were to be his staple source of income from now onwards.[5] Living in the west agreed with him, and he wrote jubilantly to Devoy in August that he had succeeded pretty well in recruiting his health and undermining the landlords at the same time.[6] According to Devoy, by July he had become engaged to be married to a sister of the John Walshe of Balla whom he describes as his cousin.[7] There is some evidence that Davitt at this time, and later, was on friendly terms with Beatrice Walshe, of Balla, a patriotic, high-spirited, and beautiful girl who was probably John Walshe's sister;[8] but if there was an engagement it must have broken down, for nothing more is heard of it.

[1] *Fall*, p. 174; S.P.O., A files, no. 590.
[2] *Fall*, pp 174–5.
[3] See above, pp 312–13.
[4] DN/3, 1 May 79; DN/5, Jan. 80; D to J. B. O'Reilly, 10 Sept. 79 (*S.C.P.*, v, 186); O'Reilly to D, 18 Oct. (*S.C.P.*, iv, 459); D to J. E. Ward, 31 Oct. (ibid); D's evidence in *S.C.P.*, ix, 456.
[5] *S.C.P.*, ix, 358.
[6] D to Devoy, 23 Aug. (*D.P.B.*, i, 453).
[7] Devoy, XVIII.
[8] D to Devoy [Feb. 79] (*D.P.B.*, i, 397); D to Sabina Davitt, 14 Nov. 81 (DP/C3); Katherine Tynan, *Twenty-five years* (1913), p. 76.

IX

The Irish National Land League, October 1879–May 1880

By the autumn of 1879 the predictions of economic disaster with which the year had opened in Ireland were seen to be amply justified. 1879 proved to be the wettest year on record and temperatures the lowest. During the six months from March to September cold rain fell on 125 days out of 183, that is, on two days out of every three.[1] The harvest of 1879, the culmination of three successive bad years, was the worst since the great famine.[2] The yield per acre of all the principal crops was dramatically below that of the three preceding years. The potato crop, ravaged by blight, amounted to only about one third of its average yield, turnips and other green crops to about one half, and oats and other cereals to about four-fifths.[3] The general economic depression in the United Kingdom was reflected in a slump in agricultural prices. The prices of oats, wheat, and barley in Ireland in 1879 were well below the average for the years 1869–76, cattle prices generally declined, and butter prices collapsed.[4] The total value of agricultural output in 1879 fell to £35.5 millions, from £43.7 in 1876, £40 in 1877, and £39.4 in 1878. Cereal crops and flax, which had been worth £6.1 millions in 1876, £5.6 in 1877, and £5.7 in 1878, fell to £4.9 in 1879. Livestock and livestock products, valued at £37.6 millions in 1876, £34.4 in 1877, and £33.7 in 1878, plunged to £30.6 in 1879. The worst disaster was to the potato crop. The tonnage of potatoes fell from 4.2 millions in 1876, 1.8 in 1877, 2.5 in 1878, to 1.1 in 1879, the yield per acre from 4.7 million tons in 1876, 2.0 in 1877, 3.0 in 1878, to 1.3 in 1879. Since for the great mass of small farmers the potato was not a cash crop but their staff of life, the loss thus involved cannot realistically be expressed in financial terms. But according to

[1] *Irish crisis*, p. 4.

[2] Appendices G1 and G2.

[3] D. B. King. *The Irish question* (London, 1882), pp 100–01.

[4] B. L. Solow, *The land question and the Irish economy, 1870–1903* (Cambridge, Mass., 1971), pp 123–5.

an official scale of prices the fall in value of the potato crop was from £14.7 millions in 1876, £10.8 in 1877, and £11.25 in 1878, to £6.77 in 1879.[1] The accumulated losses of three years depleted the savings of the strong farmer and exhausted the credit of the weak. Massive unemployment among agricultural labourers was aggravated by the depression in Britain, which cut off the normal opportunities of seasonal employment for Irish migrants in the British harvest.[2] Finally, the incessant bad weather created a fuel famine in those extensive regions where the population depended wholly or mainly on turf for their heating.

Distress was exceptionally severe in Connacht, and worst of all in Mayo. The lack of employment for migratory labourers in England was estimated to have deprived Connacht in 1879 of over £250,000 in wages.[3] The disaster to the potato crop had its most terrible effects on Connacht, where a larger proportion of the population depended on it for subsistence than in any other province. A special report, drawn up for the Irish government by the registrar general in October, reckoned that in many places in Connacht the supply of potatoes was unlikely to hold out for three months. Oats, the main cereal crop, were generally up to average, but in Connacht had failed badly. Moreover, Connacht, which had virtually no other fuel than turf for the working population, had the worst fuel shortage: less than half the normal supply had been saved and that was well below average in calorific value.[4]

To the cumulative effect of three bad years was added that of some ten years of reckless borrowing and over-expenditure by farmers and others. This borrowing was facilitated by the expansion of the joint stock banks, whose branch offices increased from 197 in 1863 to 426 in 1877 and whose competition for business encouraged an inflation of credit. This enabled thrifty men to extend their business and increase their profits but it also tempted less prudent men, including many small farmers, to live beyond their means. The same tendency was fostered by the readiness of shopkeepers and traders to supply goods on credit to the poorest farmers, who when pressed for repayment borrowed more money from a bank or opened a new credit account in another shop. The willingness of bankers and shopkeepers to allow small farmers to run up debts was strengthened by Gladstone's land act of 1870 which gave tenants a tangible interest in their holdings that creditors could accept as security for loans. Nearly half the

[1] Appendix G1. [2] *Irish crisis*, pp 6–8. [3] Ibid., p. 7.

[4] T. W. Grimshaw, *Special report on agricultural produce and fuel supply in Ireland as ascertained by inquiries made in October 1879* (Dublin, 1879; dated 3 Nov. 79 and marked 'Confidential').

occupiers of land were heavily in debt when in 1877 the banks became seriously alarmed by the bad harvest of that year and began to put a curb on further advances. By 1879 debtors found themselves under unprecedented pressure to pay existing liabilities and unable to incur new credits just when the whole country was staggering under the agricultural disasters of that year.[1]

It was repeatedly stated and widely believe in Ireland during 1879 that a catastrophe comparable with the great famine was impending. In some respects the situation was worse, in some respects better, than in 1845–9. All the principal crops suffered heavy losses, whereas in the great famine it was the potato crop alone that was destroyed; the total loss to the farmers in 1879 was reckoned to have exceeded in value that of 1846. All classes of farmers were involved in the distress of 1879, whereas in 1845–9 the victims were almost entirely the poorest classes, who depended on the potato for survival. Substantial farmers, of the class that was scarcely affected directly by the great famine, were in 1879 on the verge of bankruptcy, unable to give employment or to help their destitute countrymen. On the other hand there were factors in the 1879 situation that made it less calamitous than that of 1845–9: the total population was much smaller (about 5¼ millions as compared with 8¼ millions); the proportion of that reduced population vitally dependent on the potato was also much smaller; Indian meal was available in abundance at moderate prices; internal communication had been transformed by the creation of an extensive railway network. All this made the problem of distress in 1879 more manageable. And there were other new factors. The large range of interests affected—tenant farmers large and small, cottiers and agricultural labourers, banks, shopkeepers, traders, and moneylenders—created conditions favourable to a nation-wide movement of self-assertion very different from the fatalism and passivity shown by the peasantry in the great famine. Thanks to the increase of literacy and the widening circulation of the newspaper, public opinion could be more effectively organised than ever before. Popular leadership was forthcoming both on the local and on the national level. It was due to these conditions, and to an unprecedented outpouring of private charity from America, Australia, Great Britain, and other parts of the world, that relief measures were rapidly and effectively applied by voluntary organisations (of which the Land League served as one). By these means, augmented by government action, the hardest-hit elements in the rural

[1] Paper by Gilbert de L. Willis, formerly an official of the Munster Bank, submitted to the Cowper commission (*Report of the royal commission on the Land Law (Ireland) Act, 1885* [C4969], H.C. 1887, xxvi, 976–82.

population were saved from starvation and destitution until an abundant harvest of potatoes, in 1880, removed the fear of another great famine.

From the press and the platform the crisis of 1879 was constantly declared to be without precedent since the great famine. This is surprising because, as the *Irish Farmers' Gazette* pointed out in its issue of 6 September 1879, the crisis had a parallel less than twenty years previously. Three exceptionally wet years, 1860, 1861, and 1862, caused severe losses in crops and in livestock and livestock products. Crops, exclusive of potatoes, turnips, and hay, fell from £8.2 millions in 1860 to £5.6 in 1861 and £5 in 1862. The yield of potatoes fell from 4.3 million tons in 1859 to 2.7 million in 1860, and to 1.9 million in 1861, and rose to only 2.1 million in 1862. The output of livestock and livestock products fell in value from £25.9 millions in 1860 to £25 millions in 1861, and to £23.3 millions in 1862. There was acute distress, inability to pay rent, mounting arrears, and a sharp rise in evictions—from 571 in 1860 to 818 in 1861, 893 in 1862, 1,551 in 1863, and 1,648 in 1864, the totals for 1863 and 1864 being the highest between 1854 and 1879. The government, arguing that it would be very difficult to make special grants for relief of distress in Ireland when no such grants had been made to relieve the greater distress caused in Lancashire by the cotton famine, insisted that it was not called upon to augment the ordinary operation of the poor law system. Famine was avoided through the efforts of private charity, headed by the Mansion House Committee and the Central Relief Committee of the Society of Friends, and by the fact that imported Indian corn was at once available at low prices.[1]

The economic crisis of 1879–80 was more severe than that of 1860–62 in terms of crop losses, especially potatoes, and in the depleted value of livestock and livestock products; and it was aggravated by the general economic depression in Britain and the lack of employment there for migratory labours from Connacht. On the other hand Indian corn as an alternative food to potatoes was available more cheaply in 1879–80 than in the earlier crisis. Social suffering was probably greater in 1879–80 than in 1860–62, but both the distress and the relief measures of 1879–80 differed in degree rather than in kind from those of 1860–62. What made the later crisis unprecedented was not the distress it caused but the political reaction to that distress. A measure of the contrast with 1860–2 is the fact that parliament took

[1] J. S. Donnelly, 'The Irish agricultural depression of 1859–64' in *Irish Economic and Social History*, iii (1976), pp 33–54; below, appendices D1 and G1–2; *Hansard 3*, clxix; *Annual Register*, 1863, pt I, pp 34–5, 171–5.

no notice of the distress of those years till February 1863, and then Irish M.P.s were unable to induce the government even to appoint a select committee of inquiry into the causes of the distress, which, they alleged, was connected with the bad relations between landlords and tenants. In 1879 the distress precipitated a well-organised movement of resistance to the landlords—the 'land war'—that challenged the very authority of the government and for two years made Ireland the main preoccupation of parliament.

To radical thinkers about the land question such as Davitt the distress of 1879–80 was simply the tragic culmination of an evil system, imposed on Ireland by English conquest—a symptom, brought to a head by the current economic depression, of a deep-seated social disease, 'landlordism'. Thus William O'Brien, employed by the *Freeman's Journal* in August and September 1879 on a private commission of inquiry into the western distress, attacked the 'jaunty optimists' who claimed that conditions in Mayo, not being typical of Irish agriculture in general, could not reasonably be used to discredit the land system. O'Brien took the case of Tipperary as the antithesis of Mayo in the fertility of its soil and the wealth, skill, and traditional high spirit of its farmers, but argued that Mayo and Tipperary were nevertheless now in the same plight because 'they suffer from the same withering land laws'.[1] Davitt was in no doubt that the immediate needs were to relieve the distress and to protect impoverished tenants against eviction: the annual total of evictions had risen sharply from 406 in 1877 to 834 in 1878, and by the end of 1879 it was to reach its highest point, 1,098 since 1864; though this represented a rate of only 2.07 per 1000 holdings above one acre it was ominous evidence of the readiness of some landlords to assert their legal powers against their tenants at a time when innumerable tenants were in great distress. But relieving distress and resisting eviction would not remove the cause of the disease. The only ultimate remedy for the tenants' situation was their transformation as a body into owners of their holdings. This social revolution—'the land of Ireland for the people of Ireland'—for which the crisis of 1879 was seen to open a unique opportunity was to be achieved by a mass movement, using all possible pressures that would 'not clash defiantly with the constitution'.[2]

In inspiring and promoting such a 'war against landlordism' and in infusing it with a passionate sense of social justice Davitt by the autumn of 1879 was unrivalled. But the land war also had its political aspect, and here Parnell was supreme. 'I would not have taken off my coat and gone to this work if I had not known that we were laying the

[1] *F.J.*, 4 Sept. 79, p. 5, col. 6. [2] Above, p 317.

foundation in this movement for the regeneration of our legislative independence.'[1] This was another way of expressing Lalor's doctrine that the land question was the engine that would pull the train of self-government to its destination.[2] Security for the tenant farmers was a positive condition vital to the achievement of home rule; and a negative condition was that the power of the landlords, as the 'English garrison', had to be broken. Davitt shared this view, but went far beyond Parnell in adhering, as he still did, to the separatist aim of his fenian past; and though his energies were mainly absorbed by the open agrarian agitation he maintained close connections with the secret revolutionary movement.

It was this combination of issues that made the crisis so excruciating to landlords and to unionists generally, and that caused many people in Britain initially to believe that the distress was largely an invention of political agitators.[3] Landlords who on compassionate grounds remitted rents due in 1879–80, as large numbers of them did, found that this availed them nothing against the blanket denunciations of landlords by the Land League; and this in turn made them all the more determined to evict defaulting tenants when the distress was past. The landlords as a class felt themselves to be victims of a monstrous conspiracy, by which their property rights, their social status, and their loyalty to the union were all brutally and unjustly attacked. Beneficent landlords, such as Art McMurrough Kavanagh who prided himself on his just and paternalist rule over his numerous tenantry, found that the deference traditionally paid to them by their tenants had suddenly gone.[4] The old familiar world they had known seemed to be breaking up before their eyes in a welter of class hatred, intimidation, and violence, instigated and organised by the Land League. Agrarian outrages had increased from 236 in 1877 to 301 in 1878 and were to reach a total of 863 in 1879, the highest recorded figure, except for 1870, since 1852. Of these 863 outrages nearly half related to the last quarter of 1879, which saw the emergence of the Land League; and more than half occurred in Connacht, the heartland of the agitation.[5] Land League chiefs, and above all Davitt, who saw themselves as helping to liberate a long-suffering people from servitude to an alien and oppressive caste, claimed that the violence sprang from the injustices of the landlord system and that without the restraining influence of the league there would have been vastly more violence. The landlords,

[1] Parnell at Galway, 20 Oct. 80, in R. B. O'Brien, *Parnell*, i, 240.
[2] See above, p. 36.
[3] See, for example, *The Times*, 4 Nov. 79, editorial.
[4] Arnold-Forster, Irish journal, 7 Dec. 80.
[5] Appendices E and F.

on the other hand, believed that the increase in agrarian crime was the work of the league. What probably none of the parties in the land war understood was the complexity of the forces involved, or the significance of the fact that the economic crisis of 1879–80 came after a period (1867–76) of steadily rising agricultural production and of rising expectations on the part of the tenants. Davitt burned with indignation and compassion for the sufferings of small, poverty-stricken peasants, of whom his native Mayo afforded so many examples, but he seemed unaware of the distress of small and impoverished landlords, and unimpressed by the fact that there were many middle-sized and large tenant farmers whose improving economic interests were very different from those of the depressed tenantry of the west. What he called 'the Celtic peasantry of Ireland', to whom he dedicated his masterpiece, the *Fall of feudalism*, comprised a wide spectrum of social and economic groups, to some of which his impassioned generalisations had no real application. It is a very striking fact that this book, the most important account of the land war by a contemporary, shows relatively little concern with the economic background of the social and political transformation with which it deals.

While he tended to idealise the Land League, Davitt was by no means blind to its materialist aspect. Some years later he described the appeal that the league made to the Irish peasant mind as not 'born of the exalted patriotism of Thomas Davis'. The league, he said,

> appealed to self-interest, I admit, rather than to self-sacrifice; but who will say that in this instance the end did not justify the teaching, when no other would have aroused the tenant-farming class to an assertion of their unquestioned social rights, and a vindication of their despised and trampled manhood?

The land war was thus essentially a social revolution, but Davitt went on to state and refute the charge that it did nothing to advance the interests of nationality, claiming on the contrary that it did more to weaken alien rule in Ireland than any movement since 1798.[1]

'The Irish National Land League', like the Mayo Land League which it superseded, was essentially Davitt's creation and took on the same general characteristics as its predecessor.[2] But its actual foundation, at the meeting convened by Parnell at the Imperial Hotel, Sackville (now O'Connell) Street, Dublin, on 21 October, was a more prosaic and practical affair than that of the Mayo Land League, and was as characteristic of Parnell's style as the latter was of Davitt's. Parnell's invitation[3] had been issued to some ninety persons, well distributed

[1] *F.J.*, 3 Aug. 85, reporting a public meeting in Dublin on 1 Aug.

[2] See above, pp 317–20.

[3] Above, p. 325.

over the country outside Ulster, and to a handful of notable Irishmen resident in Britain—John Barry (London), Andrew Commins (Liverpool), John Ferguson (Glasgow), John J. Goulding and J. C. Howe (of Goulding and Howe, merchants, London),[1] James Lysaght Finigan, The O'Gorman Mahon, John O'Connor Power, and A. M. Sullivan (M.P.s, London). They were nearly all active in, or known to be favourable to, the land agitation, and nearly all of them were catholics, conspicuous exceptions being Ferguson and Rev. Isaac Nelson. The list included thirteen home rule M.P.s and twenty-three catholic clergy. A majority of those invited expressed their willingness to join the proposed committee (P. J. Smyth was an outstanding dissentient), though many regretted inability to attend the meeting on the 21st. Only some twenty-three were present at that meeting, 'for the purpose of forming a central body in connection with the present land agitation'.[2] Most of the twenty-three were from Dublin and its neighbourhood; Parnell was the only M.P., and two catholic curates, John Behan (Dublin) and Eugene Sheehy (Kilmallock), the only clergymen, among them. Preparations for the meeting, chaired by Kettle, were in the expert hands of Egan, who took care of the nine prearranged resolutions, which were duly proposed, seconded, and carried. (1) An association was formed called the Irish National Land League. (2) The objects of the league were defined as (a) 'to bring about a reduction of rack rents' and (b) 'to facilitate the obtaining of the ownership of the soil by the occupiers'. (3) These objects, it was declared, could best be attained (a) by promoting organisation among the tenant farmers; (b) by defending those who were threatened with eviction 'for refusing to pay unjust rents'; (c) by facilitating the operation, during the winter, of the 'Bright clauses' of the 1870 land act; and (d) by obtaining such a reform of the land laws as would enable every tenant to become the owner of his holding after paying 'a fair rent' for a term of years. (4) Parnell was elected president of the new league; (5) Davitt, Brennan, and Kettle were appointed its secretaries; (6) Egan, Biggar, and William Henry O'Sullivan its treasurers. (7) Parnell was requested to visit America to seek assistance from 'our exiled countrymen and other sympathisers'. (8) None of the funds of the league were to be used either to buy out any landlord or to further the interests of any candidate for election to parliament. (9) Davitt's 'Appeal to the Irish race for the sustainment of the Irish national land movement', was approved and ordered to be circulated. Finally a committee was appointed, consisting of Parnell himself and 53 persons who had accepted his

[1] O'Donnell, *Irish parl. party*, i, 164.
[2] *F.J.*, 22 Oct. 79.

invitation to serve on it. All 54 names appear on the 'appeal to the Irish race' as circulated.[1]

While the style and tone of these resolutions owed far more to Parnell than to Davitt, their substance was a triumph for Davitt. For they contained nothing less than a social revolution in germ. This is evident in the statement of means to be used for bringing about the objects of the league. The 'Bright' or land-purchase clauses in the 1870 land act provided for advances to tenants of two-thirds of the purchase money on tenancies valued at over £100 a year and of one-third on those valued at between £50 and £100, terms that left the great majority of small farmers outside the scope of the act and were unattractive to those who could qualify under it. The principle laid down by the Land League, on the other hand, while presented as merely an extension of existing land-legislation, implied the universal selling-out of tenanted land to the occupiers on favourable terms—in other words the compulsory application of the principle of state-aided land purchase, incorporated in the church disestablishment act (1869) and the 1870 land act. To reassure men with radical views on the land question, especially Americans, who would contribute nothing to the buying-out of the landlords, it was declared as a matter of principle that the league's funds would not be used for that purpose; just as advanced nationalists were assured that these funds would not be used for parliamentary electioneering.

Extreme nationalism was entrenched in the seven-man executive of the league. Its hard core was formed by Davitt and his two closest fenian associates in the land agitation, Egan and Brennan. Two other members, Biggar and O'Sullivan, were activist home rule M.P.s, the one a fenian and the other at least strongly identified with fenianism. Parnell himself, a moderate nationalist to the fenians, was an extremist to the majority of his parliamentary colleagues. The seventh member of the executive, Kettle, was a moderate home-ruler and land-reformer converted to Parnell's policy and to a radical solution of the land question.[2] He used his position as secretary of the Central Tenants' Defence Association to swing that organisation over to support of the Land League. Within two months Parnell was able to persuade the association to 'snuff themselves out'[3] in favour of the league; and a corresponding development took place in the localities, where farmers' clubs and associations became integrated into, or linked with, the league's emerging structure. Kettle was the only farmer on the executive

[1] DP/RR2; *F.J.*, 22 Oct. 79; *Irish Times*, 22 Oct.; *Nation*, 25 Oct.; *Irishman*, 25 Oct.; *Fall*, pp 171–3. None of the officers except Parnell was among the 54.

[2] Above, p. 315.

[3] W. O'Brien, *Recollections*, p. 233.

of the league. Of the others, Parnell was a landowner, Biggar and Egan had made money in business, O'Sullivan was a publican and hotel-keeper in Kilmallock (known, from his devotion to the drink interest in parliament, as 'Whiskey O'Sullivan'),[1] Brennan a clerk, and Davitt a journalist.

The committee of the league included at least two fenians, O'Connor Power and Matthew Harris, and a number of militant home-rulers, among them John Dillon, John Ferguson, J. L. Finigan, The O'Gorman Mahon, and Purcell O'Gorman, but the large majority were home-rulers distinguished not so much for their political activities as for their connection with the land agitation, such as James Daly, J. J. Louden, T. D. Sullivan, Canon Ulick Bourke, and Fr William Joyce (P.P. of Louisburgh). Altogether the committee included five Parnellite M.P.s (Nicholas Ennis, J. L. Finigan, The O'Gorman Mahon, Purcell O'Gorman, and O'Connor Power); four newspaper editors (Daly of the *Connaught Telegraph*, Richard Kelly of the *Tuam Herald*, Thomas Roe of the *Dundalk Democrat*, and T. D. Sullivan of the *Nation*); four barristers (A. Commins, J. J. Louden, E. P. M. Marum of Ballyraggett, County Kilkenny, R. H. Metge of Navan); two physicians (J. E. Kenny of Dublin, and J. R. McClosky of Derry); several business men, headed by John Ferguson of Glasgow, J. C. Howe of London, and James Rourke of the City Bakery, Dublin;[2] a hotel-keeper of Kanturk (P. F. Johnson);[3] a handful of farmers, notably William Kelly of Donabate, J. F. Grehan of Cabinteely, and Richard Lalor of Tenakill, Queen's County (brother of James Fintan Lalor); and fourteen catholic priests. While the league's executive was dominated by political activists, the committee represented a broad spectrum of nationalist thinking and a solid element of middle-class support for the land movement from men of various occupations besides farming. They were widely spread geographically—15 of them were resident in Dublin city and county, 33 in Ireland beyond, and 6 in Britain. Of the 60 'foundation members' of the league (that is, the general committee and the officers) the only protestants were Parnell himself and Ferguson.

The fact that fourteen catholic clergy—eight parish priests (including the dean of Cashel, William Quirke) and six curates—were officially identified with the league pointed the difference between it and its Mayo predecessor. The land agitation had been inspired, initiated, and led by laymen in face of hostility or aloofness from most of the

[1] *Thom 1879*, p. 406; Clifford Lloyd, *Ireland under the Land League* (1892), p. 60; Elizabeth L. Malcolm, 'The drink question in Ireland, 1856–1901' (Ph.D. thesis, University of Dublin, 1980), pp 379, 386, 406, 407, 439.

[2] Above, p. 124.

[3] Below, p. 341.

bishops but with growing support from the parochial clergy, and especially from curates. By October 1879, however, five bishops were known to approve of the agitation, five more were sympathetic to it, nine were neutral, and nine were hostile.[1] The first five were headed by T. W. Croke, the outspoken and ebullient archbishop of Cashel, who thirty years before, as curate of Charleville, had been ardently engaged in the tenant right movement. In August 1879 he had intervened with success in an ugly wrangle between Parnell and Dwyer Gray, and had publicly declared his belief in Parnell's 'chivalrous dash, devotedness, and determination'. In September Parnell had sought his support for the agitation and had met with a favourable response.[2] Like Patrick Duggan, bishop of Clonfert,[3] another of the five, Croke was to become a close personal friend and firm ally of Davitt's. The three other bishops in the group were Thomas Nulty of Meath, who had long held radical views on the land question, Patrick Dorrian of Down and Connor, and Francis MacCormack of Achonry. These five and the five episcopal sympathisers, if they did not directly encourage their clergy to play an active part in the league, did nothing to stop them from doing so. In anything they said publicly about the agitation they were highly circumspect, with the exception of Croke, whose forceful public statements on the rural distress had attracted unfavourable attention in Rome by mid-November. The pope, Leo XIII, and some of the cardinals had been informed that Croke was using violent language and expressing approval of 'a politician [Parnell] known to be a violent man and to have used language of a socialistic tendency'. Croke stoutly denied the charge and defended Parnell, fearing intervention from Rome that could only result in turning the mass of the Irish people against the church and religion. This non-interventionist attitude was shared by the archbishop of Dublin, Edward McCabe, who headed the bishops hostile to the agitation. They included the aged patriarch, John MacHale, archbishop of Tuam, John MacEvilly, bishop of Galway, and Patrick F. Moran, bishop of Ossory. Without taking the side of the landlords against the tenants, they saw the agitation as subversive of religion, morality, and the social order, and as putting power in the hands of 'Godless nobodies' tainted by fenianism and socialism—they probably had Davitt and Brennan in mind. If the Roman authorities could be quoted as opposed to the people on the land question, it would do irreparable injury to ecclesiastical

[1] Emmet Larkin, *The Roman Catholic church and the creation of the modern Irish state* (Philadelphia and Dublin, 1975), p. 24.

[2] *Fall*, pp 69–70; Mark Tierney, *Croke of Cashel*, pp 20–4, 97–100; above, p. 37.

[3] Above, p. 315.

authority and the restraining influence of the bishops.[1]

Both the episcopal supporters and opponents of the Land League had good grounds for their attitudes. For the league, alike in its programme and in the personnel of its central body, was a combination of extremism and moderation. The resulting inconsistencies and ambiguities were to become a continuing source both of bitter internal controversy and of ferocious external attack. Davitt himself, in 1884, publicly acknowledged that the founders of the league took care not to frighten away 'any timid land-reformer' and to make the league 'eminently constitutional for the double purpose of legal protection against the Castle and to enable members of parliament to defend it within the house of commons'. But what then, he asked, was the principle on which the league was founded?

> I maintain that it was the complete destruction of Irish landlordism: first, as the system which was responsible for the poverty and periodical famines which have decimated Ireland; and secondly, because landlordism was a British garrison, which barred the way to national independence.[2]

Davitt's first reason for the attack on the landlord system was the dominating idea of the land agitation, and was written into his 'Appeal to the Irish race'. His second reason was certainly in the minds of the league's founders but did not appear in their declarations.

The 'Appeal to the Irish race',[3] specially intended for Irish-Americans, was couched in Davitt's most declamatory style (O'Connor Power, no stranger to declamation himself, thought it needed to be revised and condensed[4]). It was a manifesto on the theme that 'almost all the evils' under which the people of Ireland suffered were 'referable' to an unjust land system, and could be remedied only by transferring ownership from the landlords to the occupiers. This remedy was accepted by a 'consensus of opinion' as founded on justice, reason, and expediency. It did not mean confiscation of the landlords' interest, for which a 'fair compensation' would be given. The powerful opposition that would none the less be offered by the landlords could be met in two ways: first, by organising the 600,000 landless farmers of Ireland, and those whose livelihood depended on them, in a united and determined effort to assert their rights; second, by raising a fighting-fund from among the exiled Irish all over the world, and especially from those

[1] Larkin, op. cit., pp 25–30; Tierney, op. cit., pp 98–102.

[2] D to editor of New York *Daily World*, 21 May 84, in *United Ireland*, 31 May, and in *S.C.P.*, iv, 257–9; ibid., ix, 453–4.

[3] MS in D's hand and printed copy in DP/AV; King, *Irish question*, pp 324–8, Cashman, pp 103–7; *S.C.P.*, vi, 480–82.

[4] O'Connor Power to Parnell, 20 Oct. 79 (DP/RR2).

in America, 'the great shelter-land of peoples'. And, sounding a note that was to become increasingly characteristic of his thinking, Davitt sought to enlist the support of world opinion for the Irish struggle:

Not alone to our fellow-countrymen in America, but to all whom evil laws have scattered the world over, as well as to all other nationalities who sympathise with a wronged and impoverished people who are at last resolved upon a remedy for the evils afflicting them, do we call for an advocacy of our cause.

This appeal was soon circulating widely in the Irish-American press, and, supported by personal letters from Davitt to political friends in America,[1] prepared the way for Parnell's visit. Its counterpart for internal consumption in Ireland was an address 'to the farmers of Ireland and all interested in the settlement of the land question', adopted by the league executive on 5 November, the day on which the league acquired offices at 62 Middle Abbey Street.[2] Conveying the same message in more measured terms, it claimed that the combination of the depression and the popular agitation provided a unique opportunity for a radical settlement of the land question.

The agitation for reduction of excessive rents must be sustained, so that the operation of natural causes may be asserted in bringing land to a fair valuation in order to enable its cultivators to become owners of their own farms, upon terms within the means of every occupier.

For this purpose, and to assist the victims of landlord oppression, the farmers generally were called upon to contribute whatever they could afford to the league's funds. This was no sectarian movement, but one that would benefit catholic and protestant alike, and its benefits would not be restricted to farmers and agricultural labourers but would extend to all the commercial and industrial classes.[3]

The incidental reference to agricultural labourers is significant. The league's stated programme gave no recognition to the problem of the labourers[4] as distinct from that of the tenant farmers. Some attempt to alleviate the labourers' condition had been made in the 1870 land act and subsequent legislation, but the general effect had been negligible. Efforts to obtain redress by collective action, begun in County Cork in 1869, had led in 1873 to the formation of an Irish labourers' union at Kanturk, in connection with the National Agricultural Labourers' Union that Joseph Arch had founded in England the year before. But this attempt at solidarity between agricultural labourers in Ireland and England had been quickly undermined by the divisive

[1] For example to J. B. O'Reilly and to J. J. O'Kelly, 22 Oct. 79, in *D.P.B.*, i, 455–7.

[2] Agreement between Patrick Joseph Gordon and the Land League, 5 Nov. 79, in S.P.O., I.N.L.L. and I.N.L. papers, carton 9.

[3] *F.J.*, 6 Nov.; printed copy, dated 5 Nov., in S.P.O., I.N.L.L. and I.N.L. papers, carton 9, Mallon to C.P., 10 Aug. 80.

[4] See above, p. 35.

effect of the home rule movement; and the Irish labourers' agitation, though it spread to other parts of Munster and beyond, had lost most of its force by the time the Land League emerged. The labourers, whose wretchedness was aggravated by heavy unemployment, were encouraged to see the league as a potential lever to improved conditions for themselves as well as for the farmers; and generally they supported the league, even though they suffered more at the hands of the farmers than of the landlords. The leading spirit in the agricultural labourers' union of 1873, P. F. Johnson of Kanturk, was a member of the Land League 'committee'.[1]

The league executive recognised from the start that systematic information about individual holdings throughout the country would be needed, and therefore Davitt and Brennan prepared a form for recording the following particulars: whether the holding was on lease or yearly tenancy, how long it had been in the possession of the present tenant or his family, the name of the landlord and agent, whether the landlord was resident or an absentee, the extent of the holding, the character of the land, the rent per acre, Griffiths' valuation, how often the rent had been raised since 1848, how the county cess was paid, whether the landlord or agent had to be consulted before a marriage could take place in the tenant's family. This form, approved by the executive on 5 November and ordered to be printed, was the earliest version of an instrument that was later to be developed and widely used, especially in 1881–2, by local officers of the league and of its auxiliary and successor, the Ladies' Land League, to report cases of actual or threatened eviction to the central office.[2]

The term 'Land League' has two meanings. In its original and strict sense the 'Land League' was the body founded on 21 October 1879 and located in Dublin, as distinct from the local bodies which became affiliated to it as 'branches of the Land League'. But 'Land League' is also used in a wider sense to signify the totality of the central league and its branches. This is how the term was, and is, generally used on the political level; but on the level of organisation 'Land League' generally meant only the central body. Neither in the wider nor in the restricted sense had the Land League a written constitution;[3] the omission may have been a device to make legal action against it difficult. In the absence of records[4] the nature and working of the central

[1] E. R. Hooker, *Readjustments of agricultural tenure in Ireland* (Chapel Hill, 1938), pp 175–6; Palmer, *Land League*, p. 117; Pamela L. R. Horn, 'The National Agricultural Labourers' Union in Ireland, 1873–9' in *I.H.S.*, xvii, no. 17 (Mar. 1971), pp 340–52; J. S. Donnelly, *The land and the people of nineteenth-century Cork* pp 236–8.

[2] *F.J.*, 6 Nov. 79; N.L.I., MSS 17709, 17712; Cashman, p. 231.

[3] See below, pp 346, 432, 435–6.

[4] See below, p. 360.

organisation have to be partly inferred from indirect evidence and partly reconstructed from press reports of meetings, principally those in the *Freeman's Journal* which form a continuous and informative series. What emerges is that members of the central body met at regular intervals—roughly twice a week from January to April 1880 and weekly thereafter. The place of meeting was the headquarters of the executive —at 62 Middle Abbey Street till 7 December, and from then onwards at 39 Sackville Street. There were 68 meetings from 30 December 1879 to 2 February 1881, the last at which Davitt was present. Attendance seems to have ranged from about 10 to about 40 persons, comprising some of the officers, a few members of the committee of 54, and other persons. Of the officers Parnell and Biggar each attended only 5 meetings out of 68, and O'Sullivan only 10. Davitt (when he was in Ireland), Brennan, Egan, and Kettle were nearly always present. They were unsalaried, and theoretically part-time officers, but a full-time salaried secretary (or chief clerk) was employed from the beginning—Michael Malachy O'Sullivan, of Ballinasloe, a fenian who had been involved in the land agitation since Irishtown.[1] He is recorded as present at 26 meetings, and almost certainly attended others at which his presence is not recorded. Besides the four ruling members of the executive, the most frequent attenders were M. P. Boyton, P. J. Corrigan, Patrick Cummins, Peter Daly, R. J. Donnelly, J. F. Grehan, James Murray, James Rourke, Thomas Sexton, and T. D. Sullivan. Boyton was a league organiser, Grehan was a farmer of Cabinteely, Sexton and Sullivan were journalists, and most of the others were merchants or business men—Cummins a well-to-do pawnbroker, Donnelly a wine and spirit merchant, Murray a draper, and James Rourke co-proprietor with Egan of the City Bakery.[2] The large majority of all who attended did so only once or twice, and these included representatives of local branches and parish clergy. The only clergy who attended more than twice down to 2 February 1881 were Rev. John Behan, C.C., Rev. James Canon McDermott, P.P., Rev. W. J. McKeough, P.P., and Rev. Eugene Sheehy, C.C.[3]

The status of reported meetings of the league presents some difficulty. 16 out of 68 were described as meetings of 'the committee', 3 as of 'the council', and one as of 'the executive', but there is no discernible difference between these and 'meetings of the Land League'. Indeed the reports of 2 'meetings of the Land League' (10 and 13 February) end up with the words 'the committee adjourned'; and

[1] Above, pp 289, 290, 304. [2] *Thom 1882.*

[3] See appendix H, where attendances at meetings of the central league throughout its two years (Oct. 79–Oct. 81) are tabulated.

another meeting (2 March) is described by the *Freeman's Journal* as of 'the committee' and by the *Irish Times* as of 'the Land League'. It was decided at a 'committee' on 30 December that 'committee meetings' should be held weekly, on Tuesdays, at 2 p.m., but succeeding meetings described as of 'the committee' did not recur at weekly intervals and very seldom took place on a Tuesday till 20 April, from which point onwards a meeting, whether described as of 'the committee' or of the league, was held on nearly every Tuesday, usually at 3 p.m. It follows that these meetings were of the central body, not of a committee of that body, and that the 'committee' of 54 appointed on 21 October never met as such. Meetings of the league were in effect simply meetings of the officers afforced by the attendance of such other members of the league as wished to be present. Others sometimes attended by invitation—for example, John Denvir (of Liverpool) and John Murdoch (editor of the Inverness *Highlander*). Anyone who paid a subscription of £1 could be elected to membership after being proposed and seconded by members, but a fortnight had to elapse between his nomination and his election.[1] Representatives of the press were always admitted unless they were suspected of being government note-takers. A chairman was elected for each meeting, but none of the officers ever presided (down to 2 February 1881) except Parnell (five times; that is, whenever he was present), O'Sullivan (four times), and Davitt (once). The main standing business of meetings was to receive reports from the secretary and the treasurer, to announce subscriptions and donations received, to make grants, to take decisions on special cases and important matters, to elect new members, to give advice to branches, and to shape policy for the whole organisation, central and local.

A distinctive feature of the central organisation was the dominance of the executive, which consisted of the officers meeting in private.[2] Appointed from a prepared list by those present at the inaugural meeting of the central Land League, and without any stated responsibility either to that body or to the contemplated local organisations, the executive exercised wide and undefined powers. But it did so in the light of opinions, advice, criticism, and information offered at the members' meetings, which were public in the sense that press reporters were present. Within the executive Davitt, Brennan, and Egan formed a triumvirate (duumvirate while Davitt was in America) that managed all essential business. Kettle took no share in the secretarial work, nor Biggar and O'Sullivan (both M.P.s) in the financial affairs of the league.

1 *F.J.*, 6 Nov. 79, 26 May, 2 June, 19, 27 Oct., 10 Nov. 80.
2 No records of meetings of the executive appear to have survived.

Parnell as president seems to have been content to leave the administration of the league to the triumvirate, while devoting himself to the strategy and the politics of the land war and to addressing land meetings in various parts of Ireland. Within the triumvirate Davitt specialised in organisation, Brennan in propaganda, and Egan in finance, but all three shared in league business generally. Davitt and Brennan were foremost among its orators; and Davitt became its most popular spokesman to the country at large.

For some months the executive of the league was fully occupied, first, with publicising the league and its programme, with recruiting members, encouraging the formation of branches, and promoting public meetings at which the land agitation was continued and developed in Ireland and extended to Britain by Parnell, Davitt, and others; and second, with preparations, centred on Parnell's impending mission to America, for raising funds both to support the agitation and to relieve distress. During these early months a nation-wide organisation was beginning to emerge, but it was not till 30 December that, in response to requests for guidance on the formation of branches, not only from Ireland but also from England and Scotland, the league approved a statement of 'suggestions on organisation'. Drafted by Davitt,[1] who was to describe it, and his appeal to the Irish race, as 'charters of the Land League', it was concerned both with local organisation and with principles and modes of action. If the Land League's 'code' and the constitution of its branch structure are to be sought in any single document, this is where they are to be found.

A branch of the league should be formed in every parish in Ireland or at least in every barony, with sub-branches or tenants' clubs on every large estate if possible. The initiative in forming branches should be taken by the local organisers of public meetings to agitate for rent reductions. Each branch should be managed by a committee comprising a president, treasurer, secretary and four other members, all to be elected annually by ballot. The annual subscription should be not less than one shilling for tenant farmers and labourers, and a higher rate should be fixed if the means of local farmers warranted it. Honorary membership, for merchants and other sympathisers, might be instituted at a yearly subscription of not less than ten shillings. The funds of the branches should be used to defend members resisting rack rents, arbitrary disturbance by landlords, or other injustices to tenants, on whose behalf public opinion should be appealed to or compensation claimed under the land act of 1870. Branches that voted a percentage of their funds to the central body would be entitled to assistance in

[1] MS draft in D's hand in DP/AV; *Defence*, pp 228–30.

defending such cases. Where a branch decided to bring a case to trial, and the funds in hand were inadequate, a general meeting of the branch should be called to fix a special levy for the purpose on each member. Meetings of branches could be held in the chapel yard on a Sunday if no other meeting-place was available; cases of rack-renting, contemplated evictions, and the like should then be reported, and particulars transmitted by the branch secretary to headquarters. The committee of each branch should keep a register of its members, on books to be supplied from headquarters, specifying their holdings, the names of their landlords and agents, their rents and how far these were above the government valuation, cases of rack-renting and eviction, and other information about landlord–tenant relations in the locality of the branch.[1] The committee should also organise public meetings to further the land agitation in its district and to protest against evictions. Evicted members and their families should be sheltered and provided for by their branches. No one should be allowed to become a member of any branch who took a farm from which another had been evicted for non-payment of an unjust rent. Any member guilty of bidding for or occupying such a farm, or of renting land surrendered because of excessive rent or of a landlord's refusal to accept a fair reduction of a rack rent, should be expelled 'and should be looked upon and shunned as a traitor to the interests of his fellow tenant farmers and an enemy to the welfare of his country'—or, in the terminology of a year later, he should be boycotted. No one should be allowed to become a member who assisted in serving ejectment processes, or took part in evictions, or (at sheriffs' execution sales) purchased stock or produce seized for non-payment of a rack rent. Any member guilty of such acts should be expelled and denounced.

Guidelines were added for the formation of auxiliary land clubs in cities and towns of Ireland, and in centres of Irish population in England, Scotland, America, Canada, and Australia, which, besides supporting the national land-movement in Ireland, should advocate 'the cause of labour and humanity' everywhere. Reading-rooms and libraries should, where possible, be established in connection with them, and prizes for essays on the land question should be offered, the winning essays being printed for circulation among the tenant farmers. The funds provided by subscriptions from members of these clubs should, after working expenses had been paid, be remitted to league headquarters. Land clubs outside Ireland should undertake the task of forwarding newspapers friendly to the land movement (Davitt was doubtless thinking primarily of Ford's *Irish World*) to local branches

1 See above, p. 341.

of the league in Ireland, for distribution among the poorer sections of the rural population, and should also support those of the national papers in Ireland that advocated occupying ownership. Finally land clubs in England, Scotland, and America should act as propagandist agents 'educating the people surrounding them on the claims of the people of Ireland to a free soil', and enlisting the sympathy of foreigners for the Irish tenant farmers in their struggle 'to emancipate themselves from a feudalistic land code which has been swept from the path of every other civilised people'.[1]

The foregoing 'suggestions' were adopted by the league 'pending the preparation and issuing of rules for the proper management' of the local bodies. It was not, however, till nearly a year later (9 November 1880) that 'rules for the guidance of branches'[2] were issued, and these were simply a revised version of the original 'suggestions' in so far as they related to rural Ireland. The absence of any definition of the relationship between the branches of the league and its central body may, like the absence of a written constitution for that body itself, have been calculated to put obstacles in the way of legal proceedings. But it was probably due still more to Davitt's genius as a popular organiser. He made no attempt to impose any comprehensive scheme on the rising league but merely laid down a broad pattern of local organisation, derived from six months' experience of an agitation whose origins and strength unquestionably lay in local initiative, local leadership, and a growing sense of local solidarity. Perhaps also the formation of a branch structure was allowed to take the very flexible course it did because of the multiplicity of the demands that were being made on Davitt's time and energy: he was, he wrote to Devoy on 1 November, 'running about and attending to fifty different matters'.[3] Between the founding of the Land League and the end of 1879 he spent most of his week-ends addressing land meetings in Connacht;[4] twice visited England (late October and late November), speaking at Gateshead-upon-Tyne on 30 November;[5] kept up a large correspondence, partly with individuals and partly (it was his only regular source of income) with American newspapers, chiefly the *Irish World* and the *Pilot* of Boston, to both of which he contributed regular reports on the land movement; and became again involved in the clutches of the law.

[1] *Irish National Land League: [suggestions on organisation]*, 4 pp; reprinted from *F.J.*, 31 Dec. 79; copy accompanying report of Supt John Mallon, 10 Aug. 80, in S.P.O., I.N.L.L. and I.N.L. papers, carton 9; reprinted in *S.C.P.*, iv, 420–22, vi, 114–15.

[2] See below, p. 426.

[3] *D.P.B.*, i, 460.

[4] S.P.O., R.P. 1879/20193.

[5] *D.P.B.*, i, 460, 463–4 (*not* from Paris); *Nation*, 6 Dec. 79; Cashman, pp 118–20.

From land platforms in the five counties of Connacht, Davitt repeated his message to tenants that they had a duty not to pay any rent till they had satisfied their vital needs and paid their debts to the small shopkeepers whose credit had enabled them to feed their families.[1] They must not fear, Davitt declared, that they would be turned out on the roadside to die: 'there was a spirit abroad in Ireland that would not stand that a second time in a century'.[2] Dismissing the 'exploded doctrines' about dual ownership and the '3 Fs' as a solution to the land question, he argued that the demand for peasant proprietorship had just as good a chance of being conceded, the landlords being as much opposed to the former as to the latter. The buying-out of the landlords through the amendment and extension of the Bright clauses of the 1870 land act was no chimerical proposal, but an entirely practicable plan that would change the face of Ireland in a lifetime.[3] Insisting on the abolition of landlordism was not inciting the people to sedition. He had no objection in principle to the use of force, and had not a word of apology to offer for his own revolutionary past. But illegal acts now would play into the hands of the government and the landlords; and he and his colleagues were not so foolhardy as to challenge the military power of England and get crushed in the effort. Neither were they prepared to sit down and do nothing. Instead they had chosen the middle course set by Parnell, of whom Davitt declared himself to be a 'humble follower' because he saw in Parnell 'the man whom providence had marked out to lead the Irish people to victory'.[4] The tenant farmers must stand firmly together and proclaim their principles openly before the world, conscious that their cause was also the common cause of humanity. Those who called the land movement communistic or socialistic lied in their throats. It was a moral and religious movement, supported by the majority of the patriotic priesthood of Ireland, and it had the advantage over every previous movement that it combined catholics and protestants, home-rulers and separatists, in a great effort to raise the tenant farmers in the social scale, improve their living conditions, and enable them, instead of emigrating or remaining in poverty and squalor, to live in their own country in peace and plenty. 'Therefore I say this movement is destined to triumph, no matter what action the government of Ireland may take.'[5]

[1] Carrick-on-Shannon, 14 Dec. (S.P.O., I.N.L.L. and I.N.L. papers, Speeches 1879–88, carton 2).

[2] Killala (Co. Mayo), 25 Oct. (*F.J.*, 27 Oct.).

[3] Killanin (Co. Galway), 16 Nov. (*F.J.*, 17 Nov.).

[4] Castlerea (Co. Roscommon), 7 Dec. (*F.J.*, 8 Dec.).

[5] Drumsna (Co. Leitrim), 13 Dec. (*F.J.*, 15 Dec.).

The land meetings of 1879—held in the open air, usually on Sundays, often in pouring rain—established a pattern for the movement. In point of numbers attending, frequency, enthusiasm, organisation, and dynamism combined, they were unique, recalling, but far exceeding, the mass demonstrations for repeal under O'Connell and for amnesty of fenian prisoners under Butt. In the processions to and from the place of meeting, bands playing patriotic tunes were an essential element, and so were banners and placards carrying slogans of the land movement—'The land for the people', 'Down with the land robbers', 'No more evictions', 'Emancipate the white slave', 'We are on strike against rack rents', 'Defend your birthright', 'Give us our parliament'. Horsemen in formation were often a feature of these meetings, which, even in the west, were far from being attended wholly by poverty-stricken small farmers and labourers. The platform party usually included catholic parish clergy,[1] who moved or seconded resolutions, often warning against the dangers of resort to violence. Platforms frequently proved inadequate in strength or capacity, with the result that their occupants sometimes found themselves thrown to the ground. This explains one of Parnell's rare public jokes: 'we on this platform', he said at Limerick on 31 August 1879, 'are very much in the position of the struggling tenant farmer; we find it very hard to maintain our footing'.[2] At Williamstown, County Galway, on 18 January 1880, twenty people fell through the collapsing floor of a ten-foot high platform, suffering cuts, bruises, and concussion.[3]

Though the language of the speakers was often extravagant and overheated, eliciting excited and sometimes violent responses and interjections from the audience, as a rule land meetings were orderly and peaceable. Nevertheless, clashes with the police who, armed with rifles, usually attended in some strength, were at times avoided with difficulty. The presence of police reporters in plain clothes to take official notes of the speeches could cause dangerous tension. At Castlerea, on 7 December, a fracas with the police guarding two such reporters was only averted through the strenuous efforts of Parnell and Davitt, who persuaded an angry crowd to allow the police reporters to seat themselves on the platform, behind the press reporters, while the police withdrew to a distance.[4] At Corofin, near Tuam, on 9 November, a government reporter was baffled when, towards the close of a meeting the chairman and Davitt addressed the people in Irish.[5]

[1] Of 45 major land meetings held from 25 Oct. 79 to 3 May 80 clergy were reported as present at 32.

[2] *F.J.*, 1 Sept.

[3] *F.J.*, 19 Jan. 80.

[4] *F.J.*, 8 Dec. 79; S.P.O., R.P. 1879/21609.

[5] *F.J.*, 10 Nov.

The Castlerea incident was condemned by Parnell, who believed that interference with police reporters played into the hands of the police. During discussion on the constabulary estimates in the house of commons on 30 August 1880 he protested against police provocation at land meetings, and as the result of an inquiry by the new chief secretary, Forster, Parnell was informed that if reporters were allowed a place on the platform and properly treated the ordinary police would be kept away. This was done at Ennis on 19 September, at New Ross on 26 September, and at other land meetings. But at Charleville, County Cork, on 26 September, no police being present, police shorthand-writers were rudely hustled off the platform and prevented from taking notes, despite expostulation from Sexton, who attended as delegate of the central Land League. Two days later, at one of his rare appearances at the central body, Parnell announced that if in future he found unwillingness at a land meeting to admit police reporters he would withdraw from the meeting.[1]

Meetings were sometimes called for the special purpose of demonstrating against an eviction. On such occasions tempers were apt to run high, and police protecting the sheriff or his deputy in executing an ejectment decree were sometimes attacked not only with concerted verbal abuse but with stones and other missiles. At Balla, on 22 November 1879, the intended eviction of a small farmer, Anthony Dempsey, brought on a military-style confrontation between some 8000 demonstrators, marshalled by Parnell, and 100 armed police. The latter, placed at a tactical disadvantage by an encircling movement of Parnell's forces, withdrew, leaving the demonstrators in possession of the hill on which Dempsey's cottage stood. The eviction had by that time been postponed, but a protest meeting was none the less held in the course of which Brennan made an impassioned appeal to the police not to be destroyers of their fellow Irishmen, and urged the farmers to cast out the land-grabber as an unclean thing.[2]

Such confrontations were, however, exceptional. Normally relations between the police and the crowds attending land meetings were good-humoured and even friendly. Jeremiah Stringer, a police reporter, after a painful initiation into his duties, became quite a popular figure at western land meetings.[3] Louden of Westport told the *Times*–Parnell commission that in Mayo 'there was the very best *entente* between the people and the police'. To his knowledge local police contributed

[1] *F.J.*, 27, 29 Sept. 80; cf. Arnold-Forster, Irish journal, 4 Nov.

[2] *F.J.*, 24 Nov. 79; Cashman, pp 114–16; W. O'Brien, *Recollections*, pp 231–2. An extract from Brennan's speech is given in Lyons, *Parnell*, p. 102.

[3] Below, p. 451.

to the expenses of 'a very important land meeting', and police often subscribed to the relief of people whom they had to evict.[1]

The law gave the executive no power to prevent or suppress land meetings unless they were called for the purpose of denouncing or threatening an individual or unless they appeared likely to provoke a breach of the peace. If speeches at public meetings were seen as inciting to crime it was for the executive to decide whether to prosecute the speakers.[2] A prosecution was thus brought against Davitt for a speech at a land meeting at Gurteen, County Sligo, on 2 November, as reported by a police note-taker. It was a vehement protest against a land system that threatened rural Ireland with 'another artificial famine'. Rent for land in Ireland was 'an unjust and immoral tax upon the industry of the people', through which 3000 landlords annually pocketed £20,000,000 nearly half the entire earnings of 600,000 farmers.

> The farmers must work from morn till eve to support themselves and their children, when in steps Mr Lazy Unproductive Landlord and demands almost half of the money so earned, to sustain himself in the licentious and voluptuous life he very often leads, not in Ireland but away in London, Paris, and elsewhere.

It was futile to suppose that any mere tinkering with landlord–tenant relations would provide a remedy.

> Are we here to listen to any proposal of fixity of tenure at fair rents . . .? I say no; that is fixity of landlordism, fixity of poverty and squalor, and fixity of degradation. . . . I say that . . ., in face of another impending famine too clearly visible, the time has come when the manhood of Ireland will spring to its feet and say it will tolerate this system no longer.[3]

The under-secretary, T. H. Burke, took notice of this speech and consulted the Irish law officers, who proposed to make it the subject of a prosecution. The chief secretary, James Lowther, then consulted the home secretary (R. A. Cross), who in turn consulted the English law officers. They reported (13 November) that if it were thought desirable to take action against Davitt, five options were open to the Irish government: (1) to prosecute him for seditious words, (2) to revoke his licence[4] for violating the condition that he must abstain from any breach of the law, (3) to proceed against him for not reporting to the police as required by another condition, (4) to revoke his licence by exercise of the provision declaring it revocable at the queen's pleasure, (5) to warn him that if he continued to use language such as

[1] *S.C.P.*, ix, 550.

[2] Memorandum by John Naish, legal adviser to the Irish government, 29 Dec. 80 (P.R.O., Cab. 37/4/95).

[3] S.P.O., Queen *v.* Parnell papers, 1880–81, carton 9; *F.J.*, 4 Nov. 79. [4] See above, p. 180.

that at Gurteen his licence would be revoked. Each of the first four options was open to serious objection. (1) Prosecutions for seditious language were generally undesirable, and it would be difficult both to prove the charge and to obtain a conviction from an Irish jury. (2) It was contrary to custom to revoke a licence without a fresh conviction. (3) Davitt had been allowed for nearly two years to be at large without reporting to the police.[1] (4) To revoke his licence by simple executive act without assigning any reason would be harsh and unprecedented, though it might become necessary. The law officers preferred the fifth course as most likely to succeed and to have a salutary effect on other offenders.[2]

Despite misgivings on Lowther's part, the cabinet decided to act on the advice of the Irish, and to reject that of the English, law officers.[3] Cross told Lowther privately that he would require Davitt to observe the condition of regular reporting to the police,[4] but he seems not to have done so when, on 19 November, Davitt was arrested at his lodgings in Dublin by Superintendent John Mallon on a charge of using seditious language. Two other speakers at the Gurteen meeting, James Daly of Castlebar and James Bryce Killen, a presbyterian barrister of Belfast, were simultaneously arrested on the same charge. Daly, who described himself as the 'head agitator' in Mayo,[5] was better known to Connacht audiences than Davitt, but Killen was previously unknown as a public figure. Daly at Gurteen had repeated advice he had given at Balla (15 August): if anyone was evicted it was the duty of his fellows to assemble in their thousands and reinstate him the next day.[6] Killen had concluded a fire-eating speech with the wish that everyone at the meeting were armed with a rifle; 'the days of namby-pamby speaking are over'.[7] All three men were taken to Sligo and brought before the resident magistrate. On the application of the crown solicitor they were remanded in custody and lodged in the county jail.[8]

Their arrest caused an immediate sensation. Indignation meetings were quickly organised in Dublin (21 November) and elsewhere, the Balla demonstration (22 November) being made the occasion for one of them. At the Dublin meeting, held in the Rotunda,[9] Parnell unreservedly identified himself with the cause of the arrested leaguers, and thereafter, both in Ireland and England, was their most prominent and

[1] See above, pp 194, 307–8, 323.
[2] S.P.O., R.P. 1879/10401 (1882/26234); P.R.O., H.O. 144/5/17869/22B.
[3] Lowther to Cross, 6 Dec. 79 (P.R.O., H.O. 144/1538).
[4] S.P.O., R.P., 1879/10401 (1882/26234); cf. above, p. 323.
[5] *F.J.*, 25 Nov. 79.
[6] *F.J.*, 4, 25 Nov.; cf. above, p. 314.
[7] *F.J.*, 4, 27 Nov.
[8] S.P.O., R.P. 1879/20193; *F.J.*, 20 Nov.
[9] *F.J.*, 22 Nov.

energetic champion. When the prisoners were examined before the Sligo magistrates, the proceedings received extensive publicity in the press not only of Ireland but also of Britain and America, greatly to the advantage of the league and the disadvantage of the government. This was partly because the language complained of was not essentially different from the standard rhetoric of land meetings. Then their four-day examination before the magistrates (24–8 November) was rendered farcical by the mountebank performance of the notorious John Rea, the Belfast solicitor, who was engaged (at a fee of £100) by his friend, Joseph Biggar[1] for the defence of Killen with a view to the discomfiture of the bench and the prosecution. Daly was defended by J. J. Louden and Davitt defended himself. Each day's proceedings in the court were relayed to the outside world by twenty-seven press reporters; and each day an enthusiastic procession, led by the Sligo brass band, escorted one or more of the prisoners from the prison to the courthouse in the morning, and back again to the prison in the evening, 'like a newly arrived circus company'. In all this, and in nightly protest meetings, great activity was shown by Parnell and Dillon, who lost no opportunity of spreading propaganda for the Land League. Davitt, interviewed by Albert Chester Ives, special correspondent of the New York *Herald*, described the arrests as 'a huge blunder on the part of the landlords and Dublin Castle'.[2]

The accused were successively returned for trial and released on bail, Davitt on 25 November. He conducted his own defence, showing characteristic ability in picking his way through the technicalities of legal procedure. Unable to disprove the accuracy of the official report of his speech, he denied that his words were seditious and tried to produce supporting opinions of witnesses as evidence. This, of course, was ruled by the court to be inadmissible, and Davitt's defence resolved itself into a vindication of his motives. He had not sought to promote dissension or disaffection, or to arouse class hatred, or to procure changes in the law by inciting people to lawless acts.

> The head and front of my offending is this—that I have advocated . . . peasant proprietary against the system that at present prevails . . ., and I think that, instead of my being placed here today to answer charges . . . of inciting the people to deeds of violence, it is this system of landlordism that I have denounced which should be placed in the dock to answer for the crimes . . . imputed to me in the open discussion of its effects upon the people of Ireland.[3]

On 12 December, at the winter assizes held at Carrick-on-Shannon, a grand jury found true bills against all the accused, but there the proceedings halted: on the application of the attorney general the indictments

[1] *F.J.*, 24 Nov. [2] *S.C.P.*, i, 534, 539–40. [3] *F.J.*, 26 Nov.

were transferred by a writ of *certiorari* to the court of queen's bench. Brennan, who had been arrested on 5 December and similarly charged at Castlebar before the Mayo magistrates for his speech at Balla, was treated in the same way. All four released prisoners celebrated the occasion, along with John Rea, at an exuberant demonstration at Carrick-on-Shannon on 14 December, which gave the league its first effective footing in County Leitrim.[1] The government had thus incurred a great deal of ridicule, and, far from chastening Davitt, had done much to enhance his public image and to publicise the Land League. The rejected advice of the English law officers had been vindicated.

The Sligo prosecutions were made the occasion for a propaganda drive in England, headed by a mass meeting in Hyde Park, London, on Sunday, 30 November, at which representatives of many radical and working-class organisations were present. Resolutions were adopted protesting against the arrests, expressing sympathy with the suffering people of Ireland in their present distress, and supporting the Land League's objective of peasant proprietorship.[2] On the same Sunday Parnell made what he announced as 'a seditious speech' to a monster gathering outside St George's Hall, Liverpool, and Davitt himself addressed a crowded meeting of Tyneside Irish at Gateshead on the theme that the landlord system was the root cause of Ireland's poverty and degradation. It had been responsible for the deaths of nearly two million people in the great famine, and there would never be peace in Ireland till it was abolished. 'So long as he had brain to plan, [or] hand to dare, [or] heart to feel for Ireland, so long would he stand an uncompromising enemy of landlordism.'[3] In the present crisis it was necessary to arouse in the tenant farmers such a spirit of resistance that there could be no repetition of the suicidal resignation they had shown in 1847–8; and therefore every Irishman worthy of the name should support the Land League whatever his party attachment.[4] Speaking at Birkenhead on the following night (1 December), Parnell attributed to Davitt most of the credit both for starting the league and carrying it on in face of great difficulties.[5] These speeches of Parnell's were referred both to the English and the Irish law officers, who as in

[1] S.P.O., Queen *v.* Parnell, 1880–81, carton 9. Notes by D relating to proceedings at Sligo (DA/1). *F.J.*, 25 Nov.–15 Dec. 79. Cashman, pp 116–17, *Fall*, pp 178–86.

[2] *F.J.*, 1 Dec.

[3] Cf. speech at Manchester, 21 May 82: 'So long as I have tongue to speak, or head to plan, or hand to dare for Ireland, Irish landlordism and English misgovernment in Ireland shall find in me a sleepless and incessant opponent' (Cashman, pp 167–8).

[4] *Daily Courier* (Liverpool), 1 Dec. 79; Denvir, *Life story*, pp 205–8. *Nation*, 6 Dec.; Cashman, pp 118–20.

[5] *Irishman*, 6 Dec.

Davitt's case took opposite views on whether he also should be prosecuted for sedition. The English lawyers were altogether against any action, whereas the Irish lawyers, comparing his language with that for which Davitt and the others were being prosecuted, pronounced it to be far more seditious than theirs. It was awkward, Lowther complained to Cross, when doctors thus disagreed; but the question was whether the Irish government could go on with proceedings against 'comparatively unimportant personages for "stealing a lamb", while the acknowledged leader of the whole movement is allowed to appropriate "a sheep" in broad daylight in England'. He sent the papers in the Sligo cases to Cross for study by the English law officers, but no action was brought against Parnell and the prosecutions of Davitt and his friends continued.[1] Lowther's estimate of Davitt's unimportance did little credit to his political judgment.

Ever since the formation of the league Davitt had been in communication with political friends in America—O'Reilly, O'Kelly, Devoy—about Parnell's proposed visit to America, but it had been postponed owing to the Sligo prosecutions. Davitt was anxious that Parnell should not be publicly identified with Clan na Gael, while seeking to ensure that the Clan would give him all possible help. The Clan's response was vigorous and positive: Devoy, Carroll, and others at once began to make preparations for Parnell's visit. But at the same time the trustees of the 'national fund' announced that, should the land agitation lead to an open conflict, they would use the fund to help the Irish people to 'strike down the robber rule of the landlord'; and they appealed to Irish-Americans for contributions against such an eventuality. Davitt shared Parnell's view that this announcement, which was reproduced in the Dublin press,[2] would do the Land League no good. His initial gratitude for the money advanced to him from the fund[3]—some of it used to pay the expenses of his Sligo prosecution—was soon dissipated when, in November, hints of the transaction began to be leaked to the press, to become the basis of a persistent charge that the Land League was started with money raised for the purpose of outrage and terrorism. The charge grew so galling to him that he decided to regard the loan as a personal debt, and eventually repaid it in 1880 and 1882.[4] In the context of Davitt's personality the affair had some resemblance to that of the 'pen' letter.

On 12 December Parnell was able to inform the American press that

[1] Lowther to Cross, 6 Dec. (P.R.O., H.O. 144/1538); see below, p. 364.

[2] *F.J.*, 1 Nov.

[3] Above, pp 312-13.

[4] *D.P.B.*, i, 455-7, 460-64, 468-9, 471-2; Carroll to Parnell, 5 Jan.80 (DP/A11); Cashman, pp 217-19; *Nation*, 19 Aug. 82; *S.C.P.*, ix, 454-6; *Defence*, pp 63-9; *Fall*, pp 209-10.

he and Dillon were authorised by the executive of the league to leave for New York as soon as possible.[1] They arrived there on 2 January 1880. It had been intended that they should appeal only for funds for the stated objects of the league, but the intensifying distress caused a change of plan. So their actual appeal was to be two-fold—for the relief of distress as well as for the purposes of the agitation.[2]

Throughout the last three months of 1879 innumerable voices were warning the government that emergency measures were imperative if the distress was not to get out of hand.[3] The catholic clergy, home rule M.P.s, local bodies, and the Land League itself insistently called on the government to provide employment by instituting schemes of public works.[4] But the government, suspicious of such expedients as uneconomic and inviting misappropriation of public funds, was slow to recognise the seriousness of the crisis. It had set up a commission on 14 August, under the chairmanship of the duke of Richmond, to inquire into the condition of agriculture in the United Kingdom as a whole, and though the commissioners turned their attention first to Ireland it was nearly eighteen months before they issued a preliminary report.[5] Detailed information on the state of the crops and the fuel supply was rapidly obtained by the Irish executive through the poor law inspectors and the constabulary,[6] but the conclusion was drawn that no emergency legislation was called for: the situation could be coped with by the ordinary resources of the poor law system and by increased use of the facilities available to landlords and local authorities for borrowing money for improvement projects. It was not till January 1880 that any emergency action began to be taken, and then it was only in the form of more favourable terms for borrowing from the board of works.[7] Yet by that date people in Connemara were beginning to eat their seed potatoes.[8]

By January 1880 voluntary charity had begun to be mobilised in schemes, which were to prove a spectacular success, to supply the destitute with food, clothing, and seed potatoes. The Land League, though relief of distress was no part of its official programme, was soon deeply involved in relief work. Davitt himself made a rapid tour of investigation in Mayo on 23 and 24 December, and found conditions

[1] Cashman, pp 116–17. [2] *Fall*, pp 192–4.

[3] Palmer, *Land League*, pp 78–9.

[4] For example, *F.J.*, 4, 17, 18, 24 Nov., 8, 15 Dec. 79.

[5] *Preliminary report from her majesty's commissioners on agriculture*, 14 Jan. 1881 [C 2778], H.C. 1881, xv, 1–24.

[6] T. W. Grimshaw, *Special report on agricultural produce and fuel supply in Ireland as ascertained by inquiries made in October 1879* (Dublin, 1879).

[7] Palmer, *Land League*, pp 79–80. [8] *F.J.*, 14 Jan. 80.

very grim: at Ballaghadereen there were not twenty tenants in the parish who could meet their liabilities and live through the winter; on Clare Island no rents had been paid and the tenants were holding out against the landing of any civil-bill officer or process server.[1] Davitt reported to the committee of the league on 30 December, when it was decided that, in view of the urgency of the distress, the league would undertake to receive and disburse relief funds;[2] and thus a large new field of action was opened up for it. At the same time local relief-activities were quickly improvised in many parts of the country, especially by the clergy, catholic and protestant; and two general funds were inaugurated in Dublin: on 18 December the duchess of Marlborough's fund, named after the wife of the lord lieutenant, and on 2 January the Mansion House relief fund, headed by the lord mayor of Dublin, Edmund Dwyer Gray, owner and editor of the *Freeman's Journal*. A third fund was started soon afterwards in New York by James Gordon Bennett, owner of the *Herald*, who opened the subscription list with $100,000. Parnell regarded all these funds as competitors, alleging that they were more concerned with relieving the landlords and the British government than the starving peasantry. Davitt felt that he went too far in these strictures, thereby 'arraying a phalanx of holy heroes against him'.[3] But the dual character of his appeal created inevitable difficulty: he could hardly expect to raise money, as he did, to sustain the Land League, without giving offence to those who were ready to contribute for the relief of distress only. In the event the Parnell–Dillon mission yielded (January to June 1880) about £12,000 for the league and about £60,000 for relief purposes, the latter a substantial total but much the lowest for the four principal funds.[4]

The large sums raised by these and other voluntary relief-agencies (including the Land League) during 1880, together with funds from abroad channelled through the Irish bishops and money sent directly by individuals to friends in Ireland, were estimated by the Mansion House committee to amount to about £830,000.[5] This helps to put the Parnell–Dillon mission into perspective. It was its political rather than its financial results that mattered most to the league. This first and only appearance of Parnell in America as national leader brought home to vast numbers of Americans, and more especially Irish-Americans, the nature of the new national leadership that had arisen in Ireland. In two months he and Dillon visited over sixty cities east of the

[1] DN/3, pp 43–9. [2] *F.J.*, 31 Dec. 79.

[3] D to Devoy, 6 Feb. 80 (*D.P.B.*, i, 483); *F.J.*, 7 Feb.

[4] Palmer, *Land League*, pp 84–101; *D.P.B.*, i, 475, 486–7, 490–92; *S.C.P.*, vi, 349–57, vii, 26–7; *Fall*, pp 194, 205–6, 210; Lyons, *Dillon*, pp 34–5; Lyons, *Parnell*, pp 106–8.

[5] *Irish crisis*, p. 73.

Mississippi and in Iowa, at most of which they addressed public meetings in the presence of public representatives. The legislatures of New York, Virginia, Kentucky, Wisconsin, and Iowa formally received them, and the house of representatives at Washington conferred on Parnell the rare honour of inviting him to address them. He did so on 2 February in a moderate speech that concentrated on the land question, presented, in terms of its now orthodox nationalist mythology, as dating from the first English invasions of Ireland. At Cincinnati, Ohio, on 20 February, he linked the land question with the independence question.

I feel confident that we shall kill the Irish landlord system. And when we have given Ireland to the people of Ireland, we shall have laid the foundation upon which to build our Irish nation. The feudal tenure, and the rule of the minority, have been the cornerstone of English misrule. Pull out that cornerstone . . . and you undermine English misgovernment. When we have undermined English misgovernment we have paved the way for Ireland to take her place among the nations of the earth. And let me not forget that this is the ultimate goal at which all we Irishmen aim. None of us, . . . wherever we may be, will be satisfied until we have destroyed the last link which keeps Ireland bound to England.[1]

The statement caused no particular stir at the time, but its 'last link' sentiment was to be frequently quoted against Parnell later. It was untypical of his speeches in America, and may be taken as his most distinctive gesture to Clan na Gael, to whose practical support his mission owed so much, but of whose leading members some, especially Carroll, were beginning to see the Land League as a dangerous rival.[2]

The final stage of the campaign took Parnell to Canada. Accompanied by T. M. Healy, the quick-witted and extremely able young parliamentary correspondent of the *Nation* whom he had summoned from London on 13 February to help with the secretarial work of the mission, he had two highly successful meetings at Toronto and Montreal on 7 and 8 March. At a supper in his honour after the Montreal meeting, where he had been called by Healy the 'uncrowned king of Ireland', he proposed, in a speech of unusual warmth, an extempore toast to Davitt—'the founder of the Land League' and 'the life and soul of the movement'.

Much credit had been given him [Parnell] for the progress of the present movement which he did not altogether deserve, for they must remember it was not until after long and serious consideration that he had entered into the movement, . . . being a landlord himself. But seeing the example set by other men, whose

[1] *I.W.*, 6 Mar.; quoted in *S.C.P.*, i, 195, vii, 22–3.

[2] *F.J.*, 17 Mar.; *Fall*, pp 193–206; *Defence*, pp 131–2 (not consistent with *Fall*, pp 209–10); *D.P.B.*, i, 467–8, 475–80, 484–7, 490–92, 497–8; R. B. O'Brien, *Parnell*, i, 200–04; Lyons, *Parnell*, pp 110–13.

courage and perseverance could leave no doubt of their patriotic sincerity, he had finally entered into it with a determination to see it a success.

A man of humble origin, Davitt had 'raised himself and benefited by the opportunities given him for education in a most wonderful manner'. 'Would that I could find words to express to you what I feel towards the man who has done so much in raising his country from degradation.'[1]

At Montreal Parnell learnt of Beaconsfield's decision to call a general election and at once prepared to go home, taking Healy with him but leaving Dillon to 'remain on guard' till he himself should return. Before his departure from New York on 11 March he presided at a conference of representatives of twenty-eight Irish organisations, which adopted a series of proposals tabled by him for the setting up of a land league in America. This auxiliary organisation, to be formed 'in harmony with the organisation in Ireland' was to be based on local branches, with an executive council for each state and a central council for the Union. The central council was to be the channel for forwarding official communications and funds to the Dublin executive of the Land League. A committee was to be appointed to give effect to the conference's decisions, and it was agreed that this committee should select a provisional central council, which it hastened to do, many of those selected being Parnell's nominees. This successful winding-up of Parnell's mission, in which Devoy was actively involved, seemed to Carroll to substantiate his growing fear that Parnell was bent on undermining the Clan. In withdrawing, as he now did, from Land League acitivity, Carroll was in effect expressing his realisation that the league was not the fulfilment of the new departure that he had so strongly backed in 1878–9. He was also indignant at what he saw as the 'growing flunkeyism' of Parnell's admirers.[2] But he had a special reason for hostility to Parnell.

Carroll was an ardent admirer of John Murdoch, a pioneer Scottish nationalist of heroic stature who had become imbued with Fintan Lalor's ideas about the land question. In September 1856, being then a civil servant in Dublin, Murdoch had published a series of letters in the *Nation* entitled 'The land for the people'; and since 1873, through his paper, the *Highlander*, of Inverness, he had tirelessly championed the cause of the highland crofters and of Scots-Gaelic revivalism, in combination with steady support of Irish home rule. From September

[1] *Montreal Evening Post*, 10 Mar.; *F.J.*, 14 Feb.; R. B. O'Brien, *Parnell*, i, 205–6; *Fall*, pp 206–7; Healy, *Letters and leaders*, i, 79–88; Lyons, *Dillon*, p. 35; Lyons, *Parnell*, pp 114–15.

[2] *S.C.P.*, vii, 24–5; Cashman, pp 130–33; *Defence*, pp 129–30; *Fall*, pp 209–10; *D.P.B.*, i, 499–501, 520.

1879 to April 1880 he was in America, raising funds for the *Highlander*, then in desperate financial straits. Carroll had engaged him to accompany Parnell and Dillon as an auxiliary speaker, in return for his expenses and $1000 to the *Highlander*. He had spoken eloquently on the community of suffering and of interests between Scottish and Irish tenants. But his services, in Parnell's opinion, had not justified the expense, and Parnell had felt obliged to drop him before the tour was completed. Eventually he was given some $2000 by Clan na Gael. Murdoch was a pan-Celticist of great symbolic importance for the Irish national movement, but it was importance to which Parnell was comparatively unresponsive. By contrast Murdoch was a man after Davitt's own heart; and a few years later Davitt was to campaign with Murdoch in Scotland on behalf of the crofters.[1]

The tribute paid to Davitt by Parnell at Montreal was as timely as it was just. The ten weeks of Parnell's absence showed that Davitt was indeed the dominant personality in the central organisation and direction of the Land League, with Brennan and Egan as his closest colleagues.[2] He lived under extreme pressure, his weekdays normally occupied with meetings of the league and its executive, with interminable correspondence, and with reports for American newspapers. Sundays he nearly always spent away from Dublin attending land meetings: in his diary he noted that Sunday, 29 February, was the second he had spent in Dublin since the previous July.[3] But being on the move, seeing places and people, and addressing public meetings suited his temperament no less than intensive periods of solitary work. What did not suit him, though he was a born organiser, was the grind of routine business; and this was reflected in the running of the central office of the league.

The clerical machinery of the office under his control was rudimentary—he later described it as 'slovenly'.[4] No doubt this was largely because for many months he, Brennan, and Egan combined the work of organisation, policy-making, and propaganda with sheer clerical

[1] *D.P.B.*, i, 332-3, 335, 386, 414, 415, 433-4, 459, 487, 495, 504-8, 513, 517-18, 520-34; ii, 558; *Fall*, pp 228-9; John Murdoch, Autobiography, in Mitchell Library, Glasgow; J. D. Young, 'John Murdoch, a land and labour pioneer' in *Calgacus*, i, no. 2 (summer 1975), pp 14-19; James Hunter, 'The Gaelic connection: the highlands, Ireland and nationalism, 1873-1922' in *Scottish Historical Review*, liv, 2, no. 128 (Oct. 1975), pp 179-85. I am indebted to my colleague, Rev. Terence McCaughey, for calling my attention to the article on John Murdoch, and other material relating to the Scottish crofter movement; and to Mr Owen Dudley Edwards, of the University of Edinburgh, for the loan of a typescript of Murdoch's autobiography.

[2] M. M. O'Sullivan to Matthew Harris, 28 Jan. 80 (*S.C.P.*, x, 180-81; ibid., vi, 502, ix, 458; Kettle, *The material for victory*, p. 23.

[3] DN/5, Jan.-Mar..

[4] *S.C.P.*, ix, 483.

drudgery.[1] Michael Malachy O'Sullivan, the paid secretary, who had been prominent in the land agitation from its beginnings, was privately critical, even contemptuous, of his unpaid superiors, and incurred their censure for exceeding his functions, but seems to have neglected the office routine.[2] No regular filing system was established, and no copies were kept of the hundreds of letters written by Davitt and Brennan in their own hands. A second paid officer took up duty as clerk on 1 March:[3] Joseph P. Quinn, a bright, amiable young man, like O'Sullivan was a fenian and an ex-schoolteacher, who had been involved in the Irishtown meeting.[4] He was the nucleus, and became the head, of a clerical staff which, by January 1881, had risen to some half a dozen. Davitt and his colleagues had confidence in him but he seems to have had no particular gift for running an office. The financial business of the league, in the capable hands of Egan as treasurer, was no doubt managed more efficiently. But the internal history of the central organisation, apart from the reports of meetings regularly published in the *Freeman's Journal*, is largely a blank because its records—minute books, account books, registers, letters (especially correspondence with branches), and papers—were all dispersed shortly before the league was suppressed in October 1881. Davitt, Parnell, and other officers of the league were then in prison, and Egan had moved to Paris. The records disappeared, and all that was produced before the *Times*-Parnell commission in 1889 was a few account books. It was alleged by counsel for *The Times* that the bulk of the records had been destroyed to remove incriminating evidence. Davitt treated the charge with scorn: while admitting that thousands of letters had been destroyed in the ordinary course of business, he argued that it would have been all to the league's advantage if every document it had ever possessed had been forthcoming.[5] The truth probably is that, while much was destroyed (some of it deliberately in 1881 to prevent it from falling into government hands) and much had perished through accident or neglect, much was preserved in private hands. Collections of Land League (and of Ladies' Land League) papers, largely correspondence between the central office and local branches, that have come to light in recent years[6] suggest that more material of the kind will yet be discovered.

[1] There is a reference to D's daily posting of letters at the G.P.O. in Mallon to C.P., 10 Aug. (S.P.O., I.N.L.L. and I.N.L. papers, carton 9).

[2] Above, pp 191, 289, 304; *F.J.*, 16 June 79, 17 Apr. 80; *S.C.P.*, ix, 483.

[3] Ibid.; DN/5, 1 Mar.

[4] Above, p. 285; Devoy, XVII; Healy, *Letters and leaders*, i, 175.

[5] *S.C.P.*, ix, 483; xi, 2, 380-91.

[6] N.L.I., MSS 17693-716.

In the early part of 1880, the executive of the league was simultaneously engaged in administering relief funds, in building up a structure of local branches on the lines laid down in Davitt's 'Suggestions' of 30 December,[1] and in maintaining and directing the agitation. Some local organisers were appointed, notable among them being Michael P. Boyton (an Irish-American with Kildare connections), Patrick J. Gordon (Claremorris), Matthew Harris (Ballinasloe), Patrick J. Sheridan (Tubbercurry), and John W. Walshe (Balla), who were to earn notoriety as land-leaguers. They received either salaries or expense allowances.[2] James Daly, whose *Connaught Telegraph* was one of the most ardent champions of the league, received £50 for his services at a time when his paper was in acute financial difficulty.[3] But the work of the league in the localities was very largely carried on by volunteers, among whom the catholic clergy had become a characteristic element. Parish priests and curates generally acted as distributors of relief, and where no league organisation existed this usually led to the formation of a branch in that locality.[4] The first instalment of relief money raised by Parnell in America, £500, was received by cable on 13 January and was quickly disbursed among needy tenants in Mayo and Galway. Money grants were followed by the issue of 'champion' seed potatoes for spring sowing, to replace those eaten or destroyed by blight. By 2 March 350 tons had been distributed and a further £2000 worth ordered; on 16 and 19 March further sums of £1000 were voted for the same purpose.[5]

The league was now as generally supported by the nationalist press, central and local, headed by the *Nation* and the *Irishman*, as it was generally condemned by unionist and landlord newspapers, of which the most extreme were the *Dublin Evening Mail* and the *Daily Express*. The *Nation*, the weekly edited by T. D. Sullivan, was wholly committed to the league's policy and programme. But being a weekly, with a relatively small circulation, it counted for far less than the *Freeman's Journal*, organ of moderate nationalism and most widely read of Irish dailies, which, though it had a long record of championing tenant right, had adopted an attitude of detachment, if not hostility, towards the league. The quarrelling between its editor, Gray, and Parnell, over political and personal differences, which had been composed through Archbishop Croke's intervention in the previous August,[6] was reopened

[1] Above, pp 344–6.

[2] *S.C.P.*, i, 55; iii, 604, 607, 619; vi, 507; ix, 458.

[3] Daly to D, 14 Jan. (N.L.I., MS 5930, pp 25–8).

[4] *Fall*, p. 211.

[5] DN/5, 13 Jan.–2 Mar. 80; *Defence*, p. 32; *Fall*, p. 211; *S.C.P.*, vi, 502; *F.J.*, 14 Jan.–3 Mar., 17–20 Mar.

[6] Above, pp 314, 338.

in January over Parnell's criticism of the Mansion House Relief Committee.[1] The *Freeman's* coverage of Parnell's American mission was in consequence far from adequate or sympathetic. Davitt was accused by Gray of sending false reports about the Mansion House committee to the *Irish World*, which he vehemently denied while repeating his charge that Gray was trying to make political capital out of the committee and to set the catholic bishops against Parnell.[2] At a meeting of the league on 24 February Egan attacked the *Freeman* for discriminating against individuals in its reports of land meetings. Louden expressed astonishment at the suppression of speeches by Davitt—'the originator and leader of the land agitation'—and Ferguson was indignant that 'the most important man in the land movement' was not receiving due attention. Yet Ferguson considered the *Freeman's* general coverage of the movement to be more valuable than that of all other papers in Ireland put together. He also paid tribute to the moderate unionist *Irish Times*, for its fair treatment of individuals, while complaining that it sometimes did not report a land meeting at all. Egan, endorsing this, pointed out that the *Irish Times* had sent a special correspondent to accompany Parnell in America. Louden was baffled by the tendency of the *Irish Times* to blow hot and cold on the agitation, but Ferguson felt that they need not mind articles so long as the reporting was fair. Louden asserted that the *Freeman* was 'their own' whereas the *Irish Times* did not belong to Ireland, but Egan disagreed, and Ferguson said that, while the *Freeman* was certainly the first newspaper in Ireland, the *Irish Times* was the second. A suggestion to send a deputation to protest to both papers was rejected.[3] The *Freeman's* editorial policy continued for several months to be critical of the league, but changed decisively in Parnell's favour after his election on 17 May as chairman of the parliamentary party, though it remained uncommitted to the league till November.[4] But neither before nor after May is there much evidence of any suppression of Davitt's speeches by the *Freeman*, and it is to the *Freeman's* systematic reporting of meetings of the central league that we mainly owe our knowledge of the differences between the league and the *Freeman*.

Press and pamphlet propaganda at home was powerfully augmented from America by the influence of the *Irish World*, whose circulation in Ireland had noticeably expanded during 1879 and increased enormously from early in 1880. Its editor, Ford, while continuing to publicise 'skirmishing', or urban terrorism, as a mode of attacking Britain,

[1] Above, p. 356.
[2] *Irish Times*, 27, 28 Feb.
[3] *F.J.*, 25 Feb.
[4] *F.J.*, 31 Aug., 10 Nov.; see below, pp 364, 370, 377, 378, 425.

responded with enthusiasm to the anti-rent agitation, and a fund was quickly established to 'spread the light', that is, to supply free copies of the *Irish World* to anyone in Ireland asking for them. In this way great quantities of inflammable material were regularly imported from New York and distributed in Ireland at no cost to the league.[1] But the *Irish World* also served as one of the channels through which, from mid-January, money flowed in from America to the league to sustain both its agitation and its relief measures. The bulk of this money was subscribed for relief.

No less active in the field than at headquarters, Davitt began the new year by taking part in a land meeting at Rathdrum (Parnell's town), accompanied by Egan, T. D. Sullivan, and Thomas Sexton, at which the militancy of his and other speeches was matched by the responsiveness of the audience. Two days later he set out on yet another tour in the west, and spent nine hectic days moving rapidly through Mayo and Galway, investigating local problems and speaking at land meetings. At Kilconly, between Tuam and Ballinrobe, on 4 January, he said that, hitherto, Connacht had been the speaker addressing her sister provinces, but that 1880 promised to bring the rest of Ireland, including the orange tenant farmers, into the land movement. Along the coast between Spiddal and Clifden he found that people were eating their seed potatoes. At Barnaderg, near Tuam, on 11 January, he praised the sensational and successful resistance recently offered by the people of Carraroe, including women and boys, to a process-serving operation. This encounter between sixty armed police, attempting to assert the legal right of the landlord, and a primitive community in a wild and remote part of Connemara determined to prevent the law from taking its course, soon became legendary. Since physical force was used against the process-server and his police escort, the 'battle of Carraroe' could not be regarded by the Land League as a model, but its example of collective local defiance ranked with the action at Balla on 22 November 1879[2] as a precedent for what was to become a familiar tactic of the league: the mobilising of local people to prevent or impede, short of actual conflict with the police, and bring a maximum of hostile publicity to bear upon, the service of ejectment processes and the execution of ejectment decrees for non-payment of rent.[3] The Mayo magistrates at a special session on 30 December had already warned the government that the land agitation had entered a

[1] S.P.O., R.P. 1880/5141; P. H. Bagenal, *The American Irish* (London, 1882), pp 176–90; *S.C.P.*, ix, 457–60; Palmer, *Land League*, pp 124–5. [2] Above, p. 349.

[3] DN/5, 1–12 Jan. 80; *F.J.*, 2, 5, 12, 14 Jan.; S.P.O., R.P. 1880/403, 13676; *Fall*, pp 213–19; Palmer, *Land League*, pp 148–9.

new phase: meetings 'for the purpose of terrorism' were being held wherever ejectments were to be executed.[1]

Back in Dublin Davitt was served with a writ to appear on 16 January in the Crown Office of the court of queen's bench in connection with the Gurteen meeting. He did so, along with Brennan, Daly, and Killen, but a technical hitch occurred that caused the proceedings to be postponed. He resolved not to appear again voluntarily, but in fact appearances were duly entered for all four defendants on 26 January. Legal formalities continued behind the scenes into February, but then came to a standstill, apparently owing to official bungling. So ended the only attempt of the conservative government to strike at the agitation through the courts. Cross, the home secretary took the view that the prosecutions had had a salutary effect, and decided that it would be undesirable to require Davitt to report himself regularly to the police.[2] Yet the case was not closed, but only in suspense, when the conservatives went out of office in April. Four months later Parnell in the house of commons extracted from the new attorney general, Hugh Law, the admission that the new government did not intend to carry the matter any further.[3]

Between 18 January and 2 February, Davitt was again on tour in the west.[4] At Williamstown (County Galway) on 17 January he spoke of the great work being done by Parnell in America and how splendidly it was being reported by the *Irish Times*, in contrast with the *Freeman's Journal*. It was not enough, he told his large audience, to attend such meetings and cheer; they must stand together like men in defence of their own interests. If they organised themselves in Land League branches and tenants' defence associations they would create a power that would put effective pressure on the government.[5] At Mount Partry (County Mayo), on 18 January, after stressing the principle that no one should take a farm from which a tenant had been evicted for non-payment of rent, he said that, though Ireland did not want charity from England, they were grateful to the kind-hearted English who were contributing their mite to save the people of Ireland from starvation.[6] A meeting at Straide, on 1 February, was the occasion for special tributes to his patriotism and his dedication to the improvement of his fellow men. From a platform erected on the site of the cottage where he was born, he delivered a speech that

[1] S.P.O., R.P. 1880/580.

[2] Writ of *venire facias*, 12 Jan. (DP/A11); DN/5, 14, 16 Jan.; James Daly to D, 14 Jan. (N.L.I., MS 5930); *F.J.*, 19 Jan.; *Nation*, 24, 31 Jan; S.P.O., Chief crown solicitor's papers, 1879/436, and R.P. 1880/485 (1882/26234); cf above, pp 323, 352–3.

[3] *Hansard 3*, cclvi, 416 (27 Aug.).

[4] DN/5, 18 Jan.–2 Feb.

[5] *F.J.*, 19 Jan.

[6] *F.J.*, 26 Jan.

summed up the views on the land question he had come to hold with the passionate intensity of a religious faith.

Describing the distress as 'the agony cry of the hour', and relief as the supreme object round which Irishmen of all parties must rally, Davitt nevertheless insisted that public attention must not for a moment be diverted from the primary cause of distress, the landlord system, rooted as it was in conquest and confiscation. Those who were now being denounced in the British press as ruthless agitators had been foremost in raising the cry of distress, and all the ensuing relief measures, whether voluntary or governmental, had been precipitated by them. But over and above all this the agitation had struck at 'the destroying hand of rack-renting' and had saved the farmers two or three million pounds. And 'while the rooftrees of thousands of homesteads were protected from the crowbar brigade', the civilised world had been appealed to against 'a land monopoly which is responsible for a pauperised country and every social evil now afflicting a patient and industrious people'. Proud of having rendered these services to Ireland, the Land League would not swerve one iota from its original purpose—'to haul down the ensign of land monopoly and plant the banner of "land for the people" upon the dismantled battlements of Irish landlordism'.

Against what have we declared this unceasing strife, and whence the justification for the attitude we are calling on the people to assume? . . . In the memory of many now listening to my words that peaceful little stream . . . sang back the merry voices of happy children and wended its way through a once populous and prosperous village. Now . . . the hands of the home destroyers have been here and performed their hellish work, leaving Straide but a name. . . . What wonder that . . ., standing here on the spot where I first drew breath . . ., I should swear to devote the remainder of that life to the destruction of what has blasted my early years, pursued me with its vengeance through manhood, and leaves my family in exile today . . .? . . . An average landlord may be likened to a social vulture hovering over the heads of the people. . . . The tenants in the past have stood by like a flock of frightened sheep, timid and terrified, unable to prevent this human bird of prey from devouring their own and their children's substance. . . . Is it possible that our fathers could have tolerated such a giant wrong . . . as an inevitable decree of God, to be borne in meek submission . . .? Such, however, is not our resolve. We accept no such blasphemous excuse for the abrogation of our manhood. . . .

We demand the right to live like civilised men in our [own] land; we demand the right to enjoy life here, and we are resolved to labour unitedly and unceasingly for the privilege to do so. . . . The principles upon which this land movement rests are founded upon obvious and natural justice. . . . In demanding the land for the people we are but claiming the right which is ours in virtue of our creation and the decrees of our creator. Land was created for man's sustenance, and declared to be the property of the human family, to be worked by labour and made productive in food for the children of men. To hold that, because robbery and fraud have succeeded in gaining possession of the soil of Ireland, landlordism was in the divine intention . . . is a doctrine opposed alike to reason and common sense. Landlordism has worked the deadliest wrong to our country and our race . . . Strike down this giant fraud upon a people, and peace and plenty will take the place of disturbance and starvation. Give labour its claim upon the wealth it creates, remove the restrictions which this feudal code places upon the proper cultivation of the soil of Ireland, and the charity of other lands will no more be appealed to on our behalf, or our national pride be humiliated by our being exhibited in the eyes of the world as a nation of paupers. . . . The cause of Ireland today is that of humanity and labour throughout the world, and the sympathy of all civilised people is with us in the struggle. Stand together, then, in this contest for the soil of your fatherland, and victory will soon crown your efforts with success. Remember with courage and with pride that seven hundred years of wrong [have] failed to crush the soul of Ireland.[1]

It was typical of Davitt that within a few days of this dramatic occasion he was in Paris (5–8 February), accompanied by Egan, on a mission authorised by the Land League to secure sympathetic publicity in the French press for Irish distress and the objects of the league. This move had been suggested by the fenian journalist, James J. O'Kelly, then in Paris, where the three men met. But finding that the Mansion House committee had already sent an agent, P. J. Smyth, to Paris to appeal for funds through the press, they decided not to compete, but agreed that Davitt should return in about a fortnight and in conjunction with O'Kelly (who was a good linguist) conduct a publicity campaign not only in France but also in Belgium, Spain, and probably in Italy, on behalf of the Land League. He thought of spending three or four weeks on such work. In fact he was not able to find time to revisit Paris for nearly a year. He described the state of the land movement in fenian terms in a long letter to Devoy (6 February[2]), enjoyed an evening at the Opera (7 February), and on his way back to Dublin with Egan attended a conference of the English Land Law Reform Association presided over by Charles Bradlaugh (the notorious atheist, republican, and advocate of birth control) in St James's Hall, London (10 February), to which he, Egan, and John Ferguson had been appointed delegates by the Land League. The conference adopted a programme similar to that of the league, and the solidarity between the English and Irish land movements was demonstrated at a crowded public meeting, after the conference, at which a speech by Davitt was received with enthusiasm and followed by the passing of a resolution 'that this meeting of Englishmen expresses its warm sympathy with the Irish National Land League in its efforts to destroy feudalism and plant the Irish people in the soil of their native land'. On each of three days in London (9–11 February) Davitt was present in the visitors'

[1] *F.J.*, 2 Feb.; DN/5, 1–2 Feb.

[2] See below, pp 379–80.

gallery of the house of commons to hear debates on Irish distress that were to lead to two modest relief-measures, the seed supply act (1 March)[1] and the relief of distress act (15 March),[2] the latter authorising the appropriation of £1,500,000 from the church disestablishment fund for loans to landlords and health authorities and giving poor law guardians increased powers in providing relief. He returned to Dublin on 13 February to resume the daily round of Land League business, made much more hectic by the mounting distress and interrupted by journeys into the country to attend land meetings.[3] The strain was beginning to tell on him: five times during the next few weeks he recorded himself in his diary as 'sick'.[4]

On 22 February he attended a land meeting at Knockaroe, Queen's County, along with James Redpath, John Ferguson, Richard Lalor, and others. Redpath, a well-known American journalist, was a strong and impulsive personality and an ardent social reformer, who had been involved with John Brown in the anti-slavery movement and had just arrived in Ireland as special correspondent of the New York *Tribune*. Introduced by Davitt to a meeting of the central league on 17 February, he had requested access to the league's records and had at once been granted all facilities. He sent a series of fiercely anti-landlord letters to the New York *Tribune*,[5] became passionately committed to the land movement, and was elected an honorary member of the central league on 12 October.[6] The Knockaroe meeting gave him his first experience of the league in action, and he heard Davitt declaring a ban[7] on a farm from which a tenant had been evicted:

> The landlord had thrown Malachy Kelly and his family out of their home and holding, but today you and I draw a line round this farm, and let no man dare to cross it with covetous intent if he wishes to live in peace within this county.[8]

Anyone who attempted to break this ban should be subjected to all the rigours of social ostracism. Lalor added: 'Do you see that black cloud hanging over the farm? There will always be a black cloud over it. . . . Leave the farm to the hares and rabbits, the foxes, and wild fowl if they are not afraid to alight upon it.'[9]

Davitt was absent through illness from a meeting of the league on

[1] 43 Vict., c.1.
[2] 43 Vict., c.4.
[3] D to William Haley, 7 Jan. (N.L.I., MS 3905); DN/5, 4 Feb.–18 Mar.; *F.J.*, 7, 14, 25 Feb., 5–17 Mar.; *Nation*, 7, 14 Feb.; *D.P.B.*, i, 482–4, 488–90.
[4] DN/5, 16, 19, 23, 24–5, Feb., 4 Mar.
[5] They were the basis of his book, *Talks about Ireland* (New York, 1881).
[6] *F.J.*, 18 Feb., 13 Oct.; *Fall*, pp 223–4.
[7] See above, p. 321.
[8] *Fall*, pp 224–5 (the 'speaker' was Davitt).
[9] *F.J.*, 23 Feb.; S.P.O., I.N.L.L. and I.N.L. papers, Speeches 1879–88, carton 2, p. 201.

24 February when a request from the Land Law Reform Association for a contribution to the expenses of the recent conference was considered. There was some difference of opinion between those who wanted to keep clear of even an implied affiliation with the English body and those who, with Ferguson, held that the Land Law Reform Association ought to be supported as working in a common cause with the Land League but going much further by aiming at the nationalisation of the land. Davitt would no doubt have shared Ferguson's view that the Land Law Reform Association's connection with other bodies such as the Miners' Association was an additional ground for supporting it. In the end a grant of £10 was voted.[1] This may have had something to do with the contribution of £100 made by the Durham Miners' Association to the relief fund of the league a month later.[2]

The scope of the league's activities continued to expand. A new principle was established when on 19 March the league resolved to assume responsibility for maintaining, 'no matter what the cost', the families of all persons, men, women, and young people, recently sentenced at the Castlebar assizes to stiff terms of imprisonment for resisting the serving of ejectment processes. Brennan was sent to Mayo to carry out this decision, which involved supplying food to about ten families, seeding their lands, repairing their houses, and taking care of children left without one or both parents. The precedent thus set was soon afterwards applied to a similar case in County Galway. Applications from tenants for legal assistance increasingly occupied the attention of the league executive: for example, grants were made to enable tenants to fight ejectment proceedings in the courts and to file claims under the 1870 land act for compensation for improvements. On the other hand applications for help in paying rent were firmly refused. But relief continued to be the most clamant standing business of the league executive, which found difficulty in keeping up prompt acknowledgements of money received while endeavouring to cope with the flood of applications pouring in from all quarters. A running list of moneys received, and sums voted, for relief was published in the *Freeman's Journal* and the *Irish Times*. It was a matter of pride to Davitt and his colleagues to keep the administrative costs of relief to a minimum, but they were criticised as being unsystematic in distributing relief funds and they might have done better to have spent more on building up an adequate staff. They laid down the rule that applications for relief should not be accepted from individuals but only through local committees and clergy, through whom alone relief funds

[1] *F.J.*, 25 Feb.
[2] *F.J.*, 23, 24 Mar.

should be channelled, but it was not found possible to adhere rigidly to this restriction.[1]

The Sunday land-meetings continued, and on 14 March included the novelty of a meeting in the Phoenix Park, Dublin, planned in co-operation with the trades organisations to demonstrate the community of interests between urban workers and the farmers. Some fifteen trade societies, headed by the Coalporters and each accompanied by a band, marched in procession from the assembly point in Beresford Place along the quays to the Park, escorting the speakers and organisers in three wagonettes. In the Nine Acres, within sight of the Viceregal Lodge, a huge crowd, variously estimated at between 30,000 and 70,000, gathered round one of the wagonettes that served as a platform for the speakers. Andrew Kettle presided, and the speakers included Biggar, Brennan, Daly, Davitt, Ferguson, Killen, Louden, W. H. O'Sullivan, Thomas Sexton, and J. W. Walshe. The whole operation was conducted with exemplary order, efficiency, and—despite increasing rain—success. Davitt, its principal architect, spoke first and last. The resolutions, drafted by him, and the speeches traversed well-beaten ground, and contained the whole doctrine of the Land League. It devolved on Brennan to show why the working people of Dublin should join in the movement to destroy landlordism, and he did so in terms that might have been Davitt's: the land agitation, he said, was 'a great social movement . . . against that system which in every walk of life robbed the worker of the profits of his labour'. 'It mattered not whether it were in the bogs of Connemara or in the workshops of Dublin, wherever the toiler had to contend against the heartless landlord or the exacting capitalist, the cause of labour was the same'. The *Freeman's Journal* reported all the speeches except Davitt's, and remarked that the only objectionable feature of the day's doings was the free issue of 'a somewhat blasphemous and not very brilliant burlesque' entitled *Paudeen O'Rafferty on the landlords' ten commandments*.[2] The author was Davitt and his four-page tract,[3] comprising 'the creed of the Right Hon. Lord Clan Rackrent' and the opinions on it of O'Rafferty, a supposed Mayo tenant, was neither brilliant nor essentially blasphemous, but it was vigorous anti-landlord propaganda which stressed the common interests of all workers. Davitt was later to express regret publicly for the form in which he had cast it.[4]

The Land League was faced with a new situation by the prime

[1] DN/5, 19 Mar.–17 Apr.; *F.J.*, 20 Mar.–28 Apr., 16 June; Rev. James Corbett to treasurer of Land League, 25 June (N.L.I., MS 17697).

[2] DN/5, 5, 14–15 Mar.; *F.J.*, 14 Mar.

[3] Copy in DPA.

[4] *S.C.P.*, ix, 385 (2 July 89).

minister's announcement, in a letter of 8 March to the lord lieutenant of Ireland, that parliament would shortly be dissolved. Ignoring the land question Beaconsfield declared that 'a danger in its ultimate results scarcely less disastrous than pestilence and famine' was distracting Ireland: 'a portion of its population is attempting to sever the constitutional tie which unites it to Great Britain'. This danger 'all men of light and leading' would be given an opportunity to resist in the forthcoming general election.[1] This manifesto, which brought Parnell hastening back from America, elicited a prompt response from the league. An address to the farmers, drawn up by Davitt and adopted on 12 March, sought to make the land question the vital issue for Irish electors:

> If you give your vote to a landlord candidate you are voting for famines, rack rents, evictions, workhouses and exterminations . . . Voting to return a landlord to parliament would be as stupid and suicidal as if a flock of sheep selected a wolf to guard the fold.[2]

Electioneering was no part of the league's programme, and it was bound by a resolution not to use any of its funds for that purpose,[3] but this did not prevent Egan from making Parnell a 'loan' of £2000 as an election fund[4] or the league from exerting its powerful influence in the elections on the side of the Parnellite activists within the home rule party as opposed to the moderate or whig majority of the party led by William Shaw.[5] For the contest in Ireland was not only between conservatives and liberals on the one hand and home-rulers on the other, but also between whig and Parnellite home-rulers, the one group identified with the landed interest the other with the Land League.

The outcome of the election was a small improvement in the overall majority of seats won by home-rulers (63) over conservatives and liberals (40), and a large increase in the strength of the Parnellites among the home-rulers.[6] The 40 liberals and conservatives belonged to the upper middle class, and so did 50 of the home-rulers, but the former collectively owned much greater wealth than the latter. For the first time catholics (55) outnumbered protestants (48), all but 11 of the home-rulers being catholics and all but 3 of the non-home-rulers being protestants. The decisive character of the Parnellite gains was only revealed when on 17 May Parnell was elected chairman of the party instead of Shaw, thus finally winning the struggle for leadership.

[1] *Fall*, pp 230–31. [2] *F.J.*, 13 Mar.
[3] Above, p. 336. [4] *S.C.P.*, viii, 27; *Fall*, p. 234. [5] Above, p. 297.
[6] B. M. Walker, 'Parliamentary elections, 1801–1976' in *A new history of Ireland*, ed. T. W. Moody, F. X. Martin, and F. J. Byrne, ix.

This result reflects a significant change in the social composition of the home rule party in which the landed interest had hitherto predominated: of the 34 landowners returned as home-rulers in 1874 only 14 survived the general election of 1880, and of the 23 home-rulers elected for the first time in 1880 only 3 owned any land. Of these 17 landowners only 8 owned over 1000 acres each, as compared with 18 in 1874. The minority that belonged to the lower middle class had substantially increased since 1874—from 2 to 13.[1] Instead of great landowning personages such as Col. E. R. King-Harman, George Browne, The O'Conor Don, and Kenelm Digby, the most distinctive element in the home rule party now consisted of landless newcomers such as John Barry, Andrew Commins, John Dillon, Arthur O'Connor, T. P. The O'Conor Don, and Kenelm Digby, the most distinctive element in Sullivan—all of them Parnellites. A further characteristic of the Parnellite M.P.s was that, unlike the whig home-rulers, few of them resided in their constituencies and many of them lived in England. Nearly all of them were either actively involved in, or were supporters of, the Land League. This transformation of the home rule party was due largely to the impact of the land war on the electorate, to the prestige that Parnell had acquired as president of the Land League, to the ubiquitous energy with which he fought the election, and, above all, to the backing of the league both nationally and in the constituencies. In that backing Davitt played a large and important part.

It was Davitt who drew up the Land League's address to its returning president ('another Perseus' speeding across the waters 'to save the Andromeda of nations from the political monster now threatening her with national destruction'), and who was the first to board the liner *Baltic* off Queenstown on 21 March to welcome him home. Soon Davitt was in the thick of his first experience of electioneering and finding it nearly impossible to cope with the shoal of telegrams from all parts of Ireland without neglecting the claims of the distressed—'there is no more distressed individual in all Ireland than myself' he noted in his diary for 27 March.[2]

Davitt's particular interest in the election lay in his native Mayo, where the sitting members were John O'Connor Power and George Ekins Browne. Both were home-rulers, Power well to the left of the party, Browne as much to the right. Power, from having been involved in the beginnings of the land agitation had drawn away from it, not because of lack of sympathy with its objects but because he regarded the new leadership in Mayo as a kind of intrusion—'the half dozen

[1] C. C. O'Brien, *Parnell*, ch. I; cf. above, pp 128–9.

[2] DN/5, 18–27 Mar.; address to Parnell, 21 Mar. in DP/AD.

gentlemen who have constituted themselves the "Land League of Mayo" are determined to ride roughshod over the county"[1]—and also because he resented the rising power of Parnell. It would have suited him best to have had no contest in Mayo. That was also the attitude of the local catholic clergy, who obtained a promise from Browne of 'increased parliamentary attendance and energy'. Archbishop MacHale was well known to be against a contest; and Bishop MacCormack of Achonry appealed to Davitt 'as a Mayo man, who, I know on good authority, would not be a party to lessen clerical influence even in political matters', not to 'enter the lists against the clergy'.[2] The bishop was wide of the mark. With no inhibitions about opposing clerical interests Davitt was bent on ousting Browne, as a local landowner, and thought at first of running one of the tenants lately sent to prison at the Castlebar assizes for obstructing process-servers.[3] He desisted when local nationalists pointed out that this might cause a conservative candidate to come forward and thus endanger Power's seat. Brennan was then considered, but, apart from the unlikelihood of his consenting to stand, it was felt that to force his candidature on Mayo would be unfair to priests who were supporting the Land League. Kettle and Louden were two of the names suggested, but eventually, after intensive consultation with county leaders at various places, Davitt decided that Parnell himself must be brought in to ensure Browne's defeat. Parnell, though already nominated for Cork city and Meath, agreed to stand and was nominated for Mayo (5 April) to the consternation of Browne's friends and Power's indignation. Davitt flung himself into the conflict with characteristic fervour and energy, sustaining Parnell's cause single-handed till Parnell himself arrived by special train on the eve of the poll. On polling day (11 April) Davitt acted as Parnell's personating agent, and was proud to see poor farmers making no secret of their intention to vote for Parnell. The result exceeded Davitt's expectations: Power headed the poll with 1645 votes (a victory that he attributed largely to the support of Fr John O'Malley, parish priest of The Neale),[4] but Parnell ran Power close with 1565 votes whereas Browne received only 628. It was, Davitt noted, 'a tremendous beating for Browne, office-seekers and clerical backers'. He was also elated at the unseating of The O'Conor Don in Roscommon by the Parnellite James J. O'Kelly—'great blow to catholic whiggery and landlordism', and at Parnell's triple victory—in 'rebel Cork' and 'royal Meath' as well as in 'radical Mayo'. He took particular satisfaction in the dismissal

[1] Power to Fr John O'Malley, 26 Sept. 79 (N.L.I., MS 13457).

[2] Bp MacCormack to D, 2 Apr. 80 (DP/A11).

[3] See above, p. 368.

[4] Power to Fr John O'Malley, 16 Apr. (N.L.I., MS 13457).

from County Wexford of the Chevalier Keyes O'Clery by the Parnellite candidates, John Barry and Garrett Byrne. This was the outcome of a contest in which Parnell had been mobbed by strong-arm supporters of O'Clery at Enniscorthy (28 March) and in which Davitt had indignantly but prudently intervened to prevent further violence. The Wexford election gave Parnell his first experience of being manhandled, and Davitt of being hooted, by an Irish crowd.[1]

The overall result of the general election was seen by Davitt as 'the final and successful political revolt against the landowners by the tenants' in three provinces: 'the evictors of families were themselves politically evicted'.[2] This, and the fact that in Britain the election was an overwhelming defeat for the government and brought the liberals back to power under Gladstone, from whom, of all British statesmen, Ireland had most to hope, opened up new prospects for the land movement. And this perhaps helped to offset the rueful mood in which Davitt had reflected on his thirty-fourth birthday:

> Wonder is there another of my age who had had such trials and undergone such sufferings in such time. What is the prospect of a peaceful and contented life now before me? Another term of imprisonment. Unceasing political struggles and ingratitude for services rendered. Bickerings, worry, anxiety and continued disquietude. Wonder why I cannot take life as easy as others and let politics alone. How miserably inadequate is popularity for that peace and quiet which I have always yearned for. . . . And then the possibility that all my struggling, striving etc. may not bear the fruit which I desire it should ere I quit the scene. Well, 'the rapture of pursuing is the prize the vanquished gain'.[3]

And in fact there was to be no relaxation in the tempo of his efforts till he was sent back to prison just short of a year later.

The progress of the league had now made it both necessary and possible to expand its organisation: Brennan gave up his employment with the North City Milling Company to become the league's full-time general secretary, the office staff was strengthened, and more full-time organisers were appointed. The seven-man executive (retrospectively described by Davitt as the 'governing council') was doubled in size by the addition of Dillon, Ferguson, Harris, Louden, T. P. O'Connor, Thomas Sexton, and T. D. Sullivan.[4] All the new members except O'Connor (a journalist in the London office of the New York *Herald* and successful author of a *Life of Lord Beaconsfield* (1879)[5]) were seasoned land-leaguers. Four of them—Dillon, O'Connor, Sexton, and

[1] DN/5, 28 Mar.–14 Apr.; election telegrams in DP/AC; *F.J.*, 14 Apr., 13 Aug.; *Fall*, pp 235–9.

[2] Ibid., p. 239. The statement was written in 1903, but it completely reflects Davitt's mood in 1880.

[3] DN/5, 25 Mar. 80. [4] *Fall*, p. 240; see above, p. 336. [5] *D.N.B., 1922–30.*

Sullivan—were newly-elected M.P.s, and they raised the total of M.P.s on the league's executive to exactly half (from three to seven). The executive at once prepared to take advantage of the new parliamentary situation. An address to the farmers, drafted by Davitt, and adopted on 16 April, announced the calling of a representative conference on the land question, to meet in Dublin on the 29th: now that Beaconsfield's attempt 'to shift the immediate issue at the Irish elections from the national demand for a settlement of the land question to the higher but less pressing question of self-government' had been frustrated, it was the 'imperative obligation' of the new parliament to face the land question. A committee was formed, consisting of Parnell, Davitt, Egan, Kettle, William Kelly (of Donabate, a leader among the tenant farmers of County Dublin),[1] and Louden (coopted), to prepare a scheme for the conference. In an all-night sitting at Morrison's Hotel on 24 April, at which Davitt, Louden, and Healy appear to have dominated the discussion, Parnell (according to Davitt) expressing no fixed views on how the land question should be settled, agreement was reached on a programme uncompromisingly based on the principle of universal occupying ownership.[2]

As an interim measure to meet the current emergency, the landlord's power of ejectment for non-payment of rent and for overholding (refusal of a tenant to give up his holding in response to a notice to quit) should be statutorily suspended for two years in the case of all holdings valued at £10 a year and under, and for the same period the landlord should not be entitled to a rent higher than the poor law valuation for any holding. For the permanent reform of land tenure a department or commission of land administration should be created, with full power to effect a transfer of ownership of agricultural holdings from the landlords to the occupying tenants either by voluntary or by compulsory purchase, the necessary capital being provided by the state and repayable by annuities equal to five per cent of the purchase price for thirty-five years (as in the land act of 1870[3]). If the sale were compulsory, the purchase price should be equivalent to twenty years rent at the poor law valuation. The department should be empowered to acquire any estate on the same terms and to let the holdings to tenants at a rent equal to three and a half per cent of the purchase money. Arrangements were also proposed to facilitate the sale of land: all owners of land must register their titles, together with

[1] *S.C.P.*, vii, 28; Kettle, *The material for victory*, pp 14, 17; above, p. 337.

[2] DN/5, 16 Apr. 80; *F.J.*, 17, 21, 26 Apr.; *Fall*, pp 240–42 (D's dating of meeting in Morrison's Hotel is incorrect); Healy, *Letters and leaders*, i, 92–3.

[3] See above, p. 119.

any mortgages and other charges, in a registry to be established in each county; and this, with a simplified system of conveyancing, would ensure that land could be transferred from one owner to another as cheaply as shares in a ship or money in the funds. The 'chief architect' of this scheme, Davitt says, was Louden, who had a lawyer's grasp of the land problem, but Davitt himself contributed the land-administration proposals, except the offer of twenty years purchase, which he regarded—with good reason, as it proved— as too favourable to the landlords. Though on this account he refused to sign the committee's scheme, he firmly supported it in principle as the fulfilment of the 'land for the people' doctrine.[1] Yet it contained an inner contradiction: for the concept of land as a commodity to be bought and sold in the open market as readily as moveable property was not compatible with the concept of the state as landlord, which was inherent in one of Davitt's land-administration proposals, and which might be seen as the germ of his later doctrine of national ownership of all land. Whereas his main proposals for occupying ownership prefigured the eventual settlement, his nationalisation idea was to set him apart from nearly all those with whom he was now associated in the land war.

The foregoing programme was adopted with one amendment at the land conference which met on 29 April, under the chairmanship of John Ferguson, in the Rotunda, attended by some 250 delegates (including eighteen M.P.s) from Land League branches and farmers' clubs all over Ireland. The amendment raised the maximum valuation of holdings for which immediate protection from eviction should be sought from £10 to £20. The raising of the upper limit above £10 was strenuously debated, and was strongly opposed by Matthew Harris on the ground that it would bring graziers within the scope of the proposed act. Speaking for the small farmers of the west, a class scarcely represented at the conference, he said that graziers were just as injurious to them as landlords and were detrimental to the best interests of the country.[2] Solidarity between different classes of farmers was good in principle, but the interests of graziers were as incompatible with those of small farmers as the interests of the shark with those of its prey. A sustained effort by The O'Donoghue (a Kerry landowner and M.P. for Tralee), seconded by Jeremiah Jordan (a land reformer from Enniskillen, where he was chairman of the town commissioners[3]), to commit the league to the '3 Fs', on the lines of Butt's bill of 1876,[4] instead of peasant proprietorship, was heavily defeated. The conference was reminded by W. H. O'Sullivan that nothing had been said

[1] *Fall*, pp 242–4; *S.C.P.*, vi, 489–94; vii, 28–30.
[2] See above, p. 210.
[3] *Thom, 1879*, p. 1211.
[4] See above, p. 127.

on the subject of agricultural labourers;[1] and he proposed that every farm should have one labourer's cottage of at least three rooms built on it, with half an acre of land attached, for each £50 of valuation, to be let at a rent proportional to that paid by the farmer to his landlord and not exceeding five per cent of the capital outlay on the building. The chairman ruled the proposal out of order but, commending its intention, pointed out that the contemplated department of land administration would have ample power to deal with the subject of labourers' cottages, and this was confirmed by Parnell. Finally in a resolution moved by a catholic priest, the conference reaffirmed a central principle of the land movement:

> Pending a . . . final and satisfactory reform of the Irish land system, we call upon the tenant farmers . . . to refuse to occupy any farm from which another is evicted for non-payment of unjust rent as the best check upon landlord wrong and as the best method of abolishing landlordism.

The resolutions of the conference were approved at a crowded public meeting in the Rotunda, presided over by Parnell, on the evening of the same day. The meeting was forcibly interrupted by a group of fenians protesting against the 'dictatorial proceedings' of Parnell and Davitt, 'trying to seduce the people from the straight road to independence into the corrupt and crooked ways by which renegades and persons of questionable character obtain seats in the English parliament'. The uproar they produced at the meeting probably helped rather then harmed the Land League, which could now claim a national mandate for its land reform programme, and the commitment of the Parnellite M.P.s to promoting legislation that would give effect to it, and more especially to its emergency proposals for stopping evictions.[2] The league had also in effect received a mandate to continue the agitation in the country, which had partially slowed down owing to the general election.

It had now been decided by the Land League executive that the work of organising the auxiliary movement in America, initiated by Parnell, needed special attention and that Davitt would have to be seconded for the purpose.[3] Before his departure from Queenstown on 9 May, he spoke at two further land meetings, both in Mayo. At Balla, on 1 May, the theme was the importance of promoting the programme adopted by the recent land-conference, including, as a matter of immediate urgency, legislation to suspend evictions during the present

[1] See above, pp 340–41.
[2] *F.J.*, 30 Apr.; *Fall*, pp 244–5; *S.C.P.*, vi, 494–5. 499; vii, 30–31.
[3] *D.P.B.*, i, 516; *Fall*, pp 247–8.

crisis. Louden, who chaired the meeting, opened in characteristic vein with a socio-legal point.

Why was it that a landlord had superior rights to an ordinary creditor for the recovering of his debt; . . . why was it that, whereas a shopkeeper or a moneylender could only recover his debt by civil bill process or by an action in the superior courts, the extraordinary, aye, he might say, the hellish power was given to a landlord to banish the people from their homes? Well, 22 members of parliament and 300 Irish delegates declared in the face of the world that that power must be snatched from the hands of the landlord oligarchy.

Davitt devoted most of his speech to defending the land-reform programme against an attack by the *Freeman's Journal* which had described it as 'wild and impracticable'. He had never said that the British exchequer would have at once to advance £250 millions; what the proposed department of land administration would need in order to begin the gradual creation of a peasant proprietary would be 15 or 20 millions. If evictions from holdings of £20 and under were stopped for the next two years, the small farmers could hope to be on their feet again within that time, while the better-off farmers would obtain needed relief by the requirement that rents should not exceed the poor law valuation of holdings. Thus after two years all classes of farmers would be in a position to benefit from the proposed system of land purchase. It was deplorable that the *Freeman*, which had done good service to the cause of land reform, should now be the ablest enemy of a land programme that had so strong a popular mandate. If the *Freeman* would rid itself of political jealousy and lend its powerful support to the movement led by Parnell[1] the land question could be settled in two or three years. He himself had refused to sign the land programme not because it was too extreme but because it did not go far enough. More radical than Parnell, he did not recognise any right to the soil of Ireland in the landlords, whose titles rested only on violence and the sword. If the people of Ireland were willing to give twenty years purchase for their holdings, he had no objection, but he would continue to deny that the landlords had any right to so favourable a settlement. J. J. O'Kelly, fresh from his victory over The O'Conor Don in Roscommon, made the point that, though the land agitation was primarily a social movement it would have far-reaching political effects: social enfranchisement would lead to political enfranchisement.[2]

The initiation of the agitation was commemorated by a great anniversary meeting at Irishtown on 2 May, the platform party included

[1] This contradicts what Davitt says of the capitulation of the *Freeman* to the Land League in March 1880 (*Fall*, p. 227.).

[2] *F.J.*, 3 May.

Davitt, two M.P.s—Parnell and J. J. O'Kelly— James Daly, Louden, J. W. Walshe, and the two Nallys. Davitt moved the first resolution:

that in commemorating the initiation of the national land agitation . . . we are manifesting the vitality of that movement, which during the past twelve months has shaken the feudalistic system of land laws to its foundation . . ., and demonstrated the power of the democracy of our country by the triumphs achieved over class supremacy, and the intelligence and order exhibited by the people in over one hundred great demonstrations . . .

The land movement had been attacked as communistic, but though it held an advanced position on the social question, it had absolutely no connection with communism such as had been exhibited in Paris in 1871; for Ireland was essentially a Christian country. The landlords had tried to crush the movement by intimidation—and had failed; they now tried to induce the government to crush it—and had failed; and they had been heavily defeated in the recent general election. The government's own efforts, culminating in the prosecutions initiated at Sligo, had been an egregious failure. Victory lay with the Land League, which had infused such a spirit into the tenant farmers that they had withheld between two and three million pounds of rent and thus saved themselves and their homes. Moreover the struggle for the land had been lifted out of its former insular obscurity and brought before the eyes of the world, thanks largely to Parnell's efforts. Parnell himself followed up Davitt's opening in a more practical vein, defending the land-reform programme as a moderate and realistic solution to the great question of the day, designed both to put a stop to rack-renting and to effect the gradual transfer of land to the farmers. This was not, as the *Freeman's Journal* alleged, a plan for the wholesale buying-out of the landlords; and Parnell pointed out that the power of compulsory purchase to be vested in the contemplated department of land administration was intended to be used only against rack-renting or exterminating landlords.[1]

Since the founding of the Land League the catholic parish clergy had increasingly shown solidarity with it, and among the bishops there had been a significant move to the left. Bishops such as McEvilly of Galway who had at first been inflexibly hostile began to realise that they would lose influence with their people if they did not change their attitude to the agitation, while those who had originally been neutral tended to come down on the popular side. But the bishops were far from presenting a united front to the land movement, and in the general election of 1880, while Croke and Dorrian were enthusiastic and successful supporters of the Parnellites, other bishops were

[1] *F.J.*, 3 May; *Nation*, 8 May.

involved in sharp contests on the anti-Parnellite side, especially in Wexford, Cork City, Cork County, and Roscommon.[1] One of the ironies of the election was that Parnell, having been elected in face of episcopal opposition both for Cork City and for Mayo, and with episcopal support for Meath, chose to sit for Cork and insisted on installing in his place for Mayo a presbyterian minister and land-leaguer from Belfast, Rev. Isaac Nelson, who had just been defeated in Leitrim through clerical influence. Bishop Dorrian of Down and Connor commented jubilantly on the Parnellite victories in the election:

> Ireland is erect, and the drones and lukewarm M.P.s are set aside. Some bishops and priests are shortsighted in opposing the active policy. The people see their way and must have themselves rooted in the land. They are right and will succeed.[2]

Episcopal identification with the land movement reached a high level on 30 May when Croke, in an open letter to a meeting at Emly, announced:

> There is no nation . . . that has suffered so much or so long as we have. We have borne so much, and borne it so meekly, that now that we are beginning to fret a little under our punishment and cast ourselves on a small scale into the attitude of self-defence, persons are found to call us ugly names, and words of ominous signification ['socialistic', 'communistic'], borrowed from the vicious vocabulary of the Continent, are used to designate the efforts that are being made by well-meaning men throughout the country to prevent the Irish people from perishing at home or being drafted like cattle to climes beyond the sea. There can be no sin in striving to live and wishing to die in Ireland. It is neither sin nor treason to say that where a man labours he has a right to be fed, and that it is cruel to punish a person for not paying a debt which nature has rendered it impossible for him to satisfy.[3]

This uninhibited declaration was received with enthusiasm by land-leaguers throughout Ireland and was soon circulating in Irish-America, to Davitt's great satisfaction.

Throughout the first year of the land agitation Davitt's connection with fenianism[4] was under increasing strain. He ceased to attend I.R.B. meetings, probably from the autumn of 1879, and came under attack from hard-line fenians at home while retaining the confidence of Clan na Gael. In an uninhibited letter that he wrote to Devoy during his visit to Paris in February[5] he claimed to have carried out 'the whole programme we talked so much of when we were last together'. He explained that he had as yet spent only a fraction of the money advanced by the 'national fund' for the expenses of the land agitation,[6]

[1] Larkin, *The Roman Catholic church and the modern Irish state*, pp 33–8.
[2] Dorrian to Kirby, 14 Apr. (ibid., p. 38).
[3] *F.J.*, 31 May; quoted in *Fall*, p. 262.
[4] See above, pp 302–3, 312.
[5] See above, p. 366.
[6] See above, pp 312–13.

being anxious that other sources should bear their fair share. Some £350 of the amount received remained untouched, and he asked Devoy to send no more money till further notice. The Land League was now a power in the work of famine relief, and if Parnell's American tour answered financial expectations 'we can swing along in splendid style'. There was, of course, the danger that the secret movement would suffer from 'the demoralising influences of meal and money', but during recent visits to disturbed areas in the west Davitt had found 'a great and general desire' among the people to acquire arms. He went on to speak of the arms business of the I.R.B. as though it were no less his concern than the Land League itself. John O'Connor, secretary of the I.R.B. supreme council, had obtained a 'very fair quantity' of arms, and had transferred a 'reasonable share' to the Connacht province. An. I.R.B. organiser had recently made a tour of the north of England (Davitt's own district) and had left it in very good condition. But the work of arming the organisation was impeded by the hostility of Kickham and O'Leary, representing the fenian Old Guard, to 'new departure' fenians, especially Davitt and James J. O'Kelly, of whom the latter had come to Paris on a special mission from Clan na Gael to supply arms to fenians in 'the famine districts' of the west. Davitt found the dog-in-the-manger attitude of Kickham and O'Leary to the Land League particularly hard to bear.[1] His estrangement from the I.R.B., as distinct from the fenian body in America, was brought to a head by the general election.

The I.R.B. greeted Parnell on his return from America with an address announcing that 'nationalists' had decided to take no part in the adoption, rejection, or support of parliamentary candidates in the forthcoming elections.[2] Soon afterwards the I.R.B. executive issued a statement warning members of the organisation against being 'betrayed into active participation' in these elections 'by the plausible utterances or avowals of national principles of any of the candidates'.[3] The decision to hold aloof from the elections was not strictly observed, as the violence at Enniscorthy,[4] in which fenians were involved against the Parnellite candidates, showed. The key role played by Davitt in the return of Parnell for Mayo and the election of James J. O'Kelly for Roscommon are a measure of how little both men regarded the prohibitions of orthodox fenianism. The disorder at the Rotunda meeting on 29 April,[5] during which Davitt was thrown off the platform, was largely directed against him as a renegade from orthodox fenianism, a

[1] D to Devoy, 6 Feb.; J. J. O'Kelly to Devoy, 11 Feb. (*D.P.B.*, 1, 482–4, 488–90).
[2] R. B. O'Brien, *Parnell*, i, 212–13 (21 Mar.).
[3] *S.C.P.*, vi, 498. [4] Above, p. 373. [5] Above, p. 376.

symbol of the 'new departure' that they hated and misunderstood. It is true that the I.R.B. executive soon afterwards (18 May) dissociated itself from the interrupters at this meeting, whom it described as 'a few irresponsible and unauthorised individuals', but it endorsed their denunciation of the 'new departure' fenians.[1]

By this time the I.R.B. supreme council had taken the decisive step of removing Davitt from its membership because of his connection with the land movement. The precise date of this event is not documented, but it may be taken as 8 May.[2] In thus ceasing to be a member of the supreme council, on which he had sat as representative of the north of England since January 1878,[3] Davitt continued to be a member of the I.R.B., but demoted to the ranks.[4] His breach with the supreme council was not over principle, but over policy. The ambivalence inherent in his combination of leadership of an open agrarian agitation, basing its appeal to public opinion on reason and justice, with his continued connection with a secret revolutionary movement remained. His commitment to the Land League was paramount, but the incompatibility between his public inculcation of moral force and his secret approval of supplying tenant farmers with the means of using physical force was never resolved.

[1] *Nation*, 8 May; *S.C.P.*, vi, 499–500.
[2] See below, pp. 402–3.
[3] Above, p. 187.
[4] New York *Herald*, 12 Aug.

X

With the American Land League, May–November 1880

Davitt left Queenstown according to plan, on 9 May, saddened by the sight of 'two immense ships chockfull of Irish emigrants, flying from landlordism'.[1] This third Atlantic crossing, on the Cunard liner S.S. *Gallia*, was less agreeable than his first and second. He travelled steerage and his berth was painfully near the propeller. The *Gallia*, a large, new ship,[2] was crowded, the steerage passengers were generally very dirty and untidy—especially the women, mostly young girls—and the sea was rough for the first few days. He felt thoroughly exhausted and wanted only to sleep, but it was not till the third night that he slept well. On the 13th he was up at 8.30, feeling much better; and from then onwards he enjoyed the voyage, spending most of his time promenading, talking, and eating, though he had meant to do a good deal of writing. He was soon on good conversational terms with a number of passengers. From an Australian who turned out to know Gavan Duffy he learnt of the liberal land-system and the working of responsible self-government in Victoria, and of the notorious bushranger, Ned Kelly (who was soon to be executed for his crimes).[3] Two congenial radicals, one from Sheffield, the other a Scot, strongly condemned Irish landlordism, though unsympathetic to Irish independence. Heated discussion on the independence issue with two other passengers, both Englishmen, was on one occasion continued after dinner over whiskey punch—the only contemporary indication that Davitt had acted on Devoy's advice on the use of alcohol.[4] At two concerts organised in the saloon. he created a stir by refusing to stand for 'God save the queen', and was supported by some Americans. But in general he

[1] DN/6, p. 3.

[2] 4,800 gross tonnage; built in 1879 (*Lloyd's Register of British and Foreign Shipping, 1880-81*); cf. above, pp 221–2.

[3] Convicted of murder, he was executed at Melbourne on 29 Oct. 80.

[4] See above, p. 277.

seems, as usual, to have got on well with his fellow-travellers. He landed at New York on 18 May after nine days at sea.[1]

The *Gallia* had arrived several hours early, with the result that the committee organised for his reception was not present and he was able, thankfully, to make his own way to his hotel (Merchants'). Here he was welcomed by Carroll, who was anxious that Davitt should not allow himself to be 'dazzled by the ephemeral glamour and claptrap of Parnellism'.[2] Carroll, now thoroughly hostile to the Land League, without consulting his Clan na Gael colleagues had invited John O'Leary to come over from Paris to vindicate republican orthodoxy.[3] Clan na Gael as a whole followed Devoy in supporting the Land League; and Davitt, during this second American visit as during his first, found in Devoy a strong ally and an indispensable link with the Clan. Devoy was one of several 'new departure' fenians who were among the delegates attending the first national convention of the American Land League under the chairmanship of John Boyle O'Reilly, at Trenor Hall, New York, on the day of Davitt's arrival. That evening Davitt was enthusiastically welcomed by leading delegates gathered at Everett House, who entertained him to supper and told him of their plans. Next day he attended, with Dillon, the second session of the convention and witnessed the adoption of a constitution and by-laws, and the appointment of a central council in fulfilment of the initiative taken by Parnell on 11 March,[4] for the body now called 'The Irish National Land and Industrial League of the United States'. The convention elected him secretary of the organisation and he agreed to act for the duration of his visit.[5]

That Davitt now held the key office of secretary in both the Irish and American Land Leagues was a tribute to his unique position in the land movement on both sides of the Atlantic. He had earned a high reputation during his first visit to America as a nationalist with new ideas for the regeneration of his country, but now he was received by Irish-Americans as second only to Parnell in the leadership of the Irish nation. During this second American visit, he commanded the confidence of a wide spectrum of Irish-American life. This he saw as comprising three elements: (a) conservative nationalists, strong partisans of Parnell, headed by such men as P. A. Collins of Boston, and including the catholic clergy in large numbers; (b) followers of Patrick Ford and the *Irish World*, who ardently responded to the spirit of social revolution in the land movement; (c) Clan na Gael, dominated by

[1] DN/6, pp 3-18.
[2] *D.P.B.*, i, 528; cf above, p. 358.
[3] *D.P.B.*, i, 531-5; see above, p. 380.
[4] Above, p. 358.
[5] DN/7, 18-19 May; *I.W.*, 29 May; *Nation*, 5 June; *Irishman*, 5 June; *Fall*, pp 247-8.

Devoy and committed to the Land League as a lever to their advanced political programme. Davitt was closest to the second element, while bound by institutional allegiance to the third. The Clan executive had recently issued a secret circular to its officers and members that set out with revealing clarity the Clan's attitude to the land movement. It congratulated the members on the 'magnificent success' of Parnell's mission to America while warning them to give only so much attention to 'public movements' as could be turned to the advantage of Clan na Gael and the 'real revolutionary work' that remained to be done. Wherever land leagues were formed no pains should be spared by members of the Clan to secure control of them. The work of the Clan in preparing the ground for Parnell's visit had been 'a great educating force' for themselves as well as for others. Scarcely any movement in Ireland during the past fifty years had promised more benefit to the Irish people than the present land agitation. 'It is the only really important and tangible thing that has been presented to the people, and, if successful, it will prove the most effective agency in accomplishing the greater revolution that will rid the nation entirely of foreign rule.'[1]

An immediate question dividing the supporters of the Land League was how money collected in America should be transmitted to the league's treasurer in Dublin. The conservatives wanted each branch of the American league to have the right to send their funds direct to Dublin. Clan na Gael, anxious to secure financial control and ensure unity of action, contended for a central treasury in America through which all American funds would be channelled; and Ford characteristically set up his own organisation and sent the money collected direct to Dublin, publishing a weekly list of donors and donations in the *Irish World*. At the Trenor Hall convention (in which Ford took no part) a compromise was reached between the Clan and the conservatives: all branches of the American league were indeed to send their contributions to the central treasurer, but the person appointed to that office was a priest, Rev. Lawrence Walsh, of Waterbury, Connecticut, in whom the conservatives had confidence and who favoured branch autonomy. Davitt, on good terms both with him and with Devoy and Ford, was thus favourably placed for setting about his task of propaganda and organisation.[2]

Interviewed by the *Irish World* (18 May) on the present situation at home, he described the agitation, after its resounding victory over the landlords in the recent general election, as entering a more militant

[1] *S.C.P.*, iv, 517–18; *Fall*, pp 257–8.

[2] *S.C.P.*, ix, 369–73; *Fall*, pp 250–51, 256–7; DPC/2, p. 8; Brown, *Irish-American nationalism*, pp 104–6.

phase. The people thoroughly appreciated the greatness of the challenge confronting them, and believed that the landlord system was doomed. All earnest home-rulers had thrown their energies into the struggle for the land under the incomparable leadership of Parnell, and the efforts of such men as Shaw, Mitchell Henry, and Gray to make the land issue subservient to home rule had failed. The danger of famine had passed, and Davitt had estimated that, with the money received and to be received by the various relief funds and by the catholic bishops, the distressed districts could, without any further appeal to charity, be tided over till the end of July, when a good harvest was to be expected. August should thus find the small farmers free from the demoralising effects of charity. What could they hope for from the government? Only a slight advance on the act of 1870, including an extension of land purchase that would benefit the well-to-do farmers but do nothing for the 400,000 farmers at present too impoverished to pay rent. In any case the land of Ireland, or of any other country, could not justly be sold by any one class to the detriment of the people as a whole—a fresh indication of his embryonic thinking about national ownership.[1] The agitation would continue on the old lines until landlordism was 'trampled in the dust of its own rottenness'. Unlike previous national movements in Ireland, which had all been insular and inward-looking, this one was aware of itself as part of humanity's struggle for social justice throughout the world.[2]

In his speech to the Trenor Hall convention (19 May) Davitt described the movement for the abolition of landlordism as having been initiated in America and as now extending from Dublin to San Francisco. The organisation of branches in Ireland was making rapid headway, and Ulster was following the example of the other three provinces. The league had two interrelated policies, destructive and constructive—in Ireland to hammer at the landlord system, in the house of commons to press for remedial legislation. He welcomed the new industrial clause that the American league had introduced into its programme. The one regret he expressed was at the continued hostility of the *Freeman's Journal*.[3]

Davitt's work in America had a two-fold character. For thirteen weeks he was located in New York, endeavouring to build up a central organisation for the American Land League. For twelve weeks he was on tour in New England and between New York and San Francisco, visiting innumerable centres of Irish-American population, addressing meetings, and promoting branches. He found time to spend only five

[1] Above, p. 375.

[2] *I.W.*, 29 May.

[3] New York *Star*, 20 May; *I.W.*, 29 May; Cashman, pp 136–7; *S.C.P.*, ix, 462–3.

days at his mother's home in Manayunk. Both in New York and on tour he kept in touch with the situation in Ireland and England, and especially with the central Land League in Dublin, where his trusted friend, Brennan, had taken his place as principal organiser. While fully accepted as spokesman of the home league he was in no sense its agent or delegate in America, but took his own line and on one issue at least he did not hesitate to voice criticism of colleagues at home.

After a one-day visit (20-21 May) to his mother and sisters at Manayunk, where he found the 'old lady'—she was now about 60—'looking quite strong', he began his task as secretary by engaging (21 May) an assistant, Bacon, recommended by Wendell Phillips and James Redpath (who had returned from Ireland), and spent the next week looking round for an office and publicising the Land League before large audiences at Jones's Wood, New York (23 May), Newark (24 May), and Brooklyn (26 May). The Jones's Wood meeting was an open-air welcoming, at which the chairman described Davitt as 'the William Lloyd Garrison of Ireland', and the notabilities present included Mrs Delia Tudor Parnell (Charles's mother, living at Bordentown, New Jersey), her daughter Anna, and Dillon. Anna also attended the meeting at Newark—a Clan na Gael picnic—and Davitt paid her the compliment of entrusting her with the 375 dollars raised for famine relief. In these early speeches, as generally in his speeches during this American visit, he emphasised Parnell's leadership of the land movement and the Land League's claim to the support both of constitutional and revolutionary nationalists.[1]

On 28 May he signed an agreement for an office, no. 40, University Building, Washington Square; the place was 'quiet, respectable, and cool' and the rent reasonable—300 dollars a year. He hired a janitor, furnished and equipped the office, and at once reproduced in New York the atmosphere of breathless activity of which he had been the centre in Dublin and from which his Atlantic trip had temporarily released him. But in New York he had nothing of the collective support that the Land League provided in Dublin. The central council of the American league was a façade, its members widely scattered over the Union. The only effective executive officers were Davitt himself and the treasurer, Fr Lawrence Walsh, who, at Waterbury, Connecticut, was some 100 miles away, and had enough to do in receiving and accounting for funds and forwarding money to Dublin. It devolved on Davitt, with occasional help from Devoy, Anna Parnell, and others, to carry on a multifarious correspondence, draft circulars, conduct

[1] DN/7, 20-27 May; DPC/3, pp 59-61^{v}; *Nation*, 12 June, 3 July; Cashman, p. 138 (where Anna Parnell is confused with Fanny); *S.C.P.*, vi, 105-6.

negotiations, organise branches, compile a register of branch offices, and maintain a public relations service. For some weeks he had to meet all charges out of his own pocket.[1]

Early in June, implementing a decision of the Trenor Hall convention, he drafted and issued an address from the central council 'to the Irish race in America'. The American league's aims were defined as: (1) to enlighten American public opinion on the working of the landlord system in Ireland; (2) to bring the immense moral force of that opinion to bear on the people at home, encouraging and sustaining them in their struggle with the landlords; (3) to provide the financial support needed to carry the land movement to its goal, that is, the abolition of the present land system and the establishment of a peasant proprietary. Particular purposes for which this help was sought from America by the Land League of Ireland were to enable the league (1) to extend its organisation throughout the thirty-two counties of Ireland, (2) to defend ejectment cases in the courts, (3) to protect and support families unjustly evicted or imprisoned for resisting eviction, and (4) to oppose landlord candidates for any representative position. As an addition to the 'platform' of the Land League its American auxiliary declared its conviction that the primary purpose of the land movement could be furthered by an equal concern for the protection and regulation of manufactures, mining, fishing, and commerce, 'now and for centuries past prostrated by English legislation'. For such purposes the American Land League solicited the good wishes of the American people and the earnest cooperation of the Irish race in America.[2]

This address was accompanied by a statement on local organisation and advice on how to start branches, drafted by Davitt in the light of his experience in Ireland. To initiate a branch a circular, signed by five or six influential persons, should be addressed to all representative Irishmen in a locality, inviting them to a meeting to consider the Irish Land League's appeal for help and the advisability of establishing a branch of the American Land League. As soon as a branch was established the names of its officers and other relevant information should be notified to the central office of the league. Each branch should elect a president, secretary, and treasurer annually, and, if thought desirable, an executive committee. Anyone paying an annual subscription of at least one dollar should be entitled to membership. Two members of

[1] DN/7, 28 May-16 June; DPC/2, p. 15; DPC/3, pp 59-61A; *Nation*, 3, 10 July; Anna Parnell to D, *p.* 29 June (DP/AB); *Fall*, p. 251.

[2] Printed copy in P. A. Collins papers, Boston College Library (on microfilm in N.L.I., n 4601, p 4567); reprinted in *Defence*, pp 134-8. Davitt submitted his draft for criticism to James J. McCafferty (Lowell, Mass.), president of the central council of the American league, and to J. B. O'Reilly (DN/7, 2 June).

each branch should be appointed ward organisers, to canvas for members and collect money (from both members and non-members) for transmission to Dublin through the central treasurer. In cities or counties with large Irish populations and consequently with a number of branches, it might be advisable to set up an executive committee for the area, composed of the officers of its component branches, to promote unity of action.[1]

Unity was not a distinguishing characteristic of the American Land League, which, from its beginnings, suffered from internal division, exemplified by the controversy over the transmission of funds to Ireland. The decision taken at the Trenor Hall convention was at once contested. Thus the 'Parnell Land League of New York' asserted that each branch should control its own funds, since experience of Irish national organisations in America showed that centralisation of money collected in America for an Irish purpose was open to serious abuse. The Parnell branch considered the Trenor Hall convention and the constitution it adopted to be only provisional, and looked forward to the rescinding of the centralisation plan at the next convention of the league. As this attitude was widespread, funds were in fact transmitted to Dublin both through the central treasurer and directly by branches. Moreover these were not the only channels through which American funds were to reach the Land League in Ireland: more money was to flow through Ford's *Irish World* than through any other single channel, and a second independent channel of great value was O'Reilly's *Pilot*. Davitt recognised that the financial control contemplated in the Trenor Hall constitution was unenforceable and took up a wholly pragmatic attitude towards it. The next convention of the American Land League —at Buffalo, New York, on 12-13 January 1881—was to bring the constitution into line with the facts.[2]

Davitt had not been long in America before he became involved in wrangling with two pundits of orthodox fenianism, John O'Leary and Jeremiah O'Donovan Rossa. O'Leary, who arrived in June to stay with Carroll at Philadelphia, announced that the Land League's idea of abolishing landlordism was 'claptrap'; the land question would be settled only when Ireland had achieved independence.[3] But he made no converts either at a Clan na Gael reunion in New York specially called to hear him or at a meeting of the Clan executive on 28-9 June at which Davitt was present. The case for fenian support of the Land

[1] DN/7, 31 May, 3, 9 June; P. A. Collins papers, as above; *S.C.P.*, ix, 376-8; *Defence*, pp 140-41; *Fall*, pp 250-51.

[2] DPC/2, pp 9, 25-9; *S.C.P.*, xi, 712; Brown, *Irish-American nationalism*, p. 106.

[3] *Irishman*, 3 July, quoting *Philadelphia Herald*, 14 June.

League was strongly argued by Davitt and attacked by O'Leary and Carroll (who had now resigned the chairmanship of the executive).[1] The executive decided for Davitt, who wrote jubilantly to Matthew Harris in Ballinasloe:

O'Leary . . . came from Paris to upset my Land League endeavours, but he will go back a wiser though a sadder man. Saving a few bosthoons who are following that blatant ass, Rossa, the nationalists on this side are commonsense men who hold your views and mine on the public question.[2]

O'Donovan Rossa, fanatically opposed to the Land League, had been urging 'honourable warfare' to set Ireland free;[3] and at a convention held in Philadelphia on 28–30 June he founded the 'United Irishmen of America', to reassert pure revolutionary doctrine in opposition to the deviationism of Clan na Gael, and to reactivate the skirmishing fund. His call for a new fenian body had already earned him expulsion from the Clan when the Philadelphia convention sparked off a flaming debate in the New York press, in which a central issue was his allegation that money from the skirmishing fund had been used by the Land League. Davitt, hotly denying this, declared in the New York *Herald* that, despite Rossa's apparent readiness to wallow in blood, he lacked the courage to set fire to a British haystack.[4] To Harris, Davitt described Rossa as 'a cowardly low ruffian'[5] and to Dillon he wrote that 'the O'Donovan Assa blustered a good deal but . . . refused to gobble me up'.[6]

The practical revolutionist in Davitt was disgusted even more by the gory fantasies of Rossa than by O'Leary's doctrine of endless inactivity. But he had had the satisfaction of seeing his own position strongly defended in letters to the press by two formidable spokesmen of opportunist fenianism, John Devoy writing from New York and Matthew Harris from Ballinasloe. Devoy's letter was a penetrating commentary on the connection between the land and the national movement. 'There can be no question that individually the majority of the nationalists [fenians] give an earnest and active support to the Land League, without relinquishing their own principles.' There were fenians who feared that the league was being used to sap the foundations of advanced nationalism, but Devoy, on the contrary, believed that any

[1] Devoy, *Recollections*, p. 286; *D.P.B.*, i, 534–5; Marcus Bourke, *John O'Leary* (Tralee, 1967), pp 163–4; cf. above, p. 135.

[2] D to Harris, 10 July (*S.C.P.*, iii, 608); cf. O'Reilly to Devoy, 2 Aug. (*D.P.B.*, i, 545–6).

[3] *Irishman*, 22 May.

[4] *D.P.B.*, i, 501–4; *S.C.P.*, iv, 519; *Irishman*, 22, 29 May, 19 June, 24, 31 July; DPC/2, p. 48; DN/7, 7–8 July; New York *Herald*, 9 July; *F.J.*, 20, 21, 26 July; *Nation*, 24, 31 July; *I.W.*, 28 Aug., 4 Sept.; above, pp 136, 312, 354.

[5] D to Harris, 10 July (*S.C.P.*, iii, 608).

[6] D to Dillon, 12 July (DP/BC).

attempt to do so would destroy the league, not nationalism. He scorned the theory that the Irish masses would only strive for national independence and continue to hate England if they were kept in a state of social misery; or, conversely, that a good land act would make them loyal to Queen Victoria. 'The best friend of the national cause . . . is the man who . . . does his best to lift his countrymen out of the slough of poverty, degradation and despair.' He castigated fenian critics of the league who invoked a rigid adherence to principle as an excuse for doing nothing or a cloak for personal malice, instead of helping to avert a national disaster. In the recent agrarian crisis the western landlords would have evicted their pauperised tenants wholesale, and desperate resistance would have been followed by ruthless suppression and depopulation, had not the farmers effectively combined in the league to maintain their grip on the land. The league had taught the agricultural classes their strength, had given them habits of organisation and discipline, and gone far to remove their fear of the landlords, who, through their monopoly not only of land ownership but also of county government, constituted a fundamental obstacle to independence.[1] Harris expounded the same argument in simpler but no less forceful terms.

> What is it that constitutes this island a nation? Is it not the people by whom it is inhabited? Destroy the people and you destroy the nation. Who are the destroyers of the people of this country? Are they not the landlords and all other agencies that cripple and retard industry? Who are endeavouring to save the people? Land reformers and those who, like them, strive to organise and elevate the masses. These views may be too utilitarian for some patriots, but if you ignore the utilitarian aspects of any movement . . . you take away half its strength.[2]

The two letters were reissued as a pamphlet by the Land League in Ireland.[3]

Davitt augmented this Devoy–Harris exposition in a circular of 10 July to the branches of the American Land League appealing for help for the Land League at home. The league was a temporary expedient, committed to raising the Irish farmers 'from the mire of social serfdom'. It was not intended to conflict with movements or interfere with organisations aiming at either national independence or home rule. Fenianism, it was clearly implied, in its traditional role of preparing for a war of independence, need not fear any hostility from the league, which expected similar treatment in return. The league sought to work in harmony with all friends of Ireland at home and abroad, including non-political societies. 'The cause of benevolence and temperance

[1] Devoy to editor of *Freeman*, 18 June (*F.J.*, 2 July; *S.C.P.*, ix, 387–92).

[2] Harris to editor of *Irishman*, 19 June (*Irishman*, 26 June; *S.C.P.*, iii, 605–7); cf. above, pp 275–6.

[3] *S.C.P.*, ix, 386.

among our people in America will not suffer by aiding a work which will advance the material and moral well-being of our people in Ireland.'[1]

At home the immediate question for the Land League was whether the parliamentary party could extract from the new parliament an emergency measure suspending for two years the landlords' power of ejectment on holdings valued at £20 and under, as recommended by the recent land conference[2] and adopted by the party at a meeting on 17 May at which Parnell had been elected chairman.[3] The new chief secretary for Ireland, William Edward Forster, was an ex-quaker with a distinguished record of service in quaker relief during the great famine. A dedicated reformer, one of Gladstone's most important and respected colleagues, he accepted the chief secretaryship (a lower-ranking office than he could have claimed) out of a sense of duty and the hope of doing good to a distressed country with which he had warm sympathy. He was soon anxiously aware of the difficulties of his position. The outgoing government had made no preparations to renew the existing peace preservation act, due to expire on 1 June, and for the new government to attempt its early reenactment would, he believed, occupy nearly all the parliamentary session and give a bad start to the government's relations with Ireland. Yet the country was far more disturbed than when the act was last renewed, in 1875. Resident magistrates had advised that special powers were essential to cope with the anti-rent agitation. The law required the executive to carry out ejectment decrees for non-payment of rent. 'We have no discretion as regards the humanity or moral justice of the eviction, but have simply to consider whether we will allow the law to be defied or not.' If ejectment decrees were not enforced, no rents would be paid in the district concerned; but if the law was carried out and the government was without special powers there was danger of an uprush of violence. Yet with much hesitation Forster and the lord lieutenant, Lord Cowper, agreed to take the risk of trying to govern Ireland under the ordinary law if that was what the cabinet wished. Gladstone and the majority of the cabinet were all for a conciliatory policy, and accordingly the non-renewal of the peace preservation act was announced in the queen's speech at the opening of parliament on 20 May. In the debate that followed, O'Connor Power and other Irish members called for immediate action on evictions and Forster replied that, though it would not be possible to bring in a land bill during the present short session, the government regarded the land question as the most important of all Irish questions.[4]

[1] *I.W.*, 24 July; *Nation*, 31 July; *S.C.P.*, vi, 157–8, ix, 467–8.

[2] Above, pp 374, 375.

[3] *F.J.*, 18 May.

[4] P.R.O., Cab. 37/2/23 (10 May); *Hansard 3*, cclii, 67, 127–69, 255–9 (20–21 May).

The Parnellites, by no means disarmed by this, demanded immediate action on ejectments, and caused two private members' bills to be drafted, one to suspend ejectments for two years and one to amend the land act of 1870, the first being entrusted to Dwyer Gray, the second to O'Connor Power. Gray failed in the balloting to secure a day for introducing his bill, and the government refused to give facilities for doing so, but Power succeeded by a mere chance in getting a place on the notice paper for his (28 May).[1] The bill, drafted by Dr Andrew Commins, proposed simply to repeal the clause in the land act of 1870 which debarred any claim to compensation for disturbance from a tenant ejected for non-payment of rent, with the consequence that such a tenant would be entitled to proceed against his landlord in the county court for compensation in the manner provided in the act. This proposal received a second reading on 4 June,[2] but was acceptable neither to the Land League nor to the government. Reviewing the rural situation at the beginning of June, the league was convinced that the ensuing three months would be critical for the poorer tenants who, lacking both money and credit to buy Indian meal, would be quite unable to pay rent. At a meeting on 8 June it was reported that 'ejectment processes were flying like snowflakes',[3] and that about 1000 appeals for help in defending ejectments in the courts had come in from tenants during the preceding week. Recognising that it would be financially impossible to afford such help except in special cases, and that the bulk of its resources would be needed to support the families of evicted tenants, the league decided, subject to the approval of the principal relief-committees in America, to earmark £10,000 for the evicted out of relief funds, leaving £4000–£5000 for ordinary relief. On 13 July Egan was able to report, on Davitt's authority, that there was general approval among Irish-Americans for this plan. With the eviction question thus beginning to overshadow famine relief, it is not surprising that, at a league meeting on 15 June, the parliamentary party was criticised by Louden, Kettle, Egan, and others for its failure over the suspension bill and called on it to honour its pledges without delay. O'Connor Power's bill was dismissed as utterly ineffective to meet the crying need of the farmers. If evictions continued it would not be in the power of the league to stay 'the wild justice of revenge.'[4]

This implied vote of censure produced on 19 June a sharp rejoinder from Parnell, who, explaining the constraints imposed by parliamentary forms, cogently defended the party's strategy in the house of

[1] Ibid., cclii, 740–41. [2] Ibid., cclii, 1284–1308. [3] See below, p. 417.

[4] *F.J.*, 2, 9, 16, 23 June, 7, 14 July; *Nation*, 5 June; *Irishman*, 12 June; P.R.O., Cab. 37/2/28; *Fall*, p. 263.

commons. Its intention had been, once it had got Power's bill into the committee stage, to introduce an amendment suspending ejectments for two years, thus ensuring full discussion of the evictions question. But by now the government had taken action. Disliking Power's bill for its origin, its negative character, and its intended permanence, but unwilling merely to reject it, Forster obtained the cabinet's approval for a bill to the same effect, but to expire on 31 December 1882. This reversal of the cabinet's earlier decision on the land question was to be accompanied by the appointment of 'a small strong commission' to inquire into the working of the land act of 1870. The Compensation for Disturbance (Ireland) Bill was accordingly introduced on 18 June,[1] and Parnell was able to claim the credit of forcing the government's hand and creating the opportunity of raising the suspension issue by way of amendment. This explanation was received with approval at the next meeting of the league, on 22 June, and confidence in the party was restored. Kettle used the occasion to point out that the land movement had now passed into a second phase: in the first phase the farmers had exercised their natural right of survival by withholding rent, but in so doing had put themselves in the power of the landlords, who now had the legal right to clear whole districts of their population; the second phase of the land movement, precipitated by the landlords, would be a struggle not over the tenants' inability to pay their rents but over their ability to resist wholesale eviction.[2]

Davitt in New York reacted hotly to these events. Parnell had blundered; 'for God's sake', Davitt telegraphed, 'bring forward the suspension of ejectment measure'.[3] Anna Parnell, with whom he was in close touch, reproved him for misunderstanding her brother's strategy.

> Neither you nor any of those who distinguished themselves at that meeting [of the league, on 15 June] can really know anything of the reasons for my brother's action. . . . Generalship in the house of commons is often dependent on the most trifling technicalities. . . . If a man is obliged to explain his parliamentary policy beforehand it will certainly be a very poor one.

She deplored 'that scene in the Land League' as evidence of dangerous disloyalty, which would make government and landlords happier than they had been since the league began.[4] Davitt nevertheless endorsed the league's censure of Parnell. Interviewed by an *Irish World* reporter on 16 June, he described Power's bill as 'unauthorised', and devised for the purpose of shelving the Land League's proposal. He went on to make a sustained attack on Power as 'ever a brand of discord in

[1] *Hansard 3,* ccliii, 393–4.
[2] *F.J.*, 23 June; *Irishman*, 19 June; *Nation*, 19, 26 June; P.R.O., Cab. 37/2/28 (10 June).
[3] DN/7, 16 June.
[4] Anna Parnell to D, [16 June] (DP/AB).

the national ranks' and one of the most dangerous enemies of the league, of which he was not really a member, though his name was on the original 'appeal to the Irish race'.[1] (Davitt had doubts at the time about including it.[2]) In the recent election in Mayo he had spread the rumour that Parnell's candidature was directed against him rather than against the landlord candidate, Browne, to defeat whom had been Davitt's sole reason for inducing Parnell to stand.[3] Davitt admitted to having said at Castlebar, after the election, that Mayo could have no two better representatives than Parnell and Power, but this was obvious rhetoric. Power had refused to attend the land conference and was absent from the party meeting that elected Parnell as chairman. Davitt was confident that Parnell would now correct his error by taking the first opportunity to force a suspension bill on the house of commons or effectively block its machinery with his powerful following. There was no danger of a split between the party and the league: Brennan, Egan, Kettle, and others had too much confidence in Parnell, and both he and they were too much in earnest about the land question for a split to be possible. Davitt confessed to having had a 'weakness' for Power, due to their long friendship, and their political connection, and to gratitude for Power's efforts on his behalf during his imprisonment. He had the highest opinion of his ability and capacity for vigorous action, and had cherished the hope that he would show unselfish devotion to the national cause. He now, however, was compelled to recognise 'the utter absence of that frank and honest political conduct which characterises Mr Parnell, and to class Mr O'Connor Power with that other distinguished self-seeker and egotist Mr Frank Hugh O'Donnell'.[4]

Davitt was ill-informed about Power's bill, as Power effectively pointed out in a letter of 6 July to the *Freeman's Journal* and the *Irishman*.[5] In reply (24 July) Davitt admitted and apologised for his error, but firmly adhered to his charges of political double-dealing and self-seeking. 'Not without a pang', he wrote in his diary, 'was it that I first attacked this man. Yet he has by his disgusting selfishness forced me to follow the course of all his old friends and break with him politically.'[6] It was a sad end to a relationship that went back to their boyhood days in Lancashire[7] and had continued unbroken until about a year previously. Before the land agitation began in the spring

[1] Above, pp 335–6.
[2] D to Matthew Harris, *a.* 29 Sept. 79 (*S.C.P.*, iii, 601).
[3] Cf. Healy, *Letters and leaders*, i, 92 (stating the rumour as a fact) with John Sweeney (Louisburgh) to *Freeman's Journal*, 10 Aug. 80 (*F.J.*, 13 Aug.).
[4] *I.W.*, 26 June.
[5] 10 July.
[6] DN/7, 24–5 July.
[7] Above, pp 47–8.

of 1879 Davitt had remained a steady ally of Power's despite the increasing attacks on him by fenians for his connection with the home rule movement. But in the preparations for the Irishtown meeting Davitt had found Power very reluctant to commit himself, and after his appearance at Irishtown he seldom attended a land meeting, and only after the movement had gathered momentum. His conduct in the Mayo election Davitt thought 'miserably selfish'[1] but there had been no open breach then.[2]

The polemics now exchanged across the Atlantic between the two men, like the dispute with O'Donovan Rossa, exemplified a tendency in Davitt to become embroiled in hard-hitting and acrimonious controversy. This had begun to show itself ever since his emergence as a public figure, and from time to time during the rest of his life was to make heavy demands on him, as in his later hostilities with Devoy, Parnell, Healy, William O'Brien, Bishop O'Dwyer of Limerick, and Archbishop Walsh of Dublin.

Davitt's work in New York was interrupted by a lecture tour (his fourth) in New England (16-25 June).[3] He left by night boat for Boston via Fall River on 16 June, spent two days in Boston, and on 19 June attended a Clan na Gael picnic at Lawrence where he was given 300 dollars for the league from the Father Matthew Temperance Society and met a number of old Haslingden friends.[4] Next day (20 June) he lectured at the Music Hall, Boston. Introduced by John Boyle O'Reilly as 'the author and mechanic of the Irish land agitation', he covered well-beaten ground but went on to explain just how the war for the land was being waged. If a tenant was evicted, not a man would dare, under pain of being socially ostracised, to take his farm, and the evicted family would be protected and supported by the Land League.[5] The 'crusade against landlordism' was being preached from platform, pulpit and press. Every Sunday 'little land meetings' were held in churchyards, at roadsides, and at crossroads. Wherever you met tenant farmers you found them openly discussing the land question. Throughout the civilised world the agitation was attracting attention. In denying the right of a class to monopolise the land of a country the Land League was fighting the battle of humanity.[6]

From 21 to 24 June Davitt was daily on the move in New England, travelling, in great discomfort owing to the heat and dust, largely over ground made familiar by his visits in 1878. He lectured on successive

[1] DN/6, 5 Apr.
[2] *F.J.*, 7, 11 Aug.; *Irishman*, 14 Aug.
[3] See map VII.
[4] Cf. above, p. 232.
[5] See above, p. 392.
[6] D to P.A. Collins, 7 June (P.A. Collins papers, Boston College Library, on microfilm in N.L.I., n 4601, p 4567); DN/7, 16-20 June; *I.W.*, 3 July; *Nation*, 10 July; *S.C.P.*, ix, 465-7.

days at Lowell (Mass.), Pawtucket (R.I.), Stamford (Conn.), and Blackstone (Mass.). At Pawtucket he met a 'Miss S.S.', and felt a revival of an old feeling. 'Still looking well, though like myself growing old. Wonder how I would have acted in Irish politics if I had married twelve years ago.' A tiny flowered label with the legend 'A token of love' stuck into his diary for 22 June is all that remains of this brief encounter. On 25 June he returned to New York.[1]

Warm appreciation of Davitt's work in America was expressed at a meeting of the central Land League in Dublin on 6 July by James Redpath. Davitt had considered it important that Redpath should return to Ireland and report on evictions, and for that purpose had given him the return half of his own steamship ticket.[2] Redpath told the league that Davitt had established communication with every branch of the American Land League and was rapidly organising new branches. He had succeeded better than any Irishman who had ever gone to America in uniting all the Irish organisations there, and the policy of the Land League, of which he was so effective a spokesman, was the first Irish policy that had ever commended itself to native Americans.[3]

Work in his office kept him in New York for most of the next five weeks, during which, with the consent of the central council, he completed plans for an 'organising tour'[4] to San Francisco and back.[5] He addressed a meeting at Jersey City presided over by the mayor on 26 June,[6] and on 5 July spent an uncomfortable day attending a picnic at Albany, where he spoke from beneath a shed to a large crowd in the rain. He had visited his mother only twice (20–21 May, 12–13 June) since his arrival in America when on 16 July he was summoned to Manayunk, to find her very weak but 'not seriously ill'. She feared she would not live to see Ireland, where it was her constant hope to be buried in her native Turlough: 'God grant she may live to enjoy a few years quiet and happiness in the old land after her thirty years exile from it'.[7] None the less he hurried back to New York the same evening (Friday). On Sunday, 18 July, he received a delayed telegram sent the previous night: 'come at once if you want to see her alive'. There was no train till 5.30 p.m., and he reached Manayunk three hours later to find that she had died at 3 p.m.

He was overwhelmed with sorrow and remorse:

> Oh if I had only waited . . . as I ought to have done . . . I would have been with her in her last moments. Another of my merited punishments. How little these sacrifices for the 'cause' will avail me with my enemies by and by. What a life of

[1] DN/7, 21-5 June. [2] DN/7, 15 June; see above, p. 367. [3] *F.J.*, 7 July.
[4] *Nation*, 31 July. [5] DN/7, 26 June-1 Aug.; D to Dillon, 12 July (DP/BC); *F.J.*, 24 Nov.
[6] *I.W.*, 10 July. [7] Above, p. 386. DN/7, 12-13 June, 16 July.

toil and trouble and suffering has been hers. And all this for me and through me. What a miserable life mine has been no one knows but myself.

I banished my family from England in '70 in order that I should be unfettered in the cause—that is, I sent them to America out of my way. My father died broken-hearted over my imprisonment. My poor mother suffered for me the agony which a mother must undergo at the thought of her son's treatment in prison. On my release, instead of aiding her, I spent my time and money for the same cause. I promised to take her back to Ireland and did not, and now she sleeps her last sleep beneath the same foreign sod that covers my father—while I must live to think and mourn of how I have neglected them and been the means of shortening their days. How that poor mother slaved and suffered for me the world will never know. And I have returned her no recompense—have given her no happiness for all she did for me.

Well, thank God I did see her two days before she died; and oh how glad I am that I happened to be in America when she was departing this life.

The reward of the good and the suffering is surely hers, and God in his justice and goodness will give her infinite happiness for all her trials and sorrows in this miserable world.[1]

She was buried in the churchyard of St John the Baptist Church, Manayunk, on 21 July, after requiem mass. Davitt grieved that he lacked the means to take her remains back to Turlough—'but that consolation cannot be mine'. He and his sisters had, however, the consolation of a great outpouring of sympathy from the people of Manayunk, among whom Catherine Davitt had been a general favourite—with men, women and children—during her eight years sojourn. Davitt paid her funeral expenses and debts (together about 180 dollars), and disposed of her effects among his sisters, Mary receiving her beds and clothing, Anne retaining her furniture, and Sib refusing to take anything except a few mementos.[2]

O'Reilly, condoling with Davitt, wrote: 'by losses like these we become purified and reflective, and get a glimpse, however brief, of the pettiness and selfishness of the noisy crowd around us'.[3] But within a few days of his mother's burial Davitt was again in the thick of business and of his controversy with O'Connor Power.[4] News from Ireland suggested that the compensation for disturbance bill (which passed its third reading in the commons on 26 July[5]) would be thrown out by the lords, and he hoped that this would happen, because it would 'give us another autumn, winter, and spring to kick the accursed system still more'. With an eye on Britain's troubles in the Transvaal, he made the cryptic note: 'we must carry the war into Africa'.[6] He heard a spiritualist lecturer and attended a séance conducted by a spiritualist

[1] DN/7, 18–20 July.
[2] DN/7, 21–2 July.
[3] J. B. O'Reilly to D, 30 July (DP/A26).
[4] Above, pp. 393–5.
[5] *Hansard 3*, ccliv, 1456.
[6] DN/7, 26 July.

medium, who was able to give him the name and date of death of a friend who had died eight years before.[1] He met Fanny Parnell for the first time (29 July), and found her much better-looking than he had expected: 'one of the cleverest young ladies I have yet encountered since I landed; a thorough politician; able speaker, earnest manner', and 'very inquisitive'. On 30 July he had his accounts audited in preparation for leaving New York.[2] Next day he took part in and spoke at the Irish Volunteers' annual excursion up the Hudson to Alpine Grove, a park area adjoining Excelsior Grove, which he had visited in the same company two years before.[3] The prevailing attitude to the Land League was sympathetic. There was a good deal of drinking among the excursionists but less than in August 1878. He had intended to return to New York in time to catch the 6.30 train for Wilkesbarre, but the slow progress of the boats defeated him, and it was not till 2 August that he was able to set out on his western tour.[4]

At this point the struggle in Ireland was becoming affected by the prospect of an abundant harvest. The Land League saw this not as offering the hope of a settlement but as certain to bring on a decisive confrontation with the landlords. Was the expected harvest to be surrendered to them in payment of arrears of rent by pauperised tenants who had been saved from starvation only by charitable relief from America and elsewhere? If so, their plight in the coming winter would be worse than it had been in the past six months. Were Americans to be appealed to for further charity to enable those whom they had saved from starvation to pay rent to the landlords? Alternatively, if such tenants ate the harvest and paid no rents, would the necessary resources be forthcoming for resisting wholesale eviction and supporting its victims? The government's effort to deter landlords from exercising their legal right to evict for non-payment of rent was frustrated when the house of lords overwhelmingly rejected the compensation for disturbance bill (3 August).[5] Nor did the personnel of the commission appointed by the government on 29 July to prepare the ground for new land legislation[6] inspire in the league any confidence in the government's intentions. Its chairman, the earl of Bessborough, and two of its other four members, MacMurrough Kavanagh and The O'Conor Don, were large landowners. Kavanagh and O'Conor had been unseated in the general election because of their opposition to the

[1] DN/7, 23, 27 July.
[2] DN/7, 29-30 July.
[3] Above, p. 228.
[4] DN/7, 1-2 Aug.; DP/A7, 1 Aug.
[5] Above, pp 393, 397; *Hansard 3*, cclv, 110-13 (the voting was 231 to 51).
[6] Above, p. 393.

tenant interest,[1] while William Shaw[2] was quite out of date on the land question and Baron Dowse was in the service of the government.[3]

Dillon, just returned from America, assured the league on 20 July that there was astonishing unanimity among Irish-Americans (including the catholic clergy) in support of the land movement, and that if there was any attempt to surrender the harvest to the landlords there would be an unparalleled uprising of indignation even among native Americans. No tenant supported by American charity during the past six months should be called on to pay arrears of rent, and any attempt to levy rent for 'a year of famine' should be met by 'stern and desperate resistance'. He believed that a steady income might be expected from America to 'keep up the warfare'. The league owed more than any man well knew to the exertions in America of Davitt, who, as always, had undertaken the share of the work that gave most labour and least honour. This fighting stance was welcomed by the league. Brennan reported that there were 130 branches affiliated to the central body, all of which regularly sent in a proportion of their funds and made monthly returns about events in their districts; about 100 more branches were in course of formation.[4] On 10 August Egan summed up the Land League's position in a resolution, which was carried unanimously, that

> the recent action of the English house of lords in throwing out the compensation for disturbance bill confirms us in the belief that the settlement of the Irish land question rests with the Irish people themselves. We, therefore, reiterate our call to the country to press forward with the organisation of the National Land League, to refuse to pay all unjust rent, to take no farm from which a tenant has been evicted, to buy no cattle, crops, or other property seized for rent, and to form generally an industrial union against landlord monopoly.

Egan would have liked to go further, holding that the time had come for a general strike against all rent, on the precedent of industrial strikes in England during the past twenty years, which he thought was the only way to bring landlordism to its knees. He held that they should compel the landlords to collect their rents 'at the point of the bayonet, as the tithe rents were formerly collected'.[5]

Such was the Irish background to Davitt's western tour, which occupied his next three months. It took him through the Appalachians, across the prairie and the plains of the middle west, and through the Rocky Mountains to the Pacific coast. In 1878 he had travelled less than half this distance, his furthest point west being Sedalia in central Missouri.[6] Unlike his 1878 tour, which was entirely arranged for him

[1] Above, pp 323, 372. [2] Above, pp 297, 324, 370. [3] *F.J.*, 21, 28 July, 4, 18, 25 Aug.
[4] *F.J.*, 21 July. [5] *F.J.*, 11 Aug. [6] Above, p. 241.

by Clan na Gael, he had organised this one himself, using his position as secretary of the American Land League as well as his Clan connections. His arrangements worked out satisfactorily on the whole as far as St Louis, but there he was knocked out by malaria, and from 19 August to 12 September he was mostly in bed, sick, which upset the rest of his timetable. Nevertheless the tour was a substantial success. Wherever he went among Irish-Americans he was welcomed as 'the great agitator', the heart and soul of a movement that was infusing a new spirit into Ireland. He attended innumerable meetings, large and small, delivered some twenty-five speeches and lectures, gave many interviews, made many friends, and, above all, took steps to initiate Land League branches wherever conditions were suitable, and to encourage or reanimate branches already formed. Though he did not travel under Clan na Gael sponsorship, he mixed freely with Clan members and attended Clan meetings whenever invited. Most of the 'picnics' he took part in were open-air rallies of the Clan. It was from these contacts that he obtained many of his best helpers in the task of establishing Land League branches, usually officered by Clan na Gael men.[1]

The tour can be viewed in five stages.[2] (1) The first (2–19 August) extended from New York through New Jersey, Pennsylvania, Ohio, Indiana, and Illinois to Chicago and St Louis. Davitt was enchanted by the mountain scenery in north-eastern Pennsylvania about Wilkes-barre and Scranton, but was saddened by the general depression in the mining industry of the region, in which many Irish were involved. Strangely enough, though he addressed a convention of the Catholic Total Abstinence Union at Scranton (4 August), he did not stay overnight in the town where his sister, Mary Padden, and her husband and family were living; and there is no reference to them in his diary. He made a detour south through Maryland to attend a picnic at Washington, which he now saw for the first time, before resuming his journey westwards to Chicago by way of Pittsburgh, Columbus, Cincinnati, and Indianapolis. He addressed picnics at Pittsburgh ('smoky town') and Cincinnati; at Indianapolis he was 'serenaded' in front of his hotel, where he made a speech. At these initial meetings of his tour he sounded the note that this was the last time the begging-box would go round the world for Irish farmers. If they allowed the landlords to take the present harvest out of their mouths, they deserved to starve. The Land League was now appealing for American help not for famine-relief but to fight the landlords.[3]

[1] *S.C.P.*, ix, 380, 382; Devoy, *Land of Eire*, pp 74–5.
[2] See maps VIII–X.
[3] Washington, 5 Aug. (*I.W.*, 21 Aug.); Cincinnati, 12 Aug. (*I.W.*, 28 Aug.).

He arrived at Chicago in the small hours of 14 August to find the place in the grip of an all-Union rally of freemasons; not a bed was to be had in the neighbourhood of the station nor a conveyance to other parts of the city. He had been asleep for two hours on a doorstep when a friendly Irish policeman conducted him to more confortable quarters improvised for the occasion in the outhouse of a hotel. Later that day he secured a room at Palmer House, where he had stayed in 1878.[1] At a picnic of the united Irish societies of Chicago held in Ogden's Grove, he spoke before an audience of some 8000, Alexander Sullivan[2] presiding, on the theme that, if Ireland was ever to achieve independence, she must strike off the social fetters that bound Irish brains and muscles. He felt the occasion to be a splendid success, but it left him 'sick and hoarse'. Nevertheless he lectured next evening (15 August), to a thin audience, under the auspices of the Union Stock-yards 'Spread the Light' Club—one of many such organisations formed among Irish-Americans since Parnell's visit to disseminate propaganda for the Land League in Ireland and abroad, principally through Ford's *Irish World*. The 'light' Davitt declared, had penetrated to the episcopal palace as well as the peasant's cottage, and to set against the denunciations of the archbishop of Dublin (McCabe), the archbishop of Cashel (Croke) had recently come out strongly in defence of the land movement.[3] The movement was not a war against property as such but against an anti-social monopoly rooted in English conquest and confiscation, and its ultimate object was to restore 'the old national land system', under which all land was held as national property. Aware that this concept was scarcely congenial to Americans who, having made money in Chicago, hastened to buy up land in the west, he made a distinction between American landlordism, the domestic product of a free society, and the alien feudal landlordism of Ireland. But he was not prepared to say whether it was in accordance with natural justice that land should be bought and sold like any other commodity.[4] The agitiation had reduced the value of land in Ireland from 25 to 12 years purchase; and though Parnell proposed to give the landlords 20 years purchase Davitt was in favour of offering them only six, believing as he did that they were morally entitled to no compensation at all.[5]

[1] DN/7, 2-14 Aug.; DP/A7, 2-14 Aug.; Chicago *Emerald*, 14 Aug.; *Nation*, 28 Aug.; *I.W.*, 21, 28 Aug.; *Fall*, pp 252-3.

[2] See above, pp 247-8, and Sullivan to Devoy, 2 Aug. (*D.P.B.*, i, 543-4).

[3] See *F.J.*, 31 May; *Fall*, p. 262.

[4] Cf. above, p. 385.

[5] DN/7, 14-15 Aug.; DP/A7, 14 Aug.; Chicago *Tribune*, 16 Aug.; *I.W.*, 28 Aug.; *Nation*, 4 Sept.

He spent three days (16–19 August) on the way from Chicago to St Louis, addressing picnics at Joliet and Braidwood and lecturing at Terre Haute, though continuing to feel ill and suffering from insomnia. At Joliet, near Chicago, he fell in with 'Dr Le Caron', who accompanied him to Braidwood, the small mining town where Le Caron, as a general practitioner and 'senior guardian' of the Emmet Club, the local Clan na Gael 'camp', was a popular figure among the Irish workers. He gave Davitt medicine, and the two men laid plans for a Land League branch in Braidwood, Davitt having no suspicion of Le Caron's dual personality.[1] A topic they must have discussed was the 'revelations' about the I.R.B. published in the New York *Herald* of 12 August, which Davitt had read at Chicago.

These revelations were made by Chester Ives, special correspondent in Ireland of the *Herald*,[2] as the outcome of an interview in a retired house in the suburbs of Cork, during the last week of July, with someone, unnamed, who claimed to be an active member of the I.R.B. A historical sketch of the fenian movement was followed by an account of the current state of the I.R.B., a transcript of its rules, and a record of conversation with the fenian informant. Apart from the captions there was nothing sensational about the article, which was partly well-informed reporting, partly wishful thinking, and partly analysis of the effects on the I.R.B. of the fenian deviations of the previous ten years. Both the home rule movement and, still more, the land agitation had seriously injured the 'revolutionary party'. The land agitation was a wholly selfish movement, appealing not to the patriotism of the people but to their pockets.

> The land agitators teach the people a fallacious idea that the land is theirs, that they may have it for nothing, and that the landlords are their natural enemies. We teach them that liberty and independence is theirs, and that some of the landlords may be won to our side and become our most valuable friends. . . . The landlords have money and could buy arms and would make splendid officers, and altogether we have no wish to utterly alienate them. . . . We do not favour a peasant proprietary, for peasant proprietors would inevitably become a powerful yeomanry and be the worst enemies of our cause.

It was impossible to blend a secret with a public organisation without damaging the former. Parnell had acquired an intimate knowledge of the I.R.B., and while publicly denouncing the revolutionary movement had used it both for his land agitation and for electoral purposes. In Connacht, which before the agitation had been a stronghold of nationalism, the I.R.B. had been demoralised and almost destroyed. But the tide was beginning to turn: while the Land League was weakening, the

[1] DN/7, DP/A7, 16–19 Aug. *S.C.P.*, iv, 521; ix, 380–81; *Fall*, pp 253–4; above, p. 248.
[2] Above, p. 352.

I.R.B. was again making steady progress. It had 36,000 paying members in Ireland and 11,500 in Britain; many of these were armed, and many more were being supplied with arms. Disciplinary action had been taken against several leading men, hitherto staunch revolutionists, who had deviated from principle, among them Davitt. On the eve (8 May) of his departure for America, the supreme council had decided to expel him from its membership for using his influence in the organisation for the benefit of the land agitation and for failing to attend a convention of fenian centres in the north of England (which he represented on the council), to explain his Land League activities.[1]

These disclosures filled Davitt with rage. His expulsion from the supreme council was news to him, though probably no great surprise. But what revolted him was the combination of loyalty to the 'true path' with betraying opponents to the enemy. What encouragement to the youth of Ireland to join the 'secret' movement! To Devoy he angrily attributed the disclosures to C. G. Doran, of Queenstown.[2]

> Patriotic felon-setting has been a common thing in the movement since '67. I have more than once made up my mind . . . to write a letter to the *Herald*, fix the responsibility on the patriot town-councillor [Doran], and go for the whole God-damned fraud of conspiracy in print and felon-setting patriots—ridding myself once and forever from any relationship to the I.R.B.[3]

Devoy thought that P. N. Fitzgerald, of Cork, was the culprit rather than Doran; and Davitt, admitting that it might be so, replied: 'we must find out and punish this champion of the "true path"'. Could not Ives be seized some night and forced to choose between 'divulging the name of his informant or a rope?'[4] These violent sentiments are not, of course, to be taken literally, but to be read as an outburst of Davitt's hot temper accentuated by illness; for they were written after three feverish days in a hotel bed at St Louis, where he arrived on 19 August in the throes of malaria. The same view cannot be taken of Alexander Sullivan's reaction to the *Herald* article: 'I hope to live long enough to hear of the summary disposal of the traitor who gave the *Herald* its information; the great fault with Irish revolutionary movements has been their failure to punish treason'. Sullivan felt that the I.R.B. leadership was ineffective, and condemned the expulsion of Davitt from the supreme council for his connection with the Land League, which, he admitted, was doing much good in Ireland, though he disapproved of the formation of land leagues in America as sapping the strength of Clan na Gael.[5] Davitt found that fenians in Chicago

1 New York *Herald*, 12 Aug.; *F.J.*, 23 Aug.; *Nation*, 28 Aug.

2 Above, p. 133.

3 D to Devoy, 16 Aug. (*D.P.B.*, i, 548).

4 D to Devoy, 21 Aug. (*D.P.B.*, i, 548–9).

5 Alexander Sullivan to Devoy, 4 Sept. (*D.P.B.*, i, 549–50).

and St Louis generally shared his indignation over the 'revelations'. The *Irish World* pronounced them to be true, but the press at home kept very cool and was generally sceptical about them.[1] The affair soon blew over. Davitt later learnt that Ives's informant was James or Joseph Mullett, Dublin fenians, both of whom were to be convicted in 1883 of complicity in the Phoenix Park murders.[2] What he never learnt was that a few days before he read of his expulsion from the supreme council for his fenian backsliding, Superintendent Mallon had described him to the commissioners of the Dublin Metropolitan Police as 'the soul and essence of whatever fenianism there is in the Land League'.[3]

(2) The second stage of Davitt's western tour[4] (19 August–12 September) was overshadowed by the illness that had begun at Chicago and came to a head on his arrival at St Louis. Confined to bed with malaria in Lindell House, St Louis, under the care of an Irish doctor, J. J. Kane,[5] he got up on 22 August and spoke to a large crowd in the Fair Grounds, from which the chairman of the meeting telegraphed to the Land League: '10,000 citizens of St Louis now listening to Michael Davitt send greetings to the people of Ireland and call on them to hold the harvest and starve the landlords'.[6] He returned to his hotel sick and feverish, but two days later insisted on leaving for Kansas City. The train was delayed, there was no one to receive him, and he spent part of the night vainly searching for the venue of his lecture and once again feeling ill (25 August). But he gave a successful lecture next night, stressing the vital importance for the Irish farmers of not surrendering the harvest to the landlords: 'we mean to starve landlordism into submission'. On the 27th he reached St Joseph, Missouri, to find that, through the non-arrival of a telegram, no arrangements had been made for a lecture he expected to give. He went on (28 August) to Omaha, Nebraska, where, after a lecture to an enthusiastic audience on the 29th, the pattern of his St Louis experience was repeated: he spent a fortnight[7] prostrated by malaria at Creighton House, nursed by the proprietors, a Mr and Mrs Donovan, and attended by a Dr Kauffman. By 12 September he was sufficiently recovered to leave Omaha for

[1] *F.J.*, 23 Aug.; *Irish Times*, 23 Aug.; *Daily Express*, 23, 25 Aug.; *Nation*, 28 Aug., 11 Sept.; *Irishman*, 28 Aug., 4, 18 Sept.

[2] *D.P.B.*, i, 547; *S.C.P.*, ix, 400; Tom Corfe, *The Phoenix Park murders* (London, 1968), p. 256.

[3] Mallon to C.P., 10 Aug. (S.P.O., I.N.L.L. & I.N.L. papers, carton 9).

[4] See maps IX, X.

[5] The statements in *Fall*, p. 254, about his illness in St Louis are at variance with DN/7, 19–24 Aug.

[6] *F.J.*, 25 Aug.; *I.W.*, 28 Aug., 4 Sept.; *Nation*, 11 Sept.

[7] *Fall*, p. 254, is in error in saying a month.

San Francisco, having cancelled the engagements he had made for his return journey from Omaha to New York.[1]

(3) Davitt's journey from Omaha to California[2] (12–17 September), which formed the third stage of the four, was a restorative experience, rich in sightseeing and free from speech-making. He found the grain lands of Nebraska uninteresting, and the ascent of the Rocky Mountains through Wyoming disappointing, being so gradual, though the route reached 8000 feet between Cheyenne (Wyoming) and Ogden (Utah). The descent to Ogden (14 September) in moonlight through wild, rocky canyons was a dramatic contrast. He broke his journey at Ogden to visit Salt Lake City, some 40 miles south. In this spectacular capital of the Latter-day Saints, over 4000 feet up in the Rockies, he marvelled at Brigham Young's great oval Tabernacle, seating 10,000,[3] with its rounded roof unsupported by beams or pillars and its miraculous acoustics: 'a pin dropped on a board or into a hat in front of the immense organ can be heard distinctly at the other end of the building—a distance of 230 feet'. Returning to Ogden he resumed his journey westwards, through Utah and Nevada to Reno. Approaching Reno by moonlight, seated on the platform of the car, he was enchanted by the scenery—'frowning precipices on each side of track, river bounding along over huge rocks which tumble from the mountains . . ., train sweeping along its sinuous course'. From Reno he crossed into California but, to his regret, passed through the 'grandest scenery' of all, that of the Sierra Nevada, in complete darkness. On 17 September he arrived at Sacramento, 'a lovely city' in a vine and grain country, where a deputation boarded the train to welcome him at 6 a.m., when he had just got himself out of bed.[4]

While Davitt was laid up at Omaha a new fenian 'revelation' was made in the *Irish World* by its editor, disgusted by the in-fighting over the skirmishing fund precipitated by O'Donovan Rossa.[5] Denying that the Land League had received financial support from the fund, Ford disclosed that money had been advanced to Davitt in August 1879, not for the Land League, which was not then in existence, but for the land agitation. When news of this transaction had begun to leak out, Davitt had asked the trustees of the fund to send him no more money and had committed himself to treating the advance as a personal debt to be repaid as soon as possible. The rumoured connection between the land movement and the skirmishing fund was thus publicly admitted,

[1] DN/7, DP/A7, 19 Aug.–12 Sept.; *I.W.*, 11, 18 Sept.; *Nation*, 25 Sept.; D to Devoy, 15 Sept. (*D.P.B.*, i, 551).

[2] See map X.

[3] Davitt says 12,000, which is an exaggeration.

[4] DN/7, DP/A7, 12–17 Sept.

[5] Above, p. 389.

and Davitt's acceptance of skirmishing money was for the first time explicitly made public, ironically by one of his most fervent supporters in America.[1] In his first letter to Devoy after his illness, written at Salt Lake City, he reflected ruefully:

> It's a blessing [that] there is nothing else I stand in dread of now, and that all my wrongdoings—in money matters especially—are now before the world. This exposure will frighten a good number of timid land-leaguers and place Brennan and my immediate friends in an awkward fix.

It would afford 'a rich feast to thief Pigott' and the 'yelping curs' of the *Irishman*, always eager to discredit the land movement. He went on to comment on recent evidence of Pigott's shady financial dealings and his blackmailing of home rule M.P.s who believed that the *Irishman* wielded immense influence with the fenians. He concluded in a mood of pessimism: 'my mission has been a failure and the only chance of retrieving it has been lost by my illness'.[2] But before he left America he succeeded in repaying two-thirds of the money advanced by the skirmishing fund.[3]

(4) Pessimism was conspicuously absent during the fourth stage of the tour. In contrast to the relaxed, passive, and unpublicised days of his journey from Omaha, he spent just over a week (18–26 September) in a state of intense activity and exhilirating popularity in San Francisco and its neighbourhood. Elaborate preparations, in which catholic clergy were prominently involved, were made for his reception,[4] which, a labour newspaper predicted, would be very different from the cold formality with which Rutherford Hayes, the first president of the United States to visit California, had recently been greeted. Davitt's reception would be 'as warm as the enthusiasm of a liberty-loving people can make it, because he is striving to break the chains which men of Hayes's stamp have forged for and fastened upon humanity'. 'Hayes is the representative of capitalist robbers and banking Shylocks. Davitt is the representative of labor of every kind and everywhere.'[5] Davitt's actual reception was reported by a newspaper of a different political complexion as 'the largest, finest, and most enthusiastic demonstration of the kind ever witnessed in San Francisco'; and the reporter went on to characterise him in terms that, despite their verbosity, convey something of the impact he habitually made on a large audience:

> He is a man of sterling, sober, candid, earnest aspect, and his countenance gives

[1] *I.W.*, 28 Aug., 4 Sept.; *Irishman*, 11 Sept.
[2] D to Devoy, 15 Sept. (*D.P.B.*, i, 551–3).
[3] Cashman, p. 218; *Nation*, 19 Aug. 82; *S.C.P.*, ix, 359.
[4] San Francisco *Monitor* quoted in *Nation*, 16 Oct. 80.
[5] San Francisco *Labor Tribune*, 18 Sept.

instant token of the intelligence and fervor and intensity of his mind and nature . . . He is free from the elaboration of the elocutionist, and speaks as one who has purpose in what he says and is cautious to say only what is pertinent to his subject.[1]

Davitt reached the Pacific coast at Oakland, on the eastern side of San Francisco Bay on 18 September, to be welcomed as a popular hero and lavishly entertained at the home of a wealthy Irish-American, Mrs Mary Canning. A torch-light procession accompanied him to the hall where he lectured to a crowded audience that evening. He was very favourably impressed by Oakland ('beautiful city') and its people ('all bricks'); and his visit to it was to have a determining influence on his later life. For at Oakland he first met the girl, Mary Yore, whom he was to marry on 30 December 1886. She was the niece of Mary Canning, *neé* Morgan, a famine emigrant from Meath, a strong character, self-educated and opinionated, who had settled at St Joseph, Michigan, and married an Irishman called McCann. They had no children. She and her husband set out for California by different routes, but whereas she reached her destination, he disappeared. She married as her second husband a wealthy citizen of Oakland, James Canning, and became a local celebrity, keeping open house for Irish nationalists visiting the place. Meanwhile her sister, Ellen Yore, who had also emigrated to St Joseph, had been killed in a road accident, leaving a seven-year-old daughter, Mary (born on 3 November 1861). Mary's father, John, remarried when she was thirteen, whereupon her aunt Mary, who had continued to be childless, brought her to Oakland in 1874, in effect as an adopted daughter. There was no legal adoption, but Mary Yore was generally looked upon as the daughter of the house, and Davitt describes her in his diary for 18 September as 'Miss Canning'. She was then in her eighteenth year. There is no contemporary evidence of their falling in love at this time, but later evidence suggests that they became friends during his stay in and near Oakland.[2]

Five miles of sea separated Oakland from San Francisco, on the western side of San Francisco Bay. When he crossed from Oakland by the ferry on Sunday, 19 September, a huge crowd greeted him at the landing stage. A procession, composed of the Irish organisations, civil and military, and citizens, of San Francisco, in five divisions marshalled by Thomas Desmond, a Clan na Gael man who had taken part in the *Catalpa* rescue,[3] escorted him to the Opera House, There for over an hour he spoke to a crowded and enthusiastic audience,

[1] San Francisco *Daily Examiner*, 20 Sept.

[2] DN/7, DP/A7, 18 Sept.; *I.W.*, 2 Oct.; San Francisco *Morning Call*, May 93 (DP/A50; personal information supplied by Eileen Davitt in Aug. 1940 and Dec. 1964.

[3] Above, p. 130. *D.P.B.*, i, 180, 555.

presided over by a veteran of the civil war, General William Starke Rosecrans (who confessed that he had not 'the pleasure of personally indulging in their hallowed reminiscences', and had never seen Ireland).

Six months ago, Davitt said, he would have had to speak for a famine-stricken people; today he was speaking for an Ireland that had vowed before the civilised world to suffer no more landlord-created famines. If the benefits of the present bountiful harvest, the best that Ireland had known for twelve years, were to be lost to the farmers in rents to the landlords next November, the people would be worse off next winter than last. But the landlords would not be allowed to appropriate the harvest, which they had contributed nothing to produce and on which the people depended for their very life. The people were resolved to defeat the landlords, both in the short term and in the long term, by peaceful means, unless the stupidity of the government and the vindictiveness of the landlords should drive them to desperation. The leaders of the land movement had no intention of precipitating a violent revolution. If there was any reasonable chance of winning independence by force of arms he would say to Irishmen the world over; 'clutch your rifles and strike for liberty'. But any attempt to do so now would simply be suicidal.

We are not, in 1880, going to make the mistake of 1867, because that mistake would be exactly falling into our enemies' hands. It would enable the . . . government to seize the leaders in Ireland and to suppress the . . . Land League, and put an end to a movement that is destined to attain a grand conquest in Ireland and lay the foundations of Irish independence.

Since it was not proposed to settle the question by revolutionary means, the landlords must be compensated, and last April the Land League had offered them twenty years purchase.[1] This too-liberal offer they had unanimously scouted, but he predicted that within a year they would bitterly regret their decision. The latest information he had from Ireland was that land could not be sold at ten years purchase—a tribute to the effectiveness of the agitation, which had virtually eliminated the letting of land from which a tenant had been evicted. How little the landlords appreciated these realities was shown by the recent rejection in the house of lords of the compensation for disturbance bill (4 August), after it had passed the house of commons.[2] It would have been only a small boon, and its rejection was all the more telling evidence of the landlords' 'no surrender' attitude. But the Land League had its hand on the throat of landlordism; if the landlords continued to resist the settlement offered to them and were backed up by the government, then in less than two years the tenant farmers

[1] Above, p. 374.

[2] See above, pp 393, 397, 398.

as a body would refuse to pay another penny in rent. The meeting concluded with the adoption of a telegram, prepared by General Rosecrans, to the Land League in Dublin: 'One hundred thousand people [in San Francisco] welcome Michael Davitt. Hold the harvest. No surrender to landlord tyranny.'[1]

Davitt dined that evening with the wealthy and well-placed Marquis D. J. Oliver, of the San Francisco Land League, and they discussed the question of 'property in land'. He spent much of the next few days receiving callers and laying plans. On the 20th he met the Irish demagogue, Denis Kearney, famous for his leadership of San Francisco's poor and for his superheated oratory. He delivered an address 'from the reformers of the west to Michael Davitt, the persecuted agitator and heroic apostle of the new civilisation', to which Davitt replied with unwonted astringency:

> To 'agitator' I make no objection, as every reformer must stir up and agitate the mass of his people if they are to achieve the object for which they struggle; but to the title of 'heroic apostle of the new civilisation' I can lay no particle of claim as I am too irreverent for the dignity of an apostle, and too ignorant of what is to constitute the new civilisation you credit me with propagating. I am fond of old names, about the meaning of which there can be no mistake, and I am of opinion that there can be no advantage gained for the cause of reform by enveloping ideas or clothing principles in ambiguous or new-fangled language.
>
> I am labouring for the abolition of an infamous land code which has cursed and depopulated Ireland for centuries. . . . If the overthrow of land monopoly in Ireland and the establishment of the tiller of the soil as the owner is to create . . . a 'new civilisation', then I am satisfied to be known as its advocate, not only in Ireland but in every other country afflicted with the same or a similar unrighteous system.[2]

He was well aware that California had its own landlord problem, but was not well impressed by Kearney personally—'low type of face and character'.[3] Later that day he visited a 'ladies' fair' that was raising funds to build a new church, St Brendan's. He made a supporting speech and was entertained to an 'elegant banquet'. On the 22nd he was taken for a drive round the city. He was received by the pupils of a Christian Brothers' college, St Mary's, and visited a Dominican friary. Finally he attended a crowded meeting of the local Clan na Gael camp, which expressed unanimous approval of the Land League. On the 22nd he was taken on a yachting trip round the bay and out through the Golden Gate into the Pacific, in the congenial company of Con

[1] DN/7, DP/A7, 19 Sept. 80; San Francisco *Daily Examiner*, 20 Sept.; *Monitor*, 23 Sept.; *F.J.*, 22 Sept.; *Nation*, 16 Oct.; *Irishman*, 16 Oct.

[2] Cashman, pp 141–2; San Francisco *Morning Call*, 21 Sept., quoted in *Nation*, 16 Oct.; Cork *Herald*, 22 Nov.

[3] DP/A7, 20 Sept.

O'Connor, owner of the yacht, Judge Tuohy, president of the San Francisco Land League, Thaddeus Flanagan, Marquis Oliver, and other leading members of the league. On their return they were received with a salute of cannon at the Yacht Club, where they dined. That evening Davitt gave a second lecture in the Opera House, Judge Tuohy presiding. Again the house was crowded and Davitt felt that he improved on his previous performance. On the 24th, having said farewell to Mrs Canning and Mary Yore in Oakland, he travelled some 70 miles inland to Stockton: the train was an hour late and the attendance at his lecture consequently poor, but he succeeded in forming a branch of the league. Back in San Francisco on the 25th, he visited a 'carnival of authors' ('splendid spectacle'), and (with a party that included a detective) Chinatown, where he found the opium dens revolting. He revisited St Brendan's fair and again dined with Oliver. It was typical of the spirit with which he had been received in San Francisco that when he left the city on the 26th he had a through ticket to New York in his pocket as the gift of the San Francisco Irish.[1]

(5) The final stage of Davitt's tour (26 September–18 October), covering his return to New York, was spent mainly in the western states. He broke his journey at Reno to take in Virginia City, and at Cheyenne for a lengthy detour in Colorado. He addressed meetings (26 September–10 October) at Sacramento and Vallejo (California), Virginia City (Nevada), Denver, Central City, and Leadville (Colorado), his lectures being usually followed by the formation of a league branch. At Virginia City he was the guest of J. W. Mackay 'the bonanza king', one of the Comstock lode millionaires, whom he found kind, attentive, and unassuming, 'a perfect gentleman', and popular among his workers. He attended Davitt's lecture, but regarded the land movement as a waste of effort, and thought it would be far better for the Irish to emigrate wholesale and form a New Ireland in the American west. Mackay took Davitt down one of the bonanza mines and showed him the silver workings (30 September). In Colorado Davitt saw the most unforgettable scenery of his entire tour during a four-day (8–11 October) round trip in the Rockies by the Denver and Rio Grande Railroad—from Denver (one mile high), past Pikes Peak (14,100 feet) south to the Arkansas river, west to Salida, north via Buena Vista, where he stayed a night, to Leadville, and north-east back to Denver by the South Platte river. Approaching Buena Vista:

Such stupendous rocky scenery—gorge or canyon not more than 50 yards wide and about 20 miles long! Never even imagined such piles of rocks five hundred

[1] DN/7, DP/A7, 19-26 Sept.; *Irishman*, 23 Oct.

feet high, in all formations, strata, shapes etc. . . . Scene will never fade from my memory.

Between Leadville and Denver:

Such winding of valley, river (La Platte), and railway tracks, and such combination of mountain, rock and river, with trees apparently growing from the solid rock and climbing to the summit of the boundary hills! . . . Canyon 40 miles long.

Leadville, where he found 'a splendid lot of Irishmen', he justly described as the 'magic city of the world': on a site over 10,000 feet high, immensely rich in deposits of lead and silver, it had sprung up in the previous four years from a mining camp to become a chartered city of some 35,000 inhabitants, with all public facilities.[1]

Davitt resumed his eastward journey at Cheyenne on 12 October, returning to New York by way of Omaha, Chicago, and Cleveland. He stayed overnight at Chicago (14–15 October) to see Alexander Sullivan and negotiate a commission to write letters from Ireland for the Chicago *Tribune*. He also stopped at Cleveland to give his last lecture of the tour (16 October). In a press interview there, he asserted that the tour had been 'very successful' in its purpose of building up moral and material support for the land movement. Rumours that the British government intended to prosecute the Land League leaders for seditious conspiracy had appeared in the Dublin press, and Davitt, questioned about this, said he would regard such a prosecution as 'the last kick of landlordism'.

I think nothing material will come of it. Our work is too far advanced now to be checked. . . . They may arrest the leaders, thirty-nine of us, and they may put us in prison, but that will not stop the work. If Mr Parnell and all the rest were executed or exiled it would not have the desired effect. The people themselves are . . . doing the work, and to check the agitation the whole people would have to be imprisoned or exterminated.

If the government continued to reject the united appeal of the people, then 'the justice of our principles will warrant us in using every means to enforce our reasonable demands'. He returned to New York on 18 October.[2]

Davitt's tour was essentially an organising and morale-raising effort, and its achievement was to leave throughout Irish-America from New York to San Francisco a deposit of Land League branches and a fund of enthusiasm for the land movement that was widely shared. The Irish-American and catholic press had endorsed the programme of the

[1] DN/7, 26 Sept.–11 Oct.; DP/A7, 26–7 Sept.; Denver *Daily Tribune*, 7 Oct.; *I.W.*, 23, 30 Oct.; *F.J.*, 3 Nov.

[2] DN/7, 12–18 Oct.; D to Devoy, 3 Oct. (*D.P.B.*, i, 555); *Nation*, 16 Oct.; Cleveland *Leader*, 17 Oct.

league, and catholic clergy had everywhere identified themselves with it. But, Davitt admitted, there was plenty of missionary work to be done among the American public generally, especially in combating the influence of the pro-English press. Financially the tour bears no comparison with Parnell's fund-raising mission earlier in the year. As a rule Davitt did not handle the proceeds of his lectures himself, but encouraged the local committees to transmit them either directly to Dublin or through the treasurer of the American Land League, the *Irish World*, the Boston *Pilot*, or other reputable channel. He thus could not tell how much of the American money reaching the Land League (both for relief and for the purposes of the league) was due to his efforts. The expenses of the tour were minimal, owing to the generosity of local people: for example, at St Louis his hotel bill was paid by an unnamed benefactor and Dr Kane refused to charge him; his fortnight's illness at Omaha similarly cost him nothing financially; and his railway fare was usually paid for him.[1]

He took care to maintain contact with Clan na Gael throughout his tour, winning confidence in the league among the camps whose meetings he attended. It was obviously with an eye to this Clan na Gael support that in his lectures he repeatedly used the argument: as a nationalist I approve in principle of the revolutionary movement's commitment to physical force, but as a realist I know that there is no chance of success in a shooting war with Britain, whereas immediate progress towards the goal of independence is being made by the land war. His relations with Devoy remained close, though seeds of future estrangement were planted by his departure from the Trenor Hall decision on the transmission of funds to the Land League in Dublin.[2] He expressed to Devoy his irritation with the unceasing hostility of the 'true path' patriots of the I.R.B. and their unspeakable mouthpiece, Pigott; and he was grimly amused by news that Matthew Harris and P. J. Sheridan[3] had, like himself, been expelled from the supreme council while P. W. Nally of Mayo had been added to it.[4] In a cryptic reference to 'the exterminating policy now resolved upon at home'—it is not clear whether the policy of the government or of the supreme council is meant—he told Devoy (5 October) that he would be in Ireland soon, 'and if the game of shooting or breaking up meetings is really to be played, the fun won't be all on one side'.[5]

[1] Cleveland *Leader*, 17 Oct.; Boston *Daily Globe*, 6 Nov.; Cork *Herald*, 22 Nov.; Account of income and expenditure of western tour, 1 Aug.–18 Oct. (DP/A7); Brown *Irish-American nationalism*, p. 110.

[2] Above, pp 384, 388; Devoy, *Land of Eire*, p. 74.

[3] See above, pp 312, 361.

[4] See above, pp 285, 312.

[5] D to Devoy, 3, 5 Oct. (*D.P.B.*, i, 554–5).

Davitt had promised to return to Ireland in November, which he felt sure would be a critical time, and he decided in early October to leave New York if possible by the 25th, but it proved impossible to do so till 10 November. Meanwhile the Land League in Dublin, in face of the impending prosecution (announced by the government on 23 October), urgently requested him to remain in America to continue his invaluable work there instead of returning home, where he would be the most vulnerable of the league leaders (26 October).[1] He disagreed: in a press interview at Boston on 5 November, he said that the American Land League was now an organised and nation-wide auxiliary of the Irish Land League, and his essential work in America was therefore done; he could be of more service in Ireland than in America to the cause of the tenants in the crisis now opening. The great danger was that the landlords would enforce their legal rights and that tens of thousands of small farmers, threatened with eviction, and exasperated by the prosecution of their trusted leaders, would be goaded into premature armed resistance. That was just what the establishment wanted[2] and what the Land League must do its utmost to prevent, a task in which he felt called upon to take part.[3]

Among new contacts he made on this second American visit one was to have a decisive influence on his thinking—Henry George, the Californian radical, who had written a unique work on economic theory, *Progress and poverty*. First published in an 'author's edition' of five hundred copies in August 1879, it had made a slow and disappointing start, but from January 1880, when the first regular edition appeared, it began to receive serious consideration from reviewers and to make converts on both sides of the Atlantic. Its sales expanded from 1881 till it became one of the most widely known and influential books of the world; by 1900 some two million copies of it had been sold. With great power, lucidity, and missionary fervour it argued that the root cause of poverty everywhere was private ownership of land, which had no more justification in morality or reason than private ownership of air or sunlight would have. The land of a country rightfully belonged to all the people of that country; just as everyone had an equal right to live so everyone had an equal right to land. How was this right to be made good? Not by an equal division of land, not by confiscating land from the existing landlords, but by confiscating rent and applying it to the equal benefit of all citizens. In practical terms this could be effected simply by taxing all land up to its full value,

[1] *F.J.*, 27 Oct.; Reid, *Forster*, ii, 259.
[2] Cf. above, p. 408; below, pp 429–30.
[3] Boston, *Daily Globe*, 6 Nov.; *F.J.*, 16 Nov.

exclusive of improvements, and abolishing all other taxes. The landlord's unearned increment would thus be abolished without compensation, speculation in land values would be eliminated, nothing produced by human labour would be taxed, and absolute free trade would be established. The relevance of this universal gospel to the land war in Ireland must have been plain to Davitt as soon as it impinged on him, just as he must have been responsive to George's spiritual greatness when he first met him in New York shortly before his departure for Ireland. The meeting appears to have taken place at the home of Patrick Ford, who was a firm friend and supporter of Davitt and was to become even more strongly attached to George, whose views on land monopoly he largely shared. Davitt and George became personal friends, and George was gratified by an assurance from Davitt that the Land League would push *Progress and poverty* in Britain.[1]

His last few weeks in America were full of activity. There were over a score of league branches in New York city to renew contacts with. He convened a meeting of the central council of the American league at his office on 22 October, when it was arranged that Rev. Lawrence Walsh should act as general secretary as well as treasurer 'during Davitt's absence in Ireland'. He addressed the seventh ward branch of the league in New York on 24 October, and the fifth ward branch on the 31st. On 5 November he attended a mass meeting of the Boston Land League at Faneuil Hall, Boston, and was J. B. O'Reilly's guest for dinner next evening at the Papyrus Club—'all the literary men will be there', wrote O'Reilly, inviting him, and added that the company would include Dr Lyon Playfair, deputy speaker of the house of commons, and other Englishmen. His last public appearance was at a farewell meeting on 8 November in the Cooper Institute, New York, held under the auspices of a new body, the Ladies' Land League. This, the creation of Fanny Parnell in collaboration with Ellen Ford, sister of Patrick Ford, was founded at New York on 15 October as a fund-raising organisation of women, in parallel with the main league. Its president was Mrs Parnell, with Ellen Ford and Fanny Parnell as vice-president and financial secretary respectively. Mrs Parnell made a speech (she described it as her first appearance in public) to the farewell meeting, presided over by the Hon. W. E. Robinson,[2] at which

[1] Henry George Jr, *Life of Henry George* (1900), pp 289, 310, 315-44; C. A. Barker, *Henry George* (1955), pp 320-40. D told the *Times*-Parnell commission (*S.C.P.*, ix, 432, 433, 7 July 89) that he first met George at Ford's in December 1878, but George was then living in San Francisco and it is nearly certain that D was confusing two occasions – his first interview (as distinct from meeting) with Ford and his first meeting, two years later, with George which, it is reasonable to assume, took place at Ford's.

[2] See above, p. 236.

Davitt summarised his gospel for the land and complimented the ladies on their patriotic initiative: 'when we have united the manhood and the beauty of Ireland we will be irresistible'. With what proved to be a prophetic gesture he asked whether he could say when he was back in Ireland that the league could look for active cooperation from the ladies in any emergency that might arise; to which there were answering shouts of 'yes'. He showed his sensitivity to a peculiarity of Irish-American nationalism[1] by claiming that in supporting the Land League Irish-Americans would be benefiting themselves:

> You want to be honoured among the elements that constitute this nation . . . You want to be regarded with the respect due you; that you may thus be looked on, aid us in Ireland to remove the stain of degradation from your birth.[2]

The meeting raised 1000 dollars, and presented him, as the hero of the occasion, with a 'floral ship' named 'Agitator', an address, and a testimonial. Parnell also came in for a share of the glory: a solid gold shield, with his crest and monogram surmounted by an eagle, the gift of the Wicklow men of New York, and an illuminated address conferring on him the freedom of the city of Chicago were handed over to Davitt for conveyance to him. Fanny Parnell, unable to attend the meeting owing to illness, sent Davitt her special thanks for making her organisation the last to receive an address from him, and her fear that in returning to Ireland he was rushing into great danger. She hoped that when they next met it would be on free Irish soil. A few weeks later a highly emotional poem of which he was the subject appeared in the Boston *Pilot*.[3]

He left New York on 10 November on the Cunarder, S.S. *Batavia*. She was the smallest and oldest of the four transatlantic liners on which he had travelled.[4] After a boisterous passage, in the course of which heavy seas broke into the ship and flooded cabin and berths (17 November), she made Queenstown on Saturday, 20 November. Davitt stayed that night and the next in Cork, and travelled to Dublin by the morning train on Monday.[5]

[1] See above, p. 140.

[2] *I.W.*, 13 Nov., quoted in Brown, *Irish-American nationalism*, p. 24.

[3] DN/7, 22-30 Oct.; J. B. O'Reilly to D, 2 Nov. (DP/A25); Fanny Parnell to D, 9 Nov. (DP/AV); *I.W.*, 30 Oct., 13 Nov.; Cork *Herald*, 22 Nov.; *F.J.*, 22, 24 Nov.; Boston *Pilot*, 18 Dec.; Cashman, p. 142; *Fall*, p. 256; R. F. Foster, *Charles Stewart Parnell: the man and his family* (1976), p. 245.

[4] 2,500 gross tonnage; built in 1870 (*Lloyd's Register of British and Foreign Shipping, 1880–81*); cf. above, pp 221–2, 268, 382.

[5] Cork *Herald*, 22 Nov.; *F.J.*, 22 Nov.; S.P.O., R.P. 1880/28883.

XI

The land war from August 1880 to February 1881

DAVITT had correctly judged the Irish situation in November to be critical. The harvest of 1880 ripened early, and showed distinct improvement, especially in potatoes, over that of 1879. The output of the principal crops, exclusive of potatoes, turnips, and hay rose in value from £4.9 millions in 1879 to £5.6 millions, while the vital potato crop increased from 1.11 million tons to 2.99 million and the turnip crop from 2 million tons to 4 million. In Connacht the improvement was significantly less: the increase in the tonnage of potatoes (83 per cent) was the smallest for the four provinces and was well below the national average (168 per cent).[1] Much of Connacht thus continued to be a distressed area, while everywhere the effect of three years of depression was felt in a heavy accumulation of arrears of rent owed to landlords and of debts to shopkeepers and bankers. The response of the Land League to these conditions was to take up an increasingly aggressive attitude to the landlords. By November the government of Ireland under Forster found itself driven into an intolerable position in relation both to the Land League and the landlords.

The league decided on 25 August to close its relief account,[2] and from then onwards its funds and its energies were mainly engaged in preparing for a winter struggle with the landlords in which, with strong financial support from America, it hoped to win a decisive victory. Its immediate aim was now to 'hold the harvest', that is, to induce the tenants to pay no more in rent and arrears from the sale of their produce than they could reasonably spare, having regard to their losses during the three preceding years, a plan that commonly took the form of tendering only the amount of Griffith's valuation to the landlords. This plan, which had begun to emerge in August 1879,[3] was coupled

[1] Appendix G; *Thom 1882*, pp 686-7.

[2] *F.J.*, 25 Aug. 80.

[3] Above, pp 304, 305, 317, 320-21.

with the advice, voiced by Davitt and Parnell in the following autumn,[1] that debts due to shopkeepers for necessities they had supplied on credit had a higher priority than rents. Tenants must distinguish betweeen resistance to an unjust and grasping landlord and resistance to a shopkeeper, however grasping, who had met a vital need and was not armed with the terrible engine of eviction. If a tenant could not pay what he owed a shopkeeper or a bank, he must expect to have his goods sold for the benefit of his creditors. At a meeting of the central Land League in Dublin on 19 October, Parnell cited with approval a recent occasion when a crowd that had gathered to resist the service of processes for non-payment of rent dispersed as soon as it became know that the processes were those of shopkeepers. Generally, Parnell believed, shops and banks were giving their debtors reasonable time in which to pay, but in any case the movement against rent should not be allowed to degenerate into a movement against shopkeepers and bankers.[2]

The extent of the tenants' indebtedness to landlords, shopkeepers, and bankers is, of course, not known, but indications of its magnitude are given in the report of the Mansion House Relief Committee (7 December 1880). In 1879, it was calculated, the landlords remitted at least £3,000,000 of their rents (perhaps one-fifth of the total rental). During the first seven months of 1880 some £4,000,000 of rents and debts were written off or suspended, while £500,000 was advanced by the state for buying seeds.[3] The landlords as a body had thus made substantial remissions, and had been slow to press for payment of arrears. They now regarded themselves as having the first claim on the profits of the harvest, and generally refused to accept Griffith's valuation or other diminished measure of their rents except as payments on account. Relations between landlords and tenants became more deeply embittered with the defeat of the government's compensation for disturbance bill (4 August),[4] which left the landlords legally free to assert their rights by way of eviction for non-payment of rent. Evictions, which for 1879 had shown a quarterly average of 275 and were lowest in October–December with 199, had risen to 490 in the first quarter of 1880 and to 622 in the second quarter. In the July–September quarter they stood at 629.[5] Against this trend the league braced itself, expanding and strengthening its organisation, and developing its techniques of resistance. Lawyers were engaged to

[1] *F.J.*, 22 Sept., 7, 14 Dec. 79; above, pp 321–2.
[2] *F.J.*, 20 Oct.; above, pp 347, 377.
[3] *Irish crisis*, pp 9, 73.
[4] Above, pp 398.
[5] Appendix D1; cf. above, p. 332.

defend tenants' interests in the courts: legal technicalities were exploited to defeat or delay as long as possible ejectment proceedings by landlords; and criminal charges against tenants were defended. A cardinal principle of the league, that farms from which tenants had been evicted for non-payment of unreasonable rent should be kept tenantless, was enforced against the land-grabber with increasing use of the weapon soon to be named the 'boycott'. For example, the central body of the league, on 14 September, voted £10 to the branch at Easky, County Sligo, in response to its appeal for help in establishing a new blacksmith in the town, the old one having defied the branch by continuing to work for an ostracised land-grabber.[1] Illegal practices which the league could not officially sanction but to which local branches lent timely assistance became more frequent: organised obstruction of officers of the law in carrying out ejectments, assistance to evicted tenants in reoccupying their farms, 'holding the harvest' in the literal sense of forcibly preventing landlords from seizing crops in lieu of rent, and forcible interference with sheriffs' execution sales.[2]

The frequency of land meetings and the momentum of the agitation were stepped up with the return of the home rule M.P.s to Ireland on the termination of the parliamentary session on 7 September. Parnell at Ennis, speaking of the land bill that the government was committed to bringing before parliament in the new session, assured the farmers that the benefit they would obtain from it would be proportionate to the strength of their agitation in the months ahead and to their determination

> not to pay unjust rents, . . . to keep a firm grip of your homesteads, . . . not to bid for farms from which others have been evicted, and to use the strong force of public opinion to deter any unjust men amongst yourselves—and there are many such—from bidding for such farms.

What were they to do with the 'unjust man' who flouted this public opinion? Several voices shouted 'shoot him'. Parnell retorted that there was a very much better way, and went on to urge the social excommunication of the 'land-grabber': he was to be put into a 'moral Coventry', to be treated as an outcast, a moral leper, isolated from all human and economic contacts with the community whose code he had violated.[3] There was nothing new in this doctrine; it had been implicit in the agitation since the Irishtown meeting, at which James

[1] *F.J.*, 15 Sept. 80.

[2] *F.J.*, passim; N.L.I., MSS 17693, 17697; and see above, pp 315, 350.

[3] *F.J.*, 20 Sept.; extracts in Curtis and McDowell, *Irish historical documents*, pp 260–62. Sexton, speaking on the same theme at Charleville on 26 September used the phrase 'moral Siberia' instead of Parnell's 'moral Coventry' (*F.J.*, 27 Sept.).

Daly had denounced the land-grabber.[1] Among the national leaders of the agitation Davitt was its foremost exponent: he had included it by implication in his programme for the Mayo Land League (16 August 1879),[2] and had explicitly written it into the code of the National Land League (30 December),[3] so that it had official status from then onwards. He had invoked it in a speech at Knockaroe, Queen's County, on 22 February 1880, and had cited it with approval at Boston, Mass., on 20 June.[4] Next to him, Dillon was conspicuous for his reference to it in a speech at Maryborough on 5 October 1879.[5] Brennan had voiced it at Balla, on 22 November of that year;[6] and recently J. W. Walshe at Kiltullagh, County Galway, on 22 August,[7] and James Redpath at Claremorris, County Mayo, on 12 September,[8] had spoken of it in terms very similar to those that were to be used by Parnell at Ennis. But the Ennis speech acquired a clarion-like character because of the national authority of the speaker and because the time was ripe for his message.

Within a week of the Ennis speech Captain Charles Boycott of Lough Mask House, County Mayo, became the eponymous victim of the league's most deadly weapon.[9] It was characteristic of the agitation that its most sensational episode occurred in Mayo and was an entirely local operation, directed by the Ballinrobe branch of the league under its president, Fr John O'Malley, P.P. of The Neale. Before Boycott's long and widely-publicised ordeal, which gave a new word to the English language, was over, 'boycotting' was well under way against offending landlords and their agents, and, more generally, against tenants eager to add other men's holdings to their own. Boycotting was a logical extension of the concept of the land-grabber, who was the counterpart of the blackleg or strike-breaker in the trade union struggles of industrial England which Davitt had known as a young man in Lancashire.[10] It was no great step from the concept of the boycott to that of a strike against the payment of rent until the land question was settled to the satisfaction of the tenants.

Egan had told the central league on 10 August that in his opinion the time had come for a general strike against rent on the precedent of industrial strikes in England.[11] Five days later, at a land meeting at Kildare, Dillon had called for an intensified recruiting campaign aimed

[1] Above, p. 290. [2] Above, pp 317, 319. [3] Above, p. 345.
[4] Above, pp 367, 395. [5] Above, p. 321. [6] Above, p. 349.
[7] *F.J.*, 23 Aug. [8] *F.J.*, 13 Sept.; *Fall*, pp 267–8.
[9] *Fall*, pp 274–8; Palmer, *Land League*, pp 197–210.
[10] The point is made in the context of a virulent characterisation of Davitt by F. H. O'Donnell in *Irish parl. party*, i, 500–02.
[11] Above, p. 399.

at raising the membership of the league to 300,000. When that point was reached, if the landlords still refused the 'moderate demands of the people' the league should direct the tenants 'to strike against rent altogether'.[1] Parnell at Ennis took care to convey his appreciation of these suggestions but not to commit himself on the question of a rent strike.

> It will be for the consideration of wiser heads than mine whether, if the landlords continue obdurate, . . . we shall not be obliged to tell the people of Ireland to strike against rent until this question has been settled. And if the five hundred thousand tenant farmers of Ireland struck against the ten thousand landlords, I would like to see where they would get police and soldiers enough to make them pay.[2]

In enforcing the league's policy its branches, especially in Mayo and Galway, set up courts for the trial of offenders, and in November such courts were reported to be exercising more effective authority than the courts of the state.[3] It was alleged by conservative and landlord interests that intimidation and outrage were now being fomented or encouraged by the league on such a scale that a 'reign of terror' prevailed in many parts of Ireland, especially in Connacht and Munster.[4] The figures for agrarian outrages, which for 1879 had reached a peak of 404 for the last quarter, had fallen during the first half of 1880 to 294 for January-March and to 245 for April-June. But in the third quarter they rose to 355, and in October–December were to reach the unprecedented total of 1696, a figure exceeding the total recorded by the police for any entire year since 1845. It was hardly accidental that in the same period the number of evictions plunged to 152, the lowest for any quarter since the beginning of 1879.[5] The category of agrarian crime in which the increase was greatest was that described as 'threatening letters and intimidation', which increased from 553 in 1879 to 1576 in 1880. Assaults increased from 85 to 137, incendiarism from 60 to 210, 'injury to property' from 45 to 215, injury to cattle from 25 to 101, and administering unlawful oaths from 20 to 60. On the other hand, agrarian murders decreased from 9 to 8,[6] though one of these murders (25 September), that of Viscount Mountmorres, a small landowner of County Galway, was a particularly gruesome example of rural ferocity.[7] But as a whole the statistics of agrarian crime scarcely bore out the theory of a Land League reign of terror:

[1] *F.J.*, 16 Aug.; Lyons, *Dillon*, p. 38.

[2] *F.J.*, 20 Sept.

[3] *D.P.B.*, ii, 23; *Fall*, pp 212, 311; Palmer, *Land League*, pp 167–8.

[4] Ibid., pp 161–7, 168–73; letters to W. E. Forster on the state of Ireland, 8 Oct.– 6 Nov. (P.R.O., Cab. 37/3/68).

[5] Above, p.333; appendices E1 and F.

[6] *Return of outrages reported to the Royal Irish Constabulary Office from 1 January 1844 to 31 December 1880* [C 2756], H.C. 1881, lxxvii, 909.

[7] *Fall*, p. 270; Palmer, *Land League*, pp 188–90.

many of the incidents recorded were trivial or duplicated one another; and far from being the work of the league many were examples of peasant feuding and acts of personal spite or vengeance which the league was unable to control. But undoubtedly there was a serious increase in the intimidation that was inseparable from the league's declared procedures, especially the boycott, and this in turn meant that many outrages occurred that were not reported to the police. The rising toll of personal injuries, incendiary fires, attacks on property, and of killing and maiming cattle reflected a state of tension and an atmosphere of violent excitement that were a direct outcome of the league's increasing militancy. As the frequency of land meetings increased during the last three months of 1880, the monthly rate of agrarian outrages increased still more.[1]

The increase in agrarian crime intensified the difficulties of the catholic bishops. At a meeting at Maynooth on 22 June the minority who supported Croke were able to ensure that resolutions on the land question amounted merely to generalities on the danger of using unjust or illegal remedies for admitted evils. Croke's statements on the land movement were, in McCabe's opinion, 'doing great mischief'; and his absence and that of a number of others from the next meeting of bishops at Maynooth in early September had the effect of preventing any decision being taken about the agitation. But the murder of Mountmorres caused McCabe to speak out against the Land League no less forcefully than Croke had spoken in its defence. In a pastoral letter read in the churches of the Dublin archdiocese on Sunday, 10 October, he declared that their 'unhappy country' was drinking 'the blood of her own children'. He was not counselling the people 'to lie down under their load of misery', but their cause had been stained by outrages inseparable from the inflammatory language used against landlords at many a land meeting, and the murderous interjections from the audience that went uncondemned by the platform party. Remedies for the tenants' grievances must not be sought by means that violated the laws of God and in schemes that no statesmanlike government could entertain. The government in office had abundantly proved their will to redress the wrongs of Ireland and to govern without recourse to coercion, but the response of men who claimed to be leaders of the people had been a threat to make Ireland ungovernable. And this in turn had been used by the enemies of all concession as arguments against doing justice to the tenants.[2]

[1] Palmer, *Land League*, pp 180–81; see appendix F.

[2] *F.J.*, 23 June, 11 Oct.; *Nation*, 3 July, 16 Oct.; Larkin, *Roman Catholic church . . .*, pp 42–3, 44–5, 46–7.

The archbishop's pastoral was greeted with enthusiasm by the conservative and pro-landlord press and with indignation by the Land League. Dillon, chairing a meeting of the central body on 12 October, had no fault to find with the archbishop for protesting against murders, but why should he fix on the killing of one or two landlords and remain silent on the crimes perpetrated by landlords on thousands of the poor during the last twenty years? As for trusting the liberal government rather than the Land League to bring about a satisfactory settlement, he left it to the Irish people to decide whether the archbishop of Dublin or the archbishop of Cashel was the wiser guide. Sexton strongly denied that he and other speakers from league platforms had condoned outrage: they could not be expected to take notice of every irresponsible interruption, but he himself had never spoken on the land question without warning his hearers against the folly and the evil of criminal acts. In dismissing the league's plan of settlement as chimerical, the archbishop was going beyond his proper sphere and passing a judgment on peasant proprietorship that carried no authority. T. D. Sullivan asked what attention would the tenants' plight be receiving from the British government if the league did not exist? One of the great services of the league was to convince the people that 'they have a power at their back that will plead for them, work for them, and stand up for them'; that they have no need to take up a gun to avenge their wrongs, but that their sufferings would be brought not only before the British parliament but before the world; and that in this way an unjust system would be changed.[1]

If the archbishop of Dublin was one of a very few bishops who continued to condemn the agitation explicitly, there were relatively fewer parish clergy who did so. Such an exception was Dr James Rice, P.P. of Charleville, County Cork, who, invited to preside at a local land meeting on 26 September, not only declined to do so but on that Sunday, after 8 o'clock mass, addressed his congregation for over an hour on the reasons for his refusal. He had not been consulted about the calling of the meeting, he was not convinced that the case which was the occasion for it was one of unjust eviction, and he could not endorse some of the resolutions that were to be moved. He believed that the true remedy for the tenants' grievances was not peasant proprietary but the '3 Fs'. He refused to join the cry for the annihilation of the landlords: landlords were their countrymen, many were good and humane, and some who imposed excessive rents did it in error or ignorance 'for which the land madness of some farmers and the injustice of others were mainly responsible'. What advantage would

[1] *F.J.*, 13 Oct.

it be to remove the landlords and put farmers in their place? The worst enemies of the tenants were not the landlords but the 'land sharks', the farmers who gave way to an undue passion for land. They now had as prime minister 'a most excellent and liberal man', and as chief secretary of Ireland 'a man of the highest character and honour'. These men would do their utmost to bring about a satisfactory settlement of the land question, and it was the duty of Irishmen not to frustrate their efforts by violence and extreme language. During this address a large number of Rice's hearers walked out of the church. The intended land meeting was held without him, some twenty other priests, including one of his curates, being present.[1]

In his Ennis speech on 19 September Parnell had urged that to ensure a land act satisfactory to the tenants the league's network must be extended from its existing strongholds in Connacht and Munster to cover the whole country. He and other leaders were disturbed not only by the hostility the league was encountering from protestants in Ulster but also by opposition from agricultural labourers in County Cork. A landowner in the Shanagarry area, Peter Penn-Gaskell, who had resumed possession of a farm of 24 acres from which a tenant had been evicted for non-payment of rent, began a process of letting it in small plots in conacre to a number of poor labourer-fishermen ('carberies') at rents much below what they had been paying to the local farmers. The latter tried to intimidate the labourers into giving up their plots, and, having failed to overawe the majority of them, prepared to form a branch of the Land League with a view to bringing effective pressure to bear on the offenders. A meeting was to have been held for that purpose at Shanagarry on 10 October, but at the appointed time several hundred carberies took possession of the platform and turned the occasion into a demonstration against both farmers and Land League. A spokesman for the carberies described them as 'a class of poor people who have always been trampled upon' by the farmers.

> The farmers say it is not right for . . . labourers to take land directly from the landlords . . . They insist that the land must be rented from[2] themselves, and that they must be paid double and treble the rent which we . . . are now asked to pay the landlord . . . These are the people who want a Land League in their midst and want to have the land[3] left idle in order to suit their own purposes.[4]

This demonstration elicited an important statement from Parnell at one of his rare appearances at a meeting of the central Land League.

[1] *F.J.*, 27 Sept.
[2] The printed report reads 'for', an obvious error.
[3] That is, the evicted farm.
[4] *Dublin Evening Mail*, 12 Oct., quoting *Cork Constitution*; cf. above, pp 375–6.

He hoped, he said on 19 October, that the labourers would trust the league to obtain facilities for them to acquire land, as well as for the farmers. There was plenty of land available for the purpose—perhaps four or five million acres— in the 'lighter grazing lands', which had been cleared of small tillage-farmers after the famine and had become increasingly unproductive through being too long in grass. It was a national interest to restore such lands to small farmers and labourers. This was the only real solution for the labourers' problem, and it could only be achieved through the Land League.[1] From now onwards the central body of the league showed greater concern about the labourers, and the threatened rift between them and the farmers was averted. But in the summer of 1881 labourers' grievances were to erupt in an outbreak of strikes in County Cork.[2]

The province in which the league had made least headway was, of course, Ulster, where the conflict of interests between landlords and tenants was never so bitter as in the other provinces and where the Orange Order was mobilised by the landlord and 'loyalist' interest to resist the league as subversive not only of property but of the union itself. The expedition of orange labourers from Monaghan and Cavan to save Captain Boycott's crops highlighted this attitude of Ulster unionists. Nevertheless Ulster farmers had their own grievances against their landlords. In the seventies the Ulster custom, which had given them advantages not generally enjoyed elsewhere in Ireland,[3] was shown to be no guarantee, though legalised by the 1870 land act, against rent raising, eviction, or the erosion of tenant right by landlords; and in consequence Ulster farmers had been agitating for the '3 Fs' for several years before the Land League movement began. It was an obvious interest of the league to exploit this agitation. From August onwards land meetings were held in several counties at which protestant farmers sometimes formed a substantial minority of the attendance.[4] At Belleek, County Fermanagh, on 9 November, Parnell, Dillon, O'Kelly, and Jeremiah Jordan[5] opened what Parnell described as 'the land campaign in the north of Ireland' with the argument that the Ulster custom had not saved Ulster farmers from rack-renting and eviction and that the Land League was fighting their battle and was entitled to their support.[6] The orange counter-argument was that the

[1] *F.J.*, 20 Oct.

[2] J. S. Donnelly, *The land and the people of nineteenth-century Cork* (1975), pp 238–9.

[3] Above, p. 28.

[4] Thomas MacKnight, *Ulster as it is*, i, ch. XIX–XX; R. W. Kirkpatrick, 'Landed estates in mid-Ulster and the Irish land war, 1879–85' (Ph.D. thesis, University of Dublin, 1977), pp 168–76, 432.

[5] See above, p. 375.

[6] *F.J.*, 10 Nov. 80.

league was a monstrous conspiracy against property rights, with the ulterior object of subverting protestantism, civil and religious liberty, and the British constitution.[1] The league was particularly indignant at the attempt to lead protestant farmers in Ulster astray with 'the red herring of sectarian fanaticism'.[2] Louden claimed that, in the west, the strongest supporters of the league were protestants and the worst landlords were catholics.[3]

Since the abortive prosecution of Davitt and others in November 1879 no attempt had been made by government to use the criminal law against the leaders of the league. But on 2 November 1880 Parnell and thirteen other leaguers were charged with criminal conspiracy.[4] The league reacted with defiance and intensified activity; within a week 36 new branches were formed, and, on the initiative and with the cooperation of the *Freeman's Journal*, a defence fund was started that quickly relieved the league of any embarrassment over legal costs. The *Freeman's* action was specially welcome because, as Egan was quick to point out, it proved that the most influential of national newspapers was now 'thoroughly and wholeheartedly in consort with the Land League'. Though no newspaper had given the league such full and consistent coverage, its editor, Gray, had been distinctly critical of the league and of Parnell's leadership up to the time of his election as chairman of the parliamentary party (17 May), but from then onwards the *Freeman* had given him steady support.[5] About two-thirds of the defence fund was subscribed through it and acknowledged in its columns.[6]

Among the subscribers were the catholic archbishops of Cashel and of Tuam, and the bishops of Clonfert, Cloyne, Ross and Limerick, as well as many of the parish clergy. Croke's contribution, of £30 from himself and his suffragans, was sent from Rome, where he was then making an official visit, and where he and his episcopal colleagues had delivered £8,756 to the pope as the contribution of their dioceses to Peter's Pence. In this context their subscription to the Parnell defence fund gave particular offence to McCabe, because it was popularly miscontrued as a kind of papal endorsement of Parnell's policy. Moreover Moran, bishop of Ossory, who had hitherto firmly supported his archbishop, changed his mind about the agitation in face of its progress in his own diocese. But McCabe continued to be

[1] Manifesto of Grand Orange Lodge of Ireland, 3 Nov., in *F.J.*, 9 Nov.
[2] *F.J.*, 2 Nov.
[3] *F.J.*, 10 Nov.
[4] See below, pp 427–8.
[5] *F.J.*, 10 Nov.; above, pp 361–2, 364, 377, 378.
[6] Lyons, *Parnell*, pp 139–40.

at one with Croke in advising the Roman authorities against a papal condemnation of the Land League.[1]

At the meeting of the central league, on 9 November, at which the formation of 36 new branches was announced, the long-promised 'rules for the guidance of branches' were approved. These were for the most part a repeat of Davitt's 'suggestions on organisation' of 30 December 1879, omitting the section on auxiliary land clubs.[2] That the new 'rules' differed so little from the original scheme after a year's experience of its working was a tribute to Davitt's judgment. They prescribed eleven instead of seven members as the basic minimum for a branch committee, and defined the annual subscription as one shilling for holdings of up to £5 valuation increasing by one shilling for each additional £10 of valuation. The only significant changes were those intended to strengthen and systematise the linkage between the central body of the league and the branches. The branch treasurers should issue receipts, on forms supplied by the central office, to all members on payment of their subscriptions, and the counterfoils should be forwarded to the central office. Cards of membership, provided by the central office, should be issued to all paid-up members. All affiliated branches, on the first of each month, should transmit half the funds then in hand, together with a report, to headquarters. Finally, and doubtless with an eye to the 'red herring', it was declared that 'all sectarian discussions be excluded from meetings'.[3]

The increase in centralised control of the branches was a response to the rapid expansion in their number. The same tendency produced a change in the procedure for admission to membership of the central body. Owing to the pressure of applications, it was decided on 16 November that the interval between the nomination and the election of candidates be reduced from a fortnight to a week. By this time the expansion of business had so greatly exceeded the capacity of the league's rooms in Middle Abbey Street that larger offices had become necessary. New premises were found at 39 Sackville (now O'Connell) Street, where the league met for the first time on 14 December.[4]

Viewed from the side of the government of Ireland under W. E. Forster the world of the land leaguers during the six months of Davitt's absence assumes a very different character. Relations between the chief secretary and the country he had set out hopefully to govern deteriorated

[1] Larkin, *The Roman Catholic church and the modern Irish state*, pp 48–50; Tierney, *Croke of Cashel*, p. 104.

[2] Above, pp 344–6.

[3] *F.J.*, 10 Nov.; *Nation*, 27 Dec.; *Defence*, pp 399–40.

[4] *F.J.*, 17 Nov., 8, 15 Dec.; *D.P.B.*, ii, 23.

rapidly. His unsuccessful attempt to interfere by the compensation for disturbance bill with the legal power of the landlords to evict for non-payment of rent, though it was frustrated by the house of lords,[1] earned him implacable hostility from the landlords, most of whom regarded him as betraying them to their enemies, the land-leaguers. On the other hand, his measure extending the previous government's relief act[2] by indemnifying local authorities that had exceeded their powers in advancing money and by authorising grants for public works and outdoor relief[3] did nothing to offset his growing unpopularity with the land-leaguers as he endeavoured to maintain law and order and to enforce the legal rights of both landlords and tenants. He poured police and troops into the most disturbed districts, Mayo and Galway, but outrages multiplied and spread into areas hitherto unaffected. There was a growing public clamour from landlord and conservative interests to strengthen the hands of the executive by emergency legislation, which he resisted as long as he could. But by 25 October he had reached the conclusion that, unless conditions rapidly improved, he could not face the winter without obtaining from parliament the power of discretionary arrest and imprisonment by the suspension of habeas corpus.[4]

Gladstone and most of his colleagues were very slow to admit that this odious expedient had become necessary. At Forster's instance the government had agreed, on 30 September, to mobilise the ordinary law against Parnell and other leaders of the agitation by prosecuting them for conspiracy, if the Irish law officers approved. They did approve, and on 10 October the Irish government decided on a prosecution. Forster had no confidence that criminal proceedings would materially check the outrages, and believed that the impending trial would at best result in a disagreement of the jury. Nevertheless he felt that the government was obliged to bring a prosecution: it was all they could do, in the absence of new legislation, to punish men who were 'great criminals'; it would prove that the government did not fear the agitators and would explode the landlord myth that it saw agrarian outrages as making a strong land act necessary and therefore did not regret them; it would demonstrate that 'Parnell's law' would not be allowed to supplant the law of the state, and would fully justify the government in asking parliament for special powers if the outrages continued.[5] On 2 November the Irish attorney general filed an information in the court of queen's bench charging Parnell and thirteen other land-

[1] Above, pp 393, 398.
[2] Above, p. 367.
[3] 43 & 44 Vict., c. 14 (2 Aug.).
[4] Reid, *Forster*, ii, 253–62.
[5] Reid, *Forster*, ii, 255–9, 260–1; Hamilton, *Diary*, i, 60, 65–6, 67–8.

leaguers—Biggar, Boyton, Brennan, Dillon, Egan, Gordon, Harris, J. W. Nally, Michael O'Sullivan, Sexton, Sheridan, T. D. Sullivan, John W. Walshe—with conspiracy to prevent the payment of rent that had been contracted for and generally with conspiring to impoverish the landlords and to create hostility between landlords and tenants.[1] The procedure by information meant that, in contrast with the proceedings against Davitt in 1870 and in 1879, the accused were saved the 'needless indignity' of being arrested.[2]

Long before the mammoth proceedings thus initiated came to a hearing (28 December), Forster was insisting that the suspension of habeas corpus could no longer be postponed. In a memorandum of 15 November he told members of the cabinet that the Irish government was unable to discharge 'its first duty, of protection to the person'. Few landlords or farmers were safe from personal violence if they exercised their legal rights. Rents above Griffith's valuation were being withheld by tenants, yet few defaulters were evicted. ('Parnell is quite right . . . in saying that the league has stopped evictions, though he ought to have said "the league and its attendant outrages".')[3] From 70 to 80 men were only saved from probable murder by being individually under police protection. In Galway there was a policeman for every 47 adult males, and a soldier for every 97, yet no one in that county could safely take an evicted farm.

> Large as is the police force, we have strained its strength to the utmost, and it takes months to train a policeman. We might pour in thousands of soldiers and occupy the disturbed districts as though they were an enemy's country, but these secret outrages are as difficult to deal with as a guerilla warfare. I fear no troops will prevent them, and the work is one for which our young soldiers are singularly unfitted.

A bill, suggested by Gladstone, to enable the executive to put down the Land League[4] would not meet the difficulty because, though the league stimulated men to commit outrages, its principal leaders did not themselves plan or perpetrate outrages and probably could no longer control those who did. The initiation of criminal proceedings against Parnell and others had done nothing to check outrages. So with obvious regret and reluctance Forster urged the cabinet to recall parliament on 2 December for a special session to suspend habeas corpus.[5]

The result was a ministerial crisis in which Chamberlain, supported by Bright, led the opposition to Forster's proposal, arguing that it was

[1] *F.J.*, 3 Nov., 29 Dec.; *Nation*, 6 Nov.; copy of information in DL/2.
[2] Attorney general's speech for the prosecution in *F.J.*, 29 Dec., p. 6.
[3] Forster to Gladstone, 8 Nov. (Reid, *Forster*, ii, 264).
[4] Reid, *Forster*, ii, 264–5.
[5] P.R.O., Cab. 37/4/71.

'wrong in principle and bad in policy'. If coercive legistation were necessary, it should be preceded, or at least accompanied, by redress of acknowledged grievances. Forster's statistics of agrarian crime did not prove the necessity: the actual number of serious crimes clearly due to agrarian causes was small. The suspension of habeas corpus would not be effectual: the real trouble did not come from secret societies or 'small knots of conspirators'. 'You might arrest half a county and still Captain Boycott's position would be as intolerable as ever, and Lord Leitrim's and Lord Mountmorres's murders would go unpunished.' There would be great difficulty in carrying a coercion bill through parliament; and it would be strongly opposed by sections of the liberal press. These objections would be modified, though not removed, if a strong land bill were to accompany coercion, but the government could not introduce a land bill until the Bessborough commission had reported. If it should be absolutely necessary to introduce coercion in December, Chamberlain suggested that government should at the same time bring in a short bill suspending evictions for three months.[1] Gladstone shared Chamberlain's doubts about Forster's case for coercion, which was strongly endorsed by the viceroy, but preferred, if it came to splitting the cabinet, to split with Forster rather than with Chamberlain. To avert a split Forster agreed (23 November) not to insist on recalling parliament in early December, but to carry on without special powers for a month; and the cabinet decided on 25 November to summon parliament in the first week of January. This would enable the government to proceed, if necessary, with remedial and repressive measures simultaneously.[2] In the meantime army reinforcements were sent to Ireland, and a circular was issued to the local magistrates reminding them of their powers under the existing law and exhorting them to be firm and vigilant. Simultaneously preparations went ahead for a land bill, which, Forster contended, must concede the popular demand for the '3 Fs'. Gladstone was extremely reluctant to admit that his land act of 1870 had been a failure and that some amendment of it would not suffice; and this despite the fact that the Land League had always dismissed the '3 Fs' as offering no solution and demanded the general conversion of tenants into owners as the only satisfactory basis of settlement.[3] Forster, who seems to have been in a distraught condition, was reported to have said, in applying for more troops, that the sooner civil war came the

[1] Chamberlain, *Political memoir*, pp 10–12.

[2] Hamilton, *Diary*, i, 81.

[3] Reid, *Forster*, ii, 262–73; Hamilton, *Diary*, i, 73, 74, 76–9, 80, 81, 83–4; Chamberlain, *Political memoir*, pp 8–13; J. L. Garvin, *Life of Joseph Chamberlain*, i (London, 1935), pp 325–32.

better;[1] and in Dublin Sir Thomas Steele, commander of the forces in Ireland, told Forster's adopted daughter that he fervently wished that matters would come to a head: 'I should like to have a go at the Land League'.[2]

At a press interview on the day of his arrival at Cork from America (20 November) Davitt said he believed that the land agitation would eventually result in the 'entire overthrow of landlordism'. But they should not be anxious for speedy legislation on the subject. Any bill the government might bring in next session would be only a half measure and should not be accepted as a final settlement. It would be better if legislation on the land question were postponed till the county franchise had been assimilated to the borough franchise, when an increased radical element in the house of commons would make a liberal government independent of whig support. Questioned as to American opinion on agrarian outrages he said that the London press-agency had created the impression that they were the result of Land League teaching, and it was of the greatest importance to disabuse the American mind of this fallacy. As to the impending state prosecution, he thought that it would break down, like the Sligo prosecution of 1879,[3] but that if it were carried through to the point of a conviction the land movement would go on as before. At a land meeting next day (Sunday) at Mourne Abbey, near Mallow, he developed his views on the political situation. The cabinet was divided over the issues of remedial legislation and coercion, but not even John Bright, who was far in advance of every other English statesman on the Irish land question, was sufficiently advanced to meet the wishes of the Irish people. Davitt said that he did not fear coercion but did fear that lukewarm land-reformers would throw down their arms and accept the 'dingy attempt at settlement'—the '3 Fs'—that would be offered by the government. He would oppose any such surrender:

> we can well afford to carry on this land movement until no tinkering proposal to prolong the life of landlordism by a measure of fixity of tenure and fair rents will even be offered by English statesmen. The time is not far ahead when Englishmen and Scotchmen will raise their voices also in condemnation of this remnant of feudalism and demand its banishment 'bag and baggage' from their country, as we do from ours.

In this land war the cause of the tenants, not of the landlords, was injured by acts of violence; and his American experience had convinced him that the landlords could not more effectively create sympathy for

[1] Hamilton, *Diary*, i, 83 (30 Nov. 80), 89 (17 Dec.).
[2] Arnold-Forster, Irish journal, 9 Dec.
[3] Above, pp 350–53.

themselves in America than by shooting half a dozen of their number, with a few agents thrown in, and charging the deed to the Land League. Pending a final settlement the land movement must continue with its task of teaching the people to think and act for themselves and of promoting those habits of self-reliance and organisation that could break down every obstacle in the way of Ireland's social and national regeneration.[1]

Arriving at Dublin on 22 November Davitt was met by Brennan, and taken immediately to the Land Leaque offices; and for the next ten weeks he was to be engaged incessantly in the work of the league. These ten weeks were a time of mounting tension in Ireland, and were probably the most hectic and exhausting he had yet experienced. After six months in America of almost unrelieved exertion (except when he was laid up with malaria) he resumed not only his former post at the headquarters of the league, now far more demanding than before, but also his former role of popular agitator at land meetings widely spread over the country.

He was welcomed home at the weekly meeting of the league on 23 November, and reported on his American experience. He felt satisfied with what had been done, and believed that the Land League at home, without any surrender of its independence, would benefit financially and otherwise from the support of the American Land League. The American league now had about 100 branches and the prospect of raising this total to at least 500 during the winter. Nearly all Irish organisations in America, including the Ancient Order of Hibernians and the Father Matthew[2] and other temperance societies, were in sympathy with the land movement, and the entire Irish-American catholic clergy supported it. There was, moreover, a new body, the Ladies' Land League, which, under the direction of Fanny Parnell and Ellen Ford, promised to rival the efforts of the male league in America. The question was sometimes asked in Ireland, why should Irish-Americans take such an interest in the Irish land question? The answer was threefold. First, the Irish in America had been driven from Ireland by landlordism, and it was natural that they should be eager to help in driving landlordism from Ireland. Secondly, Irish-Americans, accustomed to helping their kindred in the home country, were always responsive to a cry of general distress in Ireland. Thirdly, in helping Ireland to remove the stigma of dependence on the charity of other nations for survival, Irish-Americans were helping to ensure that they themselves would be respected in America equally with the other nationalities making up the American commonwealth. Davitt ended

[1] *F.J.*, 22 Nov. [2] Cf. above, p. 395.

by reiterating his condemnation of outrages as highly injurious to the land movement, and commended the non-violent operation against Captain Boycott as having done more for the tenants' cause than if a hundred landlords had been shot by those who resorted to the 'wild justice of revenge'.[1]

Davitt's return to Ireland had been watched by the Irish police (alerted by the British consul general at New York) from his landing at Queenstown on the 20th to his arrival at Kingsbridge, Dublin on the 22nd. From then onwards, they kept a watch on his movements without actually shadowing him.[2] He had not been included among the land-leaguers charged with conspiracy, probably because he was out of the jurisdiction when informations were filed against the accused (the 'traversers') on 2 November, and also, no doubt, because, being technically a convict on ticket of leave, his position was unique. Forster evidently regarded him as no less culpable than the others, and on his return to Ireland consulted the home secretary, Sir William Harcourt, about his ticket of leave. Harcourt was advised by the attorney general (24 November) that, though the discretionary power of the crown to revoke or alter it remained legally unimpaired, to revoke it except for breach of the express conditions on which it was granted would probably be regarded as harsh and somewhat unconstitutional. Harcourt for the moment accepted this view, but informed the Irish government (27 November) that, as the circumstances on which these conditions had been relaxed[3] no longer existed, he felt free to require their strict enforcement if so advised by the lord lieutenant.[4] On this precarious basis Davitt remained at large, without reporting to the police, for another two months.

On 30 November he presided, for the first and only occasion, at a meeting of the league in Dublin. Announcing that Sunday land-meetings were on the increase, he suggested that the central body should aim at sending a representative to every meeting. He gave notice that the executive intended shortly to propose a 'new constitution'. The meeting was told of growing orange and protestant support: no Ulster county was now without its branch and elsewhere also protestant farmers were becoming branch members. Davitt regretted that at a recent branch meeting anti-orange sentiments had been expressed, and recalled promises he had made to the American Land League that the land movement would 'build a bridge of toleration across the Boyne'. He, with Brennan, Harris, and O'Kelly were appointed a committee

[1] *F.J.*, 24 Nov.
[2] S.P.O., R.P. 1880/28883.
[3] See above, pp 194, 323, 350–51, 364.
[4] R. P. 1880/29135, 29553, 30164 (1882/26234); P.R.O., H.O. 144/5/17869/24.

to prepare an address to their northern fellow-countrymen. It was reported that ladies' branches were being formed at Croom and Askeaton in County Limerick (a week later a lady in Dublin incurred a mild reproof for trying to form a Ladies' Land League without authority[1]). Some substantial leaseholders were refusing to pay more than Griffith's valuation. A number of artisans and labourers wanted to join the central body but could not afford the £1 subscription;[2] should they not be accepted at a nominal subscription as associates? Other suggestions were that league branches should be formed in Dublin city, that O'Connell's system of repeal wardens should be introduced, and that the possibility of a 'house league' in Dublin 'against rack-rents' should be explored.'[3]

The house league idea, communicated through Davitt, was condemned by Ferguson from Glasgow as soon as he heard of it:

> Keep scientifically right. We lose educated authority if we mix up the laws of natural agents [land] with the laws of human products [houses]. Our reform of the land laws will reform the only evil existing in connection with house property, viz the land upon which houses stand.[4]

W. H. O'Sullivan raised the question again on 14 December, when he strongly attacked what he described as 'a new movement which has been started in seven or eight towns'. There was no comparison between the land question and that of urban house-rents, which depended entirely on the conditions of the market. A house league would be a dangerous distraction for the Land League, dedicated as it was to settling the great question of the land, on which merchants, shopkeepers, tradesmen, and many others depended as well as the farmers. Ferguson, who was in the chair, was able to assure O'Sullivan that the house league had been abandoned.[5]

The address to the people of Ulster that Davitt and others had been appointed to draw up was presented by him to the league and approved on 7 December. It was probably his composition. The enemies of land reform, it declared, were seeking to create disunion between north and south by charging the national movement with agrarian crime and with sectarianism. These charges were unjustified. Agrarian crime was the outcome of the land system, not of the land agitation. The agitation, far from being sectarian, was a struggle between landlord and tenant interests in which people differing in religion were involved on both sides. The last general election afforded examples, as in Mayo and Roscommon, of catholic gentlemen of old families being unseated by a catholic electorate simply because they were not sufficiently

[1] *F.J.*, 8 Dec. 80. [2] See above, p. 343. [3] *F.J.*, 1 Dec.
[4] *F.J.*, 8 Dec. [5] *F.J.*, 15 Dec.

advanced on the land question; and also of catholic voters asserting their right to differ with the highest dignatories of their church on the great question of the day. History showed that protestant farmers in Ulster during the late eighteenth century were conspicuous victims of protestant landlords, whose descendants were now foremost in hostility to the Land League. Nevertheless a landlord counter-offensive that took shape in the autumn of 1880 drew popular support mainly from Ulster protestants.

For many months the landlords had done little to combine forces against the Land League except in the field of propaganda. As early as November 1879 they had set up an 'Irish Land Committee' to publicise their case, an initiative that resulted in the presentation of a weighty body of evidence to the Richmond and Bessborough commissions and in the publication of a series of fourteen well-argued pamphlets between November 1880 and February 1882.[1] But by the autumn of 1880 more positive action was felt to be necessary: 'as there is a Land League, why is there not a Landowners' League?' The question was answered by the formation in December 1880 of two organisations to counter the work of the Land League, the Orange Emergency Committee and the Property Defence Association, the one set up by the Grand Orange Lodge of Ireland, the other by a group of landowners and agents. The two organisations did not become fully operative till after Davitt was rearrested, but from the spring of 1881 onwards were to present a serious challenge to the Land League. The Emergency Committee appealed to loyalist sentiment among middle- and working-class protestants, mainly in Ulster, against the league seen as aiming at the subversion of British authority in Ireland; the Property Defence Association, an efficient landlord body, and the better financed of the two, called for public support, regardless of creed or political opinion, 'to uphold the rights of property against organised combination to defraud'. Together the two organisations carried on a range of activities that illustrate the many-sided character of the 'land war': they supplied men to service writs and other legal processes where local officers would not risk doing so; they sent agents to attend sheriffs' auctions at which tenants' stock and interests in their farms seized for non-payment of rent were put up for sale, and to defeat the efforts of the league to stultify sales by either buying the property or ensuring a good price for it; they found tenants for evicted farms; they provided labourers, usually from Ulster, for boycotted persons and arranged for the disposal of their stock and produce; they protected labourers

[1] See bibliography, sect VI, 1.

who continued to work for their employers after being warned to leave; they helped persons whom local traders refused to supply, and traders and others who incurred financial losses through defying the league. The activity of the agents of the Emergency Committee and the Property Defence Association at sheriffs' sales raised a crucial issue for the Land League, which adopted the policy of urging tenants not to bid for their farms, as they were entitled to do, but to risk letting them go to the 'emergency men' on the assumption that the landlords would eventually have to reinstate the former tenants. The league argued that adherence to this policy would bring the landlords to their knees, because they would be unable to place new tenants on the increasing number of farms bought on their behalf. But the policy was to create problems for the league no less than for the landlords.[1]

The 'new constitution' for the league announced at its meeting on 30 November 1880, was operative by 14 December, when the weekly meeting was informed that the election of an 'executive committee' would take place a week later 'in accordance with a clause in the constitution of the Land League'. This constitution seems not to have been submitted to the league as such for approval, but to have been adopted on the sole authority of the executive. It is recorded in an undated document in Davitt's hand entitled 'Constitution of the executive council of the Irish National Land League'.[2] It was a constitution not of the league as such, which continued to be legally undefined, but of the governing body of the league; and it was not new in the sense of replacing an earlier constitution, since the governing body was now formally identified for the first time. An executive council of fifteen members was to be elected annually by the league at its second meeting in December, with power to coopt ten additional members as a reserve to fill any vacancies arising from the removal or temporary incapacity of elected members. Both elected and coopted members must be members of the league. The executive council was to elect the president, vice-president, treasurers, and secretaries of the league annually from among its own members. These officers were to be responsible to the council and the council to the league. The council was empowered to use the funds of the league as seemed to it best calculated to advance the league's objects, to recommend the removal of any of its members who should violate the league's rules or

[1] Palmer, *Land League*, ch. XI; *F.J.*, 24 May, 7, 28 June, 6, 12, 19 July, 16, 23, 31 Aug., 9, 27 Sept. 81, and passim; *Property Defence Association, Ireland, Annual Report of the committee for the year ended 30 November 1881.*
[2] DP/AV.

betray its principles, and to transfer the meetings of the executive outside Ireland in the event of 'unfair measures' being taken to injure or destroy the league.

This was the 'neat constitution' which Davitt, on 16 December, boasted privately to Devoy of having 'carried . . . by a *coup de main*'.[1] Its key feature was the executive council, in which complete control over the league was in effect vested; for this council appointed the executive officers, and they were responsible to it alone and not to the league as a whole. The responsibility of the executive council to the league, at a time when its membership was increasing rapidly, would be a much more tenuous matter. The object of these oligarchic arrangements was simply to ensure continued control of the league by the 'advanced men', who, owing to the league's very success in recruiting new members, were now, Davitt felt, in danger of being ousted by moderate elements, lay and clerical. To avert this internal danger it was only necessary to get the right men elected to the executive council; and this was done at the meeting of the league on 21 December, when the existing fourteen members of the executive (except O'Sullivan), together with James J. O'Kelly, M.P. and Dr J. E. Kenny, were elected.[2] The new executive council[3] included seven M.P.s, five of whom, together with Brennan, Egan, and Harris, were defendants in the state prosecution. The work of the executive had already been divided into five departments--finance, organisation, public policy, agriculture and labour, statistics and publication—headed respectively by Egan, Davitt, Parnell, Kettle, and Brennan,[4] and this distribution seems to have been continued by the new council. Besides what he saw as the internal danger, Davitt had in mind, in framing his constitution, the external danger that the proceedings against Parnell and the others might result in their conviction, and that the government might be stampeded by the landlords into an attempt to 'squelch' the league; this explains the provisions relating to coopted members and to the removal of the executive from Ireland in case of emergency.

By mid-December the executive was highly conscious that a confrontation between league and government was imminent. At the weekly meeting of the league on 14 December Davitt spoke for the executive in a long and critical statement on the position of the league and how best to strengthen its defences. Ireland was being presented

[1] *D.P.B.*, ii, 23.
[2] *F.J.*, 22 Dec. 80.
[3] Biggar M.P., Brennan, Davitt, Dillon M.P., Egan, Ferguson, Harris, Kettle, Kenny, Louden, O'Connor M.P., O'Kelly M.P., Parnell M.P., Sexton M.P., Sullivan M.P.; see above, pp 336, 373–4.
[4] DP/AV; *D.P.B.*, ii, 23–4.

to the world as a country in the grip of outrage and terror fomented by the league. It was their duty, as well as their interest, to refute these vicious charges: agrarian crime was grossly exaggerated, even manufactured, by the pro-landlord press, and the league was the victim, not the fomentor, of such crime. Since Irishtown, some 450 land meetings with an average attendance of 5000 had been held; if the league had appealed to the passions of the vast audience that this represented there would have been far more crime to record than their enemies alleged. In fact, during the past winter, when 800,000 people were in desperate need of food and were kept alive by public charity, only a handful of agrarian homicides had occurred. Nevertheless the executive was deeply concerned about the real increase in agrarian crime such as threatening letters, and on 13 December had issued instructions on this and other matters to organisers and officers of league branches.

These instructions, drafted by Davitt himself, began by stressing the importance of administrative efficiency and unity of purpose in the organisation. Each affiliated branch should maintain direct communication with the central executive; county centralisation and uncoordinated action by branches should alike be avoided. Every branch should take care to have its monthly report and its financial contribution sent to headquarters on the first of each month. Each branch member should pledge himself to bring in a new member till all the people of the district were enrolled. In forming new branches, only steady, reliable, and intelligent men should be appointed as officers. Men were now joining the league in substantial numbers who gave only a lukewarm allegiance to its programme and were ready to welcome such half-measures as the government was likely to propose to parliament. Such weak-kneed reformers must not be allowed to use a single branch of the league as a 'platform of compromise' with landlordism or as a lever of disunion within the movement. With this in view the executive, at a meeting on 9 December chaired by Parnell, had decided that, as soon as the government's land proposals were known, it would pronounce judgment on them; and, if thought necessary, would convoke a 'grand national convention' of league delegates to confirm its judgment and lay down policy for the coming year. The convention would consist of league delegates chosen on a basis of one delegate for every 100 membership cards issued by the central office, so that about 1000 delegates would be sent to Dublin or wherever the convention would meet. Meanwhile the officers and organisers of the league were expected to enunciate the league doctrine of no compromise or partnership with landlordism and to repudiate the doctrine of the '3 Fs' now being advocated by some landlord organs in the hope of saving a doomed system.[1]

Never, the instructions went on, was it so necessary for the farmers and labourers to keep a firm grip on their passions.

The evil system which has so long been the curse of their . . . existence is now gasping out its criminal life in face of the whole world—dethroned, discredited, and on the point of being destroyed by the stern but passionless action of a united and indignant people through the means of a bloodless revolution.

To complete the work it was only necessary for every member of the league to be true to the league's teachings and rules, and to enforce its just demands without violence or threats of violence. Violence to harmless and defenceless animals in revenge for wrongs committed by their owners was particularly to be condemned, though the executive was confident that it was not members of the league who committed such outrages, and that their reported numbers were far in excess of the truth. Branch officers were urged to inform the executive of any outrages occurring in their localities, so that press exaggerations and concoctions could be exposed. The only force sanctioned by the league was 'a fair and judicious use of the power of combination against the enemies of the people, traitors to the league, or instruments of unjust eviction or other landlord injustice'. On his own behalf Davitt added a warning on the perversion of boycotting into a means of paying off old scores between individuals. He returned to this point at the next meeting of the league, on 21 December, when he spoke out against attempts to coerce men into joining the league and against boycotting of schools because they were attended by children of land agents. His statement of 14 December was endorsed by the chairman, John Ferguson, and others, and adopted, Healy making the point that the majority of offences against animals, if not the work of the police, were committed by farmers for the purpose of obtaining compensation from the grand juries of the counties.[2]

Recalling the occasion twenty-three years later, Davitt wrote that Parnell was reluctant to agree to any statement on agrarian outrages being issued by the league, regarding them as the responsibility of the government and the landlords, but that he yielded to Davitt's argument that it was necessary, on grounds both of expediency and of principle, to denounce such outrages.[3] A highly confidential letter Davitt wrote to Devoy only two days after the meeting of 14 December presented

[1] The 'instructions' to this point, comprising the first four paragraphs, are silently omitted from the text reprinted by Davitt in *Defence*, pp 406–7, which similarly omits the last two paragraphs. The whole document, except these last two paragraphs, is reprinted in *S.C.P.*, vi, 503–6.

[2] *F.J.*, 15, 22 Dec.

[3] *Fall*, pp 286–7.

this and other matters wholly in terms of expediency. It is the last extant letter of its kind between the two men, and it was written, like that of 6 February[1], from Paris, to ensure that there would be no risk of its being opened by the police. Probably Davitt had made this quick visit abroad to prepare the way for the transfer of the league's executive to Paris in an emergency, and he contemplated going with it in that eventuality: 'I would be a fool to allow myself to be caught like a rat and be shut up for a year incapable of doing any good'. He complained to Devoy of I.R.B. hostilities against the Land League and of the murky underworld of fenianism in which he had uncovered a plot to put him 'out of the way'. By contrast he reported enthusiastically on the progress of the league. With branches in every county, a membership of nearly 200,000, organisers in all four provinces and an income of about £100 a day mostly contributed by its branches, it now virtually ruled Ireland. It was able to spend money lavishly on organisation, boycotting, relief to evicted tenants, and fighting landlords in the courts of the state. Land League courts, in which district affairs were adjudicated, were also being established everywhere. The London press declared that all the league needed to complete its control over the country was to issue its own currency. Expansion had brought its own problems, and Davitt spoke of his efforts to frustrate the influence of new elements inside the league. Many members, together with the bishops and priests 'almost to a man', would be satisfied with the '3 Fs', and he predicted a consequent split in the league, which could only be countered by a national convention on the lines decided on by the executive.[2] Meanwhile the government was under pressure from Forster and other ministers to suspend habeas corpus. If they succeeded 'the whole movement would be crushed in a month and universal confusion would reign'. Chamberlain and Dilke were holding out against coercion, and someone (unnamed) who was in Dilke's confidence had assured Davitt that if agrarian outrages diminished the government would not resort to extreme measures. 'I am necessitated, therefore, to take a conservative stand in order to stave off coercion. . . . These damned petty little outrages . . . play the devil with us on outside public opinion.' He urged Devoy not to interfere with branches of the American league sending money direct to the league in Ireland unless the government seized the league's offices, when a fund could be accumulated in America for future use. While the league was left to function it needed all the money it could get, and as long as funds were seen to be coming in from America financial support from Ireland was assured.

[1] Above, pp 366, 379–80.

[2] Above, p. 437.

On the whole, Davitt concluded, the outlook for the land movement was 'splendid'. The people were realising their collective power and learning to use it for their own benefit. The landlords were 'as meek as lambs' and were accepting Griffith's valuation 'almost universally'. The government 'does not know what the devil to do in . . . such a state of affairs as we have created'. If the movement could be carried on without government interference for another year, 'we could do almost anything we pleased. . . . The courage of the people is magnificent. All classes are purchasing arms openly.' Should habeas corpus be suspended, they might carry on the movement from London or Paris. If the government resorted to 'dragooning the people after squelching the league', something should be done by way of retaliation in England. But should the conspiracy trial break down and habeas corpus not be suspended, Davitt thought of going to America, with Brennan, for St Patrick's day, if a convention of the American league could be convoked for that date. With this in view he wrote by the same post to John Boyle O'Reilly and to Fr Lawrence Walsh.[1]

The letter to Devoy, which was published only in 1953, exposes Davitt to the imputation of lack of integrity more than any other surviving evidence for his life to this point. Its cynical tone, its mixture of flippancy and egotism, and its conspirator's jargon are in startling contrast with the passionate sincerity, the moral earnestness, the self-abandonment, and the universal appeal conveyed by his public statements of this period to the central body of the league and at land demonstrations all over the country. The jubilation with which he tells Devoy that all classes are buying arms seems hardly compatible with his public inculcation of moral force, nor his explanation that he is 'necessitated' to take a conservative line against violence with his public reprobation of agrarian outrages as not only inexpedient but morally wrong. And whereas he tells Devoy exultantly that Land League courts were being established 'everywhere', less than a month later, at the weekly meeting of the league on 12 January, he was to describe such courts as something that no one in the league had ever heard of.[2] There is here an apparent discrepancy between Davitt's private views as expressed to Devoy and his public image, especially the image that he himself did so much to build up in later years. That image finds its fullest expression in his defence of himself and the Land League, before the special commission of 1888–9, against charges of complicity in crime brought by *The Times*. If his letter of 16 December and earlier letters to Devoy had been known to the commission,

[1] D to Devoy, 16 Dec. (*D.P.B.*, ii, 21–5); see above, pp 384, 414.
[2] *F.J.*, 13 Jan. 81.

Davitt's case would have been seriously damaged, and one of the classics of the land war would have been a different book.[1]

The ambivalence in Davitt's position was nothing new, and was rooted in his commitment to what remained of the new departure.[2] But was he lacking in integrity, was he less than honest, was he self-deceived? There are no simple answers to these questions. Since his release from prison he had never concealed his continued belief in the legitimacy and the eventual necessity of using physical force in favourable circumstances to achieve national independence. He had declared that all Irishmen had the right to carry arms[3]—which, in any case, they could legally do during the intervals between the expiration of one peace preservation act in June 1880 and the coming into force of its successor in March 1881. There was a real and fundamental distinction between military action and the agrarian outrages that Davitt condemned. His approval of the use of physical force in a future war of national independence could be reconciled with his commitment to moral force in the existing land war. But there was a suggestion in his letters to Devoy of both 6 February and 16 December that moral force might at any time be replaced by physical force if circumstances should warrant it; and the same opportunism is evident in the reference to retaliatory action in England. As for Land League courts, the league obviously could not accept responsibility for courts whose existence was a direct challenge to the authority of the state. Davitt's statement at the meeting of the league on 12 January was therefore a denial of any official knowledge of these courts coupled with the implied admission that league branches did arbitrate in disputes between tenants.[4] John Ferguson, presiding at the weekly meeting of 2 February, said that no such courts had ever been established by the league, but were, if they existed, an expression of local initiative.[5] All this does not wholly dispose of the moral discrepancies in Davitt's position, but it does help to sustain the reputation he had acquired, and that was increasingly to distinguish him even in the eyes of his enemies, for integrity, honesty, and realism, against the conflicting evidence of communications with Devoy.

Devoy, indeed, seems always to have drawn out and encouraged Davitt's less admirable qualities—quickness of temper, irritability, suspicion of other men's motives, recklessness of judgment, a tendency to exaggeration, to wishful thinking, even to self-deception. Yet the

[1] *The 'Times'–Parnell commission: speech of Michael Davitt in defence of the Land League* (London, 1890).

[2] See above, pp 302–3, 379–81.

[3] See above, pp 237, 263.

[4] See below, p. 443.

[5] *F.J.*, 3 Feb. 81.

two men were temperamentally and spiritually poles apart, and their friendship, begun in August 1878, scarcely outlasted 1880. The rift that thereafter appeared was never to be repaired, and from 1882 onwards Davitt regarded Devoy as an 'implacable enemy'.[1] Perhaps this was partly due to a consciousness that he had betrayed his better self in his dealings with Devoy; for it was not characteristic of Davitt to cherish enmity. Finally, it is significant that his letters to Devoy were mostly written at times of great strain. That of 16 December, with its exaggerations, its internal contradictions, and its over-elation, is partly to be explained by the state of excessive mental stimulation and physical exertion in which he was living and from which he was only to be rescued by renewed imprisonment.

The strength of the Land League lay in local solidarity and local initiative; and Land League branches were now exercising powers that in effect encroached on those of the constituted local authorities, as when they acted as Land League courts. The principal county authority, the grand juries, were appointed by the central government and were to remain under landlord control till 1898, when their administrative powers were transferred to elected county councils. But there were local elective bodies, the boards of poor law guardians, with a relatively large electorate, on which the landlord interest still preponderated. Davitt and Devoy, in developing their new departure scheme in 1878, had clearly marked out these local bodies as areas to be brought under nationalist control.[2] At the weekly meeting of the league on 21 December, Davitt urged that the league should contest the annual elections to the boards of guardians in the following March. The idea was approved, and the local branches were advised to make preparations.[3] A more immediate concern of the league was distress among agricultural labourers resulting from unemployment, which landlord propaganda was using in an effort to sow discord between labourers and farmers. Davitt reminded the farmers that labourers were in the forefront of the agitation at the outset, and that the main beneficiaries from the movement had a duty to give the labourers employment. Parnell pointed out that the labourers would soon have the vote, and warned landlords against sacking them. Another source of division lay in efforts by moderate elements within the league to use the league's platforms for propagating the '3 Fs'. Davitt's instructions on this subject to organisers and branch officers of the league were reinforced by Parnell on 28 December, when he advised that

[1] *Defence*, p. 120; *D.P.B.*, ii, 24–5; *United Ireland*, 28 June 84.
[2] See above, pp 236–7, 237–8, 252, 261, 263, 265–6.
[3] *F.J.*, 22 Dec. 80, 12 Jan. 81.; see below, p. 480.

branches should be told to appoint as chairmen and choose as speakers for land meetings only men who would adhere strictly to the league's plan of settlement.[1]

Till December the liberal government, like its predecessor, had done nothing to prohibit, or, however extravagant the language used at them, to suppress, land meetings. But from early December meetings began to be prohibited by proclamation of the lord lieutenant and by local magistrates on the ground that they were called to threaten individuals or that they would endanger the public peace.[2] It was one indication of how extreme the tension between Land League and government had become. The league's executive believed that it was the aim of the authorities (meaning the permanent officials—'the unscrupulous ring that infest Dublin Castle',[3] not Forster or Cowper or Gladstone) to provoke, not to prevent, violence, and so to justify the use of military force against the agitation.[4] This in turn caused the central body to give increasing attention to relations with its branches. A new qualification for membership of the central body, intended to prevent men obnoxious to the branches from securing election to it, was adopted on 4 January on the motion of Brennan, seconded by Davitt: a candidate must either be a member of, or recommended by, a branch executive if a branch existed in his locality. Reporting that a reverend president of a branch had himself appointed an executive, Davitt reminded branches throughout the country that this was contrary to the rules.[5] On 12 January he urged branches in which such illegalities had occurred to communicate with the central office, which would send down an organiser to have elections carried out properly. He drew attention to the arrest and prosecution of members of the executive of the Tralee branch for participation in an alleged Land League court. The Land League had no knowledge of such courts, but, though branches should avoid acting in a way that could be construed as infringing the jurisdiction of courts of law, there was nothing illegal in their engaging in arbitration between tenants, and he thought that tenants should be encouraged to resort to such arbitration instead of wasting their money in costly and often useless litigation. P. F. Johnson, of Kanturk, warned branches against holding their meetings on licensed premises, because the police were entitled to enter such premises at all times.[6]

As Irish M.P.s were now going to London for the new and extremely critical session of parliament, and members of the central executive were involved in the trial at the Four Courts, Davitt pointed out on

[1] *F.J.*, 29 Dec. 80.
[2] P.R.O., Cab. 37/4/95; above, p. 350.
[3] *F.J.*, 5 Jan. 81.
[4] Cf. above, pp 429–30.
[5] *F.J.*, 5 Jan.
[6] *F.J.*, 13 Jan.

4 January that it would be difficult to supply speakers for land meetings;[1] branches would need to draw out local talent. He went on to enunciate emergency procedures to be applied if coercion should be stepped up. In the event of all land meetings being prohibited each branch should hold fortnightly meetings in the open air, at which routine business could be combined with speeches on matters of local or general interest affecting the land movement. If such meetings were not allowed in the open air, a hall should be hired for the purpose, and any overflow meetings should be addressed from windows. If these branch meetings were in turn prohibited, and all freedom of speech suppressed by proclamation, the only remedy would be 'illegal meetings and illegal action'. If the government suspended habeas corpus and the restraining influence of the league were thus removed, the country would be precipitated into a state of violence for which the government, not the league, would be responsible before the civilised world. Meanwhile branches should be preparing to answer a call from headquarters to send delegates to the contemplated convention to assess the government's land bill when that should be publicised. T. P. O'Connor made the point strongly that the convention would be a means of putting pressure on the Irish parliamentary party to be the spearhead of the league's land programme in the house of commons.[2] As to the timing of the convention, Davitt agreed with Parnell's view that they should wait till the government had dealt with coercion and had shown its hand on the land bill.[3]

In parallel with his sustained activity at the headquarters of the league since his return from America Davitt was away from Dublin most week-ends and at other times, addressing land meetings in all four provinces. At these meetings, he spoke with special emphasis on the need to expand the league till there was a branch in every parish, on linking the interests of the labourers with those of the farmers, on the importance of bringing in the protestant farmers of Ulster, on the danger that a sham solution of the land question—'3 Fs'—would be offered by government instead of the only real solution—occupying ownership—on agrarian violence as more damaging to the cause of the tenants than that of the landlords, on the allegations of a reign of terror propagated by enemies of the league, on the government's increasing interference with land meetings, and on the increasing numbers and presence of troops.

At Sligo on 29 November he spoke of revenge as ignoble and self-destroying: 'let the victims of the Land League movement be injustice, ignorance, social degradation, and pauperism'.[4] He was accidentally

[1] Cf. above, p. 432. [2] *F.J.*, 5 Jan. [3] *F.J.*, 13 Jan. [4] *F.J.*, 29 Nov. 80.

thrown from a car while driving to a meeting at Mitchelstown on 5 December, but escaped with a severe shaking and a cut hand, and addressed the meeting in a rousing spirit.[1] At Malahide on 6 December, addressing the first meeting to be held in County Dublin in support of the league, he claimed that the Irish land movement was now a subject of discussion in the press not only of Ireland, England, and Scotland but also of France, Germany, and the United States. The impoverished farmers of the west were the vanguard of the movement but the strong farmers of Fingal (of which Malahide was the centre) would be the heavy dragoons that would give the death-blow to landlordism. In the western agitation an indispensable part had been played by the agricultural labourers, and he himself would not have been so prominent in it had he not felt assured that in the eventual settlement the labourers would be made as independent of the farmers as the farmers would be of the landlords.[2] At Clonegall, County Carlow, on 12 December, he said that if the farmers accepted half-measures they deserved to be trampled on by landlordism, whereas, if they stuck to the Land League programme, in less than two years the landlords would be more anxious to settle than the farmers were now.[3] He administered further criticism at Blessington, County Wicklow, on 13 December. All the blame for Irish sufferings should not be attributed to land laws imposed by England. 'I would rather say that in the ignorance, the apathy, and the criminal timidity of the people of Ireland is to be found the cause of their punishment and their humiliation'; and he pointed out that 'in the county of Wicklow' three lords—Fitzwilliam, Waterford, and Downshire—claimed to own most of the land, with revenues totalling £60,000–£70,000.[4] At Rathcoole, County Dublin, on 20 December, he denounced the government for sending 700 or 800 troops the previous day to prevent a land meeting in Queen's County. But he also condemned those within the Land League who practised coercion against their fellows by misuse of boycotting; the Land League was 'a great moral organisation for a moral purpose, and must be carried on on moral lines'.[5]

On 23 December he joined in the campaign to spread the league in Ulster by speaking at a land meeting at Saintfield, County Down. Saintfield being in the heart of an orange countryside the announcement

[1] *F.J.*, 7 Dec. [2] *F.J.*, 7 Dec. [3] *F.J.*, 13 Dec.

[4] *F.J.*, 14 Dec. The three lords owned 26 per cent of Wicklow—131,692 acres out of a total of 5000,178. Just over half the county (251,950 acres) was owned by nine proprietors of over 10,000 acres each, as follows: Fitzwilliam (89,891), Powerscourt (38,725), Waterford (26,035), Wicklow (22,103), John Hugo (17,937), Carysfort (16,297), Downshire (15,766), Meath (14,717), Robert Cunninghame (10,479). Parnell's acreage was 4,678. (*Thom 1882*, p. 728)

[5] *F.J.*, 22 Dec. 80.

of an intention to hold a land League meeting there was a challenge that local orangemen endeavoured to answer, assisted by reinforcements (among them John Rea[1]) brought by special train from Belfast. But they were anticipated by the resident magistrate of Belfast, Clifford Lloyd, who, with some 600 constabulary, prevented the rival forces from making contact and enabled the land leaguers, greatly outnumbered by their would-be assailants armed with sticks and revolvers, to hold their meeting unmolested. The chairman was a local tenant farmer, James Anderson, and besides Davitt the platform party included Dillon, Biggar, Rev. James O'Boyle, parish priest of Saintfield, and Rev. Harold Rylett, unitarian minister of Moneyrea. The first resolution was a model of Ulster terseness and bite: 'that, as the Ulster custom has utterly failed to protect the property of tenants against the rapacity of landlords, the land question can be definitely settled only by making the cultivators of the soil proprietors'. Davitt supported the motion. Far from being the enemy of protestantism and of law and order the Land League was the defender of the rights of conscience and of the public peace. Had the league not been in existence there would have been twenty times more outrages than had actually occurred that winter. The league had taught the farmers a just and legal way of rescuing themselves from landlord oppression; already they had compelled rack-renting landlords to surrender over three million pounds in rent reductions, and if they fulfilled the league's programme every farmer would have it in his power to become owner of his holding. Dillon added that the league had done more for the farmers than all the tenant-right movements had done in thirty years: in that time the tenant-right organisations had never succeeded in preventing a single eviction. Clifford Lloyd, a tough and courageous upholder of the law, whose sympathies were all against the Land League, could not help being well impressed by Davitt personally: 'if he really believed all he said, it was difficult to see how he could be aught else but an ardent and uncompromising rebel'.[2] On new year's day 1881 a land meeting at Drogheda at which Davitt was to speak and which had been proclaimed by the lord lieutenant was dispersed by Lloyd, with some difficulty and uproar but no actual violence, after he had read the riot act. He spent that night in the same hotel as Davitt, and received an invitation to join him and the local Land League committee at dinner, but felt unable to accept.[3] A meeting could have been an enlightening experience for both men.

[1] Cf. above, p. 352.
[2] *F.J.*, 24 Dec.; Clifford Lloyd, *Ireland under the Land League* (1892), pp 5–13.
[3] Ibid., pp 15–16.

For as long as he was at large Davitt continued his efforts to break down denominational barriers in Ulster and foster solidarity among farmers. At Downpatrick, on 6 January, he addressed a gathering of 'about 10,000' in the presence of a large force of police under Lloyd, (who was cheered for his handling of the orange 'bludgeonmen' at Saintfield). He claimed that the intelligent farmers of Down were at one with their fellows in the rest of Ireland in regarding the '3 Fs' as Dead Sea fruit. How could a fair rent be fixed in an age of falling agricultural prices? Griffith's valuation might be a fair rent in the other provinces but in Ulster it was a rack rent. The common interest of all farmers was to hold out for a land bill that would turn the tenants into owners.[1] A meeting he was to have addressed at Magherafelt on the 8th[2] was proclaimed by the magistrates as likely to lead to a breach of the peace because a counter-meeting had been announced—got up, T. P. O'Connor alleged, by the magistrates themselves, thereby exemplifying 'the vast landlord conspiracy which sits upon the magisterial bench'.[3] On 19 January, at Letterkenny, he declared that the Boyne no longer divided Ireland, and that the people had been educated to work for social amelioration regardless of creed.[4] On the road to Strabane after the meeting he was thrown from a car in a snowstorm and had to walk to Raphoe.[5] That did not prevent him from being present next day at Ballymacnab, in north Armagh, for a land meeting that was suppressed by the local R.M. on the ground that a counter-demonstration was to be held by the local orangemen. He made his protest, and announced that he would speak next day at a meeting to be held at Kinnegoe, on the shore of Lough Neagh. Under the auspices of the Land League branch at Loughgall (the cradle of the orange movement), and the chairmanship of James Weir, master of the Kinnegoe Loyal Orange Lodge, the meeting was duly held, on 21 January, in a field belonging to Parnell's brother, John. Some 2000 farmers attended, despite arctic weather, to hear Davitt supporting a motion expressing solidarity with the league, and denouncing coercion. A short time ago, he told the assembled orangemen, the landlords would have expected them to break up this Land League meeting and throw him into the nearest river. Today they were faced with a new situation:

You are no longer the tame and superstitious fools who fought for their amusement and profit with your equally foolish and superstitious catholic fellow-workers, and allowed the landlords to pick both your pockets during the encounter. Did you ever hear tell of a catholic landlord who gave a reduction of rent to a tenant who had his head broken in a fight for the honour of the pope? Or a protestant gentleman

[1] Kirkpatrick, op. cit., p. 178; S.P.O., R.P. 1881/5487 (1882/1465).
[2] DN/8, 8 Jan. 81. [3] *F.J.*, 5 Jan. [4] *F.J.*, 21 Jan. [5] DN/8, 19 Jan.

. . . who would refuse to evict an orangeman who drank to the memory of the vanquisher of that miserable coward, King James, at the Boyne? No, my friends, the landlords of Ireland are all of one religion—their God is mammon and rack-rents, and evictions their only morality, while the toilers of the fields, whether orangemen, catholics, presbyterians, or methodists are the victims whom they desire to see fling themselves beneath the juggernaut of landlordism.

These sentiments were well received, but so also was a motion thanking John N. Richardson of Bessbrook, liberal M.P. for the county, for his untiring exertions on behalf of the tenant farmers and expressing the hope that he would adopt the Land League platform;[1] Richardson was one of the nine Ulster liberals in the house of commons who supported Forster's government and the principle of the '3 Fs'. The Kinnegoe meeting was the high-water mark of Davitt's missionary efforts in Ulster.

During January he was also active in the west and south. In County Galway the tenants of the richest landowner, the marquis of Clanricarde, had just been notified from London that unless they paid their rents in full writs would be issued against them from the Dublin courts. At a meeting of 20,000 people at Loughrea, on 2 January, Davitt declared that landlordism had received its death blow, and urged the Clanricarde tenants to stand together and tell their landlord that the time was past when they would pay rack rents.[2] On the 8th he arrived at Tralee to find that a meeting at which he was to speak had been banned by the local magistrates, and that a strong force of police and soldiers had been moved into the town. Though the meeting dispersed quietly, Davitt protested to the R.M. in charge, and contrived to make two defiant speeches, one from a wagonette and one from the window of his hotel in Tralee. He warned his hearers to avoid conflict with the law while pressing on resolutely with the land movement, and he brought a message to this effect from Timothy Harrington, the leading Land League organiser in Kerry, then under arrest in Tralee jail with other land-leaguers in connection with an alleged land court.[3] The government wanted to precipitate a bloody struggle between unarmed people and the armed forces of the state, but the people must not play into the government's hands. They had learned to keep their tempers, and their retaliation for the 'constitutional outrages' now of daily occurrence should be to secure the election as M.P.s, poor law guardians, and town commissioners of men imprisoned for Land League activities. Shopkeepers similarly imprisoned should receive four times as much custom as before.[4] Next day Davitt attended a

[1] *F.J.*, 22 Jan; *Fall*, pp 296–7.
[2] DN/8, 2 Jan.; *F.J.*, 3 Jan.; S.P.O., I.N.L.L. & I.N.L. papers, Speeches 1879–88, p. 204.
[3] See above, p. 443.
[4] *F.J.*, 10 Jan.

meeting at Thurles of the local branch of the league, chaired by Rev. James Cantwell, administrator. He said that all confidence in the so-called liberal government had been lost, but they must not allow coercion to dampen their zeal. If the local executive were arrested, the branch should ensure that their work was carried on. Davitt had called on Archbishop Croke before the meeting and dined with him afterwards.[1]

At Kilbrin, near Kanturk, County Cork, on 16 January—a bitterly cold day, with snow on the ground—he delivered a fierce attack on government policy as a yielding to the 'frenzied clamour' of the landlords. It was astonishing that so great a statesman as Gladstone should lend himself to trampling on constitutional liberty in Ireland. The irony of it was that a movement hitherto far more concerned with social needs than with national aspirations was now being supplied by government action with compelling arguments against imperial rule in Ireland. There remained only one blunder (now being advocated by the landlord press) for it to make in order to turn Irish opinion solidly in favour of legislative independence—to apply the closure against the Irish party in parliament, so forcing its members to return to Ireland for new instructions from the Irish people. In a cloudy reference to the possibility of forcible intervention from Irish-America he declared:

> If your patience becomes exhausted by government brutality . . . the world will hold England, and not you, responsible if the wolfdog of Irish vengeance bounds over the Atlantic at the very heart of that power from which it is now held back by the influence of the league; but glorious, indeed, will be our victory . . . if we can so curb our passions and control our acts in this struggle for free land as to march to success through provocation and danger without resorting to the wild justice of revenge, or being guilty of anything which could sully the character of a brave and Christian people.[2]

Perhaps the fact that the chairman was the parish priest and that ten other catholic clergy were speakers at Kilbrin helps to explain the combination of menace with moderation in what was to earn some notoriety as the 'wolfdog' speech. It was commended by the central body of the league two days later.[3]

Preparations for the trial of the Land League chiefs in the court of queen's bench had been in progress since early November. Contributions to the defence fund poured in from Ireland, Great Britain, and America, and the league's solicitor, Valentine B. Dillon, did not spare expense in recruiting a team of eminent counsel to match the attorney general and his colleagues who appeared for the crown. The hearing

[1] DN/8, 10 Jan.; *F.J.*, 12 Jan. [2] DN/8, 16 Jan.; *F.J.*, 17 Jan. [3] *F.J.*, 19 Jan.

was preceded by a judicial sensation. Lord Chief Justice May, in giving judgment in the queen's bench on 4 December against an application from the traversers for a postponement of the trial, referred to them in terms that in effect pronounced them guilty. Though he hastily corrected himself, the damage was done. At the meeting of the league on 7 December a resolution was passed condemning the 'scandalously partizan utterance' of the chief justice and recommending 'our representatives in parliament' to bring the matter before the house of commons when it reassembled. Davitt said that, instead of censuring May, they ought to pass a vote of thanks to him for turning public opinion, in England as well as in Ireland, in the traversers' favour. When the trial opened at the Four Courts, Dublin, on 28 December, May bowed before the storm he had raised: he withdrew from the bench, leaving it to his two colleagues, John D. Fitzgerald and Charles R. Barry, to conduct the trial.[1] The proceedings[2] in what proved to be the greatest state trial since that of O'Connell in 1844 occupied 20 days, from 28 December to 25 January. The prosecution was led by the attorney general, Hugh Law M.P., supported by the solicitor general, William Moore Johnson M.P., Sergeant Denis Caulfield Heron, and 5 other barristers. Francis Macdonogh, a veteran who had been a junior counsel for O'Connell thirty-six years before, headed the defence, assisted by Samuel Walker, William McLaughlin, and 6 other barristers including A. M. Sullivan M.P., of the English bar. The case for the crown, opened by the attorney general, occupied 11 days, that for the defence, opened by Macdonogh, 5½ days, Sergeant Heron's reply for the crown 1½ days, the judge's charge to the jury and the jury's response 2 days. The proceedings were conducted fairly and calmly by all parties.

The charges against the traversers, defined in nineteen counts,[3] were a summary in the prosecutor's terms of the basic procedures of the league. The traversers, 'unlawfully and wickedly' intending to impoverish and injure the landlords and frustrate the administration of justice, had combined: to incite tenants not to pay the rents they had contracted to pay, or not to pay more than Griffith's valuation; to incite tenants dispossessed for non-payment of rent to return and retake possession; to prevent persons taking or keeping farms from which others had been dispossessed for non-payment of rent; to prevent persons buying goods taken in execution for non-payment of rent; to incite people to boycott those who paid what the league held to be unjust or excessive rent, or who bought goods or stock at execution

[1] *F.J.*, 8, 29 Dec.

[2] Reported in *F.J.*, 29 Dec. 80–26 Jan. 81.

[3] Copy in DL/2.

sales, or who took farms from which tenants had been evicted, or who refused to give up such farms; and finally to create disaffection among the queen's subjects and excite hostility between landlords and tenants. The evidence produced by the prosecution in support of these charges consisted of speeches by the traversers and others, and of slogans displayed on banners and placards at land meetings, as read to the court by professional shorthand writers and police reporters, who were duly examined and cross-examined. As specimens of the speeches alleged to have inflamed the country the court had to listen for a week to a stream of repetitive and tedious rhetoric, delivered with stupefying flatness and monotony by these official witnesses.

One of the police reporters, Jeremiah Stringer, who had become well known as a target of popular abuse in the early months of the land agitation, confessed that, on one occasion, cornered in a hotel room at Shrule, he had been so frightened that he had tried to pass himself off as a reporter for the *Tipperary Advocate* when questioned by Davitt and J. W. Nally. He did not then know Davitt, as he knew him now, to be 'incapable of anything dishonourable or unfair'; and with Nally he later struck up a drinking acquaintance which gave him a kind of immunity from hostile attention. The egregious 'Scrab'[1] amiably said of him: 'he is here doing his duty and I am here doing my duty, and he is to tell the government and the Castle how the people feel'.[2] Later in the trial Nally was described by his own counsel as 'a drunken fool', whose object, if he was to be believed, was murder but whom the police did not take seriously.[3]

The story of the land war presented by the prosecution was all matter of public knowledge, and was not open to serious dispute; and the more so because the attorney general was careful to point out that conspiracy in the legal sense did not require any element of secrecy: it was a combination between two or more persons to effect an unlawful object or a lawful object by unlawful means. The case for the traversers was a sustained denial that the evidence warranted the construction put upon it by the crown. For example, the non-payment of rent was the outcome of extreme and general distress among the tenants, not of an intention to impoverish or defraud the landlords. But the defence also sought to explain the upheaval of the past two years in the context of a chronic and deep-seated conflict between landlords and tenants extending back to the eighteenth century. To prove the existence of this conflict the defence proposed to produce not only documentary evidence but also witnesses from every part of

[1] See above, pp 190, 311–12.

[2] At Westport, 17 Oct. 80 (*F.J.*, 6 Jan. 81).

[3] *F.J.*, 5, 19 Jan.

of Ireland. Justice Fitzgerald agreed that all such evidence could be admissible owing to the 'extreme generality' of the nineteenth count of the information (incitement to hostility between landlords and tenants); and, appalled at the prospect of the case dragging on indefinitely, persuaded the attorney-general to abandon that count (17 January).[1] Consequently Macdonogh dismissed his assembled army of witnesses (including a hundred inmates of Castlebar workhouse), after calling only four; and the defence resolved itself into speeches by all the defending counsel, ending with a virtuoso performance by A. M. Sullivan (20 January). Sergeant Heron then replied for the crown and Justice Fitzgerald summed up (24–5 January).

The judge did not conceal his view that, from the evidence before the court, both as to the actions and the intentions of the accused, the jury might come to the conclusion that the allegations of the prosecution were well founded. He could not say as a positive direction to the jury that, on the evidence of its rules alone, the Land League was an illegal organisation, but on the other hand he could not agree with Macdonogh that these rules showed it to be a legal organisation, and if the defendants had acted as alleged he had no hesitation in pronouncing it to be illegal under the common law. He did not intend to enter into the question of the alleged injustices of the land system, and warned the jury against doing so; that was not the concern of the court. Nevertheless he declared that the law of landlord and tenant in Ireland since 1870 was far more favourable to the occupiers than that of England or Scotland, or even that of the United States. He corrected the view widely propagated from Land League platforms that in Belgium the occupiers were all owners: on the contrary, about two-thirds of them held their farms on very short leases. While he supposed that some landlords in Ireland might have acted cruelly, the fact that over 1000 tenants out of some 500,000 or 600,000 had been evicted for non-payment of rent during the first half of 1880 was no proof of cruelty on the part of landlords as a class. He dismissed as absurd the claim that the agitation aimed at making restitution to the descendants of those dispossessed by the confiscations of the sixteenth and seventeenth centuries. They might just as well advocate restoring the 'tribal system'. Those dispossessed by the confiscations were not generally the occupiers but the landlords; and in any case a very large number of the present proprietors, being recent purchasers under the encumbered estates act, had no connection with the confiscations. Fitzgerald's final direction to the jury was legally impeccable: if the evidence for the prosecution satisfied the jury that the defendants combined to

[1] Davitt's reference in *Fall*, p. 294, to the effect of the nineteenth count is in error.

commit the acts set out in the information, the defendants were guilty of criminal conspiracy; if the evidence failed to satisfy the jury that these acts had been committed, the defendants must be acquitted on all or some of the counts in the information. It was for the jury to decide, not whether the alleged acts were criminal, but only whether they had been committed.[1] After many hours of discussion and repeated appearances before the court the jury failed to find a verdict: they were unanimous, as their foreman put it, in being unable to agree. It transpired, quite irregularly, that ten of their number were for acquittal, but that two held out for conviction. The judge therefore discharged them and the prosecution failed. This was the result that the traversers had counted on from their knowledge of the jurors, some of whom, obviously, were all along bent on acquittal, whatever the judge's direction.[2]

Davitt described the bench as 'packed' and Justice Fitzgerald's charge to the jury as 'that of a crown prosecutor'.[3] This was less than fair to both judges, but particularly to Fitzgerald, who mainly conducted the trial and whose behaviour cannot be seriously faulted on legal grounds. He showed no personal animus against the defendants or against others, such as Davitt, not named in the information but often referred to in the proceedings. He expressed appreciation of Parnell's statesmanlike qualities, acquitted him and most of the traversers of any intention to foster outrages, and distinguished sharply between them and the drunken Nally, with his 'wild and murderous speeches'. He described Davitt as 'the guiding spirit and controller' of the agitation, and, with Brennan, Harris, and others, as a land-leaguer whose ultimate aim went far beyond the abolition of landlords. He did not name him as the author of 'Paudeen O'Rafferty's ten commandments', but clearly connected him with 'this vile and blasphemous production', which the attorney general had cited as evidence of the Land League's intention to inflame passions against the landlords. Davitt did not complain of these remarks as unfair to him personally. But, as often before in his dealings with authority, his attitude to the trial was ambivalent. He regarded the court as part of a hostile establishment from which fair play was not to be expected, and thus he approved the use of underhand methods against it, as when Egan procured by bribery a copy of the brief prepared for the attorney general.[4] Yet in censoring the judge for his alleged partiality he showed that he expected impartiality from a court whose integrity he denied. His

[1] Extracts from the judge's charge are reported in *Reports of cases in criminal law*, ed. E. W. Cox and John Thompson, xiv (1882), pp 508–21.

[2] *Fall*, pp 290, 294.

[3] *Fall*, p. 294.

[4] *Fall*, pp 289–90.

ambivalence was aggravated by the anomaly of putting a social revolution on trial before a court of law, an anomaly that was to be repeated on a vastly larger scale by the *Times*-Parnell commission of 1888-9. The Land League was seeking to achieve a revolutionary end by technically legal means, but its leaders—and none more than Davitt and Parnell—knew that it was impossible to keep consistently on the right side of the law while maintaining pressure on the government. The trial was the first and only judicial test of the legality of the league, and on that issue it proved indecisive, not because of any failure on the part of the prosecution to prove its case or on the part of the judge to define the law and direct the jury, but because a majority of the jury refused to regard the actions of the Land League chiefs as criminal. Davitt hailed the outcome of the trial as one of the greatest victories yet won by the league and as showing that the government could not satisfy a jury that the league was illegal. Two of the jurymen were the object of angry demonstrations outside their homes, under the mistaken impression that they were the two who had stood out against the majority. Both Davitt and Egan publicly deplored this violation of freedom of opinion.[1]

In preparation for the new session of parliament the home rule party met in the City Hall, Dublin, on 27 December, re-elected Parnell as sessional chairman, elected Justin McCarthy as vice-chairman, elected a nine-man committee to serve as a 'cabinet' of the party, and among other matters decided that all home rule M.P.s should thenceforth sit and act together in opposition to the government.[2] The cabinet had finally approved Forster's coercion proposals on 30 December,[3] and the parliamentary session began on 6 January (a month earlier than usual) with a queen's speech which, unlike that with which the present parliament had opened (20 May 1880), was mainly concerned with the disturbed state of Ireland. Parliament would be asked to approve both a coercive and a remedial measure, the one giving the executive special powers to restore order, the other developing the principles of the 1870 land act. A measure to establish county government on representative principles, with the object of extending 'habits of local self-government' in Ireland, was also mentioned, but it became lost in the preoccupation of parliament with coercion and the land question.

[1] *F.J.*, 27 Jan. 81.

[2] *F.J.*, 28 Dec. 80. The nine elected members of the parliamentary committee were: Gray, T. P. O'Connor, A. M. Sullivan, Dillon, Arthur O'Connor, Biggar, O'Connor Power, Barry, Commins. Parnell as chairman of the party and Justin McCarthy as vice-chairman were *ex officio* members.

[3] Reid, *Forster*, ii, 284-5; Hamilton, *Diary*, i, 87, 88, 92, 95.

On coercion the Parnellites fought the government with unparalleled toughness and tenacity, using obstructionist tactics to breaking point. The debate on the address was prolonged to 20 January, by which time discussion was in progress behind the scenes to limit obstruction by the drastic expedient of a closure system. The Protection of Person and Property Bill, empowering the Irish executive to arrest and imprison without trial, for a period not extending beyond 30 September 1882, any person reasonably suspected of treasonable practices or agrarian offences, was introduced by Forster on 24 January, but it was not till 2 February, after a continuous sitting for forty-one hours, that his motion for leave to bring in the bill was carried by the action of the speaker in declaring the debate closed. Forster's argument was that a 'reign of terror' was being inflicted on Ireland by the Land League, relying on a small minority of ruthless men: members of the old ribbon and other secret agrarian societies, fenians bent on using the disorder to advance their separatist aims, and mere criminals—dissolute ruffians and blackguards. These 'village tyrants' were generally known to the police, but no one would appear in court to give evidence against them. The purpose of the bill was simply to enable the government to arrest such men and so prevent them from tyrannising over their neighbours. After a bitter and stormy passage through twenty-two sittings the bill became law on 2 March.[1] Years later Gladstone recorded that, though acquiescing in the coercion bill to avoid breaking up the government, he had not accepted Forster's 'village tyrants' thesis and believed that Forster had allowed himself to be persuaded by the permanent officials in Dublin Castle.[2]

On the promised land bill Forster had continued since October to ply Gladstone with reasons for making it 'strong', on the lines of the '3 Fs', whereas Gladstone had continued to believe that some amendment of his 1870 act would suffice. Forster's arguments were powerfully reinforced by pressure from Ulster liberal M.P.s who assured him that nothing short of the '3 Fs' would keep their constituents from joining the Land League;[3] by the report of the Bessborough commission[4] (4 January) and a minority report, drafted by Lord Carlingford, of the Richmond commission[5] (14 January); and by a memorial (21 January), signed by over 20,000 Ulster protestant farmers.[6] Intensive discussion went on within the cabinet for months before Gladstone

[1] *Hansard 3*, cclvii–cclix; Hamilton, *Diary*, i, 98–110; Reid, *Forster*, ii, 287–98; O'Connor, *Parnell movement*, pp 383–411; 44 Vict., c. 4.

[2] Morley, *Gladstone*, ii, 49–50; cf. above, p. 443.

[3] Reid, *Forster*, ii, 286. (The letter here quoted is misdated 28 Dec. 80; the actual date is 2 Dec.—Gladstone papers, B.L. Add. MS 44,158); Hamilton, *Diary*, i, 93.

[4] See above, pp 398–9.

[5] See above, p. 355.

[6] *F.J.*, 22 Jan. 81.

was finally convinced that the bill had to be 'what the brewers would call treble X'. On 7 April the revolution in his thinking on the Irish land question was revealed when he introduced his bill to reconstitute landlord–tenant relations on the principle of the '3 Fs'.[1]

But the nature of Gladstone's land bill was still a matter of speculation when Davitt ceased to be a factor in politics. Till 3 February he continued to be in the thick of the fight between the league and the government, which from 6 January was being fought simultaneously on three levels—in the Irish countryside, at the Four Courts, and at Westminster. The parliamentary party's decision of 27 December to sit in opposition had its sequel in the formal secession of Shaw and eleven other whiggish members on 16–17 January, at the height of the debate on the address. The league chose this occasion to call on all tenant farmers and voters to regard any Irish M.P. who deserted Parnell in the house of commons as having gone over to the enemy, Davitt declaring that constituents should let their representatives know what they thought of them if they voted for coercion. He was confident that the league would not be crushed by coercion and that landlordism would be overthrown.[2]

The league was in defiant mood at its next meeting (26 January) after the conspiracy trial ended. It was proposed that Davitt's Kilbrin speech should be printed and circulated, but an amendment, moved by Matthew Harris, substituting Davitt's instructions to organisers and branch officers,[3] was adopted instead. Davitt attacked Forster's speech introducing the coercion bill on 24 January as 'infamous and lying': his statistics of agrarian crime were unreliable and his use of them misleading; the league had always discountenanced intimidation; coercion would increase, not diminish, crime; it was untrue that fenians were using the league to advance their own aims—they had held aloof from the land movement just because it was constitutional.[4] Parnell in a cable to the *Irish World* (26 January) informed Irish-Americans that the government hoped to provoke a rebellion and to shoot down unarmed people 'by the thousands', that the landlords were poised to shower eviction notices on helpless tenants when the coercion bill became law, but that the people remained undaunted, that their discipline was perfect, and that, 'thanks to our American countrymen' the league had adequate funds to sustain them in the coming struggle.[5] To ensure that these funds would continue to be disbursed to evicted

[1] Hamilton, *Diary*, i, 85–96, 98–100, 107–8, 117, 121–6.
[2] *F.J.*, 17, 18, 19 Jan.
[3] See above, pp 437–8. [4] *F.J.*, 27 Jan. [5] *Fall*, pp 297–8.

tenants if the existing leaders of the league should be imprisoned, Davitt, supported by Egan, had persuaded the executive, against strong opposition from Parnell, Dillon, and Brennan, to sanction the formation of a 'provisional central committee' of ladies, headed by Anna Parnell, on the precedent of the Ladies' Land League founded at New York by Fanny Parnell in the previous October.[1] This was announced to the league on 26 January, when it was resolved that branch officers should supply names of ladies in their area willing to cooperate with Miss Parnell. The provisional committee included Mrs Anne Deane of Ballaghadereen, cousin of John Dillon, Mrs Patrick Egan, Mrs J. E. Kenny, Miss Beatrice Walshe of Balla, Mrs P. J. Sheridan of Tubbercurry, Mrs John Martin of Newry, Mrs A. M. Sullivan of London.[2] This was the beginning of the organisation shortly to become famous and formidable as the Ladies' Irish National Land League.

Writing more than twenty years later in his *Fall of feudalism* Davitt says that he now proposed, and the league executive in Dublin seriously considered, a general strike against the payment of all rent. It was agreed by the extreme element (including Davitt, Brennan, Egan, Harris, and Kettle), supported by nearly all the league organisers, that this would be the most effective way both of countering coercion and of overthrowing landlordism. The time was the more opportune for such extreme action because British power had just been challenged by a Boer rising in the Transvaal. Davitt goes on to say that he and Kettle went to London as spokesmen of the executive to consult Parnell and his principal parliamentary lieutenants on this critical question; that, at a meeting with him and six of his colleagues, held in the Westminster Palace Hotel on 3 February, it was proposed that on the day the coercion bill became law the Irish parliamentary party should withdraw in a body from Westminster, return to Ireland, and conduct a no-rent campaign, each member placing himself at the head of the league organisation in his constituency; that Parnell was not opposed to this extreme programme, but that one or two influential colleagues were very strongly so, and no decision was reached.[3]

There is no contemporary evidence for all this, but there is some corroboration in memoirs written more than ten years after the *Fall of feudalism* by Andrew Kettle, though, in his eighties, he was demonstrably confused on facts and dates, and inclined to overstate his own importance.[4] Davitt's own account is wholly inaccurate on dates:[5] two

[1] *Defence*, p. 265; *Fall*, p. 299; Kettle, *Material for victory*, p. 48; R. F. Foster, *Parnell*, pp 264–5; above, pp 414–15.

[2] *F.J.*, 27, 31 Jan.

[3] *Fall*, pp 301–2.

[4] *The material for victory*, ed. L. J. Kettle (1958), pp 39–42.

[5] Every date, explicit and implied, in *Fall*, p. 302, is wrong.

visits that he paid to London between 26 January and 2 February to see Parnell are conflated under 3 February when he was in Dublin. Nevertheless, that he proposed a general strike against rent about this time is not impugned by contemporary evidence and fits so well into the context of established facts that it may be accepted as authentic. The idea of such a strike, first formulated by Lalor in 1848, had been publicised by Ford in the *Irish World* in the seventies, and had been entertained by Land League chiefs for six months at least.[1] As recently at 17 January, in the debate on the address, Parnell had warned the government that the first arrest under the coming coercion act would be the signal for the withholding of all rent, an extreme step that he had so far successfully resisted.[2] Though Davitt had predicted on 16 December that if habeas corpus were suspended the land movement would be crushed in a month,[3] it is understandable that now, with coercion imminent and the spirit of the league running higher than ever, he should have seen in a rent strike the means of successfully defying the government. Instead of waiting to be crushed, the league should confront coercion by concerted passive resistance. He crossed to London on the evening of the 26th, and was there on the 27th and 28th.[4] It can safely be assumed that the meeting with Parnell he and Kettle describe was held at the Westminster Palace Hotel (a favourite resort of the Irish party near the Houses of Parliament) on the 27th or 28th (or possibly on both days), and that the outcome was negative.[5]

Looking back in 1903 at his failure to carry his rent strike proposal, Davitt wrote that the Land League lost its 'true revolutionary opportunity'. A no-rent campaign would have meant 'a kind of civil war' and might have led to bloodshed 'in encounters with military and police', but 'all modern Irish history' showed that 'the only way to obtain reform for Ireland was by insurrection'.[6] In January 1881, the league, he reckoned, had about a thousand branches in Ireland comprising fully 200,000 members, another 200,000 in the United States and Canada, and branches springing up in all the principal cities in Australasia which would bring the total membership of the extended league to about half a million. The country was effectively organised, and the league could count on

> at least a thousand of the truest local leaders any Irish movement of modern times ever had ready to do and dare in so promising a fight as a life-or-death combat

[1] Above, pp 36, 142, 419–20.
[2] *Hansard 3*, cclvii, 912.
[3] Above, p. 439.
[4] DN/8, 26–8 Jan. 81.
[5] This differs from Dr Lyons's account of the affair (*Parnell*, pp 146–7), in giving less weight to Kettle's testimony and more to Davitt's. The 'concentration' versus 'dispersion' debate seems to be a figment of Kettle's imagination.
[6] *Fall*, p. 301.

with landlordism offered to the Irish race, with England involved in her South African entanglements.[1]

A no-rent movement coinciding with the British disaster at Majuba Hill (27 February) would probably have won for Ireland a land act fulfilling the proposals of the land conference of 29 April, and a home rule bill anticipating that of 1886 with much more likelihood of becoming law. It was not Parnell's fault that this great opportunity was lost, but that of the 'timid and calculating constitutionalists' that made up half the Irish parliamentary party.[2] When, in the autumn, the league did declare a general rent-strike, the situation had fundamentally changed.[3]

Davitt's abortive no-rent plan, as he describes it in 1903, seems to visualise a Land League 'new departure', similar to the fenian new departure of 1878[4] in strategy and aims, and in its concept of cooperation between constitutional and revolutionary nationalists, but essentially different in that it was a plan for immediate revolutionary action to be taken by an independent, established, and open organisation with a large membership and great resources and under the direction of a national executive of which nearly half consisted of Parnellite M.P.s. But did Davitt mean, as he seems to mean, that his proposed rent-strike was intended or expected to merge into the insurrection that fenian thinking held to be inevitable? If he did he was almost certainly projecting back to 1881 his mood of 1903—of renewed disillusionment with Britain and parliamentarism induced by the Boer war and the Wyndham land act. It is more likely, however, that the bellicose terms he uses to describe his no-rent plan are not to be taken at their face value. The rent strike actually announced by the Land League in October 1881 was declared to be 'the one constitutional weapon' remaining in its hands. An insurrectionary rent-strike would have been incompatible with Davitt's public image in 1881—to orthodox fenians that of a renegade from the 'true path', to parliamentary nationalists that of a revolutionary wholly committed to constitutional action, to the great mass of tenant farmers that of a trusted champion who constantly reprobated violence. In the wealth of information that he communicated to the *Times*-Parnell commission there is not a word about his proposed rent-strike: evidently it did not fit into his picture of the land war as he saw it in 1889. He saw it in a different light when he was writing the *Fall of feudalism*.

He spent part of the evening of 27 January in the visitors' gallery of the house of commons, and had the satisfaction of hearing Henry

[1] *Fall*, p. 337.
[2] Ibid., pp 301, 309–10.
[3] Ibid., pp 301, 337–8.
[4] See above, pp 249–53.

Labouchere, the English radical, liberal M.P. for Northampton, and critic of Forster's regime, dissecting the government's outrage statistics. He returned to Dublin on the 28th.[1] On the 29th he issued a public statement from the Land League offices categorically denying a rumour that he intended to quit Ireland when the coercion bill became law.[2] Next day, at a land meeting at Borris, County Carlow, he flayed the government for a coercion policy that would be as futile as it was misconceived. 'The Chief Slanderer of Ireland, Mr Outrage Forster' had boasted of 'striking terror into what his uncouth savagery had stigmatised as the ruffian, blackguard, and scoundrel people of Ireland', but he would be made to realise that the fear of arrest had no terror for 'the Young Ireland of today'. Coercion would demonstrate that the only support for landlordism was brute force, whereas the opinion of the civilised world and the support of the new Ireland across the Atlantic were behind the Land League in its mission to win free land and happy homes for the people of old Ireland.[3] He went over to London again on the evening of the 31st to consult Parnell and other parliamentary members of the league executive about the national convention that had been contemplated since early December,[4] and it was agreed that immediate preparations should be made for convoking it. He reported this to the league on 2 February: in addition to reaffirming the national demand on the land question, the convention would show England and Forster that the local leaders were neither ruffians nor blackguards, that the league would not be terrorised by coercion, and that it condemned both coercion and outrages, real and manufactured. He proposed a revised method for electing delegates, by which branches with 500 members and under should elect one delegate and branches with over 500 members two delegates. This was approved and circulars were issued accordingly to branches, instructing them to elect their delegates within one week, so that the convention could be summoned as soon as possible after the coercion bill was passed and the land bill introduced.[5]

The coercion debate had now reached an explosive stage at Westminster, and at the meeting on 2 February the league declared that the thanks of the Irish people 'the world over' were due to Parnell and his followers for their struggle against the 'brute force' of the English majority. The conduct of Shaw and thirteen other Irish M.P.s who had deserted Parnell in face of the enemy was held up to obloquy, Davitt declaring that, as in war the penalty for such conduct was death, so in the present situation sentence of political death should be passed

[1] DN/8, 27–8 Jan. [2] *F.J.*, 29, 31 Jan.; cf. above, p. 439.
[3] *F.J.*, 31 Jan. [4] Above, pp 437, 439. [5] *F.J.*, 3 Feb.

on the renegades by their constituents without delay. At his instance the meeting recorded its gratitude to Labouchere and to Joseph Cowen, liberal M.P. for Newcastle-upon-Tyne, the staunchest and most independent English supporter of home rule and the Land League, for their efforts against coercion. He believed that arrests under the forthcoming coercion act would be far fewer than was feared, but emphasised that the league would have a clear duty to help the dependants of those arrested. The chairman of the meeting, John Ferguson, who was a warm admirer of Gladstone and Bright no less than of Davitt, spoke very gravely of the 'terrible position' into which the league was moving and which they must face 'as serious, thoughtful men, without passion, without temper, but with determination'. He was opposed to all violence and recalled Davitt's exertions to keep the agitation within constitutional lines, but he knew of no movement that had ever stirred society to its depths that was not accompanied by some excesses. Public opinion in Ireland had become wonderfully enlightened on the land question, especially in Ulster, where the change in outlook was 'astounding'. The executive had issued an address to the people of England and Scotland, on their relations with the people of Ireland, which he hoped would enlarge the scope of the enlightenment.[1] This address was the outcome of an idea of Davitt's which he had recommended in London the day before. According to Parnell he had said:

I think we have made a great mistake in not cultivating the public opinion of the English working classes, and I hope you will take steps in England to instruct the working class with regard to . . . the Irish land question.[2]

Before the meeting ended, Davitt received and read out a telegram from T. P. O'Connor,[3] reporting Gladstone's announcement to the house of commons that he intended to follow up the Speaker's revolutionary closure of the first stage of the coercion debate[4] by proposing new rules to curb obstruction. At the instance of O'Connor Power (Parnell being absent) the party had marched out of the commons' chamber in passionate protest against this 'suspension of constitutional liberty', and for the second time in a week the leaders had been faced with a proposal that the party should withdraw from parliament and return to Ireland. This time it was not to lead a rent strike but for 'a consultation with our constituents'. After heated discussion, with Parnell present, it was decided that the party must remain at Westminster and continue to offer 'dogged and relentless opposition to every step and

[1] *F.J.*, 3 Feb.

[2] *Fall*, p. 449.

[3] The original telegram is in DP/AC.

[4] Above, p. 455.

every stage of the bill'.[1] Here is further evidence that the prevailing mood of the Parnellites was against any abandonment of their parliamentary position.

The league meeting of 2 February was the last to be attended by Davitt. The government was already poised to arrest him. His statement to the central Land League on 4 January and recent speeches at Tralee and other places[2] had been brought to the notice of the house of commons on 13 January by Lord Randolph Churchill, who called on the government to cancel his ticket of leave. Forster replied that he had been kept informed of Davitt's speeches since his return from America and that the government would not hesitate to take action against him if his behaviour warranted it. But Forster was not aware that Davitt had broken any of the conditions of his licence, and to revoke it simply by the exercise of the discretionary power of the crown would be contrary to precedent.[3] His reluctance to take this course was soon to be overcome. To him as well as to his political opponents Davitt's speeches were all the more provocative because they were made at the very time that the league was on trial for just such provocation.

Harcourt, who as home secretary was the minister immediately concerned, raised the question with Selborne, the lord chancellor, who on 18 January delivered the opinion that Davitt's recent speeches were seditious and would therefore entitle the government to revoke his licence.[4] Forster, though regarding him as 'a most mischievous, not to say dangerous, agitator', still thought that this could hardly be done unless he clearly broke one of the specified conditions of the licence (19 January).[5] Lewis Harcourt, the home secretary's son and private secretary, noted in his journal for 22 January that Howard Vincent, director of the C.I.D. (Scotland Yard) was strongly opposed to arresting Davitt as likely to occasion serious outbreaks of violence.[6] On the day on which Forster introduced his coercion bill (24 January), Sir William Harcourt asked the English law officers (Henry James, attorney general, and Francis Herschell, solicitor general) for an opinion on whether the government had the legal right to revoke Davitt's licence. Their reply (26 January), differing substantially from the opinion expressed by the attorney general on 24 November 1880, and by the law officers in November 1879,[7] was in the affirmative. An

[1] *F.J.*, 3 Feb.; O'Connor, *Parnell movement*, p. 412.

[2] Above, pp 443–4, 444–9.

[3] *Hansard 3*, cclvii, 649–52.

[4] Bodleian Library, Harcourt papers, home office general correspondence, 1881, dep 95, pp 8–15.

[5] B.L., Gladstone papers, Add. MS 44,158.

[6] Bodleian Library, Harcourt papers, B I, vol. 347, p. 67; Lewis Harcourt's journal.

[7] See above, pp 432, 350–51.

absolute power of revocation was reserved to the crown by statute (27 & 28 Vict., c.47). It was assumed that this power would not be exercised without due cause, but even though the licensee had fulfilled the conditions of his licence it might properly be revoked if his conduct were adjudged by the executive to be injurious to the interests of the public. If the licence were to be revoked on the ground of breach of any of its conditions (one of them being that the licensee must abstain from any breach of the law), it was entirely within the discretion of the executive to decide whether there had been such a breach, no conviction by a court being required. Davitt's connection with the Land League and his speeches at Land meetings, did, in the law officers' opinion, amount to a legal offence and therefore to a breach of these conditions. They cited evidence produced before the court in the conspiracy trial, and Justice Fitzgerald's charge to the jury, to show that the league of which Davitt was the founder was an 'illegal confederation', that in pursuance of the objects set out in its rules Davitt had made seditious speeches—they instanced those at Irishtown (3 May 1880), Tralee (9 January 1881), and Kilbrin (16 January)—and that he had conspired with others to effect illegal objects by illegal means. Armed with this opinion Harcourt and Forster decided, with the reluctant consent of the cabinet, to arrest Davitt, and instructions were sent to Dublin accordingly on 31 January. On 2 February Davitt's licence was revoked and a warrant was issued by the home secretary to a London police magistrate, Sir James Ingham, requiring him to have Davitt arrested. Ingham accordingly issued a warrant to Chief Superintendent Williamson, of Scotland Yard (who had been involved in the original proceedings against Davitt in May 1870), directing him to effect the arrest and bring Davitt before the metropolitan police court in Bow Street.[1]

While final arrangements to arrest him were being made, Davitt was in London, and spent two hours on Tuesday, 1 February, in the Speaker's gallery of the house of commons. Two anecdotes are recorded of this occasion, one by Davitt himself, the other by Lewis Harcourt. Davitt recalled that Beaconsfield happened to be in the peers' gallery nearest to where he himself was sitting, when Harcourt (from whom Davitt heard the story years later) said to a colleague on the treasury bench: 'do you see that scoundrel next to Beaconsfield in the gallery? Well, I will have that fellow back in penal servitude tomorrow'.[2]

[1] P.R.O., H.O. 144/5/17869/25, 31; Arnold-Forster, Irish journal, 17, 31 Jan.; A. G. Gardiner, *Life of Sir William Harcourt*, i (1923), pp 423–6; above, pp 81–2.

[2] *Fall*, p. 302. Davitt does not name Harcourt, but clearly he is the 'prominent minister' referred to.

Lewis Harcourt wrote in his journal for 15 February:

> When Michael Davitt was in the house of commons about ten days ago Howard Vincent (Scotland Yard) sat by him for some time without recognising him. Labouchere came up to the gallery, and having greeted Davitt saw Vincent, upon which he said 'Mr Vincent–Mr Davitt–you are two men who ought to know one another'. I believe their faces were a sight to be seen.[1]

The arrest was not, however, made the following day, Wednesday, when Davitt was back in Dublin, but on Thursday, 3 February, as he was crossing O'Connell Bridge with Brennan and Harris about 2 p.m. after a morning's work at the offices of the league. He was escorted by a detective officer to Dublin Castle, and there handed over to two English detectives, one of them Chief Superintendent Williamson. He gave up the revolver that he carried with him, asking the police to pass it on to Brennan, which they did. After two hours at the headquarters of the Dublin Metropolitan Police he was taken by Williamson and his colleague in a cab to Kingstown, and from there, by the mailboat *Connaught*, to Holyhead, strongly guarded in a first-class cabin. The whole affair had been conducted so quietly and efficiently that there were no demonstrations, and none of his friends were allowed to see him until shortly before the departure of the mailboat at 8 p.m., when his doctor, J. E. Kenny, Brennan, and Egan were allowed into his cabin for a few minutes. They found him in good spirits, though physically worn out, having had little sleep for several nights owing to a severe cough. He described the government's action in arresting him as mean, cowardly, and vindictive, and the most stupid it had yet committed. Inquiries as to the charges on which he had been arrested, made at the Castle by his solicitor, Valentine Dillon, had consistently drawn a blank.[2]

At Holyhead he was escorted through two lines of police to the London train, where a first-class compartment was reserved for him and five of his police guards. The train was preceded by a pilot engine, a security measure normally used only for Queen Victoria. To side-step any demonstration at Euston the party left the express at Willesden junction and completed the journey to London by local train early on the morning of 4 February. Davitt was at once taken before Sir James Ingham at Bow Street police court, where Williamson produced the warrant under which he had been arrested and identified him as the Michael Davitt convicted at Old Bailey on 18 July 1870. Asked whether he wished to question the witness Davitt said 'no', but that he did wish to know why he had been arrested. The magistrate replied:

[1] Quoted in Gardiner, *Harcourt*, i, 424.

[2] *F.J.*, 4 Feb. 81; *Irish Times*, 5 Feb.; DA/1, ff 253^{v}–4.

'that is not my business. Your identity is the only thing I have to ascertain. I shall commit you.' He then signed a warrant committing Davitt to Millbank prison, to which he accordingly returned, after nearly ten years.[1] Under the continuous strain of the past eighteen hours he had been calm, collected, cheerful, and quietly defiant. The elaborate but unnecessary precautions against the possibility of a rescue were a tribute to the government's sense of his great reputation among Irishmen in Britain as well as in Ireland.[2]

In the sensation caused by Davitt's arrest the departure from Ireland of another key member of the Land League executive, the treasurer, was scarcely noticed. But Egan's move, with essential records, to Paris, where he arrived on 3 February, anticipated the danger of British government interference with the funds of the league. A special meeting of the league executive, held in Paris on 13 February, authorised Egan to make Paris the financial headquarters of the league. In that political sanctuary, Egan continued to function as treasurer of the league until it was finally succeeded in October 1882 by a new body, the National League. It was through Egan in Paris that from February onwards American money reached Ireland in a sustained flow, to provide the Land League and the Ladies' Land League with the bulk of their financial resources. Among other business at the Paris meeting of the executive Dillon was appointed to succeed Davitt as the Land League's head of organisation.[3]

[1] See above, pp 147–9.

[2] *F.J.*, 4, 5 Feb.; P.R.O., H.O. 144/5/178691 30, 31, 32, 35A, DA/1, ff 254–4v; *Fall*, pp 302–3. The telegraph office at Holyhead submitted a bill for 13*s*. 6*d*. to the home office for expenses incurred on telegrams relating to Davitt's arrest and for keeping the office open all night, but the bill was returned with a note that it should be sent to the home secretary through the postmaster general. Scotland Yard tried to get the home office to pay the £33 charged by the London and North Western Railway for the pilot engine (Scotland Yard archives, MEPO R/b 1832, 11 Feb. 81—information kindly supplied by Dr K. R. M. Short).

[3] *Fall*, pp 306, 308–9, 373; *F.J.*, 14, 17 Feb.

XII

Penal servitude again, February 1881–May 1882

DAVITT'S arrest produced predictable reactions—from Irish nationalists everywhere shock and indignation; from unionists in Britain and Ireland satisfaction that ranged from blatant rejoicing to sober approval. The *Freeman's Journal*, describing the arrest as one of those political blunders that were worse than crimes, characterised the founder of the Land League as 'the deadly enemy of crime: no man so often, so eloquently raised his voice against any act of violence or illegality'.[1] The *Nation* wrote that if the government's object was to perpetuate Irish antipathy to foreign rule it could not have chosen a more effective way than sending back to penal servitude the man who, with Parnell, 'has been more instrumental than any other living human being in rescuing the tenantry of Ireland from serfdom'. Why, in view of Forster's statement in the house of commons (13 January) that Davitt had not broken any of the conditions of his licence,[2] had he been arrested at all? If his arrest was intended to strike terror into the land-leaguers its authors would be disappointed: 'we think that Davitt's fortitude will only encourage the country to persevere in its open, legal, and determined movement for obtaining its rights'.[3] The *Newcastle Chronicle* (Joseph Cowen's paper) spoke of Davitt's great ability, high character, and personal popularity; without question he was one of the most moderate of the Land League's directors. If he had simply been detained in custody, his countrymen would perhaps not have been so much exasperated by his arrest; but to send him back to penal servitude was in their eyes an arbitrary and cruel exercise of authority.[4]

On the other hand the *Daily Express* of Dublin described the arrest as the most decisive act taken by the government to check seditious agitation and enforce respect for executive authority. By the violence

[1] *F.J.*, 4 Feb.
[2] Above, p. 462.
[3] *Nation*, 12 Feb.
[4] *Newcastle Chronicle*, quoted in *F.J.*, 8 Feb.

of his language Davitt had inflamed the passions of the multitude, inciting tenants to violate their contracts and defy the law. His recent speeches, made while the conspiracy trial was in progress, were a gross aggravation of his previous offences. As a fenian, he could have been connected with the recent threats of fenian violence in England. The wonder was that the government had shown so much forbearance towards this convicted felon on ticket of leave.[1] The London *Daily Telegraph* saw him as a link between the fenians and the open political organisation which they had so often assailed. His recent violence of language showed that he had no fear that his licence would be revoked. In revoking it the government had struck at the real leader of sedition, the man who had organised the Irish people against landlordism as an outpost of British rule.[2] The *Times* felt that his arrest would be a salutary warning to others, in whom the impunity of so notorious an offender had encouraged lawlessness. He was the most dangerous of the personalities thrown up by the present troubles in Ireland, a man who combined the roles of demagogue and conspirator. 'There are few among the patriots of the league, and still fewer among those who administer its branches, who possess the cold fanaticism, the dare-devil courage, of Michael Davitt.'[3] The *Liverpool Mercury* described him as an 'incorrigible revolutionist', whose long imprisonment seemed not to have curbed the 'impetuosity of his rebellious nature'.[4]

Davitt's arrest created a third crisis[5] for the Irish party at Westminster. When the house of commons met in the afternoon of 3 February Parnell inquired whether it was true that Davitt had been arrested, and Harcourt's 'yes sir' was greeted with a 'tempest of cheering' from liberals and radicals in which the opposition joined, though with less enthusiasm. Harcourt explained that, after consultation with the law officers and the chief secretary, he had decided that Davitt's conduct was incompatible with the conditions on which he was at large. But when Parnell demanded to know what conditions Davitt had broken, the home secretary remained silent.[6] Gladstone's attempt to go on with the next business (his anti-obstruction resolutions) precipitated a tumult of anger and exasperation from the Parnellites, in the course of which 36 of them were suspended from the service of the house for the rest of the sitting.[7] The expelled members met, and the policy of withdrawing from parliament, which had been rejected the day before, was again discussed and again rejected: if they were to obey

[1] *Daily Express*, 4 Feb. [2] *Daily Telegraph*, 8 Feb. [3] *The Times*, 5, 9 Feb.
[4] Quoted in *F.J.*, 8 Feb. [5] Cf. above, pp 461–2, 457–9. [6] *Hansard 3*, cclviii, 68.
[7] Ibid., cols 69–88; Hamilton, *Diary*, i, 105–6; O'Connor, *Parnell movement*, pp 413–17; *Memoirs*, i, 166–70.

their own feelings, Parnell told a *Freeman* interviewer, they would withdraw, but they had a disagreeable duty to perform in fighting the coercion bill in parliament and they intended to perform it.[1]

Anger at Davitt's arrest was accompanied by deep concern for the effects that prison conditions might have on him. This concern was not limited to Irish nationalists. Gladstone, who had agreed with reluctance to the arrest, expressed a feeling that was widely shared when he wrote to Harcourt: 'having put him [Davitt] out of the way of mischief, any allowable consideration for him will be so much to the good'.[2] Harcourt, though a tough and abrasive politician, was warm-hearted, and needed no prompting to bend the rules in Davitt's favour, with the result that his second period in penal servitude bears no resemblance to his first.[3] In reply to a parliamentary question from James Bryce on 7 February about Davitt's condition, Harcourt assured the house of commons that he was being treated with all possible indulgence and attention to his health.[4] Bryce, a native of Belfast, author of *The Holy Roman Empire* (1864) and one of the most intellectually eminent members of the liberal party, thought well of Davitt, whom he had met in Dublin in December, and now took a friendly interest in him as a prisoner.[5] Many other M.P.s besides those of the Irish party shared Bryce's concern. A memorial was already circulating among M.P.s requesting that Davitt should be treated as a first-class misdemeanant; and though its promoters, headed by the senior whip of the Irish party, Major J. P. Nolan, considered Harcourt's assurance of 7 February to be not unsatisfactory, it was presented to him on 10 February, signed by 104 members, mainly Irish home-rulers and British liberals and radicals (including Bradlaugh, Broadhurst, Bryce, Burt, Hopwood, Hutchinson, and Labouchere), to demonstrate their desire that Davitt should be exempted from all personal hardships not inseparable from detention.[6] His arrest was condemned as 'mean, cruel, and unjust' at a huge demonstration in Hyde Park on 13 February, called to protest against the coercion bill and interference with the freedom of parliamentary debate.[7] And the public was reminded of what he had already suffered in prison by extracts from his first pamphlet, *Prison life* (1878), serialised in the *Nation*.[8]

On 8 February an Irish member asked that Davitt's licence and the documents relating to his rearrest should be laid on the table of the

[1] *F.J.*, 4, 5, 17 Feb.; *Fall*, pp 304–5, 309–10.
[2] Gardiner, *Harcourt*, i, 425.
[3] Ibid., i, 424–5.
[4] *Hansard 3*, cclviii, 260–66.
[5] Arnold-Forster, Irish journal, 24 Dec. 80; George Fottrell to D, 10 Feb. 81 (DP/V).
[6] *F.J.*, 11 Feb.; P.R.O., H.O. 144/5/17869/44.
[7] *F.J.*, 14, 15 Feb.; *Annual Register, 1881*, pt II, p. 18.
[8] *Nation*, 12, 19, 26 Feb., 5, 12 Mar.; above, pp 199–200.

house. What conditions had he violated? Was it not contrary to all precedent to revoke a licence unless there had been a violation of its conditions? The home secretary replied that it was not customary to lay such documents on the table, but that the questioner could consult them at the Home Office. The only answer Harcourt would give to the other questions was that the crown had the unquestionable right to revoke a licence if there should seem to be good cause, that in the government's opinion there had been 'grave and sufficient cause' for revoking Davitt's, and that it would not be in the public interest to specify the reasons for its decision.[1] In other words the government had sent Davitt back to penal servitude by the exercise of that discretionary power of the crown which, Forster had admitted in the house of commons only three weeks previously, it would be unprecedented to use for such a purpose.[2] The home office was uncomfortable about this, and felt that habeas corpus proceedings might be instituted on Davitt's behalf. The warrants for his arrest and committal to Millbank had been drawn up hurriedly and contained some erasures and alterations. It was thought that fresh warrants might have to be prepared, but the attorney general decided that the verbal blemishes in them were of no importance (7 February).[3]

Harcourt was as good as his word in attending to the well-being of his prisoner. The medical officer at Millbank reported that Davitt was suffering from bronchial catarrh (an old complaint) but was fit for immediate removal to one of the 'public works' prisons (except Dartmoor). Would Portland be a suitable destination? inquired Sir Edmund Du Cane,[4] chairman of the directors of convict prisons; and would there be any danger to Davitt's health in moving him in the evening or early morning? The medical officer at Millbank approved of Portland and thought that Davitt might safely be moved there in the evening or early morning if the usual precautions applicable to invalids were taken. So on Saturday, 5 February, wearing his own clothes, Davitt was conveyed in a first-class carriage, by the 5.45 a.m. train from Waterloo, to Weymouth in Dorset, from which he completed his journey by the light railway connecting the town with the nearby 'Isle of Portland'. This rock-bound, exposed, and isolated peninsula, 4½ square miles in extent, projecting into the English Channel from the Dorset coast, to which it was barely attached by the ridge of pebbles known as Chesil Bank, had been a place of strategic importance

[1] *Hansard 3*, cclviii, 347; P.R.O., H.O. 144/5/17869/25, 32.
[2] Above, p. 462.
[3] P.R.O., H.O. 144/5/17869/25, 29, 32.
[4] See above, p. 214.

and the scene of repeated conflict from Anglo-Saxon times. It was now famous mainly for its stone-quarries, the source of a large export-trade, and for the great convict-prison, built in 1848 on rising ground in the north-east, and accommodating 1500 long-term prisoners.

On arrival just after midday Davitt was taken to the orderly room, where a good fire was burning, and examined by the medical officer, who found him to be free from any organic disease but showing the effects of loss of sleep, mental excitement, and general fatigue. His own clothes were replaced by a new suit of well-aired prison clothes, but otherwise he was exempted from indignities, such as the compulsory clipping of hair and beard, which, as he knew by bitter experience, the ordinary convict had to endure. He was placed in a central cell in the middle landing of the prison infirmary, a privileged location where, separated from the general life of the prison, he could the sooner recover from the strain of the previous two days. That afternoon he was visited by the prison governor, George Clifton, who was humane and enlightened; and excellent personal relations were established between the two men that continued throughout Davitt's sojourn in Portland. The catholic chaplain also called on him, and next day, Sunday, Davitt attended mass, being marched to the chapel after the other catholic prisoners had assembled and conducted back to the infirmary before they had left their seats. A special diet was prescribed for him which included 10 ounces of meat, 8 ounces of potatoes, 22 ounces of bread, 1 ounce of butter, 1½ ounces of sugar, ¼ ounce of tea, and 1 bottle of ale daily. Reporting all this to Sir Edmund Du Cane, Clifton wrote that Davitt seemed well content with the arrangements made for him, and that, to judge from his manner and bearing, he would conduct himself satisfactorily. Du Cane informed the home office accordingly, and instructed Clifton that Davitt was not to be moved from the infirmary without authorisation from the prison department. Davitt's temporary location in the infirmary thus became permanent, despite the fact that his health quickly improved. He was medically examined again on 9 February, when the M.O. reported that his bronchial catarrh had almost disappeared, that his coughing had ceased, and that there was no evidence of any chest disease.[1]

Davitt's first letter from Portland, written on 8 February to Tom Brennan, who was probably his closest friend, was a list of instructions. His personal effects were to be packed in boxes and entrusted to some friend in Dublin, but Brennan was to retain his books and newspaper files for his own use. His account in the National Bank was to be drawn on to pay whatever was due to his landlady, a year's subscription to

[1] P.R.O., H.O. 144/5/17869/34, 37A, 43.

the *Connaught Telegraph*, the *Mayo Examiner*, and the *Nation*, and £40 to his sister Sabina to cover the cost of erecting a plain tombstone over their mother's grave at Manayunk. A small nugget of silver that Mackay the 'bonanza king' had given him[1] and which he had promised as a contribution to the bazaar of the Convent of Mercy, Oranmore, was to be sent to Sr M. O'Hanlon, of that convent, together with one of the twenty-dollar gold pieces he had left in his trunk.[2]

He strongly resented the manner of his reimprisonment. In a petition to the home secretary, dated 24 February, he claimed that the withdrawal of his licence was a violation of the terms, expressed or implied, of his liberation in December 1877 and was in no way justified by his subsequent actions, which, as Forster had admitted in the house of commons as recently as 13 January, had not involved a breach of any of the stated conditions of the licence. His release from Dartmoor, though in the form of a ticket of leave granted to an ordinary convict, was in reality an act of amnesty. For (1) it was the result of the pressure of public opinion in Ireland and England brought to bear on Beaconsfield's government in favour of amnesty to the remaining Irish political prisoners. If this had not been so, his release would be unintelligible, as he was not entitled under the ordinary rules to a ticket of leave until he had served upwards of four more of the fifteen years of his sentence.[3] (2) The public generally acclaimed his release as an amnesty for a political offence. (3) When he was prosecuted at Sligo for alleged seditious language the government that had liberated him two years before allowed his ticket of leave to remain a dead letter, whereas an ordinary licence-holder when charged with a breach of the law would have been at once committed to prison. In the light of all this, his reimprisonment could only be explained by the assumption of an *imperium in imperio* [Dublin Castle] which could 'violate the spirit of English law' to punish twice a man who had been convicted of an 'infringement of its letter'. To justify a second imprisonment by invoking the discretionary power of the crown was to claim an arbitrary power, never previously exercised, that left the liberty of a legally-pardoned offender at the mercy of an irresponsible authority. His reimprisonment could only be explained as an unprecedented act of political vengeance, instigated by his political enemies, the Irish landlords, whose unjust privileges and despotic behaviour he had endeavoured to curtail.[4]

Harcourt made no reply to this 'solemn protest'; and there was little he could have said to refute Davitt's argument that his reimprisonment

[1] Above, p. 410.
[2] DP/A3.
[3] See above, pp 146, 180.
[4] P.R.O., H.O. 144/5/17869/51.

was arbitrary, anomalous, and unfair. His statement that he had been convicted in 1870 for an offence against the letter, rather than the spirit, of the law, was not sustainable, but it was beyond question that his release in 1877 had been a virtual amnesty. Successive governments had treated him not as an ordinary convict in the final stage of his sentence, which was technically his status, but as a political prisoner on parole. Though under police surveillance he had never been closely or vexatiously watched. His behaviour after 13 January, when Forster had said in parliament that he had not broken any of the conditions of his licence, was no different from what it had been previously. His most extreme statements could be matched in speeches by Parnell, Dillon, and the other prominent land-leaguers whom the government had unsuccessfully prosecuted; and he had been foremost in reprobating violence and counselling restraint. But there was a vital difference between Davitt's position and that of his colleagues in the Land League: he could be removed at any time by simple executive act, whereas they could not till the coercion bill became law. But could the government not have waited till then—a matter of weeks at the most—and arrested him under the coercion act, as Parnell and the others were to be arrested? In that case there would have been no question of his resuming the status and the stigma of the convict; and Kilmainham, not Portland, would have been his place of imprisonment. Was the government not acting vindictively against a political opponent in sending him back to penal servitude?

The answer to these questions is complex. Forster and Harcourt, who together were immediately responsible for Davitt's arrest, saw him as the most dangerous of the Land League chiefs; and since he was also the most vulnerable, they decided to strike at him first. His speech at Kilbrin (16 January) helped to bring matters to a head, and for a particular reason. The reference to the wolfdog of Irish-American vengeance came just at a time when an attempt to blow up the infantry barracks in Salford (14 January) and rumours of fenian attacks at other places seemed to threaten a terrorist campaign in Britain as O'Donovan Rossa's challenge to the coercion bill. Though Devoy and the executive of Clan na Gael were at one with the supreme council of the I.R.B. in condemning such activities as premature and irresponsible, Devoy was quoted as promising systematic and bloody retaliation on Britain if, as the result of coercion, Irish people were to be shot down by British soldiers.[1] Harcourt reacted angrily to such threats to the public peace of Great Britain; and Forster, who as late as

[1] *Annual Register, 1881*, pt II, pp 2-10; *Irishman*, 8, 15, 22, 29 Jan., 5, 12, 19 Feb., 5 Mar.; *The Times*, 17-18 Jan.; *D.P.B.*, ii, 29-30, 41-3; see above, pp 136, 388-9.

19 January told Gladstone that he did not feel he could have Davitt arrested unless he clearly broke one of the conditions of his licence, soon afterwards came to believe that to allow him to continue at large was to allow the law to be outrageously flouted in Ireland. His arrest was primarily a preventative measure, but there was a punitive element in it; and to the extent that this was so there was substance in his complaint that he was being punished twice for the same offence. For while he had made no secret of his continued association with the fenian movement and his continued adherence to its aims, he had not repeated any of the unlawful acts for which he had originally been convicted. But it was his identification with fenianism that gave his preeminence in the land movement its supremely sinister character in the eyes of such men as Harcourt and Forster, and that impelled them, in the political hypertension of late January 1881, to take advantage of his status as a convict on licence. In seizing this short-term advantage they blundered politically. If they had waited till March and arrested him under the coercion act, the Irish situation would hardly have worsened for Britain, and the violence of the land war might well have been lessened. By acting as they did while the coercion bill was still being fiercely debated at Westminster, they increased the bitterness of the conflict in Ireland and earned for the liberal government a new charge of ruthlessness and hypocrisy prejudicial to the remedial side of its Irish policy.

Harcourt remained unrepentant about Davitt's rearrest, but continued to keep a solicitous eye on his condition as a prisoner. The privileges initially granted to him were increased by further relaxation of the rules. His official status, that of a convict in the third class, entitled him to be visited and to write and receive letters, only once in six months.[1] In fact, during an imprisonment that lasted one year and a quarter, he was visited on six occasions at irregular intervals— on 15 February by Mrs Sullivan, on 3 March by Dr Kenny, on 2 June by Mrs Sullivan and Mrs Kenny, on 27 June by Dr Kenny, on 8 September by Archbishop Croke of Cashel and Bishop Fitzgerald of Ross, and on 10 January 1882 by Mrs Sullivan.[2] Mrs Sullivan was the Irish-American wife of A. M. Sullivan, with whom Harcourt was on friendly terms, and Mrs Kenny was the wife of Davitt's medical adviser (she had asked to be allowed to accompany her husband to Portland on 3 March, but Harcourt had politely refused).[3] All five were personal friends, and their visits, much in excess of his quota as a prisoner, must have given him great pleasure. His immediate relatives were all in

[1] Above, p. 146; P.R.O., H.O. 144/5/17869/45A, 56, 79.

[3] Ibid., nos 79, 83.

[3] Ibid., no. 52.

America, as during his Dartmoor imprisonment; and of his three sisters, only Sabina, the youngest and unmarried one, was in a position to come over, as she urgently wanted to do. In November Michael suggested that she might make the trip in the following summer,[1] but by that time he was again at large. She would, of course, have been allowed to see him. Beatrice Walshe, of Balla, now living in Dublin, was anxious to visit him, and Mrs Kenny, who had received permission from Harcourt to do so, offered to stand down in her favour (14 May), but Harcourt replied that permission could not thus be transferred. Miss Walshe, related to John Walshe and a founding member of the Ladies' Land League, was politically suspect. Mrs Sullivan and Mrs Kenny were also founding members, but Harcourt appears to have had confidence in their good faith, especially that of Mrs Sullivan.[2] Applications to visit Davitt from other friends, acquaintances, and admirers were either refused or ignored by Harcourt. A parliamentary question from Sexton, asking at what times and under what conditions M.P.s might be allowed to visit Davitt, elicited the predictable reply that the rules could not safely be set aside at the instance of any particular group, whether M.P.s or not. A personal friend, Harcourt added (he was referring to Mrs Sullivan), had been specially permitted to see him so that his friends in general might be satisfied about the state of his health. But no communication with him on public or political affairs would be allowed.[3] To this position Harcourt consistently adhered, and it explains why Davitt was not visited by Dillon, Parnell, or any other close political associate. A request from Brennan, who was managing his private affairs, for special permission to visit him was being considered by Harcourt when Brennan was arrested under the coercion act on 23 May.[4]

Eight of his letters from Portland—one to Brennan, four to Sabina, one to his eldest sister Mary, one to his Aunt Ellen, and one to Hugh King, of New York—have survived,[5] but it is evident that he wrote others. The eight were 'regulation' letters; and so doubtless were the others, for it is as good as certain that this time there was no smuggling of letters either from or to him. Only one letter received by him remains among his papers: from George Fottrell, a Dublin solicitor, who wrote on 10 February expressing the sense of shock of one who, though wholly unconnected with the Land League, appreciated the 'fearless and unselfish efforts' Davitt had made to improve the condition of

[1] D to Sabina Davitt, 14 Nov. (DP/A3).

[2] Above, pp 327, 457; Sophie O'Brien, *My Irish friends* (1937), ch. I, III.

[3] *Hansard 3*, cclviii, 635 (11 Feb.).

[4] P.R.O., H.O. 144/5/17869/56; *S.C.P.*, vi, 507.

[5] DP/A3; DA/1, ff 296–7^v, 340–40^v; *Nation*, 6 Aug.

his countrymen. He had been relieved, he said, to find that the home secretary was anxious to mitigate in every way the hardships imprisonment must entail, and that there was no fear of Davitt's being subjected to indignities such as he had suffered under his former imprisonment. The possibility of that had 'filled Ireland with dangerous anger', but Davitt would be glad to know that his inculcation of non-violence had had its effect.[1] This letter was submitted to Du Cane, who took exception to the reference to 'indignities', which, he thought, implied that Davitt's allegations on the subject had been admitted to be correct. A false impression was thus conveyed, very unfair to the prison officers concerned and very prejudicial to the public service. Harcourt brushed aside this objection, and Fottrell's letter was duly delivered to Davitt.[2] But other letters addressed to him, such as one containing a printed copy of resolutions passed at a meeting of the Pittston, Pennsylvania, branch of the American Land League, were not permitted to reach him.[3]

The indulgence shown to Davitt in the matter of visits was not allowed to defeat the government's intention to seal him off from the world of politics. Three days after his arrival at Portland Frances Sullivan sought special permission to visit him as he was a personal friend who had no relatives in England and who, when she had last seen him, appeared to be seriously ill. Harcourt at once responded sympathetically: it was his intention to have Davitt treated with all possible indulgence, he had had him placed in the infirmary for that reason, and the medical reports on him were reassuring. He was pleased to comply with Mrs Sullivan's request, and accordingly, on 15 February, she had a forty-minute interview with Davitt in the governor's room. She reported to Harcourt that he seemed much improved in health and satisfied with his treatment by the governor and the warders, but was eager to see newspapers and to be allowed to write. He complained bitterly of the unfairness of his arrest, for which he blamed Forster and officials of Dublin Castle rather than ministers in England. Mrs Sullivan gave him absolutely no political news, and as her political opinions were nearly identical with his she felt entitled, she told Harcourt, to great credit for keeping her tongue under control.[4]

Davitt's next visitor was his doctor, J. E. Kenny, of whom he had written in his letter of 8 February to Brennan:

> If Dr Kenny comes to London this week and cares to run down here, he is pretty certain to find Mr W822 at home. Visits are only for 20 minutes, and physic, not politics, must be the order of discussion. The same wicked topic is of course

[1] Fottrell to D, 10 Feb. (DP/V).
[2] P.R.O., H.O. 144/5/17869/45A.
[3] Ibid., nos 50, 66, 69.
[4] DP/UU (8, 9, 10, 11, 15, 16 Feb.).

excluded from letters, and all I can say on that head . . . is that I am boycotted with a vengeance, but am nevertheless always the same.[1]

Kenny applied to the home secretary for permission to visit Davitt in the capacity of his medical adviser (11 February), which, after consultation with Du Cane, Harcourt granted, subject to the condition that another doctor should examine him at the same time.[2] Kenny visited Portland on 3 March, in the company of Dr R. M. Gover, chief medical inspector of the prison board. He found Davitt in much better health than he had expected and felt that, being free from the hardships and rigid discipline of ordinary prison conditions, he would probably continue to improve. But this did not alter Kenny's opinion that, in view of the symptoms of lung disease Davitt had shown since his release from Dartmoor, close confinement, if prolonged, would prove very injurious to him. Besides, as soon as the excitement of the arrest and the beneficial effects of his present tranquillity had worn off, the dull routine of his life would tell heavily on him: he would be sure to suffer from depression resulting from the disuse of his mental energies and this would react injuriously on his physical condition. The best remedy (apart from liberating him) would be to enable him to employ his mind as much as possible, and this meant supplying him with books, newspapers, and writing material. Such a concession would make him comparatively happy, especially if he could look forward to release at no distant date. He felt a deep sense of grievance not so much at being imprisoned as at his imprisonment being effected by the revoking of his ticket of leave, which had consigned him again to the convict system. He had responded well to the kindness of both the governor and the medical officer of Portland, and was unwilling to be moved from that prison; but Kenny felt that Portland, though a very healthy place, was too much subject to extremes of temperature to suit a man of Davitt's physical conditon. If he had to be moved, Kenny hoped that it would not be to Dartmoor or Portsmouth prisons, both of which he loathed. Kenny reported these findings to the home secretary,[3] and communicated his general impression of Davitt's condition to the press, with some added details. He was sleeping better than before his arrest, had put on a little weight, and was in good spirits. He was allowed to spend his time as he pleased, and he spent nearly all of it in his cell, reading. The cell, ten feet long, eight feet wide, and about twelve feet high, was clean, and well heated by hot-water pipes, but its stone walls and floor were completely bare, and its only furniture was an iron bed, with seats on either side fixed to

[1] DP/A3.

[2] P.R.O., H.O. 144/5/17869/41, 49.

[3] Kenny to Harcourt, 7 Mar. (P.R.O., H.O. 144/5/17869/53).

the wall. (Compared with his cell in Dartmoor this was luxury accommodation.)[1] His current reading was a life of O'Connell, but he had access only to the books in the prison library and these, Kenny implied, would not suffice for long. During the present cold weather he was not able to take enough exercise, but he believed that he would be allowed more than the daily hour when he wanted it.[2]

Dr Kenny's wife, Lizzie, had asked to be allowed to accompany her husband to Portland, but had been politely refused by Harcourt. She however had obtained permission on her own behalf in May when Frances Sullivan again requested an interview with Davitt. Harcourt suggested that they should make a joint visit, and this the two women agreed to do. When they saw Davitt on 2 June in the presence of Governor Clifton, they found him entirely ignorant of what was going on outside. He inquired about Brennan (from whom he was expecting a visit), Dillon, and Kettle, and, as the ladies confessed to Harcourt, they broke the rules by telling him that all three, together with Fr Sheehy, were in prison. They thought it cruel that he was forbidden to see newspapers or to have writing materials, and they brought away a list of books that he hoped to be supplied with. His health was good: he was sleeping and eating well, was gaining weight, and was deeply sunburnt. This improvement owed much to the fact that, thanks to the kindness of the governor, he spent several hours a day working in the garden attached to the infirmary and had developed a lively interest in gardening. Mrs Sullivan wrote appreciatively to Harcourt that she and Mrs Kenny had received every attention from the governor and Mrs Clifton, who had entertained them to breakfast. Harcourt at once (14 June) gave permission for Davitt to have the books he requested; they included Wolfe Tone's memoirs, and a number of basic works of literature, history, and economics.[3] Thereafter he seems to have been allowed whatever reading-matter he asked for, subject to a general prohibition on newspapers and works on current politics.

A second request from Dr Kenny to visit Davitt professionally, though disapproved of by Du Cane, was granted by Harcourt (10 June) on the same condition as before. On 27 June Kenny again saw Davitt in the presence of Dr Gover and the governor. Gover was convinced by Kenny's method of examining him and by the leading questions he asked that his expressed fears for Davitt's health were not genuine; his real object was to get him out of prison, and, failing that, to bring

[1] See above, p. 150.
[2] *Nation*, 12 Mar.; *Irishman*, 12 Mar.
[3] P.R.O., H.O 144/5/17869/52, 57, 58, 59A, 60A, 61, 62.

about his transfer to Kilmainham, where his mere presence on Irish soil would be important to his countrymen, or to Woking, a weaker and more accessible prison than Portland. If, Gover advised Du Cane, Kenny should seek another interview with Davitt within the next few months, he should be refused. Harcourt ruled that Kenny should not be allowed to visit Davitt without his special permission. Kenny intended to apply again in October, but he was arrested in that month under the coercion act. On his release in February 1882 he requested leave to revisit Davitt professionally, only to receive a firm refusal from Harcourt.[1]

Gover was well pleased with Davitt's medical condition. He had steadily increased in weight from his admission to 21 May, after which a small loss (from 150 to 147 lbs) was not, as Dr Kenny professed to think, to be taken seriously but was amply explained by a temporary dyspepsia and the increased exercise Davitt was taking in the infirmary garden. There was a slight dullness at the apex of the left lung, but this was merely a trace of some old pulmonary trouble, not a symptom of any active disease. On the whole, considering both Davitt's improved health and his comparatively cheerful and contented state of mind, Gover felt that he could safely be left in Portland during the winter, subject, of course, to special medical supervision. On one point Gover took the same line as Kenny:[2] Davitt's earnest request to be allowed writing materials so that during the winter months he could express 'his ideas on politico-economical and other subjects' should be conceded. Gardening would provide him with sufficient active work during the summer, but the winter days and evenings would be very trying to a man of his mental vigour if his only occupation were to be reading. Such a concession could be justified on medical grounds, in view of Davitt's sanguine temperament, a certain eagerness and excitability in him, his extremely active life prior to his imprisonment, and the fact that at some time he had suffered from lung trouble. Gover was confident that he would not abuse the privilege, and he undertook, if allowed a certain number of sheets of writing paper each week to hand them all back to the governor for retention until his release.[3]

Du Cane, though shocked by this proposed violation of all precedent, grudgingly agreed that, with proper precautions, the privilege might be granted; the real problem would be how to prevent other prisoners from obtaining the same privilege on the same grounds. On this basis Harcourt ordered (10 July) that Davitt should be provided with writing materials.[4] In consequence, from 12 September 1881 to

[1] Ibid., nos 60, 63, 64, 87, 89.
[2] See above, p. 476.
[3] P.R.O., H.O. 144/5/17869/64.
[4] Ibid., no. 65; *Nation*, 16 July.

8 March 1882 batches of twenty blue foolscap leaves were issued to him at intervals varying from a week to a fortnight, and 358 leaves of manuscript (written on both sides of the paper from folio 120) and all initialled 'G.C.' (George Clifton) are preserved among his papers.[1] Entitled 'Jottings in solitary' and all written in his strong, clear, regular hand, they are an impressive witness to his mental activity during the autumn and winter of his time in Portland. So also is the copy of Alfred Webb's *Compendium of Irish biography* (Dublin, 1878) that its quaker author obtained permission to send to him.[2] Inscribed 'Michael Davitt, with the love and respect of the author, 10 August 1881', it was not only a treasured work of reference, but its fly-leaves, end-papers, and margins provided spaces that he filled with notes and quotations.

Davitt's isolation was the more glaring by contrast with the free and easy conditions under which land-leaguers arrested as aspects under the coercion act from early in March were held in Kilmainham jail. Could not Davitt be removed to Kilmainham? asked Joseph Cowen in the house of commons on 30 June; to which Gladstone replied that the government could not put untried prisoners on the same footing as a convict whose licence had been revoked. Cowan said he understood that Davitt was imprisoned for the purpose not of punishment but only of restraint, and Parnell asked whether Davitt was being punished for his original offence or for acts in connection with the land agitation. Gladstone refused to be drawn: he was not prepared at present to expound the rules under which convicts were released on licence.[3]

Since Davitt's arrest the Irish situation had been changing rapidly and tension between the Land League and the government had been mounting. The government's massive effort to defeat the league by the mutually conflicting methods of coercion and land reform was matched by the league's defiance of the one and its critical reaction to the other. The Protection of Person and Property Act (known simply as the coercion act), which gave the executive power to arrest on suspicion,[4] was augmented by the Peace Preservation Act (known as the arms act), prohibiting the possession of arms in proclaimed districts, empowering the government to search suspected persons and houses, and restricting the sale of arms.[5] Both measures were fiercely resisted by the Parnellites in parliament, while, outside, the league

[1] DA/1; see below, p. 505.
[2] P.R.O., H.O. 144/5/17869/67.
[3] *Hansard 3*, cclxii, 1657–9.
[4] 44 & 45 Vict., c.4 (2 Mar.).
[5] 44 & 45 Vict., c. 5 (21 Mar.).

prepared itself to withstand coercion and the expected flood of evictions. Davitt's successor in office, Dillon, of all the league chiefs was closest to him in spirit, though without his organising genius and his power of sustained exertion. Under Parnell's leadership Dillon contributed to the struggle both in the country and in parliament an intensity of self-abandoned passion comparable with Davitt's own. On a tactical level he urged league branches to declare a rent strike on estates where the landlord had made himself particularly obnoxious. If rents were reduced to the point where the tenants regarded them as just they should be paid, but the rule—pay in a body or refuse to pay in a body—must be observed. The wider the area subjected to a rent strike, the more effective the strike would be; and in the last resort, Dillon felt, a nation-wide strike might become necessary. Another close colleague of Davitt's, Brennan, developing his emergency plans, recommended branches to appoint shadow executives, to take the place of existing executives if their members should be arrested.[1]

Following up an initiative of Davitt's,[2] Parnell called on branches to take an active part in the forthcoming elections to boards of guardians, with the object of replacing agents, bailiffs, and landlord nominees with league candidates (1 March). The result was a significant increase in the tenant element on these boards, marking an important stage in a process which, within a few years, was to bring most of them, outside Ulster, under tenant control.[3] A suggestion of the league (8 February) that Parnell should conduct another campaign in America was rejected by the executive at its Paris meeting. In an open message from Paris (13 February) Parnell assured the league that American support would continue so long as the Irish people by their own exertions showed themselves worthy of it; and declared that it was his duty to remain at his post as leader at home and at Westminster. He summed up the responsibility of the tenant farmers as (1) to maintain their unity and organisation, (2) to refuse to pay unjust rents, and (3) not to take farms from which others had been unjustly evicted. Should the government's land bill fail to settle the land question, there would seem to be two courses open to the parliamentary party: withdrawal in a body from the house of commons, and 'deepening the lines and widening the area' of the agitation. Dismissing the former alternative, Parnell advocated the policy of a 'junction' between Irish nationalism and British democracy that Davitt had urged on

[1] *F.J.*, 9 Feb., 3 Mar.; above, p. 444.

[2] Above, p. 442.

[3] *F.J.*, 1, 3 Mar. See William F. Feingold, 'The tenants' movement to capture the Irish poor law boards, 1877-1886' in *Albion*, vii, no. 3 (fall 1975), pp 216-31.

1 February.[1] The most tangible result of this suggestion was a new organisation, the National Land League of Great Britain, modelled on the home league, to which it was to be an independent auxiliary, with the same general objects, but with the special aim of informing the working classes of Britain about the Irish land question and their community of interests with those of the Irish tenant farmers. It was inaugurated in London on 25 March under the presidency of Justin McCarthy, vice-chairman of the parliamentary party; at a meeting next day an executive committee that included Parnell, Biggar, Sexton, and Arthur O'Connor was elected, and Frank Byrne was appointed general secretary. From this beginning the new auxiliary spread over England and Scotland, recruited largely from Irish immigrants, closely identified with the Home Rule Confederation, and largely run by stalwarts of that body such as John Barry and John Ferguson. H. M. Hyndman, the mentor of British working men in Marxian socialism, who founded the Democratic (from 1883 the Social Democratic) Federation in June 1881 on a basis of hostility to coercion in Ireland, served on the executive of the Land League of Great Britain.[2] But the idea of an alliance between Irish nationalists and the British working classes did not materialise, and appears to have been proposed by Parnell simply as a tactical move.[3]

With the coercion act on the statute book, the continued existence of the league was threatened. It was now that Davitt's brain child, the Ladies' Land League, under the energetic leadership of the indomitable Anna Parnell, came conspicuously into action not only in providing support for families of evicted and imprisoned tenants and relief for unemployed labourers but also in the general work of the league. This drew upon the ladies a heavy rebuke from the archbishop of Dublin and the bishop of Ardagh. 'The daughters of our catholic people', Archbishop McCabe declared in a pastoral read in the Dublin churches on 13 March, 'be they matrons or virgins, are called forth, under the flimsy pretext of charity, to take their stand in the noisy arena of public life'. 'They are asked to forget the modesty of their sex and the high dignity of their womanhood by leaders who seem utterly reckless of consequences.' To this A. M. Sullivan, whose wife was a leading member of the Ladies' Land League, replied with an indignant defence of the ladies and, strict catholic though he was, sustained censure of McCabe: 'in plain truth his grace . . . does not

[1] Above, p. 461.
[2] Hyndman, *Record of an adventurous life* (1911), pp 255–7.
[3] *F.J.*, 26, 28 Mar.; *Irishman*, 2 Apr.; *Fall*, pp 227–9, 306–8, 448–9; C. C. O'Brien, *Parnell*, pp 62–3.

like the Land League or Mr Parnell, and that is the whole story' (14 March). Many of the bishops shared this view and were seriously embarrassed by McCabe's pastoral. At an episcopal meeting on 15 March it was proposed that, on political questions on which bishops held divergent views no bishop should make any public pronouncement, and that the minority should be bound by the decision of the majority. McCabe absolutely rejected any such restriction: in addressing his clergy and people he would be bound by no authority save that of the Holy Father. The proposal was dropped, and the freedom this left to individual bishops was at once exercised by the irrepressible Croke, in an open letter (17 March) to Sullivan:

I adopt, unreservedly, the sentiments you have so admirably expressed, and am delighted to find that someone of mark has at last stepped forward from the ranks of the laity to vindicate the character of the good Irish ladies who have become land leaguers and to challenge publicly the monstrous imputations cast upon them by the archbishop of Dublin. His grace will not be allowed in future, I apprehend to . . . ventilate unquestioned the peculiar political theories which he is known to hold in opposition to the cherished convictions of a great, and indeed, overwhelming majority of the Irish priests and people.[1]

Anna Parnell and her co-workers were neither abashed by Archbishop McCabe's strictures nor intimidated by the regime of coercion which began with the arrest of thirty-five minor land-leaguers (all male) in March.[2] Coercion was to be maintained by Forster with energy, determination, and distaste for the next fourteen months, without bringing the disorder in the country under control. During the second quarter of 1881 arrests rose steeply,[3] but so did agrarian outrages, while landlords, anticipating the restrictions on their legal rights provided for in the land bill that Gladstone introduced on 7 April, and emboldened by the new powers given to the government by the coercion act, evicted tenants for non-payment of rent on a scale unprecedented for any quarter since the land war began.[4] This set a pattern that broadly was to continue throughout the Forster regime. At the same time the action of the central executive was seriously weakened by the removal of Davitt's organising genius and power of control, by Egan's absence in Paris, and by the arrest of two other key men, Dillon (2 May) and Brennan (23 May). Dillon was far from being on Davitt's level as head of organisation,[5] but his successor, Sexton, was a disaster. He broke down under the strain of overwork and anxiety caused by

[1] *F.J.*, 7, 12, 16, 18 Mar.; *Fall*, pp 299-301, 314-15. Larkin, *The Roman Catholic church and the modern Irish state*, pp 96-102; Tierney, *Croke of Cashel*, pp 12-16.

[2] *List of all persons detained in prison under the statute 44 Vict., c. 4*, H.C. 1881 (171), lxxvi, 671-6 (Mar. 81).

[3] Ibid., pp 677-718 (Apr.-June 81).

[4] Appendix F.

[5] See above, pp 465, 480.

the rapidly expanding demands on the central organisation, and had to resign early in October.[1] During his tenure of office the league's executive became an object of attack, most ferociously voiced by James Daly in his *Connaught Telegraph*, on grounds of incompetence, negligence, and corruption.[2] Sexton's place was taken by Arthur O'Connor, who found the business of the league in great confusion but was in office only ten days (10–20 October) when the league was suppressed by the government.[3]

The league was threatened not only by external coercion and internal weakness but, also, and perhaps still more, by the implications of Gladstone's land bill, which was not only a great remedial measure but was also intended to deprive the league of its *raison d'être*. It provided for the setting-up of a commission of three, and the appointment of sub-commissions, to determine, as between landlords and tenants, the fair rent of agricultural holdings for periods of fifteen years; it gave security of tenure to tenants whose rents were so determined so long as these rents were paid; and it entitled tenants to sell their interest in their holdings for the best price they could get. Thus legalising the 3 Fs, it fulfilled the hopes of generations of moderate land-reformers and justified the fears of die-hard defenders of the rights of property. It improved on the land-purchase provisions of Gladstone's 1870 land act,[4] raising the proportion of the purchase price that might be advanced to tenants from two-thirds to three-quarters and retaining the repayment terms of the 1870 act. But, far from contemplating the compulsory conversion of all tenants into owners—the 'abolition of landlordism'—it provided for the development of a system of dual ownership by landlords and tenants alongside the existing landlord system. It thus failed to concede the Land League's basic demand, it threatened to divide the ranks of the tenants, and was just such a measure as Davitt had long been preparing the league and the country to reject as a settlement of the land question. It was, moreover, immensely complicated and open to criticism at many points even from those who saw it as potentially an inestimable boon for the tenants. Parnell's reaction to it was cold, cautious, and calculating: to show no gratitude and accept no responsibility for it and to be sceptical of its workability; without supporting it in principle to endeavour by amending it to make it as beneficial as possible for the tenants; while not endangering its eventual passing, to try to prevent it from undermining the league and his own authority.

Broadly this approach was endorsed by the national convention of

[1] *S.C.P.*, ix, 164–5.

[2] Palmer, *Land League*, p. 281.

[3] *S.C.P.*, viii, 416.

[4] See above, p. 119.

the league, which, long contemplated,[1] met in the Rotunda, Dublin, on 21-2 April, attended by over 1000 delegates. The convention's first decision was to call on the government to release Davitt—'the brave soldier of liberty, the patriot of humanity'—to whom the Irish nation owed a debt of gratitude that could never be repaid. Regarding the bill as wrong in principle, it pledged its members to continue the struggle for the complete emancipation of the tenant farmers. But it endorsed Parnell's proposal that the Irish parliamentary party should endeavour, at the committee stage of the bill, to secure amendments on arrears of rent and other problems, and in the event of failure to do so should work for the rejection of the bill. There was some intransigent resistance to this veiled decision to make the best of the bill. Brennan adhered to the view that the bill should be wholly rejected. Dillon argued that unless provision were made in it to wipe out the arrears of rent, the party should vote against it on the third reading. As it stood it would do nothing for the small farmers, who had started the land movement, had borne the burden and heat of the day, and were now 'steeped in arrears'. The large farmers, who had been late in joining the movement and whom alone the bill might be expected to benefit, were preparing to support it and leave their impoverished brethren to their fate. But even if the bill were improved as suggested, it stood condemned because it was based on the wrong principle; and Dillon recalled a saying of Davitt's (at Gurteen, on 2 November 1879)[2] that fixity of tenure meant fixity of landlordism. What the league had all along demanded was that every farmer should be made the owner of the farm he occupied.[3]

It was in the context of the conflict of opinion within the Land League thus indicated that Parnell conducted his subtle and devious parliamentary campaign during the months of intensive debate on the bill that followed. While only a few of the amendments he and his colleagues pressed for were accepted (the 'Healy clause', providing that a tenant's improvements should not be taken into account in assessing a fair rent, being by far the most important), they prefigured most of the land reforms to be enacted by parliament during the next quarter of a century. And Parnell's tactics helped to ensure that no substantial concessions were made to the landlords. When the bill reached its third reading on 29 July the home-rulers, except Parnell himself and six of his followers who abstained, voted with the government. The attempt of the lords to emasculate it by 'shoals of amendments' was largely defeated by the firmness and ingenuity of the

[1] See above, pp 437, 439, 460.
[2] See above, p. 000.
[3] *F.J.*, 21, 22-3 Apr.; *Nation*, 30 Apr.

government, and the bill became law on 22 August substantially as planned by its author.[1] Welcomed by all the moderate elements in the land movement, including the bishops[2] and the clergy, most of the parliamentary party, and the *Freeman's Journal*, and denounced by all the extremist elements, including the *Irish World* and a large body of Irish-American opinion, the land act posed a problem for Parnell that he met by advising the tenants not to resort to the land court until it had reached decisions on a number of test cases which it would be the duty of the league to select, after the whole question had been considered by a further convention of the league, to be held in mid-September.[3]

By that date Parnell had strengthened his position as leader by founding a weekly newspaper under his direct control, *United Ireland*. This was the outcome of negotiations with Richard Pigott for the buying-out of his weeklies, the *Irishman*, the *Flag of Ireland*, and the *Shamrock*, an object that had long been sought by nationalist leaders (including Davitt) who thoroughly distrusted the owner and editor of these self-appointed organs of advanced nationalism.[4] On 2 August Pigott sold his papers for £3,500 to the Irish National Newspaper and Publishing Company Ltd, which had been formed for the purpose by Parnell, Egan, Biggar, Justin McCarthy, Dr Kenny, Richard Lalor, and William O'Brien. O'Brien, who had made his reputation as an intense and highly articulate nationalist on the staff of the *Freeman's Journal*, and was wholly committed to Parnell's leadership, was appointed editor of *United Ireland*; from its first appearance (replacing the *Flag of Ireland*) on 13 August, it established itself as the intransigent exponent and defender of Parnellite policy.[5]

On 20 August, near the end of the parliamentary session, Parnell seized an opportunity to move in committee of supply that Davitt's rearrest was not warranted by his conduct since his release, and that the duration and nature of the imprisonment he had previously suffered warranted his liberation now. This precipitated a long and fierce debate in which Harcourt and Forster vehemently defended the government's action against Davitt, and leading members of the Irish party as vehemently attacked it and paid glowing tribute to Davitt as a man and a patriot.[6]

[1] 44 & 45 Vict., c. 49. Davitt makes the astonishing statement in *Defence*, p. 262, that the house of lords succeeded in removing the 'Healy clause', but it is, in fact, pt II, sect. VIII (9) of the act.

[2] See their statements of 26 Apr. and 28 Sept. in *F.J.*, 28 Apr., 29 Sept.

[3] Lyons, *Parnell*, pp 158–64; Hamilton, *Diary*, i, 126–61; Eversley, *Gladstone and Ireland*, ch. XV; see below, pp 492–4.

[4] See above, pp 245–6, 281.

[5] *S.C.P.*, i, 456; N.L.I., MS 8580 (8); *Irishman*, 6 Aug.; *Fall*, pp 332–3; W. O'Brien, *Recollections*, ch. XIII.

[6] *Hansard 3*, cclxv, 510–51.

Parnell opened the debate with a review of Davitt's political behaviour since his release from Dartmoor. He quoted from nine of his speeches between 21 November and 16 January to show that they were characterised by moderation and by admonitions to refrain from illegality and outrage. His power as a public speaker, his earnestness and energy, his wonderful belief in his cause, his great influence with Irishmen, all would doubtless have earned him arrest, but the government might have detained him under the coercion act in an honourable manner instead of resorting to the mean and contemptible expedient of revoking his licence. Harcourt, in defence of the government, quoted the 'pen' letter (15 December 1869), recalled the horror it had aroused in the trial judge (18 July 1870),[1] and attributed to it the severity of the sentence on Davitt. Why the late government had released him, or why it had waived the condition of reporting to the police, Harcourt did not know and regretted that no responsible member of the opposition was present to explain. Being at large by special grace and favour Davitt had been under the greater obligation to behave himself; his position had resembled that of a prisoner of war who, liberated on parole, was bound in honour not to make war on the enemy. Yet after a year of release he had returned from America an avowed fenian,[2] with the Land League, modelled on the fenian organisation, and intimately related to it, in his pocket. He would like to see a disavowal of fenianism from gentlemen opposite, but that would be very inconvenient for them and might stop American supplies to the league. Davitt and other members of both the league and the fenian organisation spoke with two voices: with one, professing to be the most innocent and quiet people in the world, they preached excellent sermons; with another they threatened civilised society with speeches such as Davitt's at Kilbrin. Would any government tolerate such language from a fenian convict? He was convinced that Davitt had founded and conducted the Land League as an instrument of fenianism. If the government had not arrested him it would have been said that they were afraid of him and his 'braggart talk'. The atrocious language of these 'assassin conspirators' was just as detestable to the American as to the British government.[3]

In Davitt's defence Healy contended that Forrester had been discredited by his own story of the 'pen' letter and that circumstances suggested that he was an informer.[4] It was the present government,

[1] Above, pp 60-61, 102.

[2] Harcourt quoted from Davitt's speech at Milltown (15 June 1879; see above, pp 306-7) as evidence of this.

[3] Notes for Harcourt's speech are in Bodleian Library, Harcourt papers, home office general correspondence, 1881, dep. 95, pp 17-27.

[4] See above, pp 62, 111.

not its predecessor, that had dropped the proceedings in the queen's bench against Davitt.[1] It had shown malignity in revoking his ticket of leave instead of arresting him under the coercion act. Though he was in prison, Davitt's name had a potency with his countrymen that the government would have reason to regret. Justin McCarthy expressed high admiration for him: 'he combined a remarkable power of practical organisation down to the mastery of the meanest detail with a certain antique grandeur of patriotic purpose'. He was better qualified to keep the peace in Ireland amid the hottest agitation than a hundred ministers holding such views as Harcourt's. John Barry, who claimed to be one of Davitt's oldest friends, pointed out that the Land League, far from being modelled on the fenian organisation, had been angrily denounced by fenians just because of its open and constitutional character. Philip Callan, an anti-Parnellite and anti-Land League home-ruler said that nothing would tend to produce goodwill and commend the land bill in Ireland more than Davitt's release. J. A. Blake, who was similarly opposed to the league, believed that if Davitt had not been arrested Forster would have had a much easier task and Kilmainham jail would not contain so many suspects. F. H. O'Donnell accused Harcourt of gross misrepresentation in associating the Land League with the dynamite school merely because some extremists had joined in the agitation, and he drew a telling parallel with the movement of national liberation in Italy, which Harcourt so much admired. T. P. O'Connor asked whether there was any other state in Europe, apart from Russia, where a man, released from prison for a political offence, could be again imprisoned for the same offence. No man was more imbued with 'pure and honest political feeling' than Davitt.

Forster wound up the debate with a short speech endorsing Harcourt's case in much more sober tones, but conceding that Davitt's language occasionally showed a nobility of feeling which prompted the hope that some day he might become a more useful member of society. No doubt there was much in his early life for which allowance should be made in judging him. But at the time of his arrest it was clear to the government that he was 'the main conductor' of an agitation that endangered life and property, perhaps more than he intended. If they had allowed a convict with an unexpired sentence to be a principal instigator of disorder, their efforts to restore order would not have been taken seriously by the public.

The debate was listened to by a very thin house, and on a division Parnell's motion was lost by 61 votes to 19.

[1] Above, p. 364.

Healy's damning reference to Forrester in the debate was probably the cause of two letters to the *Freeman* of 22 and 23 August from Forrester himself, then apparently in Dublin. Denying that it was his evidence that had convicted Davitt in 1870, he implied that the conviction was wholly due to the evidence of the informer, Corydon. He offered 'a few facts' about the trial that were a tissue of lies, misrepresentations, and conceit, and went well with his fatuous demand that Gladstone, Forster, and Harcourt should 'produce the full minutes of the evidence' on which Davitt had been convicted; for Davitt's continued imprisonment was 'weighing upon the souls of his friends'.[1] Forrester was obviously no less vain, foolish, and self-deceived than when, a decade before, he had had so malign an influence on Davitt's career.

The first substantial piece of news to reach Davitt in Portland was brought by two unexpected visitors, Archbishop Croke of Cashel and one of his diocesan bishops, William Fitzgerald, of Ross, on 8 September. They had applied to Harcourt only four days beforehand for permission, which had immediately been granted.[2] Croke, apparently without expostulation from Governor Clifton, conveyed to Davitt the gist of the land act, and the impression that he wanted Davitt to agree with his own and Parnell's opinion that, while the agitation should be kept up pending a final settlement in accordance with the programme of the league, the act should be given a fair trial as an instalment of justice to the tenants. Davitt, of course, fully approved of continuing the agitation but was unwilling to commit himself to even a qualified approval of the act, being ignorant of its full scope. He objected to it on the fundamental ground that it sought to reconcile the irreconcileable interests of 'a rent-extracting landlord who produced nothing and a rent-paying tenant who produced everything'. The act seemed to offer some relief to the large farmers—those best able to take care of themselves—but, lacking any effective remedy for the problem of accumulated arrears of rent, left the poorer tenants—the majority—unprotected against a crushing burden. The commissioners and sub-commissioners appointed under the act were apparently all lawyers and land agents—'a nice lot of rogues into whose hands farmers and landlords have been placed by Mr Gladstone's second attempt to patch up a peace in the agrarian war of Ireland'. The general effect of the act, he thought, would be to plague the country with litigation and leave the land question where it was.[3]

[1] *F.J.*, 22 Aug. 81.
[2] P.R.O., H.O. 144/5/17869/70.
[3] DA/1, ff 255-5^{v}, 261-2.

This criticism of the land act, recorded in Davitt's prison journal, was in agreement with the views that Brennan, Dillon, and other hard-line critics of the act within the Land League had been, and were, expressing. In later years Davitt was to admit that he and his colleagues underestimated the value of what he called Gladstone's 'remedial set-off to coercion'.

In a time of less passion in Ireland, the magnitude and importance of the measure would have been more fully recognised and acknowledged by the Irish leaders, for the bill was a legislative sentence of death by slow processes against Irish landlordism.[1]

Its introduction of dual ownership made the position of the landlords progressively less attractive, and this soon led to legislation, promoted by conservative governments, extending and improving its land purchase provisions and thus facilitating the buying-out of their holdings by tenants, a development that eventually achieved the essential purpose of the Land League. But in his prison reflections on the act, Davitt did not foresee this long-term result. In any case he no longer looked to occupying ownership as the goal of the land movement. Instead he became convinced that the 'abolition of landlordism' could only be truly realised by the abolition of private ownership of land altogether. He had travelled a long way in his thinking since his part-authorship of the programme adopted by the land conference of 29 April 1880.[2] He can hardly have communicated his new vision to Croke, for the archbishop, who described him as 'that sagest, that truest, that best, that most patriotic of men' brought out of Portland the belief that Davitt had expressed approval of the land act.[3]

Davitt's health continued to be good,[4] and as he told his sister Sabina in a letter of 14 November, his spirits were 'considerably above proof'. He sent her a draft for $100 for 'Christmas comforts' and showed a caring interest in his two married sisters, their husbands and families. He was anxious to know whether 'the future candidate for the presidency', his nephew and namesake 'of noisy reputation', was able to talk. Michael Davitt Crowley,[5] son of Anne and Edward, was aged three, and now had a sister, Kathleen, born at Manayunk on 13 November 1880, three days after Davitt's second visit to America had ended with his departure from New York. Mary and Neil, at Scranton, had had a ninth child, Elizabeth, born to them on 1 March 1879; as their seventh, Michael, like their firstborn, had died in infancy,

[1] *Fall*, p. 317.
[2] *Nation*, 29 Nov., 31 Dec.; above, pp 374–5.
[3] DA/1, ff 261-2; *Nation*, 10, 17 Sept.; *United Ireland*, 10, 17 Sept.; *Irishman*, 15 Oct. p. 243.
[4] P.R.O., H.O. 144/5/17869/72.
[5] See above, p. 230.

they now had seven children, ranging from two to fifteen, to fend for, and their life continued to be a grinding struggle.[1] But the eldest child, James, was now an apprentice in the printing office of the *Scranton Times*.[2] Sabina herself, aged thirty-one, was still unmarried, and was to remain so. Davitt's only literate sister, she had established herself in a clerical post and was in relatively comfortable circumstances. She wished to visit her brother, and Michael suggested that she should spend a month or six weeks in Europe visiting Portland, Haslingden, and Ireland in the summer of 1882. In six months he would send her the price of a return ticket; and he hoped that she could take back with her to Manayunk all his personal belongings, at present in the keeping of the Misses Walshe, whom he was anxious to relieve of the inconvenience. Sabina agreed to this plan.[3]

Permission to visit Davitt was again sought by Frances Sullivan, in November. Harcourt had recently refused similar requests from J. J. Louden and Alfred Webb; and though he told Mrs Sullivan that it would be too great a departure from the prison rules to allow her another visit then, he encouraged her to apply later (22 November). Soon afterwards he turned down an application from Rev. Harold Rylett, unitarian minister of Moneyrea, County Down, and a prominent land-leaguer, with whom Davitt had become friendly during his campaigning in Ulster in December 1880.[4] Davitt remained unvisited from 8 September to 10 January, the longest interval between any two visits he had experienced while in Portland. This seems not to have irked him; he was well aware of his privileged position. To the pleasure of working in his garden, the companionship of the birds ('a most interesting lot of chums they are and no mistake'), and virtually unrestricted reading (except on current affairs), he was now allowed to add the satisfaction of daily writing. He enjoyed the splendid views of sea and land, of chalky cliffs and wave-beaten coastline, that the commanding position of the prison offered.[5] Above all he appreciated the personality and behaviour of the prison governor: 'we have not as yet', he wrote in mock-heroic style on 1 January 1882, 'been introduced to the governor, but a gentleman named Mr Clifton has never ceased to treat us in a most kind and gentlemanly manner since the time of our arrival'.[6]

[1] See above, pp 22-3, 169, 170-71.

[2] *Portrait and biographical record of Lackawanna county, Pennsylvania* (New York and Chicago, 1897), p. 342.

[3] Sabina Davitt to D, 14 Nov. 81, 11 Apr. 82 (DP/A3).

[4] P.R.O., H.O. 144/5/17869/72, 77, 78, 80; DP/UU; *Nation*, 29 Nov., 31 Dec. 81; above, p. 446.

[5] See his word-picture in *Leaves*, ii, 255.

[6] DA/1, f. 254v.

Nevertheless, on 25 December 1881 he could not help reflecting ruefully that it was his eighth Christmas day spent in prison, and that he had to count on three more before he would be due for release. As often before he saw himself as a man prone to misfortune. Nevertheless

as the widow said when being condoled with on the death of her husband, 'there is no help for misfortune but to marry again'; and, translated to apply to my situation, there is nothing for it but to 'bate no jot of heart or hope' in the service of justice and humanity, in prison or out.[1]

On new year's day he recalled:

On January 1st 1872 I was 'doing bread and water in Dartmoor.[2] As I am privileged to write this in the prison infirmary, Portland, I have, in the space of ten years passed . . . from the 'chokey' to the 'farm'. It's a sign of progress.[3]

His mood as he contemplated 1882 was calm and hopeful.

May this year, which recalls a bright little chapter of Irish history [1782], bring peace and some prospect of prosperity to poor distracted Ireland, and may it see tyranny and injustice humbled throughout the world, to the exaltation of justice and the cause of humanity. Amen.[4]

Frances Sullivan on 2 January renewed her request to visit Davitt, which Harcourt at once granted, though refusing a plea from Lizzie Kenny for permission to accompany her.[5] The fifteen-minute interview was held on 10 January in the governor's room and in his presence, but he did not intervene except when 'dangerous subjects' were mentioned. Mrs Sullivan found Davitt in excellent health and spirits. He presented her with a bouquet of pansies and wallflowers from his garden, in which he took intense pleasure. A thrush that had become his domestic pet and companion had left him, but its place had been taken by a sparrow, which had nested just outside his cell and came in every day to be fed. He knew nothing of what was going on outside apart from having heard of the assassination of President Garfield (who had died on 19 September). He wondered why Dr Kenny had not been to see him again, and Mrs Sullivan (as she admitted to Harcourt) divulged the fact that he, along with Parnell, Dillon, and O'Kelly, were 'under Mr Forster's protection'. Davitt also, it would seem, learnt from her that a no-rent manifesto had been issued by the league's executive.[6] He spoke of Forster as 'a thoroughly good-natured man', but, 'the best-intentioned statesman in the world would be ruined by a few months' contact with Dublin Castle'. He asked whether any of 'the ladies' had

[1] DA/1, ff 241–2^{v}.
[2] See above, p. 158. Davitt wrote '1871', but this was an obvious slip.
[3] DA/1, f. 253.
[4] Ibid.
[5] P.R.O., H.O. 144/5/17869/83, 84; DP/UU.
[6] Below, pp 494–5.

been arrested, and was glad to learn that Anna Parnell was still 'to the fore'. He had still not seen the land act, and knowing only what the archbishop had told him about it could neither approve nor disapprove of it. He was very eager to study it and also *Hansard* for last session, which, as 1881 had now passed into history, Harcourt might be prepared to regard as off the forbidden list. He showed a passionate concern about outrages on people and animals, which Mrs Sullivan admitted to be still prevalent in Ireland; and with great energy and vehemence denounced the perpetrators of deeds that, under the name of agrarianism, were simply private crime. In particular, the maiming and mutilation of animals was a crime so cruel and cowardly that it could not be too severely punished.

Some of this Mrs Sullivan conveyed to the press, with the further information that piles of Christmas cards and presents addressed to him were lying in the prison undelivered. Alfred Webb had inquired on 14 December whether Davitt would be allowed to receive Christmas cards, and Harcourt had given the non-committal reply that all communications must conform to the prison rules.[1] What happened to the accumulation of Davitt's Christmas mail is not known. Mrs Sullivan did not refer to it in her letter to Harcourt about her visit, though she did not conceal her feelings about Davitt's imprisonment.

> I wish Dublin castle was pulled down and all the officials paid off. The best Englishman would be spoiled there. Drummond was a Scotchman but I fear there are few like him. I am quite sure that Mr Davitt could have kept more peace and order than all the soldiers and police in Ireland.

She conveyed Davitt's plea for *Hansard* and offered to provide it herself if permission were granted.[2] Permission was eventually granted (Harcourt sardonically told the house of commons that reading *Hansard* would be an additional punishment[3]), but the nine volumes for 1881 did not reach Portland till just after Davitt's release on 6 May.[4]

The second national convention on the land act, held at the Rotunda on 15-17 September 1881, had declared through innumerable voices and with strong professions of loyalty to Davitt's teaching, that it condemned the act, based as it was on the principle of a joint proprietorship of landlord and tenant in the soil. No settlement could be satisfactory that did not abolish landlordism 'root and branch'. At the

[1] P.R.O., H.O. 144/5/17869/81.

[2] Frances Sullivan's notes of her interview with D [10 Jan. 82] (DP/UU); Frances Sullivan to Harcourt, 10 Jan. (DP/UU; P.R.O., H.O. 144/5/17869/83); DA/1, f. 261; *Nation*, 14, 21 Jan.; *Irishman*, 14 Jan., p. 460.

[3] *Hansard 3*, cclxvii, 1277 (20 Mar.).

[4] *S.C.P.*, ix, 394.

same time the mood of the delegates was overwhelmingly in favour of not missing any advantages the act might have to offer. A representative of the *Irish World*, speaking for 'a great Irish-American constituency', protested against any compromise with the land act, and a telegram from Patrick Ford, in the name of eight hundred branches of the American league, called on the convention to 'unfurl the banner of no rent' and to 'hold the harvest' if they did not wish to dishearten American supporters. Nevertheless, after tough and protracted debate extending over most of its first and second days, the convention adopted two resolutions embodying Parnell's plan of 'testing the act':[1] the league should bring a number of selected cases before the land court, while the farmers should refrain from entering into engagements to pay rent for a longer period than one year. This was the most crucial decision of the convention. Other resolutions, carried without opposition, ranged over a wide field. Ireland's right to self-government was affirmed, coercion was denounced, and the release of Davitt, 'the pioneer of the land movement', and all others imprisoned for the same cause was demanded. Much of the third day was devoted to the claims of labour. Parnell strongly contended that it was the duty as well as the interest of the farmers to promote better housing and better treatment for agricultural labourers, who had rendered such valuable services to the land movement. The landlords were simulating interest in their welfare in an effort to detach them from the farmers, yet the labourers had manfully withstood temptation and now were entitled to their reward. Farmers should make as much use as possible of the clause in the land act facilitating the assignment of plots to, and the building of cottages for, agricultural labourers.[2] Pending further legislation to enable labourers to become owners of land, each farmer should set aside half an acre for every 25 acres of tilled land (or the grass of a cow) for the use of each labourer employed on his farm and a member of the league, and the rent payable by the labourer for his plot should not exceed that paid by the farmer to his landlord. Irish M.P.s were requested to press for the inclusion, in the county government bill promised for next session, of provisions empowering county boards to acquire land by compulsory purchase for the benefit of labourers and to undertake arterial drainage and other works of public improvements that would stimulate the demand for labour. All members of the league were recommended to use Irish-manufactured goods and

[1] See above, p. 485.

[2] Sect. XVIII, XIX, and XXXI; these provisions were extended by an act of 18 Aug. 82 'to amend the provisions of the Land Law (Ireland) Act, 1881, relating to labourers' cottages and allotments'. Davitt was wrong in stating (*Fall*, p. 768) that the land act of 1881 did nothing for agricultural labourers.

all branches to encourage home industries. To enable the league 'to keep pace with' the movement for developing Ireland's resources and fostering her industry the executive of the league was authorised to establish 'an industrial and labour department' in the central office. As a demonstration that 'the industrial and labour movements' were now 'under the supervision and within the jurisdiction' of the league, its title was expanded to read 'Irish National Land League and Industrial Union'. Finally, the 'rules for the guidance of branches'[1] were amended: (1) the membership subscription was redefined as one shilling a year for each £5 of valuation; (2) each branch should transmit its funds to headquarters as soon as they were collected, deducting only one quarter, instead of one half, for local expenses. The latter change was made necessary, Parnell explained, because during the previous year branches had retained as much of their income as they pleased, transmitting to the central executive only from 20 per cent to 25 per cent.[2]

It seemed to Forster that Parnell's object was not really to test the land act but to defeat it, and he convinced Gladstone that the only alternative to allowing the Land League to usurp the government of Ireland was to arrest Parnell and the other leaders still at large. So Parnell was arrested on 13 October, to be followed to Kilmainham jail by Sexton and J. P. Quinn on the 14th, and by Dillon (who had been released on 7 August), William O'Brien, and James J. O'Kelly on the 15th.[3] The retort of the imprisoned leaders was a manifesto, in which, as the executive of the league 'forced to abandon the policy of testing the land act', they called on the tenant farmers 'to pay no rents under any circumstances to their landlords until the government relinquishes the existing system of terrorism and restores the constitutional rights of the people'. Written by O'Brien in his best pyrotechnic style, the manifesto was signed by Parnell, Kettle, Brennan, Dillon, and Sexton, all in Kilmainham, and in addition bore the names of Davitt and Egan. It declared that a rent strike was 'the one constitutional weapon' left in the hands of the league, but that it was 'the strongest, the swiftest, the most irresistible of all'. The farmers were assured that it was as lawful 'to refuse to pay rents as it is to receive them'; that against the passive resistance of an entire population military power had no weapons; that the government could no more evict, than it could imprison, the whole nation; that the funds of the league would be poured out unstintedly in support of all who might have to endure eviction; and that 'our exiled brothers in America may be relied upon

[1] Above, p. 426.
[2] *F.J.*, 16, 17, 19 Sept.; *Nation*, 24 Sept.; *Irishman*, 24 Sept.
[3] *F.J.*, 14, 15, 17 Oct.; Reid, *Forster*, ii, 339–55; Lyons, *Parnell*, pp 168–9.

to contribute, if necessary, as many millions of money as they have contributed thousands to starve out landlordism and bring English tyranny to its knees'.

Landlordism is already staggering under the blows which you have dealt it amid the applause of the world. One more crowning struggle for your land, your homes, your lives—a struggle in which you have all the memories of your race, all the hopes of your children, all the sacrifices of your imprisoned brothers, all your cravings for rent-enfranchised land, for happy homes and national freedom to inspire you—one more heroic effort to destroy landlordism at the very source and fount of its existence and the system which was and is the curse of your existence will have disappeared forever. The world is watching to see whether all your splendid hopes and noble courage will crumble away at the first threat of a cowardly tyranny.[1]

This sensational statement was issued to the public on 18 October by the central body of the league, at whose weekly meeting, presided over by Rev. James Cantwell (Archbishop Croke's administrator), it was read.[2] Its thinking, as distinct from its rhetoric, was that of the left wing in the Land League, headed by a group within the executive—Brennan, Egan, Kettle, and Sexton—which, for an obvious reason, was to be known as the 'Kilmainham party'. There was nothing new in the idea of a rent strike,[3] but two at least of those who signed the manifesto, Parnell and Dillon, were far from whole-hearted in launching one now; and Davitt, had it been possible to consult him, would probably have refused to sign it. Dillon's objection was that it was unrealistic, a declaration of war without the means of waging war. The attitude of Parnell, concerned, as he was, not only for the land movement but for his own position as national leader, is more difficult to interpret, but the weight of evidence[4] is all against his sharing the faith of the 'Kilmainham party' in the no-rent doctrine. The manifesto was, of course, vociferously acclaimed by advanced opinion at home and in America, but all the moderate elements in the land movement, including the great bulk of the catholic clergy, condemned it. The *Freeman's Journal*, predictably, voiced this condemnation, and the *Nation*, rather surprisingly, took the same line. It was no surprise that Archbishop McCabe denounced the manifesto as having 'at once assailed the eternal law of God and struck at the foundations on which society rests—the rights of property . . . If the notice to pay no rents be not the teaching of communism, communism is yet to be defined.'[5] But it came as a shock to land-leaguers when Archbishop Croke announced: 'against the committal of the people of this country . . . to the doctrine of non-payment of rent, though but for a specified time, I must, and

[1] *F.J.*, 19 Oct. [2] Ibid. [3] See above, pp 419, 480.
[4] Analysed in Lyons, *Parnell*, pp 172-5. [5] King, *Irish question*, pp 333-4.

hereby do, enter my solemn protest'. Nearly all the bishops except Nulty agreed with him.[1] Between the extremists who welcomed the manifesto and the moderates who rejected it Parnell had little room for manoeuvre. As a gesture to his left wing it served his interests, and since it was bound to fail it would not endanger whatever advantages the land act offered. In prison he could not be held responsible for its failure. Aware that the league was demoralised and disintegrating, he believed that the agitation was 'breaking fast',[2] and that it would subside in a few months, during which it would suit him politically to be imprisoned. After that he would be released, and would accept accomplished facts without loss of face. If while he was in prison his place was taken by 'Captain Moonlight'[3] that would be Forster's responsibility and would only enhance his own image.

Davitt, whose name was added to the manifesto by Brennan, relying on the intimate friendship between them, knew nothing of it till three months after it was issued. Interviewed about it in July 1882, two months after his release from Portland, he said: 'while I admit its great success so far as results are concerned, I think that it dulled a weapon which could have been used to give the final blow to landlordism'. Had the league waited until two or three hundred thousand tenant farmers were ready to obey it, a million people would have been evicted and a situation created in which the government would have been compelled to surrender.[4] This was a singularly ill-informed and unrealistic judgment. Davitt made a quite different assessment of the manifesto in 1903, when, viewing it in the perspective of his history of the land war, he described it as 'an act of desperation, prompted by the high-handed policy which had superseded the ordinary powers of the law'. It gave the impression of being also an act of retaliation on the part of a man 'unfairly fought by his assailants, who strikes back blindly and passionately', not 'a blow of cool and calculating purpose'. Davitt had urged Parnell and his parliamentary colleagues to strike just such a blow in January.[5] But now the land act had become law, the national leader was a prisoner, and the hour of opportunity had passed: 'the no-rent shell fired from Kilmainham would only demoralise and could not explode; its fuse had fallen off'.[6] This judgment is sound on the timing and effect of the manifesto, and also in regarding it as in some degree Parnell's reprisal for the outrage to his pride that his summary arrest inflicted. But that it was motivated by passion, rather than political calculation, on Parnell's

[1] Tierney, *Croke of Cashel*, p. 130.
[2] Lyons, *Parnell*, p. 175.
[3] Ibid., p. 168.
[4] Cashman, p. 229.
[5] Above, pp 457–9.
[6] *Fall*, pp 337–8.

part is hardly tenable. Writing in 1903, Davitt may well have been unduly influenced by his experience of the lengths to which wounded pride had driven Parnell in the last great crisis of his life.

The meeting of the league on 18 October was its last. To Forster the manifesto gave an 'excellent excuse'[1] for a step which he had hitherto hesitated to take, but which he now lost no time in taking. On 20 October he issued a proclamation, drafted with admirable terseness and clarity by the law officers, declaring the league to be 'an unlawful and criminal association', in that it had (A) sought to effect its purposes by (1) an organised system of intimidation, (2) attempting to obstruct process-serving and the execution of the queen's writs, (3) attempting to deter the queen's subjects from fulfilling their contracts, following their lawful callings, and generally exercising their lawful rights, and (B) that it had now avowed its intention to prevent the payment of all rent. The public was warned that all meetings to carry out the purposes of the league were unlawful and criminal, and would be prevented, and if necessary dispersed by force; and all persons who had become connected with the league were warned to disconnect themselves from it.[2] Forster had taken this action on his own responsibility, counting on Gladstone's backing. This he at once received, despite the fact that Gladstone, only a few months previously, had admitted in the house of commons: 'we are not able to say that, according to the actual law of the land, the Land League is an illegal organisation'.[3] Yet somewhat to Forster's surprise the proclamation was not challenged on legal grounds, and the central body of the Land League ceased to exist. Nearly all its leading men were either in prison or were shortly to be arrested; Egan, Biggar, Healy, T. P. O'Connor and Arthur O'Connor remained at large, but outside Ireland. There was talk of moving the headquarters to Holyhead, Liverpool, or Paris, but in fact the Ladies' Land League took over the functions of the suppressed body, operating from the league's offices in 39 Sackville Street and continuing to use, or dispersing, or destroying, the league's records.[4]

During the six months that followed the suppression of the league, Parnell's prediction that the agitation would quickly subside was no more fulfilled than Forster's hopes of eradicating the 'village tyrants'. Far from subsiding, the land war became more inflamed than ever as local leaders of the league were brought into the net of arrests in

[1] Forster to Gladstone, 20 Oct. (Reid, *Forster*, ii, 357).

[2] *Proclamation by the lord lieutenant of Ireland dated 20 October 1881* [C 3125], H.C. 1882, lv, 275–7.

[3] *Hansard 3*, cclxii, 111 (9 June).

[4] Reid, *Forster*, ii, 360–63; Arnold-Forster, Irish journal, 20–21 Oct.; *S.C.P.*, viii, 430–33; *Fall*, p. 339; Eversley, *Gladstone and Ireland*, pp 172–3.

increasing numbers. By the end of January 1882, 512 suspects were held in prison, though many of the original detainees had been released.[1] If Forster's theory about the 'village tyrants' being generally known to the police[2] had been sound, they should have constituted the bulk of the detainees, and agrarian outrages should have sharply declined. But in fact the detainees were local activists openly involved in carrying out the league's policy rather than terrorists and mere criminals who operated in secret; and the number of outrages in the last quarter of 1881 was only marginally lower than in that of 1880, the worst since the beginning of 1879. During the first quarter of 1882 there was some decrease in the total, but even so it was the third highest for the entire land war. Evictions, which had reached a peak in the summer of 1881, fell substantially during the last quarter of that year; yet their total for 1881 was higher than for any year since 1853. They rose to unprecedented heights during the first and second quarters of 1882,[3] which reflected the alarm of landlords at the rent reductions effected by the new land court, and their consequent reluctance to write off arrears.

The land court had begun its work on the day on which the Land League was proclaimed, and it was soon apparent, first that tenants were resorting to it in great numbers, ignoring the league's advice, and, second, that 'judicial rents' generally meant substantially reduced rents.[4] The land act was thus detaching from the league tenants who were not disqualified by arrears of rent from invoking it. At the same time the efforts of Anna Parnell and the Ladies' Land League to carry out the intended rent-strike proved that there was no general will among tenants to resist the payment of rents as such. The evicted tenants whose distress the ladies showed energy, audacity, and resourcefulness in relieving were poverty-stricken tenants unable to pay; tenants able to pay and refusing, in obedience to the manifesto, to do so were, in Anna Parnell's experience, a rare phenomenon. Indeed, one of the problems for the ladies was to prevent the money they disbursed for the relief from finding its way as rent into the pockets of the landlords.[5] Though much of their work was humanitarian—assisting

[1] *List of all persons detained in prison [on 1 February 1882] under the statute 44 Vict., c. 4*, H.C. 1882 (1), lv, 685–712.

[2] Above, p. 455.

[3] Appendix F.

[4] *Return of the number of cases lodged and disposed of in the court of the Irish land commission in each month from 1 October 1881 to 31 March 1882*, H.C. 1882 (171), lv, 311–14.

[5] For an account of Anna Parnell's astringent treatment of the land war—'The tale of a great sham'—see my article 'Anna Parnell and the Land League' in *Hermathena: a Dublin University review*, no. cxvii (1974), pp 5–17; and for an informative study of Anna Parnell and the Ladies Land League see R. F. Foster, *Parnell*, pp 260–84.

evicted familes, including the provision of temporary housing in the form of prefabricated wooden huts, and caring for imprisoned 'suspects' and their families, the militancy and recklessness of the ladies helped to keep the political temperature high and greatly aggravated Forster's difficulties: for example, with extreme nerve and ingenuity they maintained the circulation of *United Ireland*, which William O'Brien contrived to go on editing from Kilmainham, in the teeth of the government's efforts to suppress it, and after it had to be printed in various cities in England and Scotland, and in Paris. Forster was goaded into arresting some of the ladies and many more showed themselves eager for martyrdom.[1] The boast in the no-rent manifesto about financial support from America was partially vindicated: the third convention of the American Land League, held at Chicago on 30 November–2 December and attended by T. P. O'Connor, T. M. Healy, and Rev. Eugene Sheehy as delegates of the home league endorsed the manifesto; and Egan in Paris was able to keep the Ladies' Land League well supplied with American funds for sustaining the land war.[2] But all this could not conceal the fact that the no-rent manifesto was an egregious failure and the land act an increasing success.

The great defect of the act, as Parnell and the Land League had insistently pointed out during its passage through parliament, was that it left unprotected the large mass of small farmers who, overwhelmed by arrears, were the worst casualties of agricultural depression and land war combined. Over 100,000 such tenants were in arrears of rent for up to three years prior to 1881: they were therefore excluded from the benefits of the act, and were exposed to the danger of mass eviction on a scale unparalleled since the famine 'clearances'. In Parnell's opinion this was the root cause of the prevalent agrarian crime. The small and poor tenants, 'in self-protection' were 'banding themselves together to intimidate the larger tenants from paying'.[3]

Davitt had no more visitors after Mrs Sullivan; an application from Dr Kenny (17 February 1882) to visit him professionally was rejected by Harcourt,[4] who told the house of commons that Kenny was unfit to form an unprejudiced judgment on the effect of imprisonment on Davitt's health.[5] A request from Henry George, who was then

[1] Cashman, pp 231–3; *Defence*, pp 264–9; *Fall*, pp 340–42; W. O'Brien, *Recollections*, pp 376–85; S.P.O., R.P. 1883/25439.

[2] *Irishman*, 10 Dec. 81, p. 370; *Defence*, pp 147–8; 267–8; *Fall*, pp 340–41, 365–6, 373.

[3] R. B. O'Brien, *Parnell*, i, 386, quoting *S.C.P.*, vii, 45.

[4] Above, pp 477–8.

[5] *Hansard 3*, cclxvii, 1275–6 (20 Mar. 82).

campaigning in England on the land question, was also refused.[1] If news of the political world outside filtered through to Davitt there is no evidence of it. But in that world he was far from being forgotten. In Ireland, Britain, and America appreciative references to him and demands for his release were common form at public demonstrations of support for the land agitation. When A. M. Sullivan, who had suffered a heart attack the previous year, resigned his seat for Meath county early in 1882, the bishop of the diocese, Nulty, convened a meeting of his clergy at Navan on 14 February, at which Davitt was recommended for election if eligible, and, if not, Patrick Egan. On 22 February Davitt and Egan were both nominated, but when it was certain that there would be no third candidate Egan's nomination was withdrawn and Davitt was declared elected. The election was declared void by the house of commons because Davitt was a convict, and at a subsequent election, on 14 April, a home-ruler, Edward Sheil, was returned unopposed. But both in Meath and at Westminster the occasion drew out strong expressions of regard for Davitt. Very Rev. John Duncan, P.P. of Trim, declared his election to be a warning to government that the more they sought to degrade and persecute Davitt, the dearer he would be to the people of Ireland. Rev. Michael Woods, Navan, saw the election as a protest by the people of Meath against coercion and as a symbol of their resolve to carry out Davitt's programme of making the land the property of those who worked it. Although he was 'a pinioned eagle', he was 'the royal eagle of Meath . . . spreading his wings over the tenant farmers of Ireland and protecting them against their natural enemies'.[2]

A copy of the record of Davitt's conviction at Old Bailey in July 1870 was laid before the house of commons on 27 February,[3] and a debate ensued next day on the motion that he was incapable of being a member. Much of it turned on legal points, and the precedents of O'Donovan Rossa (1869) and John Mitchell (1875) were discussed. But politically the only important point raised was the plea that Davitt should be granted a free pardon and thus be enabled to take the place in parliament that his constituents sought for him. Joseph Cowen described him as one of those men who, in any great social and political upheaval, always came to the surface as embodying the ideas, hopes, and aspirations of people in the mass. Davitt articulated the feelings of the Irish peasantry. His courage, self-sacrifice, integrity,

[1] Henry George to Harcourt, 30 Mar. (P.R.O., H.O. 144/5/17869/90).

[2] *F.J.*, 23 Feb.; *Irishman*, 18, 25 Feb.; Walker, *Parliamentary election results*, p. 128.

[3] P.R.O., H.O. 144/5/17869/88; *Copy of the record of the conviction and of the judgment . . . against Michael Davitt and another . . . July 1870*, H.C. 1882 (66), lv, 147–60; *Hansard 3*, cclxvi, 1804–17 (27 Feb. 82).

and 'moral chivalry' had won for him the confidence of his colleagues and would ensure the undying gratitude of his country. His release would be the most effective message of peace the government could send to a disturbed and afflicted country. Cowen was the most conspicuous English supporter of the Land League; but the leader of the anti-Parnellite home-rulers, William Shaw, unexpectedly took the same line about Davitt. He had had several conversations with him, the last on the evening before his arrest, and he had seldom met anyone of such mental power, honesty, and earnestness. Shaw did not agree with all his views but he was certain that Davitt's presence in the house of commons would be 'of very great importance'. The motion was carried by 208 to 20.[1] Reflecting on the debate, one of Gladstone's private secretaries, E. W. Hamilton, noted in his diary: 'to Davitt no doubt is due the credit of the original organisation of the Land League, and . . . without him it never would have developed to the pitch it since has attained'. In releasing him in 1877, the late government, and more particularly Cross, Beaconsfield's home secretary, must bear a large share of responsibility for the evils of the land war.[2]

Davitt's health continued to be good during the rigours of a Portland winter,[3] and his morale remained unimpaired despite the prospect of three more solitary years in prison, so different from the gregarious existence Parnell and his friends were leading in Kilmainham. Since in fact he was to be released in a few months, it was probably more beneficial to him to be where he was than to have been with the others in Kilmainham; there, in a constant hubbub, he would have been unable to relax and would have had little opportunity for reading and still less for writing. As it was, he was able, in solitude, to view life philosophically, to recharge his mental batteries by reading and reflection, and to write his 'Jottings in solitary', substantial portions of which were to be published in 1885 as *Leaves from a prison diary*. The book is in the form of a series of 'lectures' to a young blackbird, which, rescued in the nick of time from the infirmary cat, had been presented to him by the governor soon after his arrival at Portland. He won the bird's confidence so successfully that 'Joe' would awaken him in the morning, perch on his plate as he ate his porridge, fetch and carry small objects like a well-trained dog, and spend the night on the post of his bedstead.[4] This was presumably the bird that Mrs

[1] *Hansard 3*, cclxvi, 1842–69 (28 Feb.).
[2] Hamilton, *Diary*, i, 232.
[3] P.R.O., H.O. 144/5/17869/87; *Nation*, 25 Mar.
[4] *Leaves from a prison diary, or lectures to a solitary audience* (2 vols, London, 1885), i, pp vii–viii.

Sullivan described as a thrush. In the autumn Joe had taken flight,[1] at just about the time that Davitt began his 'Jottings in solitary', so that Joe's role as the constant audience of Davitt's 'lectures' is largely imaginary. But Davitt's delight in the companionship of birds was a reality that recalls Francis of Assisi. 'You will be surprised', he wrote to his Aunt Ellen in Washington on 30 January, 'to learn that I have got a large family to look after'.

Perhaps you do not like sparrows? . . . There are few birds of which I am so fond as the self-sufficient, saucy little 'street arabs' of the feathered world. I am on the most intimate terms of friendship with about one hundred of the happiest, noisiest, most playful, and most love-making sparrows. . . . Never have I witnessed such scenes of love-making, successful wooing, and conjugal felicity as fall beneath my observation almost every day.[2]

He had now changed his mind about Sabina's visit: from what Mrs Sullivan had let slip about the Ladies' Land League he decided that Ireland in 1882 was too dangerous a place for his strong-minded and devoted sister, and therefore postponed her visit.[3] In April he received news from Sabina that Neil Padden, Mary's husband, had died at Scranton on 6 March after a short illness.[4] He at once obtained Governor Clifton's permission for a special letter to Mary, which he sent through Sabina, then in New York. The best way to show her regard for Neil's sterling qualities was not to yield to useless repining. Neil's life had been 'a sacrifice in the battle for daily bread' which all industrial workers were 'compelled to wage with the callous agencies of inhuman greed'. But worse might have happened. 'Your children are not helpless orphans while your life is spared . . . and while there are those living who will not see them in want so long as they are unable to provide for themselves'. He sent her a draft for $100 to help to meet immediate needs.

Let me know your plans, and be sure to tell me how I can assist you in furthering them. I shall not always be as helplessly placed as I now am, and when I am free again rely upon me to render you all assistance I can in supporting your family. Any debts that poor Neil may have contracted when out of work I will cheerfully pay.

He concluded with a characteristic admonition.

When we find ourselves confronted with misfortune it becomes a question of conquering or being conquered, and only those who lose hope in God and confidence in themselves are ever vanquished in the struggle. . . . Remember how bravely our poor mother acted when she had to provide for us all, how courageously she met every reverse and beat down despair in the darkest hour of trial.[5]

[1] Ibid., ii, 254–6. [2] D to Aunt Ellen, 30 Jan. 82 (DA/1, ff 296–7A).
[3] Ibid.; D to Sabina Davitt, 11 Apr. (DP/A3). [4] *Scranton Republican*, 17 Mar.
[5] D to Sabina Davitt and to Mary Padden, 24 Apr. (DP/A3).

Mary had in fact plenty of the same metal in her, as well as being shrewd and resourceful, and she successfully reared and educated all her seven surviving children, most of whom lived to a great age. Her eldest son, James, was to become a local personality in Scranton as proprietor of the popular and successful 'Padden's Hotel', which he opened in 1891 and where his mother lived with him till her death in 1905.[1]

Davitt's generosity in sending money to his sisters—it must have come out of his savings, which cannot have been very large—was matched by his fastidiousness about accepting money himself. Early in February, the Fifth Ward branch of the American Land League in New York placed to his credit in a New York savings bank the sum of $633, the proceeds of an entertainment the branch had organised. Davitt obtained special permission to reply to the letter conveying the news.

> Service on behalf of one's country is never truly noble or elevating unless accompanied by the conviction that we are the creditors and not the pensioners of our fatherland. As I am wholly unconscious of any pecuniary loss . . . that should call for such action as that of the Fifth Ward branch . . . on my account, neither can I imagine any contingency in my personal affairs as likely to arise pending my release from prison that will need any monetary assistance outside of my own resources.

For the past fifteen years he had considered himself as 'engaged for life in the service of Ireland'. If, while he was immobilised, a situation should arise in which the money in question could be regarded as representing service he would gladly render if at liberty, the Fifth Ward branch should use it in that context to advance the interests and well-being of the Irish people.[2] This rather convoluted refusal of a 'testimonial' to his public services set a precedent to which he was to adhere for the rest of his life. Two earlier and more ambitious attempts to reward him had come to nothing, apparently because their promoters had been persuaded that he would refuse the contemplated gift. The first was a proposal by the Society of St Patrick of Montreal to buy him a 'homestead' in that city; the second a fund started by a group of land-leaguers in Wicklow to buy him an estate in that county.[3] He seems not to have known of either attempt.

The process of self-education in which the years in Dartmoor had marked so important a stage was continued under incomparably more favourable conditions in Portland. Probably in no other period of

[1] *Portrait and biographical record of Lackawanna county, Pennsylvania*, p. 342; Scranton, Pa, Records of the Cathedral Cemetery.

[2] D to Hugh King, New York, 24 Feb. (DA/1, ff 340–40^{v}). *Nation*, 1 Apr.

[3] *Nation*, 26 Mar. 81; *F.J.*, 26, 30 Aug.

similar length throughout his life did he have such facilities for uninterrupted reading as during his fifteen months in Portland. In Dartmoor it was only during intervals between spells of fatiguing manual work that he was allowed to read, and then only in the poor light and general discomfort of a cell very different from the one he occupied in the infirmary block at Portland. In Dartmoor he had to content himself with the resources of the prison library; in Portland he could supplement the library's stock with books from outside. The only real restriction on his reading-matter, the prohibition on newspapers and works on current politics, was an unintended blessing, since it helped him to see himself and his preoccupation with the Irish problem with the greater clarity and detachment. He was already a well-read man when he found himself in Portland, and he used his opportunities there to deepen and extend his command of general literature, of social sciences, and of history. To judge from the literary quotations and references in his Portland writings, he found most pleasure in the masters of English literature from Shakespeare onwards to Wordsworth and Coleridge, Dickens, and Charles Reade; but he also shows an acquaintance with a number of French, Italian, German, and Spanish writers. How far he depended on translations is not known, but it is clear that he had a working knowledge of French and Spanish, and could read at least a little German and Italian. He seems also to have understood some Latin. He transcribed, along with an unidentified translation, the Latin poem attributed to St Francis Xavier, 'O deus ego amo te', and also a Spanish version of the same poem with a translation by himself. He has few quotations from the Bible. While he evidently enjoyed poetry, drama, and the novel, the writers that he chiefly studied were historians—Thiers, Thierry, Guizot, Macaulay, Froude, Lecky, and Gavan Duffy; and social scientists—Auguste Comte, Herbert Spencer, Thorold Rogers, Émile de Laveleye, and especially John Stuart Mill, Joseph Kay (author of *Free trade in land*, 1879), and Henry George. Among works of reference he relied heavily on the encyclopaedic *Thom's Official Directory of . . . Great Britain and Ireland*, Webb's serviceable *Compendium of Irish biography*, and on parliamentary papers.

The most important new influence that emerges in his thinking in Portland was that of his American friend, Henry George. Davitt had read *Progress and poverty* twice before his return to penal servitude, but there is no evidence of its impact on him until he was again in prison, when he reread it twice. By the end of 1880 George had come to see Ireland as 'the theatre' of the 'world-wide drama of the land question'. He had written a pamphlet, *The Irish land question: what it involves and how alone it can be settled*, applying his teaching to the Irish situation. The pamphlet was published in New York, London, Manchester, and Glasgow in March 1881, but it seems not to have reached Davitt while in Portland, doubtless because it came under the forbidden category of 'current politics'.[1]

This wide-ranging but purposeful reading is reflected in the remarkable corpus of writing entitled 'Jottings in solitary' that he was able to bring with him out of Portland[2]—a miscellany of essays, narratives, notes, and extracts, with, as epigraph, two sayings in Irish translated as—'Neither praise nor dispraise thyself' and 'Character is better than wealth'. Davitt took this writing seriously and he may well have had publication in mind as he wrote. The Central News had announced in July 1881 that he intended to write a book of 'a political and historical character', to be published simultaneously in Ireland and America.[3] Mrs Sullivan reported after her visit of 10 January that he had written 320 pages of what would be 'an interesting addition to our national literature'.[4] Being from its very nature discursive, uneven, and lacking any unifying structure, Davitt's prison miscellany was unpublishable as a whole; and, experienced journalist that he was, Davitt can never have thought otherwise. But this does not mean that he did not see parts of it as material for a potential book. The great bulk of it consists of (1) essays on criminal life and character (between a quarter and a third of the whole miscellany), and (2) studies in Irish history, politics, and society (well over a half). Nearly all the former and a small portion of the latter were to be published in 1885, with other writing, as *Leaves from a prison diary*—his first book.[5] The rest of the miscellany consists of a short opening narrative of the first four and a half years of Davitt's life,[6] a few diary entries and copies of letters sent, and essays and notes on the history of conquests, on the dispersion of the Jews, on secret societies in modern Europe, on the religions of the Japanese, and on John Henry Foley (the sculptor) and William Lloyd Garrison (the abolitionist).

The miscellany contains Davitt's first sustained writing on general topics and shows a distinct advance in his facility as a writer and his power of assembling large masses of material. In parts, especially in 'Criminal life and character', it has a lightness of touch wholly absent from his first publication, *Prison life* (1878); on the other hand it is

[1] Henry George Jr, *Life of Henry George*, pp 345–8, 380; see above, pp 413–14.

[2] See above, pp 478–9.

[3] *Nation*, 16 July 81; see above, p. 478.

[4] *Nation* and *Irishman*; 14 Jan. 82. The actual total in terms of pages was 425, in terms of folios 260.

[5] See my introduction to the reprint of *Leaves* (Shannon, 1972), p. ix.

[6] Incorporated in ch. I above.

not free from the diffuseness and stilted diction of his oratorical style.[1] It includes his views, committed to paper in the space of six months, on all the major questions with which he had been concerned. His wide range of interests in history, literature, and current affairs is reflected in the variety of the topics he treats, and his treatment reveals a powerful, orderly, and richly stocked mind. His personality shines through the miscellany, not only in its fragments of autobiography but in the autobiographical quality of nearly all the rest of its contents. Thus the studies on criminal life and character are based on, and provide evidence for, his first term of imprisonment; the Irish studies express his philosophy of Irish history or are related to his mission as a nationalist and land reformer; his educational proposals recall his youth in Haslingden, and his essay on secret societies has echoes of his career in the I.R.B. And as a whole the miscellany is documentary evidence of the ferment of his ideas during his thirty-fifth year. His 'Criminal life and character'[2] is drawn almost entirely from his prison experience in Clerkenwell, Newgate, Millbank, Portsmouth, and, above all, Dartmoor; he saw little of prisoners and ordinary prison-life in Portland. But the treatment is quite different from that of his first pamphlet—which was reprinted in April, and again in June 1882, by J. J. Lalor, of Dublin, together with the text of his examination before the Kimberley commission.[3] The added maturity and worldly wisdom that nearly four years of political activity had given him, together with the effect of the sustained reading and reflection that made Portland a blessing in disguise, are evident in the good humour, the tolerance, the insight, the compassion, the detachment, and the sense of proportion with which he deploys the experience of prisoners and prison life he had bought so dearly during 1870–77. His sketches of personalities and incidents of those years have a freshness and colour that owe much to his sense of the ludicrous, which, he thankfully acknowledges, has served him through life as a sixth sense and has relieved even his darkest hours in captivity.[4]

Starting from the official classification of convicts according to their behaviour in prison, he identifies types of convicts in each class according to the crimes for which they were convicted. A wide spectrum of criminals is thus rapidly presented, ranging from petty thieves, confidence-tricksters, forgers, and bigamists to imposters, blackmailers, and murderers. This systematic treatment is enlivened with many

[1] See above, p. 203.

[2] DA/1, ff 162^{v}–252^{v}; *Leaves*, i, 11–211.

[3] *The prison life of Michael Davitt, related by himself* . . . (Dublin, Apr. 1882; later editions, June 1882, 1886); *Nation*, 8 Apr. 82; above, pp 199–200, 211.

[4] DA/1, ff 161–2^{v}.

illustrative examples, among them 'Sir Roger Tichborne', the notorious 'claimant', who was a fellow-prisoner with Davitt for two years (1874–6) in Dartmoor: he was generally accepted by the convicts as genuine and became the recognised authority on all manner of questions 'from the merits of the skilly to the evils of trial by jury, or from the partisanship of judges to the quality of the shin-of-beef soup'.[1]

There are interesting generalisations on aspects of criminal character and convict behaviour. Murderers are usually among the best-behaved convicts, 'bruisers' (those convicted of robbery with violence, usually in association with female confederates) among the worst. The really hardened, irreclaimable criminal will never commit murder, having too wholesome a fear of being 'topped'. Murder is ordinarily the outcome of the passions of revenge and jealousy or of social and political wrong, and is more often traceable to some derangement of the nobler impulses than to the more debased appetites. It is the most heinous of crimes; but the most infamous of criminals, and those held in most contempt by convicts generally, are, in Davitt's opinion, the blackmailers of homosexuals (he does not use the word)—usually elderly men. The great mass of convicts are thieves, burglars, and swindlers of all kinds. Among them, more than among any class of men outside prison, there is constant talk of 'rights', of 'law', of 'justice', and of appeals to the home secretary.

> While boasting of having committed crimes that were never brought to light, and while planning the perpetration of similar ones when they will be restored to liberty, these men, in the same breath, will inveigh against their convictions with genuine indignation, and threaten to expose judge, jury, detectives, and prison authorities for having acted contrary to law the moment they were in a position to do so.[2]

If Davitt sensed the parallel between this situation and his own case as a political prisoner,[3] he gives no sign of it. But his scheme of treatment does not provide for the problem of the political prisoner; what he is concerned with is crime and punishment as a social problem, and he is constantly aware of relations between criminals and their social environment. The society against which these modern Ishmaelites have turned their hands deserves in some degree the attacks to which they subject it, because it has allowed ignorance and poverty in cities and towns 'to perfect their work of demoralisation in the creation of habitual thieves and vagabonds under its very eyes'.[4] In his *Leaves from a*

[1] DA/1, f. 193; *Leaves*, p. 79.
[2] DA/1, f. 221; *Leaves*, i, 140.
[3] Above, pp 198, 211–12.
[4] DA/1, f. 163; *Leaves*, i, 12.

prison diary Davitt was to develop this line of thought by proposing as the best of preventatives of crime both a comprehensive reform and extension of the educational system and fundamental remedies for the evils of poverty.

For the imprisoned criminal he believes that the most effective medium of reform is a judiciously selected library, well-stocked with novels in which 'truth and honesty are made to triumph . . . , and the precepts and duties of religious, moral, and industrial citizenship are held up as the standard of social obligations and the surest guarantee of worldly happiness and prosperity'.[1] It is only what prisoners read that can come between them and their thoughts of crime, past and prospective; and in this connection he gives the highest praise to a number of well-known serial publications—*Cassell's Family Magazine*, with its select stories and charming pictures of home life, *Chambers' Journal* and *Chambers' Papers for the People*, and others more directly religious in tone such as *Leizure Hours*, *Sunday at Home*, and *Good Words*. The drawback to the latter is that they have a sectarian stamp, and are therefore banned by the catholic chaplains. The only catholic serial to be found in prison libraries, *The Lamp*, is no adequate alternative for catholic prisoners. After good fiction Davitt rates as a reformative influence biographies of 'illustrious and remarkable men', and he thinks that half a prison library should be stocked with such books, which provide moral instruction by example, not by precept. Direct moral and religious teaching he regards as useless, despite the pains taken by the prison authorities to cater for the religious life of all denominations. Most convicts have a completely cynical attitude to religion, and declare their denomination or profess conversion to another denomination for quite extraneous reasons, such as the wish to be with a 'chum', or for the sake of variety, or, in the case of catholics, to have access to serial publications in the prison library.[2] But Scottish presbyterians will never turn catholic, nor Irish, as distinct from other, catholics, protestant, no matter how often they may be 'lagged'. Such religious 'consistency' does not, however, imply that Irish catholics and Scottish presbyterians are less prone to crime that those indifferent to religion.

In the second main component of Davitt's prison miscellany, his Irish studies, the topics are often controversial and the tone, though generally restrained and good-humoured, is at times emotive and polemical, in contrast with the coolness and detachment of his 'Criminal life and character'. After sketching the broad cultural effects of

[1] DA/1, f. 229^{v}; *Leaves*, i, 183.
[2] Cf. above, pp 148–9.

the invasions of Europe by Teutons, Celts, Saracens, and Tartars, and of the New World by Spaniards and Portuguese, he declares:

of all the races which are known in history as conquerors—that is robbers and murderers on a gigantic scale—the one which has most signally failed in impressing either its civilisation or religion upon the victims of its lust of powers in the Anglo-Saxon.[1]

This is the more surprising because the political institutions of England were infinitely superior to those of the other conquering powers. The essential cause of England's failure to implant her civilisation on conquered peoples he finds in a ruthless disregard by her ruling classes for every consideration other than British interests narrowly conceived, and he takes British India as the classic example. This 'British interests' concept is crucially exemplified in foreign relations, where popular sympathy with national liberation struggles abroad has been frequently negated by the foreign policy of the government.[2]

In Ireland, the rejection of English civilisation has been due not to the vitality of the native system nor to any inherent antagonism of Celts to Anglo-Saxons, but to that same inhuman, relentless, and undeviating pursuit of British interests.

The two most powerful motives which determine the . . . character of the Irish people have always been, and are still, an enthusiastic fidelity to their national faith and passionate attachment to the soil of Ireland, forming the two most prominent features of Irish civilisation for over a thousand years. Yet it has been England's one grand object to detach them from the one and deprive them of all claim or title to the other. Three hundred years of religious persecution . . . succeeds only in rooting the catholic church more firmly on Irish soil today than among any other nation in the world. . . . The 'land war' has been equally long, equally unjust, sanguinary, and impolitic on the part of England . . . , while the resistance offered to the feudal system from its first introduction into Ireland to the present hour has been equally determined, unceasing, and heroic. . . .[3]

Had England in her conquest of Ireland allowed the Irish people to remain owners of their land and in the peaceful exercise of their religion

there is every probability that Ireland would be today in reality and not [only] in name 'an integral part of the British empire', and my countrymen as submissive to English rule as those of their kilted and Cambrian race north of the Tweed and west of the Severn.[4]

As it is, the only great victory won by English civilisation in Ireland has been the supplanting of the Irish by the English language; and this, he believes, must be attributed to the teaching of the catholic church in Ireland during the half-century before the famine.[5]

In the long history of Anglo-Irish relations Davitt sees the episode

[1] DA/1, f. 20. [2] DA/1, ff 18-36. [3] DA/1, ff 40-40^{v}.
[4] DA/1, f. 39. [5] DA/1, ff 37-40^{v}.

of 'Grattan's parliament' as a unique example of the regenerating power of self-government. Though that parliament was only the instrument of protestant ascendancy, the remarkable social progress that Ireland made during the eighteen years (1782–1800) of legislative independence indicates what a native legislature, constituted on liberal principles, would be able to do for Ireland, and explains why Irishmen continue to cherish the memory of Grattan's parliament. But the narrowness of its base was a fatal weakness. There was no one among the leaders of the Volunteers, least of all the commander-in-chief, Lord Charlemont, to play the part of a Washington or a Bolivar. It is really England, not Ireland, that should honour Charlemont's memory, for it was due mainly to him that the Volunteers did not become 'the army of Irish liberation'.[1] Grattan, the leader of the movement for legislative independence, was a patriot of an altogether different stamp, who might have become the real liberator of his country had his mind not been formed in a legal mould. 'Lords and lawyers', Davitt observes, 'make the worst of leaders'.[2] He is glad that with the advance of democratic principles in Ireland, no lord, even though he could claim descent from Niall of the Nine Hostages, has the remotest chance of defeating a commoner in any electoral contest depending on the votes of the 'purely Celtic people'. He hopes that lawyer leadership has ceased with Butt, though no doubt the legal profession—'parasites of justice and truth'—will continue to play a part in Irish politics.[3] Returning to Grattan's parliament, he condemns the Volunteers for throwing away an opportunity, never likely to recur, of using their power to consolidate the legal victory of 1782 on a basis of effective political independence. Their failure to grasp that opportunity opened the way for the union of 1800, imposed on Ireland by a British government fearful that an Irish parliament might endanger the British connection and anxious to humble a people that had profited from Britain's difficulties in 1782. It was for this nefarious purpose that the government, by unheard of cruelties, goaded the Irish people into revolt in 1798, thereby providing a pretext for abolishing the Irish parliament. The union Davitt sees as one of the most disastrous events in Irish history.[4]

As to the existing government of Ireland Davitt makes a telling comparison between conditions in Ireland and in England by imagining what it would be like for Englishmen to be ruled from Dublin by Irishmen and anti-English Englishmen through a 'London Castle' ring. This elaborate and successful piece of political satire is presented as a corrective to the mistaken belief of Englishmen that Ireland enjoys

[1] DA/1, f. 324^{v}.
[2] DA/1, f. 326.
[3] DA/1, f. 326^{v}.
[4] DA/1, ff 321–38, 341–52.

the same constitution as that of England.[1] While thus high-lighting the anti-national character of the government in Ireland Davitt reiterates his view that the causes of Irish disaffection lie not so much in the denial of national independence as in practical grievances springing from misgovernment. Had Wales and Scotland after their union with England been treated in a similar manner to Ireland, both countries would now be as troublesome to England as Ireland was.[2]

Davitt sees the Anglo-Irish question in the perspective of the struggles of European nations for social and political progress, in which, he claims, an important part has been played by secret revolutionary societies, though they are now generally condemned.The fenian movement thus appears in the context of the Illuminati of Bavaria, the Tugendbund of Prussia, and the Carbonari of Naples, but he has little to say about fenianism except with reference to the charge of assassination. Murder—'the foulest crime which it is in the power of man to commit, whether the victim be king, statesman, or mechanic'[3]—admits of no defence, but the killing of despotic rulers or their instruments by decrees of secret tribunals ought to be viewed in relation to the murders that are a commonplace of every large city, and that vastly outnumber political murders. Foul and unnatural murders are recorded once or twice every week in England without arousing comment,

> but let a rack-renting landlord be shot in Ireland by a supposed decree of the ribbon secret society, or the vengeance of the Carbonari or Nihilist tribunals fall upon a victim in Italy, Germany, France, or Russia, and a shudder runs through the length and breadth of 'Society' at such diabolical deeds being perpetuated in the noontide glare of nineteenth-century civilisation.[4]

The very existence, and the misdeeds, of secret societies are a necessary consequence of the monopoly of power and wealth by the privileged few, to the injury, unhappiness, and discontent of the great majority. The most frequent victims of secret societies are spies and informers, and considering the great number of them the remarkable fact is how few have been assassinated. Though scores of informers appeared at the trials of fenians in and after 1865, the only one who met a violent end was the universally execrated Constable Talbot. This fact, Davitt says, refutes the slander about fenian 'assassinating committees'. But he says nothing about the right claimed by the supreme council, under the I.R.B. constitution of 1869, to execute members found guilty of treason; nor about the implication in his own 'pen' letter that killing traitors was accepted doctrine among fenians.[5]

[1] DA/1, ff 84–98, corresponding generally with *Leaves*, ii, 170–210.
[2] DA/1, ff 83, 84. [3] DA/1, ff 46, 47. [4] DA/1, f. 48.
[5] DA/1, ff 41–60, 301–12^{v}; see above, pp 58, 60.

While fenianism and his fenian past came in for only passing attention, Davitt shows a professional politician's interest in Ireland's parliamentary representation. He tabulates the M.P.s elected and the candidates defeated in the general election of 1880, the votes cast for each, the number of voters, and the total population of each constituency, and other particulars, and combines this information (evidently derived from *Thom* and from official returns in parliamentary papers) with comments on the political character of each member and his constituency based on personal knowledge of the parliamentary scene down to 1 February 1881.[1] The constituencies and their members are classified as (1) national and land-reforming, (2) whig or liberal, and (3) tory or landlord, for which Davitt's statistics may be summarised as follows:

character of representation	constituencies				
	counties	towns	university	total	M.P.s
national and land-reforming	23	15	–	38	65
whig or liberal	3[2]	4	–	7	11
tory or landlord	6[3]	12	1	19	27
	32	31	1	64	103

Of the 65 members returned on the national ticket, 22 have deserted the national party and gone over, overtly or covertly, to the whigs or have otherwise proved unfaithful to their pledges and their constituents. They include: George Errington (Co. Longford), Mitchell Henry (Co. Galway), F. H. O'Donnell (Dungarvan), W. H. O'Shea (Co. Clare), O'Connor Power (Co. Mayo), William Shaw (Co. Cork), and P. J. Smyth (Co. Tipperary). 'One-third of the whole turned traitors!' Davitt notes, 'whom it would be a pleasure to kick out next general election'.[4]

His comments on individual home-rulers are incisive and generally critical: E. Dwyer Gray—'able, adroit, and ambitious'; Major J. P. Nolan—'an army officer; should be permitted to keep to his military duties'; T. P. O'Connor—'able, ambitious, needs care; [holds] English radical more than Irish national opinions'; F. H. O'Donnell—'a most accomplished fraud, dishonest, treacherous, and aiming for office';

[1] DA/1, ff 256-60^v.
[2] Donegal, Londonderry, Monaghan.
[3] Antrim, Down, Armagh, Fermanagh, Tyrone, and Dublin.
[4] Cf. C. C. O'Brien, *Parnell*, pp 11-35.

W. H. O'Sullivan—'weak, but afraid to go wrong'; O'Connor Power—'renegade to former nationalist principles: unscrupulously ambitious and untrustworthy'; Charles Russell—'lawyer, but honest as a lawyer looking for promotion can be'; P. J. Smyth—'Irish national Don Quixote'. Only a few members receive unqualified approval: John Barry—'strong, honest and reliable'; J. G. Biggar—'staunch'; J. L. Finigan—'reliable'; Richard Lalor—'honesty personified'; Arthur O'Connor—'able, adroit, and reliable'; Sexton—'honest, reliable, and promising'; and, above all, Parnell—'sans peur et sans reproche'. Healy (who was returned for Wexford at a by-election in November 1880) is described as 'earnestness run riot; honest without judgment or discretion'; J. J. O'Kelly as 'crotchety, but reliable, honest, and able'; and Dillon as 'thoroughly honest and unselfish, but wanting in habits of reflection and calculation; liable to make mistakes and regret them; slight overdose of sincerity'.

Reviewing the political character of the constituencies Davitt has some interesting comments on the influence of the catholic clergy in the counties. In Cavan the landlord party is very active; priests and nationalists must keep united to retain their hold on the constituency. In Cork the priests are very active, some of them strongly opposed to the national party, and need very careful handling; farmer-voters are intelligent and indoctrinated with the new ideas on land reform. Leitrim is a 'retrograde' constituency owing to the hostility of the priests and division in the national ranks. Louth is controlled by advanced nationalists and priests; it could be won by two strong land-reformers not objectionable to the priests. Mayo is the most radical and independent of all constituencies. Nationalists united can carry both seats; the priests are jealous of nationalist influence but some of them 'go with it'. Meath is 'thoroughly reliable'; priests control elections but act in accordance with prevailing national sentiment. Roscommon, despite the hostility of the bishop and all the priests, is democratic and independent. In Tipperary, which is 'national and reliable' the controlling influence is the archbishop of Cashel.

Davitt is keenly aware of the limited nature of the electorate and assembles some telling statistics on the subject. Using the census of 1871 he arrives at a total electorate equivalent to 4 per cent of the population, and sets this against a corresponding figure of 11 per cent for England and Wales. Developing the comparison he shows that the combined electorate of Belfast and the nine other parliamentary boroughs of Ulster, with a population of 261,946, is 6,327 less than that of Wednesbury (Staffs.) and Dudley (Worcs.), with a population of 199,058. Similarly Dublin and the eight other Leinster boroughs, with a population of 346,823 have 9,068 fewer electors than those of Hull, with a population of 123,408. The two provinces of Leinster and Munster, comprising 18 counties, with a population of 2,674,054, have 6,218 fewer electors than the two counties of Cheshire and Derbyshire, with a population of 912,218. The entire electorate of Connacht, with a population of 881,553, is only 18,258, or 1,718 less than that of Stoke-on-Trent, with a population of 130,985.[1] These contrasts are partly accounted for by differences in the franchise as between Ireland and Britain but also by the greater wealth per head of population in Britain than in Ireland.

Irish poverty was inseparable, in Davitt's mind, from Irish ignorance, and a substantial section of his miscellany is devoted to 'the education of the Irish citizen'.[2] He acknowledges the benefit that fifty years of the 'national schools' have brought to 'young Ireland', and he describes the intermediate education act of 1878, which had instituted a system of state support for secondary schools, as 'one of the best measures of its kind we have yet received from Westminster'.[3] But he considers that the teachers under the 'national board' are grossly underpaid, averaging only £40 a year for men and £33 a year for women. The corresponding figures for England are £121 and £72, and for Scotland £139 and £72. The disparity is even greater than these figures show, because a far lower proportion of teachers are given rent-free houses in Ireland than in Britain. Still more deplorable is the lack of 'evening schools' in Ireland such as the mechanics' institutes provide for working classes of England and Scotland. Thanks to the dedicated efforts of Sir James Kay-Shuttleworth and his associates, these institutions have been the principal means of forming the intelligent industrial character for which the skilled artisans of the north of England have a world-wide reputation. Davitt recalls his own indebtedness to 'The Mechanics' of Haslingden, attendance at which marked the line between the 'sober, industrious, and intelligent working-men' of the town and the rest.[4] How much good might have been done for rural Ireland by comparable institutions, and what an opportunity the Land League has missed by not extending its action into the field of popular education. He himself had intended to propose such a development on his return from his second visit to America, but he had been frustrated by the rapid advance of government policy towards coercion and by his own arrest. Something more than a change in the land

[1] Davitt's figures are broadly in agreement with those of B. M. Walker, 'The Irish electorate, 1868–1915' in *I.H.S.*, xviii, no. 71 (Mar. 1973), pp 359–406. But Davitt puts the electorate of England and Wales as 11 per cent of the population whereas Dr Walker puts it at 9 per cent.

[2] DA/1, ff 121–60^{v}. [3] Ibid., f. 121. [4] DA/1, ff 122–2^{v}; see above, pp 20–21.

system of Ireland is needed if the great natural intelligence of the Irish peasantry is to be brought to bear on their primitive agriculture and the wretchedness and squalor of their living conditions, unparalleled in the civilised world. The practical education on which the well-being of the peasantry of France, Belgium, the Rhineland, Saxony, and Switzerland is founded points the moral.

With a faith in the regenerative power of self-help and education like that of Thomas Davis, Davitt goes on to sketch a model for 'A People's Institute'. In every barony an institute should be established by voluntary effort as a centre of light and leading for the locality, under the management of an elected baronial committee. Modest buildings, erected as far as possible by volunteer labour, should provide for a library, reading rooms, and lecture rooms. The working capital for this and for books, furniture, and other equipment, he reckons at £35,000 for the whole country, and this might be raised by a levy of twopence per head of the population of each barony, assisted by outside sympathisers and a grant of £5,000 from the Land League. The institute would provide evening classes in the rudiments of education, to be conducted by volunteer teachers as a labour of love. Teaching in agricultural science and in the use of fertilisers and machines would be given by permanent lecturers, whose salaries could be met out of a fund to be raised by a central committee in Dublin, probably with government support. Heating, lighting, and general maintenance of the institutes would be the responsibility of the local committees. Each institute would organise a plan of 'homestead reform', aimed at abolishing such abuses as housing animals with people and keeping dung-heaps close to cabin-doors, and at promoting improvements in the multitude of single-roomed mud cabins lacking windows and chimney. The effect of such reforms on the health and morale of the peasantry could be spectacular; and Davitt visualises schemes for promoting further improvements in existing dwellings and the building of new ones. Local 'inspection and encouragement committees' should be appointed each year to make the rounds of the barony and see to the carrying out of homestead reform where most needed. Prizes could be offered annually for the best house-improvements, internal and external, which would be sure to rouse a healthy spirit of emulation. All this can be done here and now.

> Waiting for the abolition of landlordism won't do. I don't believe in the waiting policy . . . 'Act, act in the living present' wherever humanity is suffering either from the injustice of evil laws or through the prevalence of habits and customs born of such laws for ages until they seem to be a defect in the character of those who practice them.[1]

[1] DA/1, f. 128.

After a long systematic exposition of order, progress, and civilisation, Davitt concludes that 'much has to be done in merely extending to the many what is as yet but enjoyed by the "better to do" portion of society'. Judged by most of the criteria of a progressive civilisation, Ireland is far behind contemporary nations. The remedy lies, on the one hand in the abolition of land monopoly, and on the other in a variety of practical reforms from improvements in the rewards offered to primary teachers to better housing and fostering the industrial powers of the people.

Finally, the Irish studies component of Davitt's prison miscellany includes 'Random thoughts on the Irish land war'.[1]

Why should English statesmen or English public opinion be anxious to maintain Irish landlordism? Because it is held to be essential to the continuance of England's power in Ireland, and because the landlords are the element most loyal to the English crown. Both these arguments Davitt sweeps aside. The concept of 'the garrison' is an English popular fallacy. If the real garrison of 20,000 soldiers and 12,000 military police were withdrawn tomorrow, how long would the sham garrison of landlords be able to maintain itself against the people whom it has wronged and outraged? The boasted loyalty of the landlords is simply the self-interest of a privileged class: 'they hold the land that formerly belonged to the Irish nation, and could not be otherwise than grateful to the power which guarantees them in its possession'.[2]

In upholding landlordism in Ireland England is responsible for social, political, and economic effects disastrous to her own interests. The system stands condemned before the bar of public opinion for its social consequences—a diminishing population, widespread destitution, increasing pauperism, periodical famine, a million people living in unhealthy hovels, and the physical deterioration resulting from this and from inadequate diet. Of the total rental (£10,000,000) extracted annually by the landlords, not more than one-eighth can be credited to their investment, care, enterprise, or superintendence; nothing worth placing on record is returned by them to justify their annual plunder—no outlay on improving the soil, or on helping tenants to introduce new agricultural methods, or on providing better housing, or on schools, colleges, or hospitals. This leads to Davitt's central doctrine on rent, already voiced on many a Land League platform: rent for land cultivated by the labour of the occupier or by his labour and capital, independent of all outlay, supervision, or risk by the landlord, is legalised robbery.

Socially, then, England has governed Ireland for the least good and

[1] DA/1, ff 261-95, 316-16v.

[2] DA/1, f. 265v.

the greatest misery of the greatest number of the Irish people. Politically, she has imposed a land system on Ireland that has prevented the Irish from ever becoming reconciled to English law and government.

Never has landlordism succeeded in obtaining a moral recognition from the Irish people—not for a single hour has the Irishman ceased to look upon the landlord as an enemy and the law by which he was compelled to part with most of his earnings in the shape of rent but as the detestable instrument by which himself and his family were impoverished and his country ruined.[1]

Finally, landlordism has been economically ruinous. It discourages industry and thrift by depriving the farmers of security for the fruits of their labour, leaves the land grossly underdeveloped, and takes a large annual toll of the country's wealth through absenteeism. If the land were freed from this incubus its productivity would be immensely increased and the area under crops could be doubled. Instead of having a diminishing population, Ireland would be able to support from 12 to 15 millions on a standard of living comparable with that of continental countries where feudalism has been abolished.

On social, political, and economic grounds alike the continued existence of landlordism cannot be rationally defended by England. That the system still continues is due largely to the failure of the Land League to present its case effectively before English public opinion, which alone can decide the fate of Irish landlordism. The league, embracing 'the manhood and intelligence of Ireland, and the services of two-thirds of her public men and representatives', made full use of the unique combination of circumstances offered by the crisis of 1879–80 to drive the landlords out of most of their entrenchments in Ireland, but allowed the landlords to turn the whole battery of English public opinion against the agitation. They did this through their influence with the press in London, 'the greatest centre of press-association in the world'. Writers and reporters belonging to the *Dublin Evening Mail*, the *Daily Express*, and the *Irish Times* were the 'Dublin correspondents' of *The Times, Standard*, and *Daily Telegraph*, and of most of the large English provincial and Scottish papers. They reflected the views of the landlord press to which they were attached, and the landlord interest thus succeeded in dominating opinion in England. This in turn decisively affected foreign opinion, which takes its tone from the London press. Had the Land League recognised the vast importance of outside opinion, it would have set up a press agency in London, organised public meetings there and at all great centres of population in England, and issued a stream of publications, through

[1] DA/1, f. 270v.

all of which the justice and practicability of its demands could have been ventilated, debated, and defended. Instead the landlord interest has been given virtually a free hand to inflame anti-Irish prejudice in England, so crudely exemplified in popular cartoons of the Irish countryman as a simian monstrosity, 'a "missing link" type of being in the evolution of species'.[1] What Ireland might have won if the Land League had given proper attention to English opinion can be conjectured from the measure of reform the government has felt compelled to concede despite the storm of misrepresentation raised against the league in England.

English opinion has also been dangerously prejudiced against the land movement by the prevalence of agrarian outrages. Davitt has no doubt that, in general, they are 'deeds of despair' springing directly from landlordism, and he quotes well-informed British authority in support of this view. Thomas Drummond, under-secretary for Ireland in 1835-40, referring to an agrarian murder in Tipperary, told the magistrates of that county: 'property has its duties as well as its rights; to the neglect of those duties . . . is to be mainly ascribed that diseased state of society in which such crimes take their rise'[2] (22 May 1838). John Bright, paragon of Victorian radicalism with a deep concern for Ireland, a champion of peasant proprietorship and author of the land-purchase clauses in the land act of 1870, asking why the perpetrators of a particular agrarian murder were never brought to justice answered:

> [It is] because of the sympathy . . . on the part of the great bulk of the population with those who, by these dreadful acts of vengeance, are supposed to be the conservators of the rights of the tenant, and supposed to give him that protection which imperial legislation has denied. . . . Don't let us disguise it from ourselves, there is a war between landlord and tenant, a war as fierce and relentless as though it were carried on by force of arms.[3]

One class of agrarian crime, the mutilation of cattle, is directly encouraged by the law that empowers the grand jury of the county in which the outrage is committed to award compensation to the owner of the injured animals by levying a fine on the locality concerned. Helpless animals are thus attacked in the same spirit in which buildings are deliberately set on fire by their owners in order to secure the insurance money. But animals are also victimised at the instigation of landlords in order to raise a storm of prejudice in the English mind against the tenants; and Davitt solemnly asserts that the majority of outrages on animals have been thus motivated. For whatever reason

[1] DA/1, f. 286. On this 'simianisation of Paddy' see L. P. Curtis, *Apes and angels; the Irishman in Victorian caricature* (Washington D.C., 1971).

[2] DA/1, f. 288v.

[3] DA/1, ff 288v-9v.

these horrible brutalities are committed, the culprits place themselves outside the pale of human sympathy and deserve to be 'branded with some indelible mark of public execration'.[1]

Englishmen generally view the land question with reference only to the particular situation that has forced them to give attention to it, whereas Irish land reformers are constrained to see it in the context of 'a train of retrospective ruin',[2] and set little value on temporary expedients. Davitt gives Gladstone little credit for the 1881 act. Instead of grappling courageously with the 'festering social cancer' of landlordism, he has repeated his previous error and produced a second 'experimental measure' that leaves the essential disease untouched. Landlord and tenant, instead of being legally divorced, are handed over to universal litigation, and the farmers are expected to see their interests protected by a land court composed of lawyers and land agents. As well might the fly seek protection by accepting the spider's invitation to his parlour.

Davitt's final view of how the 'foul, pestiferous social rinderpest' of landlordism can be really abolished was first recorded in his 'Jottings' on 7 September after Archbishop Croke had brought him news of the land act. Instead of the futile complexities and ingenuities of the act, 'how simply just it would have been' he writes,

> to have declared the land of Ireland to be national property with the state as the only landlord; to pension off, out of the revenues of the land, the ten thousand individuals whose interests . . . constitute the one grand evil that afflicts the people . . .; to give security from wrong and disturbance to the tillers of the soil by the removal of every other power that stands between them and the protection of the state; and finally, when landlords should be compensated and the treasury reimbursed for its expenses in the process of settlement, to abolish rent, fix a reasonable tax upon the land, and allow the revenue from this tax to be employed in developing the general resources of the country and in defraying the expenses of the civil administration.[3]

In concluding his 'Random thoughts on the land war' on 15 February, he spelt out this plan with some amendment: starting from the proposition that in strict justice the landlords are not entitled to even their fares from Kingstown to Holyhead, he concedes that, according to 'conventional or political justice', they must be compensated for the loss of their interest in the soil. This he puts at £7,000,000 annually, or half the total annual value of all the land, the other half being the proper share of the farmers whose labour and capital have given the land its present value. Reckoning the landlords' share to be worth 20 years purchase, or £140,000,000, Davitt would raise this sum by

[1] DA/1, f. 293v.
[2] DA/1, f. 294v.
[3] DA/1, f. 255v.

public loan at 3 per cent interest or £4,200,000 a year. Annual contributions to a sinking fund to repay the capital in 50 years would add £2,8000,000, giving a total of £7,000,000 which would be covered to the existing public revenue of Ireland. The civil administration of Ireland, central and local, would be met out of a tax of 10 per cent on all land values: the farmers would thus pay as land tax only half what they now pay as rent, and after the liquidation of the loan raised to buy-out the landlords the land tax would be the only source of public revenue.[1]

This plan, with further modification in detail, Davitt was to offer to the world on his release from Portland as a new social gospel and as the true meaning of the battle cry of the Land League—'the land for the people'. His argument for it, as developed in speeches and publications during the next few years,[2] was that occupying ownership, the stated aim of the Land League, would not achieve the 'land for the people', and that national ownership would do so with inestimable advantages for the whole community. Occupying ownership would be merely landlordism in a new form. The multiplication of landowners would not remove the evils inherent in the private ownership of land: it would not get rid of rent, which would simply be changed into a capital sum to be paid by the purchaser; it would create a new landed interest to add to the conservative forces in society; it would do nothing to prevent speculation in land values inflated through the growth of towns and other causes independent of the labour of the farmers; and it would do nothing for agricultural labourers or industrial workers. 'By what right are the public funds and the public credit to be utilised for the benefit of a section of the community merely? If public money or public credit is to be used at all, it ought to be used for the public good.'[3] On the other hand, under national ownership the land would become the national inheritance, administered by the state 'with a single eye to the welfare of the entire people'.[4] The taxation of land up to its full value exclusive of improvements would give all citizens a share in its benefits, abolishing all other taxes and putting an end to speculation in land values. The farmer would have an absolute property in the product of his labour and a virtual freehold in his farm subject to the payment of his tax and the observance of certain conditions: (1) the land should be cultivated; (2) it should not be subdivided beyond certain limits; (3) it should not be larger in size than the farmer could manage personally; (4) the state should

[1] DA/1, ff 316–16v; 320–20v.

[2] See especially the speeches of 21 May and 6 June 82 reported in Cashman, pp 156–85 (many passages reproduced from 'Random thoughts'), and *Leaves*, ii, 69–86, 93–9.

[3] *Leaves*, ii, 99.

[4] Ibid., p. 73.

have the right to authorise the working of mines and minerals in it, compensating the farmer for disturbance or injury to his occupancy. The operation of the land tax would bring under cultivation large areas now lying waste or used only as game preserves; while the increased revenue of the state would enable it to advance large sums for land reclamation and out of the reclaimed land to create small holdings on which people able and willing to work them, such as agricultural labourers, could be settled. The mineral resources of the country would be fully exploited. National wealth would greatly increase and would be more equitably distributed. Opportunities for employment, agricultural and industrial, would be multiplied, and wages would rise. The state would have the means to promote better housing for the poorer classes and to improve and expand education and other social services. All these beneficial changes would go far to abolish poverty and the crime that springs from poverty and social discontent.

Davitt's prison miscellany as a whole is pervaded by a preoccupation with the betterment of his fellow men. National independence is not so much an end in itself as a means of achieving social justice and material progress. The social reforms he demands he wants to see 'here and now', not postponed till Ireland has her own government. Thus he would rather see the entire soil of Ireland administered by a British state than left in the hands of Irish landlords. This attitude, as soon as he made it public after his release from Portland, earned him strong censure from nationalists. John O'Leary expressed the opinion that Davitt 'was not a nationalist at all in any sense intelligible to us [fenians], but only some sort of an internationalist or socialist, in some sense not intelligible even to himself'.[1] Though he was not, and was never to become, a socialist in any ideological sense, the rest of his life was to show that he had outgrown the romantic nationalism of his youth.

In his reforming ideas on such problems as crime and punishment, popular education, rural poverty and housing, and above all, on the ownership and occupation of land, he was a man in advance of his time. His doctrine of national ownership and the taxation of land values was so far in advance that it was generally dismissed as utopian. Only in England did it win converts to any appreciable extent. In Ireland, and in Irish-America, it was generally rejected. Parnell characteristically declared: 'I cannot see how it could ever come in Ireland within the region of practical politics'.[2] As a scheme for the compulsory buying-out

[1] Quoted in Brown, *Irish-American nationalism*, p. 127.
[2] New York *Herald*, 18 June 82.

of landlords as a class it prefigured proposals for a final settlement of the land question that began to be seriously considered by British statesmen and economists in the context of the home rule debate of 1886.[1] But national ownership of the land, which from now onwards was to be one of Davitt's most cherished principles, was generally felt to be a staggering departure from his previous commitment to occupying ownership, towards which the tide of Irish popular opinion had now irresistibly set. When he said on 6 June 1882 that there was 'not a particle more of difference of opinion' between himself and Parnell on the land question than there had been 'when we first stood together on a public platform in Westport three years ago',[2] it was another instance of his wishful thinking.

Davitt was not so much an original thinker as extraordinarily responsive to new ideas and quick to absorb them into his own thinking. Intimations of his national ownership doctrine may be discerned in occasional undefined references to holding land from the state that appear in his speeches in America during the autumn of 1878. It was in America, through the influence of Lalor and Mill on Devoy, that he seems first to have taken up the concept of public ownership of land in a pre-conquest Gaelic Ireland.[3] Patrick Ford's crusade in the *Irish World* against land monopoly was an influence in the same direction.[4] The idea of land nationalisation, a legacy of Bronterre O'Brien and the chartists, was in the air in England when Davitt attended the Land Law Association's Conference in London in February 1880.[5] His land administration scheme, adopted at the land conference of 29 April 1880, visualised the state as acquiring land and letting it to tenants.[6] During his recent visit to America he gave further signs that he favoured state ownership.[7] But before his Portland imprisonment he had not made any explicit statement on land nationalisation, and was universally regarded by the farmers as committed to occupying ownership—or, as he more often, but less accurately, described it, peasant proprietorship. It was his reading and reflection in solitude that caused the idea of nationalisation to crystallise in his mind as the master-key to the land problem. His principal inspiration was undoubtedly Henry George. He may have been influenced by Alfred

[1] *Fall*, pp 504–13.

[2] Cashman, p. 177. They had been on the same platform in St James's Hall, London, on 9 Mar. 1878 and at St Helens, Lancs., on 12 May, but it was at Westport that they first shared an *Irish* platform.

[3] Above, pp 232–3, 237, 238, 262–31.

[4] Above, p. 142.

[5] E. Eldon Barry, *Nationalisation in British politics: the historical background* (1966). ch. 1–2; above, pp 366, 368.

[6] Above, pp 374–5.

[7] Above, pp 385, 401.

Russel Wallace,[1] the eminent naturalist who was first president of the English Land Nationalisation Society, founded in 1881. And he must have known that Bishop Nulty of Meath, one of the most outstanding clerical supporters of the Land League, believed in land nationalisation. In April 1880 Nulty had addressed a pastoral letter to his diocesan clergy and laity in which he declared:

The land of every country is the common property of the people of that country, because its real owner, the creator who made it, has transferred it as a voluntary gift to them. *Terram dedit filius hominum.* Now as every individual is a creature and child of God, and as all his creatures are equal in his sight, any settlement of the land of a country that would exclude the humblest man . . . from a share in the common inheritance would be not only an injustice and a wrong to that man but, moreover, would be an impious resistance to the benevolent intentions of his creator.[2]

There is no evidence that Davitt had read Marx or that he owed anything directly to socialist theory. He no doubt owed something to the socialist sympathies of Thomas Brennan, and to the radical views on the taxation of land values held by John Ferguson, both men being among his closest friends and colleagues in the Land League. Brennan was later described by Parnell as having been one of a land nationalisation group within the league.[3] But, though Davitt was to assert that he was a 'land nationaliser' before ever he met George or read his book,[4] it is obvious that the immediate source of his nationalisation doctrine was *Progress and poverty*—in its analysis of the injustice and inexpediency of private property in land, and in its remedy of taxing all land up to its full value exclusive of improvements. He differs essentially from George only in holding that all land should be directly owned and administered by the state, and that the existing owners should be compensated.

Davitt's new thinking on the land question was presented to the world a month after he emerged from Portland as simply his 'definition' of 'the land for the people'—'the charter cry of the Land League'. The task of definition, too long postponed, had become imperative now that a temporary cessation of hostilities gave an opportunity to discuss the terms of a final settlement of the land war.[5] In fact, however, his land nationalisation scheme, was not so much a 'definition' of his previous doctrine, as the formulation of a new vision.

[1] Author of 'How to nationalise the land: a radical solution of the Irish problem' in *Contemporary Review*, xxxviii, Nov. 1880, pp 716–36, and *Land nationalisation: its necessity and its aims . . .* (London, 1882).

[2] Thomas Nulty, *Letter to the clergy and laity of the diocese of Meath*, dated Kells, Apr. 80.

[3] *S.C.P.*, vii, 46 (30 Apr. 89).

[4] *S.C.P.*, ix, 419 (3 July 89).

[5] Speech at Liverpool, 6 June, in Cashman, p. 177.

The 'land for the people' doctrine as he had used it to inspire popular resistance to the landlords was steeped in a nationalist mythology that he had done more than any other national leader to foster and articulate. He had presented 'landlordism' as a system of private ownership of land imposed on Ireland by English conquest and confiscation, and supplanting a Gaelic system under which the land belonged to the 'clan', every man having a right to share in the use of it. The landlords were a privileged class of alien and ruthless usurpers to whom the mass of the people had become enslaved as tenants at will. The landlords contributed almost nothing to the improvement and cultivation of the land, but as rent-chargers they appropriated most of the wealth produced by the labour and capital of the tenants. Their power of rack-renting and eviction hung like a menacing cloud over the lives of the tenants, and its exercise was responsible for banishing hundreds of thousands of them from their homes. The tenants had never recognised the landlords' legal rights over the land as having any moral validity. They regarded the landlords as their natural enemies, against whom the guerilla violence of agrarian secret societies was legitimate warfare. Landlordism was the fundamental cause of economic and social ruin to Ireland, and the great famine was its predictable and most catastrophic outcome. The crisis of 1879–80 was the climax of thirty years of post-famine landlordism; and the Land League expressed the determination of the tenants to break the evil system once and for all by recovering for themselves the rights of their ancestors to the soil.

In making this formidable indictment of the land system Davitt seems never to have questioned his basic assumptions about the landlords; and his tremendous generalisations about rack rents, evictions, and agrarian outrages took no account of actual rent levels, of regional variations, of divergent interests between classes of tenants, and of improving conditions in rural society between the famine and 1878. It was as if all the tenant farmers of Ireland were in the situation of the poorest peasants of Connacht under the worst of landlords. In characterising the landlords as the descendants of the English conquerors of Ireland he ignored, among other things, that substantial element, mostly Irish, who had purchased their land since 1849 through the encumbered estates court.

On the other hand his remedy of land nationalisation was even more remote from the actual Ireland than his mythology of landlordism. It had no roots in Irish tradition. The idea of public ownership of land in pre-conquest Ireland was no more necessary to it than the concept of the landlords as aliens. His nationalisation scheme was based on a philosophy of land in relation to the whole population, not simply to the owners and occupiers. Its central principles were no more applicable to Ireland than to England and Scotland, and it was addressed in the first instance to British audiences and the British reading public. It called on the tenant farmers to abandon their most passionately held aspiration—to own the land they occupied—in accordance with a theory of the common good that meant nothing to them. The 'land for the people' gospel as he had preached it responded to this aspiration and was at the same time essentially nationalist, since it identified landlordism with the English conquest of Ireland. His land nationalisation doctrine was in principle not nationalist at all, but, as John O'Leary declared, essentially socialist and internationalist. It was a doctrine that sought to harmonise and cater equally for the interests of all classes of workers, rural and urban. Whatever its weakness as an economic theory or a plan of action it expressed an ideal of social justice that had its roots in Davitt's own experience and personality. In combining the cause of farmers, agricultural labourers, and industrial workers it epitomised what was to be a central theme of his whole subsequent career.

Davitt seems never to have faced the contradiction between nationalism and land nationalisation. It was spelt out by Henry George in the pamphlet on the Irish land question that he published in March 1881,[1] soon after Davitt was sent back to prison

> It is the fashion of Land League orators and sympathising newspapers . . . to talk as if the distress and disquiet in Ireland were caused by British oppression . . . But while it is true that in the past Ireland has been deeply wronged and bitterly oppressed by England, it is not true that there is—in an economic sense at least—any peculiar oppression of Ireland by England now. . . . The Irish land system, which is so much talked of as though it were some peculiarly atrocious system, is essentially the same land system which prevails in all civilised countries.[2]

When Justice Fitzgerald, in his charge to the jury at the state trial of the land leaguers, remarked that the land laws of Ireland since 1870 were more favourable to the tenant than those of Great Britain, Belgium, or the United States, he was right. If Ireland tomorrow were to become a state of the American union, the gain would be to the landlords, the loss to the tenants.[3] The fact that Ireland was a conquered country and that centuries ago the native inhabitants were expropriated by the conquerors had nothing to do with the real land question of today. England too was a conquered country. That Irish land titles rested on force and fraud was true; but so did land titles in

[1] Above, pp 504–5.
[2] *The Irish land question*, p. 1; above, p. 452.
[3] *Irish land question*, pp 1-2.

every country. The Irish land system was the general system of modern civilisation. Rack-renting, the fixing of rent for short terms by competition, was more common in the United States than in Ireland, where it was probably true, as the apologists for landlordism claimed, that land was largely under-rented. This was borne out by the peculiar bitterness of complaints against middlemen, such as tenant farmers who sublet patches at twice the rent they themselves paid their landlords,[1] and against speculative purchasers of encumbered estates who managed them solely for profit.

But if the land system in Ireland was essentially the same as that which prevailed elsewhere, how was it that it did not produce the same results everywhere? George answered that it did everywhere produce the same *kind* of results, that Irish poverty and distress, however grievous, were not peculiar. Its cause, the ownership by some of the people of the land on which, and from which, the whole people must live, everywhere produced similar evils—the hideous squalor of London and Glasgow slums, want jostling luxury in the streets of New York, children doomed to stunting toil in the mills of Massachusetts.[2] In this perspective the Irish land movement assumed a significance and a dignity that no struggle for 'mere national independence' could have. So far the movement had been conducted in the interests merely of the tenant farmers; it promised nothing to the labouring and artisan classes. But the moment it ceased to be for the benefit of a class and became a movement for the benefit of all the working classes it would become the van of a world-wide struggle. To identify it with nationalism was to diminish it fatally: indiscriminate denunciation of England, so common at Land League meetings, was 'the very madness of folly'. 'The greatest enemy of the people's cause is he who appeals to national passion and excites old hatreds.' Let the land-leaguers follow the example of the German social democrats and be leaguers first and Irishmen afterwards.[3] Home rule, in so far as it meant self-government, was good, but talk of Irish independence was as harmful as it was wild and vain. It was not with the English people that the Irish people had cause of quarrel, but with a system that oppressed both. The way to fight the system most effectively was to unite the masses against it. The greatest blow that could be struck against landlordism would be 'to carry this land agitation into England, not as a mere Irish question but as an English question as well'.[4]

[1] See Charlotte G. O'Brien, 'The Irish "poor man"' in *Nineteenth Century*, viii, no. 46 (Dec. 80), p. 876.

[2] *Irish land question*, pp 3-4, 6, 15.

[3] Ibid., pp 15, 34-6.

[4] Ibid., p. 37.

This was the strategy that Davitt set about pioneering, after his release from Portland, in association with Henry George himself, who had come to Ireland as a special correspondent of the *Irish World* in October 1881. It is not surprising that nationalist opponents should have taunted him with having been captured by Henry George and the *Irish World.* What is surprising is that he abandoned neither his nationalism nor his land nationalisation.

The last entry in Davitt's prison miscellany is a gloomy reflection on his thirty-sixth birthday (26 March 1882). He would not, he wrote, be thirty-six if he could help it, any more than he would choose the companionship of whitewashed walls and the ceaseless censorship of his writing. He recalled a passage in 'grand old Will Shakespeare':

> I have done no harm but I remember now
> I am in this earthly world, where to do harm
> Is often laudable; to do good sometime
> Accounted dangerous folly.[1]

Between laudable harm and dangerous folly he had no hesitation in choosing the latter, though he was not going to acquiesce in a state of society that produced the moral anomaly of such a choice. Reviewing the course of his life, of which he could recollect every year after the first five, he saw a generally happy childhood prematurely ending at nine, followed by thirteen comparatively happy years of toil as a wage-earner for his family (interrupted by the loss of his right arm at eleven and by four subsequent years of unexpected schooling), followed by fourteen years wholly devoted to the service of Ireland, nearly nine of which he had spent in prison in consequence of his 'dangerous folly'.[2] He wondered whether he would see another birthday. In fact he was to see twenty-four.

His thirty-seventh birthday was to be spent in prison.[3] but not in Portland and not in connection with his original conviction. He was released from Portland on 6 May as a result of communications between Parnell and Gladstone that disclosed an identity of interests between them and made the continued imprisonment of Parnell and his colleagues irrelevant. From the reassembling of parliament on 7 February it was evident that a change in government policy towards Ireland was impending. The government was increasingly troubled about the coercion regime and embarrassed by the continued imprisonment of 'suspect' land-leaguers, three of them (Parnell, Dillon,

[1] DA/1, ff 358–8^{v}; the quotation (word-perfect except that 'sometime' is rendered 'sometimes') is from a speech by Lady Macduff in *Macbeth*, act IV, sc. ii. I owe its identification to my friend, Professor J. K. Walton.

[2] I have modified Davitt's own periodisation, which is confused by an attempt to fit his previous life into four periods of nine years.

[3] See below, p. 597.

and O'Kelly) prominent M.P.s. It was becoming divided over Forster's insistence that steps would have to be taken to replace the coercion act, due to expire in September, by new coercive measures. Forster came increasingly under fire not only from the Irish party and from English radicals but also from conservatives. Gladstone's mind was moving in the opposite direction from Forster's. When the question of home rule was raised in the house of commons on an amendment to the address, moved by P. J. Smyth, he said in the house of commons (9 February) that he would be glad to consider any practicable plan of local government for Ireland that would reduce the excessive centralisation of business in London and would at the same time maintain the supremacy of parliament, but that no such plan had hitherto been forthcoming from the home-rulers.[1] On the land question he condemned the action of the house of lords in setting up a committee of inquiry (24 February) into the working of the land act which was the retort of the landowning interest to the rent-reductions that were being made by the sub-commissioners under the act.[2] But he was impressed by the fact that conservative opinion was now setting in favour of land purchase: the principal recommendation of the lords' committee was to be that the state should facilitate the conversion of tenants into owners by advancing the whole of the purchase money and in other ways increasing the incentives offered to tenants to buy out their holdings.[3] A leading conservative, W. H. Smith, gave notice of his intention to propose a measure 'to facilitate the transfer of ownership of land to occupiers on terms which would be just and reasonable to the existing landlords' (16 March).[4] Gladstone turned his attention to the subject, and this led him to draft a plan for elected provincial councils to be responsible for the purchase of land for resale to the occupying tenants (just as, four years later, he was to couple a comprehensive measure of land purchase to his home rule bill). To Forster he wrote on 12 April that 'until we have seriously responsible bodies to deal with us in Ireland, every plan we frame comes to Irishmen . . . as an English plan'.

> If we say we must postpone the question till the state of the country is more fit for it, I should answer that the least danger is going forward at once. It is liberty alone that fits men for liberty. This proposition . . . has its bounds, but it is far safer than the counter doctrine—wait till they are fit . . .
>
> For the Ireland of today the first question is the rectification of the relations between landlord and tenant, which happily is going on; the next is to relieve

[1] *Hansard 3*, cclxvi, 260-6.

[2] Ibid., pp 889-978, 1075-6, 1501-22.

[3] *First report from the select committee of the house of lords on land law (Ireland)*, pp iii-ix, H.C. 1882 (249), xi (28 Apr. 82).

[4] *Hansard 3*, cclxvii, 752, 1029.

Great Britain from the enormous weight of the government of Ireland unaided by the people, and from the hopeless contradiction in which we stand while we give a parliamentary representation, hardly effective for anything but mischief without the local institutions of self-government which it presupposes, and on which alone it can have a sound and healthy basis.[1]

The government was thus assuming a more conciliatory attitude towards Ireland, and on the land question both British parties were moving towards the Land League's plan of settlement, the conversion of tenants into owners. The imprisoned Parnell was kept well-informed of these changes no less than of the state of Ireland.

Recognising that the no-rent manifesto was a failure and the land act a success in so far as tenants were in a position to invoke its benefits, he framed a bill, of which notice was given in the house of commons as early as 8 February over the names of John Redmond, Parnell, Healy, Sexton, and Justin McCarthy, to remedy what he and his colleagues held to be the deficiencies of the act—principally the lack of provision for small tenants in arrears of rent, the exclusion of leaseholders, the insufficient attractiveness of the land-purchase provisions, and the inadequacy of the clauses relating to tenants' improvements.[2] Amended on these points, the land act could, he believed, be made the basis of a practical settlement of the land question, and the land war could thus be ended. Disgusted by the violence and the drift to anarchy that the successors (headed by his sister and the Ladies' Land League) of the imprisoned land-leaguers were unable to control, he decided that the time had come for him to reassert his authority. During an absence from Kilmainham prison on parole (10-24 April), he entered into communication with Gladstone through intermediaries—W. H. O'Shea, Justin McCarthy, and Joseph Chamberlain—on the theme that if the government were at once to announce a satisfactory plan of settling the paramount problem of arrears, he and his colleagues would be in a position to have the no-rent manifesto withdrawn and to do their utmost to stop outrage and intimidation. No plan would be satisfactory that did not compulsorily wipe off all arrears accrued up to 1 May 1881 by a payment, not exceeding one year's rent, from the tenant, a gift, similarly limited, from the state, and the remission of the balance by the landlord. With the prospect of an early return of normal conditions in Ireland Parnell would hope that the government 'would allow the coercion act to lapse and govern the country by the same laws as England'.[3] This would enable the Parnellites 'to cooperate cordially for the future with the liberal party

[1] Morley, *Gladstone*, iii, 58-9.
[2] *A bill to amend the Land Law (Ireland) Act, 1881*, H.C. 1882 (2), iii, 11-20.
[3] Parnell to Justin McCarthy, 26 Apr. (R. B. O'Brien, *Parnell*, i, 341-2).

in forwarding liberal principles'.[1] Gladstone was quickly persuaded that Parnell, far from being the cynical extremist he had supposed, was really a moderate, now anxious to co-operate with the government in making the most of the land act. When Redmond's amending bill came up for a second reading on 26 April, he welcomed it as evidence of the Irish party's new attitude to the land act and declared the government's intention to deal with the arrears question on an equitable basis and in accordance with Irish public opinion. Healy, Sexton, Shaw, and others responded in appreciative terms. On 2 May the cabinet agreed, Forster resigning, that the three imprisoned M.P.s should be released immediately and that the list of suspects should be examined with a view to releasing all persons listed who were not held to be associated with crime. As soon as business permitted, a bill would be proposed to parliament to strengthen the ordinary law for the security of life and property in Ireland, and the government would 'reserve their discretion' as to renewing the coercion act.[2] The queen reluctantly assented, while expressing apprehension.[3] In announcing the cabinet's action to the house of commons the same day (2 May), Gladstone declared that it was not the outcome of 'any negotiation, promise, or engagement whatsoever'.[4] And it was true that the Kilmainham treaty was not so much a compact between Parnell and Gladstone as their mutual recognition that they had a common and immediate interest in the settlement of the arrears question, the restoration of order in Ireland, and the phasing out of coercion.[5]

Davitt was not imprisoned as a 'suspect' under the coercion act, but it was obvious that he would now have to be released. Parnell, in his communications with O'Shea, while not raising the question of his own release, had been emphatic about the importance of releasing Davitt if Ireland was to be pacified. When Parnell arrived in London on Thursday, 4 May, and learnt from O'Shea that Davitt was indeed to be released, he asked O'Shea to inform the home secretary that it would be inexpedient if the release were to take place before he had seen Davitt and apprised him of the new political situation. O'Shea explained this to Harcourt, who agreed to defer the release till Saturday.[6]

[1] Parnell to W. H. O'Shea, 28 Apr. (ibid., pp 343–4). [2] Morley, *Gladstone*, iii, 65.

[3] Hamilton, *Diary*, i, 262, 263; Philip Guedalla, *The queen and Mr Gladstone*, (1933) ii.

[4] *Hansard 3*, cclxviii, 1968.

[5] Ibid., cclxvi–cclxix; Hamilton, *Diary*, i, 220–63; Chamberlain, *Political memoir*, pp 29–50; O'Connor, *Parnell movement*, pp 454–60; Reid, *Forster*, ii, 424–44; *S.C.P.*, i, 343–53, 372–8 (O'Shea's evidence, 31 Oct. 88); R. B. O'Brien, *Parnell*, i, 335–50; Eversley, *Gladstone and Ireland*, pp 187–204; Hammond, *Gladstone and the Irish nation*, pp 252–82; C. C. O'Brien, *Parnell*, pp 75–9; Lyons, *Parnell*, pp 189–204.

[6] O'Shea to Chamberlain, 23 Apr. 82 (Chamberlain, *Political memoir*, pp 39–40); *S.C.P.*, i, 345–6, 350, 352, 353, 372, 378.

In the house of commons on 4 May, in reply to a question from Joseph Cowen, Harcourt announced that the government had decided to release Davitt for the same reasons as had induced it to release Parnell, Dillon, and O'Kelly. He would be released on the same conditions as the late government had attached to his release from Dartmoor in December 1877, and, he presumed, for the same reason—that it could be done consistently with the public safety. In other words Davitt would again be a convict at large on ticket of leave. Cowen gave notice that he intended to ask whether, since Davitt's land policy had been accepted by the government and adopted in the report of the house of lords' committee on the working of the land act, the government would advise the queen to grant a free pardon to the founder of the Land League, so that Davitt might enter parliament and defend his doctrine now accepted on all sides.[1] There was no response from the government to this quip, but before the night was out Harcourt received a telegram from the queen: 'Is it possible that M. Davitt, known as one of the worst of the treasonable agitators, is also to be released? I cannot believe it. Three suspects were spoken of, but no one else.' She continued after Davitt had been released to express indignation, eliciting from Harcourt a soothing letter and the assurance that Davitt was using his influence against outrage.[2]

On the morning of Saturday, 6 May, Davitt was enjoying the sun in the infirmary garden at Portland when a smiling Governor Clifton brought him a letter from Parnell, conveying the news that he was to be liberated and that Parnell and Dillon would arrive at Portland that afternoon to accompany him to London.[3] Parnell was not apt to make such a gesture out of pure affection and his visit to Portland was a measure of the importance he attached to Davitt's reaction to the new deal. Parnell arrived at 3 p.m., not only with Dillon, but also with O'Kelly. In the presence of the governor, Davitt declared that he intended to ignore entirely the conditions of the new ticket of leave now issued to him.[4] At his request the governor sent for the catholic chaplain, Rev. Thomas Matthews,[5] to receive the thanks of the visitors for his kindness to Davitt. The visitors were then shown Davitt's cell and the infirmary garden, Dillon remarking that the cell was larger than the one he himself had occupied in Kilmainham. After leaving the prison Davitt asked to see Mrs Clifton to thank her for her attention to the friends who had visited him from time to time and to

[1] *Hansard 3*, cclxix, 97.

[2] Gardiner, *Harcourt*, i, 434–5; Guedalla, *The queen and Mr Gladstone*, ii, 189.

[3] Parnell to Davitt, 5 May (*Fall*, p. 135).

[4] See plate XI.

[5] DP/X.

introduce Parnell and his colleagues to her. This the governor permitted. Before departing from Portland Davitt expressed his satisfaction with his treatment in the prison and his gratitude to the governor and other officers for their consistent consideration and courtesy. A final medical examination showed him to be in good health. He was subject to attacks of dyspepsia that readily disappeared under treatment. He had slight bronchial catarrh. There was an old patch of consolidated lung-tissue on his left side, which diminished expansion, but otherwise his chest was healthy. His general condition had much improved and he had gained twelve pounds in weight since entering Portland. All this was duly reported to the home office through Sir Edmund Du Cane, who, months later, raised a technical query about the case. In the ordinary way, as a released convict, Davitt would be listed in the issue of the Habitual Criminals Register for the current year; was an exception to be made in his favour? What was done when he was released from Dartmoor, asked Harcourt? His name appeared in the register for that year, replied Du Cane. Follow the same course, Harcourt ruled (1 December 1882).[1]

In the train, returning to London with his three companions, Davitt learnt why all four were again at large, Parnell, uncharacteristically, doing most of the talking. We have only Davitt's account, written years afterwards, of what Parnell said, but there is no reason to doubt its substantial accuracy.

> We are on the eve of something like home rule. Mr Gladstone has thrown over coercion and Mr Forster, and the government will legislate further on the land question. The tory party are going to advocate land purchase, almost on the lines of the Land League programme, and I see no reason why we should not soon obtain all we are looking for in the league movement. The no-rent manifesto had failed and was withdrawn. A frightful condition of things prevailed in Ireland during the last six months.[2]

He went on to denounce the Ladies' Land League, speaking of anarchy 'as if he were a British minister bringing in a coercion bill'.

> I never saw him so wild and angry; the Ladies' Land League had . . . taken the country out of his hands and should be suppressed. I defended the ladies, saying that, after all, they had kept the ball rolling while he was in jail. 'I am out now', said he, 'and I don't want them to keep the ball rolling any more. The league must be suppressed, or I will leave public life.'[3]

Then in playful vein he talked of a future 'home rule cabinet', casting Sexton as chancellor of the exchequer, Dillon as home secretary, O'Kelly as head of a national police force, and Davitt as director of prisons. He spoke highly of Lord Frederick Cavendish, the new chief

[1] P.R.O., H.O. 144/5/17869, 93, 97.
[2] *Fall*, p. 355.
[3] R. B. O'Brien, *Parnell*, i, 364.

secretary, as one of the most modest and best men in the house of commons and thoroughly committed to the new policy. And thus they arrived in London, to be welcomed by a host of friends and escorted to the Westminster Palace Hotel. There, some two hours later, they received the shattering news that Lord Frederick and the under-secretary, Thomas Henry Burke, had been assassinated in the Phoenix Park, Dublin, that evening.[1]

[1] *S.C.P.*, ix, 394; *Fall*, pp 355–7.

Epilogue: After the 'Kilmainham treaty'

THE 'Kilmainham treaty' began a new era in Davitt's life. It ensured not only his release from Portland but his return to Irish politics in circumstances in which he was certain to be politically opposed to Parnell and the majority of nationalists.

The release of the Land League chiefs symbolised a great and far-reaching gain for the land movement as interpreted by Parnell. Within a few months the land act was complemented by a settlement of the arrears question essentially on Parnell's terms,[1] at considerable cost to the state and, in principle, at definite cost to the landlords, who, however, in practice benefited to the extent of two years' rent that they otherwise had little hope of recovering. The tenants in greatest need—those whose annual rent was less than £30—were thus relieved of a crushing burden and enabled to apply to the land courts to have their rents judicially fixed. Other parts of Parnell's programme were realised within a few years. Land purchase was set on a new and hopefull course in 1885 by the Ashbourne[2] act, which for the first time, provided for the advance of the entire purchase money by the state, instead of three-quarters, as under the 1881 act. Leaseholders were brought within the scope of the latter act in 1887.[3] Parnell in effect called off the land war after securing an immediate settlement of the arrears question for some 130,000 small and poor tenants and accepting as a long-term settlement of the land question the development of dual ownership under the land act and of occupying ownership through an improved system of land purchase. On that basis he snuffed out the Ladies' Land League, turned his back once and for all on land agitation, and sought to steer the national movement into a wholly parliamentary channel with home rule as its primary objective. His

[1] 45 & 46 Vict., c. 47 (18 Aug. 82).
[2] 48 & 49 Vict., c. 73 (14 Aug. 85).
[3] 50 & 51 Vict., c. 33 (23 Aug. 87).

assessment of the situation in which he made the 'Kilmainham treaty' proved to be sound. The combination of dual ownership and occupying ownership was to be broadly the pattern on which the land question was to work itself out until the final stage, after 1921, of compulsory purchase of all tenanted land from the landlords. The Land League's programme was thus ultimately fulfilled.

That could not be foreseen in 1882, and conflict between landlords and tenants was to erupt intermittently during Davitt's lifetime. But there was never again to be a land war on the scale of that conducted by Davitt's Land League. The land war of 1879–82 was decisive in several fundamental ways. The legal powers of the landlords over their lands were irremediably restricted, and without compensation, through the operation of the land act. Age-long habits of deference towards the landlords were broken by the sense of collective power that the Land League's teaching and action aroused in the tenants. The social ascendancy of the landlords received blows from which it never recovered. And the tenants as a body became unshakeably attached to the cause of home rule, now seen to be inseparable from their cause as farmers—a change whose full effect was to be harvested, after the small farmers and labourers were enfranchised by the electoral reform act of 1884, in every general election from 1885 onwards. The land war was thus a watershed both in the democratising of Irish society and in its advance towards national independence. Finally, although the Land League was proclaimed and its central organisation suppressed in October 1881, its branches remained in being, reemerging a year later as branches of the new central organisation, the National League, and continuing the tradition of an Irish shadow government, over against the British government, of Ireland.[1]

The war had been fought on three levels—open agitation and associated procedures (including the defence of tenants in the courts) conducted or supported by the Land League; underground action by fenians and agrarian secret societies; parliamentary action by militant home-rulers in the house of commons. The overwhelming momentum of the movement in 1879–82 had been due to this unique combination of forces. Parnell had been the acknowledged link between the first and the third level. Davitt had been a vague and unacknowledged link between the first level and fenians operating on the second. But neither Davitt nor Parnell was in control of the agrarian secret societies, except in the sense that their power in the localities was generally in inverse proportion to the power of the Land League. A higher total of agrarian

[1] *Fall*, p. 380; T. W. Moody, 'Anna Parnell and the Land League' in *Hermathena*, no. cxvii (summer 1974),]. 11; below, pp 543–5.

outrages was recorded for the six months from October 1881 to March 1882, during which both Davitt and Parnell were in prison, than for any period of the same length during the land war; and the total for 1881, during eleven months of which Davitt was in prison, was the highest ever recorded. Parnell emerged from Kilmainham determined not only to damp down agrarian agitation but to do all in his power to suppress 'Captain Moonlight'; and Davitt, though eager to maintain the connection between parliamentary action and agrarian agitation, was scarcely less hostile to secret action than Parnell himself. The total of agrarian outrages fell sharply during the second quarter of 1882 (from 1440 during the first quarter to 1141), and the fall continued for the rest of the year and during the whole of 1883: the total for October–December of that year, 154, was the lowest for any quarter since April–June 1879.[1]

For Davitt a long process of disillusionment with, and disengagement from, the fenian organisation was brought to a decisive point by the Park murders. 'I wish to God I had never left Portland' was his first reaction to the news, and he took the lead in drawing up a 'manifesto to the people of Ireland', signed by himself, Parnell, and Dillon, which condemned the 'horrible deed' and was widely publicised in Great Britain, Ireland, and America. The final passage, written by A. M. Sullivan, though felt to be perilous to the signatories, was added on Davitt's insistence that it was absolutely necessary to prove the sincerity of the condemnation:

> We feel that no act has ever been perpetrated in our country during the exciting struggles for social and political rights of the past fifty years that has so stained the name of hospitable Ireland as this cowardly and unprovoked assassination of a friendly stranger, and that, until the murderers of Lord Frederick Cavendish and Mr Burke are brought to justice, that stain will sully our country's name.[2]

On 11 May Davitt had an interview with Howard Vincent, director of the C.I.D.: as reported by Vincent he declared that he was no longer a fenian, that his life was in extreme danger, that before his recommittal 'his assassination had been resolved upon' by a secret society,[3] that he had been saved by his imprisonment, and that he was now prepared to 'assist the authorities by every means in his power'; he believed the murders to be the work not, as he had been supposed, of Rossa—that 'arch-scoundrel'—who lacked the courage to organise it—

[1] Appendix F.

[2] *F.J.*, 8 May 82; *United Ireland*, 13 May; *S.C.P.*, i, 353–4; vi, 526; vii, 49; vii, 107–10; ix, 394–5; Bodleian Library, Harcourt papers, B I, vol. 351, p. 48: Lewis Harcourt's journal, 15 May; *Fall*, p. 350.

[3] Cf. above, p. 439.

but of 'a few desperate ruffians' who were still in Dublin.[1] Vincent's account of Davitt's admissions may not have been literally accurate, but it is clear that the interview occurred and it may be accepted that Davitt expressed extreme revulsion against the activities of secret societies and repudiation of all further connection with fenianism. This is in line with the open breach with Devoy[2] that was evident by July when, during a third visit to America, Davitt insisted on repaying out of his own pocket the balance of the money confidentially advanced to him by the 'national' (or 'skirmishing') fund through Devoy in August 1879 for the purposes of the land agitation. The loan had been made public and used as evidence of a connection between the Land League and O'Donovan Rossa's terrorist agency, which was now earning lurid notoriety in Britain. On 13 July, in New York, Davitt paid off the full amount outstanding, in the presence of W. K. Redmond, and obtained a receipt from Devoy on behalf of the fund.[3] 'Thank heaven', he wrote in his diary, 'I've done with that infernal transaction. I have never regretted any act of my political life so much . . . Am almost without a cent today, but feel happy in having that weight removed from me.'[4]

While Davitt was now on much the same ground as Parnell in relation to the secret societies, he and his closest colleagues in the land war—Dillon, Brennan, and Egan—and Parnell's own sister, Anna, as head of the Ladies' Land League, held that Parnell had surrendered to the government on terms that fell far short of the league's basic demand and had disbanded his fighting forces when victory was almost within sight. Twenty-one years later, in his *Fall of feudalism*, Davitt's final judgment was still that Parnell should have allowed the agitation to continue. English rule had never been so demoralised since 1798 nor so fiercely and effectively assaulted. The country was 'absolutely ungovernable', and an organisation with nearly a million members throughout the world 'stood behind Parnell's lead'. The need for decentralisation of authority in the government of Ireland was recognised by Gladstone, and a scheme of provincial councils was in contemplation that must lead to the delegation of power to a national council, as was to be proposed in 1886 in the first home rule bill. There would have been far less opposition to the bill from English public opinion

[1] Bodleian Library, Harcourt papers: C. E. H. Vincent to Harcourt, 11 May (printed in Lyons, *Parnell*, p. 231); B I, vol. 351, p. 24: Lewis Harcourt's journal, 11 May; Hamilton, *Diary*, i, 271.

[2] See *S.C.P.*, ix, 433–4.

[3] *D.P.B.*, ii, 124–5; Cashman, p. 218; *Nation*, 19 Aug.; see above, pp 312–13, 354, 389, 405–6.

[4] DN/9, 14 July.

if the Castle system and landlordism had been still more 'battered and broken' in 1882 than it actually was.[1] But how, it may be asked, could the land war have been carried to the conclusion desired by Davitt while he himself, Parnell, and the other leaders were in prison? Davitt's speculation on what might have happened if Parnell had acted differently should be compared with the opinion he expressed in July 1882 on the misused potentiality of the no-rent manifesto,[2] and with what he says in the *Fall of feudalism* about the rejection of his rent-strike proposal in January 1881.[3]

While Davitt and his associates deplored the 'Kilmainham treaty, as a surrender to the government, it was seen by government opponents, British and Irish, as a surrender to Parnell. That, of course, was Forster's position. On the day the 'treaty' was approved by the cabinet he was asked in private conversation by an independent M.P. 'how far is it politic to purchase an immediate cessation of outrage and apparent pacification of Ireland by the unconditional surrender of the suspects?'. He replied:

> Such a course would be a tremendous step towards home rule. It would be equivalent to admitting that these men are what they claim to be—but are not—the leaders and representatives of the Irish people, and that the government released them in order to effect what it cannot accomplish itself—the pacification of Ireland and the maintenance of law and order.[4]

This amounted to a sound forecast of the way in which Gladstone's mind was to move during the next four years, and was the exact reverse of Davitt's assessment of the effect of the 'treaty' on the home rule demand.

In Ireland the 'treaty' was widely acclaimed as a victory for Parnell. Nevertheless Parnell's disengagement from the land war placed him politically in serious danger from the Land League left, headed by Davitt and Dillon and strongly supported in Irish-America by the *Irish World*. In surmounting this danger and establishing his authority as national leader more firmly than ever, Parnell owed much to the assassinations in the Phoenix Park, which at first threatened to overwhelm him, and to the behaviour of Davitt and Dillon. The Park murders (which turned out to be the work of a secret terrorist group, the Irish National Invincibles) precipitated a new and more draconic coercion act[5] but did not permanently interrupt the Kilmainham understanding. By discrediting the extreme revolutionary element in the national movement they helped, in nationalist eyes, to justify

[1] *Fall*, pp 363–4. [2] Above, p. 496. [3] Above, pp 457–9.
[4] Arnold-Forster, Irish journal, 30 Apr. 82.
[5] 45 & 46 Vict., c. 25 (12 July 82).

Parnell's shift to moderation, while the parliamentary resistance that he and his followers inevitably presented to coercion served to sustain his reputation as a fighter and to maintain national solidarity. But these considerations would have counted for far less in his favour if Davitt and Dillon, with their passionate commitment to the 'abolition of landlordism', had led a left-wing revolt against the Kilmainham 'surrender'.

In fact they did not. Dillon, after a few months of uneasy cooperation with Parnell, announced on 25 September that he intended to withdraw from Irish politics 'for the next few years', and did so, leaving Ireland in November. The reason he gave was his weakened health, but inability to accept the Kilmainham policy was beyond doubt another, and perhaps the determining, reason.[1] His withdrawal weakened Parnell's party but removed a potential danger. Davitt's opposition to the 'treaty' was more complicated and potentially more dangerous.

The 'treaty' ran counter to the main current of Davitt's thinking on the land question. In a speech at Manchester on 21 May he said that Gladstone deceived himself egregiously if he believed that the Land League movement was about to efface itself because he had been converted to Parnell's views on the arrears question and had accepted 'the services of a Mr O'Shea in effecting the treaty of Kilmainham'. The Land League movement was organised to bring about the complete abolition of Irish landlordism, and until that was achieved there could be no alliance between the people of Ireland and the British liberal party.[2] This rejection of the 'treaty' was, however, mitigated by Davitt's reluctance to cause a breach with Parnell and by Parnell's tact and consideration in handling Davitt. Davitt went on to give Parnell an immeasurable advantage when, at Liverpool on 6 June,[3] he revealed in full detail that the abolition of landlordism meant ownership of the land by the state, not by the occupiers. The utter unacceptability of this doctrine both in Ireland and in Irish-America, and Parnell's consummate skill in exploiting the fact ensured the failure of Davitt's attempt to revive the land war. He quickly recognised that both Ireland and Irish-America were stony ground for his land nationalisation gospel, though for the next few years he continued to preach it in England and Scotland, where he helped to promote the cause of radical reform of the land laws. On the other hand Parnell's own conservatism responded to that of the tenant farmers in their overmastering passion to become owners of their farms. Occupying ownership, the

[1] Lyons, *Dillon*, pp 66–70; *Parnell*, pp 229–30.

[2] Cashman, p. 163.

[3] Cashman, pp 171–85.

Land League's stated aim, was a more conservative concept than the dual ownership of the land act, and this the landowners were quick to realise, as their swing in favour of land purchase early in 1882 showed: a multiplicity of small landowners would strengthen the principle of private ownership of land and act as a shock absorber to further attacks on 'landlordism'. This was why Davitt's opposition to the 'Kilmainham treaty' went far beyond criticism of Parnell's tactics; it was a protestation of his wider vision of a regenerated Ireland from which the whole working population would benefit, and which, he believed, the progress of the land war had made attainable. That he was politically wrong does not negate the significance in principle of the stand he made. He never ceased to believe in land nationalisation as the only ultimate solution of the land problem, and near the end of his life, while admitting his failure to convert Irishmen to his gospel, he wrote: 'I still hold fondly and firmly to this great principle, and I believe a national ownership to be the only true meaning of the battle-cry of the Land League—the Land for the People'.[1]

After a disillusioning visit to America (June-July 1882),[2] in which, however, he obtained Irish-American support for the resumption of a militant policy on the land question, he produced a plan for an updated and expanded version of the original league, to be called 'The National Land and Industrial Union of Ireland'. This was to be a democratic organisation with a comprehensive programme—'to improve the social and political condition of the Irish people'—combining the exclusively agrarian purpose, as officially defined, of the defunct Land League with a wide range of other objects characterised as social, industrial, educational, and political. Under all these heads the influence of Davitt's thinking and writing in Portland is apparent. The primary object of the new body—'the complete abolition of the landlord system'—was intended to leave the way open to land nationalisation: in Davitt's original draft the phrase was followed by 'and the substitution of such a one as shall make the land of Ireland the property of the people of Ireland', but he had struck out these words.[3] The other social objects of the union were the amelioration of the conditions of agricultural labourers and improved housing for the people. The industrial objects were the revival of manufacturing industries, the development of fisheries, improvement in agricultural methods, and the establishment of a cooperative land and labour association, with a capital of £1,000,000 in shares of £1 each, for the purchase of

[1] *Some suggestions for a final settlement of the land question* (1902), pp 6-7.
[2] *Fall*, pp 366-7; Brown, *Irish-American nationalism*, pp 127-30.
[3] DP/AV.

unoccupied and waste land on which to place labourers and evicted tenants. The educational objects of the union were to improve the scientific and practical education of the artisan and labouring classes by the establishment of Mechanics' Institutes[1] throughout the country; and to encourage the cultivation of national literature and the Irish language. Finally the political objects of the new body were defined as repeal of the act of union, national self-government, and, pending its attainment, improved parliamentary representation and payment of nationalist M.P.s; the abolition of the grand jury system of county government; and improved representation on all local bodies. All these necessary reforms were to be demanded on the ground of their reasonableness and justice, and were to be advanced by legal and constitutional means in such a way as to obtain the sympathy and moral support of external public opinion for a nation's efforts to change a destiny of poverty and discontent into one of prosperity and happiness. To convince the British parliament, through which these reforms were mainly to be obtained, of their necessity and expediency, the Irish people must be united in 'an open, national organisation' wholly non-sectarian, and democratic. With a four-tier branch-structure based on parishes, electoral districts, counties, and provinces, it was to be governed by a central executive council, of 25 members, five elected by a convention of county delegates in each of the four provinces and five coopted. It is deeply significant that, unlike the Land League, in which the central executive was elected by a Dublin body, unconnected organically with the local branches, Davitt's proposed 'union' was to have its central executive and its branches integrated on every level in a representative structure.[2]

Davitt had presented this scheme to Parnell on his return to London from America on 3 August. He found Parnell 'decidedly against any attempt to revive the Land League movement', believing that a good deal had been gained for Ireland, fearing the effects of the coercion act, and holding that the country needed rest from agitation. Parnell was convinced that, for the next three years at least, during which the coercion act would be in force, the national movement would have to behave with caution. So he refused to discuss Davitt's new proposals; 'there is very little backbone in this man after all', Davitt confided to his diary (3 August). But Parnell was far from being inactive. He took steps to meet the danger presented by the Land Corporation, a landlord syndicate formed in July by Art MacMurrough Kavanagh with the special object of protecting tenants who occupied evicted farms

[1] Cf. above, pp 514–15.
[2] DP/AV; Cashman, pp 254–6.

and consequently furthered evictions. At a public meeting in the Mansion House, Dublin, on 17 August, the Mansion House Committee for the Relief of Evicted Tenants was set up under the chairmanship of the lord mayor, Charles Dawson, M.P. A second initiative in which Parnell was involved concerned agricultural labourers. The Irish Labour and Industrial Union was founded at a meeting in the Antient Concert Rooms, Dublin, on 21 August, with the object, Parnell announced, of promoting and harmonising the interests of agricultural labourers and urban workers. The labourers had played a vital part in the agitation of the past few years from which tenant farmers had gained so much. 'In prudence no less than in common gratitude' the national credit was pledged to securing the following benefits for the labourers: (1) plots of ground and improved dwellings, and generally better treatment from their employers; (2) legislation to enable labourers to acquire land; (3) extension of the parliamentary franchise to them, and the creation of local government boards, in the election of which they would take part, with power of compulsory purchase of land for them; (4) encouragement of native industries and consequent enlargement of employment opportunities. Parnell urged the labourers to show moderation in pressing their claims, to keep within the law, and to avoid conflict with the farmers. All this is in line with his previous attitude to the labourers and to the danger of a breach between them and the farmers.[1] His plan, while expanding the clause in Davitt's scheme that dealt with labourers, left the land question in general and the home rule question to be dealt with separately. An executive committee was appointed, under Parnell's presidency, that included Davitt, Dillon, and Matthew Harris.[2]

Further negotiations between Davitt and Parnell led to a private meeting between the two, together with Dillon and Brennan, held at Parnell's home, Avondale, on 13 September, at which Parnell was persuaded to launch a new national organisation on the basis of a compromise between his and Davitt's views on the land question. Under this 'Avondale treaty' Parnell was to summon a national conference to consider a programme for the intended organisation in which the land policy would be defined by Parnell and Davitt's proposals on other matters would be included. Davitt agreed not to divide the conference over land nationalisation, while reserving the right to advocate that doctrine on any public platform afterwards. In the invitations to the conference issued on 18 September its general object was stated to be 'the uniting together on one central platform of the

[1] See above pp 423–4, 492–3.

[2] *Nation*, 12, 19, 26 Aug.; *Fall*, p. 370; W. O'Brien, *Recollections*, pp 456–8, 461.

various movements and interests that are now appealing to the country for separate sanction and support'.[1]

The programme and the constitution for submission to the national conference was drafted by T. M. Healy and Timothy Harrington under Parnell's vigilant eye.[2] The objects of the new body, 'The Irish National League', were summarised as (1) national self-government, (2) land-law reform, (3) local self-government, (4) extension of the parliamentary and municipal franchises, (5) the development and encouragement of the labour and industrial interests of Ireland, with emphasis on improving the conditions of agricultural labourers. Davitt's 'complete abolition of the landlord system' was replaced by the aim of amending the land act in relation to land purchase, leaseholders, and the protection of tenants' improvements as proposed in Parnell's bill of 8 February.[3] The programme broadly followed Davitt's plan as to agricultural labourers, the purchase of unoccupied and waste land for resale or reletting to small farmers and labourers, the revival of manufactures, national self-government, improved parliamentary representation, and reformed local government. It developed his suggestions on local self-government by proposing the creation of elected county boards and the transfer to them of powers now exercised by the grand juries and other local bodies and by the central government; the election by county boards of the members of central administrative bodies such as the local government board, at present nominated by the crown; and the substitution of local for central control of the police. On the other hand it entirely omitted his proposals as to housing in general, fisheries, agricultural methods, education, the encouragement of Irish literature and language, and the payment of M.P.s. Finally a constitution was proposed that was to give the parliamentary party effective control over the governing body, which in Davitt's scheme was to be democratically elected. The new league was to consist of local branches and a central governing council, which was to comprise 30 members, 20 to be elected by county conventions and 10 by the parliamentary party; pending its election the council's powers were to be exercised by an 'organising committee' of 30, consisting of 5 members of the Mansion House Committee for the Relief of Evicted Tenants, 5 members of the executive of the Labour and Industrial Union, 5 members of the council of the Home Rule League, and 15 elected members.[4]

The national conference, held in The Antient Concert Rooms,

[1] DN/9, 12-13 Sept.. *Fall*, pp 371-2.
[2] *Fall*, pp 374-5.
[3] See above, p. 592.
[4] *Nation*, 21 Oct.

Dublin on 17 October, was well attended by delegates from all over Ireland, and both the old Land League element and the parliamentary interest were strongly represented. Davitt believed that he could have carried advanced proposals on the land question if his hands had not been tied by the 'Avondale treaty'. He had no difficulty in persuading the conference to add to the industrial clauses of the league's programme a statement that its branches should encourage mechanics' institutes and working-men's clubs and reading-rooms 'to enable the artizans and labourers of Ireland to improve their education'. A second point in his scheme that had been omitted from Parnell's document—payment of nationalist M.P.s—was also adopted. So too was Matthew Harris's proposal that a special tax should be levied on grassland so as to penalise large grazing-farmers, described by a speaker as 'the curse of the country, second only to landlords'. When the constitution of the league came under discussion Davitt felt free to propose an amendment that would have made the council a wholly elected body of 32 members, one from each county. This was well supported, but was countered by two objections: first it would give disproportionate weight to counties in Ulster, some of which, with only one or two branches of the league, would have equal representation with southern counties with three or four hundred; second, it amounted to a vote of no confidence in Parnell and his party. Davitt was disgusted by the 'ugly discussion' on Ulster and by the tactics of Healy and T. P. O'Connor in raising the no-confidence issue. 'The slavish name-worshippers who would have voted for my amendment turned with characteristic Irish fickleness to support the 'name' when their clannishness was appealed to by a treacherous argument.' But to avoid a split he withdrew his amendment and agreed to a compromise: the council should consist of 48 members, 1 elected by each county and 16 by the parliamentary party. Apart from these changes the programme and the constitution for the National League as presented by Parnell to the conference were adopted, and thus in effect the 'Kilmainham treaty' was ratified.[1]

The discussion on the composition of the council, though heated and at some points even embittered, proved to have no practical effect. For the council in fact was never to be elected. Instead, the government of the league was to remain in the hands of the temporary organising committee dominated by members of the parliamentary party under Parnell's chairmanship.[2] In its oligarchic character the new league

[1] DN/9, 17 Oct.; *F.J.* 18 Oct.; W. O'Brien, *Recollections*, pp 466-70. In *Fall*, pp 375-7 Davitt gives the text of the National League's constitution as amended at the conference but omits the conference's amendments to the league's programme. This the more surprising because, as correspondent of the New York *Daily News*, he sent the amended text of both documents to that paper on 21 Oct.

[2] C. C. O'Brien, *Parnell*, pp 127-8.

did not differ greatly from the central body of the old league,[1] but unlike the Land League the National League was designed to serve chiefly as an electoral machine for the parliamentary party. It soon absorbed Butt's Home Rule League.

The conference received a letter from Egan in Paris to Parnell announcing his intention to resign the treasurership of the Land League and conveying a summary of his receipts and expenditure during his three years in office. He reckoned that his total receipts amounted to about £245,000, of which about £50,000 had been spent on relief of distress, over £15,000 on the state trial, and nearly £148,000 on the work of the league and of the Ladies' Land League in supporting evicted tenants, meeting legal costs, providing temporary housing, and generally in carrying on the organisation. This left a balance in hand of £31,900. In thus rendering an account of his stewardship, Egan took care to express his confidence in Parnell's leadership: 'never since I have taken a part in politics have I felt more hopeful of the long struggle for Ireland's national rights'.[2] The acceptance of Egan's letter by the conference and an enthusiastic vote of thanks for his services may be taken as the voluntary winding-up of the Land League, as distinct from its suppression by government a year before. The Ladies' Land League, under pressure from Parnell, had dissolved itself in August.[3]

Davitt saw the outcome of the national conference of 17 October as 'a veritable new departure'; and we may regard the conference as putting an end to the new departure of which he himself, as father of the Land League, was the author, and which was the third and culminating innovation in Irish politics since 1870.[4] He later described the founding of the National League, with some justice, as 'the complete eclipse, by a purely parliamentary substitute, of what had been a semi-revolutionary organisation, . . . the overthrow of a movement and the enthronement of a man'.[5] This statement, written in 1903, fairly represents the view he held, but did not so forcibly express, in 1882; yet he accepted membership of the organising committee of the National League, supported its programme and that of its successors, and steadily upheld Parnell's leadership until the O'Shea divorce scandal split the parliamentary party. In this apparent paradox lies a clue to all Davitt's subsequent political behaviour and an illustration of an aspect of his personality. A man of great independence of mind and of great moral courage in the defence of his ideas, he was also modest

[1] See above, pp 341–3.
[2] *F.J.*, 18 Oct.; *Fall*, pp 372–4.
[3] R. F. Foster, *Parnell*, pp 276–8.
[4] Above, pp 325–6.
[5] *Fall*, pp 377–8.

and self-critical, devoid of personal ambition, and almost obsessively anxious not to divide the national forces.

None of his contemporaries had a higher appreciation than Davitt of Parnell's greatness as a leader, however critical he might at times be of Parnell's policy. No one more clearly distinguished between Parnell's own restrained and tolerant conduct as leader, until the divorce crisis, and the cult of Parnellism sedulously fostered by his brilliant lieutenants, especially T. M. Healy, T. P. O'Connor, Thomas Sexton, and William O'Brien—who, having 'preached Parnell's autocracy as a dogma of absolute political faith for nearly ten years', led the revolt against their 'uncrowned king' in 1890.[1] Davitt, while detesting this personality cult, cooperated fully with Parnell in the 'liberal alliance' and the struggle for Gladstonian home rule, and in countering the attempts of *The Times* to ruin Parnell and the home rule cause through the special commission of 1888, whose proceedings culminated in the exposure of the Pigott forgeries. But when Parnell's ten years' old adultery with O'Shea's wife was disclosed in ignominious detail through the divorce court in November 1890, Davitt did not hesitate to demand Parnell's temporary retirement on the ground that he had deceived his colleagues and was morally disgraced. He was greatly troubled by the split and the chronic in-fighting that ensued, and he rendered valuable service to the home rule cause in the negotiations leading to party reunion in 1900.

In backing the home rule demand that was the primary concern of the parliamentary party Davitt did not renounce his fenian ideal of complete independence for Ireland. But he saw home rule as the largest measure of self-government that could be obtained in the early future, and as an advance that would be of inestimable value to Ireland. He was prevailed upon, in the interest of home rule, to become a member of parliament, and sat for North Meath in 1892, for North-east Cork in 1893 and for Mayo in 1895–9. He made a deep impression on the house of commons by a speech in which he welcomed Gladstone's home rule bill of 1893 as a 'pact of peace' between England and Ireland. He did valuable work in committee on the prisons bill of 1898, and in the same year had the satisfaction of helping to place on the statute book the local government bill which replaced the oligarchic grand-jury system by elected county and district councils. But he was not happy as a parliamentarian: his temperament, the previous course of his life, and his views about parliamentary action, were not conducive to success in the house of commons.

The attempt of the National League and its successors to contain

[1] *Fall*, p. 378.

the national movement within the limits of parliamentary politics was not compatible with his conception of the relationship that should exist between national action in and outside parliament. In a letter to Bishop Nulty thanking the electors of Meath for electing him as their M.P. while he was in Portland, he said in 1882 that, from the last general election, Ireland had a truly national and trustworthy party at Westminster that was rendering indispensable service, but that extra-parliamentary exertion was also necessary and that this 'could be more efficiently performed and would better command the cooperation and confidence of our people if undertaken by men who would be above the suspicion of parliamentary aspirations'.

> I have endeavoured to prove myself one of such men; and I think the history of the Land League movement will show how much can be done for Ireland by an organisation that is wielded in conjunction with, but not in subordination to, the labours of its advocates in the English parliament.[1]

Thus, on the land question, while always ready to exert himself to obtain the maximum of advantage for the tenants through the parliamentary party, he engaged spasmodically in agrarian agitation on the old lines, on occasions when agrarian distress flared up again. In November 1882, he made an extremist speech at Navan that earned him a further term of imprisonment—seventeen weeks (4 February–4 June 1883) in Richmond Bridewell, Dublin—his fourth, and, as it proved his last, and his only imprisonment to be served in an Irish jail.[2] During evictions that he witnessed at Bodyke, County Clare, in June 1887, his anger became so uncontrollable that he publicly expressed shame for having ever counselled the people to refrain from violence and illegality: 'would to God we had the . . . weapons by which freemen in America and elsewhere have struck down tyranny'.[3] But this was an obvious aberration, brought on by the extreme heat of the moment; and in fact Davitt used his great influence to prevent clashes with the officers of the law—and raised a fund for the relief of the evicted tenants.[4] His occasional sallies into agrarian agitation were less significant than his decision, despite his protestation of 1882 to the Meath electors, to enter parliament.

His distinctive role in public life from 1882 onwards was that of a free-lance—as nationalist, labour leader, democratic reformer, humanitarian, and internationalist—and a fearless critic and arduous educator

1 D to Bp Nulty, 14 May (*F.J.*, 16 May).

2 DL/3. He was charged under the same statute (34 Edward III, c.1, 1360) that was invoked against Forrester in December 1870 (above, p. 63), but refused to give bail to be of good behaviour.

3 *F.J.*, 3 June 87.

4 *F.J.*, 4, 6 June; DP/A17–A18; DN/59A; *S.C.P.*, ix 525–6.

of the national movement. No public figure commanded greater respect and affection among the Irish masses than the 'father of the Land League'. But though he continued to have a political force to be reckoned with throughout his remaining twenty-four years, he was never again to exercise power at the centre of Irish affairs as he had done in 1879–81. On the other hand he was to become well and widely known outside Ireland—as a platform speaker, especially to working men, in Britain and in America (which he visited eight times from 1882 to 1904), as a correspondent for American newspapers and the *Melbourne Advocate*, and as the author of six substantial books.

The general trend of his political thinking and action was leftward. In Ireland he had a special concern for the condition of agricultural labourers, in whose interest he founded at Cork an Irish Democratic and Trade and Labour Federation (21 January 1891). For the general election of 1892 he recommended seven labour men as labour-nationalist candidates for Irish constituencies, and two of these were returned to parliament. But his labour interests found their main outlet in Britain, where much of his time and energy were given to helping the rising labour movement, both as an end in itself and as a means of promoting that alliance between Irish nationalism and British democracy that he had suggested to Parnell in February 1881 and that Parnell had endorsed but later rejected. From 1882 onwards he was the most striking exponent of the idea that the democratisation of the United Kingdom parliament and the winning of home rule for Ireland were the common interest of working men, both British and Irish. In his self-appointed task of preaching this gospel in Britain he made full use of his doctrine of land nationalisation as a link between the cause of 'the land for the people' and the interests of all workers. At Inverness on 4 November 1882 he drew a warm response from a large public meeting when he applied the doctrine to the rising crofter agitation in Scotland, which had been encouraged by the Irish Land League movement.[1] He helped in the initiation of a land movement in Wales which brought about a 'Welsh Land, Commercial and Labour League' in 1887.[2] He started and edited in London in 1890 a pioneer weekly, the *Labour World* as 'a journal of progress for the masses', but after eight months (September 1890–May 1891) found the burden too great. His involvement in British politics in the labour and 'lib.-lab.' interest reached an appropriate climax in the general election of January 1906, when, a few month before his death, he contributed

[1] DN/9, 4 Nov.; DPC/3, ff 25v–26; Roy Douglas, *Land, people, and politics . . . in the United Kingdom, 1878–1952* (London, 1976), pp 63–5.

[2] DN/15, 14 Feb. 84; Douglas, op. cit., pp 97–9.

conspicuously to the labour successes that made the election a landmark in labour history.[1]

The range of his interests and sympathies expanded with increasing age. He had the idea of securing the return to parliament for an Irish constituency of Dadabhai Naoroji, an Indian resident in London, so as to give a direct voice in the house of commons to Indian nationalism, but the practical difficulties were too great. He was invited to preside at the Indian National Congress of 1894 at Madras, but declined on the ground that his presence would be too serious a risk for Congress to take.[2] A lecture tour in Australia and New Zealand in 1895 brought him into contact with the vigorous young democracies in those countries, where the immigrant Irish presented striking contrasts with their counterparts in America. In 1900 he was commissioned by American newspapers to go out to South Africa and report on the Boer war from the standpoint of the Boers, whose cause he indignantly championed against what he regarded as outrageous imperalist aggression on Britain's part. His international reputation as a journalist was again recognised when, in 1903, he investigated an anti-Semitic outbreak at Kishineff, in the Russian province of Bessarabia, for the New York *American*. This experience roused his compassionate interest in the Jewish problem, for the study of which a visit to the Holy Land in 1885 had prepared the way. He became 'a convinced believer in the remedy of Zionism' and a formidable enemy of anti-Semitism. When in January 1904 a priest in Limerick preached an anti-Semitic sermon, Davitt effectively denounced him, and the hostilities against local Jews that followed the sermon, as a national disgrace.[3] He returned to Russia in June 1904 to report on the growing political tensions that in the following January were to erupt at St Petersburg in the 'revolution of 1905'. This brought him back to Russia for the third time as a newspaper reporter. Both in 1904 and 1905 he visited Tolstoy at Yasnia, and talked with him about the Irish struggle for independence.

Contributions to newspapers constitute a large part of Davitt's writing, which was his principal source of livelihood till near the end of his life. But he also found time and energy to write six books, in addition to numerous pamphlets and articles in periodicals. *Leaves from a prison diary* (1885) was, as we have seen,[4] largely the fruit of his thinking and writing in Portland. His *Defence of the Land League*

[1] This phase of Davitt's career is treated in my 'Michael Davitt and the British labour movement, 1882-1906' in *Transactions of the Royal Historical Society*, 5th series, iii, 53-76 (1952).

[2] *F.J.*, 28 May 88; Naoroji to D, 2 Oct. 94 (DP/W), 15 Jan. 96 (DP/X); DN/27, 3-5 Oct. 94.

[3] Louis Hyman, *The Jews of Ireland* . . . (1972), p. 216.

[4] Above, pp 501, 505, 506-8.

(1890) is a reprint of the speech he delivered before the special commission in October 1889 in reply to the charges of complicity in crime brought by *The Times* against the leaders of the land war. *Life and progress in Australasia* (1898) is an appreciative account of his experience of Australia and New Zealand during his lecture tour of 1895. *The Boer fight for freedom* (1902) is a narrative of the war based largely on information obtained from Boer sources and from his own observations in the Transvaal and the Orange Free State in March–May 1900. The story is continued down to March 1902, two months before the peace treaty, in the form of annals derived from the press. The Kishineff assignment led to *Within the pale: the true story of anti-Semitic persecution in Russia* (1903), a moving report of his findings and an eloquent plea for Zionism.

Finally, his largest and most important book, *The fall of feudalism, or the story of the Land League revolution* (1904) is a history of the land war in historical perspective and carried down to 1903. It contains a wealth of information on its subject, and is an indispensable source not only for the history of the land war but also for its mythology. It is generally accurate in its statements of fact, is well, though not consistently, documented, and, considering that Davitt was so deeply involved in the story, is remarkably detached and fair except where 'landlordism' is directly concerned: here it is nearer to polemic than to history. Its merit as history is seen at its best in the treatment of Butt and of Parnell, who fill large spaces in it: here the book attains a very high level of sympathy, appreciation, objectivity, and fairmindedness. It is rich in character sketches, telling incidents, and amusing anecdotes, but Davitt's attention is never distracted from the wood by the trees. The book shows a gift for synthesis, percipient generalising, lateral thinking, and orderly construction that lift it far above any comparable work by its author's contemporaries. Its style is uneven, at times pedestrian, but on the whole highly readable, and well adapted in pace, tension, and dramatic emphasis to the changing character of its subject. For a book written in less than a year (1903) it is a miraculous performance.

Taken together Davitt's books are a monument to his enormous energy, power of concentration, and fluency as a writer, largely self-educated. All of them have a strong, though restrained, autobiographical quality; the first two and the last are essential material for the subject of this book.

Davitt at thirty-six, viewed in the perspective of his career as a whole, had made his greatest contribution to shaping his country's future.

His work as reformer, teacher, writer, and prophet of a new Ireland lay ahead, but its foundations were well established in his character, personality, experience, and thinking.

Warm-hearted, generous, ardent, and impulsive, he was also strong-willed, idealistic, self-reliant, and in some ways austere. He had immense courage, physical and moral: he could endure physical suffering and hardship with stoical calm and he could challenge and shock majority opinions and prejudices regardless of the cost in popularity. In this quality of moral courage he stands alone among the Irish public men of his time with the possible exception of John Dillon. Yet he was self-critical, often lacked self-confidence, and had not a trace of self-importance or arrogance. He believed that he was prone to misfortune and had some grounds for the belief, as in his early association with Forrester, his arrest and trial in 1870, his loan from the 'skirmishing fund', and his relations with Devoy. He had virtually no home life between 1870, when his family moved to Pennsylvania just before he moved to Dartmoor, and 1886, when he married Mary Yore, the Irish-American of Oakland, California, whom he had met there in 1880.[1] She brought him enduring happiness and the peace and support of a stable home. They had five children,[2] two of them, Cahir and Robert Emmet, happily still alive.

His personal life was ruled by the simple code of duty in which he had been reared, but he was not dour or censorious. His attitude to the place of women in society, as shown by his institution of the Ladies' Land League, was far in advance of his time. He was abstemious in his habits, and held that Ireland's greatest enemy, along with moral cowardice, was drink. His health was generally good, but not robust; yet, except when in prison, he lived an intensely strenuous life, physical and mental. His longest periods of relaxation down to May 1882 were during his four Atlantic crossings and the time he spent in the infirmary garden at Portland. Though he suffered many a disappointment and defeat he was fundamentally a hopeful man, who never lost his faith in human goodness and the power of reason; yet he was pensive and given to questioning the value of his own efforts and repining at the fate that doomed him to a life of politics. But he could never disengage himself from the dust and heat and unending pressures of political life; for he was a dedicated public man, a people's tribune, whose vital energies were committed to the self-consuming task of

[1] Above, p. 407.

[2] Kathleen (1888-95), Michael (1890-1928), Eileen (1892-1974), Cahir (b. 1894), Robert Emmet (b. 1899). Kathleen died in childhood, Michael and Robert became doctors, Eileen a school teacher, and Cahir a lawyer and president of the high court of Ireland.

changing society in the interests of the common man, especially the weak and the oppressed. Yet he was never a monomaniac or a bore. He could laugh at himself as well as criticising his own shortcomings, he was friendly and sociable, enjoyed good conversation with all sorts of people, and had a keen sense of the ludicrous. He was fiercely independent in money matters, earning a modest and precarious livelihood by his exertions as a journalist and public speaker. The only testimonial to his unpaid public services that he could be induced to accept was the gift to his wife, on the occasion of their marriage, of a house at Ballybrack—'Land League Cottage'—which was their home from 1887 to 1895. As their children grew up he was usually under financial strain, but his wife received help occasionally from her wealthy Californian aunt, Mary Canning, and from her in 1904 inherited enough to enable the Davitts to live in solid comfort in Dalkey, a neighbourhood that Michael loved. His independence of spirit was also shown in his attitude to his physical handicap; he wanted no special privileges because he lacked a right arm, having from his boyhood learnt astonishing resourcefulness and skill in making his left arm serve the purpose of two. He could tie his own bootlaces and in later life even coped with a bow tie. He wrote a firm, clear hand.

He was a truth-loving man, yet was often involved in situations where it was difficult to be strictly truthful. He had the revolutionary conspirator's ambivalence towards the law, which he was ready to invoke in the letter in defence of his rights while violating it in spirit. The influence of his early experience in the fenian underworld clung to him in a tendency to suspect the motives of political associates, in a certain evasiveness, and in discrepancies between his public and his private statements. He sometimes lapsed into wishful thinking, even self-deception. His habit of reinterpreting his past actions and attitudes in accordance with altered conditions was partly the outcome of a longing for integrity in his political conduct, partly of his quickness of response to the appeal or challenge of a new situation. It was also related to the fact that he was a man with an unquenchable interest in ideas, and that his own ideas were not static but evolving. Henry George, who greatly admired him, thought him 'a very impressionable man'.[1] His conscience was too tender and active for his comfort as a politician, and he suffered from its prickings in ways unknown to political contemporaries such as Parnell. What most immediately impressed people meeting him for the first time was his passionate sincerity.

In the fierce campaigning, on the platform and in the press, in

[1] George to Patrick Ford, 27 May 82 (New York Public Library, Henry George papers).

which he had been engaged since 1878 and which was to continue throughout his life, he was apt to let his feelings run away with him and to attack his opponents with violence of language and wild exaggeration. To the landlord class he appeared as the most dangerous and sinister of the land-leaguers. Yet in an elemental conflict over the most vital of human interests, control of land, his great influence was exerted on the side of restraint rather than of excess. He never desisted from his mission to destroy 'landlordism', but generally it was a system, and landlords as a class, that he attacked, not individuals. He well deserved the reputation he came to acquire of being a clean fighter. He was not apt to harbour anger or malice against individuals (Devoy was one of the conspicuous exceptions), and was quick to forgive a personal slight or injury.

Temperamentally a fighter and always convinced of the morality of using physical force as a last resort in a just cause, he devoted his energies after 1877 to persuading and inspiring his countrymen to combine in a disciplined organisation to effect a social revolution by non-violent means. Insisting that the demands of the tenants were founded on morality and natural justice, he counselled them to refrain from violence, which could only weaken their cause in the eyes of an awakened public opinion. He had no doubt that landlords as a class were greedy, oppressive, idle, unproductive—economically, socially, and (he was apt to add), morally, worthless—and that landlordism was the great curse of Ireland that must be removed if she were ever to enjoy social health and peace. Though the land war was not free from violence, and still less from near-violent intimidation, he had good grounds for holding that so great a revolution as the Land League had brought about had never been so free from bloodshed.

He was an instructed and during most of his life an orthodox and practising catholic. He could be militant in defence of catholic interests, as when, in 1868 he defeated an attack by protestant bigots on St Mary's Church, Haslingden. He appreciated the immense social and moral importance of the catholic church in Irish society. But he was no zealot. Towards the end of his life he ceased to be a communicant, while continuing to attend mass with his family. But he became reconciled to the catholic church during his last illness. He was completely free from sectarian feeling, and accepted diversity of religious denominations as a fact of life, like difference of sex. He was no anti-clerical, and had close and friendly relations with individual catholic clerics, most notably Archbishop Croke of Cashel and Bishop Duggan of Clonfert. In his relations with the catholic clergy he had no sense of awe; accepting their authority in the sphere of faith and morals, he was ready at all times to challenge and reject their opinions and activities in politics, and to dispute the boundary between their proper field of authority and the field in which they should count for no more than the laity. This was the orthodox fenian position, maintained with unabated tenacity by Davitt till the end of his life. During his last few months he was hotly engaged in a public controversy on educational policy with two formidable prelates, O'Dwyer, bishop of Limerick, and Walsh, archbishop of Dublin. In a letter to the rector of Westport, Canon J. O. Hannay ('George Birmingham'), he blamed, next to English misrule, the educational system for the 'criminal misuse' by Irish farmers of some of the best land in Europe:

It has scarcely any relation to the industrial needs of the country, and yet, because it is supposed to be, in some mysterious way, a safeguard for 'faith and morals', our bishops—and I fear yours too—are standing in the way of efficient reform. One would like to know . . . what the devil's private view about 'faith and morals' that are protected by ignorance and a slovenly social life really is.[1]

He was a rare combination of revolutionary and reformer, of idealist and realist, of dogmatist and pragmatist. In his youthful involvement in politics he was a revolutionary both in the object he pursued and in the means he was committed to using. In his later years, from 1882 onwards, he was a radical reformer, working for great social and political improvements in instalments and by constitutional means. Between these two phases of his life, from 1878 to 1882, the revolutionary and the reformer in him interacted in a dynamic and ambivalent combination. After the crisis of the land war the revolutionary was never extinguished, but while continuing to cherish revolutionary objectives —complete national independence and national ownership of the land— he devoted himself to working within the law for social and political changes that fell far short of these but were realisable in the 'living present'. He had an instinctive loathing for terrorism as an instrument of revolution. In his youth he saw himself as a soldier in an Irish revolutionary army; but to him, as to Stephens, Kickham, O'Leary, and the other founding fathers of fenianism, the role of soldiers in a war of national liberation was wholly different from, and incompatible with, that of the urban terrorists who, under the auspices of O'Donovan Rossa and Clan na Gael, conducted a dynamite campaign in 1881–7 against London and other British cities. Davitt made his attitude to this campaign clear in a letter of 25 March 1883.

Principles of reform intelligently and fearlessly propagated are far more destructive to unjust and worn-out systems than dynamite bombs, which only kill individuals

[1] D to Rev. J. O. Hannay, 4 Apr. 1906 (DP/YY; quoted in Sheehy-Skeffington, *Michael Davitt* (new ed., 1967), p. 208.

or knock down buildings but do no injury to oppressive institutions. . . . The dynamite theory is the very abnegation of mind, the surrender of reason to rage, of judgment to blind, unthinking recklessness.[1]

Though he was never a pacifist, and in times of crisis carried a revolver (as did Parnell), he was never involved in physical conflict and shed no man's blood.

Intellectually he was well endowed. His prodigious activity as a public man, as a writer, and as a speaker was energised by a powerful, perceptive, resourceful, and resilient mind. He had a genius for organisation, uniquely exemplified in the Land League, but also in his arms traffic of 1870 and in the ease and efficiency with which, from 1878, he managed his many journeys in various parts of the world. He was well able to cope with the practical business of life, but also tireless in acquiring new knowledge and new skills, through reading and observation. He read avidly and adventurously, and in his frequent travelling was always alert to new scenes and developments. He showed scholarly ability in the assembling and interpreting of evidence, and he had the faculty of conceptual thinking. He was not outstanding as an original thinker but was a sensitive receiver of ideas and a skilful adapter and transmitter of them. As a people's educator in public affairs he had no rival in Ireland. And in his faith in the value of popular education for the social regeneration of Ireland he was unequalled among his political contemporaries.

Unique in many ways in the Ireland of his day, he conformed to no Irish prototype. He was the only man of working-class origins ever to have attained the top level of national leadership, and he retained that distinction throughout his life. But his culture was middle-class. Never a social climber, he had close relations with men and women of all social levels and walks of life. He was courteous and approachable, refined in his manner and bearing, and of cultivated tastes, especially in books, gardening, travel, and music. In his travels he always had an eye for natural beauty.

His personality shines through the distinctive character of his nationalism. He inherited from his parents a traditional sense of Irish identity and the collective emotions that went with it, especially the peasant's attitude to land and landlords. Reared in the extreme republican school, in his youth he saw it as the first duty of a patriotic Irishman to prepare for rebellion against British authority. In his maturity, like Fintan Lalor before him, he came to regard social revolution as more fundamental than political revolution. The emancipation of the

[1] *Glasgow Herald*, 25 Mar. 83; *S.C.P.*, vi, 617–20; *Defence*, pp 407–8.

small tenant from the power of the landlord was a more vital and urgent need than, and would be a powerful lever to, self-government. The fight against poverty, ignorance, social servility, and low standards, and for an improving, self-reliant, self-advancing, democratic society could be fought here and now, and victories could be won pending the achievement of national independence. The outcome of the land war and every subsequent democratic reform in Davitt's lifetime substantiated this concept of national progress. The nation as a political abstraction was empty and futile; 'his Ireland', as Keir Hardie said in an obituary appreciation, 'was the actual flesh and blood Ireland'.[1] His heart was always with the cause of the poor and the oppressed. The independent Irish nation of his dreams was a society absolutely committed to promoting human welfare and social justice as well as to democratic government. That was essentially why his doctrine of national ownership of all land became integral to this thinking about the nation. For it was in his view the only way in which the whole nation, urban as well as rural, could share in the benefits of the land, which was the national inheritance. Land, which no man had created, which was vital to all life, and which was fixed in quantity, could not justly be the absolute property of any man, or left exposed to the greed and acquisitiveness of the speculator. The emancipated tenant would be as secure in the occupancy of his farm as under private ownership, but the evils inseparable from private ownership would be banished and the national life would be invigorated and enriched by making the land the property of the whole nation.

The Irish nation of Davitt's ideal was to be a tolerant, pluralist (he did not, of course, use the word), outward-looking, democratic community, in which the separate strands and traditions of the past would be united, and the old sectarian and cultural divisions healed, in co-operative effort for the common good. In achieving that cooperation, nationalisation of the land was more important than nationalisation of the government. It followed from this concept of the nation, and from his awareness and growing knowledge of the world outside Ireland, that his nationalism was complemented by an internationalism. In the land war he constantly sounded the note that the cause of the small farmers was the cause of struggling humanity, and the centrality of social justice in his nationalism ensured that he could never be blind to the common interests of working people everywhere. That was why he never tired of preaching that the Irish quarrel was with British rule, not with the British people, and that the working masses in both islands had a common interest in striving for democracy throughout

[1] *Labour Leader*, 8 June 1906.

the United Kingdom and for national self-government for Ireland. The rights that he claimed for Ireland he claimed for all struggling nations, whatever their race or religion or history.

Davitt's most distinctive achievement was crowded into the sixteen months from October 1879 to February 1881 when, as 'father of the Land League' he led an uprising of tenant farmers that effected revolutionary changes in Irish society. The legal relations between landlords and tenants were revolutionised by the land act of 1881–which, as Gladstone admitted in the house of commons, would not have been on the statute book without the Land League.[1] The psychological relations between landlords and tenants were revolutionised by the spirit of collective resistance that the Land League infused among the farmers, a spirit that Davitt with his 'gospel of manhood' was foremost in promoting. His sixteen months of Land League activity did incomparably more to advance the interests of the Irish nation as he conceived them than his five years of service in the I.R.B. and his consequent seven years of penal servitude. Yet without his fenian background and connections he could not have brought to the land movement the indispensable support that it received from fenians. Devoy shared with him the authorship of the 'new departure' in fenian policy, but the adaptation of the new policy to the interests of the land war was Davitt's doing. He did not initiate the land agitation: that was the work of James Daly, Matthew Harris, O'Connor Power, J. J. Louden, and other Connacht tenant-righters. But he was quick to realise the explosive character of the situation in the west that caused these men to summon the Irishtown meeting. He was quick to grasp the potentiality of the procedure they had pioneered and to organise it effectively, first on a regional and then on a national scale. It was Davitt who canalised the agitation and brought it to the point at which Parnell felt compelled to commit himself to it if the national movement was not to bypass him. In directing and administering the Land League Davitt was associated with a small number of able and dedicated men, principally Egan, Brennan, and Kettle, who, with Dillon, Sexton, and others, carried on the organisation while Davitt was in America and after he was rearrested. In shaping the strategy of the land war Parnell probably counted for more than Davitt, and it was Parnell's statesmanship that ended the war with a peace settlement highly advantageous to the tenants. On the other hand Davitt counted for more than Parnell in ensuring vital support for the Land League from Irish-America: it was Davitt above all the league leaders who

[1] *Hansard 3*, cccxli, 1686–7 (3 Mar. 90).

typified for Irish-Americans the struggle for the land in Ireland. Both Davitt and Parnell sought to stamp the land movement with a national rather than a class character, even though, in fact, it involved a social revolution. On the one hand, they saw the landlords collectively as outside the nation, and on the other they were concerned to prevent cleavages between farmers and labourers, and between well-to-do and poor farmers from injuring the solidarity of the league. They were well aware of the importance of urban middle-class support. They differed profoundly in that Parnell wanted to stop the war as soon as he was convinced that the vital interests of the farmers were secured, whereas Davitt wanted to carry on the war until 'landlordism' was 'abolished'. The conception, organisation, and inspiration of the Land League were peculiarly Davitt's work, but in the leadership of the farmers in the land war, the greatest mass movement in modern Irish history, both men were indispensable. The success of the land war is conceivable without Egan, or Brennan, or Kettle, or Dillon, but not without both Davitt and Parnell.

Davitt had defects that impaired his effectiveness as a politician and prevented him from ever seeing himself as a potential rival or successor to Parnell—faults of judgment, lack of confidence in himself, over-sensitivity, impulsiveness, a tendency to extend his energies over too wide a field, and the absence of that mysterious power of command that Parnell so superbly possessed. These defects were least detrimental to his effectiveness during the land war, when he achieved his greatest tangible success in a partnership with Parnell that came near to perfection on both sides. But in the estimation of Irishmen and of innumerable others all over the world his faults counted for very little in the scale against his great-heartedness, his self-sacrifice, and his invincible courage. He did not seek power or glory or money but he won gratitude and respect and love in full measure.

APPENDICES

A LANDOWNERS, 1870

Source: *Copy of a return of the names of proprietors and the area and valuation of all properties in the several counties in Ireland held in fee or perpetuity, or on long leases at chief rents . . .*, H.C. 1876 (412), lxxx, 395-580.

	landowners		properties	
size of estate in acres	number	%	acres	%
20,000 and over	110	0.57	4,151,142	20.71
20,000-10,000	192	0.99	2,607,719	13.01
10,000 and over	302	1.56	6,758,861	33.72
10,000-5,000	440	2.28	3,071,471	15.32
5,000-2,000	1,246	6.46	3,872,611	19.32
2,000-1,000	1,773	9.19	2,474,756	12.34
1,000-10,000	3,459	17.93	9,418,838	46.98
1,000-500	2,633	13.65	1,871,171	9.33
500-100	6,975	36.16	1,764,838	8.80
100 and below	5,919	30.69	233,864	1.17
1,000 and below	15,527	80.50	3,869,873	19.30
total	19,288		20,047,572	

General Valuation Office, Dublin, July 1870

B TENANTS, 1870-71

1 *TENANTS CLASSIFIED ACCORDING TO SIZE OF HOLDINGS, 1871*

Source: 'Approximate return of the number of occupiers resident in each county and province in 1871, classified according to the total extent of land they held, without any reference to the townland, barony, county, or province in which the portions of land are situated' in *The agricultural statistics of Ireland for 1871* [C762], H.C. 1873, lxix, 375.

holdings classed according to size in acres	number of occupiers in each class	% of total occupiers
not exceeding 1	47,030	8.70
above 1 and not exceeding 5	67,054	12.44
above 5 and not exceeding 15	152,987	28.39
above 15 and not exceeding 30	124,457	23.10
not exceeding 30	391,528	72.66
above 30 and not exceeding 50	65,427	12.14
above 50 and not exceeding 100	50,286	9.33
above 30 and not exceeding 100	115,713	21.47

above 100 and not exceeding 200	20,421	3.79
above 200 and not exceeding 500	8,672	1.61
above 500	2,499	0.46
above 100	31,592	5.86
total	538,833	

2 TENURE OF HOLDINGS, 1870

Source: *Returns showing the number of agricultural holdings in Ireland and the tenure by which they are held by the occupiers* [C32], H.C. 1870, lvi, 737-56.

province	A leasehold and other fixed tenancies	B tenancies from year to year and at will	C total holdings	B as % of C
Ulster	45,179	205,549	250,728	82
Leinster	39,342	100, 744	140,086	72
Munster	52,244	93,468	145,712	64
Connacht	18,933	126,778	145,711	87
Ireland	155,698	526,539	682,237	77

Tenancies in col.A comprise: leaseholds for years–61,335; leaseholds for lives–63,759; perpetuities–10,298; holdings in occupation of proprietors–20,217; undescribed–89.

C AGRICULTURAL LABOURERS, 1871

Source: (A) *Census of Ireland, 1871*; (B) *Agricultural statistice of Ireland for 1871.*

province	A total labourers	B total occupiers above 1 acre	C A as % of B
Ulster	194,077	182,019	106.6
Leinster	162,951	95,763	170.2
Munster	185,377	100,853	183.8
Connacht	124,139	113,168	109.7
Ireland	666,544	491,803	135.5

D EVICTIONS, 1849-83

Source: *Return, by provinces and counties . . . of cases of evictions which have come to the knowledge of the constabulary in each of the years from 1849 to 1880 (inclusive),* H.C. 1881 (185), lxxvii, 725-48.'Return by provinces and counties compiled from returns made by the inspector general of the Royal Irish Constabulary of cases of evictions in each of the years 1849 to 1886 inclusive and of agrarian and general crime', in *S.C.P.*, vii, 177-81.

1 ALL IRELAND

The column on the extreme right is based on the totals for agricultural holdings in the first and sixth years of each decade given in the Irish agricultural statistics (see bibliography, V 1 (d) as follows:

1851	570,338	1871	544,142
1856	556,015	1876	529,320
1861	568,484	1881	526,743
1866	549,392		

year	families evicted			persons evicted			evictions per 1000 holdings above one acre
	gross total	readmitted	net total	gross total	readmitted	net total	
1849	16,686	3,302	13,384	90,440	18,375	72,065	23.5
1850	19,949	5,403	14,546	104,163	30,292	73,871	25.5
1851	13,197	4,382	8,815	68,023	24,574	43,449	15.5
1852	8,591	2,041	6,550	43,494	11,334	32,160	11.5
1853	4,833	1,213	3,620	24,589	6,721	17,868	6.4
1854	2,156	331	1,825	10,794	1,805	8,989	3.2

1855	1,849	525	1,324	9,338	2,841	6,497	2.3
1856	1,108	230	878	5,114	1,166	3,948	1.6
1857	1,161	242	919	5,475	1,252	4,223	1.7
1858	957	237	720	4,643	1,211	3,432	1.3
1859	837	346	491	3,872	1,564	2,308	0.9
1860	636	65	571	2,985	274	2,711	1.0
1861	1,092	274	818	5,288	1,324	3,964	1.4
1862	1,136	243	893	5,617	1,218	4,399	1.6
1863	1,734	183	1,551	8,695	812	7,883	2.7
1864	1,924	276	1,648	9,201	1,312	7,889	2.9
1865	942	183	759	4,513	856	3,657	1.3
1866	795	185	610	3,571	862	2,709	1.1
1867	549	90	459	2,489	411	2,078	0.8
1868	637	122	515	3,002	548	2,454	0.9
1869	374	63	311	1,741	313	1,428	0.6
1870	548	104	444	2,616	527	2,089	0.8
1871	482	114	368	2,357	535	1,822	0.7
1872	526	118	408	2,476	537	1,939	0.8
1873	671	152	519	3,078	709	2,369	1.0
1874	726	200	526	3,571	997	2,574	1.0
1875	667	71	596	3,323	387	2,936	1.1
1876	553	85	468	2,550	383	2,167	0.9
1877	463	57	406	2,177	277	1,900	0.8
1878	980	146	834	4,679	763	3,916	1.6
1879	1,238	140	1,098	6,239	663	5,576	2.1
1880	2,110	217	1,893	10,457	1,021	9,436	3.6
1881	3,415	194	3,221	17,341	1,085	16,256	6.1
1882	5,201	198	5,003	26,836	833	26,003	9.5
1883	3,643	226	3,417	17,855	1,069	16,786	6.5

EVICTIONS, 1849-83 (*continued*)

2 BY PROVINCES

	ULSTER		LEINSTER		MUNSTER		CONNACHT	
year	net evic-tions	per 1000 holdings above one acre	net evic-tions	per 1000 holdings above one acre	net evic-tions	per 1000 holdings above one acre	net evic-tions	per 1000 holdings above one acre
1849	1,534	7.3	2,554	20.8	6,169	51.0	3,127	27.2
1850	1,575	7.5	2,836	23.7	6,407	53.0	3,728	31.9
1851	821	3.9	2,204	17.9	3,306	35.6	2,484	21.2
1852	643	3.1	1,435	11.7	2,135	17.6	2,337	20.0
1853	379	1.8	960	7.8	894	7.4	1,387	11.9
1854	198	0.9	443	3.6	541	4.5	643	5.5
1855	119	0.6	362	2.9	244	2.0	599	5.1
1856	86	0.4	223	1.9	221	1.9	348	3.0
1857	90	0.4	388	3.3	167	1.4	274	2.3
1858	113	0.6	207	1.8	115	1.0	287	2.4
1859	82	0.4	106	0.9	136	1.2	167	1.4
1860	119	0.6	145	1.2	147	1.3	160	1.4
1861	173	0.8	216	1.9	251	2.1	178	1.4
1862	127	0.6	256	2.2	234	2.0	276	2.2
1863	304	1.5	353	3.0	385	3.3	509	4.0
1864	301	1.5	294	2.5	439	3.7	614	4.9
1865	229	1.1	185	1.6	123	1.0	222	1.8
1866	119	0.6	161	1.4	158	1.4	172	1.4
1867	77	0.4	117	1.0	80	0.7	185	1.5
1868	152	0.8	94	0.8	82	0.7	187	1.6
1869	73	0.4	104	0.9	62	0.5	72	0.6
1870	100	0.5	125	1.1	104	0.9	115	1.0
1871	73	0.4	82	0.7	89	0.8	124	1.0
1872	96	0.5	54	0.5	93	0.8	166	1.4
1873	90	0.5	119	1.1	162	1.4	139	1.1
1874	133	0.7	97	0.9	127	1.1	169	1.4
1875	86	0.4	117	1.0	136	1.2	257	2.1
1876	137	0.4	111	1.0	119	1.1	101	0.9
1877	60	0.3	136	1.3	108	1.0	102	0.9
1878	83	0.4	216	2.0	207	1.8	328	2.8
1879	165	0.9	305	2.8	360	3.2	268	2.3
1880	445	2.4	419	3.8	664	5.9	365	3.1
1881	606	3.2	655	6.0	641	5.7	767	6.4
1882	1,136	6.0	1,009	9.4	1,434	12.8	1,430	11.9
1883	619	3.3	601	9.6	1,242	11.1	956	8.0

E AGRARIAN OUTRAGES, 1849-83

Sources: S.P.O., Returns of agrarian outrages specially reported in each county to the constabulary, 1849-83; *Return of [agrarian] outrages reported to the Royal Irish Constabulary from 1 January 1844 to 31 December 1880* [C2756], H.C. 1881, lxxvii, 887-914. 'Return by provinces and counties . . . of cases of evictions . . . and of agrarian and general crime' [as for table D above].

1 ALL IRELAND

	number of agrarian outrages	agrarian outrages as a percentage of total crime	agrarian outrages per 1,000 holdings above one acre
1849	957 (15)	6.33	1.7
1850	1,362 (18)	12.75	2.4
1851	1,013 (12)	11.75	1.8
1852	913 (6)	11.75	1.6
1853	469 (1)	8.75	0.8
1854	334 (5)	7.00	0.6
1855	255 (6)	6.00	0.5
1856	287 (6)	6.75	0.5
1857	194 (4)	4.75	0.4
1858	235 (6)	6.75	0.4
1859	221 (5)	6.00	0.4
1860	232 (4)	6.75	0.4
1861	229 (4)	6.20	0.4
1862	363 (8)	8.25	0.6
1863	349 (2)	9.11	0.6
1864	304 (2)	10.25	0.5
1865	178 (4)	6.00	0.3
1866	87 (0)	4.50	0.2
1867	123 (2)	4.45	0.2
1868	160 (4)	6.25	0.3
1869	767 (10)	24.25	1.4
1870	1,329 (7)	30.50	2.4
1871	373 (6)	12.75	0.7
1872	256 (5)	7.75	0.5
1873	254 (5)	11.00	0.5
1874	213 (5)	10.00	0.4
1875	136 (11)	6.75	0.3
1876	212 (5)	10.75	0.4
1877	236 (5)	10.25	0.5
1878	301 (8)	11.75	0.6
1879	863 (10)	24.50	1.6
1880	2,585 (8)	45.65	4.9
1881	4,439 (22)	58.50	8.4
1882	3,433 (27)	54.25	6.5
1883	870 (2)	34.25	1.7

The figures in parentheses are for agrarian homicides. The totals for agrarian outrages in 1869 and 1870 are inflated owing to the use of a new method of computing these outrages introduced by the police in 1869 and abandoned in 1871 (see above pp 32-3).

AGRARIAN OUTRAGES, 1849–83 (*continued*)

2 BY PROVINCES

	ULSTER		LEINSTER		MUNSTER		CONNACHT	
year	total outrages	per 1000 holdings above one acre	total outrages	per 1000 holdings above one acre	total outrages	per 1000 holdings above one acre	total outrages	per 1000 holdings above one acre
1849	160	0.76	286	2.33	377	3.12	134	1.15
1850	403 (4)	1.92	408 (7)	3.32	377 (5)	3.12	174 (2)	1.49
1851	312 (4)	1.49	343 (5)	2.79	251 (3)	2.07	107	0.92
1852	278 (2)	1.32	329 (1)	2.68	190 (3)	1.57	116	0.99
1853	146	0.70	167 (1)	1.36	97	0.80	59	0.50
1854	116 (2)	0.55	91	0.74	75 (1)	0.62	52 (2)	0.44
1855	72 (2)	0.34	51 (1)	0.42	79 (1)	0.65	53 (2)	0.45
1856	80 (3)	0.39	78	0.66	70 (1)	0.60	59 (2)	0.50
1857	46 (1)	0.23	66 (1)	0.56	47 (1)	0.40	35 (1)	0.30
1858	72	0.35	64 (1)	0.54	46 (1)	0.39	53 (4)	0.45
1859	75	0.37	73 (4)	0.62	38 (1)	0.32	35	0.30
1860	61 (3)	0.30	68	0.58	49 (1)	0.42	54	0.46
1861	60 (1)	0.29	85 (1)	0.73	49 (2)	0.42	35	0.28
1862	82	0.39	96 (2)	0.82	96 (4)	0.81	89 (2)	0.71
1863	73 (1)	0.35	109 (1)	0.93	90	0.76	77	0.61
1864	64	0.31	99 (2)	0.85	70	0.59	71	0.56
1865	47	0.23	52 (2)	0.44	36 (1)	0.31	43 (1)	0.33
1866	28	0.14	28	0.25	16	0.14	15	0.12
1867	48 (1)	0.24	33	0.29	27 (1)	0.24	15	0.12
1868	49	0.24	60 (1)	0.53	20 (3)	0.18	31	0.26
1869	99	0.49	289 (3)	2.46	82 (3)	0.72	297 (3)	2.46
1870	98	0.49	335 (2)	2.94	90 (3)	0.80	806 (2)	6.66
1871	60 (1)	0.31	122 (2)	1.09	63 (1)	0.55	128 (2)	1.05
1872	55 (2)	0.28	85 (1)	0.76	50 (1)	0.44	66 (1)	0.54
1873	32 (1)	0.16	59 (1)	0.53	99 (2)	0.86	64 (3)	0.53
1874	60 (1)	0.31	57 (1)	0.51	46 (2)	0.40	50 (1)	0.41
1875	44 (4)	0.22	29 (2)	0.27	38 (2)	0.33	25 (3)	0.21
1876	64 (1)	0.34	50 (2)	0.46	70 (1)	0.62	28 (1)	0.24
1877	52 (2)	0.28	45 (1)	0.41	45 (2)	0.40	94	0.79
1878	57 (3)	0.30	86 (1)	0.79	74 (4)	0.66	84	0.71
1879	109 (3)	0.58	147 (4)	1.35	136 (2)	1.20	471 (1)	3.96
1880	259 (1)	1.37	351 (1)	3.22	1,018 (3)	9.01	957 (3)	8.04
1881	414 (1)	2.20	833 (4)	7.79	1,957 (8)	17.47	1,235 (9)	10.29
1882	320	1.70	732 (2)	6.84	1,500 (10)	13.39	881 (15)	7.34
1883	89	0.47	184	1.72	446 (11)	3.98	151	1.26

F EVICTIONS AND AGRARIAN OUTRAGES, QUARTERLY, BY PROVINCES, 1878-83

Sources: S.P.O., Returns of agrarian outrages 1878-83; returns of evictions and agrarian outrages published in parliamentary papers listed in bibliography V 1(e) and (f).

province	evictions					outrages				
	Jan.-Mar.	Apr.-June	July-Sept.	Oct.-Dec.	year	Jan.-Mar.	Apr.-June	July-Sept.	Oct.-Dec.	year
					1878					
Ulster	28	27	20	8	83 (10%)	7	20	19	11	57 (19%)
Leinster	48	90	57	21	216 (26%)	16	37	16	15	84 (28%)
Munster	47	67	52	41	207 (25%)	14	21	23	15	73 (25%)
Connacht	60	159	45	64	328 (39%)	25	25	11	22	83 (28%)
total	183	343	174	134	834	62	103	69	63	297
					1879					
Ulster	34	71	29	31	165 (15%)	13	34	6	56	109 (13%)
Leinster	63	96	89	57	305 (28%)	23	29	20	76	148 (17%)
Munster	77	104	101	78	360 (33%)	29	25	34	47	135 (16%)
Connacht	87	83	65	33	268 (25%)	37	102	90	233	462 (54%)
total	261	354	284	199	1098	102	190	150	412	854
					1880					
Ulster	96	122	172	55	445 (24%)	41	21	31	166	259 (10%)
Leinster	127	100	134	58	419 (22%)	41	31	58	221	351 (14%)
Munster	186	248	210	20	664 (35%)	50	66	122	781	1019 (39%)
Connacht	81	152	113	19	365 (19%)	162	127	144	528	961 (37%)
total	490	622	629	152	1893	294	245	355	1696	2590

EVICTIONS AND AGRARIAN OUTRAGES (*continued*)

province	evictions					outrages				
	Jan.–Mar.	Apr.–June	July–Sept.	Oct.–Dec	year	Jan.–Mar.	Apr.–June	July–Sept.	Oct.–Dec.	
					1881					
Ulster	160	416	364	218	1158 (36%)	80	83	106	145	414 (9%)
Leinster	58	159	262	176	655 (20%)	101	145	218	369	833 (19%)
Munster	56	175	267	143	641 (20%)	289	491	433	744	1957 (44%)
Connacht	44	265	295	163	767 (24%)	299	272	303	361	1235 (28%)
total	318	1015	1188	700	3221	769	991	1060	1619	4439
					1882					
Ulster	435	334	267	94	1130 (23%)	129	113	41	21	304 (9%)
Leinster	183	279	338	209	1009 (20%)	301	260	111	56	728 (22%)
Munster	331	456	466	181	1434 (29%)	615	448	261	155	1479 (44%)
Connacht	350	582	317	181	1430 (29%)	372	320	113	53	858 (26%)
total	1299	1651	1388	665	5003	1417	1141	526	285	3369
					1883					
Ulster	144	216	166	93	619 (18%)	33	26	21	9	89 (10%)
Leinster	205	153	140	103	601 (18%)	54	46	43	41	184 (21%)
Munster	238	410	356	238	1242 (36%)	133	121	115	77	446 (51%)
Connacht	177	367	243	168	955 (28%)	53	40	31	27	151 (17%)
total	764	1146	905	602	3417	273	233	210	154	870

There are small discrepancies between the figures for agrarian outrages compiled monthly by the Royal Irish Constabulary, which are reproduced here, and the annual figures subsequently published (see table E).

All figures for evictions are net (that is, tenants later reinstated are deducted from the gross totals) except for the quarter April–June 78 in Connacht. Here 91 families evicted on Inishboffin, who were readmitted as caretakers and subsequently recognised as tenants, are included in the total, which should in reality be 68 (H.C. 1880 (254 sess. 2), lx, 363).

G AGRICULTURAL OUTPUT, 1851–83

1 *VALUE OF TOTAL AGRICULTURAL OUTPUT, 1871–83*

Sources: Irish agricultural statistics (see bibliography, V 1 (d); series of agricultural prices prepared by T. W. Grimshaw, registrar general, for the Cowper commission (H.C. 1887, xxvi, 960–67). The table has been supplied by Dr W. E. Vaughan, and is based on material in his Ph.D. thesis, 'A study of landlord and tenant relations between the famine and the land war, 1850–78' (University of Dublin, 1973), pp 33–5, 336–58. It embodies a new approach to the calculation of agricultural output, which hitherto has been expressed as the combined value of all the crops and all the livestock in each year. His figures for tillage are an estimate of the wheat, oats, barley, and flax sold by farmers, and therefore do not include potatoes, turnips, mangel wurzels, and hay, the great bulk of which was consumed on the farm. These fodder crops are regarded as realising their value through the sale of the livestock that consumed them. Under livestock he includes cattle (2+ years old, 1–2 years old, and calves), all sheep except breeding ewes, and pigs. Livestock products include butter, wool, and eggs. The resulting figures, while not claiming to be an exact measure of value, are offered as a realistic index of changes in the total value of agricultural output and of the relative values of tillage and livestock production.

year	tillage £ millions	livestock and livestock products £ millions	total £ millions	year	tillage £ millions	livestock and livestock products £ millions	total £ millions
1851	7.3	14.6	21.9	1868	8.9	27.4	36.3
1852	6.9	14.8	21.7	1869	7.5	28.6	36.1
1853	11.3	19.0	30.3	1870	6.7	31.7	38.4
1854	11.9	22.2	34.1	1871	6.1	33.1	39.2
1855	12.9	23.1	36.0	1872	5.4	34.4	39.8
1856	8.7	24.1	32.8	1873	4.9	34.8	39.7
1857	7.4	24.9	32.3	1874	6.3	35.8	42.1
1858	7.2	25.6	32.8	1875	6.6	35.8	42.4
1859	7.1	26.9	34.0	1876	6.1	37.6	43.7
1860	8.2	25.9	34.1	1877	5.6	34.4	40.0
1861	5.6	25.0	30.6	1878	5.7	33.7	39.4
1862	5.0	23.3	28.3	1879	4.9	30.6	35.5
1863	7.3	22.3	29.6	1880	5.6	31.3	36.9
1864	7.8	25.0	32.8	1881	5.7	30.8	36.5
1865	9.0	29.3	38.3	1882	4.7	34.1	38.8
1866	9.1	31.8	40.9	1883	4.3	34.3	38.6
1867	8.6	24.9	33.5				

AGRICULTURAL OUTPUT, 1851-83 (*continued*)

2 *TONNAGE AND VALUE OF POTATO CROP, 1847-83*

Source: as for preceding table.

year	million tons	price per ton £	value £ millions	year	million tons	price per ton £	value £ millions
1847	2.0	5.50	11.25	1866	3.1	3.75	11.63
1848	–	6.33	–	1867	3.1	4.35	13.49
1849	4.0	4.67	18.79	1868	4.1	3.85	15.79
1850	4.0	4.75	19.13	1869	3.4	2.85	9.69
1851	4.4	3.80	16.72	1870	4.2	4.00	16.80
1852	4.3	5.00	21.50	1871	2.8	4.25	11.90
1853	5.7	4.85	27.65	1872	1.8	6.75	12.15
1854	5.1	6.50	33.15	1873	2.7	4.85	13.10
1855	6.2	4.65	28.83	1874	3.6	3.10	11.16
1856	4.4	3.25	11.30	1875	3.5	3.50	12.25
1857	3.5	5.50	19.25	1876	4.2	3.50	14.70
1858	4.9	3.15	15.44	1877	1.8	6.00	10.80
1859	4.3	3.85	16.56	1878	2.5	4.50	11.25
1860	2.7	5.75	15.53	1879	1.1	6.15	6.77
1861	1.9	4.90	9.31	1880	3.0	3.10	9.30
1862	2.1	3.90	8.19	1881	3.4	4.00	13.60
1863	3.4	2.75	9.35	1882	2.0	3.60	7.20
1864	4.3	2.85	12.26	1883	3.5	4.30	15.10
1865	3.9	3.15	12.29				

3 *TONNAGE OF POTATO CROP, BY PROVINCES, 1875–83*

Source: Irish agricultural statistics (see bibliography V 1 (c)).

	ULSTER		LEINSTER		MUNSTER		CONNACHT	
year	million tons	percentage change	million tons	percentage change	million tons	percentage change	million tons	percentage change
1875	1.34		0.67		0.83		0.67	
1876	1.61	+ 19.6	0.73	+ 8.6	0.87	+ 4.6	0.95	+ 42.3
1877	0.61	– 61.9	0.37	– 49.4	0.42	– 51.8	0.36	– 62.3
1878	1.11	+ 84.3	0.48	+ 29.1	0.38	– 10.1	0.55	+ 53.0
1879	0.35	– 70.8	0.23	– 50.8	0.30	– 20.9	0.23	– 58.3
1880	1.15	+ 226.2	0.61	+ 161.5	0.81	+ 169.9	0.42	+ 82.8
1881	1.30	+ 13.0	0.67	+ 10.2	0.81	+ 0.5	0.65	+ 55.2
1882	0.65	– 50.0	0.44	– 34.0	0.53	– 34.4	0.38	– 42.3
1883	1.27	+ 94.7	0.68	+ 53.1	0.85	+ 59.2	0.66	+ 79.0

ALL IRELAND

year	million tons	percentage change
1875	3.51	
1876	4.15	+ 18.3
1877	1.76	– 57.7
1878	2.53	+ 43.8
1879	1.11	– 55.9
1880	2.99	+ 168.1
1881	3.43	+ 15.0
1882	1.99	– 41.9
1883	3.45	+ 73.1

H ATTENDANCE AT MEETINGS OF CENTRAL LAND LEAGUE, DUBLIN, 21 OCTOBER 1879–18 OCTOBER 1881

Source: Reports of meetings in *Freeman's Journal*, *Irish Times*, and *Nation*.

	21 Oct. 79	(a) 30 Dec. 79– 11 May 80	(b) 18 May– 16 Nov. 80	(c) 23 Nov. 80– 2 Feb. 81	(d) 4 Feb.– 18 Oct. 81	total
total number of meetings	1	30	27	11	38	107
Begg, Garrett (Dublin)	–	–	–	2	25	27
Begg, G., jr	–	–	–	–	3	3
Begg, James (Cabra)	–	–	–	–	4	4
Behan, Rev. John, C.C. (Dublin)	1	6	1	–	1	9
Biggar, J. G., M.P. (Belfast)	–	2	1	2	2	7
Birmingham, J. A. (Tullamore)	–	–	–	4	9	13
Boyton, Michael P.	–	3	22	7	2	34
Brennan, Thomas (Dublin)	1	22	24	10	13	70

ATTENDANCE AT MEETINGS OF CENTRAL LAND LEAGUE (*continued*)

	21 Oct. 79	(a) 30 Dec. 79- 11 May 80	(b) 18 May- 16 Nov. 80	(c) 23 Nov. 80- 2 Feb. 81	(d) 4 Feb.- 18 Oct. 81	total
total number of meetings	1	30	27	11	38	107
Brenon, E. St J. (Dublin)	–	11	–	–	–	11
Briody, Rev. P. (Mountnugent)	–	–	2	–	3	5
Burke, James	–	–	3	2	3	8
Burton, Henry M.	–	–	–	–	8	8
Butterfield, John J. (Newry, organiser)	–	–	–	–	7	7
Byrne, Garrett, M.P. (Wicklow)	–	–	1	1	1	3
Campbell, Henry	–	–	–	–	4	4
Cantwell, Rev. James, Adm. (Thurles)	–	1	–	–	3	4
Carpenter, Thomas (Drogheda)	–	–	–	–	3	3
Clancy, J. J. (Dublin)	–	1	2	5	21	29
Clarke, James (Coralstown, Westmeath)	–	–	–	–	4	4
Clinton, John, P. L. G.	–	–	–	–	8	8
Cobbe, W. H. (Portarlington)	1	1	3	6	7	18
Condron, John D.	–	–	–	–	7	7
Connolly, Rev. W. F. (Athboy)	–	–	–	–	3	3
Cooke, Rev. Edward (Kingscourt)	–	–	–	–	3	3
Corrigan, P. J. (Dublin)	–	24	8	4	17	53
Coyne, Rev. W., Adm. (Rosscahill)	–	–	1	–	2	3
Crilly, Daniel	–	–	–	–	4	4
Cummins, Patrick, P. L. G. (Dublin)	1	17	13	5	8	44
Daly, John (Howth)	–	–	–	4	19	23
Daly, Peter (Howth)	–	14	8	6	18	46
Davitt, Michael	1	24	–	11	–	36
Delany, Rev. F., P.P. (Clonegall)	–	–	1	2	2	5
Delany, George	1	–	–	1	1	3
Delany, Rev. James E., C.C. (Clonegall)	–	–	–	–	3	3
Dennehy, William	–	–	–	1	3	4
Dillon, John (Dublin)	1	–	6	3	12	22
Dillon, William (Dublin)	1	–	–	–	–	1
Donaghy, J. M. (St James's branch, Dublin)	–	–	–	–	13	13
Donnelly, R. J. (Dublin)	1	24	20	7	19	71
Doriss, William (Dublin)	–	–	–	–	24	24
Duff, Matthew (Swords)	–	–	–	–	3	3
Dunne, Laurence	–	–	–	–	4	4
Egan, Dr Dillon (New York)	–	–	–	–	5	5
Egan, Patrick (Dublin)	1	23	24	11	–	59
Egan, Patrick[1]	–	–	–	–	3	3

[1] Not the Land League treasurer.

Fagan, Rev. J. P., P.P. (Kilbeg)	–	–	–	–	3	3
Farragher, P. J.	–	–	–	–	6	6
Farrelly, Owen P.	–	–	–	–	4	4
Fegan, Laurence (Stackallen)	–	–	–	–	3	3
Ferguson, John (Glasgow)	–	2	3	2	5	12
Finegan, B. (Lr Gardiner St, Dublin)	–	–	–	–	4	4
Finigan, J. L., M.P. (London)	–	1	1	–	1	3
Fitzpatrick, J.	–	–	–	3	–	3
Fitzpatrick, T. E.	–	–	–	4	3	7
Flanagan, Michael	–	–	–	–	4	4
Flanagan, William	–	–	–	–	3	3
Foley, Patrick	–	–	–	–	3	3
Fredricks, Sabin (Democratic Federation)	–	–	–	–	6	6
Fullam, Francis (Stamullan)	–	–	–	–	4	4
Fullam, Patrick (Donore)	–	–	–	–	7	7
Gartland, James (Kilbeg)	–	–	–	–	3	3
Gill, Christopher (Dundalk)	–	–	–	–	11	11
Gilligan, Philip (Dublin)	–	–	–	1	9	10
Gordon, P. J. (Middle Abbey St, Dublin)	–	–	1	–	3	4
Grehan, James	–	–	–	–	4	4
Grehan, James F., P.L.G. (Cabinteely)	1	22	19	7	26	75
Grehan, Myles	–	–	–	–	4	4
Grehan, P.	–	1	3	–	1	5
Grehan, Thomas (Loughlinstown)	1	7	7	2	13	30
Harrington, Timothy (Tralee)	–	–	1	–	4	5
Harris, Matthew (Ballinasloe)	–	–	2	7	6	15
Healy, T. M., M.P. (Dublin)	–	1	–	5	12	18
Heffernan, John T. (Kildare)	–	–	1	–	4	5
Hoare, E. J. (Castledermot)	–	–	–	–	3	3
Hogan, F.	–	–	–	–	7	7
Hollywood, E. (Dublin)	–	–	–	–	3	3
Humphreys, Rev. M., C.C. (Clonoulty)	–	–	–	–	4	4
Jeffers, Andrew (Arran Quay branch, Dublin)	–	–	–	–	6	6
Johnson, P. F. (Kanturk)	–	–	1	1	1	3
Jones, George (Navan)	–	–	1	2	4	7
Kearns, Joseph (St James.s branch, Dublin)	–	–	–	–	6	6
Keelan, Patrick (Carrickmacross)	–	–	–	–	3	3
Kelleher, E. B. (treas., St James's branch, Dublin)	–	–	–	–	6	6
Kelly, M. J.	–	–	–	–	10	10
Kelly, Thomas (Ballymore Eustace)	–	–	–	–	3	3
Kelly, William, P.L.G. (Donabate)	1	9	3	–	–	13
Kennedy, Edward (Mountbrown)	–	–	–	–	11	11
Kenny, Dr J. E. (Dublin)	1	2	5	3	8	19
Kenny, Rev. M. J.	–	–	2	–	5	7

ATTENDANCE AT MEETINGS OF CENTRAL LAND LEAGUE (*continued*)

	21 Oct. 79	(a) 30 Dec. 79– 11 May 80	(b) 18 May– 16 Nov. 80	(c) 23 Nov. 80– 2 Feb. 81	(d) 4 Feb.– 18 Oct. 81	total
total number of meetings	1	30	27	11	38	107
Kenny, Dr R. D.	–	–	1	2	–	3
Kenny, Dr R. F.	–	–	2	1	2	5
Kettle, A. J., P.L.G. (Artane)	1	21	24	10	17	73
Kettle, Patrick (Swords)	–	–	–	–	9	9
Killen, J. B., B.L.	–	1	5	3	10	19
Kirby, Michael (Quinlan's Castle)	–	–	–	–	3	3
Lalor, Richard, M.P. (Tenakill)	–	4	2	–	1	7
Larkin, P. O'Neill (*Irish World*, N.Y.)	–	–	–	–	11	11
Louden, J. J., B.L. (Westport)	–	5	2	1	15	23
Leggatt, J. J.	–	–	–	–	3	3
Lennon, D. (Tullow)	–	–	–	1	4	5
Long, Patrick (Swords branch)	–	–	–	–	3	3
Lynam, James, P.L.G. (Tullamore; president, Ballycumber branch)	–	–	–	–	7	7
McCabe, Patrick (Balbriggan)	–	–	2	2	10	14
McCartan, Michael (Downpatrick)	–	–	–	–	6	6
McCarthy, James (Drogheda)	–	7	14	5	15	41
McCarthy, William	–	2	3	–	–	5
McCourt, Laurence, P.L.G.	1	3	1	1	1	7
McDermott, Rev. Canon James (Kilmore)	–	3	2	–	–	5
McGough, John	–	–	–	2	1	3
McGrath, P., P.L.G. (Ballingarry)	–	–	–	–	9	9
McHugh, Edward	–	–	8	5	2	15
McHugh, J. B., B.L. (Glasnevin)	–	6	8	5	3	22
McHugh, R., T.C. (Navan)	–	–	–	–	3	3
McInerney, M. C., B.L.	–	–	–	–	6	6
McKenna, James (Howth)	–	–	–	1	18	19
McKenna, Joseph (Swords)	–	–	–	–	5	5
McKenna, Thomas J. (Howth)	–	–	–	2	5	7
McKeogh, Rev. L. J., P.P. (Ballinasloe)	–	1	1	1	–	3
McLaughlin, P. J. (Ballinrobe)	–	–	1	1	2	4
Maguire, James P. (Rooskey)	–	1	2	2	3	8
Mangan, Patrick (C.S. Parnell branch, Dublin)	–	–	–	–	8	8
Masterson, J. E. (sec., Thomas Sexton branch, Dublin))	–	–	–	–	4	4
Matthews, Thomas (Balbriggan)	–	1	8	4	3	16
Moloney, W. F. (Dublin)	–	–	–	1	27	28
Monks, E.	–	–	–	–	4	4
Monks, J. (Blackrock)	–	–	–	–	5	5

Moran, Denis (Arran Quay branch, Dublin)	—	—	—	—	8	8
Moran, Rev. Philip (Finea)	—	—	2	—	1	3
Muldoon, John (Crumlin)	—	—	—	—	3	3
Mullaly, Henry Joseph (Dunlavin)	—	—	1	2	5	8
Murphy, D. (St Andrew St, Dublin)	—	—	—	—	3	3
Murphy, Rev. Gregory, P.P. (Newtownbarry)	—	—	—	—	3	3
Murray, James (Dublin)	—	12	22	4	15	53
Nolan, T. J. (Baltinglass)	—	—	—	—	3	3
O'Brien, William (*United Ireland*)	—	—	—	—	3	3
O'Connor, Arthur, M.P. (London)	—	—	1	1	4	6
O'Connor, James	1	—	—	1	—	2
O'Connor, T. P., M.P. (London)	—	—	5	1	4	10
O'Doherty, J. E. (solr, Derry)	—	—	—	—	3	3
O'Donoghue, Denis	—	—	—	—	5	5
O'Kelly, J. J., M.P.	—	1	2	2	7	12
O'Neill, Fergus (Baldoyle)	—	2	—	2	6	10
O'Neill, James (Malahide)	—	—	2	1	10	13
O'Neill, James (Rathgar)	—	—	—	—	3	3
O'Neill, John	—	—	—	2	9	11
O'Neill, Joseph (Kinsealy)	—	1	2	6	4	13
O'Neill, M.	—	—	1	1	1	3
O'Neill, Patrick (Kinsealy)	—	1	—	3	18	22
O'Neill, T.	—	—	—	—	15	15
O'Neill, William (Kinsealy)	—	8	7	1	12	28
O'Neill, William P.	—	—	—	—	3	3
O'Quinn, J.	—	2	1	—	—	3
O'Reilly, Charles (Artane)[1]	—	—	—	2	4	6
O'Reilly, Michael T. (Dublin)	—	—	—	—	17	17
O'Reilly, Thomas F.	—	—	—	—	15	15
O'Rourke, James	—	4	6	1	—	11
O'Sullivan, M. M.	—	9	12	5	1	27
O'Sullivan, W. H., P.L.G., M.P. (Kilmallock)	—	5	4	1	1	11
O'Toole, G. (Baltinglass)	—	—	—	—	3	3
Park, Henry (organiser)	—	—	—	—	4	4
Parnell, C. S., M.P. (Rathdrum)	1	2	2	1	5	11
Pearson, J.	—	—	—	—	5	5
Peyton, James (treas., John Dillon branch, Dublin)	—	—	—	—	4	4
Quinn, J. O'D.	—	4	—	—	—	4
Quinn, J. P.	—	—	3	6	36	45
Rafferty, James (president, John Dillon branch, Dublin)	—	—	—	—	3	3
Rea, John (sec., Charleville branch, Co. Cork)	—	—	—	—	3	3
Redlington, J.	—	1	1	1	2	5
Redpath, James (U.S.A.)	—	—	7	—	4	11

[1] This may be the same person as Charles Reilly (see below).

ATTENDANCE AT MEETINGS OF CENTRAL LAND LEAGUE (*continued*)

	21 Oct. 79	(a) 30 Dec. 79–11 May 80	(b) 18 May–16 Nov. 80	(c) 23 Nov. 80–2 Feb. 81	(d) 4 Feb.–18 Oct. 81	total
total number of meetings	1	30	27	11	38	107
Reilly, Charles (Artane)[1]	1	–	–	–	8	9
Roche, Dr John (Kingstown)	–	8	6	–	1	15
Roe, Thomas, (Dundalk)	1	1	–	4	6	12
Rourke, James (Dublin)	1	3	20	5	21	50
Ryan, Thomas	1	–	–	–	–	1
Rylett, Rev. Harold (Moneyrea, Co. Down)	–	–	–	–	13	13
Sexton, Thomas, M.P. (London)	–	14	9	6	25	54
Sheehy, Rev. Eugene (Kilmallock)	1	5	–	2	3	11
Sheridan, P. J. (Tubbercurry)	–	–	3	6	3	12
Stinson, J.	–	–	–	–	3	3
Sullivan, T. D., M.P. (Dublin)	1	18	10	6	17	52
Sweeney, Patrick (Eyrecourt)	–	–	–	1	2	3
Sweetman, John	1	–	–	–	–	1
Teeling, Charles	–	–	–	–	3	3
Tighe, James	–	–	–	–	4	4
Tormey, Rev. Dr Michael, P.P. (Beauparc)	–	–	–	–	4	4
Tyrrell, P. A. (sec., Arran Quay branch, Dublin)	–	–	–	–	17	17
Tuite, Rev. T., Adm. (Stamullan)	–	–	–	1	25	26
Varian, A. J. (Dublin)	–	–	–	1	25	26
Wall, J. M.	–	–	–	–	16	16
Walsh, R. D. (Dublin)	–	–	1	2	7	10
Walshe, John W. (Balla)	–	1	10	10	2	23
White, P. J. (sec., Clara branch)	–	–	–	–	5	5
Woods, Christopher D. (Chancery Place, Dublin)	–	–	–	1	8	9
Woods, Rev. M., C.C. (Navan)	–	–	–	–	3	3

[1] This may be the same person as Charles O'Reilly (see above).

All persons recorded as present at the inaugural meeting of the league are listed. Otherwise only those with a recorded attendance of not fewer than three meetings are included. The 106 ordinary meetings are grouped in periods in relation to Davitt's whereabouts as follows: (a) before his mission to the U.S., (b) during his absence in the U.S., (c) from his return from the U.S. to his arrest, (d) from his arrest to the suppression of the league.

The meeting of 27 January 1880 was followed by three adjourned sessions, on 29 and 30 January and on 3 February, to make arrangements for the Phoenix

Park demonstration (14 March). These meetings have not been taken into account in the table. Not all who attended meetings are mentioned in the published reports, but the indications are that very few names were omitted. Names are not always given in precise detail: 'Mr' is sometimes given instead of a Christian name or an initial, clergy are often described simply as 'Rev.', and this sometimes involves uncertainty of identification. Places of residence or names of Land League branches from which attenders were delegates are often stated, and such particulars are included in parenthesis in the list.

The total number of persons listed is 194. Several hundred other persons attended not fewer than two meetings each. Of the 190 persons who attended not fewer than three meetings, only 71 attended at least 10 meetings, only 31 at least 20 meetings, and only 15 at least 35 meetings or one-third of the total. Attenders, especially in 1881, came from residences widely dispersed over the country, but, as might be expected, the most frequent attenders lived in Dublin city and its neighbourhood. The fifteen with the highest attendance, who constituted the hard core of attenders and included the most active members of the executive, are listed in the following table. The attendance of Davitt and other members of the executive is also given as a percentage of the number of meetings which it was possible for them to attend, that is, when they were not absent on league business or in prison.

Attendance of those recorded as present at not less than 35 out of 107 meetings

	no. of meetings attended	percentage of total meetings attended	total of possible attendances	percentage of possible attendances
Brennan	70	66%	84	79%
Corrigan	53	50%		
Cummins	44	41%		
Daly, P.	46	43%		
Davitt	36	34%	43	84%
Donnelly	71	67%		
Egan	59	56%	70	84%
Grehan, J. F.	75	71%		
Kettle	73	69%	85	86%
McCarthy, J.	41	38%		
Murray	53	50%		
Quinn, J. P.	45	42%		
Rourke	50	47%		
Sexton	54	50%	105	51%
Sullivan	52	49%		

The reported attendance at meetings was much higher in 1881 than in 1880, but the great bulk of the increased attendance was of persons appearing only once, and a great many of these were representatives from local branches. Many new names appear in 1881, including many clergy. Of persons attending at least one-third of the meetings held after Davitt's arrest, about half had seldom or never previously attended: Garrett Begg, John Daly, J. M. Donaghy, William Doriss, James McKenna, W. F. Moloney, Patrick O'Neill, T. O'Neill, M. T. O'Reilly, T. F. O'Reilly, Rev. Harold Rylett, Rev. T. Tuite, P. A. Tyrrell, A. J. Varian,

ATTENDANCE AT MEETINGS OF CENTRAL LAND LEAGUE (*continued*)

J. M. Wall. J. P. Quinn, who succeeded M. M. O'Sullivan as paid secretary or chief clerk and had the highest total of attendances in the post-Davitt period, had been a frequent attender since 28 December 1880.

Members of the 'provisional central committee' of what was to become the Ladies' Land League attended meetings of the central league as follows:

Attendance of women at meetings in January and February 1881

	26 Jan.	4 Feb.	16 Feb.
Burke, Mrs J.	x		
Byrne, Miss H.	x	x	x
Cantwell, Miss		x	
Deane, Mrs A.	x		
Dillon, Mrs	x		
Egan, Mrs P.	x		
Kenny, Mrs J. E.	x	x	
Lynch, Miss		x	x
Maloney, Mrs W. F.	x	x	x
Parnell, Anna		x	x
Sullivan, Mrs A. M.	x	x	
Walshe, Beatrice	x	x	

BIBLIOGRAPHY

Sections II–VIII of this bibliography comprise sources, sections X and XI secondary works; sections I and IX combine materials in both categories, either because they are inseparable or because it would be pointless or misleading to separate them. On the other hand, later writings by contemporaries (section IX) are distinguished from contemporary writings (section VI), because the two can differ so greatly in value as historical evidence. While items classifiable in more than one section are normally entered only in the section to which they most distinctively belong, some, because of their importance in more than one category, or for convenience of reference, appear more than once. The assignment of items to subsections in section VI and as between section IX 2 and section X is in some cases a matter of judgment on the intentions of the writers.

Sections I–III are intended to be comprehensive; all other sections relate to that part of Davitt's life covered by this book. All the material used is listed; and other material is included as a guide to the further study of Irish revolution, political and agrarian.

No publications later in date than 1979 (except the last item on p. 633) are included.

I PUBLICATIONS ON DAVITT

In chronological order. In addition to writings primarily about Davitt this section includes some other works which have a special bearing on his career.

A new song on the arrests of Messrs Davitt, Daly, and Killen. [Nov. 1879.]
Ballad in 6 stanzas and chorus, beginning: 'All Irishmen have heard of our brothers who have cared'. (DP/Z)

'Michael Davitt', by A. J. H. Duganne. [1880.]
Undated and unidentified press-cutting, probably American. 6 stanzas beginning: 'God keep you Michael Davitt'. (DP/Z)

'A greeting to Michael Davitt', by Lucy McEwen. [1880.]
Undated and unidentified American press-cutting, probably from Boston *Pilot.* 7 stanzas beginning: 'Far over the ocean's billows'. (DP/Z)

'All hail! Michael Davitt: lines respectfully dedicated to the Irish agitator, on his visit to Blackstone', by Patrick Carpenter. Waterford, Mass., 23 June 1880.
Unidentified press-cutting, probably from Boston *Pilot.* 11 stanzas beginning: 'No haughty knight with nodding plume'. (DPC/2, 41)

'Michael Davitt', by Fanny Parnell. In Boston *Pilot*, 18 Dec. 1880.
6 stanzas beginning: 'Out from the grip of the slayer'. (DP/Z)

Davitt's life, in sunshine and shade, by One who knew him. Pp 72. Dublin, 1881.
Printed by W. J. Alley & Co., 9 Ryder's Row, Capel Street.

A new song on Michael Davitt: air—Garryowen. [Aug. 1881.]
Ballad in 7 stanzas beginning: 'Then up with the flag raised by Davitt our head'; with woodcut of Davitt's head and shoulders. (DP/Z)

Michael Davitt, Land League leader: a poem, by A country curate. Pp 32. Dublin: M. H. Gill, 1881.
Preface dated July 1881. Poem begins 'You set your banner 'gainst the wind'.

The life of Michael Davitt, with a history of the rise and development of the Irish National Land League, by D. B. Cashman. Boston, Mass.: Murphy & McCarthy, 1881.
See above, p. xix.

The life of Michael Davitt, founder of the National Land League, by D. B. Cashman, *to which is added The secret history of the Land League*, by Michael Davitt. London: R. & T. Washbourne Ltd. [1882.]
This is an augmented edition of the preceding item. The 'secret history' is a report of interviews given by Davitt in America to Balch, a representative of the New York *Daily World*, in July 1882, and published in that paper on 9 and 16 July. The book was later reissued as a 'Cameron and Ferguson edition'.

Release of M[ichae]l Davitt (founder of the Land League). [May 1882.]
Ballad in 5 stanzas beginning: 'You sons of Erin's Isle'; with woodcut of Davitt's head and shoulders identical with that on *A new song on Michael Davitt* [Aug. 1881], above. In the Johnson collection of printed ephemera in the Bodleian Library; copy supplied by L. P. Curtis. (DP/Z)

The land of Eire: the Irish Land League, its origin, progress and consequences, . . ., by John Devoy, New York: Patterson & Neilson, 1882.
See above, p. xix. The above title applies only to pt I (pp 1-92) of the book. Pts II and III comprise a descriptive guide-book to Ireland; see below, p. 612.

Letter of John Devoy to editor of New York *Daily World*. Reprinted in *Nation*, 19 Aug. 1882.

Correcting a statement by Davitt, in New York *Daily World*, as to money received by him from the national fund.

Letter of John Devoy to editor of *Irish Nation* (New York). Reprinted in *United Ireland*, 28 June 1884.

Fiercely critical of Davitt.

A wondrous life: story of Michael Davitt, factory boy, fenian organiser, convict prisoner, Land League chief, and tribune of the Irish people, being the chief episodes in his life of sufferings, struggles and triumphs. Pp 39. Glasgow and London: Cameron & Ferguson. [1885.]

Pp 19-28 are an abridgement of *The prison life of Michael Davitt, related by himself* [1878]; see below, III 2.

'Phrenology of Irish leaders'. In *Phrenological Magazine*, new series, iii, July 1887, pp 281-3.

Short estimates of Davitt, T. D. Sullivan, Healy, Dillon, and Parnell.

'Lines suggested by reading Michael Davitt's Leaves from a Prison Diary', by the Dowager Countess Russell. Sept. 1887. (DP/TT)

'Davitt', by Robert Blake (20 Grand Parade, East Putney). 1893.

4 stanzas beginning 'Not yet! Not ruin yet! This as he rose'. (DP/Z)

The life of Charles Stewart Parnell, 1846-1891, by R. Barry O'Brien. 2 vols. London: Smith, Elder & Co., 1898.

'Parnell and the fenians', by John Devoy. In *Chicago Journal*, 24 Mar. 1899.

Review of preceding, with special reference to the Davitt-Devoy-Parnell negotiations of 1879.

'The exile from Mayo', by Stephen Gwynn. [1906.]

10 stanzas beginning: 'He sickened when the springtime had scarce clothed the hedge with green' (DP/Z, DPC/33). One of many memorial verses, collected in DP/Z and DPC/29-33.

'The last of the Irish rebels', by T. P. [O'Connor]. In *T.P.'s Weekly*, 8 June 1906, pp 733-6.

One of many memorial articles, collected in DPC/29-33.

'Davitt's career', by John Devoy. Pts I–XVII, in *Gaelic American* (New York), 9 June-3 Nov. 1906; reprinted in *Irish Freedom*, 1913-14.

See above, p. xix; relates only to 1878-9 (DP/AA5)

Michael Davitt: revolutionary, agitator, and labour leader, by Francis Sheehy-Skeffington. Introduction by Justin McCarthy. London: T. Fisher Unwin, 1908. Reprinted, with introduction by F. S. L. Lyons, London: MacGibbon & Kee, 1967.

See above, p. xx.

'Michael Davitt: a text for a revolutionary lecture', by James Connolly. In *The Harp* (New York), Aug. 1908; reprinted in James Connolly, *Selected political writings*, ed. Owen Dudley Edwards and Bernard Ranson (London: Cape, 1973), pp 209-14.

'Michael Davitt (1846-1906)', by Francis Sheehy-Skeffington. In *Dictionary of national biography, 1901-11* (London: Smith Elder, 1912), i, 476-80.

Chief and tribune: Parnell and Davitt, Dublin and London: Maunsell & Co., 1919.
See above, pp xx-xxi.

Michael Davitt, by J. W. Good. Pp 14. Dublin, 1921.

'Irishmen in English prisons: XI Michael Davitt', by P. S. O'Hegarty. In *Weekly Freeman*, 1 Oct. 1921.

'Michael Davitt and Haslingden', by Briar (pseudonym of A. J. Chappell). In *Accrington Observer and Times*, 18, 25 July, 1 Aug. 1925.
Other articles by Briar on Davitt, with special reference to Haslingden, appeared in *Haslingden Observer*, 27 July 1925, and 2, 9, 16, 23, 30 Mar., 6 Apr. 1946.

'Michael Davitt in penal servitude, 1870-77', by T. W. Moody. In *Studies*, xxx, no. 120 (Dec. 1941), pp 517-30; xxxi, no. 121 (Mar. 1942), pp 16-30.

'Michael Davitt and the "pen" letter', by T. W. Moody. In *Irish Historical Studies*, iv, no. 15 (Mar. 1945), pp 224-53.

'Michael Davitt, 1846-1906: a survey and appreciation', by T. W. Moody. In *Studies*, xxxv, no. 138 (June 1946), pp 199-208; no. 139 (Sept. 1946), pp 325-34; no. 140 (Dec. 1946), pp 433-8.

'The new departure in Irish politics, 1878-9', by T. W. Moody. In *Essays in British and Irish history in honour of James Eadie Todd*, ed. H. A. Cronne, T. W. Moody, and D. B. Quinn (London: Frederick Muller, 1949), pp 303-33.

'Michael Davitt and the British labour movement, 1882-1906', by T. W. Moody. In *Transactions of the Royal Historical Society*, 5th series, iii, 53-76 (1953).

'Michael Davitt', by T. W. Moody. In *Leaders and workers*, ed. J. W. Boyle (Cork: Mercier Press, [1965]), pp 47-55.

Irish-American nationalism, 1870-1890, by Thomas N. Brown. Philadelphia and New York: Lippincott, 1966. (Critical Periods of History)

'Irish-American nationalism', by T. W. Moody. In *Irish Historical Studies*, xv, no. 60 (Sept. 1967), pp 438-45.
Review-article on preceding.

John Dillon: a biography, by F. S. L. Lyons. London: Routledge & Kegan Paul, 1968.

Introduction by T. W. Moody to reprint of Davitt's *Leaves from a prison diary* (Shannon: Irish University Press, 1972).

Michael Davitt, a son of the Irish people, 1846-1906: pages of life and struggle, by Valeriya Emmanuilovna Kunina. Moscow: Publishing House 'Mysl', 1973.
A study of Davitt in Russian. The title is a translation.

'Michael Davitt: the "preacher of ideas", 1881-1906', by James M. Cahalan. In *Éire-Ireland*, xi, no. 1 (spring 1976), pp 13-33.

Charles Stewart Parnell, by F. S. L. Lyons. London: Collins, 1977.

'The treason trial of Michael Davitt', by Cahir Davitt. In *Irish Times*, 30 Apr. 1979.
Judge Cahir Davitt, Michael's second son.

Michael Davitt and Haslingden . . . by John Dunleavy. 12 pp typescript. Haslingden Local History Society, 1979.

II THE DAVITT PAPERS

The collection, on deposit in the library of Trinity College, Dublin, covers Davitt's life from 1870. It consists predominantly of unpublished manuscripts, with a substantial element of press-cuttings and other printed material. Letters from and to him, diaries, note-books, accounts, press-cutting books, documents relating to legal proceedings, unpublished autobiographical writings, published pamphlets and articles, and much other material, both manuscript and printed, constituted Davitt's papers at the time of his death. It was far from complete, especially in respect of letters, both those he had written and those he had received. The gaps were diminished and the whole collection enriched by the efforts of his widow, Mary Davitt, in recovering, through appeals in the public press and otherwise, letters of her husband surviving in the hands of his correspondents and their families—for example his sister, Sabina, and three close friends of his later years, Richard McGhee, James Collins, and John Dillon. In some cases the original letters were presented to her outright, in others she had them copied and returned. Mary Davitt's intention was to prepare the way for an 'official' biography of her husband, to be written by J. G. Swift McNeill, a project that came to nothing. Further material has been recovered by Davitt's son, Judge Cahir Davitt, and by the present writer; and this is now included in the collection in series I (see below).

The collection has been arranged by the present writer in seven series as follows.

I Letters from and to Davitt, 1870-1906, and papers (including press cuttings) by and relating to him, 1863-1923 (DP).

Separate items in packets, each containing a group of letters or papers. This was the organisation of the bulk of the letters and papers when I received them. The materials in each packet now form an ordered group, and the packets are designated, without reference to date or topic, as A-Z, AA-ZZ, AB-AZ, BC-BZ, A2-A97, AA1-AA6.

II Davitt's diaries and note-books etc., 1877-1906 (DN):

Diaries and records of tours and other special occasions, 1877-1906 (DN/1-DN/53A).

Notes of letters for newspapers, 1883-95 (DN/54-DN/56).

Accounts, 1882-95 (DN/57-DN/63).

III Davitt's press-cutting books etc., 1878-1923 (DPC).

DPC/1-28 cover 1878-1904; DPC/29-32, for 1906, consist of obituary notices, and DPC/33 of obituary notices and miscellaneous material, 1883-1923. There are many gaps in these books, partly accounted for by cuttings removed and separately preserved in series I.

IV Material (MS and printed) relating to legal proceedings, 1879-92 (DL):

Prosecution of Davitt for speech at Gurteen, 1879-80 (DL/1).

Prosecution of Parnell and other land-leaguers for conspiracy, 1880-81 (DL/2).

Prosecution of Davitt for speech at Navan, 1882-3 (DL/3).

The *Times*-Parnell commission, 1888-90 (DL/4).

Material relating to the above is also in series I.

Libel action by Davitt against *Irish Independent*, 1892, and related papers (DL/5).

V Davitt's autobiographical writings, 1881-1904 (DA):

'Jottings in solitary', MS written in Portland prison, 12 Sept. 1881-May 1882 (DA/1).

358 folios on official blue foolscap paper, each folio initialled 'GC' (George Clifton), the governor of Portland prison; see above, pp 478-9.

Autobiographical sketches, in MS and TS (DA/2-8).

Written in 1894-5 and 1900-04, for publication in newspapers and eventually as a book, these sketches seem never to have been completed or published. They are generally (except the 1884-5 portion) very slight, and are far from adding up to an autobiography. There is also autobiographical material in series I (DP/T).

VI Pamphlets and articles, by Davitt and others, 1880-1904 (DPA).

See below, III 2 and 4.

VII Photographs of Davitt, and of relatives and friends, 1863/4-1906, and miscellanea (DPG).

III PUBLICATIONS OF DAVITT

1 VERSES

'The traitor's doom'. Haslingden, 18 Dec. [1868]. In *Universal News* (London), 26 Dec. 1868, p. 18.

Begins: 'The moon her silvery light had hid behind a darkening cloud'.

'A pleasant quarrel, dedicated to all Irish lovers'. Haslingden, 9 Jan. [1869]. In *Universal News*, 16 Jan. 1869, p. 4.

11 stanzas beginning: 'Good morning to you, Tim Delaney'.

'The long-expected day'. Haslingden, 30 Jan. 1869. In *Universal News*, 13 Feb. 1869, p. 14.

6 stanzas beginning: 'The stalwart sons of Ireland'.

'A soldier's life for me'. Haslingden, 11 May 1869. In *Universal News*, 15 May 1869, p. 7.

6 stanzas beginning: 'Let those who lead a life of riot, and pleasures seek to find'. Davitt's initials only are given under this poem.

'Christmas musings in prison, 1875'. In *Irishman*, 12, 19, 26 Feb. 1881. (DP/AA)

In 5 sections, showing a variety of metrical forms: (1) Past and present, (2) Flight from despair, (3) A felon's home, (4) Visions of Erin, (5) The sword. See above, p. 174.

Irish felon's song, or Innisfail. Single sheet, printed in Haslingden, Mar. 1877. (DP/A5)

5 stanzas beginning: 'In England's felon garb we're clad'; reprinted, in Cashman, pp 15-16, and in J. B. O'Reilly, *The poetry and song of Ireland* (New York, 2nd ed., [1889], p. 1025. See above, p. 174.

2 *PAMPHLETS*

The prison life of Michael Davitt, related by himself. Pp 40. [London, 1878.]

Dated London, March 1878; published before 6 May (see above, p. 199). No copy of the original has been found; the above particulars are derived from item 3 below. Extracts serialised in *Nation*, 12, 19, 26 Feb., 5, 12 Mar. 1882. Abridged version in Cashman (above, I, [1882]), pp 23–43; another abridgement in *A wondrous life* (above, [1885]), pp 19–38.

Paudeen O'Rafferty on the landlords' ten commandments, dedicated to exterminators & rack-renters, as also to the people who work: the creed of the Right Hon. Lord Clan Rack-rent, earl of Idleness and Viscount Absentee. Pp 4 [Dublin, 1880.] (DPA)

Issued at the land meeting held in Phoenix Park, Dublin, on 14 Mar. 1880.

The prison life of Michael Davitt, related by himself, together with his evidence before the house of lords[sic] commission on convict prison life. Pp [iv], 40, 58. Dublin: J. J. Lalor, April 1882. Later editions, June 1882, 1886.

A combination of his first pamphlet (pp 1–40) with a separately paged reprint (pp 1–53) of his examination before the Kimberley commission (H.C. 1878–9, xxxvii, 515–45; see above, pp 211–17 and below, p. 596), together with extracts (pp 54–8) from speeches, 5 Oct. 1879–30 June 1881, 'in which he strongly condemns the committing of outrages'.

The Land League proposal: a statement for honest and thoughtful men. Printed for gratuitous circulation by the author. Pp 32. Glasgow and London: Cameron & Ferguson, 1882. (DPA)

An address delivered in the Free Trade Hall, Manchester, on 21 May 1882.

The Castle government of Ireland: a lecture by Mr Michael Davitt. For gratuitous circulation. Pp 16. Glasgow and London: Cameron & Ferguson, [1882]. (DPA)

A lecture delivered at Foresters' Hall, Clerkenwell, on behalf of the fund for Maurice Collins, on 23 Oct. 1882.

Land nationalisation, or national peasant proprietary, Michael Davitt's lectures in Scotland: the principles of radical reform in the land laws. Pp 32. Glasgow and London: Cameron & Ferguson, [1882]. (DPA)

Lectures delivered, 25 Oct.–8 Nov. 1882.

Speech of Michael Davitt at the meeting in favour of land nationalisation held at St James's Hall, October 30th 1883. Pp 16. London: Land Reform Union, [1883]. (DPA)

Landlordism, low wages and strikes. Pp 4. London: English Land Restoration League, ([Leaflet], no. 21). (DPA)

Reprint of letter to editor of *Daily Chronicle*, 23 Aug.

Home rule: speeches of Earl Spencer and Right Hon. John Morley, M.P., at Newcastle, April 21, and of Michael Davitt at Glasgow, April 20, 1886, in support of Mr Gladstone's home rule bill. Pp 31. Printed, Glasgow, [1886]. (DPA)

Davitt's speech, pp 23–31.

Reasons why home rule should be granted to Ireland: an appeal to the common-sense of the British democracy. Pp 8. London: National Press Agency, [1886]. (DPA)

Mr Michael Davitt's reply to the Irish chief secretary's misstatements, delivered on December 18th, 1887. Pp 15. Manchester: Manchester and District Home Rule Union, 1887/8. (DPA)
Lecture in Free Trade Hall, Manchester.

'Unionists' brought to book. Pp 22. London: Irish Press Agency, 1888. (The Irish Question, no. 27) (DPA)

G.A.A. rule book. Preface by Davitt. Dublin, 1888.

The settlement of the Irish question: a speech by Mr Michael Davitt M.P. on April 11th, 1893, in the house of commons on the second reading of the home rule bill. London: Liberal Publication Department, 1893. (DPA)

Ireland's appeal to America. Pp 24. London: John Denvir (Denvir's Monthly Irish Library, Book of the Month, March 1902). (DPA)
Address at Chicago on 15 Aug. 1901.

Some suggestions for a final settlement of the land question. Pp 39. Dublin: Gill, 1902. (DPA)
Oct. 1902

3 *CONTRIBUTIONS TO NEWSPAPERS*

Besides a host of polemical contributions (1878–1906) to the *Freeman's Journal*, the *Irishman*, the *Nation*, and other newspapers, Davitt supplied letters and articles on commission to the following:

Irish World (New York), 1879–80, 1887.
Pilot (Boston, Mass.), 1879
San Francisco Chronicle, 1880 (DPC/6), 1883.
New York Daily News, 1882 (DPC/6).
Chicago Daily News, 1883.
Cincinnati Commercial Gazette, 1883.
Melbourne Advocate, 1883–1903 (DPC/6, 16, 26).
Montreal Post, 1883–4 (DPC/6).
New Orleans Times Democrat, 1883–4, 1885–7.
Philadelphia Times, 1883–4 (DPC/6).
New York Sun, 1885–6, 1893.
Frisco Examiner, 1887.
Daily Chronicle (London), 1893–5.
Westminster Gazette, 1894–5.

Davitt founded, edited, and was a large contributor to the following weekly:

The Labour World. Edited by Michael Davitt. London, 1890–91. Vol. i, nos 1–26, 26 Sept. 1890–14 Mar. 1891; vol. ii, nos 27–32, 21 Mar.–25 Apr. 1891.
Published on Saturdays, with a special Sunday edition down to 22 Mar. 1891. From 29 Mar. the Sunday edition appeared as the *Sunday World* (see below), and from 28 Mar. the *Labour World* carried the secondary title: *a journal devoted to the interests of all who toil.* Davitt resigned the editorship with no. 32 (25 Apr. 1891), the paper continuing for five further issues (nos 33–7, 2–30 May) under the editorship of H. W. Massingham. Davitt contributed 'Current topics' to nos 33–4.

The Sunday World: politics, literature, labour, athletics, the drama, social reform, London, 1891. Vol. ii, nos 28–37, 29 Mar.–31 May.

Sunday edition of the *Labour World*, containing less labour news and more matter of wider interest. It carried the same enumeration as the corresponding issues of the *Labour World* and was under the same editorship.

4 *ARTICLES IN PERIODICALS*

The punishment of penal servitude. In *Contemporary Review*, xliv, Aug. 1883, pp 169–82.

Reprinted in *Leaves from a prison diary* (1885), i, 225–51.

The Irish social problem. In *To-day*, new series, i, no. 4 (Apr. 1884), pp 241–55.

Irish conservatism and its outlooks. In *Dublin University Review*, Sept. 1885, pp 93–108.

Mr Giffen and the Irish question. In *Contemporary Review*, xlix, Apr. 1886, pp 501–12.

The Irish landlords' appeal for compensation. In *Contemporary Review*, liii, Apr. 1888, pp 594–607.

The report of the Parnell commission. In *Nineteenth Century*, xxvii, no. 157 (Mar. 1890), pp 357–83.

Retiring the landlord garrison. In *Nineteenth Century*, xxvii, no. 159 (May 1890), pp 779–94.

The latest Midlothian campaign. In *Nineteenth Century*, xxviii, no. 165 (Nov. 1890), pp 854–60.

Remedies for Irish distress. In *Contemporary Review*, lviii, Nov. 1890, pp 625–33.

Impressions of the Canadian north-west. In *Nineteenth Century*, xxxi, no. 182 (Apr. 1892), pp 631–47.

La question d'Irlande. In *Revue de Famille*, Apr. 1892, pp 394–409.

Le Caron's (re-published) story. In *The Speaker*, 29 Oct. 1892, pp 521–4.

The priest in politics. In *Nineteenth Century*, xxxiii, no. 191 (Jan. 1893), pp 139–55.

Fabian fustian. In *Nineteenth Century*, xxxiv, no. 202 (Dec. 1893), pp 849–59.

The evicted tenants' problem. In *Nineteenth Century*, xxxv, no. 206 (Apr. 1894), pp 560–73.

Home rule and labour representation. In *The Speaker*, Apr. 1894, pp 465–6.

Criminal and prison reform. In *Nineteenth Century*, xxxvi, no. 214 (Dec. 1894), pp 875–89.

The crimes of Irish landlordism. In *Irish Bits: a journal of Irish wit, romance and scenery*, iv, no. 100 (13 Aug. 1898), pp 588–90.

Speech at Straide, 1 Feb. 1880.

What I think of the English. In *The Universal Magazine* (Birmingham), i, no 5 (July 1900), pp 425–6.

Les États-Unis et l'Europe. In *Minerva: revue des lettres et des arts* (Paris), 15 Nov. 1902, pp 280–92.

The Irish national assembly. In *Independent Review*, v, Apr. 1905, pp 284–98.

5 BOOKS

Leaves from a prison diary; or lectures to a solitary audience. 2 vols: i, pp xv, 251; ii, pp xi, 256. London: Chapman and Hall, 1885. Cheap edition, in one volume, pp xvi, 352; London: Chapman and Hall, 1885. New cheap edition in one volume, pp 311, illus., paper cover; New York, 1886 (Ford's National Library). Reprint of original edition, with introduction (pp vii–xiv) by T. W. Moody; 2 vols in 1, Shannon: Irish University Press, 1972.

The 'Times'-Parnell commission: speech delivered by Michael Davitt in defence of the Land League. Carefully revised. Pp xiv, 414. London: Kegan Paul, Trench, Trubner & Co., 1890.

A reprint of the speech, with revisions, from *S.C.P.* x, 422–636, xi, 1–26 (24–31 Oct. 1889).

Life and progress in Australasia. Pp xx, 470, 2 maps. London: Methuen, 1898.

The Boer fight for freedom. Pp xii, 603, illus., maps. New York and London: Funk & Wagnalls Co., 1902.

Within the pale: the true story of anti-Semitic persecution in Russia. Pp xiv, 300. London: Hurst & Blackett, 1903.

The fall of feudalism in Ireland: or the story of the Land League revolution. Pp xviii, 752. London and New York: Harper Bros, 1904. Reprint, with introduction (pp v–x) by Seán Ó Lúing; Shannon: Irish University Press, 1970.

A copy of the book, inscribed 'To Lenin/Michael Davitt/1904', is in Lenin's library in the Kremlin, Moscow, where it forms part of a collection of about 30 books presented to Lenin by their authors. I am indebted for this information to my colleague James Buckley, who inspected the inscribed copy in March 1974.

IV MANUSCRIPT SOURCES OTHER THAN THE DAVITT PAPERS

1 DUBLIN

STATE PAPER OFFICE

Chief secretary's office

Registered papers, 1867–82.

Chief secretary's office: Police and crime division

Government files memoranda.

Fenianism, index of names, 1866–71 (1 vol.).

Abstracts of cases of persons arrested under habeas corpus suspension act, 1866–8 (3 vols and index vol.).

Description of fenian suspects, 1871–80 (1 vol.).

Photographs of fenians discharged from custody, 1866–70 (1 vol. and 4 cartons).

Fenian papers, 1866–74, 1879:
F1-F5076 (1866–7)
5R-9134R (1868–74)
9135R (30 Sept. 1879).

Fenian papers: A files, 1877–83 (nos 500–784).

Returns of outrages, 1848–93 (4 vols).
Printed but not published. Includes annual, monthly, and county statistics of agrarian outrages; vol. 4, covering 1877–82, also includes monthly reports on these outrages.

Arrests under Protection of Person and Property Act, 1881–2 (5 vols).

Crime branch, special papers (C.B.S.): B files 1881–4 (nos 9–268).

Irish National Land League and Irish National League papers, 1879–88 (10 cartons).

Chief crown solicitor's department

Chief crown solicitor's papers, 1859–90.

Queen *v.* Parnell papers, 1880–81 (11 cartons).

See also below, under National Library of Ireland.

PUBLIC RECORD OFFICE

Incumbered estates court rentals, 1850–85 ('O'Brien rentals').
Another copy in National Library of Ireland.

Wills, and administration and related papers.
Davitt's will (1 Feb. 1904): Principal Probate Registry, will of Michael Davitt, proved 21 July 1906.

REGISTRY OF DEEDS

Estate of Bourke, of Oldtown Cottage, Ballindine, Co. Mayo: 1857/19/7, 1859/1/11, 1873/6/293, 1873/34/91, 1877/29/211, 1879/17/157, 1880/40/107, 1881/38/287.

NATIONAL LIBRARY OF IRELAND

Papers relating to the Land League and the Ladies' Land League: MSS 842, 2070, 8167, 8291, 8574, 8583, 8933, 9219, 9281, 9283, 10700, 11289, 13503, 17693–7, 17699–17716, 17794, 17805, 18456.

Anna Parnell, 'The tale of a great sham' [the Land League], Oct. 1907: MS 12144.

Devoy papers: MSS 18001–158.

P. A. Collins papers (microfilm of originals in Boston (Mass.) College Library): n. 4601 p. 4567.

Croke papers (microfilm of originals in Archbishop's House, Thurles): n 5710–13.
TS catalogue by Dom Mark Tierney.

Harrington papers: MS 8580.

J. F. X. O'Brien papers: MS 13457.

Michael MacDonagh papers: MS 11445.

William Haley papers: MS 3905.

J. P. Quinn letters: MS 5930.

Memoirs of Mrs William O'Brien: MS 8507.

Letters of Davitt to publishers, 1890, 1893, 1903: MS 18575.

Chief secretary's office: Irish news-cuttings, with some annotations, 1880–1920. 196 vols. ILB 0822.
Vols 40–42: May–Dec. 1880, 1881–3.

Queen *v.* Parnell and others: [*Reports by police reporters of speeches at Land League meetings, 1880*]. Pp 1725 in 4 vols. ILB 343.

Queen *v.* Parnell and others: Briefs, evidence, extracts from *Hansard*, reports of speeches at Land League meetings, and reports of proceedings in court of queen's bench, 1879–81. V. B. Dillon & Co., solicitors for the traversers. 7 vols of MS and printed material (chiefly newspaper extracts). ILB 343.

NATIONAL MUSEUM OF IRELAND

Davitt to John Walshe, 9 Aug. 1878

Gold watch presented to Davitt by the Irish nationalists of Burnley district, Lancs., on 22 Mar. 1878, and given to the National Museum by his son, Judge Cahir Davitt, in Oct. 1972.

DUBLIN PUBLIC LIBRARIES: ARCHIVES DIVISION (CITY HALL)

Records of the Mansion House Committee for the Relief of Distress in Ireland, 1880.
A voluminous collection, for which a full analytical catalogue has recently been compiled by the archivist, Miss Mary Clark.

LIBRARY OF TRINITY COLLEGE

Dillon papers: MSS 6455-6909

FRIENDS' HISTORICAL LIBRARY, 6 EUSTACE STREET

Alfred Webb. Autobiography. 1904-5.

IN PRIVATE OWNERSHIP

Florence Arnold-Forster. My Irish journal: a record—from the inside—of the chief secretary's experiences in Dublin and London during the bad times 1880-1882 . . . TS. 6 vols.

The property of Mrs Veronica Rowe, granddaughter of the author. The diary has been prepared for publication by Oxford University Press under the editorship of T. W. Moody and Richard Hawkins.

Charles Guilfoyle Doran. Letters and papers, 1869-1903.

See T. W. Moody and Leon Ó Broin, 'The I.R.B. supreme council, 1868-78' in *Irish Historical Studies*, xix, no. 75 (Mar. 1975), pp 286-7, 290-97. These papers are now the property of Mr John C. Elliott.

2 *BELFAST*

PUBLIC RECORD OFFICE OF NORTHERN IRELAND

Letter book of Home Government Association and of Home Rule League, 1873-8 (D213)

Documents relating to Land League in D1163, D1308, D1481, and T2355.

3 *TUAM (CO. GALWAY)*

ST JARLATH'S COLLEGE

Fee-payment books, 1838-67, 1867-80.

4 *LONDON*

PUBLIC RECORD OFFICE

Census returns, 1851: township of Haslingden, Lancs. (H.O. 107/2250-1/477/4a-4b).

Census returns, 1861: township of Haslingden, Lancs. (RG9/3060-1/477/4a-4b).

Home office papers:
Fenian activities, 1865-70 (H.O. 45/O.S. 7799)
Political prisoners and amnesty agitation, 1869-86 (H.O. 45/9329-31/19461)
Books for libraries of convict prisons, 1856-78 (H.O. 45/9455/71414)
Attested lists of convicts, 1870-76 (H.O. 8/186-207)
Quarterly returns from convict prisons, in large folio volumes
Criminal registers, 1870 (H.O. 27/156)
Prison registers and returns, Millbank prison, 1865-74 (H.O. 24/10-11)
Papers of Sir Robert Anderson, 1868-1906 (H.O. 144/1538)
Michael Davitt's imprisonment, 1871-82 (H.O. 144/5/17869)
Relief of distress in Connemara, 1880 (H.O. 45/9587/89099)
Famine relief fund, 1880-81 (H.O. 45/9587/89099A)
Petition of Irish landowners on working of land act, 1882 (H.O. 45/9618/A14298).

Foreign office records: General correspondence, U.S.A., series II (F.O.5).

Cabinet papers, 1880-82 (Cab. 37/1-7).

CENTRAL CRIMINAL COURT (OLD BAILEY)

Indictments, 11 July 1870, Reg. *v*. Wilson and Davitt (107).

BRITISH LIBRARY

Gladstone papers.

5 *OXFORD*

BODLEIAN LIBRARY

Harcourt papers.

6 *HASLINGDEN (LANCS.)*

REGISTER OFFICE

Records of births, marriages, and deaths.

PUBLIC LIBRARY

Haslingden Institute, members' subscription book, 1846-67 (Reference Department, local collection).

ST MARY'S CHURCH (R.C.)

Records of baptisms, marriages, and deaths.
Records of confirmations.

IN PRIVATE OWNERSHIP

Distributors' register of hawkers' licences, 1 Aug. 1849—14 July 1864 (the property of Mr John Driver, newsagent, Bury Road, Haslingden).

7 LIVERPOOL

CENTRAL LIBRARY

Reports of Head constable of Liverpool to watch committee, 1857–69 (352 POL/ 2/1–5).

8 GLASGOW

MITCHELL LIBRARY

John Murdoch. Autobiography.

9 WASHINGTON (D.C.)

NATIONAL ARCHIVES

Passenger arrival lists, port of New York.
Population census schedules.

10 NEW YORK

PUBLIC LIBRARY

Henry George papers.

11 SCRANTON (PA)

CITY HALL, DEPARTMENT OF HEALTH

Death records.

CATHEDRAL CEMETERY

Burial records.

12 MANAYUNK (PHILADELPHIA)

ST JOHN THE BAPTIST'S CHURCH (R.C.)

Records of baptisms, marriages, and deaths.

V PRINTED RECORDS

1 PARLIAMENTARY PAPERS

A date in round brackets at the end of any entry is that on which the relevant paper was ordered by the house of commons to be printed. A date in square brackets in the same position is that printed in a command paper.

(a) POPULATION

The census of Ireland for the year 1851. Pt I [*Area, population, and houses*]: vol. i, *Leinster*, H.C. 1852-3, xci, 1-376; vol. ii, *Munster*, H.C. 1852-3, xci, 379-758; vol. iii, *Ulster*, H.C. 1852-3, xcii, 1-333; vol. iv, *Connaught*, H.C. 1852-3, xcii, 335-581. Pt II [*Agricultural produce*], H.C. 1852-3, xciii. Pt III [*Disease*], H.C. 1854, lviii, 1-154. Pt IV [*Ages and education*], H.C. 1856, xxix, 1-260. Pt V [*Deaths*], H.C. 1856, xxix, 261-824, xxx. Pt VI: *General report*, H.C. 1856, xxxi.

— *1861.* Pt I [*Area, population, and houses*]: vol. i, *Leinster*, H.C. 1863, liv, 1-379; vol. ii, *Munster*, H.C. 1863, liv, 381-763; vol. iii, *Ulster*, H.C. 1863, liv, 1-336; vol. iv, *Connaught, and summary for Ireland*, H.C. 1863, lv, 341-594. Pt II [*Ages and education*], H.C. 1863, lvi-lvii. Pt III [*Vital statistics*], H.C. 1863, lviii, 1-510. Pt IV [*Religious professions, education, and occupations*], H.C. 1863, lix-lx. Pt V: *General report*, H.C. 1863, lxi.

— *1871*, Pt I [*Area, houses, and population; ages, civil condition, occupations, birthplaces, religion, and education*]: vol. i, *Leinster*, H.C. 1872, lxvii; vol. ii, *Munster*, H.C. 1873, lxxii, pt i, pt ii, 1-475; vol. iii, *Ulster*, H.C. 1874, lxxiv, pt i; vol. iv, *Connaught, and summary tables for Ireland*, H.C. 1874, lxxiv, pt ii. Pt II [*Vital statistics*], H.C. 1873, lxxii, pt ii, lxxiv, pt iii. Pt III: *General report*, H.C. 1876, lxxxi.

— *1881.* Pt I [*Area, houses, and population; ages, civil or conjugal condition, occupations, birthplaces, religion, and education*]: vol. i, *Leinster*, H.C. 1881, xcvii; vol. ii, *Munster*, H.C. 1882, lxxvii; vol. iii, *Ulster*, H.C. 1882, lxxviii; vol. iv, *Connaught*, H.C. 1882, lxxix. Pt II, *General report*, H.C. 1882, lxxvi, 385-851.

Fourteenth detailed report of the registrar general of marriages, births, and deaths in Ireland, 1877 [etc.] [C2301], H.C. 1878-9, xix, 523-655 [etc.].

(b) POLITICAL PRISONERS AND CONVICT PRISONS

Report of the directors of convict prisons . . . for the year 1870 [etc.] [C449], H.C. 1871, xxxi, 1-630 [etc.].

Report of the commissioners on the treatment of the treason-felony convicts in the English convict prisons [3880], H.C. 1867, xxxv, 673-98. (8 June 1867)

Return of the names and sentences of the fenian convicts now proposed to be released, stating what portion of their sentences is unexpired and distinguishing between those confined in Australia and those in Great Britain and Ireland, H.C. 1868-9 (72), li, 531-2. (10 Mar. 1869)

Return of the names and sentences of the fenian convicts not proposed to be released, stating what portion of their sentences is unexpired, and distinguishing between those confined in Australia and those in Great Britain and Ireland, H.C. 1868-9 (125), li, 533-6. (6 Apr. 1869).

Report of the commissioners appointed to inquire into the treatment of treason-felony convicts in English prisons, together with appendix and minutes of evidence [C319], H.C. 1871, xxxii, 1-60; [C319-I], H.C. 1871, xxxii, 61-602. (Devon comm. rep., 20 Sept. 1870).

Return of the names of the fenian convicts recently released, showing in each case the offence, the date of conviction, the sentences, the term of sentence unexpired, the cost of passage money provided, and the total expense incurred in connection with the release, H.C. 1871 (144), lviii, 461-2. (31 Mar. 1871)

Returns of the names, the dates of conviction, and the sentences of the Irish convicts still remaining under punishment in English goals or in the penal settlements, for complicity in one or other of the offences known as the Manchester rescue or the Clerkenwell outrage . . ., H.C. 1871 (430), lxviii, 463-4. (8 Aug. 1871)

Returns of the names of any persons now suffering imprisonment on account of their conviction . . . of the murder of Sergeant Brett at Manchester, 1867 . . ., H.C. 1874 (119) liv, 493-4. [17 Apr. 1874]

Copies of the record of the conviction of William O'Mara Allen, Michael Larkin, William Gould, Thomas McGuire, and Edward Shore . . . for the murder of Sergeant Brett; . . . and of the conviction of Michael Davitt and John Wilson at the Central Criminal Court in the month of July 1870, H.C. 1877 (424), lxix, 361-4.

Return of the various diets . . . which have been in use for civil and for military prisoners at Millbank and at other civil prisons . . . since 1870 inclusive, H.C. 1877 (204) lxix, 717-66.

Inquiry as to the alleged ill-treatment of the convict Charles McCarthy in Chatham convict prison [C1978], H.C. 1878, lxiii, 769-96.

Further papers relative to the case of the late Sergeant McCarthy [C1987-I], H.C. 1878, lxiii, 797-800.

Report of the commissioners appointed to inquire into the working of the penal servitude acts [C2368], H.C. 1878-9, xxxvii, 1-66; [C2368-I], H.C. 1878-9, xxxvii, 67-770; [C2368-II], H.C. 1878-9, xxxviii. (Kimberley comm. rep., comm. rep., 14 July 1879).

Return . . . of the conditional pardons granted to persons convicted of treason-felony and other offences of a political character since and including the year 1865, H.C. 1881 (208), lxxvi, 381-90. (6 May 81).

Third report of the general prisons board, Ireland, 1880-81 [C3067], H.C. 1881, li, 665-800.

Fourth report of the general prisons board, Ireland, 1881-2 [C3360], H.C. 1882, xxxiii, 661-808.

Copy of the record of the conviction and of the judgment of the queen against Michael Davitt and another, tried at the Central Criminal Court on 11 July 1870, H.C. 1882 (66), lv, 147-60. (27 Feb. 82)

Correspondence respecting the imprisonment in Ireland . . . of naturalized citizens of the United States [C3193], H.C. 1882, lxxx, 9-52.
8 June 81-19 Apr. 82.

Protection of Person and Property Act, 1881: reglations made by the lord lieutenant . . . for the treatment . . . of persons arrested and committed to prison . . ., H.C. 1881 (130), lxxvi, 667-70. (14 Mar. 81)

—; *list of all persons detained in prison under the statute 44 Vict., c.4*, H.C. 1881 (171), lxxvi, 671-6. (7 Apr. 81)

—:—, H.C. 1881 (209), lxxvi, 677-84. (6 May 81)

—: —, H.C. 1881 (273), lxxvi, 685-98. (6 June 81)

—: —, H.C. 1881 (316), lxxvi, 699-718. (5 July 81)

—: —, H.C. 1881 (372), lxxvi, 719-40. (3 Aug. 81)

—: *return of all persons who have been or are in custody . . . up to 31 March 1882*, H.C. 1883 (156), lv, 635-52. (21 Apr. 82)
Includes dates of arrest and release.

—; *list of all persons detained in prison . . . [on 1 February 1882]*, H.C. 1882 (1), lv, 685-712. (7 Feb. 82)

—:— *[on 1 March 1882]*, H.C. 1882 (1-I), lv, 713-44. (7 Mar. 82)

—:— *[on 1 April 1882]*, H.C. 1882 (1-II), lv, 745-74. (3 Apr. 82)

—:— *[on 1 May 1882]*, H.C. 1882 (1-III), lv, 775-96. (4 May 82)

—:— *[on 1 June 1882]*, H.C. 1882 (1-IV), lv, 797-812. (5 June 82)

—:— *[on 1 July 1882]*, H.C. 1882 (1-V), lv, 813-24. (4 July 82)

—:— *[on 1 August 1882]*, H.C. 1882 (1-VI), lv, 825-34. (4 Aug. 82)

(c) LANDLORD-TENANT RELATIONS

Report from her majesty's commissioners of inquiry into the state of the law and practice in respect of the occupation of land in Ireland, H.C. 1845 (605), xix, 1-56; (606), xix, 57-1183; (616), xx, 1-1168; (657), xxi, 1-1004; (672), xxii, 1-224; (673), xxii, 225-725. (Devon comm. rep., 14 Feb. 45)

Digest of evidence taken before her majesty's commissioners of inquiry into the state of the law and practice in respect to the occupation of land in Ireland. By J. P. Kennedy. Dublin: pt I, 1847; pt II, 1848.

Two reports for the Irish government on the history of the landlord and tenant question in Ireland, with suggestions for legislation: first report made in 1859, second in 1866, by W. Neilson Hancock, LL.D. [4204], H.C. 1868-9, xxvi, 1-70.

Reports from the poor law inspectors in Ireland as to the existing relations between landlord and tenant in respect of improvements on farms, drainage, reclamation of land, fencing, planting, etc.; also as to the existence (and to what extent) of the Ulster tenant-right in their respective districts etc. [C31], H.C. 1870, xiv, 37–192.

Reports from her majesty's representatives respecting the tenure of land in the several countries of Europe, pt I 1869 [C66], H.C. 1870, lxvii, 1–548; pt II 1869–70 [C75], H.C. 1870, lxvii, 549–930.

Return for the year 1870 of the number of landed proprietors in each county classed according to residence, showing the extent and value of the property held by each class—resident on or near the property . . ., H.C. 1872 (167), xlvii, 775–84. (23 Apr. 72)

Copy of the letter of instruction issued by the Irish government to the poor law inspectors relative to the return of landed proprietors (Ireland) lately issued, H.C. 1872, xlvii, 785–6. (21 June 72)

Report from the select committee of the house of lords on the Landlord and Tenant (Ireland) Act 1870 . . ., H.C. 1872 (403), xi, 1–360. (Chelmsford comm. rep., 17 July 72)

Return of owners of land of one acre and upwards in the several counties, counties of cities, and counties of towns in Ireland . . . [C1492], H.C. 1876, lxxx, 61–394. [20 Apr. 76]

Copy of a return of the names of proprietors and the area and valuation of all properties in the several counties in Ireland held in fee or perpetuity, or on long leases at chief rents . . ., H.C. 1876 (412), lxxx, 395–580. (10 Aug. 76)

Summary of the returns of owners of land in Ireland, showing with respect to each county, . . . (1) the number of owners below an acre . . . (13) of 100,000 [acres] and upwards, H.C. 1876 (422), lxxx, 35–60. (11 Aug. 76)

Report from the select committee on Irish land act, 1870 . . ., H.C. 1877 (328), xii, 1–304; H.C. 1878 (249), xv, 1–466. (Shaw-Lefevre comm. rep.)

Supplement to the return of owners of land in the several counties, counties of cities, and counties of towns in Ireland, presented to both houses of parliament in the session of 1876 . . . [C2022], H.C. 1878, lxxix, 501–10.

Preliminary report from her majesty's commissioners on agriculture [C2778], H.C. 1881, xv, 1–24. (Richmond comm. rep., 14 Jan. 81)

Minutes of evidence taken before her majesty's commissioners on agriculture [C2778–I], H.C. 1881, xv, 25–1126.

Digest and appendix to part I of evidence taken before the royal commission on agriculture, together with reports of the assistant commissioners [C2778–II]. H.C. 1881, xvi, 1–840.

Royal commission on agriculture, preliminary report of the assistant commissioners for Ireland [C2951], H.C. 1881, xvi, 841–8.

Minutes of evidence taken before her majesty's commissioners on agriculture, vol. ii [C3096], H.C. 1881, xvii.

[Final] report from her majesty's commissioners on agriculture [C3309], H.C. 1882, xiv, 1–44 (11 July 1882).

Minutes of evidence taken before her majesty's commissioners, vol. iii [C3309-I], H.C. 1882, xiv, 43-492.

Digest of minutes of evidence (parts I and III) taken before her majesty's commissioners on agriculture, with appendix [C3309-II], H.C. 1882, xiv, 493-673.

Royal commission on agriculture, reports of the assistant commissioners, southern district of England [C3375 I-C3375 VI], H.C. 1882, xv, 1-718.

Report of her majesty's commissioners of inquiry into the working of the Landlord and Tenant (Ireland) Act, 1870, and the acts amending the same [C2779], H.C. 1881, xviii, 1-72. (Bessborough comm. rep., 4 Jan. 81)

—, vol. ii: *Digest of evidence, minutes of evidence, part I* [C2779-I], H.C. 1881, xviii, 73-970.

—, vol. iii: *Minutes of evidence, part II* [C2779-II], H.C. 1881, xix, 1-824.

—, vol. iv: *Index to evidence and appendices* [C2779-III], H.C. 1881, xix, 825-920.

First report from the select committee of the house of lords on land law (Ireland) . . ., H.C. 1882 (249), xi, 1-545. (Cairns comm. rep., 28 Apr. 82)

Second report . . ., H.C. 1882 (379), xi, 547-904. (1 Aug. 82)

Third report . . ., H.C. 1883 (204), xiii, 443-653. (10 May 83)

Fourth report . . ., H.C. 1883 (279), xiii, 655-742. (9 July 83)

Report of the royal commission on the Land Law (Ireland) Act, 1881, and the Purchase of Land (Ireland) Act, 1885 [C4969], H.C. 1887, xxvi, 1-24. (Cowper comm. rep., 21 Feb. 87)

—, vol. ii: *Minutes of evidence and appendices* [C4969^{I}], H.C. 1887, xxvi, 25-1107.

—, vol. iii: *Index to evidence and appendices* [C4969^{II}], H.C. 1887, xxvi, 1109-1240.

—, vol. iv: *Report by Thomas Knipe* [C5015], H.C. 1887, xxvi, 1241-8.

Report of the select committee on land acts (Ireland) . . ., H.C. 1894 (310), xiii, i-lix, 1-846. (Morley comm. rep., 20 Aug. 94)

(d) AGRICULTURAL STATISTICS

Returns of agricultural produce in Ireland in the year 1847 [923,1000], H.C. 1847-8, lvii.

— *1848* [1116], H.C. 1849, xlix.

— *1849* [1245], H.C. 1850, li.

— *1850* [1404], H.C. 1851, l.

— *1851* [1589], H.C. 1852-3, xciii.

— *1852* [1714], H.C. 1854, lvii.

— *1853* [1865], H.C. 1854-5, xlvii.

— *1854* [2017], H.C. 1856, liii.

— *1855* [2174], H.C. 1857 sess. 1, xv.

— *1856* [2289], H.C. 1857-8, lvi.

The agricultural statistics of Ireland for the year 1857 [2461], H.C. 1859, xxvi.
— *1858* [2599], H.C. 1860, lxvi.
— *1859* [2763], H.C. 1861, lxii.
— *1860* [2997], H.C. 1862, lx.
— *1861* [3156], H.C. 1863, lxix.
— *1862* [3286], H.C. 1864, lix.
— *1863* [3456], H.C. 1865, lv.
— *1864* [3766], H.C. 1867, lxxi.
— *1865* [3929], H.C. 1867, lxxi.
— *1866* [3958-II], H.C. 1867-8, lxx.
— *1867* [4113-II], H.C. 1868-9, lxii.
— *1868* [C3], H.C. 1870, lxviii.
— *1869* [C239], H.C. 1871, lxix.
— *1870* [C463], H.C. 1872, lxiii.
— *1871* [C762], H.C. 1873, lxix.
— *1872* [C880], H.C. 1874, lxix.
— *1873* [C1125], H.C. 1875, lxxix.
— *1874* [C1380], H.C. 1876, lxxviii.
— *1875* [C1568], H.C. 1876, lxxviii.
— *1876* [C1749], H.C. 1877, lxxv.
— *1877* [C1938], H.C. 1878, lxxvii.
— *1878* [C2347], H.C. 1878-9, lxxv.
— *1879* [C2534], H.C. 1880, lxxvi.
— *1880* [C2932], H.C. 1881, xciii.
— *1881* [C3332], H.C. 1882, lxxiv.
— *1882* [C3677], H.C. 1883, lxxvi.
— *1883* [C4069], H.C. 1884, lxxv.

Returns showing the number of agricultural holdings in Ireland and the tenure by which they are held by the occupiers [C32], H.C. 1870, lvi, 737-56.

Return of agricultural holdings in Ireland compiled by the local government board . . . from returns furnished by the clerks of the poor law unions . . . in January 1881 [C2934], H.C. 1881, xciii, 793-806.

Agricultural statistics, Ireland, report and tables relating to migratory agricultural labourers [C2809], H.C. 1881, xciii, 807-24.

(e) EVICTIONS

Return by provinces and counties . . . of cases of eviction which have come to the knowledge of the constabulary in each of the years 1849 to 1880 inclusive, H.C. 1881 (185), lxxvii, 725-48. (8 Apr. 81)

Copy of return . . . of cases of eviction which have come under the knowledge of the constabulary, showing the number of families evicted in each county of Ireland in each of the four quarters of . . 1877, 1878, 1879, first quarter of . . 1880, and up to 20 June 1880, H.C. 1880 (254 sess. 2), lx, 361-4. (1 July 80)

Return . . . of cases of eviction which have come to the knowledge of the constabulary in each quarter of the year ended 31 December 1880 . . . in each county in Ireland . . ., H.C. 1881 (2), lxxvii, 713–20. (6 Jan. 81)

— *31 December 1881 . . .*, H.C. 1882 (9), lv, 229–36. (7 Feb. 82)

— *31 December 1882 . . .* [C3465], H.C. 1883, lvi, 99–105. [24 Jan. 83]

Return of cases of eviction which have come to the knowledge of the constabulary in the quarter ended 31 March 1883 . . . in each county . . . [C3579], H.C. 1883 lvi, 107–10. [11 Apr. 83]

— *30 June 1883 . . .* [C3770], H.C. 1883, lvi, 111–14. [6 July 83]

— *30 September 1883 . . .* [C3892], H.C. 1884, lxiv, 407–10. [11 Oct. 83]

— *31 December 1883 . . .* [C3893], H.C. 1884, lxiv, 411–14. [22 Jan. 84]

(f) AGRARIAN CRIME

See also p. 590: Returns of outrages, 1848–93.

Return of [agrarian] outrages reported to the Royal Irish Constabulary office from 1 January 1844 to 31 December 1880 [C2756], H.C. 1881, lxxvii, 887–914. (8 Jan. 81)

Monthly totals, classified into (1) offences against the person, (2) against property, (3) against the public peace, and (4) threatening letters.

Return of all agrarian outrages which have been reported by the Royal Irish Constabulary between 1 January 1879 and 31 January 1880, giving particulars of crimes, arrests, and results of proceedings . . . H.C. 1880 (131), lx, 199–289. (15 Mar. 80)

Summary by months and counties on pp 288–9.

Return of the number of agrarian offences in each county . . . in each month of . . . 1880, distinguishing offences against the person, offences against property, and offences against the public peace . . ., H.C. 1881 (12), lxxvii, 619–34. (13 Jan. 81)

— *1881 . . .*, H.C. 1882 (8), lv, 1–16. (7 Feb. 82)

— *during January 1882*, H.C. 1882 (116), lv, 29–32. (14 Mar. 82)

— *during February 1882*, H.C. 1882 (117), lv, 33–6. (14 Mar. 82)

— *during March 1882*, H.C. 1882 (142), lv, 37–40. (3 Apr. 82)

— *during April 1882*, H.C. 1882 (182), lv, 41–4. (9 May 82)

— *during May 1882*, H.C. 1882 (216), lv, 45–8. (2 June 82)

— *during June 1882* [C3267], H.C. 1882, lv, 49–51. [1 July 82]

— *during July 1882* [C3323], H.C. 1882, lv, 53–5. [Aug. 82]

— *during October 1882* [C3412], H.C. 1882, lv, 57–9. [1 Nov. 82]

Return of the number of agrarian outrages [in each county] which were reported to the inspector general of the Royal Irish Constabulary during the month of February 1883 [C3511], H.C. 1883, lvi, 13–15. [2 Mar. 83]

— *during . . . March 1883* [C566], H.C. 1883, lvi, 17–19. [2 Apr. 83]

— *during . . . April 1883* [C3608], H.C. 1883, lvi, 21–3. [30 Apr. 83]

— *during . . . May 1883* [C3664], H.C. 1883, lvi, 25–7. [1 June 83]

— *during . . . June 1883* [C3681], H.C. 1883, lvi, 29–31. [2 July 83]

— *during . . . July 1883* [C3743], H.C. 1883, lvi, 33–5. [1 Aug. 83]

— *during . . . August, September, October, November and December 1883* [C3894], H.C. 1884, lxiv, 13–23. [1 Sept., 1 Oct., 1 Nov., 1 Dec. 83, 2 Jan. 84]

Return of the number of persons receiving special police protection in each county in Ireland on 31 December 1880, H.C. 1881 (1), lxxvi, 641–2. (6 Jan. 81)

Return showing for each month of the years 1879 and 1880 the number of Land League meetings and agrarian offences reported to . . . the Royal Irish Constabulary in each county throughout Ireland, H.C. 1881 (5), lxxvii, 793–804. (6 Jan. 81)

Proclamation by the lords justices and general governors of Ireland dated 14 October 1881 warning all persons that certain forms of intimidation practised in many parts are unlawful and criminal . . . [C3124], H.C. 1882, lv, 271–4.

Proclamation by the lord lieutenant of Ireland dated 20 October 1881 relative to an association styling itself the Irish National Land League [C3125], H.C. 1882, lv, 275–7.

(g) RELIEF OF DISTRESS

Correspondence relative to measures for the relief of distress in Ireland, 1879–80 [C2483], H.C. 1880, lxii, 157–86.
Sept. 79–Jan. 80.

Further correspondence relative to measures for the relief of distress in Ireland, 1879–80 [C2506], H.C. 1880, lxii, 187–94.
Feb. 1880

Copy of circular of 7 February 1880, issued by the local government board for Ireland, to boards of guardians, relating to the relief to families of persons occupying land, H.C. 1880 (9), lxii, 337–8. (10 Feb. 80)
Interpreting quarter-acre clause of 25 & 26 Vict., c.83.

Report from Captain Digby Morant, Senior Naval Officer at Galway, on the relief of distress on the west coast of Ireland [C2671], H.C. 1880, lxii, 195–202. [4 Aug. 80]

Return of all applications from landed proprietors and sanitary authorities in scheduled unions for loans under the notices of the commissioners of public works in Ireland, dated 22 November 1879 and 12 January 1880, respectively . . ., H.C. 1880 (154), lxii, 209–16. (24 Mar. 80)

Return of the loans applied for and granted in each of the various unions in Ireland scheduled as distressed . . ., up to . . . 29 February 1880, H.C. 1880 (158), lxii, 283–8. (29 Mar. 80)

Returns of numbers in receipt of relief in the several unions in Ireland on 1 January, 1 March, and 1 June in 1878, 1879, and 1880, H.C. 1880 (420 sess. 2), lxii, 289-316. (7 Sept. 80)

Return showing the unions and electoral divisions scheduled by the local government board for Ireland under the Seed Supply (Ireland) Act, 1880, H.C. 1880 (299 sess. 2), lxii, 339-44. (21 July 80)

Return of the names of landowners and sanitary authorities who have obtained loans under the provisions of the Relief of Distress (Ireland) Act, . . . 1880 . . ., H.C. 1881 (99), lvii, 653-704. (23 Feb. 81)

Annual report of the local government board for Ireland . . . [C2926], H.C. 1881, xlvii, 269-304. [16 Apr. 81]
Covers relief work, Feb. 80-Feb. 81.

Appendix to the annual report of the local government board for Ireland . . . [C2926-I], H.C. 1881, xlvii, 305-560.

Report of the joint committee selected from the committees of the Duchess of Marlborough Relief Fund and the Dublin Mansion House Fund for the Relief of Distress in Ireland to administer the sum of 100,000 dollars voted by the parliament of the Dominion of Canada towards the relief of distress in Ireland, H.C. 1881 (326), lxxv, 859-94. (12 July 81)

Return showing the amount allowed for relief works in Ireland, the amount authorised to be expended, and the amount expended up to the present date, H.C. 1881 (274), lvii, 705-6. (27 July 81)

(h) LAND ACT 1881, AND ARREARS ACT 1882

Copy of form of delegation by land commission to sub-commission, H.C. 1882 (102), lv, 309-10. (7 Mar. 82)

Return giving the names of the gentlemen appointed to be assistant commissioners under the Land Law (Ireland) Act, 1881 . . ., H.C. 1882 (150), lv, 287-90. (20 Apr. 82)

Return of the number of cases lodged and disposed of in the court of the Irish land commission in each month from 1 October 1881 to 31 March 1882, H.C. 1882 (171), lv, 311-14. (28 Apr. 82)

Return, according to provinces and counties, of judicial rents fixed by sub-commissions and civil bill courts, as notified to the Irish land commission up to, and including, 28 January 1882 [C3120], 1882, H.C. lvi, 1-95 [the first of a monthly series].

Copy of treasury minute, dated 16 June 1882, stating the method on which it is proposed to provide money for the purposes of the Arrears of Rent (Ireland) Bill, H.C. 1882 (324), lv, 75-82. (16 June 82)

Copy of treasury minute on arrears of rent in Ireland, dated 26 June 1882, H.C. 1882 (256), lv, 69-74. (1 July 82)

Copy of recommendations made to the government by the land commission as to an amendment of those clauses of the land act affecting leaseholders and labourers, H.C. 1882 (329), lv, 323-6. (31 July 82)

Arrears of Rent (Ireland) Act, 1882: return of . . . applications lodged and disposed of in the court of the Irish land commission up to and including 30 November 1882 [C3483], H.C. 1883, lvi, 37-41 [the first of a monthly series]. [2 Dec. 82]

Arrears of Rent (Ireland) Act, 1882: return of payments made to landlords by the Irish land commission . . .; and also a return of rent charges cancelled . . . [C4059], H.C. 1884, lxiv, 97-405.

Return showing, according to provinces and counties, the number of cases in which judicial rents have been fixed by all the methods provided by the land law acts for a first and second statutory term repectively, to 31 December 1902 . . ., H.C. 1903 (91), lvii, 373-8. (25 Mar. 1903)

(i) MISCELLANEOUS

Reports of the inspectors of factories to her majesty's principal secretary of state for the home department for the half year ending 31 October 1855 [2031], H.C. 1856, xviii, 211-333.

— *31 October 1857* [2314], H.C. 1857-8, xxiv, 661-717.

Report . . . from the select committee on general valuation etc. (Ireland) . . . H.C. 1868-9 (362), ix, 1-258.

Index to the report from the select committee on general valuation etc. (Ireland), H.C. 1868-9 (362-I0, ix, 259-304.

Report from the select committee of the house of lords on Irish grand jury law, H.C. 1881 (430), xi, i-xx, 1-549. (25 Aug. 81)

Correspondence respecting the publication in the United States of incitements to outrage in England [C3194], H.C. 1882, lxxx, 53-8.
June 81, 27 July 82.

First annual report of the congested districts board for Ireland, 1893 [C6908], H.C. 1893-4, lxxi, 525-82.

Royal commission on congestion in Ireland, appendix to the ninth report: minutes of evidence (taken in Co. Mayo, 21 August-3 September 1907) [Cd 3845], H.C. 1908, xli, 487-845.

2 *RECORDS OF PARLIAMENT*

(a) PARLIAMENTARY PROCEEDINGS

Hansard's parliamentary debates, third series, vols cxcix-cclxxv, 1870-82. London, 1870-82.

Journals of the house of commons, vols 125-37, 1870-82.

Lucy, Henry W. *A diary of two parliaments*: [i] *The Disraeli parliament, 1874-80*; [ii] *The Gladstone parliament, 1880-85*. 2 vols, London, 1885-6.

(b) ACTS OF PARLIAMENT

1793 Irish convention act, 33 Geo. III, c. 29 [Ire.].

1848 Treason-felony act., 11 Vict., c.12, 22 Apr.

1849 Incumbered Estates (Ireland) Act, 12 & 13 Vict., c.77, 28 July

1853 Act to substitute in certain cases other punishments in lieu of transportation, 16 & 17 Vict., c.99, 20 Aug.

1857 Act amending the preceding, 20 & 20 Vict., c.3, 26 June

1858 Landed Estates (Ireland) Act, 21 & 22 Vict., c.72, 2 Aug.

1860 Tenure and Improvement of Land (Ireland) Act, 23 & 24 Vict., c.153, 28 Aug. ('Cardwell's act')

1860 Landlord and Tenant Law Amendment (Ireland) Act, 23 & 24 Vict., c.154, 28 Aug. ('Deasy's act')

1864 Act to amend penal servitude acts, 27 & 28 Vict., c.47, 26 July

1866 Suspension of habeas corpus act, 29 Vict., c.4, 18 Feb.

1868 Representation of the People (Ireland) Act, 31 & 32 Vict., c.44, 13 July

1869 Irish church disestablishment act, 32 & 33 Vict., c.42, 26 July

1870 Peace Preservation (Ireland) Act, 33 Vict., c.9, 4 Apr.

1870 Landlord and Tenant (Ireland) Act, 1870, 33 & 34 Vict., c.46, 1 Aug. (first Gladstone land act)

1871 Protection of Life and Property in Certain Parts of Ireland Act, 34 & 35 Vict., c.25, 16 June ('Westmeath act')

1872 Ballot Act, 35 & 36 Vict., c.33, 18 July

1875 Peace Preservation (Ireland) Act, 38 Vict., c.4, 22 Apr.

1879 Act repealing Irish convention act of 1793, 42 & 43 Vict., c.28, 21 July

1880 Seed Supply (Ireland) Act, 43 Vict., c.1, 1 Mar.

1880 Relief of Distress (Ireland) Act, 43 Vict., c.4, 15 Mar.

1880 Relief of Distress (Ireland) Amendment Act, 43 & 44 Vict., c.14, 2 Aug.

1881 Protection of Person and Property Act, 44 & 45 Vict., c.14, 2 Aug.

1881 Peace Preservation (Ireland) Act, 44 & 45 Vict., c.5, 21 Mar.

1881 Land Law (Ireland) Act, 44 & 45 Vict., c.49, 22 Aug. (second Gladstone land act)

1882 Prevention of Crime (Ireland) Act, 45 & 46 Vict., c.25, 12 July

1882 Arrears of Rent (Ireland) Act, 45 & 46 Vict., c.47, 18 Aug.

1882 Labourers' Cottages and Allotments (Ireland) Act, 45 & 46 Vict., c.60, 18 Aug.

1883 Labourers (Ireland) Act, 46 & 47 Vict., c.60, 25 Aug.

1885 Purchase of Land (Ireland) Act, 48 & 49 Vict., c.73, 14 Aug. (Ashbourne act)

1887 Land Law (Ireland) Act, 50 & 51 Vict., c.33, 23 Aug.

1891 Purchase of Land (Ireland) Act, 54 & 55 Vict., c.48, 5 Aug.

1898 Criminal Evidence Act, 61 & 62 Vict., c.36, 12 Aug.

1898 Local Government (Ireland) Act, 61 & 62 Vict., c.37, 12 Aug.

(c) PARLIAMENTARY BILLS

1876 A bill to amend the laws relating to the tenure of land in Ireland, H.C. 1876 (10), iii, 415–42; brought in by Isaac Butt and others (9 Feb.)
Embodying the 3 Fs.

1877 A bill [as preceding]. H.C. 1877 (2), iii, 33–60; brought in by Isaac Butt and others (9 Feb.)
As preceding bill.

1880 A bill to make temporary provision with respect to disturbance in certain cases of ejectment for non-payment of rent in certain parts of Ireland, H.C. 1880 (232), i, 427–30; brought in by W. E. Forster (18 June)

1880 [The foregoing as amended in committee], ibid., pp 431–4 (19 July)

1880 [The foregoing as amended in committee and on consideration as amended], ibid., pp 435–8 (22 July)

1882 A bill to amend the Land Law (Ireland) Act, 1881, H.C. 1882 (2), lii, 11–20; brought in by John Redmond, C. S. Parnell, T. M. Healy, Thomas Sexton, and Justin McCarthy (9 Feb.)

3 RECORDS OF LEGAL PROCEEDINGS

(a) QUEEN *v.* DAVITT AND WILSON, 1870

The Times, 16 May–15 June, 16–19 July 1870; and other newspapers (see above, pp 81–102).

Central criminal court, sessions paper, Besley mayor, seventh session . . . 1870, minutes of evidence, vol. lxxii, London, [1870].

Reports of cases in criminal law, argued and determined in all the courts in England and Ireland, vol. xi (1867–71). *Ed.* Edward W. Cox. London, 1871.

(b) QUEEN *v.* DAVITT AND OTHERS, 1879

Freeman's Journal, 20 Nov.–13 Dec. 1879.

(c) QUEEN *v.* PARNELL AND OTHERS, 1880–81

See also above, II, series IV; and IV 1 (National Library of Ireland).

Freeman's Journal, 29 Dec. 1880–26 Jan. 1881.

Reports of cases in criminal law, argued and determined in all the courts in England and Ireland, vol. xiv (1877–82). *Ed.* E. W. Cox and John Thompson. London, 1882.

(d) 'THE TIMES'-PARNELL COMMISSION, 1889–90

Special commission act, 1888: reprint of the shorthand notes of the speeches, proceedings, and evidence taken before the commissioners appointed under the above-named act. 12 vols, London, 1890.

Report of the special commission, 1888 [C5891], H.C. 1890, xxvii, 477-640.

Russell, Sir Charles. *The Parnell commission: the opening speech for the defence.* London, 1889.

James, Sir Henry. *The work of the Irish leagues: the speech of . . . Sir Henry James . . . replying in the Parnell commission inquiry.*

See also above, III 5, and below, VI 4.

Macdonald, John. *Diary of the Parnell commission.* Revised from the *Daily News.* London, 1890.

4 OTHER PRINTED RECORDS

General valuation of rateable property in Ireland, [under] acts 15 & 16 Vic., c.63, 17 Vic., c.8, 19 & 20 Vic., c.63. 202 vols, Dublin, 1852-64.
'Griffith's valuation'.

The I.R.B. supreme council, 1868-78. *Ed.* T. W. Moody and Leon Ó Broin. In *Irish Historical Studies*, xix, no. 75 (Mar. 1975), pp 286-332.

Proceedings of the home rule conference held at the Rotunda, Dublin, on the 18th, 19th, 20th and 21st November 1873 . . . Dublin, 1874.

Special report on agricultural produce and fuel supply in Ireland, as ascertained by inquiries made in October 1879, with appendix. By T. W. Grimshaw, registrar general for Ireland. Dublin, 1879.

The Irish crisis of 1879-80: proceedings of the Dublin Mansion House Relief Committee. Dublin, 1881.

Reports on the condition of the peasantry of Mayo in 1880. By J. A. Fox. 3rd ed. Dublin: Mansion House Relief Committee, [1880].

Reports of meetings of the central body of the Irish National Land League, 21 Oct. 1879-18 Oct. 1881. In *Freeman's Journal*, 22 Oct. 1879-19 Oct. 1881, and other newspapers (see above, appendix H).

Irish National Land League of the U.S., reports of conventions, 1881-3. No. 1, Buffalo, N.Y., 12-13 Jan. 1881 (Richmond, Va, 1881); no. 2, Washington, D.C., 12-13 Apr. 1882 (Buffalo, 1882); no. 3, Philadelphia, 25 Apr. 1883 (Buffalo, 1883).

Property Defence Association, Ireland, annual report of the committee for the year ended 30 November 1881 [etc.]. Dublin, 1881-8.

Report of the proceedings of the great aggregate meeting of the Irish landlords held in Dublin . . . 3 January 1882 . . . Dublin, 1882.

Private letters from the British embassy in Washington to the foreign secretary, Lord Granville, 1880-1885. *Ed.* Paul Knaplund and Carolyn M. Clewes. In *Annual Report of the American Historical Association, 1941* (Washington, D.C., 1942).

An army on police work, 1881-2: Ross of Bladensburg's memorandum. *Ed.* Richard Hawkins. In *Irish Sword*, xi, no. 43 (winter, 1973), pp 75-117.

The Dublin Gazette, published by authority.

Register of admissions to the Honourable Society of the Middle Temple, from the fifteenth century to the year 1944. 3 vols, London, [1950].

Irish historical documents, 1172-1922. Ed. Edmund Curtis and R. B. McDowell. London, 1943.

VI PRINTED CONTEMPORARY WORKS OTHER THAN DAVITT'S

1 *PAMPHLETS AND POLEMICAL ARTICLES*

Argyll, *duke of.* See Campbell, G.D.

Arnold, Matthew. The incompatibles. In *Nineteenth Century*, ix, no. 50 (Apr. 1881), pp 709-26, no 52 (June 1881), pp 1026-43.

Arnold-Forster, Hugh Oakeley. *The truth about the Land League.* London: National Press Agency, for the Property Defence Association, 1882. 2nd ed., 1882; 3rd ed., 1883. The lst ed., published on 1 Apr. 82, appeared under the pseudonym 'One who knows'. The author was an adopted son of the chief secretary, who, however, knew nothing about the pamphlet before its publication.

Atkins, T. D. *The case of Ireland stated.* London, 1881.

Bagenal, Philip H. *The Irish agitator in parliament and on the platform: a complete history of Irish politics for the year 1879.* Dublin, 1880.

— *Parnellism unveiled: or the land-and-labour agitation of 1879-80.* Dublin, 1880.

— *The American-Irish and their influence on Irish politics.* London, 1882.

— Uncle Pat's cabin. In *Nineteenth Century*, xii, no. 70 (Dec. 1882), pp 925-38.

Battersby, T. S. F. *The secret policy of the land act: compensation to landlords the corollary to the land act.* Dublin, 1882.

Belmore, *earl of.* See Lowry-Corry, S.R.

Bernard, W. L. *The Irish land question: suggestions for the extended establishment of a peasant proprietary in Ireland.* Dublin, 1880.

Bourke, *Very Rev.* Ulick J. *A plea for the evicted tenants of Mayo.* Dublin, 1883,

Butt, Isaac. *Land tenure in Ireland: a plea for the Celtic race.* Dublin, 1866.

— *The Irish people and the Irish land: a letter to Lord Lifford.* Dublin, 1867. See Hewitt, James, *Viscount Lifford.*

— *Ireland's appeal for amnesty: a letter to the Right Honorable W. E. Gladstone, M.P.* Glasgow and London, 1870.

— *Irish federalism: its meaning, its objects, and its hopes.* Dublin, 1870. 3rd ed., 1870; 4th ed., 1874.

Buxton, Sidney C. *The Irish land bill of 1870 and the lords' and tories' amendments thereon.* London, 1881.

Campbell, George Douglas, *duke of Argyll*. The new Irish land bill. In *Nineteenth Century*, ix, no. 51 (May 1881), pp 880–904.
See Shaw-Lefevre, G. J.

Clancy, J. J. (ed.). *The Land League manual*. New York, 1881.

Clark, G. B. *A plea for the nationalisation of the land*. London, 1882.

Comfort, G. F. *The land trouble in Ireland*. Syracuse, 1881.

Condemnation of crime, compiled from speeches delivered at meetings of the Land League and National League in Ireland, 1879–1887. Dublin and London: Irish Press Agency, 1888.

A continental observer. The Irish question. In *Contemporary Review*, xl, Nov. 1881, pp 736–87.

Conyngham, David P. *Ireland, past and present, embracing a complete history of the land question . . .; also A very full and complete history of the penal laws, by Parnell, and Talks about Ireland, by Redpath*. New York, 1884.

Cusack, Mary Frances Clare. *The famine in Ireland: thanks and appeal to munificent America.* [Kenmare, 1880.]

— *The case of Ireland stated: a plea for my people and my race.* Dublin, 1880. London, 1881.

— *The present case of Ireland plainly stated: a plea for my people and my race.* New York, 1881

Errington, George. *The Irish land question: a question in practical politics . . .* London, 1880.

Fitzgerald, Peter, *knight of Kerry*. Irish land agitation. In *Nineteenth Century*, vii, no. 37 (Mar. 1880), pp 492–502.
A reply to John O'Connor Power; see below.

Fitzpatrick, Bernard, *Baron Castletown. The BAC of the Irish land question.* London, 1881.

Flatley, P. J. *Ireland and the Land League: key to the Irish question.* Intro. by the Hon. Wendell Phillips. Boston, 1881.

Froude, J. A. Ireland. In *Nineteenth Century*, viii, no. 43 (Sept. 1880), pp 341–69.

George, Henry. *The Irish land question: what it involves and how alone it can be settled: an appeal to the Land Leagues.* New York and London, 1881.

Gibbons, T. A. *Irish land and Irish landlords.* New York, 1880.

Godkin, James, *The land war in Ireland: a history for the times.* London, 1870.

Gray, *Sir* John. *The Irish land question: speech of Sir John Gray, delivered in the Free Trade Hall, Manchester, on 18 October 1869.* London and Dublin, 1869.

Healy, T. M. *Why there is an Irish land question and an Irish Land League.* New York, 1881.

Hewitt, James, *Viscount Lifford. A plea for Irish landlords: a letter to Isaac Butt Esq.* Dublin, 1867.
See Butt, Isaac.

Higgins, Charles. *The Irish land question: facts and arguments.* Manchester, 1881.

Hodgkin, Howard. *Irish land legislation and the royal commissions.* London, 1881.

Irish Land Committee. *The land question, Ireland: confiscation or contract?* London and Dublin, November 1880.

— *The land question, Ireland.* No. I: *Notes upon the government valuation of land in Ireland, commonly known as 'Griffith's valuation'.* London and Dublin, November 1880.

— — No. II: *The anarchy in Ireland.* London and Dublin, December 1880.

— — No. III: *Facts and figures.* London and Dublin, December 1880.

— — No. IV: *French opinion on the Irish crisis.* London and Dublin, [December 1880].

— — No. V: *Arrested progress.* London and Dublin, January 1881.

— — No. VI: *Lord Dufferin on the Three Fs.* London and Dublin, January 1881.

— — No. VII: *Mr Gladstone and the Three Fs.* London and Dublin, February 1881.

— — No. VIII: *Mr Bonamy Price on the Three Fs.* London and Dublin, February 1881.

— — No. IX: *Mr Gladstone's commissioners and Mr Gladstone.* London and Dublin, March 1881.

— — No. X: *Mr Gladstone's bill.* London and Dublin, April 1881.

— — No. XI: *Foregone conclusions: the Bessborough commission.* London and Dublin, April 1881.

— — No. XII: *The Richmond commission: notes on Lord Carlingford's report.* London and Dublin, June 1881.

— — No. XIII: *More facts and figures: evictions.* London and Dublin, July 1881.

— — No. XIV: *The working of the land law act.* London and Dublin, February 1882.

Lalor, James Fintan. *Writings.* Introduction by John O'Leary. Dublin, 1895.

— *James Fintan Lalor, patriot and political essayist. Ed.* Lilian Fogarty. Dublin and London, 1918.

Lavelle, *Rev.* Patrick. *The Irish landlord since the revolution, with notes of ancient and modern tenures in various countries.* Dublin, 1870.

Leech, H. B. Are the Irish landowners entitled to compensation? In *Contemporary Review,* xli, Mar. 1882, pp 462–74.

Lifford, *Viscount.* See Hewitt, James.

Lowry-Corry, Somerset Richard, *earl of Belmore.* Fair play to landlords. In *Nineteenth Century,* xii, no. 65 (July 1882), pp 120–30.

McCarthy, J. G. *Irish land questions plainly stated and answered.* London, 1870.

McCarthy, Justin. The landowners' panic. In *Nineteenth Century,* viii, no. 42 (Aug. 1880), pp 305–12.

— Ireland in '48 and Ireland now. In *Nineteenth Century,* viii, no. 46 (Dec. 1880), pp 861–75.

Mahaffy, J. P. The Irish landlords. In *Contemporary Review,* xli, Jan. 1882, pp 160–76.

Monsabré, J. M. L. *Pour L'Irlande: allocution prononcée dans l'église de la Madeleine à Paris le 18 Avril 1880 . . ., rendu au profit des victimes de la famine en Irelande.* Paris, [1880].
N.L.I., Ir 280 P 163.

Monteagle, *Baron*. See Spring Rice, Thomas.

Montgomery, Hugh de F. *Irish land and Irish rights.* London, 1881.

Morley, John. Irish revolution and English liberalism. In *Nineteenth Century*, xii, no. 64 (Nov. 1882), pp 647–66.

Nulty, *Most Rev.* Thomas, *bishop of Meath. Letter to the clergy and laity of the diocese of Meath* (Kells, Apr. 1880).
Reprinted in *Cause of poverty explained; land nationalization the only true remedy* . . . [1887/8], N.L.I., P 200. P.1: introduction; p. 2: 'Back to the land' from *Eagle & County Adviser*, 12 Nov. 1887; pp 3–6: 'Bishop Nulty's essay on land nationalization', Apr. 1880; pp 7–8: 'Speech of Michael Davitt at St James's Hall', 30 Oct. 1883 (see III 2).

— *The land agitation in Ireland: letter . . . to the clergy and laity of the diocese of Meath* (Mullingar, Feb. 1881). Manchester, [1881].

O'Brien, Charlotte G. The Irish 'poor man'. In *Nineteenth Century*, viii, no. 46 (Dec. 1880), pp 876–87.

— The emigration and waste-land clauses [of the land bill]. In *Fortnightly Review*, xxix, no. 174 (June 1881), pp 757–66.

O'Connor, T. P. The Land League and its work. In *Contemporary Review*, xxxviii, Dec. 1880, pp 981–99.

Parnell, C. S. The Irish land question. In *North American Review*, cxxx, Apr. 1880, pp 388–406.

Parnell, Fanny. *The hovels of Ireland.* Preface by C. S. Parnell. New York 1880.

Philip, Kenward. *Boycotting: or avenging Ireland's wrongs* . . . New York, 1881.

Pim, Jonathan. *Ireland and the imperial parliament.* Dublin, 1871.

'Political economy'. *The Irish landlord and his accusers, with an account of misguided legislation and consequent demoralization and danger.* Dublin, 1882.

Power, John O'Connor. The Irish land agitation. In *Nineteenth Century*, vi, no. 34 (Dec. 1879), pp 953–67.
See above, Fitzgerald, Peter, *knight of Kerry*.

Redpath, James. *Talks about Ireland.* New York, 1881.
Dedication to Davitt, 10 May 1881.

Richardson, R. *The Irish land question.* London, 1881.

Russell, Charles (later *Baron Russell of Killowen*). *New views on Ireland; or Irish land: grievances, remedies.* London, 1880.
Reprinted from the London *Daily Telegraph*, for which Russell was special correspondent.

Russell, Robert. *Ulster tenant right for Ireland.* Edinburgh and London, 1870.

Shaw-Lefevre, G. J. (later *Baron Eversley*). The duke of Argyll and the Irish land bill. In *Nineteenth Century*, ix, no. 52 (June 1881), pp 1044–65.
See Campbell, George Douglas, *duke of Argyll*.

Smith, Samuel. *The nationalisation of land*. London, 1884.

Spring Rice, Thomas, *Baron Monteagle*. Abolition of landlords. In *Nineteenth Century*, ix, no. 48 (Feb. 1881), pp 372–84.

Thornton, W. E. *A plea for peasant proprietorship*. London, 1874. New ed., New York, 1881.

Traill, Anthony. A conservative view of the Irish land bill. In *Fortnightly Review*, xxix, no. 174 (June 1881), pp 741–56.

Trench, C. E. *Are the landlords worth preserving?* Dublin, 1881.

Wakefield, E. T. *The disaffection in Ireland: its cause and its cure*. Dublin, 1882.

Wallace, Alfred Russel. How to nationalise the land: a radical solution of the Irish problem. In *Contemporary Review*, xxxviii, Nov. 1880, pp 716–36.

— *Land nationalisation: its necessity and its aims* . . . London, 1882.

Walters, J. T. *Ireland's wrongs and how to mend them*. London, 1874.
Advocating peasant proprietorship.

2 *NARRATIVES AND REPORTS*

Becker, Bernard H. *Disturbed Ireland: being the letters written during the winter of 1880–81*. London, 1881.
By a special commissioner of the London *Daily News*.

Blake, *Sir* Henry A. *Pictures from Ireland*. By Terence McGrath (*pseudonym*). London, 1880.

Cant-Wall, Edward. *Ireland under the land act: letters contributed to the 'Standard' newspaper*. London, 1882.

Devoy, John. *The land of Eire: the Irish Land League, its origin, progress and consequences, preceded by a concise history of the various movements which have culminated in the last great agitation, with a descriptive and historical account of Ireland from the earliest period to the present day*. New York, [1882].

Dun, Finlay. *Landlords and tenants in Ireland*. London, 1881.
Reprint of reports to *The Times* during the winter of 1880–81.

Hoare, E. J. *The legion of honour*. Dublin, 1883.
On Land League, Ladies' Land League, and imprisoned 'suspects'.

Houston, Mrs M. C. *Twenty years in the wild west, or life in Connaught*. London, 1879.

Jones, W. Bence. *The life's work in Ireland of a landlord who tried to do his duty*. London, 1880.
See O'Leary, *Rev.* John.

— My answer to opponents. In *Contemporary Review*, xl, Aug. 1881, pp 246–56.

McGrath, Terence, *pseudonym*, see Blake, *Sir* Henry A.

Maguire, J. F. *The Irish in America*. London, 1868. Reprint, New York, [1969].

Morris, W. O'Connor. *Letters on the land question of Ireland*. London, 1870.
Letters written between Aug. 1869 and Jan. 1870 by special commissioner of *The Times* and published in that paper.

O'Brien, R. Barry. *The parliamentary history of the Irish land question from 1829 to 1869; and the origin and results of the Ulster custom*. London, 1880.

— *Fifty years of concessions to Ireland, 1831–1881*. 2 vols. London, [1883–4].

O'Brien, William. *Christmas on the Galtees: an inquiry into the condition of the tenantry of Mr Nathaniel Buckley*. By the special correspondent of the *Freeman's Journal*. Dublin: Central Tenants' Defence Association, 1878.
Reprinted from *F.J.*, 27 Dec. 1877–5 Jan. 1878.

— Our land commission, nos I–VIII. In *F.J.*, 25 Aug.–9 Sept. 1879.

O'Leary, *Rev.* John. Mr Bence Jones's story of his experiences in Ireland. In *Contemporary Review*, xl, July 1881, pp 127–49.

— Mr Bence Jones's answer to opponents examined. In *Contemporary Review*, xl, Sept. 1881, pp 479–89.

Sullivan, Alexander Martin. *New Ireland*. London, 1877; new ed., with a sequel on 1877–82, [1882].

Sullivan, M. F. *Ireland of today*. Philadelphia, 1881.

Shaw-Lefevre, G. J. (later *Baron Eversley*). *Incidents of coercion: a journal of visits to Ireland in 1882 and 1888*. London, 1888.

Tuke, James Hack. *A visit to Connaught in the autumn of 1847: a letter addressed to the central relief committee of the Society of Friends, Dublin*. London, 1847.

— *Irish distress and its remedies: a visit to Donegal and Connaught in the spring of 1880*. London, 1880.

3 STUDIES

Arnold, Arthur. *Free land*. London, 1880.

Blackwood, Frederick Temple Hamilton-Temple, *Lord Dufferin* (later *marquis of Dufferin and Ava*). *Irish emigration and the tenure of land in Ireland*. London, 1867.

Blake, *Sir* Henry A. The Irish police. In *Nineteenth Century*, ix, no. 48 (Feb. 1881), pp 385–96.

Broderick, George C. *The Irish land question: past and present*. London, 1881.

— The Irish land act of 1881: its origin and its consequences. In *Fraser's Magazine*, xxv, Jan. 1882, pp 91–106.

Butt, Isaac. *Fixity of tenure: heads of a suggested legislative enactment*. Dublin, 1866.

— *A practical treatise on the new law of compensation to tenants in Ireland and other provisions of the Landlord and Tenant Act 1870, with an appendix of statutes and rules*. Dublin, 1871.

Caird, *Sir* James. *The Irish land question*. London, 1869.

— *The landed interest and the supply of food*. London, 1878. 4th ed., 1880.

Cairns, J. E. *Essays in political economy, theoretical and applied*. London, 1873.

Campbell, George. *The Irish land*. London and Dublin, 1869.

— The land legislation for Ireland. In *Fortnightly Review*, xxix, no. 169 (Jan. 1881), pp 18–34.

De Moleyns, Thomas. *The landowners's and agents' practical guide* . . . 7th ed., 1878; 8th ed., by H. W. Quill and F. P. Hamilton, 1899.

Du Cane, *Sir* E. F. *An account of the manner in which sentences of penal servitude are carried out in England*. London, 1872. New ed., 1882.

— *The punishment and prevention of crime*. London, 1885.

Dublin Review. The landlord and tenant question in Ireland. In *Dublin Review*, xiv, Jan. 1870, pp 165–84.

— The distress of Ireland. In *Dublin Review*, 3rd series, i, Apr. 1880, pp 464–91.

— The Land League and the land act. In *Dublin Review*, 3rd series, vii, Jan. 1882, pp 208–38.

Dufferin, *Lord*. See Blackwood, F. T. H.-T.

Edinburgh Review. The Irish land question. In *Edinburgh Review*, cxxxi, no. 267 (Jan. 1870), pp 257–304.

— Irish discontent. In *Edinburgh Review*, clv, no. 317 (Jan. 1882), pp 155–85.

Fitzgibbon, Gerald. *Ireland in 1868* . . . London, 1868.

Fournier, Paul *La question agraire en Irlande*. Paris, 1882.

Fraser's Magazine. Ireland and the land question. In *Fraser's Magazine*, N.S., i, no. 1 (Jan. 1870), pp 121–42.

George, Henry. *Progress and poverty: an inquiry into the cause of industrial depressions and of increase of want with increase of wealth: the remedy*. Author's ed., New York, 1879. First regular ed., New York, 1880; London, 1881.

Grimshaw, Thomas Wrigley. *Facts and figures about Ireland: part I, comprising a summary and analysis of the principal statistics of Ireland for the past fifty years, 1841–1890; part II, comprising comparative statistics of Irish counties . . . . ., 1841–1891* . . . Dublin, 1893.

Hancock, W. Neilson. *Report on the landlord and tenant question in Ireland from 1860 till 1866; with an appendix containing a report on the question from 1835 till 1859*. Dublin, 1866.

— Migratory labourers from Mayo to England. In *Journal of the Statistical and Social Inquiry Society of Ireland*, viii, pt 56 (Apr. 1880), pp 52–78.

Healy, T. M. *The tenant's key to the land law act, 1881*. Dublin, 1881.

Hutton, H. D. The Stein-Hardenberg land legislation: its basis, development, and results in Prussia. In *Transactions of the National Association for the Promotion of Social Science, Belfast meeting, 1867*. London, 1868.

— *Proposals for the creation of a farmer proprietary in Ireland*. London, 1868.

Kay, Joseph. *Free trade in land*. Preface by John Bright. London, 1879.

King, D. B. *The Irish question*. New York, 1882.

Leadam, I. S. *Coercive measures in Ireland, 1830–1880*. London, 1880.

Leslie, T. E. Cliffe. *Land systems and industrial economy of Ireland, England, and continental countries*. London, 1870.

— The Irish land question. In *Fraser's Magazine*, N.S., xxii, Dec. 1880, pp 828–42.

Longfield, Mountifort. The tenure of land in Ireland. In *Systems of land tenures in various countries*, ed. J. W. Probyn (London, 1881), pp 1–92.

— Land tenure in Ireland. In *Fortnightly Review*, xxviii, no. 164 (Aug. 1880), pp 137–46.

Maclagan, Peter, M.P. *Land culture and land tenure in Ireland: the results of observation during a recent tour in Ireland.* Edinburgh, 1869.

Marx, Karl, and Engels, Frederick. *On Ireland* London, 1971.
A collection of letters, articles, and pamphlets, including Engels's 'History of Ireland' and 'Notes for the history of Ireland'.

Mecredy, Thomas T., *and* Mecredy, James. *A practical guide to the Land Law (Ireland) Act, 1881* . . . Dublin, 1881.

Mill, J. S. *England and Ireland*. London, 1868.

— *Chapters and speeches on the Irish land question: reprinted from 'Principles of political economy' and Hansard's debates*. London, 1870.

Morris, W. O'Connor. *The Irish land act, with a full commentary and notes*. Dublin, 1870.

Murphy, J. N. *Ireland, industrial, political and social*. London, 1870.

Nolan, Francis, *and* Kane, R. R. *The statutes relating to the law of landlord and tenant in Ireland* . . . Dublin, 1871; 3rd ed., 1878.

O'Brien, Murrough. Irish rents, improvements, and landlords. In *Fortnightly Review*, xviii, no. 166 (Oct. 1880), pp 409–21.

O'Brien, R. Barry. *The Irish land question and English public opinion.* Dublin, 1880.

O'Grady, Standish. The Irish small farmer. In *Fortnightly Review*, xxvii, no. 160 (Apr. 1880), pp 568–79.

— *The crisis in Ireland*. Dublin, 1882.

Probyn, J. W. (ed.). *Systems of land tenure in various countries* . . . London, 1870. Revised ed., 1881.

Richey, A. G. *The Irish land laws*. London, 1880.

Samuelson, *Sir* Bernard, M.P. *Studies of the land and tenantry of Ireland*. London, 1870.

Seebohm, Frederic. The land question. In *Fortnightly Review*, N.S., vi, no. 36 (Dec. 1869), pp 626–40.

— The historical claims of tenant right. In *Nineteenth Century*, ix, no. 47 (Jan. 1881), pp 19–36.

Shaw, J. J. The nationalisation of the land. In *Journal of the Statistical and Social Inquiry Society of Ireland*, viii, pt 62 (July 1884), pp 492–508.

Shaw-Lefevre, G. J., M.P. (later *Baron Eversley*). *The working of the Bright clauses of the Irish land act, 1870.* Dublin, 1879.

— *Freedom of land.* London, 1880.

—*English and Irish land questions: collected essays.* London, 1881.

Sigerson, George. *History of the land tenures and land classes of Ireland. . . .* London, 1871.

Tuke, James Hack. Irish emigration. In *Nineteenth Century*, ix, no. 48 (Feb. 1881), pp 358–71.

— Emigration from Ireland. In *Contemporary Review*, xli, Apr. 1882, pp 694–714.

Walsh, *Rev.* William J. (later *archbishop of Dublin*). *A plain exposition of the Irish land act of 1881.* Dublin, 1881.

Watt, William. *Economic aspects of recent legislation.* London, 1885.
On land acts of 1870 and 1881.

4 *LETTERS, DIARIES, AND SPEECHES*

Blunt, Wilfrid Scawen. *The land war in Ireland . . .* London, 1912.
Mainly Blunt's diaries for 1885–8.

Bright, John. *Speeches on questions of public policy. Ed.* J. E. Thorold Rogers. Vol. i. London, 1868.

Chamberlain, Joseph. *A political memoir, 1880–1892. Ed.* C. H. D. Howard. London, 1953.
Contains various letters of 1880–82.

Devoy, John. *Devoy's post bag, 1871–1928. Ed.* William O'Brien and Desmond Ryan. 2 vols. Dublin, 1948, 1953. Reprint, Dublin, 1979.
From the Devoy papers in the National Library of Ireland.

Forster, William Edward. Letters, in T. Wemyss Reid, *Life of . . . W. E. Forster* (2 vols, London, 1888).

Gladstone, Herbert. Herbert Gladstone, Forster, and Ireland, 1881–2. *Ed.* A. B. Cooke and J. R. Vincent. In *Irish Historical Studies*, xvii, no. 68 (Sept. 1971), pp 521–48; xviii, no. 69 (Mar. 1972), pp 74–89.

Gladstone, William Ewart. *Gladstone's speeches . . . Ed.* A. Tilney Bassett. London, 1916.

— *The queen and Mr Gladstone. Ed.* Philip Guedalla. 2 vols. London, 1933.

Hamilton, *Sir* E. W. *The diary of Sir Edward Walter Hamilton, 1880–1885. Ed.* Dudley W. R. Bahlman. 2 vols. Oxford, 1972.

Jones, Ernest. *Ernest Jones, chartist: selections from the writings and speeches of Ernest Jones.* With introduction and notes by John Saville. London, 1952.

Kirby, *Rev.* Tobias. Irish College, Rome, Kirby papers: guide to material of public and political interest, 1862-83. *Ed.* Patrick J. Corish. In *Archivium Hibernicum*, xxx (1972), pp 29-115.

O'Reilly, John Boyle. *Life of John Boyle O'Reilly, by J. J. Roche, together with his complete poems and speeches, edited by Mrs John Boyle O'Reilly.* New York and London, 1898.

O'Sullivan, W. H. *Speeches in and out of parliament.* Dublin, 1880.

Parnell, Charles Stewart. Letters, in Katharine O'Shea, *Charles Stewart Parnell: his love story and political life.* 2 vols. London, 1914.

— *Mr Parnell's speeches, letters, and public utterances (out of parliament) in the United Kingdom, from 17th April 1879 to [18th September] 1888.* Dublin, printed by R. D. Webb and Son, for use before the Special Commission, 24 Jan. 1889.

Victoria, *Queen. The letters of Queen Victoria.* 2nd series, 1862-85. *Ed.* G. E. Buckle. 3 vols. London, 1926-8.

— *The queen and Mr Gladstone. Ed.* Philip Guedalla. 2 vols. London, 1933.

5 OTHER CONTEMPORARY PUBLICATIONS

Ancient laws of Ireland: Seanchus Mor. Vol. i, with preface by W. Neilson Hancock; vol. ii, with preface by W. Neilson Hancock and Thaddeus O'Mahony. Dublin, 1865, 1869.

Forrester, Ellen, Arthur, *and* Fanny. *Songs of the rising nation.* Glasgow and London, 1869.

Harris, W. F. Vernon. *Dartmoor prison, past and present*, Plymouth: Wm. Brendon, [*c*.1876].

Kickham, Charles. *Sally Cavanagh, or the untenanted graves: a tale of Tipperary.* Dublin, 1869.
First published serially in *Hibernian Magazine*, 3rd series, nos 1-6 (July-Dec. 1864).

— *Knocknagow, or the homes of Tipperary.* Dublin, 1873; many later editions.
Ch. 1-36 published serially in the *Emerald* (New York) and the *Shamrock* (Dublin), Mar.-Sept. 1870.

Lander, E. *The Birmingham gun trade.* Birmingham, 1865.

O'Reilly, John Boyle. *Songs from the southern seas and other poems.* Boston (Mass.), 1873.

— *Moondyne: a story from the underworld.* Boston, 1880.

— (ed.). *Songs, legends, and ballads.* Boston, 1878. 5th ed., 1882.

— (ed.). *The poetry and song of Ireland.* New York, 2nd ed., [1889].

Trollope, Anthony. *The land leaguers.* 3 vols. London, 1883.
Unfinished at Trollope's death. Contains ch. I-XLVIII and part of ch. XLIX; was to have run to 60 chapters.

VII CONTEMPORARY NEWSPAPERS AND MAGAZINES

1 NEWSPAPERS

See also above, III 3 and IV 1 (National Library of Ireland)
Accrington Times.
Bacup Times.
Belfast. *Belfast News Letter.*
— *Northern Whig.*
— *Banner of Ulster.*
— *Ulster Examiner.*
— *Morning News.*
Birmingham Daily Gazette.
Blackburn Standard.
Blackburn Weekly Times.
Boston (Mass.). *Daily Globe.*
— *The Pilot.*
Burnley Free Press.
Castlebar. *Connaught Telegraph.*
Chicago. *Chicago Journal.*
— *The Emerald.*
— *Tribune.*
Cleveland Leader.
Cork. *Cork Examiner.*
— *The Herald.*
Denver. *Daily Tribune.*
Downpatrick. *Down Independent.*
Dublin (daily). *Daily Express.*
— *Dublin Evening Mail.*
— *Freeman's Journal.*
— *Irish Times.*
— *Saunders News Letter.*
Dublin (weekly). *Flag of Ireland.*
— *The Irishman.*
— *The Irish People.*
— *The Nation.*
— *United Ireland.*
— *Weekly Freeman.*
— *Weekly Irish Times.*
— *Weekly News.*
Dubuque (Iowa). *Daily Herald.*
— *Daily Telegraph.*
Glasgow, *Evening Citizen.*
— *Glasgow Herald.*
Haslingden Chronicle and Ramsbottom Times.
Haslingden Guardian.
Inverness. *The Highlander.*
Leeds, *Leeds Mercury.*
— *Yorkshire Post and Leeds Intelligencer.*
Little Falls (N.Y.). *Catholic Telegraph.*

Liverpool. *Daily Courier.*
— *Liverpool Daily Post.*
— *Liverpool Mercury.*
London. *Daily News.*
— *Daily Telegraph.*
— *Illustrated London News.*
— *Morning Post.*
— *Pall Mall Gazette.*
— *Punch.*
— *The Standard.*
— *The Tablet.*
— *The Times.*
— *The Universe.*
— *Universal News.*
Manayunk Sentinel.
Manchester. *Examiner and Times.*
— *Manchester Courier and Lancashire General Advertiser.*
— *Manchester Guardian.*
Montreal Evening Post.
Newark (N.J.). *Newark Morning Register.*
New York. *Daily World.*
— *The Herald.*
— *Irish American.*
— *Irish Nation.*
— *Irish World.*
— *The Star.*
— *Weekly Union.*
Newcastle-upon-Tyne. *Newcastle Chronicle.*
— *Newcastle Daily Journal.*
— *Newcastle Daily Telegraph.*
— *Newcastle Examiner.*
Paris. *Le Monde Illustré.*
Preston Herald.
San Francisco. *Daily Examiner.*
— *Labor Tribune.*
— *Monitor.*
— *Morning Call.*
St Helen's Newspaper and Advertiser.
Scranton Republican.
Sheffield Telegraph.

2 *MAGAZINES*

Contemporary Review (London).
Dublin Review (London and Dublin).
Edinburgh Review (Edinburgh and London).
Fortnightly Review (London).
Fraser's Magazine (London).
Irish Ecclesiastical Record (Dublin).
Journal of the Statistical and Social Inquiry Society of Ireland (Dublin).
Nineteenth Century (London).

VIII CONTEMPORARY WORKS OF REFERENCE

The Annual Register: a review of public events at home and abroad, for the year 1863 [etc.]. New series, London, 1864- . .

Bateman, John. *The great landowners of Great Britain and Ireland: a list of all owners of three thousand acres and upwards, worth £3000 a year. . . .* London, 1878; 4th ed., 1883, reprinted, with introduction by David Spring, Leicester, 1971.

Belfast and Province of Ulster Post Office Directory and Official Guide. Belfast, 1870- (annual).

The Catholic Directory, Ecclesiastical Register and Almanac. London, 1838- (annual).

De Burgh, U. H. Hussey. *The landowners of Ireland: an alphabetical list of owners of estates of 500 acres or £500 valuation and upwards, in Ireland.* Dublin, 1878.

Dod's Parliamentary Companion. London, 1865- (annual).

Encyclopaedia Britannica. 9th edition. London, 1875-85.

Foster, Joseph. *Men-at-the-bar: a biographical hand list of the members of the various inns of court.* London, 1885.

Gray, O. W., & Son. *The national atlas . . . of the United States. . . .* Philadelphia, 1881 ed.

Handbook for travellers in Ireland. 3rd ed. London: John Murray, 1871.

Irish Catholic Directory, Almanac and Registry. New series, Dublin, 1870- (annual).

Lancashire. *Slater's Commercial Directory and Topography of Lancashire.* Manchester, 1856.

— *Post Office Directory of Lancashire.* London, 1858.

— *Post Office Directory of Liverpool and Manchester.* London, 1864.

— *Slater's Royal National Commercial Directory of Lancashire.* Manchester, 1865, 1869.

Lewis, Samuel. *Topographical dictionary of Ireland . . .* 2 vols. London, 1837.

Lloyd's Register of British and Foreign Shipping, 1878-9 [etc.]. London, 1878- .

Men and Women of the Time: a dictionary of contemporaries. . . . London, 1875-99 (incorporated in *Who's Who*).

New York. *Hudson by Daylight: map from New York Bay to head of tidewater.* New York: Wm F. Link, for the office of New York and Albany Day Line Steamers. 1878.

Newspaper Press Directory and Advertisers' Guide, containing full particulars of every newspaper, magazine, review and periodical published in the United Kingdom. . . . London, 1846- (annual).

Philadelphia. *Philadelphia City Directory*. 1872-82.

— Westcott, Thompson. *Guide to Philadelphia and vicinity: a new handbook for strangers and citizens, expressly designed for the use of those visiting the international exhibition.* Philadelphia, 1875.

— *Philadelphia and its environs illustrated.* New ed., Philadelphia, 1887.

Philips' handy atlas of the counties of Ireland. Constructed by John Bartholomew; revised by P. W. Joyce. London, 1884.

The Queen's University calendar, 1882: a supplement to the preceding series of calendars. Dublin, 1882.

Scranton City Directory. 1867–95.

Slater's Royal National Directory of Ireland. . . . Manchester, [1881].

The Statesman's Year Book. London, 1864– (annual).

Thom's Irish Almanac and Official Directory of the United Kingdom of Great Britain and Ireland, for the year 1844 [etc.]. Dublin, 1844– (annual).
Title altered in 1881 to *Thom's Official Directory* . . .

Who's Who: an annual biographical dictionary. . . . London, 1897– .

Who was who, 1897–1916. London, 1920.
—, *1916–28.* London, 1929.

IX LATER WRITINGS BY CONTEMPORARIES

1 *MEMOIRS AND AUTOBIOGRAPHIES*

Anderson, *Sir* Robert. *Sidelights on the home rule movement.* London, 1906.

— *The lighter side of my official life.* London, 1910.

Bussy, F. M. *Irish conspiracies: recollections of John Mallon (the great Irish detective) and other reminiscences.* London, 1910.

[Callow, Edward]. *Five years' penal servitude.* By One who has endured it. London, 1877; New ed., 1878.

Chamberlain, Joseph. *A political memoir, 1880–92. Ed.* C. H. D. Howard, London, 1953.

Collins, James T. *Life in old Dublin: historical associations of Cook Street; reminiscences of a great tribune.* Dublin, 1913.
Reminiscences (pp 179–94) are of Isaac Butt.

Cowper, Earl. *Memoir of Earl Cowper.* By his wife. London, 1913. Privately printed.

Cusack, Mary F. C. *The nun of Kenmare: an autobiography.* London, 1889.

Daly, John. Recollections. In *Irish Freedom*, 1912–13.

Devoy, John. *Recollections of an Irish rebel . . . a personal narrative.* New York, 1929. Reprint, with introduction by Seán Ó Lúing, Shannon, 1969.

Duffy, Charles Gavan. *My life in two hemispheres.* 2 vols. London, 1898. Reprint, with introduction by J. H. Whyte, Shannon, 1969.

Hamilton, John. *Sixty years' experience as an Irish landlord: memoirs of John Hamilton, D.L., of St Ernan's, Donegal. Ed. Rev.* H. C. White, London, 1894.

Healy, Timothy Michael. *Letters and leaders of my day.* 2 vols. London, [1928]; New York, 1929.

Hussey, S. M. *The reminiscences of an Irish land agent: being those of S. M. Hussey.* Compiled by Home Gordon. London, 1904.

Hyndman, Henry Mayers. *Record of an adventurous life.* London, 1911.

— *Further reminiscences.* London, 1912.

Kettle, Andrew J. *The material for victory: being the memoirs of Andrew J. Kettle. Ed.* L. J. Kettle. Dublin, 1958.

Le Caron, Henri (i.e. Thomas Billis Beach). *Twenty-five years in the secret service.* London, 1892; 12th ed., 1893.

Lloyd, Clifford. *Ireland under the Land League: a narrative of personal experiences.* London, 1892.

McCarthy, Justin. *Reminiscences.* 2 vols. London, 1899.

— *The story of an Irishman.* London, 1904.

Morley, John, *Viscount. Recollections.* 2 vols. London, 1917.

O'Brien, William. *Recollections.* London, 1905.

— *The Parnell of real life.* London, 1926.

O'Connor, Thomas Power. *C. S. Parnell: a memory.* London, 1891.

— *Memoirs of an old parliamentarian.* 2 vols. London, 1929.

O'Donovan Rossa, Jeremiah. *O'Donovan Rossa's prison life: six years in English prisons.* New York, 1874. Later ed. (entitled *Irish rebels in English prisons: a record of prison life*), New York, [1882].

— *Rossa's recollections, 1838 to 1890; childhood, boyhood, manhood . . .* New York, 1898. Reprint, with introduction by Seán Ó Lúing, Shannon, 1972.

O'Leary, John. *Recollections of fenians and fenianism.* 2 vols. London, 1896. Reprint, with introduction by Marcus Bourke, Shannon, 1969.

Orpen, *Sir* William. *Stories of old Ireland and myself.* London, 1924.

O'Shea, Katharine (Mrs Charles Stewart Parnell). *Charles Stewart Parnell: his love story and political life.* 2 vols. London, 1914.

Parnell, John Howard. *Charles Stewart Parnell: a memoir.* London, 1916.

Pigott, Richard. *Personal recollections of an Irish national journalist.* Dublin, 1883. Reprint, Cork, 1979.

Robinson, Henry A. *Memories wise and otherwise.* London, 1923.

— *Further memories of Irish life.* London, 1924.

Ryan, Mark Francis. *Fenian memories. Ed.* T. F. O'Sullivan. Dublin, 1945.

Sullivan, Timothy Daniel, *Recollections of troubled times in Irish politics.* Dublin, 1905.

Sweeney, John. *At Scotland Yard: being the experiences during twenty-seven years' service of John Sweeney, late detective-inspector, criminal investigation department, New Scotland Yard.* London, 1904.

Tynan, Katharine. *Twenty-five years: reminiscences.* London, 1913.

— *Memories.* London, 1924.

Wallace, Alfred Russel. *My life: a record of events and opinions.* London, 1905.

2 NARRATIVES AND STUDIES

See also X 2

Daunt, William J. O'Neill. *Eighty-five years of Irish history, 1800–85.* 2 vols. London, 1886.

Denieffe, Joseph. *A personal narrative of the Irish Revolutionary Brotherhood... from 1865 to 1867.* New York, 1906. Reprint, with introduction by Seán Ó Lúing, Shannon, 1969.

Denvir, John. *The life story of an old rebel.* Dublin, 1910; new ed., 1914. Reprint, with introduction by Leon Ó Broin, Shannon, 1972.

— *The Irish in Britain from the earliest times to the fall and death of Parnell.* London, 1892.

Duffy, Charles Gavan. *Four years of Irish history, 1845-9 . . .* London, 1883.

— *The league of north and south: an episode in Irish history, 1850–1854.* London, 1886.

Forrester, Arthur M. The romance of fenianism. In *Irish Weekly Independent*, 4, 11 Aug., 22, 29 Sept., 13, 20 Oct., 1894.

McCarthy, Justin Huntly. *An outline of Irish history from the earliest times to the present day.* London, [1883].

— *Ireland since the union: sketches of Irish history from 1798 to 1886.* London, 1887.

McCarthy, Michael J. F. *The Irish revolution.* Vol. i: *The murdering time, from the Land League to the first home rule bill.* Edinburgh and London, 1912. All published.

McWade, R. M. *The uncrowned king: the life and public services of the hon. Stewart Parnell.* Philadelphia, 1891.

O'Brien, William. Was fenianism ever formidable? In *Contemporary Review*, lxxi, May 1897, pp 680–93.

O'Connor, T.P. *The Parnell movement: with a sketch of Irish parties from 1843.* London, 1886. Revised ed., 1887.

—, and McWade, Robert. *Gladstone, Parnell and the great Irish struggle . . . with biographies of Parnell, Davitt, Egan, and very many others.* Philadelphia, 1888.

O'Donnell, Frank Hugh. *A history of the Irish parliamentary party.* 2 vols. London, 1910.

Sheehan, D. D. *Ireland since Parnell.* London, 1921.

Tynan, Patrick J. P. ('Number One'). *The Irish National Invincibles and their times.* English ed., London, 1894.

X HISTORICAL WORKS

1 GENERAL HISTORY

Beckett, J. C. *The making of modern Ireland, 1603–1923.* London, 1966.

Cullen, L. M. *An economic history of Ireland since 1660.* London, 1972.

Kee, Robert. *The green flag: a history of Irish nationalism.* London, 1972.

Lampson, G. Locker. *A consideration of the state of Ireland in the nineteenth century.* London, 1907.

Lee, Joseph. *The modernisation of Irish society, 1848–1918.* Dublin, 1973. (The Gill History of Ireland, ed. James Lydon and Margaret MacCurtain)

Lyons, F. S. L. *Ireland since the famine.* London, 1971.

MacDonagh, Oliver. *Ireland: the union and its aftermath.* Englewood Cliffs, N.J., 1968. Revised ed., London, 1977.

Mansergh, P. N. S. *The Irish question, 1840–1921.* London, 1940 (under the title *Ireland in the age of reform and revolution*). 3rd ed., 1975.

O'Farrell, P. J. *Ireland's English question: Anglo-Irish relations, 1534–1970.* London, 1971.

— *England and Ireland since 1800.* London, 1975.

Strauss, Emil. *Irish nationalism and British democracy.* London, 1951.

2 BIOGRAPHY AND STUDIES RELATED TO INDIVIDUALS

Dictionary of national biography. Ed. Sir Leslie Stephen. 66 vols. London, 1885-1901. Reprint, with corrections, 22 vols, London, 1908–9, etc.

Dictionary of American biography. Ed. Allen Johnson and Dumas Malone. 20 vols. New York and London, 1928–37.

Alfred Webb. *A compendium of Irish biography* . . . Dublin, 1878.

Henry Boylan. *A dictionary of Irish biography.* Dublin, 1978.

D. J. O'Donoghue. *The poets of Ireland: a biographical and bibliographical dictionary of writers of English verse.* 2nd ed. Dublin, 1912; reprint, 1962.

Frederick Boase. *Modern English biography.* 6 vols. London, 1892-1921.

Michael McDonagh. *Irish graves in England.* Dublin, 1888. (*Evening Telegraph*, reprints, vi).

Butt. White, Terence de Vere. *The road of excess.* Dublin, [1946].

— Thornley, D. A. *Isaac Butt and home rule.* London, [1964].

Chamberlain. Garvin, J. L., and Amery, Julian. *The life of Joseph Chamberlain.* Vol. i, 1836-85. London, 1932.

— Fraser, Peter. *Joseph Chamberlain, radicalism and empire, 1868-1914.* London, 1966.

Croke. Tierney, Mark. *Croke of Cashel: the life of Archbishop Thomas William Croke, 1823-1902.* Dublin, 1976.

Davis. Moody, T. W. *Thomas Davis, 1814-45* . . . Dublin 1945.

— Moody, T. W. Thomas Davis and the Irish nation. In *Hermathena*, ciii (1966), pp 5-31.

Devoy. Ryan, Desmond. *The phoenix flame: a study of fenianism and John Devoy.* London, 1937.

— Ó Lúing, Seán. *John Devoy.* Baile Átha Cliath, 1961.

Dillon. Lyons, F. S. L. *John Dillon: a biography.* London, 1968.

Disraeli. Moneypenny, W. F., and Buckle, G. E. *The life of Benjamin Disraeli, earl of Beaconsfield.* 2nd ed. 6 vols in 2. London, 1929.

— Blake, Robert. *Disraeli.* London, 1966.

Duggan. Brett, *Rev.* Thomas. *Life of Patrick Duggan, bishop of Confert.* Dublin, 1921.

Ford. Rodechko, James P. *Patrick Ford and his search for America: a case study of Irish-American journalism, 1870-1913.* New York, 1976.

Forster. Reid, T. Wemyss. *Life of the Right Honourable William Edward Forster.* 2 vols. London, 1888.

George. George, Henry, jr. *The life of Henry George.* New York, 1900.

— Barker, Charles Albro. *Henry George.* New York, 1955.

Gladstone. Morley, John. *The life of William Ewart Gladstone.* 3 vols. London, 1903.

— Shaw-Lefevre, G. J., *Baron Eversley. Gladstone and Ireland: the Irish policy of parliament from 1850-1894.* London, 1912.

— Hammond, J. L. *Gladstone and the Irish nation.* London, 1938. Reprint, with introduction by M. R. D. Foot, London, 1964.

— Hammond, J. L., and Foot, M. R. D. *Gladstone and liberalism.* New ed., London, 1970.

— Steele, E. D. Gladstone and Ireland. In *Irish Historical Studies*, xvii, no. 65 (Mar. 1970), pp 58-88.

Harcourt. Gardiner, A. G. *The life of Sir William Harcourt.* 2 vols. London, 1923.

Hartington. Holland, Bernard H., *Life of Spencer Compton, eighth duke of Devonshire.* 2 vols. London, 1911.

Healy. Sullivan, Maev. *No man's man.* Dublin, 1943.

Kickham. Comerford, R. V. *Charles J. Kickham: a study in Irish nationalism and literature.* Portmarnock, Co. Dublin, 1979.

Labouchere. Thorold, Algar Labouchere. *The life of Henry Labouchere.* London, 1913.

Lucan. Woodham-Smith, Cecil. *The reason why.* London, 1953.

MacHale. O'Reilly, Bernard. *John MacHale, archbishop of Tuam: his life, times, and correspondence.* 2 vols. New York, 1890.

Morley. Hamer, D. A. *John Morley: liberal intellectual in politics.* Oxford, 1968.

Murdoch. Young, J. D. John Murdoch, a land and labour pioneer. In *Calgacus: the Scottish review of politics, current affairs, history, and the arts,* 1, no. 2 (summer 1975), pp 14–19.

Nugent. Bennet, John. *Father Nugent of Liverpool.* Liverpool, 1949.

O'Brien. MacDonagh, Michael. *The life of William O'Brien, the Irish nationalist: a biographical study of Irish nationalism, constitutional and revolutionary.* London, 1928.

O'Leary. Bourke, Marcus. *John O'Leary: a study in Irish separatism.* Tralee, 1967.

O'Reilly. Roche, J. J. *Life of John Boyle O'Reilly.* . . . New York and London, 1891.

— McMenamin, F. G. *The American years of John Boyle O'Reilly, 1870–90.* New York, 1976.

Parnell, Anna. Moody, T. W. Anna Parnell and the Land League. In *Hermathena,* cxvii (1974), pp 5–17.

Parnell, Charles Stewart. O'Brien, R. Barry. *The life of Charles Stewart Parnell, 1846–1891.* 2 vols. London, 1898. Reprint, New York, 1969.

— O'Hara, M. M. *Chief and tribune: Parnell and Davitt.* Dublin, 1919.

— O'Brien, Conor Cruise. *Parnell and his party, 1880–90.* Oxford, 1957. Corrected impression, 1964.

— Lyons, F. S. L. The economic ideas of Parnell. In *Historical Studies,* ii, ed. Michael Roberts (London, 1959), pp 60–78.

— Lyons, F. S. L. The political ideas of Parnell. In *Historical Journal,* xvi, no. 4 (Dec. 1973), pp 749–75.

— Foster, R. F. *Charles Stewart Parnell: the man and his family.* Hassocks, Sussex, 1976.

— Lyons, F. S. L. *Charles Stewart Parnell.* London, 1977.

Stephens. Ryan, Desmond. *The fenian chief: a biography of James Stephens.* Introduction by Patrick Lynch. Dublin, 1967.

Vincent. Jeyes, S. H., and How, F. S. *Life of Sir Howard Vincent.* London, 1912.

Walsh. Walsh. P. J. *William J. Walsh, archbishop of Dublin.* Dublin, 1928.

3 *THE CATHOLIC CHURCH AND IRELAND*

Corish, Patrick J. Political problems, 1860–78. In *A history of Irish catholicism*, ed. Patrick J. Corish, v, ch. 3. Dublin, 1963.

Larkin, Emmet. *The Roman Catholic church and the creation of the modern Irish state, 1878–1886.* Philadelphia and Dublin, 1975.

Norman, E. R. *The catholic church and Ireland in the age of rebellion, 1859–1873.* London, 1965.

Whyte, J. H. The influence of the catholic clergy on elections in nineteenth-century Ireland. In *English Historical Review*, lxxv, no. 295 (Apr. 1960), pp 239–59.

Woods, C. J. The catholic church and Irish politics, 1879–92. Ph.D. thesis, University of Nottingham, 1968.

4 *THE IRISH IN AMERICA*

Brown, Thomas N. The origins and character of Irish-American nationalism. In *Review of Politics*, xviii, no. 3 (July 1956), pp 327–58.

— *Irish-American nationalism, 1870–1890.* Philadelphia and New York, 1966. (Critical Periods of History)

Broehl, Wayne G. *The Molly Maguires.* Cambridge, Mass., 1965.

Edwards, Owen Dudley. American diplomats and Irish coercion, 1880–83. In *Journal of American Studies*, i, no. 2 (Oct. 1967), pp 213–32.

Edwards, R. Dudley. Parnell and the American challenge to Irish nationalism. In *University Review* (Dublin), ii, no. 2, pp 47–64 [1958].

Joyce, W. L. *Editors and ethnicity: a history of the Irish-American press, 1848–1883.* New York, 1976.

Moody, T. W. Irish-American nationalism. In *Irish Historical Studies*, xv, no. 60 (Sept. 1967), pp 438–45.

O'Grady, J. P. *Irish-Americans and Anglo-American relations, 1880–1888.* New York, 1976.

Roohan, J. E. *American catholics and the social question, 1865–1900.* New York, 1976.

Shannon, W. V. *The American-Irish.* New York, 1963. Revised ed., 1966.

Wittke, Carl. *The Irish in America.* Baton Rouge, La, 1956.

5 *THE FENIAN MOVEMENT*

Corfe, Tom. *The Phoenix Park murders: conflict, compromise and tragedy in Ireland, 1879–82.* London, 1968.

D'Arcy, William. *The fenian movement in the United States: 1858–1886.* Washington, D.C., 1947.

Mac Giolla Choille, Breandán. Fenian documents in the State Paper Office. In *Irish Historical Studies*, xvi, no. 63 (Mar. 1969), pp 258–84.

Moody, T. W. (ed.). *The fenian movement.* Cork, 1968.

Ó Broin, Leon. *Fenian fever: an Anglo-American dilemma.* London, 1971.

— *Revolutionary underground: the story of the Irish Republican Brotherhood, 1858-1924.* Dublin, 1976.

Ryan, Desmond. *The phoenix flame: a study of fenianism and John Devoy.* London, 1937.

Short, K. R. M. *The dynamite war: Irish-American bombers in Victorian Britain.* Dublin, 1979.

University Review: organ of the Graduates Association of the National University of Ireland, iv, no. 3 (winter 1967).

Issue devoted to articles on fenian history.

6 THE HOME RULE MOVEMENT AND THE IRISH PARLIAMENTARY PARTY

McCaffrey, L. J. Home rule and the general election of 1874. In *Irish Historical Studies,* ix, no. 34 (Sept. 1954), pp 190-212.

— *Irish federalism in the 1870s: a study in conservative nationalism.* Philadelphia, 1962. (Transactions of the American Philosophical Society, new series, vol. lii, pt 6)

MacDonagh, Michael. *The home rule movement.* Dublin, 1920. (Modern Ireland in the Making)

O'Brien, Conor Cruise. *Parnell and his party, 1880-90.* Oxford, 1957; corrected impression, 1964.

Thornley, D. A. The Irish conservatives and home rule. In *Irish Historical Studies,* xi, no. 43 (Mar. 1959), pp 200-22.

— *Isaac Butt and home rule.* London, 1964.

Whyte, J. H. *The independent Irish party, 1850-59.* London, 1958.

— *The Tenant League and Irish politics in the eighteen-fifties.* Dundalk, 1963. (Dublin Historical Association pamphlet)

7 THE LAND

Bailey, W. F. *The Irish land acts: a short sketch of their history and development.* Dublin, 1917.

Bew, Paul. *Land and the national question.* Dublin, 1978.

Bonn, M. J. *Modern Ireland and her agrarian problem.* London, 1906.

Buckley, K. The fixing of rents by agreement in Co. Galway, 1881-5. In *Irish Historical Studies,* vii, no. 27 (Mar. 1951), pp 149-79.

Donnelly, J. S., jr. *The land and the people of nineteenth-century Cork: the rural economy and the land question.* London and Boston, 1975. (Studies in Irish History, 2nd series, ed. T. W. Moody and others, ix)

— The Irish agricultural depression of 1859-64. In *Irish Economic and Social History,* ii (1976), pp 33-54.

Hooker, Elizabeth R. *Readjustments of agricultural tenure in Ireland.* Chapel Hill (N.C.), 1938.

Kirkpatrick, R. W. Landed estates in mid-Ulster and the Irish land war, 1879-85. Ph.D. thesis, University of Dublin, 1976.

Lane, P. G. The social impact of the encumbered estates court on Counties Galway and Mayo, 1849-58. M.A. thesis, National University of Ireland (University College, Dublin), 1969.

Montgomery, W. E. *The history of land tenure in Ireland* . . . Cambridge, 1889.

O'Brien, R. Barry. *The parliamentary history of the Irish land question from 1829 to 1869; and the origin and results of the Ulster custom.* London, 1880.

O'Neill, Brian. *The war for the land in Ireland.* With an introduction by Peadar O'Donnell. New York, 1933.

Pomfret, John E. *The struggle for land in Ireland, 1800-1923.* Princeton, 1950.

Solow, Barbara L. *The land question in the Irish economy, 1870-1903.* Cambridge (Mass.), 1971. (Harvard Economic Studies, cxxxix)

Steele, E. D. Ireland and the empire in the 1860s: imperial precedents for Gladstone's first Irish land act. In *Historical Journal,* xi, 64-83 (1968).

— J. S. Mill and the Irish question: the principles of political economy, 1848-1865. In *Historical Journal,* xiii, 216-36 (June 1970).

— *Irish land and British politics: tenant right and nationality, 1865-1870.* Cambridge, 1974.

Vaughan, W. E. A study of landlord and tenant relations in Ireland between the famine and the land war, 1850-78. Ph.D. thesis, University of Dublin, 1973.

— Landlord and tenant relations between the famine and the land war, 1850-78. In L. M. Cullen and T. C. Smout (ed.), *Comparative aspects of Scottish and Irish economic and social history, 1600-1900* (Edinburgh, [1978]), pp 216-26.

Whyte, J. H. Landlord influence on elections in Ireland, 1760-1885. In *English Historical Review,* clxxx (Oct. 1965), pp 740-60.

Barry, E. Eldon. *Nationalisation in British politics: the historical background.* London, 1965.

Dewey, Clive. Celtic agrarian legislation and the Celtic revival: the historicist implications of Gladstone's Irish and Scottish land acts 1870-1886. In *Past and Present,* no. 64 (Aug. 1974), pp 30-70.

Douglas, Roy. *Land, people & politics: a history of the land question in the United Kingdom, 1878-1952.* London, 1976.

Hanham, H. J. The problem of Highland discontent, 1880-1885. In *Transactions of the Royal Historical Society,* 5th series, xix (1970), pp 21-65.

Hunter, James. The Gaelic connection: the Highlands, Ireland, and nationalism, 1873-1922. In *Scottish Historical Review,* liv, no. 158 (Oct. 1975), pp 178-204.

— The politics of Highland land reform, 1873-1895. In *Scottish Historical Review,* liii, no. 155 (Apr. 1974), pp 45-68.

Mackenzie, Alexander. *History of the Highland clearances.* Inverness, 1883.

MacPhail, I. M. M. The Napier commission. In *Transactions of the Gaelic Society of Inverness,* xlviii (1972-4), pp 435-72.

Orwin, C. S., and Whetham, E. H. *A history of British agriculture, 1846-1914.* London, 1964.

Prothero, R. E. *Baron Ernle. English farming, past and present.* With introductions by G. E. Fussell and C. R. McGregor. London, 1912. 6th ed., 1961.

Shaw-Lefevre, G. J. (later *Baron Eversley*). *English and Irish land questions: collected essays.* London, 1881.

— *Agrarian tenures: a survey of the laws and customs relating to the holding of land in England, Ireland, and Scotland, and of the reforms therein during recent years.* London, 1893.

Thompson, F. M. L. Land and politics in England in the 19th century. In *Transactions of the Royal Historical Society,* 5th series, xv (1965), pp 23-44.

8 THE 'NEW DEPARTURE' AND THE LAND LEAGUE

Bew, Paul. *Land and the national question.* Dublin, 1978.

Brown, Thomas N. *Irish-American nationalism, 1870-1890.* Philadelphia and New York, 1966. (Critical Periods of History)

Clark, Samuel D. The land war in Ireland. Ph.D. thesis, Harvard University (Cambridge, Mass.), 1973.

— The social composition of the Land League. In *Irish Historical Studies,* xvii, no. 68 (Sept. 1971), pp 447-69.

— The political mobilization of Irish farmers. In *Canadian Review of Sociology and Anthropology,* xii (4, pt 2, 1975), pp 483-99.

— The importance of agrarian classes. In *British Journal of Sociology,* xxix, no. 1 (Mar. 1978), pp 22-40.

— *Social origins of the Irish land war.* Princeton, 1979.

Moody, T. W. The new departure in Irish politics, 1878-9. In *Essays in British and Irish history in honour of James Eadie Todd,* ed. H. A. Cronne, T. W. Moody, and D. B. Quinn. (London, 1949), pp 303-33.

— Irish-American nationalism. In *Irish Historical Studies,* xv, no. 60 (Sept. 1967), pp 438-45.

Palmer, Norman Dunbar. *The Irish Land League crisis.* New Haven, 1940. (Yale Historical Publications, Miscellany XXXVII)

9 PRISONS AND PENAL SERVITUDE

Callow, Edward. See IX 1

Clarke, Thomas James. *Glimpses of an Irish felon's prison life.* With an introduction by P. S. O'Hegarty. Dublin, 1922.
First published as articles in *Irish Freedom*, 1912-13.

O'Donovan Rossa. See IX 1.

Phelan, Jim. *Jail journey.* London, 1940.

Macartney, Wilfrid. *Walls have mouths: a record of ten years' penal servitude.* London, 1936.

Griffiths, Arthur. *Memorials of Millbank, and chapters in prison history.* New edition, London, 1884.

— *The chronicles of Newgate.* 2 vols. London, 1884.

Harris, W. F. Vernon. *Dartmoor prison, past and present.* Plymouth, [*c.*1876].

Ives, George. *A history of penal methods.* London, 1914.

Ruggles-Brise, *Sir* Evelyn. *The English prison system.* London, 1921.

10 LOCAL STUDIES

Aspin, Christopher. *Haslingden, 1800–1900: a history.* Haslingden, 1962.

Craft, *Rev.* David, and others. *History of Scranton, Penn.* Dayton, Ohio, 1891.

Daly, John, and Weinberg, Allen. *Genealogy of Philadelphia county subdivisions*, City of Philadelphia, Department of Records, 1966.

Dunham, Keith. *The gun trade of Birmingham: a short historical note of some of the more interesting features of a long-established industry.* Birmingham, 1955. Reprint, with corrections, 1968.

Hitchcock, F. L. *History of Scranton and its people.* 2 vols. New York, 1914.

Iarlaith: St Jarlath's College, Tuam, past pupils' magazine. Tuam, 1955.

Lowe, W. J. The Irish in Lancashire, 1846–71: a social history. Ph.D. thesis, University of Dublin, 1974.

Moody, T. W., and Beckett, J. C. (ed.) *Ulster since 1800: a political and economic survey.* London, 1954. 2nd printing, with corrections, 1957.

— *Ulster since 1800: a social survey.* London, 1957. 2nd printing, with corrections, 1958.

Portrait and biographical record of Lackawanna County, Pennsylvania. New York and Chicago, 1897.

Throop, B. H. *A half century in Scranton.* Scranton, 1895.

Victoria history of the county of Lancaster. Ed. W. Farrer and J. Brownbill. 8 vols. London, 1906-12.

11 OTHER SPECIAL STUDIES

Bailey, W. F. *Local and centralised government in Ireland: a sketch of the existing system.* London, 1888.

Black, R. D. C. *Economic thought and the Irish question, 1817–70.* Cambridge, 1960.

Clarkson, J. D. *Labour and nationalism in Ireland.* New York, 1925. Reprint, New York, 1970.

Cole, G. D. H. *Chartist portraits.* London, 1941.

Comerford, Richard Vincent. Irish nationalist politics, 1858–70. Ph.D. thesis, University of Dublin, 1977.

Curtis, L. P., jr. *Apes and angels: the Irishman in Victorian caricature.* Washington, 1971.

Denvir, John. *The Irish in Britain, from the earliest times to the fall and death of Parnell.* London, 1892. 2nd ed., 1894.

Feingold, William L. The tenants' movement to capture the Irish poor law boards, 1877–1886. In *Albion, including the Proceedings of the Conference on British Studies at its regional and national meetings,* vii, no. 3 (Fall 1975), pp 216–31.

Handley, James E. *The Irish in modern Scotland.* Cork, 1947.

Hawkins, Richard. Government versus secret societies: the Parnell era. In T. D. Williams (ed.), *Secret societies in Ireland* (1973), pp 100–12.

— Liberals, land, and coercion in the summer of 1880: the influence of the Carraroe ejectments. In *Journal of the Galway Archaeological and Historical Society,* xxxiv (1975), pp 40–57.

Hyman, Louis. *The Jews of Ireland. . . .* Shannon, 1972.

Jackson, John Archer. *The Irish in Britain.* London, 1963.

Leo, Mary. The influence of the fenians and their press on public opinion in Ireland, 1863–70. M. Litt. thesis, University of Dublin, 1976.

Malcolm, Elizabeth Letitia. The drink question in Ireland, 1856–1901. Ph.D. thesis, University of Dublin, 1980.

Moody, T. W. *The Times* versus Parnell and Co., 1887–90. In *Historical Studies,* vi, ed. T. W. Moody (London, 1968), pp 147–82.

Morgan, K. O. *Wales in British politics, 1868–1922.* Cardiff, 1963.

XI BIBLIOGRAPHIES AND LATER WORKS OF REFERENCE

Carty, James. *Bibliography of Irish history, 1870–1911.* Dublin, 1940 (National Library of Ireland).

Bibliography of British history, 1851–1914, issued under the direction of the American Historical Association and the Royal Historical Society of Great Britain. Compiled and edited by H. J. Hanham. Oxford, 1976.
The section on Ireland (pp 1173–238) is comprehensive and invaluable.

Brown, Stephen J. *A guide to books on Ireland.* Part I: *Prose literature, poetry, music, and plays.* Dublin, 1912.

MacWhite, Eóin. A guide to Russian writing on Irish history. In *Melbourne Slavonic Studies,* no. 3 (1969), pp 40–96.

Writings on Irish history, 1936– . In *Irish Historical Studies,* i, no. 1 (Mar. 1938)– .

Select bibliography of publications on Irish economic and social history published in 1973 [etc.]. In *Irish Economic and Social History,* i (1974)– .

Vaughan, W. E., and Fitzpatrick, A. J. *Irish historical statistics: population, 1821–1971.* Dublin, 1978 (New History of Ireland Ancillary Publications II).

Walker, B. M. *Parliamentary election results in Ireland, 1801–1922.* Dublin, 1978 (New History of Ireland Ancillary Publications IV).

MacLysaght, Edward. *Irish families: their names, arms, and origins.* Dublin, 1957.

—— *More Irish families.* Galway and Dublin, 1960.

—— *Supplement to Irish families.* Dublin, 1964.

Freeman, T. W. *Ireland: a general and regional geography.* London, 1950. 4th ed., 1972.

Hajducki, S. Maxwell. *A railway atlas of Ireland.* Newton Abbot, 1974.

Census of Ireland: 1901: general topographical index . . . to the townlands and towns of Ireland, and indices to the parishes, baronies, poor law unions . . ., [Cd 2071], H.C. 1904, cix.

Hickey, D. J., and Doherty, J. E. *A dictionary of Irish History since 1800.* Dublin, 1980.

MAPS

showing places mentioned in the text

Railways c. 1880
N
Giant's Causeway
Portrush
Inishowen
Mulroy Bay
DERRY
LONDONDERRY
ANTRIM
Letterkenny
DONEGAL
Raphoe
Strabane
Carrickfergus
BELFAST
Hannahstown
Moneyrea
TYRONE
Ballyshannon
Belleek
Lough Erne
Kinnegoe
Saintfield
Loughgall
Armagh
DOWN
Downpatrick
FERMANAGH
Enniskillen
MONAGHAN
ARMAGH
Sligo
LEITRIM
Bessbrook
Newry
Camlough
Clones
SLIGO
MAYO
Boyle
Carrick-on-Shannon
Drumsna
Cavan
CAVAN
LOUTH
Dundalk
Straide
Castlebar
Westport
Castlerea
ROSCOMMON
LONGFORD
Slane
Drogheda
Navan
MEATH
Trim
Tuam
WESTMEATH
Athlone
Donabate
Malahide
Howth
Maynooth
DUBLIN
Kingstown
Dalkey
Rathcoole
GALWAY
Ballinasloe
KINGS CO.
KILDARE
Kildare
Bray
Blessington
Tenakill
Maryborough
QUEENS CO.
Knockaroe
WICKLOW
Rathdrum
Avondale
CLARE
Ennis
Tullow
Ballyragget
CARLOW
Arklow
Kilkenny
Clonegall
TIPPERARY
KILKENNY
Thurles
Borris
LIMERICK
Askeaton
Enniscorthy
Cashel
Croom
Emly
WEXFORD
Kilmallock
Cahir
New Ross
Charleville
Galtees
Portlaw
Waterford
Tralee
Mitchelstown
Newmarket
Kanturk
WATERFORD
Mallow
Mourne Abbey
Dungarvan
Killarney
Ballyknockane
KERRY
CORK
Queenstown
Shanagarry
0 Miles 50
0 Kms 80

I Ireland

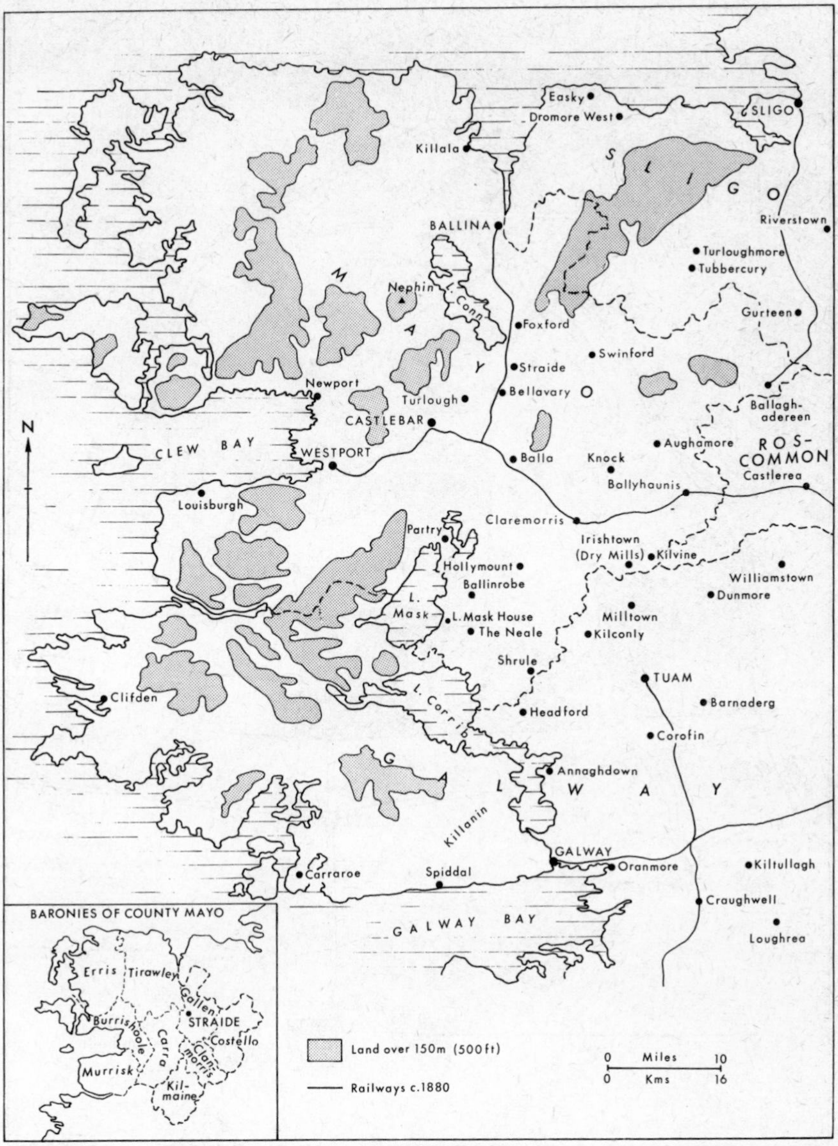

II West Connacht

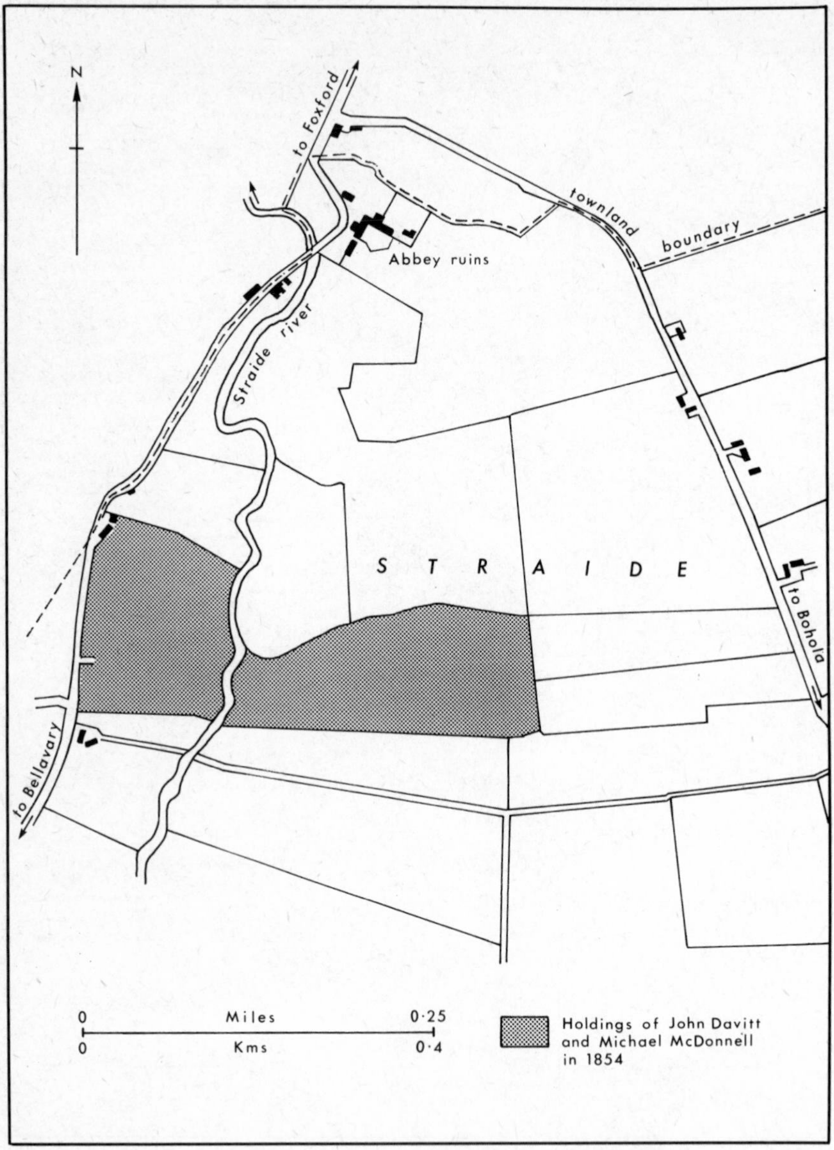

III Part of the Knox estate in the townland of Straide in 1854 (from map accompanying rental for sale of part of Knox estate in encumbered estates court on 15 June 1854; see above, pp 6–7)

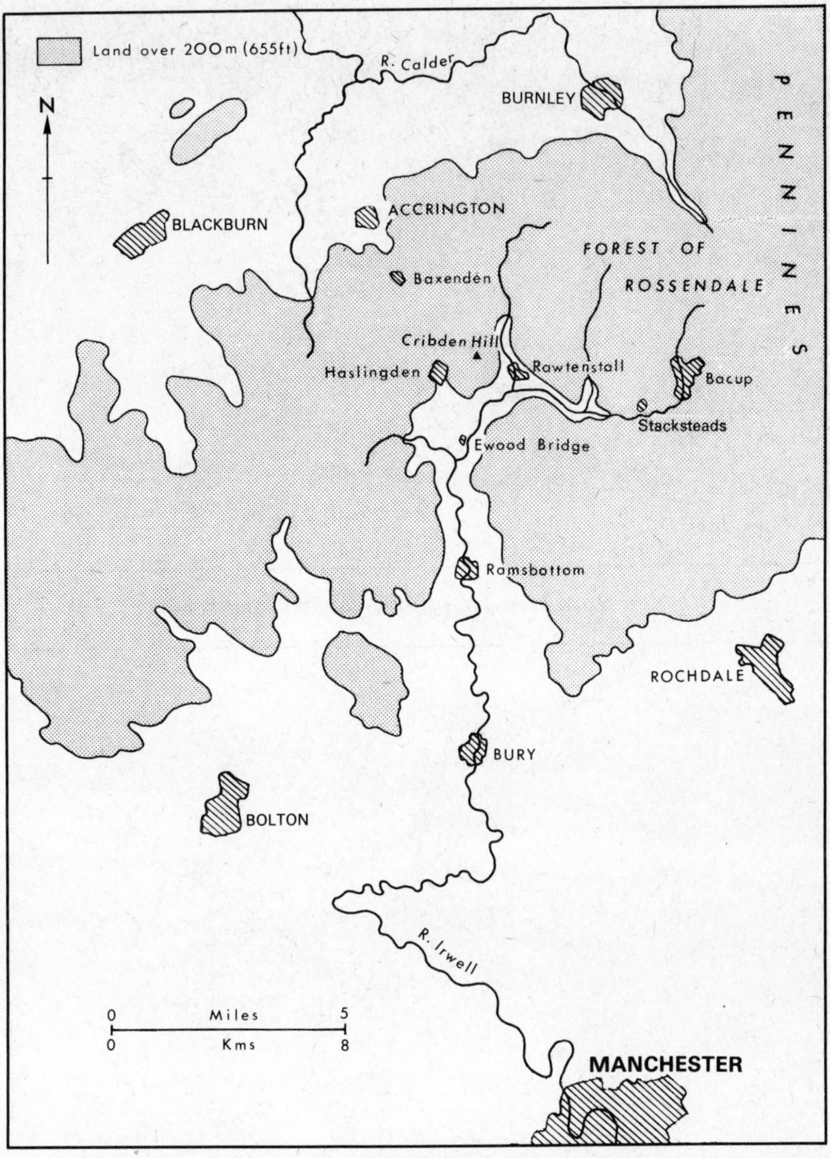

IV The neighbourhood of Haslingden, Lancashire. Urban areas (hatched) are shown as in the first-edition maps of the ordnance survey, *c*.1850

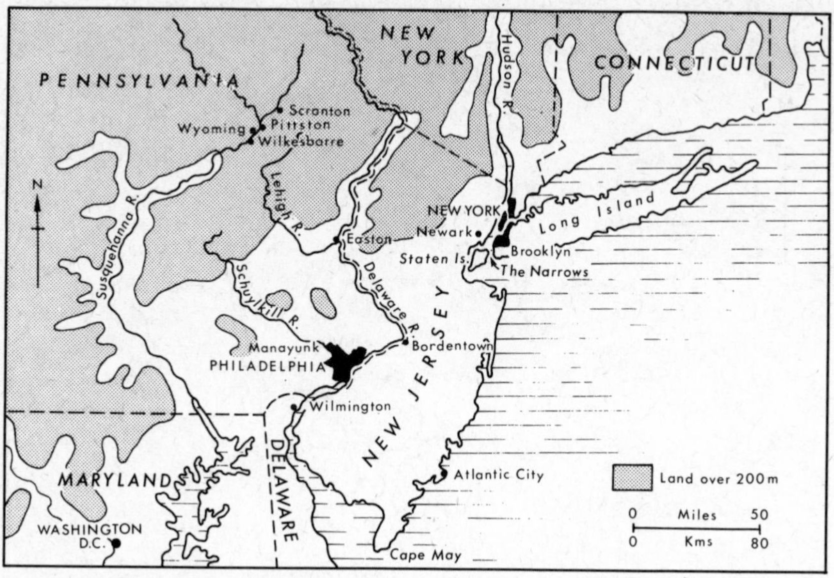

V New York, New Jersey, and eastern Pennsylvania

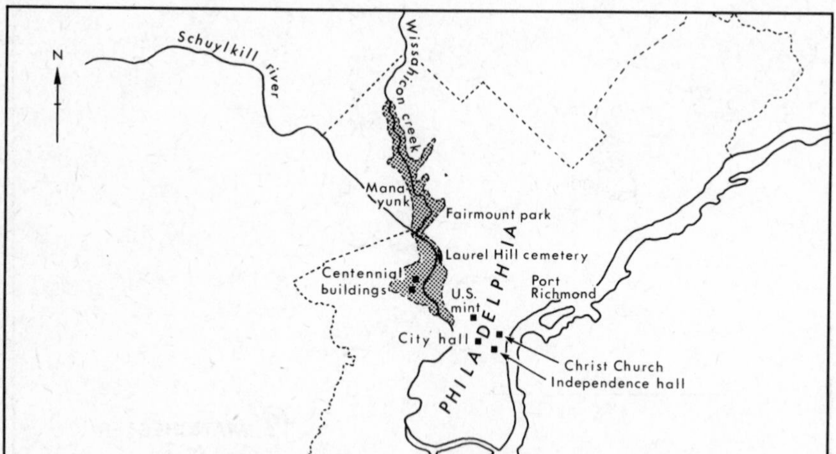

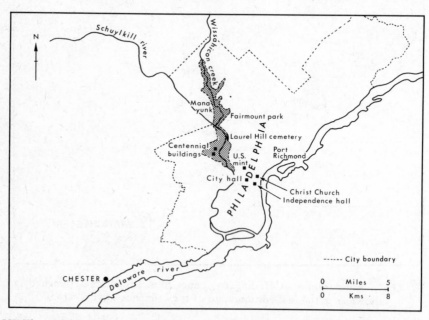

VI The neighbourhood of Manayunk, Philadelphia, 1878–80 (From maps of Philadelphia, 1879, in Gray, *National atlas . . . of the United States* (Philadelphia, 1881) and maps in *Encyclopaedia Britannica*, 9th ed., xviii (1885), p. 736 and facing plate)

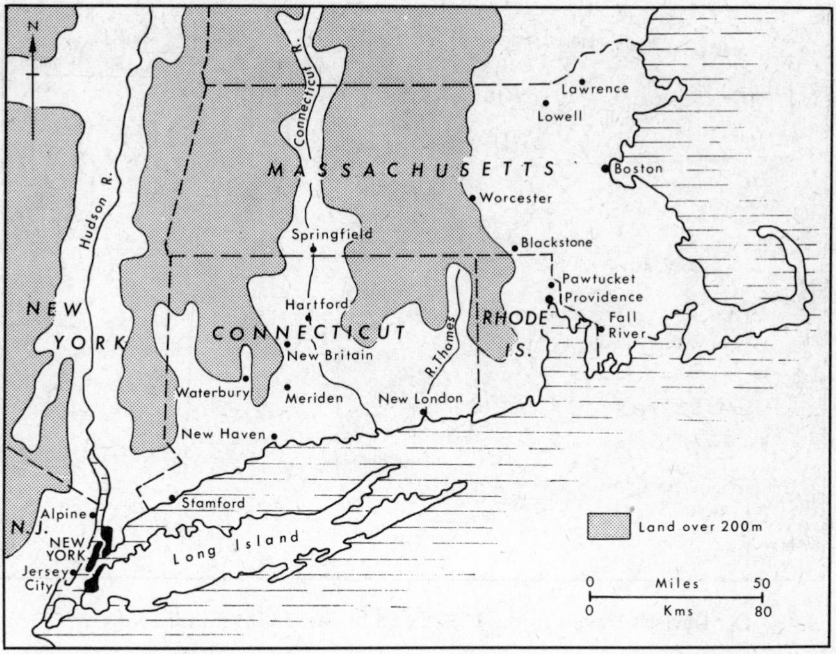

VII Davitt's travels in the U.S.A., 1878 and 1880; New York and New England

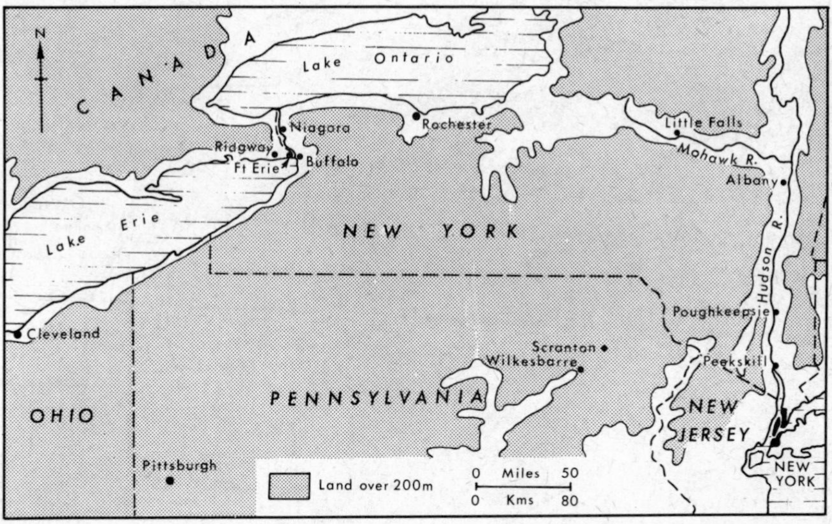

VIII Davitt's travels in the U.S.A., 1878 and 1880: New York to Ohio

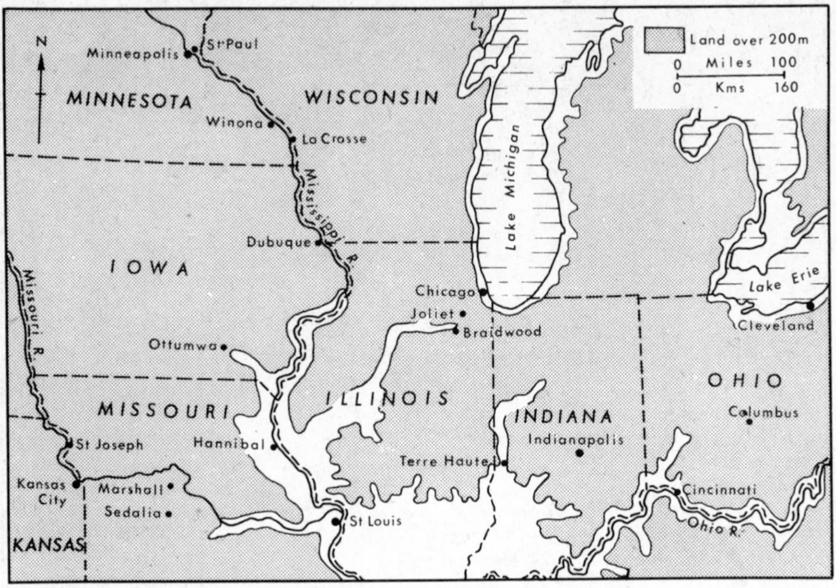

IX Davitt's travels in the U.S.A., 1878 and 1880: middle west

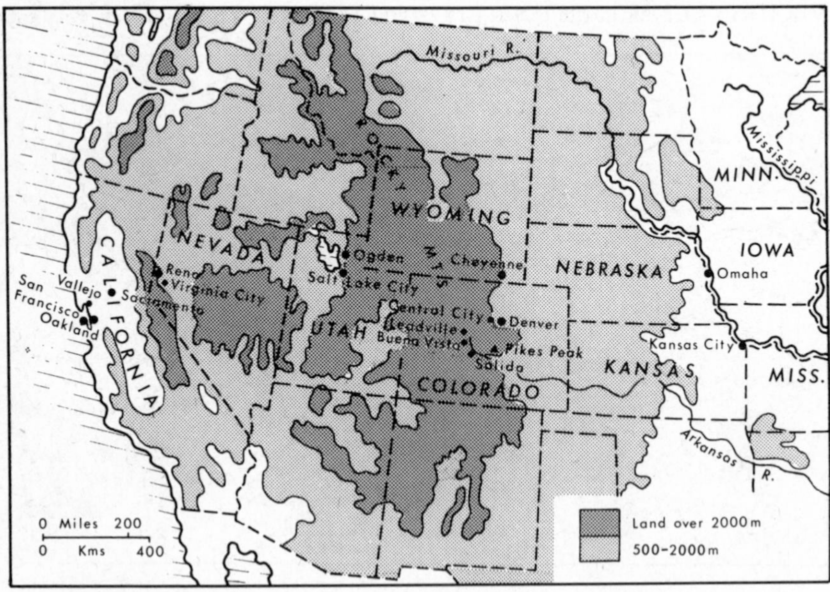

X Davitt's travels in the U.S.A., 1880: the Mississippi to San Francisco

INDEX

The following abbreviations are used in addition to those listed above, pp xi–xiv.

A.G.	attorney general	D.M.P.	Dublin Metropolitan Police
abp	archbishop	H.C.	House of Commons
app.	appendix	Ire.	Ireland
b.	born	K'ham treaty	'Kilmainham treaty'
bp	bishop	L.L.	Land League
chmn	chairman	L.L.L.	Ladies' Land League
commn	commission	mtg	meeting
cttee	committee	new dep.	new departure
d.	died	P.L.G.	poor law guardian

Dates are given in the form: 18.5.57; 12.68 - 5.69

The index is divided into two parts: part I covers the career and personality of Michael Davitt and certain related topics, part II all other subjects.

Cross-references are kept to a minimum, but many subjects are indexed under more than one heading.

PART I MICHAEL DAVITT

career, 1846-65: birth and birthplace, 1; parents, 5–6; father's holding, 6–7; parentage and upbringing compared with Parnell's, 7–8; family evicted (1850), 8–9; emigrates to Haslingden, Lancs., 9–10; D ill with measles, 11; life at Rock Hall, 12; inherits peasant tradition of hatred of 'landlordism', 14, 33–4; finds employment as mill-hand (1855), 15–17; loses his right arm in factory accident (18.5.57), 17–18; schooling resumed (1857–61), 18–19; employed by local postmaster (1861), 19–20; early skill as printer, 20; attends evening classes, 20–21; in contact with Ernest Jones, chartist, 21–2; his sister Mary marries and emigrates to Scranton, Pa, 22–3

—, 1865–70: joins I.R.B. in Rossendale, Lancs. (1865), 43–4; his fenian associates, 44–8; takes part in attempted raid on Chester castle (11.2.67), 48–9; attitude to Manchester rescue (18.9.67) and to Clerkenwell explosion (13.12), 52; confirmed, 52; defends St. Mary's church, Haslingden (1868), 52–3; organising secretary and arms agent of I.R.B. for England and Scotland (1868), 53; his poems in *Universal News* (12.68 - 5.69), 53–4; his fenian activities (1869), 54–5; under police observation (from 1.69), 55–6, 57; opposes Forrester's demand for killing of alleged traitor, 58–9; his 'pen' letter to Forrester (15.12), 59–62; finds bailsmen for Forrester, 65; closely watched by police, 66–7; takes over Forrester's functions in I.R.B. (1.70), 66; police report on his family and friends in Haslingden, 67; his traffic in arms for I.R.B., 67–9; his connection with John Wilson, 69; his arms traffic discovered by police, 69–77; arrested at Paddington station, London (14.5), 77–9, 81; his parents and sisters move to Scranton, Pa, 79

—, July 1870: his examination before Marylebone police court (5–6.70), 81–4; in prison awaiting trial (6–7.70), 84–6; trial at Old Bailey (15, 16, 18.7), 86–102; his appeal on behalf of Wilson, 101–2, 103, 105, 110; sentenced to 15 years penal servitude, 102–3; his